STUDY GUIDE

STUDY GUIDE

Richard O. Straub

University of Michigan, Dearborn

to accompany

PSYCHOLOGY
TENTH EDITION IN MODULES

David G. Myers

WORTH PUBLISHERS

Study Guide
by Richard O. Straub
to accompany
Myers: **Psychology, Tenth Edition in Modules**

© 2013, 2010, 2007, 2004, 2001 by Worth Publishers

All rights reserved. No part of this publication may be reproduced, stored
in a retrieval system, or transmitted in any form or by any means, electronic,
mechanical, photocopying, or otherwise, without the prior written permission
of the publisher.

Printed in the United States of America

ISBN 13: 978-1-4641-0846-4
ISBN 10: 1-4641-0846-3

First printing

Cover: *Woman's face:* © Tanner Productions/Corbis; *Trees:* Photodisc; *Drops of water/ripples:* Photodisc; *Human eye:* Digital Vision/Getty Images; *Cat:* Eric Isselée/Shutterstock; *Bride/groom:* bluehand/Shutterstock; *Sleeping baby:* Courtesy Kevin Feyen; *Smiling girl:* Tim Gainey/Alamy; *Man with glasses:* Tristan Savatier/Getty Images; *Rose:* Frank Chmura/Alamy; *Robins:* Lightscapes Photography Inc./Corbis; *Brain:* From Mapping the Mind, Rita Carter (c) 1989 University of California Press; *Elephant:* Johan Swanepoel/Alamy.

Worth Publishers
41 Madison Avenue
New York, New York 10010
www.worthpublishers.com

Contents

Preface

This Study Guide is designed for use with *Psychology, Tenth Edition in Modules,* by David G. Myers. It is intended to help you learn material in the textbook, to evaluate your understanding of that material, and then to review any problem areas.

This Study Guide offers many useful features. Each module includes a review test: In addition to questions asking about facts and definitions, several items evaluate your understanding of the module's broader conceptual material and its application to real-world situations. At the back of each module are the correct answers, as well as complete explanations not only of why the answer is correct but also of why the other choices are incorrect.

The module review is organized by major text section. For each section the fill-in and essay-type questions are organized under a learning objective.

General Internet Resources

To obtain general information about psychology-related topics, you might want to consult some of the following Web sites.

Russ Dewey's Psych Web is an effort to compile a great deal of information for psychology students and teachers, including self-quizzes, lists of psychology journals on the Web, self-help resources, tip sheets for psychology majors, and psychology departments on the Internet. Psych Web is available at the following site: www.psychwww.com.

Deborah Kelley-Milburn and Michael A. Milburn's "Cyberspace: Resources for Psychologists on the Internet" (Psychological Science, [1995, July], Volume 6, 203–211) is another excellent resource. This review provides helpful information on Listservs, Usenet groups, electronic journals and newsletters, databases, grant and job information, and library catalogues.

Both the American Psychological Association (APA) and the American Psychological Society (APS) have Internet services. These services provide not only information about their organizations but also selected articles from their main journals, information about current research in the discipline, and links to other science-related sites on the Internet. Their locations are as follows:

APA: www.apa.org and APS: www.psychologicalscience.org

Finally, and perhaps most important, is Psychtalk, a list for students interested in discussion topics and controversies related to psychology. Topics that have been discussed over the past few years include child abuse, the nature-nurture issue, homosexuality, and pornography. To subscribe, send a message to:
psychtalk-request@fre.fsu.umd.edu
The message should read "subscribe psychtalk (your name)."

Acknowledgments

I would like to thank all the students and instructors who used this Study Guide in its previous editions and provided such insightful and useful suggestions. Special thanks are also due to Betty Shapiro Probert for her extraordinary editorial contributions and to Don Probert for his skill and efficiency in the composition of this guide. I would also like to thank Sharon Prevost, Julio Espin, and Stacey Alexander of Worth Publishers for their dedication and energy in skillfully coordinating various aspects of production. Most important, I want to thank Jeremy, Rebecca, Melissa, and Pam for their enduring love and patience.

Richard O. Straub

The Story of Psychology

MODULE OVERVIEW

Psychology's historical development and current activities lead us to define the field as the science of behavior and mental processes. Module 1 discusses the development of psychology from ancient times until today and the range of behaviors and mental processes being investigated by psychologists in each of the various specialty areas. In addition, it introduces the biopsychosocial approach that integrates the three main levels of analysis followed by psychologists working from the seven major perspectives. Next is an overview of the diverse subfields in which psychologists conduct research and provide professional services.

Module 1 concludes with a Close-Up explaining how to get your study of psychology off on the right foot by learning (and pledging to follow!) the SQ3R study method. This study method is also discussed in the essay at the beginning of this Study Guide.

NOTE: Answer guidelines for all Module 1 questions begin on page 9.

MODULE REVIEW

First, skim each section, noting headings and boldface items. After you have read the section, review each objective by answering the fill-in questions that follow it. In some cases, Study Tips explain how best to learn a difficult concept and Applications help you to know how well you understand the material. As you proceed, evaluate your performance by consulting the answers on page 9. Do not continue with the next section until you understand each answer. If you need to, review or reread the section in the textbook before continuing.

What Is Psychology?

Objective 1-1: Describe some important milestones in psychology's early development.

1. The Greek naturalist and philosopher _____ developed early theories about _____ , _____ _____ , _____ , _____ and _____ .

2. The first psychological laboratory was founded in 1879 by Wilhelm _____ . His student _____ introduced the school of _____ , which explored the basic elements of mind using the method of _____ . This method proved _____ (reliable/unreliable).

3. Under the influence of evolutionary theorist Charles Darwin, philosopher-psychologist _____ assumed that thinking developed because it was _____ . As a _____ , he focused on how mental and behavioral processes enable the organism to adapt and survive. In 1890, he published the first psychology textbook.

4. The first female president of the American Psychological Association was _____ . The first woman to receive a Ph.D. in psychology was _____ , who was the second female APA president and author of *The Animal Mind*.

Objective 1-2: Describe how psychology continued to develop from the 1920s through today.

5. In its earliest years, psychology was defined as the science of _____ life. From the 1920s into the 1960s, psychology in America was redefined by _____ and _____ as the science of _____ behavior.

6. The other major force was Freudian psychology, which emphasized the ways our _____ thought processes and our _____ responses to childhood experiences affect our behavior.

7. As a response to Freudian psychology and to _____ , which they considered too mechanistic, pioneers _____ and _____ forged _____ psychology. This new perspective emphasized the _____ potential of _____ people.

8. During the 1960s, psychology underwent a _____ revolution as it began to recapture interest in how our _____ processes and retains information. The study of brain activity linked with mental activity is called _____ _____ .

9. The text author defines *psychology* as the scientific study of _____ and _____ processes. In this definition, "behavior" refers to any action that we can _____ and _____ , and "mental processes" refers to the internal, _____ _____ we _____ from behavior.

10. As a science, psychology is less a set of findings than a way of _____ _____ .

APPLICATIONS:

11. *Psychology* is defined as the "science of behavior and mental processes." Wilhelm Wundt would have omitted which of the following words from this definition?
    a. science
    b. behavior and
    c. and mental processes
    d. Wundt would have agreed with the definition as stated.

12. Jawan believes that psychologists should go back to using introspection as a research tool. This technique is based on
    a. survey methodology.
    b. experimentation.
    c. self-examination of mental processes.
    d. the study of observable behavior.

13. Dharma's term paper on the history of American psychology notes that
    a. psychology began as the science of mental life.
    b. from the 1920s into the 1960s, psychology was defined as the scientific study of observable behavior.
    c. contemporary psychologists study both overt behavior and covert thoughts.
    d. all of these statements are true.

14. During his presentation on the history of psychology, Sanjay notes that Darwin's theory led most directly to the development of the school of
    a. structuralism.
    b. behaviorism.
    c. functionalism.
    d. humanism.

15. The psychological views of William James are to those of Edward Titchener as _____ is to _____ .
    a. nature; nurture
    b. nurture; nature
    c. structuralism; functionalism
    d. functionalism; structuralism

Contemporary Psychology

16. The historical roots of psychology include the fields of _____ and _____ .

17. Some early psychologists included Ivan Pavlov, who pioneered the study of _____ ; the personality theorist _____ ; and Jean Piaget, who studied _____ .

18. Worldwide, the number of psychologists is
_____ (increasing/decreasing).
Thanks to international publications and meetings, psychological science is also

_____ .

Objective 1-3: Summarize the nature–nurture issue in psychology.

19. The nature–nurture issue is the controversy over
the relative contributions of _____
and _____ .

20. The Greek philosopher who assumed that character and intelligence are inherited is
_____ . The Greek philosopher
who argued that all knowledge comes from sensory experience is _____ .

21. In the 1600s, the views of the Greek philosophers
were revived by _____ , who
believed that most knowledge comes in through
the senses, and _____ , who
believed that some ideas are innate.

22. In 1859, naturalist _____
explained species variation by proposing the
process of _____ , which works
through the principle of _____

_____ .

23. Although the debate continues, we will see that
_____ works on what
_____ endows and that every
_____ event is simultaneously a
_____ event.

STUDY TIP: The nature–nurture issue is psychology's
biggest and most persistent debate. Psychologists
explore the issue by asking, for example, how differences in intelligence, personality, and psychological
disorders are influenced by heredity and by environment. Today, contemporary science recognizes that
nurture works on what nature endows. Our species is
biologically endowed with an enormous capacity to
learn and to adapt. Moreover, every *psychological
event is simultaneously a biological event.*

APPLICATION:

24. The philosophical views of John Locke are to
those of René Descartes as _____ is to

_____ .
   a. nature; nurture
   b. nurture; nature
   c. rationality; irrationality
   d. irrationality; rationality

Objective 1-4: Describe psychology's three main levels of analysis and related perspectives.

25. Each person is a complex _____
that is part of a larger _____

_____ and at the same time composed of smaller systems. For this reason,
psychologists work from three main

_____ of _____ :
biological , _____ , and

_____-_____ ,
which together form an integrated

_____ approach to the study of
behavior and mental processes.

26. Psychologists who study how the body and brain
enable emotions, memories, and sensory experiences are working from the _____
perspective.

27. Psychologists who study how natural selection
influences behavior tendencies are working from
the _____ perspective, whereas
those concerned with the relative influences of
genes and environment on individual differences
are working from the _____

_____ perspective.

28. Psychologists who believe that behavior springs
from unconscious drives and conflicts are working from the _____
perspective.

29. Psychologists who study the mechanisms by
which observable responses are acquired and
changed are working from the

_____ perspective.

30. The _____ perspective explores
how we encode, process, store, and retrieve
information.

31. Psychologists who study how thinking and behavior vary in different situations are working from the _____-_____ perspective.

32. The different perspectives on the big issues _____ (contradict/complement) one another.

STUDY TIP: This section describes a number of perspectives in psychology. Keep in mind that each perspective is nothing more than how certain psychologists feel behavior and mental processes should be investigated. For example, a clinical psychologist could approach the study of abnormal behavior from any of the perspectives discussed. Typically, however, psychologists work from a combination of perspectives rather than exclusively from only one. To deepen your understanding of the various perspectives, review the following chart. In the first column are listed psychology's contemporary perspectives. In the second column are listed historical roots and the pioneers who contributed to each modern-day perspective and the subfield that derives from it. As you work through the chapters, you might want to annotate this chart to include what you know about these psychologists.

Perspective	Historical Roots and Pioneers
Neuroscience	Aristotle (perception, emotion), Wundt
Evolutionary	Darwin, Freud
Behavior Genetics	Darwin
Psychodynamic	Aristotle (personality), Freud
Behavioral	Aristotle (learning), Pavlov, Watson, Skinner
Cognitive	Aristotle (memory), Wundt (quantifying mental processes), Piaget
Social-Cultural	Piaget, Rogers, Maslow

APPLICATIONS:

33. Professor Gutierrez, who believes that human emotions are best understood as being jointly determined by heredity, learning, and the individual's social and cultural contexts, is evidently a proponent of the
    a. psychodynamic perspective.
    b. biopsychosocial approach.
    c. evolutionary perspective.
    d. neuroscience perspective.

34. In concluding her report on the "nature–nurture issue in contemporary psychology," Karen notes that
    a. most psychologists believe that nature is a more important influence on the development of most human traits.
    b. most psychologists believe that nurture is more influential.
    c. the issue is more heatedly debated than ever before.
    d. nurture works on what nature endows.

35. Dr. Waung investigates how a person's interpretation of a situation affects his or her reaction. Evidently, Dr. Waung is working from the _____ perspective.
    a. neuroscience   c. cognitive
    b. behavioral   d. social-cultural

36. The psychological perspective that places the MOST emphasis on how observable responses are learned is the _____ perspective.
    a. behavioral   c. behavior genetics
    b. cognitive   d. evolutionary

37. During a dinner conversation, a friend says that the cognitive and behavioral perspectives are quite similar. You disagree and point out that the cognitive perspective emphasizes_____, whereas the behavioral perspective emphasizes

_____ .

    a. conscious processes; observable responses
    b. unconscious processes; conscious processes
    c. overt behaviors; covert behaviors
    d. introspection; experimentation

38. Concerning the major psychological perspectives on behavior, the text author suggests that
    a. researchers should work within the framework of only one of the perspectives.
    b. only those perspectives that emphasize objective measurement of behavior are useful.
    c. the different perspectives often complement one another; together, they provide a fuller understanding of behavior than provided by any single perspective.
    d. psychologists should avoid all of these traditional perspectives.

Objective 1-5: Identify psychology's main subfields.

39. Psychologists may be involved in conducting

_____ _____,

which builds psychology's knowledge base, or

_____ _____,

which seeks solutions to practical problems.

40. Psychologists who help people cope with problems in living are called _____ psychologists. Psychologists who study, assess, and treat troubled people are called _____ psychologists.

41. Medical doctors who provide psychotherapy and treat physical causes of psychological disorders are called _____ .

42. The subfield of_____ scientifically explores human strengths and human flourishing.

43. Psychologists who work to create healthy social and physical environments are called

_____ .

APPLICATIONS:

44. Terrence wants to talk to a professional to help him cope with some academic challenges he's facing. You recommend that he contact a(n)
    a. industrial-organizational psychologist.
    b. developmental psychologist.
    c. counseling psychologist.
    d. psychiatrist.

45. Dr. Aswad is studying people's enduring inner traits. Dr. Aswad is most likely a(n)
    a. clinical psychologist.
    b. psychiatrist.
    c. personality psychologist.
    d. industrial-organizational psychologist.

Close-Up: Improve Your Retention— and Your Grades!

Objective 1-6: Explain how psychological principles can help you learn and remember.

46. Repeated _____ and

_____ of material improves retention of information. This phenomenon is called the _____ _____ .

47. To master any subject, you must

_____ process it.

48. The _____ study method incorporates five steps: **a.** _____ ,
    b. _____ , **c.** _____ ,
    d. _____ , and
    e. _____ .

List five additional study tips identified in the text.

a. _____

b. _____

c. _____

d. _____

e. _____

APPLICATIONS:

49. Your roommate announces that her schedule permits her to devote three hours to studying for an upcoming quiz. You advise her to
    a. spend most of her time reading and rereading the text material.
    b. focus primarily on her lecture notes.
    c. space study time over several short sessions.
    d. cram for three hours just before the quiz.

50. A fraternity brother rationalizes the fact that he spends very little time studying by saying that he "doesn't want to peak too soon and have the test material become stale." You tell him that
    a. he is probably overestimating his knowledge of the material.
    b. if he devotes extra time to studying, his retention of the material will be improved.
    c. the more often students test themselves on the material, the better their exam scores.
    d. all of these statements are true.

51. Brad, who prepares for exams simply by reading the textbook assignment several times, evidently has not heard about
    a. functionalism
    b. positive psychology.
    c. the testing effect.
    d. the nature–nurture issue.

PROGRESS TEST

Multiple-Choice Questions

Circle your answers to the following questions and check them with the answers beginning on page 11. If your answer is incorrect, read the explanation for why it is incorrect and then consult the text.

1. In its earliest days, psychology was defined as the
    a. science of mental life.
    b. study of conscious and unconscious activity.
    c. science of observable behavior.
    d. science of behavior and mental processes.

2. Who would be most likely to agree with the statement, "Psychology should investigate only behaviors that can be observed"?
    a. Wilhelm Wundt
    b. Sigmund Freud
    c. John B. Watson
    d. William James

3. Today, *psychology* is defined as the
    a. science of mental phenomena.
    b. science of conscious and unconscious activity.
    c. science of behavior.
    d. science of behavior and mental processes.

4. Who introduced the early school of structuralism?
    a. Edward Titchener
    b. Wilhelm Wundt
    c. William James
    d. Mary Whiton Calkins

5. Who wrote the early textbook *Principles of Psychology*?
    a. Wilhelm Wundt   c. Jean Piaget
    b. Ivan Pavlov   d. William James

6. Psychologists who study the degree to which genes influence our personality are working from the _____ perspective.
    a. behavioral   c. behavior genetics
    b. evolutionary   d. neuroscience

7. Which of the following exemplifies the issue of the relative importance of nature and nurture on our behavior?
    a. the issue of the relative influence of biology and experience on behavior
    b. the issue of the relative influence of rewards and punishments on behavior
    c. the debate as to the relative importance of heredity and instinct in determining behavior
    d. the debate as to whether mental processes are a legitimate area of scientific study

8. The seventeenth-century philosopher who believed that the mind is blank at birth and that most knowledge comes through sensory experience is
    a. Plato.   c. René Descartes.
    b. Aristotle.   d. John Locke.

9. Which seventeenth-century philosopher believed that some ideas are innate?
    a. Aristotle   c. René Descartes
    b. Plato.   d. John Locke.

10. Which psychological perspective emphasizes the interaction of the brain and body in behavior?
    a. neuroscience
    b. cognitive
    c. behavioral
    d. behavior genetics

11. A psychologist who explores how Asian and North American definitions of attractiveness differ is working from the _____ perspective.
    a. behavioral   c. cognitive
    b. evolutionary   d. social-cultural

12. A psychologist who conducts experiments solely intended to build psychology's knowledge base is engaged in
    a. basic research.
    b. applied research.
    c. industrial-organizational research.
    d. clinical research.

13. Psychologists who study, assess, and treat troubled people are called
    a. basic researchers.
    b. applied psychologists.
    c. clinical psychologists.
    d. psychiatrists.

14. Today, psychology is a discipline that
    a. connects with a diversity of other fields.
    b. is largely independent of other disciplines.
    c. is focused primarily on basic research.
    d. is focused primarily on applied research.

15. (Close-Up) In order, the sequence of steps in the SQ3R method is
    a. survey, review, retrieve, question, read.
    b. review, question, survey, read, retrieve.
    c. question, review, survey, read, retrieve.
    d. survey, question, read, retrieve, review.

16. Psychologists who study how brain activity is linked to memory, perception, and other thought processes are called
    a. humanistic psychologists.
    b. psychiatrists.
    c. clinical psychologists.
    d. cognitive neuroscientists.

17. The first psychology laboratory was established by _____ in the year _____ .
    a. Wundt; 1879   c. Freud; 1900
    b. James; 1890   d. Watson; 1913

18. Who would be most likely to agree with the statement, "Psychology is the science of mental life"?
    a. Wilhelm Wundt
    b. John Watson
    c. Ivan Pavlov
    d. virtually any American psychologist during the 1960s

19. In psychology, *behavior* is best defined as
    a. anything a person says, does, or feels.
    b. any action we can observe and record.
    c. any action, whether observable or not.
    d. anything we can infer from a person's actions.

20. Carl Rogers and Abraham Maslow are most closely associated with
    a. cognitive psychology.
    b. behaviorism.
    c. psychodynamic theory.
    d. humanistic psychology.

21. In defining *psychology*, the text notes that psychology is most accurately described as a
    a. way of asking and answering questions.
    b. field engaged in solving applied problems.
    c. set of findings related to behavior and mental processes.
    d. nonscientific approach to the study of mental disorders.

22. Two historical roots of psychology are the disciplines of
    a. philosophy and chemistry.
    b. physiology and chemistry.
    c. philosophy and biology.
    d. philosophy and physics.

23. The Greek philosopher who believed that intelligence was inherited was
    a. Aristotle.   c. Descartes.
    b. Plato.   d. Simonides.

24. The way we encode, process, store, and retrieve information is the primary concern of the _____ perspective.
    a. neuroscience   c. social-cultural
    b. evolutionary   d. cognitive

25. Which of the following individuals is also a physician?
    a. clinical psychologist
    b. experimental psychologist
    c. psychiatrist
    d. biological psychologist

26. Dr. Jones' research centers on the relationship between changes in our thinking over the life span and changes in moral reasoning. Dr. Jones is most likely a
    a. clinical psychologist.
    b. personality psychologist.
    c. psychiatrist.
    d. developmental psychologist.

27. Which subfield is most directly concerned with studying human behavior in the workplace?
    a. clinical psychology
    b. personality psychology
    c. industrial-organizational psychology
    d. psychiatry

28. Dr. Ernst explains behavior in terms of different situations. Dr. Ernst is working from the _____ perspective.
    a. behavioral   c. social-cultural
    b. evolutionary   d. cognitive

29. Which perspective emphasizes the learning of observable responses?
    a. behavioral   c. neuroscience
    b. social-cultural   d. cognitive

30. A psychologist who studies how worker productivity might be increased by changing office layout is engaged in _____ research.
    a. applied   c. clinical
    b. basic   d. developmental

31. (Close-Up) A major principle underlying the SQ3R study method is that
    a. people learn and remember material best when they actively process it.

b. many students overestimate their mastery of text and lecture material.
c. study time should be spaced over time rather than crammed into one session.
d. overlearning disrupts efficient retention.

32. The biopsychosocial approach emphasizes the importance of
    a. different levels of analysis in exploring behavior and mental processes.
    b. basic research over pure research.
    c. pure research over basic research.
    d. having a single academic perspective to guide research.

Matching Items

Match each psychological perspective, school, and subfield with its definition or description.

Terms

_____ 1. neuroscience perspective
_____ 2. social-cultural perspective
_____ 3. psychiatry
_____ 4. clinical psychology
_____ 5. behavior genetics perspective
_____ 6. behavioral perspective
_____ 7. industrial-organizational psychology
_____ 8. cognitive perspective
_____ 9. basic research
_____ 10. applied research
_____ 11. evolutionary perspective
_____ 12. psychodynamic perspective
_____ 13. positive psychology
_____ 14. community psychology
_____ 15. behaviorism
_____ 16. cognitive neuroscience

Definitions or Descriptions

a. behavior in the workplace

b. how people differ as products of different environments

c. the study of practical problems

d. the scientific study of the strengths and virtues of human functioning

e. the mechanisms by which observable responses are acquired and changed

f. how the body and brain create emotions, memories, and sensations

g. how we encode, process, store, and retrieve information

h. the view that psychology should be an objective science that avoids reference to mental processes

i. how natural selection favors traits that promote the perpetuation of one's genes

j. the study, assessment, and treatment of troubled people

k. brain activity linked with perception, thinking, memory, and language

l. the disguised effects of unfulfilled wishes and childhood traumas

m. adds to psychology's knowledge base

n. how people interact with their social environment and how social institutions affect individuals and groups

o. how much genes and environment contribute to individual differences

p. the medical treatment of psychological disorders

True–False Items

Place a T or an F in the blank next to each statement.

_____ 1. Psychology's three main levels of analysis often contradict each other.

_____ 2. The primary research tool of the first psychologists was the experiment.

_____ 3. The subject matter of psychology has changed over the history of the field.

_____ 4. Every psychological event is simultaneously a biological event.

_____ 5. Today, most psychologists work within the behavioral perspective.

_____ 6. The major perspectives in psychology contradict one another.

_____ 7. (Close-Up) Repeated self-testing and rehearsal promotes better retention than rereading.

_____ 8. (Close-Up) Overlearning hinders retention.

_____ 9. A major goal of psychology is to teach us how to ask important questions and to think critically as we evaluate competing ideas.

_____ 10. The school of structuralism fell from favor in part because the method of introspection was unreliable.

Essay Question

Explain how researchers working from each of psychology's major perspectives might investigate an emotion such as love. (Use the space below to list the points you want to make, and organize them. Then write the essay on a separate piece of paper.)

TERMS AND CONCEPTS TO REMEMBER

Using your own words, on a separate piece of paper write a brief definition or explanation of each of the following.

1. behaviorism
2. humanistic psychology
3. cognitive neuroscience
4. psychology
5. nature–nurture issue
6. natural selection
7. levels of analysis
8. biopsychosocial approach
9. basic research
10. applied research
11. counseling psychology
12. clinical psychology
13. psychiatry
14. positive psychology
15. community psychology
16. testing effect
17. SQ3R

ANSWERS

Module Review

What Is Psychology?

1. Aristotle; learning; memory; motivation; emotion; perception; personality
2. Wundt; Edward Titchener; structuralism; introspection; unreliable
3. William James; adaptive; functionalism
4. Mary Calkins; Margaret Floy Washburn
5. mental; John B. Watson; B. F. Skinner; observable
6. unconscious; emotional
7. behaviorism; Carl Rogers; Abraham Maslow; humanistic; growth; healthy
8. cognitive; mind; cognitive neuroscience
9. behavior; mental; observe; record; subjective experiences; infer

10. asking and answering questions

11. **b.** is the answer.
a. As the founder of the first psychology laboratory, Wundt certainly based his research on the scientific method.
c. The earliest psychologists, including Wilhelm Wundt, were concerned with the self-examination of covert thoughts, feelings, and other mental processes.

12. **c.** is the answer.

13. **d.** is the answer.

14. **c.** is the answer. Like Darwin, James assumed that thinking, like smelling, developed because it was adaptive.

15. **d.** is the answer. James emphasized the adaptive value of our thoughts and behaviors (functionalism). Titchener used the method of introspection to examine the basic contents of the mind (structuralism).
a. & b. The text does not discuss the views of these psychologists regarding the nature–nurture issue.

Contemporary Psychology

16. biology; philosophy

17. learning; Sigmund Freud; children

18. increasing; globalizing

19. biology; experience

20. Plato; Aristotle

21. John Locke; René Descartes

22. Charles Darwin; evolution; natural selection

23. nurture; nature; psychological; biological

24. **b.** is the answer. Locke believed that all knowledge comes from experience (nurture). Descartes believed that some ideas are innate (nature).

    c. & d. The text does not discuss the views of these philosophers regarding this issue.

25. system; social system; levels; analysis; psychological; social-cultural; biopsychosocial

26. neuroscience

27. evolutionary; behavior genetics

28. psychodynamic

29. behavioral

30. cognitive

31. social-cultural

32. complement

33. **b.** is the answer.

a., c., & d. Each of these perspectives is too narrow to apply to Professor Gutierrez's belief. Moreover, the psychodynamic perspective (a.) emphasizes unconscious processes, in which Professor Gutierrez has not expressed a belief.

34. **d.** is the answer. Because both nature and nurture influence most traits and behaviors, the tension surrounding this issue has dissolved.

35. **c.** is the answer.
a. This perspective emphasizes the influences of physiology on behavior.
b. This perspective emphasizes environmental influences on observable behavior.
d. This perspective emphasizes how behavior and thinking vary across situations and cultures.

36. **a.** is the answer.

37. **a.** is the answer.
b. Neither perspective places any special emphasis on unconscious processes.
c. Neither perspective emphasizes covert behaviors.
d. Introspection was a research method used by the earliest psychologists, not those working from the cognitive perspective.

38. **c.** is the answer.
a. The text suggests just the opposite: By studying behavior from several perspectives, psychologists gain a fuller understanding.
b. & d. Each perspective is useful in that it calls researchers' attention to different aspects of behavior. This is equally true of those perspectives that do not emphasize objective measurement.

39. basic research; applied research

40. counseling; clinical

41. psychiatrists

42. positive psychology

43. community psychologists

44. **c.** is the answer.
a. Industrial-organizational psychologists study and advise on behavior in the workplace.
b. Developmental psychologists investigate behavior and mental processes over the life span.
d. Psychiatrists are medical doctors who treat medical disorders. There is no indication that Terrence is suffering from a medical disorder.

45. **c.** is the answer.
a. Clinical psychology is concerned with the study and treatment of psychological disorders.
b. Psychiatry is the branch of medicine concerned with the physical diagnosis and treatment of psychological disorders.

d. Industrial-organizational psychologists study behavior in the workplace.

Close-Up: Improve Your Retention—and Your Grades!

46. self-testing; rehearsal; testing effect
47. actively
48. SQ3R; a. survey; b. question; c. read; d. retrieve; e. review
    a. Distribute study time.
    b. Process class information actively.
    c. Overlearn material.
    d. Learn to think critically.
    e. Be a smart test-taker.
49. **c.** is the answer.
    a. To be effective, study must be active rather than passive in nature.
    b. Most exams are based on lecture and textbook material.
    d. Cramming hinders retention.
50. **d.** is the answer.
51. **c.** is the answer.

Progress Test

Multiple-Choice Questions

1. **a.** is the answer.
   b. Psychology has never been defined in terms of conscious and unconscious activity.
   c. From the 1920s into the 1960s, psychology was defined as the scientific study of observable behavior.
   d. Psychology today is defined as the scientific study of behavior and mental processes. In its earliest days, however, psychology focused exclusively on mental phenomena.

2. **c.** is the answer.
   a. Wilhelm Wundt, the founder of the first psychology laboratory, was seeking to measure the simplest mental processes.
   b. Sigmund Freud developed an influential theory of personality that focused on unconscious processes.
   d. William James, author of the early textbook *Principles of Psychology,* was a philosopher and was more interested in mental phenomena than observable behavior.

3. **d.** is the answer.
   a. In its earliest days psychology was defined as the science of mental phenomena.
   b. Psychology has never been defined in terms of conscious and unconscious activity.

   c. From the 1920s into the 1960s, psychology was defined as the scientific study of behavior.
4. **a.** is the answer.
5. **d.** is the answer
   a. Wilhelm Wundt founded the first psychology laboratory.
   b. Ivan Pavlov pioneered the study of learning.
   c. Jean Piaget was this century's most influential observer of children.
6. **c.** is the answer.
7. **a.** is the answer. Biology and experience are internal and external influences, respectively.
   b. Rewards and punishments are both external influences on behavior.
   c. Heredity and instinct are both internal influences on behavior.
   d. The legitimacy of the study of mental processes does not relate to the internal/external issue.
8. **d.** is the answer. For Locke, the mind at birth was a blank sheet.
   a. Plato assumed that much of intelligence is inherited and therefore present at birth. Moreover, he was a philosopher of ancient Greece.
   b. Aristotle held essentially the same viewpoint as Locke, but he lived in the fourth century B.C.E.
   c. Descartes believed that knowledge does not depend on experience.
9. **c.** is the answer.
   a. Aristotle was a philosopher in ancient Greece who would have agreed with Locke that knowledge comes from experience.
   b. Plato assumed that character and intelligence are inherited.
   d. Locke believed that the mind is a blank sheet at birth.
10. **a.** is the answer.
    b. The cognitive perspective is concerned with how we encode, process, store, and retrieve information.
    c. The behavioral perspective studies the mechanisms by which observable responses are acquired and changed.
    d. The behavior genetics perspective focuses on the relative contributions of genes and environment to individual differences.
11. **d.** is the answer.
    a. Behavioral psychologists investigate how learned behaviors are acquired. They generally do not focus on subjective opinions, such as attractiveness.
    b. The evolutionary perspective studies how natural selection favors traits that promote the perpetuation of one's genes.

c. Cognitive psychologists study the mechanisms of thinking and memory, and generally do not investigate attitudes. Also, because the question specifies that the psychologist is interested in comparing two cultures, d. is the best answer.

12. **a.** is the answer.
b. & c. Applied and industrial-organizational psychologists tackle practical problems.
d. Clinical psychologists (and researchers) focus on treating troubled people.

13. **c.** is the answer.
d. Psychiatrists are medical doctors rather than psychologists.

14. **a.** is the answer.
c. & d. Psychologists are widely involved in *both* basic and applied research.

15. **d.** is the answer.

16. **d.** is the answer.

17. **a.** is the answer.

18. **a.** is the answer.
b. & d. John Watson, like many American psychologists during this time, believed that psychology should focus on the study of observable behavior.
c. Because he pioneered the study of learning, Pavlov focused on observable behavior and would certainly have *disagreed* with this statement.

19. **b.** is the answer.

20. **d.** is the answer.

21. **a.** is the answer.
b. Psychology is equally involved in basic research.
c. Psychology's knowledge base is constantly expanding.
d. Psychology is the *scientific study* of behavior and mental processes.

22. **c.** is the answer.

23. **b.** is the answer.
a. Aristotle believed that all knowledge originates with sensory experience.
c. Descartes was a philosopher of the seventeenth century.
d. Simonides was a well-known Greek orator.

24. **d.** is the answer.
a. The neuroscience perspective studies the biological bases for a range of psychological phenomena.
b. The evolutionary perspective studies how natural selection favors traits that promote the perpetuation of one's genes.

c. The social-cultural perspective is concerned with variations in behavior across situations and cultures.

25. **c.** is the answer. After earning their M.D. degrees, psychiatrists specialize in the diagnosis and treatment of mental health disorders.
a., b., & d. These psychologists generally earn a Ph.D. rather than an M.D.

26. **d.** is the answer. The emphasis on change during the life span indicates that Dr. Jones is most likely a developmental psychologist.
a. Clinical psychologists study, assess, and treat people who are psychologically troubled.
b. Personality psychologists study our inner traits.
c. Psychiatrists are medical doctors.

27. **c.** is the answer.
a. Clinical psychologists study, assess, and treat people with psychological disorders.
b. & d. Personality psychologists and psychiatrists do not usually study people in work situations.

28. **c.** is the answer.
a. Psychologists who follow the behavioral perspective emphasize observable, external influences on behavior.
b. The evolutionary perspective focuses on how natural selection favors traits that promote the perpetuation of one's genes.
d. The cognitive perspective places emphasis on conscious, rather than unconscious, processes.

29. **a.** is the answer.

30. **a.** is the answer. The research is addressing a practical issue.
b. Basic research is aimed at contributing to the base of knowledge in a given field, not at resolving particular practical problems.
c. & d. Clinical and developmental research would focus on issues relating to psychological disorders and life-span changes, respectively.

31. **a.** is the answer.
b. & c. Although each of these is true, SQ3R is based on the more *general* principle of active learning.
d. In fact, just the opposite is true.

32. **a.** is the answer.
b. & c. The biopsychosocial approach has nothing to do with the relative importance of basic research and applied research and is equally applicable to both.
d. On the contrary, the biopsychosocial approach is based on the idea that single academic perspectives are often limited.

Matching Items

1. f	7. a	13. d
2. b	8. g	14. n
3. p	9. m	15. h
4. j	10. c	16. k
5. o	11. i	
6. e	12. l	

True–False Items

1. F	5. F	9. T
2. F	6. F	10. T
3. T	7. T	
4. T	8. F	

Essay Question

A psychologist working from the neuroscience perspective might study the brain circuits and body chemistry that trigger attraction and sexual arousal. A psychologist working from the evolutionary perspective might analyze how love has facilitated the survival of our species. A psychologist working from the behavior genetics perspective might attempt to compare the extent to which the emotion is attributable to our genes and the extent to which it is attributable to our environment. A psychologist working from the psychodynamic perspective might search for evidence that a person's particular emotional feelings are disguised effects of unfulfilled wishes. A psychologist working from the behavioral perspective might study the external stimuli, such as body language, that elicit and reward approach behaviors toward another person. A psychologist working from the cognitive perspective might study how our thought processes, attitudes, and beliefs foster attachment to loved ones, and a psychologist working from the social-cultural perspective might explore situational influences on attraction and how the development and expression of love vary across cultural groups.

Terms and Concepts to Remember

1. **Behaviorism** is the view that psychology should focus only on the scientific study of observable behaviors without reference to mental processes.
2. **Humanistic psychology** is a historically significant perspective that emphasized the growth potential of healthy people.
3. **Cognitive neuroscience** is the interdisciplinary study of how brain activity is linked with cognition (including thinking, language, memory, and perception).
4. **Psychology** is the science of behavior and mental processes.
5. The **nature–nurture issue** is the controversy over the relative contributions that genes (nature) and experience (nurture) make to the development of psychological traits and behaviors.
6. **Natural selection** is the principle that those traits of a species that contribute to reproduction and survival are most likely to be passed on to succeeding generations.
7. Psychologists analyze behavior and mental processes from differing complementary views, or **levels of analysis,** from biological to psychological to social-cultural.
8. The **biopsychosocial approach** is an integrated perspective that focuses on biological, psychological, and social-cultural levels of analysis for a given behavior or mental process.
9. **Basic research** is pure science that aims to increase psychology's scientific knowledge base rather than to solve practical problems.
10. **Applied research** is scientific study that aims to solve practical problems.
11. **Counseling psychology** is the branch of psychology that helps people with challenges in their daily lives and in achieving greater well-being.
12. **Clinical psychology** is the branch of psychology concerned with the study, assessment, and treatment of people with psychological disorders.
13. **Psychiatry** is the branch of medicine concerned with the physical diagnosis and treatment of psychological disorders.
14. **Positive psychology** is the scientific study of the strengths and virtues of human functioning that help people and communities thrive.
15. **Community psychology** is the branch of psychology concerned with how people interact with their social environments and how social institutions affect individuals and groups.
16. The **testing effect** (also called the *retrieval practice effect* or *test-enhanced learning*) refers to the beneficial effects on memory of actively retrieving, rather than simply reading, information.
17. **SQ3R** is a study method consisting of five steps: *s*urvey, *q*uestion, *r*ead, *r*etrieve, and *r*eview.

Thinking Critically With Psychological Science

MODULE OVERVIEW

Module 2 explains the limits of intuition and common sense in reasoning about behavior and mental processes. To counteract our human tendency toward faulty reasoning, psychologists adopt a scientific attitude that is based on curiosity, skepticism, humility, and critical thinking.

Module 2 concludes with a discussion of several questions people often ask about psychology, including why animal research is relevant, whether laboratory experiments are ethical, whether behavior varies with culture and gender, and whether psychology's principles don't have the potential for misuse.

NOTE: Answer guidelines for all Module 2 questions begin on page 18.

MODULE REVIEW

First, skim each section, noting headings and boldface items. After you have read the section, review each objective by answering the fill-in questions that follow it. In some cases, Study Tips explain how best to learn a difficult concept and Applications help you to know how well you understand the material. As you proceed, evaluate your performance by consulting the answers beginning on page 18. Do not continue with the next section until you understand each answer. If you need to, review or reread the section in the textbook before continuing.

The Need for Psychological Science

Objective 2-1: Explain how hindsight bias, overconfidence, and the tendency to perceive order in random events illustrate why science-based answers are more valid than those based on intuition and common sense.

1. The tendency to perceive an outcome that has occurred as being obvious and predictable is
called the _____
_____ . This phenomenon is
_____ (rare/common) in
_____ (children/adults/both children and adults).

2. Our everyday thinking is also limited by
_____ in what we think we know.

3. Most people are _____
(better/worse/equally wrong) in predicting their social behavior.

4. Another common tendency is to perceive order in
_____ _____ .

5. Patterns and streaks in random sequences occur
_____ (more/less) often than people expect, and they _____ (do/do not) appear random.

Objective 2-2: Explain how the three main components of the scientific attitude relate to critical thinking.

6. The scientific approach is characterized by the attitudes of _____ ,
_____ , and
_____ .

7. Scientific inquiry thus encourages reasoning that examines assumptions, discerns hidden values, evaluates evidence, and assesses conclusions, which is called _____
_____ .

STUDY TIP: Try applying a scientific attitude toward how you evaluate your knowledge of psychology in preparation for an upcoming quiz or exam. As is true of researchers, many students develop a false sense of overconfidence in their mastery of course material. Be skeptical! Remain humble! You'll likely do better.

APPLICATIONS:

8. The scientific attitude in psychology refers to the fact that
   a. psychologists study only observable behaviors.
   b. psychologists study thoughts and actions with an attitude of skepticism and derive their conclusions from direct observations.
   c. psychological research should be free of value judgments.
   d. all of these statements are true.

9. The scientific attitude of humility is based on the idea that
   a. researchers must evaluate new ideas and theories objectively rather than accept them blindly.
   b. scientific theories must be testable.
   c. simple explanations of behavior make better theories than do complex explanations.
   d. researchers must be prepared to reject their own ideas in the face of conflicting evidence.

Frequently Asked Questions About Psychology

Objective 2-3: Explain the value of simplified laboratory conditions in illuminating everyday life.

10. In laboratory experiments, psychologists' concern is not with specific behaviors but with the underlying theoretical _____ .

11. Psychologists conduct experiments on simplified behaviors in a laboratory environment to gain _____ over the many variables present in the "real world." In doing so, they are able to test _____ _____ of behavior that also operate in the real world.

Objective 2-4: Discuss whether psychological research can be generalized across cultures and genders.

12. Culture refers to the enduring _____ , _____ , _____ , and _____ shared by a large group of people and passed on from one generation to the next.

13. Although specific attitudes and behaviors vary across cultures, the underlying _____ are the same. For instance, throughout the world people diagnosed with _____ exhibit the same _____ malfunction. Likewise, similarities between the _____ far outweigh differences.

Objective 2-5: Explain why psychologists study animals, and describe the ethical guidelines that safeguard human and animal research participants.

14. Many psychologists study animals because they are fascinating. More important, they study animals because of the _____ (similarities/differences) between humans and other animals. These studies have led to treatments for human _____ and to a better understanding of human functioning.

15. Some people question whether experiments with animals are _____ . They wonder whether it is right to place the _____ of humans over those of animals.

16. Opposition to animal experimentation also raises the question of what _____ should protect the well-being of animals.

17. The ethics code of the _____ _____ _____ urges researchers to obtain participants' _____ _____ and fully _____ people after the research.

Describe two other ethical guidelines for psychological research.

Objective 2-6: Discuss whether psychology is free of value judgments.

18. Psychologists' values _____ (do/ do not) influence their theories, observations, and professional advice.

19. Although psychology _____ (can/cannot) be used to manipulate people, its purpose is to _____ .

APPLICATIONS:

20. Your best friend criticizes psychological research for being artificial and having no relevance to behavior in real life. In defense of psychology's use of laboratory experiments you point out that
    a. psychologists make every attempt to avoid artificiality by setting up experiments that closely simulate real-world environments.
    b. psychologists who conduct basic research are not concerned with the applicability of their findings to the real world.
    c. most psychological research is not conducted in a laboratory environment.
    d. psychologists intentionally study behavior in simplified environments in order to gain greater control over variables and to test general principles that help to explain many behaviors.

21. A friend majoring in anthropology is critical of psychological research because it often ignores the influence of culture on thoughts and actions. You point out that
    a. there is very little evidence that cultural diversity has a significant effect on specific behaviors and attitudes.
    b. most researchers assign participants to experimental and control conditions in such a way as to fairly represent the cultural diversity of the population under study.
    c. it is impossible for psychologists to control for every possible variable that might influence research participants.
    d. even when specific thoughts and actions vary across cultures, as they often do, the underlying processes are much the same.

PROGRESS TEST

Multiple-Choice Questions

Circle your answers to the following questions and check them with the answers on page 19. If your answer is incorrect, read the explanation for why it is incorrect and then consult the text.

1. The scientific attitude of skepticism is based on the belief that
    a. people are rarely candid in revealing their thoughts.
    b. mental processes can't be studied objectively.
    c. the scientist's intuition about behavior is usually correct.
    d. ideas need to be tested against observable evidence.

2. Psychologists' personal values
    a. have little influence on how their experiments are conducted.
    b. do not influence the interpretation of experimental results because of the use of statistical techniques that guard against subjective bias.
    c. can bias both scientific observation and interpretation of data.
    d. have little influence on investigative methods but a significant effect on interpretation.

3. Juwan eagerly opened an online trading account, believing that his market savvy would allow him to pick stocks that would make him a rich day trader. This belief best illustrates
    a. a scientific attitude.
    b. critical thinking.
    c. hindsight bias.
    d. overconfidence.

4. Which statement about the ethics of experimentation with people and animals is FALSE?
    a. The same processes by which humans learn are present in rats, monkeys, and other animals.
    b. Views on whether it is right to place the well-being of humans above that of animals are the same in every culture.
    c. The American Psychological Association and the British Psychological Society have set strict guidelines for the care and treatment of human and animal subjects.
    d. Most psychological studies are free of such stress as the delivery of electric shock.

5. Which of the following BEST describes the hindsight bias?

  a. Events seem more predictable before they have occurred.

  b. Events seem more predictable after they have occurred.

  c. A person's intuition is usually correct.

  d. A person's intuition is usually not correct.

6. Debriefing refers to

  a. the perception that two negatively correlated variables are positively correlated.

  b. explaining the purpose of a research study after its conclusion.

  c. an insignificant correlation.

  d. a correlation that equals –1.0.

Matching Items

Match each psychological perspective, school, and subfield with its definition or description.

Terms

_____ **1.** culture
_____ **2.** hindsight bias
_____ **3.** critical thinking
_____ **4.** informed consent
_____ **5.** debrief

TERMS AND CONCEPTS TO REMEMBER

Using your own words, on a separate piece of paper write a brief definition or explanation of each of the following.

1. hindsight bias

2. critical thinking

3. culture

4. informed consent

5. debriefing

ANSWERS

Module Review

The Need for Psychological Science

1. hindsight bias; common; both children and adults

2. overconfidence

3. equally wrong

7. Which of the following is true, according to the text?

  a. Because laboratory experiments are artificial, any principles discovered cannot be applied to everyday behaviors.

  b. Psychological science demonstrates why we cannot rely on intuition and common sense.

  c. Psychology's theories reflect common sense.

  d. Psychology has few ties to other disciplines.

Definitions or Descriptions

  a. giving research participants information that enables them to choose whether to participate

  b. shared ideas and behaviors passed from one generation to the next

  c. explaining the purpose of a research study after its conclusion

  d. "I-knew-it-all-along" phenomenon

  e. reasoning that does not blindly accept arguments

4. random events

5. more; do not

6. curiosity; skepticism; humility

7. critical thinking

8. **b.** is the answer. Psychologists approach their studies of behavior and mental processes with attitudes of curiosity, skepticism, and humility.

  a. Psychologists study both overt (observable) behaviors and covert thoughts and feelings.

  c. Psychologists' values definitely do influence their research.

9. **d.** is the answer.

  a. This follows from the attitude of skepticism, rather than humility.

  b. & **c.** Although both of these are true of the scientific method, neither has anything to do with humility.

Frequently Asked Questions About Psychology

10. principles

11. control; general principles

12. ideas; behaviors; attitudes; traditions
13. processes; dyslexia; brain; genders
14. similarities; diseases
15. ethical; well-being
16. safeguards
17. American Psychological Association; informed consent; debrief

Ethical guidelines require investigators to protect research participants from harm and discomfort and treat information obtained from participants confidentially.

18. do
19. can; enlighten
20. **d.** is the answer.
21. **d.** is the answer.
    a. In fact, just the opposite is true.
    b. Actually, psychological experiments tend to use the most readily available people, often white North American college students.
    c. Although this may be true, psychological experiments remain important because they help explain underlying processes of human behavior everywhere. Therefore, d. is a much better response than c.

Progress Test

Multiple-Choice Questions

1. **d.** is the answer.
2. **c.** is the answer.
   a., b., & d. Psychologists' personal values can influence all of these.
3. **d.** is the answer.
   a. & b. Both of these answers reflect the opposite of Juwan's thinking.
   c. This is the tendency to believe, after learning an outcome, that one could have foreseen it.
4. **b.** is the answer. Just the opposite is true. Cultures differ in their views about valuing human well-being over animal well-being.
5. **b.** is the answer.
   a. The phenomenon is related to hindsight rather than foresight.

c. & d. The phenomenon doesn't involve whether the intuitions are correct but rather people's attitude that they had the correct intuition.
6. **b.** is the answer.
7. **b.** is the answer.
   a. In fact, the artificiality of experiments is part of an intentional attempt to create a controlled environment in which to test theoretical principles that are applicable to all behaviors.
   c. Some psychological theories go against what we consider common sense; furthermore, on many issues that psychology addresses, it's far from clear what the "common sense" position is.
   d. Psychology has always had ties to other disciplines, and in recent times, these ties have been increasing.

Matching Items

1. b
2. d
3. e
4. a
5. c

Terms and Concepts to Remember

1. **Hindsight bias** refers to the tendency to believe, after learning an outcome, that one would have foreseen it; also called the *I-knew-it-all-along phenomenon.*
2. **Critical thinking** is careful reasoning that examines assumptions, discerns hidden values, evaluates evidence, and assesses conclusions.
3. **Culture** is the enduring behaviors, ideas, attitudes, and traditions shared by a large group of people and transmitted from one generation to the next.
4. **Informed consent** is the ethical practice of giving research participants enough information to enable them to choose whether they wish to take part in a study.
5. **Debriefing** is the ethical practice of explaining a study, including its purpose and any deceptions, to participants after they have finished.

Research Strategies: How Psychologists Ask and Answer Questions

CHAPTER OVERVIEW

Module 3 describes the scientific method. It then explains how psychologists employ the research strategies of description, correlation, and experimentation in order to objectively describe, predict, and explain behavior.

The next section discusses how statistical reasoning is used to help psychologists describe data and to generalize from instances. To describe data, psychologists often rely on measures of central tendency such as the mean, median, and mode, as well as variation measures such as the range and standard deviation. Statistical reasoning also helps psychologists determine when it is safe to generalize from a sample to the larger population.

Module 3 introduces a number of concepts and issues that will play an important role in later modules. Pay particular attention to the strengths and weaknesses of descriptive and correlational research. In addition, make sure that you understand the method of experimentation, especially the importance of control conditions and the difference between independent and dependent variables. Finally, you should be able to discuss three important principles concerning populations and samples, as well as the concept of significance in testing differences.

NOTE: Answer guidelines for all Module 3 questions begin on page 31.

MODULE REVIEW

First, skim each section, noting headings and bold-face items. After you have read the section, review each objective by answering the fill-in and essay-type questions that follow it. In some cases, Study Tips explain how best to learn a difficult concept and Applications help you to know how well you understand the material. As you proceed, evaluate your performance by consulting the answers beginning on page 31. Do not continue with the next section until you understand each answer. If you need to, review or reread the section in the textbook before continuing.

How *Do* Psychologists Ask and Answer Questions?

Objective 3-1: Describe how theories advance psychological science.

1. Psychological science uses the _____ _____ to evaluate competing ideas. Psychologists make careful _____ and form _____ , which are _____ based on new _____ .

2. An explanation using an integrated set of principles that organizes and predicts behaviors or events is a _____ . Testable predictions that allow a scientist to evaluate a theory are called _____ . These predictions give direction to _____ .

3. To prevent theoretical biases from influencing scientific observations, research must be reported precisely—using clear _____ _____ of all concepts—so that others can _____ the findings.

4. The test of a useful theory is the extent to which it effectively _____ a range of self-reports and observations and implies clear _____ .

5. Psychologists conduct research using _____ , _____ , and _____ methods.

Objective 3-2: Describe how psychologists use case studies, surveys, and naturalistic observation to observe and describe behavior, and explain the importance of random sampling.

6. The research strategy in which one or more individuals is studied in depth in order to reveal universal principles of behavior is the

   _____ _____ .

7. Although case studies can suggest _____ for further study, a potential problem with this method is that any given individual may be _____ .

8. The research method in which people or animals are directly observed in their natural environments is called _____

   _____ .

9. Using naturalistic observation, researchers have found that people are more likely to laugh in _____ situations than in _____ situations. Also, using observations of walking speed and the accuracy of public clocks, researchers have concluded that the pace of life _____ (varies/ does not vary) from one culture to another.

10. The method in which a group of people is questioned about their attitudes or behavior is the _____ . An important factor in the validity of survey research is the _____ of questions.

11. We are more likely to overgeneralize from samples we observe, especially _____ ones.

12. Surveys try to obtain a _____ sample, one that will be representative of the _____ being studied. In such a sample, every person _____ (does/does not) have a chance of being included.

13. Large, representative samples _____ (are/are not) better than small ones.

14. Case studies, surveys, and naturalistic observation do not explain behavior; they simply _____ it.

APPLICATIONS:

15. Your roommate is conducting a survey to learn how many hours the typical student studies each day. She plans to pass out her questionnaire to the members of her sorority. You point out that her findings will be flawed because
   a. she has not specified an independent variable.
   b. she has not specified a dependent variable.
   c. the sample will probably not be representative of the population of interest.
   d. of all of these reasons.

16. A professor constructs a questionnaire to determine how students at the university feel about nuclear disarmament. Which of the following techniques should be used to survey a random sample of the student body?
   a. Every student should be sent the questionnaire.
   b. Only students majoring in psychology should be asked to complete the questionnaire.
   c. Only students living on campus should be asked to complete the questionnaire.
   d. From an alphabetical listing of all students, every tenth (or fifteenth, e.g.) student should be asked to complete the questionnaire.

Objective 3-3: Describe positive and negative correlations, and explain how correlational measures can aid the process of prediction but not provide evidence of cause-effect relationships.

17. When changes in one factor are accompanied by changes in another, the two factors are said to be _____ , and one is thus able to _____ the other. The statistical expression of this relationship is called a _____ _____ . A graphical representation of this relationship is called a _____ .

18. If two factors increase or decrease together, they are _____ _____ . If, however, one decreases as the other increases, they are _____ _____ . Another way to state the latter is that the two variables relate _____ .

19. A negative correlation between two variables does not indicate the _____ or _____ of the relationship. Nor does correlation prove _____ ; rather, it merely indicates the possibility of a _____ -_____ relationship.

If your level of test anxiety goes down as your time spent studying for the exam goes up, would you say these events are positively or negatively correlated? Explain your reasoning.

20. A correlation between two events or behaviors means only that one event can be

_____ from the other.

21. Because two events may both be caused by some other _____ , a correlation does not mean that one _____ the other. For this reason, correlation thus does not enable _____ .

STUDY TIP: Many students find the concept of correlation confusing. A common mistake is the belief that a negative correlation indicates a weak or absent relationship between two variables. Remember that correlation does not prove causation; rather, it indicates the degree to which you can predict changes in one variable from another. The strength of a correlation, indicated by a numerical value, is independent of the direction (positive [+] or negative [–]) of the relationship. A negative correlation simply means that two variables change in opposite directions, such as when sales of hot chocolate decrease as the average daily temperature increases.

APPLICATIONS:

22. A researcher was interested in determining whether her students' test performance could be predicted from their proximity to the front of the classroom. So she matched her students' scores on a math test with their seating position. This study is an example of
    a. experimentation.
    b. correlational research.
    c. a survey.
    d. naturalistic observation.

23. If eating saturated fat and the likelihood of contracting cancer are positively correlated, which of the following is true?
    a. Saturated fat causes cancer.
    b. People who are prone to develop cancer prefer foods containing saturated fat.
    c. A separate factor links the consumption of saturated fat to cancer.
    d. None of these statements are necessarily true.

24. If height and body weight are positively correlated, which of the following is true?
    a. There is a cause-effect relationship between height and weight.
    b. As height increases, weight decreases.
    c. Knowing a person's height, one can predict his or her weight.
    d. All of these statements are true.

Objective 3-4: Explain how experiments help researchers isolate cause and effect, focusing on the characteristics of experimentation that make this possible.

25. To isolate _____ and _____ , researchers control for other _____ .

26. Research studies have found that breast-fed infants _____ (do/do not) grow up with higher intelligence scores than those of infants who are bottle-fed with cow's milk. To study cause-effect relationships, psychologists conduct _____ . Using this method and _____ assigning participants to groups, a researcher _____ the factor of interest while _____ _____ (controlling) other factors.

27. If a _____ changes when an _____ factor is varied, the researcher knows the factor is having an _____ .

28. An experiment must involve at least two conditions: the _____ condition, in which the experimental treatment is present, and the _____ condition, in which it is absent.

29. To ensure that the two groups are identical, experimenters rely on the _____ _____ of individuals to the experimental conditions.

30. The factor that is being manipulated in an experiment is called the _____ variable. The measurable factor that may change as a result of these manipulations is called the _____ variable. Other factors that can potentially influence the results of an experiment are called _____ _____ .

31. When neither the participants nor the person collecting the data knows which condition a participant is in, the researcher is making use of the _____-_____ procedure.

STUDY TIP: Students often confuse independent variables and dependent variables. Remember that independent variables are manipulated (controlled) directly by the researcher to determine how they affect dependent variables. Dependent variables are the behaviors and mental processes that psychologists are trying to understand. In a sense, dependent variables *depend* on the actions of independent variables. When you are struggling to distinguish two variables, ask yourself, "Which of these two variables can affect the other?" Consider, for example, a researcher investigating caffeine and reaction time. After randomly assigning different students to groups that drink a highly caffeinated drink and a weakly caffeinated drink, she measures each student's speed in pushing a button in response to a signal light. Which variable is the independent variable, and which is the dependent variable? If the answer is not obvious, try the test question, "Which variable can affect the other?" Clearly, reaction time cannot affect caffeine. So, in this example, the dose of caffeine is the independent variable and reaction time is the dependent variable.

32. Researchers sometimes give certain participants a pseudotreatment, called a _____ , and compare their behavior with that of participants who receive the actual treatment. When merely thinking that one is receiving a treatment produces results, a _____ _____ is said to occur.

33. The aim of an experiment is to _____ a(n) _____ variable, measure the _____ variable, and _____ all other variables.

Explain at least one advantage of the experiment as a research method.

STUDY TIP/APPLICATIONS: The concepts of control and operational definition are important in experimental research. In an experiment, researchers strive to hold constant (control) the possible effects of all variables on the dependent variable, except the one that is being manipulated (independent variable). Operational definitions, which were explained earlier, are like recipes for measuring a variable so that other researchers can replicate your results. They are much more precise than dictionary definitions. For example, the dictionary might define intelligence as "the capacity to reason." Because this definition is too vague for research purposes, a psychologist might create the operational definition of intelligence as "a person's answers to a specific set of IQ test questions." Test your understanding of these important concepts by completing the following exercises.

34. You decide to test your belief that men drink more soft drinks than women by finding out whether more soft drinks are consumed per day in the men's dorm than in the women's dorm. Your belief is a(n) _____ , and your research prediction is a(n) _____ .
    a. hypothesis; theory
    b. theory; hypothesis
    c. independent variable; dependent variable
    d. dependent variable; independent variable

35. The concept of control is important in psychological research because
    a. without control over independent and dependent variables, researchers cannot describe, predict, or explain behavior.
    b. experimental control allows researchers to study the influence of one or two independent variables on a dependent variable while holding other potential influences constant.

    c. without experimental control, results cannot be generalized from a sample to a population.

    d. of all of these reasons.

36. Martina believes that high doses of caffeine slow a person's reaction time. To test this belief, she has five friends each drink three 8-ounce cups of coffee and then measures their reaction time on a learning task. What is wrong with Martina's research strategy?

    a. No independent variable is specified.

    b. No dependent variable is specified.

    c. There is no control condition.

    d. There is no provision for replication of the findings.

37. Rashad, who is participating in a psychology experiment on the effects of alcohol on perception, is truthfully told by the experimenter that he has been assigned to the "high-dose condition." What is wrong with this experiment?

    a. There is no control condition.

    b. Rashad's expectations concerning the effects of "high doses" of alcohol on perception may influence his performance.

    c. Rashad was given a placebo, so the results may be tainted.

    d. All of these statements are correct.

38. Which of the following procedures is an example of the use of a placebo?

    a. In a test of the effects of a drug on memory, a participant is led to believe that a harmless pill actually contains an active drug.

    b. A participant in an experiment is led to believe that a pill, which actually contains an active drug, is harmless.

    c. Participants in an experiment are not told which treatment condition is in effect.

    d. Neither the participants nor the experimenter knows which treatment condition is in effect.

SUMMARY STUDY TIP: As we will note through this Study Guide, preparing a table to summarize what you have learned about a topic is a good way to promote understanding. The text includes a table that compares the three research methods. Without looking at the text, try to complete that table on your own (on the next page). We've partially filled in a couple of column entries for you.

COMPARING RESEARCH METHODS

Research Method	Basic Purpose	How Conducted	What Is Manipulated	Weaknesses
Descriptive	observations	Do case studies, surveys, or naturalistic	Nothing	
Correlational	To detect naturally			
Experimental	To explore			

Statistical Reasoning in Everyday Life

Objective 3-5: Describe the three measures of central tendency, and discuss the relative usefulness of the two measures of variation.

39. Researchers use _____ to help them see and interpret their observations.

40. Once researchers have gathered their _____ , they must _____ them. One simple way of visually representing data is to use a

_____ _____ .

It is important to read the _____

_____ and note the

_____ to avoid being misled by

misrepresented data.

41. The three measures of central tendency are the

_____ , the _____ ,

and the _____ .

42. The most frequently occurring score in a distribu-

tion is called the _____ .

43. The mean is computed as the _____

_____ of all the scores divided by

the _____ of scores.

44. The median is the score at the _____

percentile.

45. When a distribution is lopsided, or

_____ , the _____

(mean/median/mode) can be biased by a few

extreme scores.

46. Averages derived from scores with

_____ (high/low) variability are

more reliable than those with _____

(high/low) variability.

47. The measures of variation include the

_____ and the

_____ _____ .

48. The range is computed as the _____

_____ .

49. The range provides a(n) _____

(crude/accurate) estimate of variation because it

_____ (is/is not) influenced by

extreme scores.

50. The standard deviation is a _____

(more accurate/less accurate) measure of varia-

tion than the range. Unlike the range, the

standard deviation _____

(does/does not) use information from each score

in the distribution.

51. The symmetrical, bell-shaped distribution in

which most scores fall near the

_____ with fewer and fewer near

the extremes is called the _____

_____ .

APPLICATIONS:

52. The football team's punter wants to determine
how consistent his punting distances have been
during the past season. He should compute the
   a. mean.   c. mode.
   b. median.   d. standard deviation.

53. Esteban refuses to be persuaded by an adver-
tiser's claim that people using their brand of
gasoline average 50 miles per gallon. His decision
probably is based on
   a. the possibility that the average is the mean,
      which could be artificially inflated by a few
      extreme scores.
   b. the absence of information about the size of
      the sample studied.
   c. the absence of information about the variation
      in sample scores.
   d. all of these statements.

54. Bob scored 43 out of 70 points on his psychology exam. He was worried until he discovered that
most of the class earned the same score. Bob's
score was equal to the
   a. mean.   c. mode.
   b. median.   d. range.

55. The four families on your block all have annual
household incomes of $25,000. If a new fam-
ily with an annual income of $75,000 moved in,
which measure of central tendency would be
most affected?
   a. mean   c. mode
   b. median   d. standard deviation

Objective 3-6: Explain how we know whether an
observed difference can be generalized to other
populations.

56. It is safer to generalize from a _____

sample than from a _____ sample.

57. Averages are more reliable when they are based

on scores with _____ (high/low)

variability.

58. Small samples provide a _____

(more/less) reliable basis for generalizing than

large samples.

59. Tests of statistical _____ are used

to estimate whether observed differences are

real—that is, to make sure that they are not

simply the result of _____ varia-

tion. The differences are probably real if the

sample averages are _____ and

the difference between them is _____ (relatively small/relatively large).

60. Statistical significance does not necessarily indicate the importance or _____ significance of a difference or result.

APPLICATION

61. Dr. Salazar recently completed an experiment in which she compared reasoning ability in a sample of females and a sample of males. The means of the female and male samples equaled 21 and 19, respectively, on a 25-point scale. A statistical test revealed that her results were not statistically significant. What can Dr. Salazar conclude?
    a. Females have superior reasoning ability.
    b. The difference in the means of the two samples is probably due to chance variation.
    c. The difference in the means of the two samples is reliable.
    d. She cannot reach any of these conclusions.

PROGRESS TEST

Multiple-Choice Questions

Circle your answers to the following questions and check them with the answers beginning on page 33. If your answer is incorrect, read the explanation for why it is incorrect and then consult the text.

1. After detailed study of a gunshot wound victim, a psychologist concludes that the brain region destroyed is likely to be important for memory functions. Which type of research did the psychologist use to deduce this?
   a. the case study   c. correlation
   b. a survey   d. experimentation

2. In an experiment to determine the effects of exercise on motivation, exercise is the
   a. control condition.
   b. intervening variable.
   c. independent variable.
   d. dependent variable.

3. To determine the effects of a new drug on memory, one group of people is given a pill that contains the drug. A second group is given a sugar pill that does not contain the drug. This second group constitutes the
   a. random sample.   c. control group.
   b. experimental group. d. test group.

4. *Theories* are defined as
   a. testable propositions.
   b. factors that may change in response to manipulation.
   c. statistical indexes.
   d. principles that help to organize observations and predict behaviors or events.

5. A psychologist studies the play behavior of young children by watching groups during recess at school. Which type of research is being used?
   a. correlation
   b. case study
   c. experimentation
   d. naturalistic observation

6. To ensure that other researchers can repeat their work, psychologists use
   a. control groups.
   b. random assignment.
   c. double-blind procedures.
   d. operational definitions.

7. Which of the following is NOT a basic research technique used by psychologists?
   a. description
   b. replication
   c. experimentation
   d. correlation

8. If shoe size and IQ are negatively correlated, which of the following is true?
   a. People with large feet tend to have high IQs.
   b. People with small feet tend to have high IQs.
   c. People with small feet tend to have low IQs.
   d. IQ is unpredictable based on a person's shoe size.

9. Which of the following would be best for determining whether alcohol impairs memory?
   a. case study   c. survey
   b. naturalistic observation d. experiment

10. Well-done surveys measure attitudes in a representative subset, or _____ , of an entire group, or _____ .
    a. population; random sample
    b. control group; experimental group
    c. experimental group; control group
    d. random sample; population

11. What is the mean of the following distribution of scores: 2, 3, 7, 6, 1, 4, 9, 5, 8, 2?
    a. 5   c. 4.7
    b. 4   d. 3.7

12. What is the median of the following distribution of scores: 1, 3, 7, 7, 2, 8, 4?
    a. 1
    b. 2
    c. 3
    d. 4

13. What is the mode of the following distribution: 8, 2, 1, 1, 3, 7, 6, 2, 0, 2?
    a. 1
    b. 2
    c. 3
    d. 7

14. Which of the following is important when generalizing from a sample to the population?
    a. the sample be representative of the population
    b. the sample be large
    c. the scores in the sample have low variability
    d. all of these conditions exist

15. When a difference between two groups is statistically significant, this means that
    a. the difference is statistically real but of little practical significance.
    b. the difference is probably the result of sampling variation.
    c. the difference is not likely to be due to chance variation.
    d. all of these statements are true.

16. A lopsided set of scores that includes a number of extreme or unusual values is said to be
    a. symmetrical.
    b. normal.
    c. skewed.
    d. dispersed.

17. Which of the following is the measure of central tendency that would be most affected by a few extreme scores?
    a. mean
    b. range
    c. median
    d. mode

18. Which of the following research methods does NOT belong with the others?
    a. case study
    b. survey
    c. naturalistic observation
    d. experiment

19. To prevent the possibility that a placebo effect or researchers' expectations will influence a study's results, scientists employ
    a. control groups.
    b. experimental groups.
    c. random assignment.
    d. the double-blind procedure.

20. In an experiment to determine the effects of attention on memory, memory is the
    a. control condition.
    b. intervening variable.
    c. independent variable.
    d. dependent variable.

21. Which of the following is NOT characteristic of a normal curve?
    a. The distribution is bell-shaped and symmetrical.
    b. Most scores fall near the mean.
    c. About 95 percent of all scores fall within one standard deviation on either side of the mean.
    d. The distribution describes many types of psychological data.

22. The procedure designed to ensure that the experimental and control groups do not differ in any way that might affect the experiment's results is called
    a. variable controlling.
    b. random assignment.
    c. representative sampling.
    d. stratification.

23. In generalizing from a sample to the population, it is important that
    a. the sample be representative.
    b. the sample be nonrandom.
    c. the sample not be too large.
    d. all of these conditions exist.

24. The strength of the relationship between two vivid events will most likely be
    a. significant.
    b. positive.
    c. negative.
    d. overestimated.

25. Which type of research would allow you to determine whether students' grades accurately predict later income?
    a. case study
    b. naturalistic observation
    c. experimentation
    d. correlation

26. In a test of the effects of air pollution, groups of students performed a reaction-time task in a polluted or an unpolluted room. To what condition were students in the unpolluted room exposed?
    a. experimental
    b. control
    c. randomly assigned
    d. dependent

27. To study the effects of lighting on mood, Dr. Cooper had students fill out questionnaires in brightly lit or dimly lit rooms. In this study, the independent variable consisted of
 a. the number of students assigned to each group.
 b. the students' responses to the questionnaire.
 c. the room lighting.
 d. the subject matter of the questions asked.

28. What is the mode of the following distribution of scores: 2, 2, 4, 4, 4, 14?
 a. 2   **c.** 5
 b. 4   **d.** 6

28. What is the mean of the following distribution of scores: 2, 5, 8, 10, 11, 4, 6, 9, 1, 4?
 a. 2   **c.** 6
 b. 10   **d.** 15

30. What is the median of the following distribution: 10, 7, 5, 11, 8, 6, 9?
 a. 6   **c.** 8
 b. 7   **d.** 9

31. Which of the following is the measure of variation that is most affected by extreme scores?
 a. mean   **c.** mode
 b. standard deviation **d.** range

32. The set of scores that would likely be most representative of the population from which it was drawn would be a sample with a relatively
 a. large standard deviation.
 b. small standard deviation.
 c. large range.
 d. small range.

33. If a difference between two samples is NOT statistically significant, which of the following can be concluded?
 a. The difference is probably not a true one.
 b. The difference is probably not reliable.
 c. The difference could be due to sampling variation.
 d. All of these conclusions can be reached.

Matching Items

Match each psychological perspective, school, and subfield with its definition or description.

Terms

_____ **1.** median
_____ **2.** placebo effect
_____ **3.** mode
_____ **4.** range
_____ **5.** standard deviation
_____ **6.** scatterplot
_____ **7.** mean
_____ **8.** measures of central tendency
_____ **9.** measures of variation

Definitions or Descriptions

 a. the mean, median, and mode
 b. the difference between the highest and lowest scores
 c. the arithmetic average of a set of scores
 d. the range and standard deviation
 e. the most frequently occurring score
 f. the middle score in a distribution
 g. a graphed cluster of dots depicting the values of two variables
 h. a measure of variation based on every score
 i. experimental results caused by expectations alone

Matching Items

Match each term with its definition or description.

Terms

_____ 1. hypothesis
_____ 2. theory
_____ 3. independent variable
_____ 4. dependent variable
_____ 5. experimental group
_____ 6. control group
_____ 7. case study
_____ 8. survey
_____ 9. replication
_____ 10. random assignment
_____ 11. experiment
_____ 12. double-blind

Definitions or Descriptions

a. an in-depth observational study of one person
b. the variable being manipulated in an experiment
c. the variable being measured in an experiment
d. testable proposition
e. repeating an experiment to see whether the same results are obtained
f. the process in which research participants are selected by chance for different groups in an experiment
g. an explanation using an integrated set of principles that organizes observations and predicts behaviors or events
h. the research strategy in which the effects of one or more variables on behavior are tested
i. the "treatment-present" group in an experiment
j. the research strategy in which a representative sample of individuals is questioned
k. experimental procedure in which neither the research participant nor the experimenter knows which condition the participant is in
l. the "treatment-absent" group in an experiment

Essay Question

Elio has a theory that regular exercise for 1 month can improve thinking. Help him design an experiment evaluating this theory. (Use the space below to list the points you want to make, and organize them. Then write the essay on a separate piece of paper.)

TERMS AND CONCEPTS TO REMEMBER

Using your own words, on a separate piece of paper write a brief definition or explanation of each of the following.

1. theory
2. hypothesis
3. operational definition
4. replication
5. case study
6. naturalistic observation
7. survey
8. population
9. random sample
10. correlation
11. correlation coefficient
12. scatterplot
13. experiment
14. experimental group
15. control group
16. random assignment
17. double-blind procedure

18. placebo effect
19. independent variable
20. confounding variable
21. dependent variable
22. mode
23. mean
24. median
25. range
26. standard deviation
27. normal curve
28. statistical significance

ANSWERS

Module Review

How Do Psychologists Ask and Answer Questions?

1. scientific method; observations; theories; revised; observations
2. theory; hypotheses; research
3. operational definitions; replicate
4. organizes; predictions
5. descriptive; correlational; experimental
6. case study
7. hypotheses; atypical
8. naturalistic observation
9. social; solitary; varies
10. survey; wording
11. vivid
12. random; population; does
13. are
14. describe
15. **c.** is the answer. The members of one sorority are likely to share more interests, traits, and attitudes than will the members of a random sample of college students.
    a. & b. Unlike experiments, surveys do not specify or directly manipulate independent and dependent variables. In a sense, survey questions are independent variables, and the answers, dependent variables.
16. **d.** is the answer. Selecting every tenth person would probably result in a representative sample of the entire population of students at the university.
    a. It would be difficult, if not impossible, to survey every student on campus.
    b. Psychology students are not representative of the entire student population.
    c. This answer is incorrect for the same reason as b. This would constitute a biased sample.
17. correlated; predict; correlation coefficient; scatterplot
18. positively correlated; negatively correlated; inversely
19. strength; weakness; causation; cause-effect
    This is an example of a negative correlation. As one factor (time spent studying) increases, the other factor (anxiety level) decreases.
20. predicted
21. event; caused; explanation
22. **b.** is the answer.
    a. This is not an experiment because the researcher is not manipulating the independent variable (seating position); she is merely measuring whether variation in this factor predicts test performance.
    c. If the study were based entirely on students' self-reported responses, this would be a survey.
    d. This study goes beyond naturalistic observation, which merely describes behavior as it occurs, to determine if test scores can be predicted from students' seating position.
23. **d.** is the answer.
    a. Correlation does not imply causality.
    b. Again, a positive correlation simply means that two factors tend to increase or decrease together; further relationships are not implied.
    c. A separate factor may or may not be involved. That the two factors are correlated does not imply a separate factor. There may, for example, be a direct causal relationship between the two factors themselves.
24. **c.** is the answer. If height and weight are positively correlated, increased height is associated with increased weight. Thus, one can predict a person's weight from his or her height.
    a. Correlation does not imply causality.
    b. This situation depicts a negative correlation between height and weight.
25. cause; effect; factors
26. do; experiments; randomly; manipulates; holding constant
27. behavior; experimental; effect
28. experimental; control
29. random assignment
30. independent; dependent; confounding variables
31. double-blind

32. placebo; placebo effect

33. manipulate; independent; dependent; control
Experimentation has the advantage of increasing the investigator's control of both relevant and irrelevant variables that might influence behavior. Experiments also permit the investigator to go beyond observation and description to uncover cause-effect relationships in behavior.

34. **b.** is the answer. A general belief such as this one is a theory; it helps organize, explain, and generate testable predictions (called hypotheses) such as "men drink more soft drinks than women."
c. & d. Independent and dependent variables are experimental treatments and behaviors, respectively. Beliefs and predictions may involve such variables, but are not themselves those variables.

35. **b.** is the answer.
a. Although the descriptive methods of case studies, surveys, naturalistic observation, and correlational research do not involve control of variables, they nevertheless enable researchers to describe and predict behavior.
c. Whether a sample is representative of a population, rather than control over variables, determines whether results can be generalized from a sample to a population.

36. **c.** is the answer. To determine the effects of caffeine on reaction time, Martina needs to measure reaction time in a control, or comparison, group that does not receive caffeine.
a. Caffeine is the independent variable.
b. Reaction time is the dependent variable.
d. Whether Martina's experiment can be replicated is determined by the precision with which she reports her procedures, which is not an aspect of research strategy.

37. **b.** is the answer.
a. The low-dose comparison group is the control group.
c. Rashad was not given a placebo.

38. **a.** is the answer.
b. Use of a placebo tests whether the behavior of a research participant, who mistakenly believes that a treatment (such as a drug) is in effect, is the same as it would be if the treatment were actually present.
c. & d. These are examples of *blind* and *double-blind* control procedures.

STUDY TIP: COMPARING RESEARCH METHODS (For your convenience the text table is repeated here.)

Research Method	Basic Purpose	How Conducted	What Is Manipulated	Weaknesses
Descriptive	To observe and record behavior observations	Do case studies, surveys, or naturalistic	Nothing may be misleading	No control of variables; single cases
Correlational	To detect naturally occurring relationships; to assess how one variable predicts another	Collect data on two or more variables; no manipulation	Nothing	Does not specify cause and effect
Experimental and effect	To explore cause factors; use random	Manipulate one or more variable(s) assignment	The independent results may not generalize	Sometimes not feasible; to other contexts; not ethical to manipulate certain variables

Statistical Reasoning in Everyday Life

39. statistics

40. data; organize; bar graph; scale labels; range

41. mode; median; mean

42. mode

43. total sum; number

44. 50th

45. skewed; mean

46. low; high

47. range; standard deviation

48. difference between the lowest and highest scores

49. crude; is

50. more accurate; does

51. mean; normal curve (normal distribution)

52. **d.** is the answer. A small or large standard deviation indicates whether a distribution is homogeneous or variable.

a., b., & c. These statistics would not give any information regarding the consistency of performance.

53. d. is the answer.

54. c. is the answer.
a. The mean is computed as the sum of the scores divided by the number of scores.
b. The median is the midmost score in a distribution.
d. The range is the difference between the highest and lowest scores in a distribution.

55. a. is the answer. The mean is strongly influenced by extreme scores. In this example, the mean would change from $25,000 to (75,000 + 25,000 + 25,000 + 25,000 + 25,000)/5 = $35,000.
b. & c. Both the median and the mode would remain $25,000, even with the addition of the fifth family's income.
d. The standard deviation is a measure of variation, not central tendency.

56. representative; biased

57. low

58. less

59. significance; chance; reliable; relatively large

60. practical

61. b. is the answer.
a. If the difference between the sample means is not significant, then the groups probably do not differ in the measured ability.
c. When a result is not significant it means that the observed difference is unreliable.

Progress Test

Multiple-Choice Questions

1. a. is the answer. In a case study, one person is studied in depth.
b. In survey research, a group of people is interviewed.
c. Correlations identify whether two factors are related.
d. In an experiment, an investigator manipulates one variable to observe its effect on another.

2. c. is the answer. Exercise is the variable being manipulated in the experiment.
a. A control condition for this experiment would be a group of people not permitted to exercise.
b. A confounding variable is a variable other than those being manipulated that may influence behavior.

d. The dependent variable is the behavior measured by the experimenter—in this case, the effects of exercise.

3. c. is the answer. The control condition is that for which the experimental treatment (the new drug) is absent.
a. A random sample is a subset of a population in which every person has an equal chance of being selected.
b. The experimental condition is the group for which the experimental treatment (the new drug) is present.
d. "Test group" is an ambiguous term; both the experimental and control group are tested.

4. d. is the answer.
a. Hypotheses are testable propositions.
b. Dependent variables are factors that may change in response to manipulated independent variables.
c. Statistical indexes may be used to test specific hypotheses (and therefore as indirect tests of theories), but they are merely mathematical tools, not general principles, as are theories.

5. d. is the answer. In this case, the children are being observed in their normal environment rather than in a laboratory.
a. Correlational research measures relationships between two factors. The psychologist may later want to determine whether there are correlations between the variables studied under natural conditions.
b. In a case study, one subject is studied in depth.
c. This is not an experiment because the psychologist is not directly controlling the variables being studied.

6. d. is the answer.

7. b. is the answer. Replication is the repetition of an experiment to determine whether its findings are reliable. It is not a research method.

8. b. is the answer.
a. & c. These answers would have been correct had the question stated that there is a *positive* correlation between shoe size and IQ. Actually, there is probably no correlation at all!

9. d. is the answer. In an experiment, it would be possible to manipulate alcohol consumption and observe the effects, if any, on memory.
a., b., & c. These answers are incorrect because only by directly controlling the variables of interest can a researcher uncover cause-effect relationships.

10. d. is the answer.
a. A sample is a subset of a population.

b. & c. Control and experimental groups are used in experimentation, not in survey research.

11. **c.** is the answer. The mean is the sum of scores divided by the number of scores. [(2 + 3 + 7 + 6 + 1 + 4 + 9 + 5 + 8 + 2)/10 = 4.7.]

12. **d.** is the answer. When the scores are put in order (1, 2, 3, 4, 7, 7, 8), 4 is at the 50th percentile, splitting the distribution in half.

13. **b.** is the answer. The mode is the most frequently occurring score. Because there are more "2s" than any other number in the distribution, 2 is the mode.

14. **d.** is the answer.

15. **c.** is the answer.
    a. A statistically significant difference may or may not be of practical importance.
    b. This is often the case when a difference is not statistically significant.

16. **c.** is the answer.

17. **a.** is the answer. As an average, calculated by adding all scores and dividing by the number of scores, the mean could easily be affected by the inclusion of a few extreme scores. (p. 34)
    b. The range is not a measure of central tendency.
    c. & d. The median and mode give equal weight to all scores; each counts only once and its numerical value is unimportant.

18. **d.** is the answer. Only experiments can reveal cause-effect relationships; the other methods can only *describe* relationships.

19. **d.** is the answer.
    a. & b. The double-blind procedure is one way to create experimental and control groups.
    c. Research participants are randomly assigned to either an experimental or a control group.

20. **d.** is the answer.
    a. The control condition is the comparison group, in which the experimental treatment (the treatment of interest) is absent.
    b. Memory is a directly observed and measured dependent variable in this experiment.
    c. Attention is the independent variable, which is being manipulated.

21. **c.** is the answer. Only about 68 percent of all cases in a normal curve fall within one standard deviation on either side of the mean.

22. **b.** is the answer. If enough participants are used in an experiment and they are randomly assigned to the two groups, any differences that emerge between the groups should stem from the experiment itself.
    a., c., & d. None of these terms describes precautions taken in setting up groups for experiments.

23. **a.** is the answer.
    b. & c. Large, random samples are more likely to be representative of the populations from which they are drawn.

24. **d.** is the answer. Because we are sensitive to dramatic or unusual events, we are especially likely to perceive a relationship between them.
    a., b., & c. The relationship between vivid events is no more likely to be significant, positive, or negative than that between less dramatic events.

25. **d.** is the answer. Correlations show how well one factor can be predicted from another.
    a. Because a case study focuses in great detail on the behavior of an individual, it's probably not useful in showing whether predictions are possible.
    b. Naturalistic observation is a method of describing, rather than predicting, behavior.
    c. In experimental research the effects of manipulated independent variables on dependent variables are measured. It is not clear how an experiment could help determine whether IQ tests predict academic success.

26. **b.** is the answer. The control condition is the one in which the treatment—in this case, pollution—is absent.
    a. Students in the polluted room would be in the experimental condition.
    c. Presumably, all students in both conditions were randomly assigned to their groups. Random assignment is a method for establishing groups, rather than a condition.
    d. The word *dependent* refers to a kind of variable in experiments; conditions are either experimental or control.

27. **c.** is the answer. The lighting is the factor being manipulated.
    a. & d. These answers are incorrect because they involve aspects of the experiment other than the variables.
    b. This answer is the dependent, not the independent, variable.

28. **b.** is the answer.

29. **c.** is the answer. The mean is the sum of the scores divided by the number of scores (60/10 = 6).

30. **c.** is the answer. When the scores are put in order (5, 6, 7, 8, 9, 10, 11), 8 is at the 50th percentile, splitting the distribution in half.

31. **d.** is the answer. Since the range is the difference between the highest and lowest scores, it is by definition affected by extreme scores.
    a. & c. The mean and mode are measures of central tendency, not of variation.

b. The standard deviation is less affected than the range because, when it is calculated, the deviation of every score from the mean is computed.

32. **b.** is the answer. Averages derived from scores with low variability tend to be more reliable estimates of the populations from which they are drawn. Thus, a. and c. are incorrect. Because the standard deviation is a more accurate estimate of variability than the range, d. is incorrect.

33. **d.** is the answer. A difference that is statistically significant is a true difference, rather than an apparent difference due to factors such as sampling variation, and it is reliable.

Matching Items

1. f		**6.** g	
2. i		**7.** c	
3. e		**8.** a	
4. b		**9.** d	
5. h			

Matching Items

1. d	**5.** i	**9.** e
2. g	**6.** l	**10.** f
3. b	**7.** a	**11.** h
4. c	**8.** j	**12.** k

Essay Question

Elio's hypothesis is that daily aerobic exercise for one month will improve memory. Exercise is the independent variable. The dependent variable is memory. Exercise could be manipulated by having people in an experimental group jog for 30 minutes each day. Memory could be measured by comparing the number of words they recall from a test list studied before the exercise experiment begins, and again afterward. A control group that does not exercise is needed so that any improvement in the experimental group's memory can be attributed to exercise, and not to some other factor, such as the passage of one month's time or familiarity with the memory test. The control group should engage in some nonexercise activity for the same amount of time each day that the experimental group exercises. The participants should be randomly selected from the population at large, and then randomly assigned to the experimental and control groups.

Terms and Concepts to Remember

1. A **theory** is an explanation using an integrated set of principles that organizes observations and predicts behaviors or events.

2. A **hypothesis** is a testable prediction, often implied by a theory. Testing the hypothesis helps scientists to test the theory.

   Example: To test his theory of why people conform, Solomon Asch formulated the testable **hypothesis** that an individual would be more likely to go along with the majority opinion of a large group than with that of a smaller group.

3. An **operational definition** is a precise statement of the procedures (operations) used to define research variables.

4. **Replication** is the process of repeating an experiment, often with different participants and in different situations, to see whether the basic finding generalizes to other people and circumstances.

5. The **case study** is an observation technique in which one person is studied in great depth in the hope of of revealing universal principles.

6. **Naturalistic observation** involves observing and recording behavior in naturally occurring situations without trying to manipulate and control the situation.

7. The **survey** is a technique for ascertaining the self-reported attitudes or behaviors of a representative, random sample of people.

8. A **population** consists of all the members of a group being studied.

9. A **random sample** is one that is representative because every member of the population has an equal chance of being included.

10. **Correlation** is a measure of the extent to which two factors vary together, and thus of how well either factor predicts the other.

11. The **correlation coefficient** is a statistical measure of the relationship between two things. It can be positive or negative (from –1 to +1).

    Example: If there is a positive correlation between air temperature and ice cream sales, the warmer (higher) it is, the more ice cream is sold. If there is a negative correlation between air temperature and sales of cocoa, the cooler (lower) it is, the more cocoa is sold.

12. A **scatterplot** is a depiction of the relationship between two variables by means of a graphed cluster of dots.

13. An **experiment** is a research method in which a researcher directly manipulates one or more factors (independent variables) to observe the effect on some behavior or mental process (the dependent variable); experiments therefore make it possible to establish cause-effect relationships.

14. The **experimental group** in an experiment is one in which participants are exposed to the independent variable being studied.

    Example: In the study of the effects of a new drug on reaction time, participants in the **experimental group** would actually receive the drug being tested.

15. The **control group** in an experiment is one in which the treatment of interest, or independent variable, is withheld so that comparison to the experimental condition can be made.

    Example: The **control group** in an experiment testing the effects of a new drug on reaction time would be a group of participants given a placebo (inactive drug or sugar pill) instead of the drug being tested.

16. **Random assignment** is the procedure of assigning participants to the experimental and control conditions by chance, thus minimizing preexisting differences between those assigned to the different groups.

17. A **double-blind procedure** is an experimental procedure in which both the experimenter and the research participants are ignorant (blind) about whether the research participants have received the treatment or a placebo. It is used to prevent experimenters' and participants' expectations from influencing the results of an experiment.

18. The **placebo effect** occurs when the results of an experiment are caused by expectations alone.

19. The **independent variable** of an experiment is the factor being manipulated and tested by the investigator.

    Example: In the study of the effects of a new drug on reaction time, the drug is the **independent variable**.

20. In an experiment, a **confounding variable** is a factor other than the independent variable that might influence the results.

21. The **dependent variable** of an experiment is the factor being measured by the investigator, that is, the factor that may change in response to manipulations of the independent variable.

    Example: In the study of the effects of a new drug on reaction time, the participants' reaction time is the **dependent variable**.

22. The **mode** is the most frequently occurring score in a distribution; it is the simplest measure of central tendency to determine.

23. The **mean** is the arithmetic average in a distribution; the measure of central tendency computed by adding the scores in a distribution and dividing by the number of scores.

24. The **median**, another measure of central tendency, is the score that falls at the 50th percentile, cutting a distribution in half.

    Example: When the **mean** of a distribution is affected by a few extreme scores, the **median** is the more appropriate measure of central tendency.

25. The **range** is a measure of variation computed as the difference between the highest and lowest scores in a distribution.

26. The **standard deviation** is a computed measure of how much scores in a distribution deviate around the mean. Because it is based on every score in the distribution, it is a more precise measure of variation than the range.

27. The **normal curve** (*normal distribution*) is the symmetrical, bell-shaped distribution describing many types of psychological data, in which most scores fall near the mean, with fewer and fewer at the extremes.

28. **Statistical significance** means that an obtained result, such as the difference between the averages for two samples, very likely reflects a real difference rather than sampling variation or chance factors. Tests of statistical significance help researchers decide when they can justifiably generalize from an observed instance.

Neural and Hormonal Systems

MODULE OVERVIEW

Module 4 is concerned with the body's neural systems, which provide the basis for all human behavior. Under the direction of the brain, the nervous and endocrine systems coordinate a variety of voluntary and involuntary behaviors and serve as the body's mechanisms for communication with the external environment.

NOTE: Answer guidelines for all Module 4 questions begin on page 44.

MODULE REVIEW

First, skim each section, noting headings and bold-face items. After you have read the section, review each objective by answering the fill-in and essay-type questions that follow it. In some cases, Study Tips explain how best to learn a difficult concept and Applications help you to know how well you understand the material. As you proceed, evaluate your performance by consulting the answers beginning on page 44. Do not continue with the next section until you understand each answer. If you need to, review or reread the section in the textbook before continuing.

STUDY TIP: Many students find the technical material in Modules 4–6 difficult to master. Not only are there many terms for you to remember, but you must also know the organization and function of the various divisions of the nervous system. Learning this material will require a great deal of active processing, testing yourself frequently to be sure you know and understand the many structures and their functions. Working the module reviews several times, drawing and labeling brain diagrams, making flash cards, and mentally defining the terms are all useful techniques for learning this type of material.

Biology, Behavior, and Mind

Objective 4-1: Explain why psychologists are concerned with human biology.

1. In the most basic sense, every idea, mood, memory, and behavior that an individual has ever experienced is a _____ phenomenon.

2. The theory that linked our mental abilities to bumps on the skull was _____ . Although its popularity faded, this theory focused attention on the _____ of _____ .

3. Researchers who study the links between biology and behavior are working from the

   _____ _____ .

4. We are made up of smaller and smaller _____ ; we are also part of larger _____ . Thus, we are _____ systems.

APPLICATIONS:

5. Someone working from the biological perspective would be more likely to study
   a. how you learn to express emotions.
   b. how to help people overcome emotional disorders.
   c. life-span changes in the expression of emotion.
   d. the chemical changes that accompany emotions.

6. Which of the following was a major problem with phrenology?
   a. It was "ahead of its time" and no one believed it could be true.
   b. The brain is not neatly organized into structures that correspond to our categories of behavior.
   c. The brains of humans and animals are much less similar than the theory implied.
   d. All of these were problems with phrenology.

7. Cite some possible areas a person working from the biological perspective would be likely to study.

Neural Communication

Objective 4-2: Describe the parts of a neuron, and explain how its impulses are generated.

8. Our body's neural system is built from billions of nerve cells, or _____ .

9. Identify the major parts of the neuron diagrammed below.
   a. _____   c. _____
   b. _____   d. _____

10. The extensions of a neuron that receive messages from other neurons are the _____ . The extension of a neuron that transmits information to other neurons is the _____ . Some of these extensions are insulated by a fatty tissue called the _____ _____ , which helps speed the neuron's impulses.

11. The neural impulse, or _____ _____ , is a brief electrical charge that travels down a(n) _____ .

12. The fluid interior of a resting axon carries mostly _____ (positively/negatively) charged ions, while the fluid outside has mostly _____ (positively/negatively) charged ions. This polarization, called the _____ _____ , occurs because the cell membrane is _____ _____ .

13. An action potential occurs when the first part of the axon opens its gates and _____ (positively/negatively) charged ions rush in, causing that part of the neuron to become _____ . During the resting pause following an action potential, called the _____ _____ , the neuron pumps _____ (positively/negatively) charged ions back outside the cell.

14. To trigger a neural impulse, _____ signals minus _____ signals must exceed a certain intensity, called the _____ . Increasing a stimulus above this level _____ (will/will not) increase the neural impulse's intensity. This phenomenon is called an _____-_____-_____ response.

15. The strength of a stimulus _____ (does/does not) affect the intensity of a neural impulse. A strong stimulus _____ (can/cannot) trigger more neurons to fire.

Objective 4-3: Describe how nerve cells communicate with other nerve cells.

16. The junction between two neurons is called a _____ , and the gap is called the _____ _____ . This discovery was made by _____ .

17. The chemical messengers that convey information across the gaps between neurons are called _____ . These chemicals bind to receptor sites and unlock tiny channels, allowing

electrically charged _____ to enter the neuron.

18. Neurotransmitters influence neurons either by _____ or _____ their readiness to fire. Excess neurotransmitters are reabsorbed by the sending neuron in a process called _____ .

Outline the sequence of reactions that occur when a neural impulse is generated and transmitted from one neuron to another.

Objective 4-4: Describe how neurotransmitters influence behavior, and explain how drugs and other chemicals affect neurotransmission.

19. A neurotransmitter that is important in muscle contraction is _____ ; it is also important in learning and _____ .

20. Naturally occurring opiatelike neurotransmitters that are present in the brain are called _____ . When the brain is flooded with drugs such as _____ or _____ , it may stop producing these neurotransmitters.

21. Drugs that produce their effects by mimicking neurotransmitters are called _____ . Drugs that block neurotransmitters' functioning by occupying their _____ _____ are called _____ . Although certain _____ drugs create a temporary "high" by mimicking the endorphins, the poison _____ produces paralysis by blocking the activity of the neurotransmitter ACh.

STUDY TIP: To understand the relationships among excitatory and inhibitory synapses, threshold, and the all-or-none response, you should think of the neuron as a simple switch that is always either "on" or "off." This "all-or-none" response is in contrast to the graded, "partially on" response of the more complex dimmer switch. Whether the all-or-none response occurs depends on whether the input to the neuron is sufficient to allow it to reach its threshold—much as a simple light switch requires a certain amount of force to operate. In the neuron's case, the "force" refers to the combination of excitatory inputs (which promote a response) and inhibitory inputs (which promote the neuron's remaining in its resting state).

APPLICATIONS:

22. Several shy neurons send an inhibitory message to neighboring neuron Joni. At the same time, a larger group of party-going neurons sends Joni excitatory messages. What will Joni do?
    a. fire, assuming that her threshold has been reached
    b. not fire, even if her threshold has been reached
    c. enter a refractory period
    d. become hyperpolarized

23. I am a relatively fast-acting chemical messenger that influences muscle action, learning, and memory. What am I?
    a. dopamine   c. acetylcholine
    b. a hormone   d. glutamate

24. Since Malcolm has been taking a drug prescribed by his doctor, he no longer enjoys the little pleasures of life, such as eating and drinking. His doctor explains that this is because the drug
    a. triggers release of dopamine.
    b. inhibits release of dopamine.
    c. triggers release of ACh.
    d. inhibits release of ACh.

25. Lolita is feeling depressed for no particular reason. It is possible that she has an undersupply of _____ .

26. Punjab had lunch at the local Chinese restaurant. Afterward, he suffered a migraine, most likely caused by an _____ of _____ .

The Nervous System

Objective 4-5: Describe the functions of the nervous system's main divisions, and identify the three main types of neurons.

27. Taken altogether, the neurons of the body form the _____ _____ .

28. The brain and spinal cord form the _____ nervous system. The neurons that link the brain and spinal cord to the rest of the body form the _____ nervous system.

29. Axons are bundled into electrical cables called _____ , which link the CNS with muscles, glands, and sense organs. Information arriving in the brain and spinal cord from the body's tissues and sensory receptors travels in _____ neurons. Instructions from the brain and spinal cord are sent to the body's tissues via _____ neurons. The neurons that enable internal communication within the brain and spinal cord are called

_____ .

30. The division of the peripheral nervous system that enables voluntary control of the skeletal muscles is the _____ nervous system.

31. Involuntary, self-regulating responses—those of the glands and muscles of internal organs—are controlled by the _____ nervous system.

32. The body is made ready for action by the _____ division of the autonomic nervous system.

33. The _____ division of the autonomic nervous system produces relaxation.

Describe and explain the sequence of physical reactions that occur in the body as an emergency is confronted and then passes.

34. The brain's neurons cluster into work groups called _____ _____ .

35. Automatic responses to stimuli, called _____ , illustrate the work of the _____ _____ . Simple pathways such as these are involved in the _____-_____ response and in the _____ reflex.

Beginning with the sensory receptors in the skin, trace the course of a spinal reflex as a person reflexively jerks his or her hand away from an unexpectedly hot burner on a stove.

STUDY TIP: To keep the various functions of the peripheral nervous system (PNS) straight, remember that the PNS consists of two main divisions: somatic and autonomic. The somatic ("S") division primarily regulates "S functions," such as the *senses* and *skeletal* muscles. The autonomic ("A") division regulates *automatic* ("A") physical systems that do not require conscious attention. These include breathing, heart rate, and digestion, to name a few.

APPLICATIONS:

36. You are sitting at your desk at home, studying for an exam. No one else is home, but you hear creaking floorboards. You sneak downstairs, only to discover your parents have returned home early. Describe and explain the sequence of physical reactions that occurred in your body as you felt fear and then relief.

37. You are able to pull your hand quickly away from hot water before pain is felt because

   a. movement of the hand is a reflex that involves intervention of the spinal cord only.

   b. movement of the hand does not require intervention by the central nervous system.

   c. the brain reacts quickly to prevent severe injury.

   d. the autonomic division of the peripheral nervous system intervenes to speed contraction of the muscles of the hand.

38. Following Jayshree's near-fatal car accident, her physician noticed that the pupillary reflex of her eyes was abnormal. This MAY indicate that Jayshree's _____ _____ _____ was damaged in the accident.

39. Your brother has been taking prescription medicine and experiencing a number of unpleasant side effects, including unusually rapid heartbeat and excessive perspiration. It is likely that the medicine is exaggerating activity in the

   a. central nervous system.

   b. sympathetic nervous system.

   c. parasympathetic nervous system.

   d. somatic nervous system.

The Endocrine System

Objective 4-6: Describe the nature and functions of the endocrine system and its interaction with the nervous system.

40. The body's chemical communication network is called the _____ _____ . This system transmits information through chemical messengers called _____ at a much _____ (faster/slower) rate than the nervous system, and its effects last _____ (a longer time/a shorter time).

41. In a moment of danger, the autonomic nervous system orders the _____ glands to release _____ and _____ . These hormones increase _____ _____ , _____ _____ , and _____ _____ .

42. The most influential gland is the _____ , which, under the control of an adjacent brain area called the _____ , helps regulate

_____ and the release of hormones by other endocrine glands. The hormone _____ enables contractions associated with birthing, milk flow during nursing, and orgasm. It also promotes _____ _____ .

Write a paragraph describing the feedback system that links the nervous and endocrine systems.

APPLICATIONS:

43. I am a relatively slow-acting (but long-lasting) chemical messenger carried throughout the body by the bloodstream. What am I?

   a. a hormone   **c.** acetylcholine

   b. a neurotransmitter   **d.** dopamine

44. A bodybuilder friend suddenly seems to have grown several inches in height. You suspect that your friend's growth spurt has occurred because he has been using drugs that affect the

   a. pituitary gland.   **c.** adrenal glands.

   b. pancreas.   **d.** parathyroids.

PROGRESS TEST

Multiple-Choice Questions

Circle your answers to the following questions and check them with the answers beginning on page 45. If your answer is incorrect, read the explanation for why it is incorrect and then consult the text.

  1. The axons of certain neurons are covered by a layer of fatty tissue that helps speed neural transmission. This tissue is

   a. dopamine.

   b. the myelin sheath.

   c. acetylcholine.

   d. an endorphin.

2. Heartbeat, digestion, and other self-regulating bodily functions are governed by the
   a. voluntary nervous system.
   b. autonomic nervous system.
   c. sympathetic division of the autonomic nervous system.
   d. somatic nervous system.

3. A strong stimulus can increase the
   a. speed of the impulse the neuron fires.
   b. intensity of the impulse the neuron fires.
   c. number of times the neuron fires.
   d. threshold that must be reached before the neuron fires.

4. The pain of heroin withdrawal may be attributable to the fact that
   a. under the influence of heroin the brain ceases production of endorphins.
   b. under the influence of heroin the brain ceases production of all neurotransmitters.
   c. during heroin withdrawal the brain's production of all neurotransmitters is greatly increased.
   d. heroin destroys endorphin receptors in the brain.

5. The effect of a drug that is an antagonist is to
   a. cause the brain to stop producing certain neurotransmitters.
   b. mimic a particular neurotransmitter.
   c. block a particular neurotransmitter.
   d. disrupt a neuron's all-or-none firing pattern.

6. Which is the correct sequence in the transmission of a simple reflex?
   a. sensory neuron, interneuron, sensory neuron
   b. interneuron, motor neuron, sensory neuron
   c. sensory neuron, interneuron, motor neuron
   d. interneuron, sensory neuron, motor neuron

7. In a resting state, the axon is
   a. depolarized, with mostly negatively charged ions outside and positively charged ions inside.
   b. depolarized, with mostly positively charged ions outside and negatively charged ions inside.
   c. polarized, with mostly negatively charged ions outside and positively charged ions inside.
   d. polarized, with mostly positively charged ions outside and negatively charged ions inside.

8. Dr. Hernandez is studying neurotransmitter abnormalities in depressed patients. She would most likely be working from a _____ perspective.
   a. personality
   b. phrenology
   c. psychoanalytic
   d. biological

9. Voluntary movements, such as writing with a pencil, are directed by the
   a. sympathetic nervous system.
   b. somatic nervous system.
   c. parasympathetic nervous system.
   d. autonomic nervous system.

10. A neuron will generate action potentials when it
    a. remains below its threshold.
    b. receives an excitatory input.
    c. receives more excitatory than inhibitory inputs.
    d. is stimulated by a neurotransmitter.

11. Which is the correct sequence in the transmission of a neural impulse?
    a. axon, dendrite, cell body, synapse
    b. dendrite, axon, cell body, synapse
    c. synapse, axon, dendrite, cell body
    d. dendrite, cell body, axon, synapse

12. Chemical messengers produced by endocrine glands are called
    a. agonists.
    b. neurotransmitters.
    c. hormones.
    d. enzymes.

13. In the brain, learning occurs as experience strengthens certain connections in cell work groups called
    a. action potentials.
    b. neural networks.
    c. endocrine systems.
    d. dendrites.

14. When Sandy scalded her toe in a tub of hot water, the pain message was carried to her spinal cord by the _____ nervous system.
    a. somatic
    b. sympathetic
    c. parasympathetic
    d. central

15. Which of the following are governed by the simplest neural pathways?
    a. emotions
    b. physiological drives, such as hunger
    c. reflexes
    d. movements, such as walking

16. Melissa has just completed running a marathon. She is so elated that she feels little fatigue or discomfort. Her lack of pain is probably the result of the release of
    a. ACh.
    b. endorphins.
    c. dopamine.
    d. norepinephrine.

17. The myelin sheath that is on some neurons
    a. increases the speed of neural transmission.
    b. slows neural transmission.
    c. regulates the release of neurotransmitters.
    d. prevents positive ions from passing through the membrane.

18. I am a relatively fast-acting chemical messenger that affects mood, hunger, sleep, and arousal. What am I?
    a. acetylcholine
    b. dopamine
    c. norepinephrine
    d. serotonin

19. The neurotransmitter acetylcholine (ACh) is most likely to be found
    a. at the junction between sensory neurons and muscle fibers.
    b. at the junction between motor neurons and muscle fibers.
    c. at junctions between interneurons.
    d. in all of these locations.

20. The gland that regulates body growth is the
    a. adrenal.
    b. thyroid.
    c. hypothalamus.
    d. pituitary.

21. Epinephrine and norepinephrine are _____ that are released by the _____ gland.
    a. neurotransmitters; pituitary
    b. hormones; pituitary
    c. neurotransmitters; thyroid
    d. hormones; adrenal

22. The effect of a drug that is an agonist is to
    a. cause the brain to stop producing certain neurotransmitters.
    b. mimic a particular neurotransmitter.
    c. block a particular neurotransmitter.
    d. disrupt a neuron's all-or-none firing pattern.

Essay Question

Discuss how the endocrine and nervous systems become involved when a student feels stress—such as that associated with an upcoming final exam. (Use the space below to list the points you want to make, and organize them. Then write the essay on a separate sheet of paper.)

TERMS AND CONCEPTS TO REMEMBER

Using your own words, on a piece of paper write a brief definition or explanation of each of the following terms.

1. biological perspective
2. neuron
3. dendrites
4. axon
5. myelin sheath
6. action potential
7. threshold
8. synapse
9. neurotransmitters
10. reuptake
11. endorphins
12. nervous system
13. central nervous system (CNS)
14. peripheral nervous system (PNS)
15. nerves
16. sensory neurons
17. motor neurons
18. interneurons
19. somatic nervous system
20. autonomic nervous system

21. sympathetic nervous system
22. parasympathetic nervous system
23. reflex
24. endocrine system
25. hormones
26. adrenal glands
27. pituitary gland

ANSWERS

Module Review

Biology, Behavior, and Mind

1. biological
2. phrenology; localization; function
3. biological perspective
4. subsystems; systems; biopsychosocial
5. **d.** is the answer. Someone working from the biological perspective studies the links between biology (chemical changes in this example) and behavior (emotions in this example).
   a., b., & c. Experimental, clinical, and developmental psychologists would be more concerned with the learning of emotional expressions, the treatment of emotional disorders, and life-span changes in emotions, respectively.
6. **b.** is the answer.
   a. "Ahead of its time" implies the theory had merit, which later research clearly showed it did not. Moreover, phrenology was accepted as an accurate theory of brain organization by many scientists.
   c. Phrenology said nothing about the similarities of human and animal brains.
7. A person working from the biological perspective might study chemical changes that accompany emotions, how muscle tension varies with facial expression, how heart rate changes as people become angry, and so on.

Neural Communication

8. neurons
9. **a.** dendrites
   b. cell body
   c. axon
   d. myelin sheath
10. dendrites; axon; myelin sheath
11. action potential; axon
12. negatively; positively; resting potential; selectively permeable

13. positively; depolarized; refractory period; positively
14. excitatory; inhibitory; threshold; will not; all-or-none
15. does not; can
16. synapse; synaptic cleft (gap); Sir Charles Sherrington
17. neurotransmitters; atoms
18. exciting; inhibiting; reuptake

A neural impulse is generated by excitatory signals minus inhibitory signals exceeding a certain threshold. The stimuli are received through the dendrites, combined in the cell body, and electrically transmitted in an all-or-none fashion down the length of the axon. When the combined signal reaches the end of the axon, chemical messengers called neurotransmitters are released into the synaptic cleft, or gap, between two neurons. Neurotransmitter molecules bind to receptor sites on the dendrites of neighboring neurons and have either an excitatory or inhibitory influence on that neuron's tendency to generate its own neural impulse.

19. acetylcholine (ACh); memory
20. endorphins; heroin; morphine
21. agonists; receptor sites; antagonists; opiate; curare
22. **a.** is the answer.
    b. Because she has reached her threshold, she will probably fire.
    c. The refractory period is a resting period. Because Joni has received a large number of excitatory messages, she will not be at rest.
    d. *Hyperpolarization* is not a term.
23. **c.** is the answer.
24. **b.** is the answer.
    a. By triggering release of dopamine, such a drug would probably enhance Malcolm's enjoyment of the pleasures of life.
    c. & d. ACh is the neurotransmitter at synapses between motor neurons and muscle fibers.
25. norepinephrine. An undersupply can cause depression.
26. oversupply; glutamate. Glutamate is in MSG, which is sometimes used in Chinese cooking. Glutamate can cause migraines because an oversupply can overstimulate the brain.

The Nervous System

27. nervous system
28. central; peripheral
29. nerves; sensory; motor; interneurons
30. somatic

31. autonomic

32. sympathetic

33. parasympathetic

The sympathetic division of the autonomic nervous system becomes aroused in response to an emergency. The physiological changes that occur include accelerated heartbeat, elevated blood sugar, slowing of digestion, and increased perspiration to cool the body. When the emergency is over, the parasympathetic nervous system produces the opposite physical reactions.

34. neural networks

35. reflexes; spinal cord; knee-jerk; pain

From sensory receptors in the skin the message travels via sensory neurons to an interneuron in the spinal cord, which in turn activates a motor neuron. This motor neuron causes the muscles in the hand to contract, and the person jerks his or her hand away from the heat.

36. When you hear the creaking, you become afraid. The sympathetic division of your autonomic nervous system becomes aroused, causing these physiological changes: accelerated heartbeat, elevated blood sugar, increase in blood pressure, slowing of digestion, and increased perspiration to cool the body. When you realize it's only your parents, your parasympathetic nervous system produces the opposite physical reactions, calming your body.

37. **a.** is the answer. Because this reflex is an automatic response and involves only the spinal cord, the hand is jerked away before the brain has even received the information that causes the sensation of pain.

b. The spinal cord, which organizes simple reflexes such as this one, is part of the central nervous system.

c. The brain is not involved in directing spinal reflexes.

d. The autonomic nervous system controls the glands and the muscles of the internal organs; it does not influence the skeletal muscles controlling the hand.

38. autonomic nervous system

39. **b.** is the answer. Sympathetic arousal produces several effects, including accelerated heartbeat and excessive perspiration.

a. & d. Activation of the central nervous system and the somatic nervous system does not have these effects.

c. Arousal of the parasympathetic nervous system would have effects opposite to those stated.

The Endocrine System

40. endocrine system; hormones; slower; a longer time

41. adrenal; epinephrine; norepinephrine; heart rate; blood pressure; blood sugar

42. pituitary; hypothalamus; growth; oxytocin; pair bonding, group cohesion, and social trust

The hypothalamus in the brain influences secretions by the pituitary. The pituitary regulates other endocrine glands, which release hormones that influence the brain, which directs behavior.

43. **a.** is the answer.

b., c., & d. Acetylcholine and dopamine are fast-acting neurotransmitters released at synapses, not in the bloodstream.

44. **a.** is the answer. Hormones of the pituitary gland regulate body growth.

b. The pancreas regulates the level of sugar in the blood.

c. The adrenal glands produce hormones that provide energy during emergencies; they are not involved in regulating body growth.

d. The parathyroids help regulate the level of calcium in the blood.

Progress Test

Multiple-Choice Questions

1. **b.** is the answer.
   a. Dopamine is a neurotransmitter that influences movement, learning, attention, and emotion.
   c. Acetylcholine is a neurotransmitter that triggers muscle contraction.
   d. Endorphins are opiatelike neurotransmitters linked to pain control and to pleasure.

2. **b.** is the answer. The autonomic nervous system controls internal functioning, including heartbeat, digestion, and glandular activity.
   a. The functions mentioned are all automatic, not voluntary, so this answer cannot be correct.
   c. This answer is incorrect because most organs are affected by both divisions of the autonomic nervous system.
   d. The somatic nervous system transmits sensory input to the central nervous system and enables voluntary control of skeletal muscles.

3. **c.** is the answer. Stimulus strength can affect only the number of times a neuron fires or the number of neurons that fire.
   a., b., & d. These answers are incorrect because firing is an all-or-none response, so intensity

remains the same regardless of stimulus strength. Nor can stimulus strength change the neuronal threshold or the impulse speed.

4. **a.** is the answer. Endorphins are neurotransmitters that function as natural painkillers. When the body has a supply of artificial painkillers such as heroin, endorphin production stops.
   b. The production of neurotransmitters other than endorphins does not cease.
   c. Neurotransmitter production does not increase during withdrawal.
   d. Heroin makes use of the same receptor sites as endorphins.

5. **c.** is the answer.

6. **c.** is the answer. In a simple reflex, a sensory neuron carries the message that a sensory receptor has been stimulated to an interneuron in the spinal cord. The interneuron responds by activating motor neurons that will enable the appropriate response.

7. **d.** is the answer.

8. **d.** is the answer. Biological psychologists study the links between biology (in this case, neurotransmitters) and psychology (depression, in this example).

9. **b.** is the answer.
   a., c., & d. The autonomic nervous system, which is divided into the sympathetic and parasympathetic divisions, is concerned with regulating basic bodily maintenance functions.

10. **c.** is the answer.
    a. An action potential will occur only when the neuron's threshold is *exceeded.*
    b. An excitatory input that does not reach the neuron's threshold will not trigger an action potential.
    d. This answer is incorrect because some neurotransmitters inhibit a neuron's readiness to fire.

11. **d.** is the answer. A neuron receives incoming stimuli on its dendrites and cell body. These electrochemical signals are combined in the cell body, generating an impulse that travels down the axon, causing the release of neurotransmitter substances into the synaptic cleft or gap.

12. **c.** is the answer.
    a. Agonists are drugs that excite neural firing by mimicking a particular neurotransmitter.
    b. Neurotransmitters are the chemicals involved in synaptic transmission in the nervous system.
    d. Enzymes are chemicals that facilitate various chemical reactions throughout the body but are not involved in communication within the endocrine system.

13. **b.** is the answer.
    a. Action potentials are neural impulses that occur in all forms of communication in the nervous system.
    c. The endocrine system is the body's glandular system of chemical communication.
    d. Dendrites are the branching extensions of neurons that receive messages from other nerve cells.

14. **a.** is the answer. Sensory neurons in the somatic nervous system relay such messages.
    b. & c. These divisions of the autonomic nervous system are concerned with the regulation of bodily maintenance functions such as heartbeat, digestion, and glandular activity.
    d. The spinal cord itself is part of the central nervous system, but the message is carried to the spinal cord by the somatic division of the peripheral nervous system.

15. **c.** is the answer. As automatic responses to stimuli, reflexes are the simplest complete units of behavior and require only simple neural pathways.
    a., b., & d. Emotions, drives, and voluntary movements are all behaviors that are much more complex than reflexes and therefore involve much more complicated neural pathways.

16. **b.** is the answer. Endorphins are neurotransmitters that function as natural painkillers and are evidently involved in the "runner's high" and other situations in which discomfort or fatigue is expected but not experienced.
    a. ACh is a neurotransmitter involved in muscular control.
    c. Dopamine is a neurotransmitter involved in, among other things, movement.
    d. Norepinephrine is an adrenal hormone released to help us respond in moments of danger.

17. **a.** is the answer.
    c. & d. Myelin sheaths are not involved in regulating the release of neurotransmitters.

18. **d.** is the answer.

19. **b.** is the answer. ACh is a neurotransmitter that causes the contraction of muscle fibers when stimulated by motor neurons. This function explains its location.
    a. & c. Sensory neurons and interneurons do not directly stimulate muscle fibers.

20. **d.** is the answer. The pituitary regulates body growth, and some of its secretions regulate the release of hormones from other glands.

a. The adrenal glands are stimulated by the autonomic nervous system to release epinephrine and norepinephrine.
b. The thyroid gland affects metabolism, among other things.
c. The hypothalamus, which is not a gland, regulates the pituitary but does not itself directly regulate growth.

21. **d.** is the answer. Also known as adrenaline and noradrenaline, epinephrine and norepinephrine are hormones released by the adrenal glands.

22. **b.** is the answer.
    a. Abuse of certain drugs, such as heroin, may have this effect.
    c. This describes the effect of an antagonist.
    d. Drugs do not have this effect on neurons.

Essay Question

The body's response to stress is regulated by the nervous system. As the date of the exam approaches, the stressed student's cerebral cortex activates the hypothalamus, triggering the release of hormones that in turn activate the sympathetic branch of the autonomic nervous system and the endocrine system. The autonomic nervous system controls involuntary bodily responses such as breathing, heartbeat, and digestion. The endocrine system contains glands that secrete hormones into the bloodstream that regulate the functions of body organs.

In response to activation by the hypothalamus, the student's pituitary gland would secrete a hormone which in turn triggers the release of epinephrine, norepinephrine, and other stress hormones from the adrenal glands. These hormones would help the student's body manage stress by making nutrients available to meet the increased demands for energy stores the body often faces in coping with stress.

These hormones activate the sympathetic division of the autonomic system, causing increased heart rate, breathing, and blood pressure and the suppression of digestion. After the exam date has passed, the student's body would attempt to restore its normal, pre-stress state. The parasympathetic branch of the autonomic system would slow the student's heartbeat and breathing and digestive processes would no longer be suppressed, perhaps causing the student to feel hungry.

Terms and Concepts to Remember

1. The **biological perspective** is concerned with the links between biology and behavior.
2. The **neuron**, or nerve cell, is the basic building block of the nervous system.
3. The **dendrites** of a neuron are the bushy, branching extensions that receive messages from other nerve cells and conduct impulses toward the cell body.
4. The **axon** of a neuron is the extension that sends impulses to other nerve cells or to muscles or glands.
5. The **myelin sheath** is a layer of fatty tissue that segmentally covers many axons and helps speed neural impulses.
6. An **action potential** is a neural impulse generated by the movement of positively charged atoms in and out of channels in the axon's membrane.
7. A neuron's **threshold** is the level of stimulation required to trigger a neural impulse.
8. A **synapse** is the junction between the axon tip of the sending neuron and the dendrite or cell body of the receiving neuron. The tiny gap at this junction is called the *synaptic gap* or *cleft*.
9. **Neurotransmitters** are chemicals that are released into synaptic gaps and so transmit neural messages from neuron to neuron.
10. **Reuptake** is the absorption of excess neurotransmitters by a sending neuron.
11. **Endorphins** are natural, opiatelike neurotransmitters linked to pain control and to pleasure.

    Memory aid: <u>End</u>orphins *end* pain.
12. The **nervous system** is the speedy, electrochemical communication system, consisting of all the nerve cells in the peripheral and central nervous systems.
13. The **central nervous system (CNS)** consists of the brain and spinal cord; it is located at the *center*, or internal core, of the body.
14. The **peripheral nervous system (PNS)** includes the sensory and motor neurons that connect the central nervous system to the body's sense receptors, muscles, and glands; it is at the *periphery* of the body relative to the brain and spinal cord.
15. **Nerves** are bundles of neural axons, which are part of the PNS, that connect the central nervous system with muscles, glands, and sense organs.
16. **Sensory neurons** carry information from the sensory receptors to the central nervous system for processing.
17. **Motor neurons** carry information and instructions for action from the central nervous system to muscles and glands.

18. **Interneurons** are the neurons of the central nervous system that link the sensory and motor neurons in the transmission of sensory inputs and motor outputs.

19. The **somatic nervous system** is the division of the peripheral nervous system that enables voluntary control of the skeletal muscles; also called the skeletal nervous system.

20. The **autonomic nervous system** is the division of the peripheral nervous system that controls the glands and the muscles of internal organs and thereby controls internal functioning; it regulates the *automatic* behaviors necessary for survival.

21. The **sympathetic nervous system** is the division of the autonomic nervous system that arouses the body, mobilizing its energy in stressful situations.

22. The **parasympathetic nervous system** is the division of the autonomic nervous system that calms the body, conserving its energy.

23. A **reflex** is a simple, automatic response to a sensory stimulus; it is governed by a very simple neural pathway.

24. The **endocrine system**, the body's "slower" chemical communication system, consists of glands that secrete hormones into the bloodstream.

25. **Hormones** are chemical messengers, mostly manufactured by the endocrine glands, that are produced in one tissue and circulate through the bloodstream to their target tissues, on which they have specific effects.

26. The **adrenal glands** produce epinephrine and norepinephrine, hormones that prepare the body to deal with emergencies or stress.

27. The **pituitary gland**, under the influence of the hypothalamus, regulates growth and controls other endocrine glands; it is a sort of master gland.

Tools of Discovery and Older Brain Structures

MODULE OVERVIEW

Knowledge of the workings of the brain has increased with advances in neuroscientific methods. These include the EEG, PET scans, MRI scans, and, most recently, fMRI, which allows researchers to view brain activity as a person performs a task.

The older brain structures—the brainstem and limbic system—function in much the same way for us as they did for our distant ancestors. These structures sustain basic life functions and enable memory, emotions, and basic drives.

NOTE: Answer guidelines for all Module 5 questions begin on page 52.

MODULE REVIEW

First, skim each section, noting headings and boldface items. After you have read the section, review each objective by answering the fill-in and essay-type questions that follow it. In some cases, Study Tips explain how best to learn a difficult concept and Applications help you to know how well you understand the material. As you proceed, evaluate your performance by consulting the answers beginning on page 52. Do not continue with the next section until you understand each answer. If you need to, review the section in the textbook before continuing.

The Tools of Discovery: Having Our Head Examined

Objective 5-1: Describe several techniques for studying the brain's connections to behavior and mind.

1. Researchers sometimes study brain function by producing _____ or by selectively destroying brain cells. The oldest technique for studying the brain involves _____ _____ of patients with brain injuries or diseases.

2. The _____ is an amplified recording of the waves of electrical activity that sweep across the brain's surface.

3. The technique depicting the level of activity of brain areas by measuring the brain's consumption of glucose is called the _____ _____ .

Briefly explain the purpose of the PET scan.

4. A technique that produces clearer images of the brain (and other body parts) by using magnetic fields and radio waves is known as _____ .

5. By comparing scans taken less than a second apart, the _____ _____ detects oxygen-laden bloodflow to the part of the brain thought to control the bodily activity being studied. Using this technique, researchers found that bloodflow to the back of the brain _____ (increases/decreases) when people view a scene because that is where _____ information is processed.

STUDY TIP/APPLICATIONS: To help keep the various research methods for studying the brain straight, think of the methods as falling into two categories: (1) those that measure ongoing electrical or metabolic brain activity in real time (EEG, PET scan, fMRI) and (2) those that merely provide a momentary picture of the brain's anatomical structure (MRI).

6. a. Which method would be most useful to a neurologist attempting to locate a tumor in a patient's brain?

    _____

    b. Which method would be most useful to a researcher attempting to pinpoint the area of the brain that is most critical to speaking aloud?

    _____

    c. What are some other instances when a researcher would be best advised to use methods that give a picture of the brain's structure?

    d. What are some other instances when a researcher would be best advised to use methods that measure brain activity?

Older Brain Structures

Objective 5-2: Describe the components of the brainstem, and summarize the functions of the brainstem, thalamus, and cerebellum.

7. The oldest and innermost region of the brain is the _____ .

8. At the base of the brainstem, where the spinal cord enters the skull, lies the _____ , which controls _____ and _____ . Just above this part is the _____ , which helps coordinate movements.

9. Nerves from each side of the brain cross over to connect with the body's opposite side in the _____ .

10. At the top of the brainstem sits the _____ , which serves as the brain's sensory switchboard, receiving information from all the senses except _____ and routing it to the regions dealing with those senses. These egg-shaped structures also receive replies from the higher regions, which they direct to the _____ and to the _____ .

11. The finger-shaped network of neurons, the _____ _____ , is contained inside the brainstem and plays an important role in controlling _____ . Electrically stimulating this area will produce an _____ animal. Lesioning this area will cause an animal to lapse into a _____ .

12. At the rear of the brainstem lies the _____ . It influences one type of _____ _____ and memory. It also helps us judge time, modulate our _____ , and discriminate sounds and textures; and it coordinates voluntary movement and _____ control.

13. The lower brain functions occur without _____ effort, indicating that our brains process most information _____ (inside/outside) of our awareness.

Objective 5-3: Describe the structures and functions of the limbic system.

14. Between the brainstem and cerebral hemispheres is the _____ system. One component of this system that processes conscious memories is the _____ (see a in drawing).

15. Aggression or fear will result from stimulation of different regions of the lima-bean-sized neural clusters, the _____ (see b).

16. We must remember, however, that the brain _____ (is/is not) neatly organized into structures that correspond to our categories of behavior. For example, aggressive behavior _____ (does/does not) involve neural activity in many brain levels.

17. Below the thalamus is the _____ (c), which regulates bodily maintenance behaviors such as _____ , _____ ,

_____ _____ , and

_____ behavior. This area also

regulates behavior by secreting _____

that enable it to control the _____

gland. Olds and Milner discovered that this

region also contains _____ centers,

which animals will work hard to have stimulated.

18. Some researchers believe that alcohol dependence, drug abuse, binge eating, and other _____ disorders may stem from a

genetic _____

_____ _____

in the natural brain systems for pleasure and well-being.

APPLICATIONS:

19. The part of the human brain that is most like that of a fish is the
   a. cortex.
   b. limbic system.
   c. brainstem.
   d. right hemisphere.

20. If Dr. Rogers wishes to conduct an experiment on the effects of stimulating the reward centers of a rat's brain, he should insert an electrode into the
   a. thalamus.
   b. amygdala.
   c. hypothalamus.
   d. brainstem.

21. In primitive vertebrate animals, the brain primarily regulates _____ ; in lower mammals, the brain enables _____ .
   a. emotion; memory
   b. memory; emotion
   c. survival functions; emotion
   d. reproduction; emotion

22. A scientist from another planet wishes to study the simplest brain mechanisms underlying emotion and memory. You recommend that the scientist study the
   a. brainstem of a frog.
   b. limbic system of a dog.
   c. hypothalamus of a monkey.
   d. hypothalamus of a human.

23. Dr. Frankenstein made a mistake during neurosurgery on his monster. After the operation, the monster "saw" with his ears and "heard" with his eyes. It is likely that Dr. Frankenstein "rewired" neural connections in the monster's
   a. hypothalamus.   c. amygdala.
   b. cerebellum.   d. thalamus.

PROGRESS TEST

Multiple-Choice Questions

Circle your answers to the following questions and check them with the answers on page 53. If your answer is incorrect, read the explanation for why it is incorrect and then consult the text.

1. The brain research technique that involves monitoring the brain's usage of glucose is called (in abbreviated form) the
   a. PET scan.   c. EEG.
   b. fMRI.   d. MRI.

2. Though there is no single "control center" for emotions, their regulation is primarily attributed to the brain region known as the
   a. limbic system.   c. brainstem.
   b. reticular formation.   d. cerebellum.

3. Following a head injury, a person has ongoing difficulties staying awake. Most likely, the damage occurred to the
   a. thalamus.   c. reticular formation.
   b. hypothalamus.   d. cerebellum.

4. The technique that uses magnetic fields and radio waves to produce computer images of structures within the brain is called
   a. the EEG.   c. a PET scan.
   b. a lesion.   d. MRI.

5. Jessica experienced difficulty keeping her balance after receiving a blow to the back of her head. It is likely that she injured her
   a. medulla.   c. hypothalamus.
   b. thalamus.   d. cerebellum.

6. Moruzzi and Magoun caused a cat to lapse into a coma by severing neural connections between the cortex and the
   a. reticular formation.   c. thalamus.
   b. hypothalamus.   d. cerebellum.

Matching Items

Match each structure or technique with its corresponding function or description.

Structures

_____	1. hypothalamus
_____	2. lesion
_____	3. EEG
_____	4. fMRI
_____	5. reticular formation
_____	6. MRI
_____	7. thalamus
_____	8. cerebellum
_____	9. amygdala
_____	10. medulla
_____	11. brainstem

Functions or Descriptions

a. amplified recording of brain waves
b. technique that uses radio waves and magnetic
fields to image brain anatomy
c. serves as sensory switchboard
d. contains reward centers
e. tissue destruction
f. technique that uses radio waves and magnetic
fields to show brain function
g. helps control arousal
h. influences rage and fear
i. regulates breathing and heartbeat
j. enables coordinated movement
k. oldest part of the brain

TERMS AND CONCEPTS TO REMEMBER

Using your own words, on a piece of paper write a
brief definition or explanation of each of the following
terms.

1. lesion
2. electroencephalogram (EEG)
3. PET (positron emission tomography scan)
4. MRI (magnetic resonance imaging)
5. fMRI (functional magnetic resonance imaging)
6. brainstem
7. medulla
8. thalamus
9. reticular formation
10. cerebellum
11. limbic system
12. amygdala
13. hypothalamus

ANSWERS

Module Review

The Tools of Discovery: Having Our Head Examined

1. lesions; clinical observation
2. electroencephalogram (EEG)

3. PET (positron emission tomography) scan

By depicting the brain's consumption of temporarily
radioactive glucose, the PET scan allows researchers
to see which brain areas are most active as a person
performs various tasks by tracking the gamma rays
released. This provides additional information on the
specialized functions of various regions of the brain.

4. MRI (magnetic resonance imaging)

5. functional MRI; increases; visual

6. **a.** MRI
b. PET scan
c. to study developmental changes in brain structure, to compare brain anatomy in women and
men
d. to learn which areas of the brain become active
during strong emotions, to determine whether
brain activity is abnormal in people suffering
from dementia (memory and language problems)

Older Brain Structures

7. brainstem
8. medulla; breathing; heartbeat; pons
9. brainstem
10. thalamus; smell; medulla; cerebellum
11. reticular formation; arousal; alert (awake); coma
12. cerebellum; nonverbal learning; emotions;
balance
13. conscious; outside
14. limbic; hippocampus
15. amygdala

16. is not; does

17. hypothalamus; hunger; thirst; body temperature; sexual; hormones; pituitary; reward

18. addictive; reward deficiency syndrome

19. **c.** is the answer. The brainstem is the oldest and most primitive region of the brain. It is found in lower vertebrates, such as fish, as well as in humans and other mammals. The structures mentioned in the other choices are associated with stages of brain evolution beyond that seen in the fish.

20. **c.** is the answer. As Olds and Milner discovered, electrical stimulation of the hypothalamus is a highly reinforcing event because it is the location of the animal's reward centers. The other brain regions mentioned are not associated with reward centers.

21. **c.** is the answer.
    d. Reproduction is only one of the basic survival functions the brain regulates.

22. **b.** is the answer. The hippocampus of the limbic system is involved in processing memory. The amygdala of the limbic system influences fear and anger.
    a. The brainstem controls vital functions such as breathing and heartbeat; it is not directly involved in either emotion or memory.
    c. & d. These answers are incorrect because the hypothalamus directs several maintenance activities and drives, not emotions and memory.

23. **d.** is the answer. The thalamus relays sensory messages from the eyes, ears, and other receptors to the appropriate projection areas of the cortex. "Rewiring" the thalamus, theoretically, could have the effects stated in this question.
    a., b., & c. These brain structures are not directly involved in brain processes related to sensation or perception.

Progress Test

Multiple-Choice Questions

1. **a.** is the answer. The PET scan measures glucose consumption in different areas of the brain to determine their levels of activity.
   b. The fMRI compares MRI scans taken less than a second apart to reveal brain structure and function.

   c. The EEG is a measure of electrical activity in the brain.
   d. MRI uses magnetic fields and radio waves to produce computer-generated images of soft tissues of the body.

2. **a.** is the answer.
   b. The reticular formation is linked to arousal.
   c. The brainstem governs the mechanisms of basic survival—heartbeat and breathing, for example—and has many other roles.
   d. The cerebellum coordinates movement output and balance.

3. **c.** is the answer. The reticular formation plays an important role in arousal.
   a. The thalamus relays sensory input.
   b. The hypothalamus directs several maintenance activities.
   d. The cerebellum is involved in coordination of movement output and balance.

4. **d.** is the answer.
   a. The EEG is an amplified recording of the brain's electrical activity.
   b. A lesion is destruction of tissue.
   c. The PET scan is a visual display of brain activity that detects the movement of a radioactive form of glucose as the brain performs a task.

5. **d.** is the answer. The cerebellum is involved in the coordination of voluntary muscular movements.
   a. The medulla regulates breathing and heartbeat.
   b. The thalamus relays sensory inputs to the appropriate higher centers of the brain.
   c. The hypothalamus is concerned with the regulation of basic drives and emotions.

6. **a.** is the answer. The reticular formation controls arousal via its connections to the cortex. Thus, separating the two produces a coma.
   b., c., & d. None of these structures controls arousal. The hypothalamus regulates hunger, thirst, sexual behavior, and other basic drives; the thalamus is a sensory relay station; and the cerebellum is involved in the coordination of voluntary movement.

Matching Items

1. d	**5.** g	**9.** h
2. e	**6.** b	**10.** i
3. a	**7.** c	**11.** k
4. f	**8.** j	

Terms and Concepts to Remember

1. A **lesion** is destruction of tissue; studying the consequences of lesions in different regions of the brain—both surgically produced in animals and naturally occurring—helps researchers to determine the normal functions of these regions.

2. An **electroencephalogram (EEG)** is an amplified recording of the waves of electrical activity of the brain. *Encephalo* comes from a Greek word meaning "related to the brain."

3. The **PET (positron emission tomography) scan** measures the levels of activity of different areas of the brain by tracing their consumption of a radioactive form of glucose, the brain's fuel.

4. **MRI (magnetic resonance imaging)** uses magnetic fields and radio waves to produce computer-generated images that show brain structures more clearly.

5. In a **fMRI (functional magnetic resonance imaging)**, MRI scans taken less than a second apart are compared to reveal bloodflow and, therefore, brain function.

6. The **brainstem**, the oldest and innermost region of the brain, is an extension of the spinal cord and is the central core of the brain; its structures direct automatic survival functions.

7. Located in the brainstem, the **medulla** controls breathing and heartbeat.

8. Located atop the brainstem, the **thalamus** routes incoming messages to the appropriate cortical centers and transmits replies to the medulla and cerebellum.

9. Also part of the brainstem, the **reticular formation** is a nerve network that plays an important role in controlling arousal.

10. The **cerebellum** processes sensory input and coordinates movement output and balance.

11. The **limbic system** is a neural system associated with emotions such as fear and aggression and basic physiological drives.
    Memory aid: Its name comes from the Latin word *limbus*, meaning "border"; the **limbic system** is at the border of the brainstem and cerebral hemispheres.

12. The **amygdala** is part of the limbic system and influences the emotions of fear and aggression.

13. Also part of the limbic system, the **hypothalamus** regulates hunger, thirst, body temperature, and sexual behavior; helps govern the endocrine system via the pituitary gland; and contains the so-called reward centers of the brain.

The Cerebral Cortex and Our Divided Brain

MODULE OVERVIEW

Module 6 is concerned with the structures and functions of the brain's ultimate control and information-processing center, the cerebral cortex. Studies of split-brain patients have given researchers a great deal of information about the specialized functions of the brain's right and left hemispheres.

Many students find the technical material in this module difficult to master. Learning this material will require a great deal of rehearsal. Working the module review several times, drawing and labeling brain diagrams, and mentally reciting terms are all useful techniques for rehearsing this type of material.

NOTE: Answer guidelines for all Module 6 questions begin on page 60.

MODULE REVIEW

First, skim each section, noting headings and bold-face items. After you have read the section, review each objective by answering the fill-in and essay-type questions that follow it. In some cases, Study Tips explain how best to learn a difficult concept and Applications help you to know how well you understand the material. As you proceed, evaluate your performance by consulting the answers on page 60. Do not continue with the next section until you understand each answer. If you need to, review the section in the textbook before continuing.

The Cerebral Cortex

Objective 6-1: Identify the various regions of the cerebral cortex, and describe their functions.

1. The most complex functions of human behavior are linked to the most developed part of the brain, the _____ _____ .

This thin layer of interconnected neural cells is the body's ultimate control and

_____-_____ center.

2. Compared with the cortexes of lower mammals, the human cortex has a _____ (smoother/more wrinkled) surface. This _____ (increases/decreases) the overall surface area of our brains.

3. The cells that support, protect, and nourish cortical neurons are called _____ _____ . These cells may also play a role in _____ and _____ .

4. Each hemisphere's cortex is subdivided into four lobes, separated by prominent _____ , or folds. List the four lobes of the brain.

   a. _____   c. _____
   b. _____   d. _____

5. Electrical stimulation of one side of the _____ cortex, an arch-shaped region at the back of the _____ lobe, will produce movement on the opposite side of the body. The more precise the control needed, the _____ (smaller/greater) amount of cortical space occupied.

6. Researchers investigating _____-_____ _____ believe that one day mind-reading computers may enable paralyzed people to control machines directly with their _____ . Clinical trials involving _____ _____ are now under way for people. For example, recording

electrodes implanted in the _____ _____ of a 25-year-old man's brain have enabled him to mentally control a TV, draw shapes on a screen, and play video games.

7. At the front of the parietal lobes lies the _____ cortex, which, when stimulated, elicits a sensation of _____ . The more sensitive a body region, the greater the area of _____ _____ devoted to it.

8. Visual information is received in the _____ lobes, whereas auditory information is received in the _____ lobes.

9. Areas of the brain that don't receive sensory information or direct movement but, rather, integrate and interpret information received by other regions are known as _____ _____ . Approximately _____ of the human cortex is of this

type. Such areas in the _____ lobe are involved in judging, planning, and processing of new memories and in some aspects of personality. In the _____ lobe, these areas enable mathematical and spatial reasoning, and an area of the _____ lobe enables us to recognize faces.

10. Although the mind's subsystems are localized in particular brain regions, the brain _____ (does/does not) act as a unified whole.

APPLICATIONS:

11. Raccoons have much more precise control of their paws than dogs. You would expect that raccoons have more cortical space dedicated to "paw control" in the _____ of their brains.
    a. frontal lobes   c. temporal lobes
    b. parietal lobes   d. occipital lobes

12. In the diagrams to the right, the numbers refer to brain locations that have been damaged. Match each location with its probable effect on behavior.

Location		Behavioral Effect
_____ 1.		a. vision disorder
_____ 2.		b. insensitivity to touch
_____ 3.		c. motor paralysis
_____ 4.		d. hearing problem
_____ 5.		e. split brain
_____ 6.		f. altered personality

The Brain's Plasticity

Objective 6-2: Discuss the brain's ability to reorganize itself, and define *neurogenesis*.

13. The quality of the brain that makes it possible for undamaged brain areas to take over the functions of damaged regions is known as _____ . This quality is especially apparent in the brains of _____ (young children/adolescents/adults).

14. Although severed neurons usually _____ (will/will not) regenerate, some neural tissue can _____ in response to damage. The form of therapy aimed at helping to reprogram a damaged brain is called _____- _____ therapy. New evidence suggests that adult mice, birds, monkeys, and humans _____ (can/cannot) generate new brain cells through a process called _____ . Research also reveals the existence of master _____ cells in the human embryo that can develop into any type of brain cell.

Our Divided Brain

Objective 6-3: Explain how split-brain research helps us understand the functions of our left and right hemispheres.

15. The brain's two sides serve differing functions, which is referred to as hemispheric specialization, or _____ . Because damage to the _____ hemisphere will impair such important functions as reading, writing, speaking, arithmetic reasoning, and understanding, the _____ hemisphere was thought to be a subordinate or minor hemisphere.

16. In treating several patients with severe epilepsy, Philip Vogel and Joseph Bogen separated the two hemispheres of the brain by cutting the _____ _____ . When this structure is severed, the result is referred to as a _____ _____ .

17. In a split-brain patient, only the _____ hemisphere will be aware of an unseen object held in the left hand. In this case, the person would not be able to _____ the object. When different words are shown in the left and right visual fields, if the patient fixates on a point on the center line between the fields, the patient will be able to say only the word shown on the _____ .

Explain why a split-brain patient would be able to read aloud the word *pencil* flashed to his or her right visual field, but would be unable to identify a *pencil* by touch using only the left hand.

18. When the "two minds" of a split brain are at odds, the _____ hemisphere tries to rationalize what it doesn't understand. The _____ hemisphere often acts on autopilot. This phenomenon demonstrates that the _____ mind _____ (can/cannot) control our behavior.

APPLICATIONS:

19. To pinpoint the location of a tumor, a neurosurgeon electrically stimulated parts of the patient's sensory cortex. If the patient was conscious during the procedure, which of the following was probably experienced?
    a. "hearing" faint sounds
    b. "seeing" random visual patterns
    c. movement of the arms or legs
    d. a sense of having the skin touched

20. A split-brain patient has a picture of a knife flashed to her left hemisphere and that of a fork to her right hemisphere. She will be able to
    a. identify the fork using her left hand.
    b. identify a knife using her left hand.
    c. identify a knife using either hand.
    d. identify a fork using either hand.

21. Dr. Johnson briefly flashed a picture of a key in the right visual field of a split-brain patient. The patient could probably

    a. verbally report that a key was seen.
    b. write the word key using the left hand.
    c. draw a picture of a key using the left hand.
    d. do none of these things.

Right-Left Differences in the Intact Brain

22. Deaf people use the _____ hemisphere to process sign language.

23. Although the _____ hemisphere is better at making literal interpretations of language, the _____ hemisphere excels in making inferences, modulating our _____ , orchestrating our sense of _____ , and perceiving objects.

24. (Close-Up) In all cultures of the world, most of the human population is _____ (right/left-handed). Genetic factors _____ (play/do not play) a role in handedness. This handedness bias is unique to humans and to our nearest _____ relatives.

APPLICATION:

25. Anton is applying for a technician's job with a neurosurgeon. In trying to impress his potential employer with his knowledge of the brain, he says, "After my father's stroke I knew immediately that the blood clot had affected his left cerebral hemisphere because he no longer recognized a picture of his friend." Should Anton be hired?

    a. Yes. Anton obviously understands brain structure and function.
    b. No. The right hemisphere, not the left, specializes in picture recognition.
    c. Yes. Although blood clots never form in the left hemisphere, Anton should be rewarded for recognizing the left hemisphere's role in picture recognition.
    d. No. Blood clots never form in the left hemisphere, and the right hemisphere is more involved than the left in recognizing pictures.

PROGRESS TEST

Multiple-Choice Questions

Circle your answers to the following questions and check them with the answers beginning on page 60. If your answer is incorrect, read the explanation for why it is incorrect and then consult the text.

1. Which of the following is typically controlled by the right hemisphere?
    a. language
    b. learned voluntary movements
    c. arithmetic reasoning
    d. perceptual tasks

2. The increasing complexity of animals' behavior is accompanied by an
    a. increase in the size of the visual cortex.
    b. increase in the depth of the corpus callosum.
    c. increase in the size of the frontal lobes.
    d. increase in the amount of association area.

3. An experimenter flashes the word FLYTRAP onto a screen facing a split-brain patient so that FLY projects to her right hemisphere and TRAP to her left hemisphere. When asked what she saw, the patient will
    a. say she saw FLY.
    b. say she saw TRAP.
    c. point to FLY using her right hand.
    d. point to TRAP using her left hand.

4. Cortical areas that are not primarily concerned with sensory, motor, or language functions are
    a. called projection areas.
    b. called association areas.
    c. located mostly in the parietal lobe.
    d. located mostly in the temporal lobe.

5. The visual cortex is located in the
    a. occipital lobe.   c. frontal lobe.
    b. temporal lobe.   d. parietal lobe.

6. Which of the following is typically controlled by the left hemisphere?
    a. making inferences
    b. word recognition
    c. the left side of the body
    d. perceptual skills

7. In the brain, I outnumber neurons. I also provide nutrients to the neurons and help remove excess neurotransmitters. I am a
    a. hormone.   c. glial cell.
    b. myelin sheath.   d. gland.

8. Research has found that the amount of representation in the motor cortex reflects the
   a. size of the body parts.
   b. degree of precise control required by each of the parts.
   c. sensitivity of the body region.
   d. area of the occipital lobe being stimulated by the environment.

9. The nerve fibers that enable communication between the right and left cerebral hemispheres and that have been severed in split-brain patients form a structure called the
   a. temporal lobes.
   b. association areas.
   c. corpus callosum.
   d. parietal lobes.

10. Beginning at the front of the brain and moving toward the back of the head, then down the skull and back around to the front, which of the following is the correct order of the cortical regions?
    a. occipital lobe; temporal lobe; parietal lobe; frontal lobe
    b. temporal lobe; frontal lobe; parietal lobe; occipital lobe
    c. frontal lobe; occipital lobe; temporal lobe; parietal lobe
    d. frontal lobe; parietal lobe; occipital lobe; temporal lobe

11. Following a nail gun wound to his head, Jack became more uninhibited, irritable, dishonest, and profane. It is likely that his personality change was the result of injury to his
    a. parietal lobe.
    b. temporal lobe.
    c. occipital lobe.
    d. frontal lobe.

12. Three-year-old Marco suffered damage to the speech area of the brain's left hemisphere when he fell from a swing. Research suggests that
    a. he may never speak again.
    b. his motor abilities may improve so that he can easily use sign language.
    c. his right hemisphere may take over much of the language function.
    d. his earlier experience with speech may enable him to continue speaking.

Matching Items

Match each structure or term with its corresponding function or description.

Structures or Terms

_____ 1. right hemisphere
_____ 2. temporal lobes
_____ 3. occipital lobes
_____ 4. plasticity
_____ 5. neurogenesis
_____ 6. association areas
_____ 7. left hemisphere
_____ 8. glial cells

Functions or Descriptions

a. the formation of new neurons
b. specializes in rationalizing reactions
c. support cells of the nervous system
d. specializes in spatial relations
e. brain areas containing the auditory cortex
f. brain areas containing the visual cortex
g. the brain's capacity for modification
h. brain areas involved in higher mental functions

TERMS AND CONCEPTS TO REMEMBER

Using your own words, on a piece of paper write a brief definition or explanation of each of the following terms.

1. cerebral cortex
2. glial cells
3. frontal lobes
4. parietal lobes
5. occipital lobes
6. temporal lobes
7. motor cortex
8. sensory cortex
9. association areas
10. plasticity
11. neurogenesis
12. corpus callosum
13. split brain

ANSWERS

Module Review

The Cerebral Cortex

1. cerebral cortex; information-processing

2. more wrinkled; increases

3. glial cells; learning; thinking

4. fissures
   a. frontal lobe
   b. parietal lobe
   c. occipital lobe
   d. temporal lobe

5. motor; frontal; greater

6. brain-computer interface; thoughts; cognitive neural prosthetics; motor cortex

7. sensory; touch; sensory cortex

8. occipital; temporal

9. association areas; three-fourths; frontal; parietal; temporal

10. does

11. **a.** is the answer. The motor cortex, which determines the precision with which various parts of the body can be moved, is located in the frontal lobes.
    b. The parietal lobes contain the sensory cortex, which controls sensitivity to touch.
    c. The temporal lobes contain the primary projection areas for hearing and, on the left side, are also involved in language use.
    d. The occipital lobes contain the primary projection areas for vision.

12. Brain Damage Diagram

1. a	4. d
2. h	5. e
3. c	6. f

The Brain's Plasticity

13. plasticity; young children

14. will not; reorganize; constraint-induced; can; neurogenesis; stem

Our Divided Brain

15. lateralization; left; right

16. corpus callosum; split brain

17. right; name; right

The word *pencil* when flashed to a split-brain patient's right visual field would project only to the opposite, or left, hemisphere of the patient's brain. Because the left hemisphere contains the language control centers of the brain, the patient would be able to read the word aloud. The left hand is controlled by the right hemisphere of the brain. Because the right hemisphere would not be aware of the word, it would not be able to guide the left hand in identifying a pencil by touch.

18. left; right; unconscious; can

19. **d.** is the answer. Stimulation of the sensory cortex elicits a sense of touch, as the experiments of Penfield demonstrated.
    a., b., & c. Hearing, seeing, or movement might be expected if the temporal, occipital, and motor regions of the cortex, respectively, were stimulated.

20. **a.** is the answer. The left hand, controlled by the right hemisphere, would be able to identify the fork, the picture of which is flashed to the right hemisphere.

21. **a.** is the answer. The right visual field projects directly to the verbal left hemisphere.
    b. & c. The left hand is controlled by the right hemisphere, which, in this situation, would be unaware of the word since the picture has been flashed to the left hemisphere.

Right-Left Differences in the Intact Brain

22. left

23. left; right; speech; self

24. right; play; primate

25. **b.** is the answer.
    a., c., & d. The left hemisphere does not specialize in picture recognition. And blood clots can form anywhere in the brain.

Progress Test

Multiple-Choice Questions

1. **d.** is the answer.
   a. In most persons, language is primarily a left hemisphere function.
   b. Learned movements are unrelated to hemispheric specialization.
   c. Arithmetic reasoning is generally a left hemisphere function.

2. **d.** is the answer. As animals increase in complexity, there is an increase in the amount of association area.
   a. The visual cortex is not related to the complexity of an animal's behavior.
   b. The corpus callosum connects the brain's two hemispheres; it's not necessarily related to more complex behaviors.

c. The frontal lobe is concerned with personality, planning, and other mental functions, but its size is unrelated to intelligence or the complexity of behavior.

3. **b.** is the answer.

4. **b.** is the answer. Association areas interpret, integrate, and act on information from other areas of the cortex.

5. **a.** is the answer. The visual cortex is located at the very back of the brain.

6. **b.** is the answer.

   a., c., & d. making inferences, perceptual skills, and the left side of the body are primarily influenced by the right hemisphere.

7. **c.** is the answer.

   a. Hormones are secreted by endocrine glands directly into the bloodstream.

   b. Myelin sheath is the fatty tissues that intermittently surrounds the axons of neurons.

   d. Glands are part of the endocrine system.

8. **b.** is the answer.

   c. & d. These refer to the sensory cortex.

9. **c.** is the answer. The corpus callosum is a large band of neural fibers linking the right and left cerebral hemispheres. To sever the corpus callosum is in effect to split the brain.

10. **d.** is the answer. The frontal lobe is in the front of the brain. Just behind is the parietal lobe. The occipital lobe is located at the very back of the head and just below the parietal lobe. Next to the occipital lobe and toward the front of the head is the temporal lobe.

11. **d.** is the answer. As demonstrated in the case of Phineas Gage, injury to the frontal lobe may produce such changes in personality.

    a. Damage to the parietal lobe might disrupt functions involving the sensory cortex.

    b. Damage to the temporal lobe might impair hearing.

    c. Occipital damage might impair vision.

12. **c.** is the answer.

Matching Items

1. d
2. e
3. f
4. i
5. a
6. k
7. b
8. c

Terms and Concepts to Remember

1. The **cerebral cortex** is a thin intricate covering of interconnected neural cells atop the cerebral hemispheres. The seat of information processing, the cortex is responsible for those complex functions that make us distinctively human.

   Memory aid: Cortex in Latin means "bark." As bark covers a tree, the **cerebral cortex** is the "bark of the brain."

2. More numerous than cortical neurons, the **glial cells** of the brain guide neural connections, provide nutrients and insulating myelin, and help remove excess ions and neurotransmitters.

3. Located at the front of the brain, just behind the forehead, the **frontal lobes** are involved in speaking and muscle movements and in making plans and judgments.

4. Situated between the frontal and occipital lobes, the **parietal lobes** contain the sensory cortex, which receives sensory input for touch and body position.

5. Located at the back and base of the brain, the **occipital lobes** contain the visual cortex, which receives information from the eyes.

6. Located on the sides of the brain, the **temporal lobes** contain the auditory cortex, which receive information from the ears.

   Memory aid: The **temporal lobes** are located near the *temples.*

7. Located at the back of the frontal lobe, the **motor cortex** controls voluntary movement.

8. The **sensory cortex** is located at the front of the parietal lobes, just behind the motor cortex. It registers and processes body touch and movement sensations.

9. Located throughout the cortex, **association areas** of the brain are involved in higher mental functions, such as learning, remembering, and abstract thinking.

   Memory aid: Among their other functions, **association areas** of the cortex are involved in integrating, or *associating*, information from different areas of the brain.

10. **Plasticity** is the brain's capacity for modification, as evidenced by brain reorganization following damage (especially in children).

11. **Neurogenesis** is the formation of new neurons.

12. The **corpus callosum** is the large band of neural fibers that links the right and left cerebral hemispheres. Without this band of nerve fibers, the two hemispheres could not interact.

13. **Split brain** is a condition in which the major connections between the two cerebral hemispheres (the corpus callosum) are severed, literally resulting in a split brain.

Brain States and Consciousness

MODULE OVERVIEW

Consciousness—our awareness of ourselves and our environment—can be experienced in various states. Module 7 examines how researchers in the relatively new field of cognitive neuroscience have demonstrated our two-track mind, our ability to simultaneously process information at conscious and unconscious levels, as well as our tendency to miss changes in our environment. Selective attention illustrates our conscious information processing.

NOTE: Answer guidelines for all Module 7 questions begin on page 65.

MODULE REVIEW

First, skim each section, noting headings and bold-face items. After you have read the section, review each objective by answering the fill-in and essay-type questions that follow it. In some cases, Study Tips explain how best to learn a difficult concept and Applications help you to know how well you understand the material. As you proceed, evaluate your performance by consulting the answers on page 65. Do not continue with the next section until you understand each answer. If you need to, review the section in the textbook before continuing.

Defining Consciousness

Objective 7-1: Describe the place of consciousness in psychology's history.

1. The study of _____ was central in the early years of psychology and in recent decades, but for quite some time it was displaced by the study of observable _____ .

2. Advances in neuroscience made it possible to relate _____ _____

to various mental states; as a result, psychologists once again affirmed the importance of

_____ .

Define consciousness in a sentence.

3. The interdisciplinary study of how brain activity is linked with mental processes is called

_____ _____ .

The Biology of Consciousness

Objective 7-2: Explain what is meant by "dual processing," as revealed by today's cognitive neuroscience.

4. Much of our everyday thinking, feeling, and acting operates outside of our _____ awareness.

5. Unconscious information processing occurs _____ on _____ (sequential/parallel) tracks.

6. The principle that information is often processed on separate _____ and _____ tracks is called

_____ _____ .

7. The condition in which a person responds to a visual stimulus without consciously experiencing it is called _____ .

8. Our vision is actually a _____ -_____ system with a visual _____ track enabling us to recognize things and plan future actions and a visual _____ track guiding our moment-to-moment movements.

9. Solving new problems _____ (requires/does not require) conscious attention.

Selective Attention

Objective 7-3: Discuss how much information we can attend to at once.

10. When we focus our conscious awareness on a particular stimulus, we are using

_____ _____ .

11. Your ability to attend to only one voice among many is called the _____

_____ _____ .

12. When researchers distracted participants with a counting task, the participants failed to notice a gorilla-suited assistant who passed through, thus displaying _____ _____ .
Two specific forms of this phenomenon are

_____ _____ and

_____ _____ .

13. Some stimuli are so powerful they demand our attention, causing us to experience

_____-_____ .

APPLICATIONS:

14. Concluding his presentation on levels of information processing, Miguel states that:
    a. humans process both conscious and unconscious information in parallel.
    b. conscious processing occurs in parallel, while unconscious processing is sequential.
    c. conscious processing is sequential, while unconscious processing is parallel.
    d. all information processing is sequential in nature.

15. When we become absorbed in reading a book, we do not hear the people talking around us. This *selective attention* is most accurately defined as
    a. the focusing of conscious awareness on a particular stimulus.
    b. our awareness of ourselves and our environment.
    c. failing to see visible objects when our attention is directed elsewhere.
    d. separating our conscious awareness to focus on two tasks at the same time.

PROGRESS TEST

Multiple-Choice Questions

Circle your answers to the following questions and check them with the answers on page 65. If your answer is incorrect, read the explanation for why it is incorrect and then consult the text.

1. As defined by the text, *consciousness* includes which of the following?
    a. focused attention
    b. sleeping
    c. hypnosis
    d. all of these conditions

2. Which of the following best illustrates dual processing?
    a. While at the movies, Jack notices the one person scowling when everyone else was laughing.
    b. Despite the loud conversations around her, Karen is able to concentrate on what her friend is saying.
    c. At the soccer game, Gavin misses seeing a goal kick when his cell phone rings.
    d. While listening to the symphony, Marisol concentrates on what the pianist plays while automatically responding to the tempo and theme of the overall performance.

3. At its beginning, psychology focused on the study of
    a. observable behavior.
    b. consciousness.
    c. abnormal behavior.
    d. all of these behaviors.

4. The perceptual error in which we fail to see an object when our attention is directed elsewhere is
    a. dual processing.
    b. inattentional blindness.
    c. perceptual adaptation.
    d. divided consciousness.

5. *Consciousness* is defined in the text as
    a. mental life.
    b. selective attention to ongoing perceptions, thoughts, and feelings.
    c. information processing.
    d. our awareness of ourselves and our environment.

Matching Items

Match each term with its appropriate definition or description.

Definitions or Descriptions

_____ 1. simultaneous unconscious and conscious tracks
_____ 2. study of how brain activity is linked to mental activity
_____ 3. unconscious response to a visual stimulus
_____ 4. focusing conscious awareness on a particular stimulus
_____ 5. our awareness of ourselves and our environment

Terms

a. cognitive neuroscience
b. dual processing
c. consciousness
d. selective attention
e. blindsight

TERMS AND CONCEPTS TO REMEMBER

Using your own words, on a separate piece of paper write a brief definition or explanation of each of the following terms.

1. consciousness
2. cognitive neuroscience
3. dual processing
4. blindsight
5. selective attention
6. inattentional blindness
7. change blindness

ANSWERS
Module Review

Defining Consciousness

1. consciousness; behavior
2. brain activity; cognition

Consciousness is our awareness of ourselves and our environment.
3. cognitive neuroscience
4. conscious
5. simultaneously; parallel
6. conscious; unconscious; dual processing
7. blindsight
8. dual-processing; perception; action
9. requires

Selective Attention

10. selective attention
11. cocktail party effect
12. inattentional blindness; change blindness; choice blindness
13. pop-out
14. **c.** is the answer.
15. **a.** is the answer.
    b. This is the definition of consciousness.
    c. This defines inattentional blindness.
    d. In selective attention, awareness is focused on one stimulus.

Progress Test

Multiple-Choice Questions

1. **d.** is the answer.
2. **d.** is the answer.
   a. Jack apparently is experiencing pop-out.
   b. Karen is demonstrating selective attention.
   c. Gavin's experience is an example of inattentional blindness.
3. **b.** is the answer.
   a. The behaviorists' emphasis on observable behavior occurred much later in the history of psychology.
   c. Psychology has never been primarily concerned with abnormal behavior.
4. **b.** is the answer.
5. **d.** is the answer.

Matching Items

1. b
2. a
3. e
4. d
5. c

Terms and Concepts to Remember

1. For most psychologists, **consciousness** is our awareness of ourselves and our environment.
2. **Cognitive neuroscience** is the interdisciplinary study of the links between brain activity and cognition.
3. **Dual processing** is the principle that information is often simultaneously processed on separate conscious and unconscious tracks.
4. **Blindsight** is a condition in which a person responds to a visual experience without consciously experiencing it.
5. **Selective attention** is the focusing of conscious awareness on a particular stimulus.
6. **Inattentional blindness** is a perceptual error in which we fail to see visible objects when our attention is directed elsewhere.
7. **Change blindness** occurs when we fail to notice changes in the environment.

Sleep and Dreams

MODULE OVERVIEW

Module 8 examines sleep and dreaming. Most of the terminology in this module is introduced in the section on Biological Rhythms and Sleep. Doing the module review several times and rehearsing the material frequently will help you to memorize all the terms associated with the stages of sleep.

NOTE: Answer guidelines for all Module 8 questions begin on page 73.

MODULE REVIEW

First, skim each section, noting headings and bold-face items. After you have read the section, review each objective by answering the fill-in and essay-type questions that follow it. In some cases, Study Tips explain how best to learn a difficult concept and Applications help you to know how well you understand the material. As you proceed, evaluate your performance by consulting the answers beginning on page 73. Do not continue with the next section until you understand each answer. If you need to, review or reread the section in the textbook before continuing.

Biological Rhythms and Sleep

Objective 8-1: Describe how our biological rhythms influence our daily functioning

1. Our bodies' internal "clocks" control several

   _____ _____ .

2. The sleep-waking cycle follows a 24-hour clock
   called the _____

   _____ .

3. Body temperature _____
   (rises/falls) as morning approaches and

begins to _____ (rise/fall) again before we go to sleep.

4. When people are at their daily peak in circadian arousal, _____ is sharpest and

   _____ is most accurate.

5. Our circadian rhythm is altered by

   _____ and _____ .

Objective 8-2: Describe the biological rhythm of our sleeping and dreaming stages.

6. The sleep cycle consists of _____
   distinct stages.

7. The rhythm of sleep cycles was discovered when Aserinsky noticed that, at periodic intervals during the night, the _____ of a sleeping child moved rapidly. This stage of sleep, during which _____ occur, is called

   _____ _____ .

8. The relatively slow brain waves of the awake but relaxed state are known as _____
   waves. As you grow tired, you slip into

   _____ .

9. During non-REM stage 1 sleep, people often experience _____ sensations similar to _____ . These sensations may later be incorporated into

   _____ .

10. The bursts of brain-wave activity that occur during NREM-2 sleep are called _____

    _____ .

11. Large, slow brain waves are called
_____ waves. They occur in
non-REM stage _____ , which is
therefore called _____-
_____ sleep. A person in the latter
stage of sleep generally will be _____
(easy/difficult) to awaken. It is during this stage
that children may wet the bed or begin

_____ .

Describe the bodily changes that accompany REM
sleep.

APPLICATIONS:

14. Match the sleep stage with a description of that
stage or an activity that occurs then.

Sleep Stage

_____ 1. NREM-1 sleep
_____ 2. NREM-2 sleep
_____ 3. NREM-3 sleep
_____ 4. REM sleep

15. Given that REM is referred to as *paradoxical
sleep*, which of the following is true about what
happens when Nicholas dreams that he is running
around the school track?

   a. Studies of people deprived of REM sleep indicate that REM sleep is unnecessary.
   b. The body's muscles remain relaxed while other
   body systems are active.
   c. It is very easy to awaken a person from REM
   sleep.
   d. The body's muscles are very tense while the
   brain is in a nearly meditative state.

16. Although her eyes are closed, Adele's brain is
generating bursts of electrical activity. It is likely
that Adele

   a. is in deep sleep.
   b. is at the peak of her circadian rhythm.
   c. is in REM sleep.
   d. has been deprived of sleep for 24 hours.

12. During REM sleep, the motor cortex is
_____ (active/relaxed), while
the muscles are _____ (active/
relaxed). This creates the disturbing experience
of _____ _____ ,
and for this reason, REM is often referred to as
_____ sleep.

13. The sleep cycle repeats itself about every
_____ minutes. As the night progresses, deep NREM-3 sleep becomes
_____ (longer/briefer) and REM
periods become _____
(longer/briefer). Approximately
_____ percent of a night's sleep is
spent in REM sleep.

Description or Example

   a. Bonita dreams that she's dancing with Orlando
   Bloom at a grand ball.
   b. Manfred feels like he's floating above the bed.
   c. Rapid, rhythmic brain-wave activity indicates you
   are clearly asleep.
   d. You are in slow-wave sleep and you do not
   awaken easily.

What Affects Our Sleep Patterns?

Objective 8-3: Explain how biology and environment
interact in our sleep patterns.

17. Newborns spend nearly _____
(how much?) of their day asleep, while adults
spend no more than _____ .

18. Sleep patterns are influenced by
_____ , as indicated by the fact that
sleep patterns among _____
(identical/fraternal) twins are very similar. Sleep
is also influenced by _____ , as
indicated by the fact that people now sleep
_____ (more/less) than they did a
century ago.

19. Our biological clock is reset each day by exposure to _____ _____ , which triggers proteins in the _____ of the eyes to signal the brain's _____ _____ (a), which causes the brain's _____ gland (b) to increase or decrease its production of _____ (c).

Sleep Theories

Objective 8-4: Describe sleep's functions.

20. Two possible reasons for sleep are to _____ us and to help us _____ by restoring and repairing _____ tissue. Animals with high waking _____ produce an abundance of chemical _____ that are toxic to _____ . Sleep also facilitates our _____ of the day's experiences and stimulates _____ thinking.

21. During deep sleep, a growth hormone is released by the _____ gland. Adults spend _____ (more/less) time in deep sleep than children and so release _____ (more/less) growth hormone.

22. (Close-up) Exercise _____ (improves/disrupts) sleep and _____ (improves/disrupts) athletic performance. The optimal exercise time is _____ .

APPLICATIONS:

23. Concluding her presentation on contemporary theories of why sleep is necessary, Marilynn makes all of the following points except that
a. sleep may have evolved because it kept our ancestors safe during potentially dangerous periods.
b. sleep gives the brain time to heal, as it restores and repairs damaged neurons.
c. sleep encourages growth through a hormone secreted during NREM-3.
d. slow-wave sleep provides a "psychic safety valve" for stressful waking experiences.

24. Arsenio is participating in a sleep experiment. While he sleeps, a PET scan of his brain reveals increased activity in the amygdala of the limbic system. This most likely indicates that Arsenio is in _____ sleep.

Sleep Deprivation and Sleep Disorders

Objective 8-5: Describe the effects of sleep loss, and identify the major sleep disorders.

25. Allowed to sleep unhindered, most people will sleep _____ (how many?) hours a night.

26. Students who sleep _____ (how many?) or fewer hours each night have a higher risk of _____ than those who sleep _____ hours or more.

27. Another effect of sleep deprivation is to promote weight gain by increasing the hormone _____ and decreasing the hormone _____ . Another is that sleep deprivation may suppress the functioning of the body's _____ system and increase the risk of _____ _____ _____ . Another indication of the hazards of this state is that the rate of _____ tends to increase immediately after the spring time change in Canada and the United States.

28. A persistent difficulty in falling or staying asleep is characteristic of _____ . Sleeping pills and alcohol may make the problem worse since they tend to _____ (increase/reduce) REM sleep.

State several tips for those suffering from insomnia.

29. The sleep disorder in which a person experiences uncontrollable sleep attacks is _____ . People with severe cases of this disorder may collapse directly into _____ sleep and experience a loss of _____ _____ . This disorder may be linked to low levels of the neurotransmitter _____ , which is linked to alertness.

30. Individuals suffering from _____ _____ stop breathing while sleeping. This disorder is especially prevalent among _____ _____ .

31. The sleep disorder characterized by extreme fright and rapid heartbeat and breathing is called _____ _____ . Unlike nightmares, these episodes usually happen early in the night, during NREM-_____ sleep. The same is true of episodes of _____ and _____ , problems that _____ (run/do not run) in families. These sleep episodes are most likely to be experienced by _____ (young children/adolescents/older adults), in whom this stage tends to be the _____ and _____ .

APPLICATIONS:

32. Norbert's wife complains that she has to stay up all night to be sure he starts breathing again each time he stops breathing for a minute or so. So, Norbert consults his doctor and learns that he is suffering from
    a. sleep apnea.   c. night terrors.
    b. narcolepsy.   d. insomnia.

33. A person who falls asleep in the midst of a heated argument probably suffers from
    a. sleep apnea.   c. night terrors.
    b. narcolepsy.   d. insomnia.

Dreams

Objective 8-6: Describe the most common content of dreams.

34. Dreams experienced during _____ sleep are vivid, emotional, and bizarre.

35. On average, people spend _____ (how many?) years of life in dreams.

36. For both men and women, 8 in 10 dreams are marked by _____ (positive/negative) emotions, such as fears of being

    _____

    _____ .

37. Most dreams _____ (incorporate/ do not incorporate) traces of previous days' experiences.

38. While we sleep, our mind _____ (monitors/does not monitor) stimuli in the environment.

Objective 8-7: Identify proposed explanations for why we dream.

39. Freud referred to the actual content of a dream as its _____ content. Freud believed that this is a censored, symbolic version of the true meaning, or _____ content, of the dream.

40. According to Freud, most of the dreams of adults reflect _____ wishes and are the key to understanding inner _____ . To Freud, dreams serve as a psychic _____ _____ that discharges otherwise unacceptable feelings.

41. Researchers who believe that dreams serve an _____-processing function receive support from the fact that REM sleep facilitates

    _____ .

42. Brain scans confirm the link between _____ sleep and _____ .

43. Other theories propose that dreaming serves some _____ function, for example, that REM sleep provides the brain with needed _____ . Such an explanation is supported by the fact that _____ (infants/adults) spend the most time in REM sleep.

44. Still other theories propose that dreams are elicited by random bursts of _____ activity originating in lower regions of the brain, such as the _____ . According to one version, dreams are the brain's attempt to make sense of this activity. The bursts have been shown by PET scans to be given their emotional tone by the brain's _____ system, especially the _____ . Other theorists see dreams as a natural part of brain _____ and _____ development.

45. Researchers agree that we _____ (need/do not need) REM sleep. After being deprived of REM sleep, a person spends more time in REM sleep; this is the _____ _____ effect.

46. REM sleep _____ (does/does not) occur in other mammals. Animals such as fish, whose behavior is less influenced by learning, _____ (do/do not) dream. This finding supports the _____-_____ theory of dreaming.

APPLICATIONS:

47. Barry has participated in a sleep study for the last four nights. He was awakened each time he entered REM sleep. Now that the experiment is over, Barry will most likely show a(n) _____ (increase/ decrease) in REM sleep, a phenomenon known as _____ _____ .

48. Bahara dreams that she trips and falls as she walks up the steps to the stage to receive her college diploma. Her psychoanalyst suggests that the dream might symbolize her fear of moving on to the next stage of her life—a career. The analyst is evidently attempting to interpret the _____ content of Bahara's dream.

49. Six-month-old Piper spend two-thirds of the day sleeping and most of that time in REM sleep. Her 25-year-old mother sleeps only 8 hours with fewer hours in REM sleep than her daughter. According to a physiological theory of dreaming, this makes sense because the brain activity associated with REM sleep
    a. fixes the day's activities in memory.
    b. gives meaning to random neural activity.

c. provides the brain with periodic stimulation.
d. keeps the infant in deep sleep.

PROGRESS TEST

Multiple-Choice Questions

Circle your answers to the following questions and check them with the answers beginning on page 74. If your answer is incorrect, read the explanation for why it is incorrect and then consult the text.

1. The cluster of brain cells that control the circadian rhythm is the
   a. amygdala.
   b. suprachiasmatic nucleus.
   c. NPY.
   d. pineal.

2. Sleep spindles predominate during which stage of sleep?
   a. NREM-1   c. NREM-2
   b. NREM-3   d. REM sleep

3. During which stage of sleep does the body experience increased heart rate, rapid breathing, and genital arousal?
   a. NREM-2   c. NREM-1
   b. NREM-3   d. REM sleep

4. The sleep cycle is approximately _____ minutes.
   a. 30   c. 75
   b. 50   d. 90

5. The effects of chronic sleep deprivation include
   a. suppression of the immune system.
   b. diminished productivity.
   c. depression.
   d. all of these effects.

6. One effect of sleeping pills is to
   a. decrease REM sleep.
   b. increase REM sleep.
   c. decrease NREM-2 sleep.
   d. increase NREM-2 sleep.

7. People who heard unusual phrases prior to sleep were awakened each time they began REM sleep. The fact that they remembered less the next morning provides support for the _____ theory of dreaming.
   a. manifest content
   b. physiological
   c. information-processing
   d. cognitive development

8. According to Freud, dreams are
   a. a symbolic fulfillment of erotic wishes.
   b. the result of random neural activity in the brainstem.
   c. the brain's mechanism for self-stimulation.
   d. the disguised expressions of inner conflicts.

9. Which of the following is NOT a theory of dreaming mentioned in the text?
   a. Dreams facilitate information processing.
   b. Dreaming stimulates the developing brain.
   c. Dreams result from random neural activity originating in the brainstem.
   d. Dreaming is an attempt to escape from social stimulation.

10. The sleep-waking cycles of young people who stay up too late typically are _____ hours in duration.
    a. 23   c. 25
    b. 24   d. 26

11. Which of the following statements regarding REM sleep is true?
    a. Adults spend more time than infants in REM sleep.
    b. REM sleep deprivation results in a REM rebound.
    c. People deprived of REM sleep adapt easily.
    d. Sleeping medications tend to increase REM sleep.

12. A person whose EEG shows a high proportion of alpha waves is most likely
    a. dreaming.   c. in NREM-3 sleep.
    b. in NREM-2 sleep.   d. awake and relaxed.

13. Circadian rhythms are the
    a. brain waves that occur during deep sleep.
    b. muscular tremors that occur during opiate withdrawal.
    c. regular body cycles that occur on a 24-hour schedule.
    d. brain waves that are indicative of NREM-2 sleep.

14. Which of the following is NOT an example of a biological rhythm?
    a. the circadian rhythm
    b. the 90-minute sleep cycle
    c. the four sleep stages
    d. sudden sleep attacks during the day

15. Which of the following is characteristic of REM sleep?
    a. genital arousal
    b. increased muscular tension
    c. night terrors
    d. alpha waves

16. According to one physiological theory, dreaming represents
    a. the brain's efforts to integrate unrelated bursts of activity in visual brain areas with the emotional tone provided by limbic system activity.
    b. a mechanism for coping with the stresses of daily life.
    c. a symbolic depiction of a person's unfulfilled wishes.
    d. an information-processing mechanism for converting the day's experiences into long-term memory.

Matching Items

Match each term with its appropriate definition or description.

Definitions or Descriptions

_____ 1. surface meaning of dreams
_____ 2. deeper meaning of dreams
_____ 3. stage of sleep associated with delta waves
_____ 4. stage of sleep associated with muscular relaxation
_____ 5. sleep disorder in which breathing stops
_____ 6. sleep disorder occurring in NREM-3 sleep
_____ 7. disorder in which sleep attacks occur
_____ 8. twilight stage of sleep associated with imagery resembling hallucinations
_____ 9. brain wave of awake, relaxed person
_____ 10. sleep stage associated with dreaming
_____ 11. theory that dreaming reflects our erotic drives
_____ 12. brain-wave activity during NREM-2 sleep

Terms

a. NREM-1 sleep
b. manifest content
c. narcolepsy
d. sleep apnea
e. NREM-3 sleep
f. REM sleep
g. latent content
h. night terrors
i. Freud's theory
j. alpha
k. sleep spindle
l. REM

TERMS AND CONCEPTS TO REMEMBER

Using your own words, on a separate piece of paper write a brief definition or explanation of each of the following terms.

1. circadian rhythm

2. REM sleep

3. alpha waves

4. sleep

5. hallucinations

6. delta waves

7. insomnia

8. narcolepsy

9. sleep apnea

10. night terrors

11. dream

12. manifest content

13. latent content

14. REM rebound

ANSWERS
Module Review

Biological Rhythms and Sleep

1. biological rhythms

2. circadian rhythm

3. rises; fall

4. thinking; memory

5. age; experience

6. four

7. eyes; dreams; REM sleep

8. alpha; sleep

9. hypnagogic; hallucinations; memories

10. sleep spindles

11. delta; 3; slow-wave; difficult; sleepwalking

During REM sleep, brain waves become as rapid as those of NREM-1 sleep, heart rate rises and breathing becomes more rapid and irregular, and genital arousal and rapid eye movements occur.

12. active; relaxed; sleep paralysis; paradoxical

13. 90; briefer; longer; 20 to 25

14. 1. b   3. d
    2. c   4. a

15. **b.** is the answer. Although the body is aroused internally, the messages of the activated motor cortex do not reach the muscles.

    a. Studies of REM-deprived people indicate just the opposite.

    c. It is difficult to awaken a person from REM sleep.

    d. Just the opposite occurs in REM sleep: the muscles are relaxed, yet the brain is aroused.

16. **c.** is the answer. The rapid eye movements of REM sleep coincide with bursts of activity in brain areas that process visual images.

What Affects Our Sleep Patterns?

17. two-thirds; one-third

18. genes; identical; culture; less

19. bright light; retinas; suprachiasmatic nucleus; pineal; melatonin

Sleep Theories

20. protect; recuperate; brain; metabolism; free radicals; neurons; memory; creative

21. pituitary; less; less

22. improves; improves; late afternoon or early evening

23. **d.** is the answer. Freud's theory proposed that dreams, which occur during fast-wave, REM sleep, serve as a psychic safety valve.

24. REM. The amygdala is involved in emotion, and dreams during REM sleep often tend to be emotional.

Sleep Deprivation and Sleep Disorders

25. 9

26. 5; depression; 8

27. ghrelin; leptin; immune; high blood pressure; accidents

28. insomnia; reduce

Tips for promoting healthy sleep include exercising during the day, avoiding caffeine after early afternoon and food and drink before bedtime, sleeping on a regular schedule, and relaxing before bedtime.

29. narcolepsy; REM; muscular tension; orexin

30. sleep apnea; overweight men

31. night terrors; 3; sleepwalking; sleeptalking; run; young children; lengthiest; deepest

32. **a.** is the answer. With sleep apnea, the person stops breathing for a minute or so, then is awakened by decreased blood oxygen that forces him or her to snort in the air. This happens hundreds of times each night.

33. **b.** is the answer. Narcolepsy is characterized by uncontrollable sleep attacks.

    a. Sleep apnea is characterized by the temporary cessation of breathing while asleep.

    c. Night terrors are characterized by high arousal and terrified behavior, occurring during NREM-3 sleep.

    d. Insomnia refers to chronic difficulty in falling or staying asleep.

Dreams

34. REM

35. six

36. negative; attacked, pursued, or rejected, or of experiencing misfortune

37. incorporate

38. monitors

39. manifest; latent

40. erotic; conflicts; safety valve

41. information; memory

42. REM; memory

43. physiological; stimulation; infants

44. neural; brainstem; limbic; amygdala; maturation; cognitive

45. need; REM rebound

46. does; do not; information-processing

47. increase; REM rebound

48. latent. The analyst is evidently trying to go beyond the events in the dream and understand the dream's hidden meaning, or the dream's latent content.

49. **c.** is the answer.

Progress Test

Multiple-Choice Questions

1. **b.** is the answer.
   a. The amygdala is an emotion center in the limbic system.
   c. NPY is a brain chemical that has been found to be reduced in rats who prefer alcohol to water.
   d. The pineal is a gland that produces the sleep-inducing hormone melatonin.

2. **a.** is the answer.
   b. Delta waves predominate during NREM-3.
   c. NREM-2 is characterized by sleep spindles.
   d. Faster, nearly waking brain waves occur during REM sleep.

3. **d.** is the answer.
   a., b., & c. During non-REM stages 1–3 heart rate and breathing are slow and regular and the genitals are not aroused.

4. **d.** is the answer.

5. **d.** is the answer.

6. **a.** is the answer. Like alcohol, sleeping pills carry the undesirable consequence of reducing REM sleep and may make insomnia worse in the long run.
   b., c., & d. Sleeping pills do not produce these effects.

7. **c.** is the answer. They remembered less than if they were awakened during other stages.

8. **a.** is the answer. Freud saw dreams as psychic safety valves that discharge unacceptable feelings that are often related to erotic wishes.
   b. & c. These physiological theories of dreaming are not associated with Freud.
   d. According to Freud, dreams represent the individual's conflicts and wishes but in disguised, rather than transparent, form.

9. **d.** is the answer.
   a., b., & c. Each of these describes a valid theory of dreaming that was mentioned in the text.

10. **c.** is the answer. We can reset our biological clocks by adjusting our sleep schedules. Thus, young adults adopt something closer to a 25-hour day by staying up too late to get 8 hours of sleep.

11. **b.** is the answer. Following REM deprivation, people temporarily increase their amount of REM sleep, in a phenomenon known as REM rebound.
    a. Just the opposite is true: the amount of REM sleep is greatest in infancy.
    c. Deprived of REM sleep by repeated awakenings, people return more and more quickly to the REM stages after falling back to sleep. They by no means adapt easily to the deprivations.
    d. Just the opposite occurs: they tend to suppress REM sleep.

12. **d.** is the answer.
    a. The brain waves of REM sleep (dream sleep) are more like those of Stage 1 sleepers.
    b. Stage 2 is characterized by sleep spindles.
    c. NREM-3 is characterized by slow delta waves.

13. **c.** is the answer.

14. **d.** is the answer.

15. **a.** is the answer.
    b. During REM sleep, muscular tension is low.
    c. Night terrors are associated with NREM-3 sleep.

d. Alpha waves are characteristic of the relaxed, awake state.

16. **a.** is the answer.
    b. & c. These essentially Freudian explanations of the purpose of dreaming are based on the idea that a dream is a psychic safety valve that harmlessly discharges otherwise inexpressible feelings.
    d. This explanation of the function of dreaming is associated with the information-processing viewpoint.

Matching Items

1. b	**6.** h	**11.** i
2. g	**7.** c	**12.** k
3. e	**8.** a	
4. f	**9.** j	
5. d	**10.** l	

Terms and Concepts to Remember

1. A **circadian rhythm** is any regular bodily rhythm, such as body temperature and sleep-wakefulness, that follows a 24-hour cycle.

   Memory aid: In Latin, *circa* means "about" and *dies* means "day." A **circadian rhythm** is one that is about a day, or 24 hours, in duration.

2. **REM sleep** is the sleep stage in which the muscles are relaxed but other body systems are active, and vivid dreaming occurs; also known as *paradoxical sleep*.

   Memory aid: **REM** is an acronym for rapid eye movement, the distinguishing feature of this sleep stage that led to its discovery.

3. **Alpha waves** are the relatively slow brain waves characteristic of an awake, relaxed state.

4. **Sleep** is the natural, periodic, easily reversible loss of consciousness, on which the body and mind depend for healthy functioning.

5. **Hallucinations** are false sensory experiences that occur without any sensory stimulus.

6. **Delta waves** are the large, slow brain waves associated with deep sleep.

7. **Insomnia** is a sleep disorder in which the person regularly has difficulty in falling or staying asleep.

8. **Narcolepsy** is a sleep disorder in which the victim suffers sudden, uncontrollable sleep attacks, often characterized by entry directly into REM.

9. **Sleep apnea** is a sleep disorder in which the person ceases breathing while asleep, briefly arouses to gasp for air, falls back asleep, and repeats this cycle throughout the night.

Example: One theory of the sudden infant death syndrome is that it is caused by **sleep apnea**.

10. A person suffering from **night terrors** experiences episodes of high arousal with apparent terror. Night terrors usually occur during NREM-3 sleep.

11. **Dreams** are sequences of images, emotions, and thoughts, the most vivid of which occur during REM sleep.

12. In Freud's theory of dreaming, the **manifest content** is the remembered story line.

13. In Freud's theory of dreaming, the **latent content** is the underlying but censored meaning of a dream.

Memory aids for 18 and 19: *Manifest* means "clearly apparent, obvious"; *latent* means "hidden, concealed." A dream's **manifest content** is that which is obvious; its **latent content** remains hidden until its symbolism is interpreted.

14. **REM rebound** is the tendency for REM sleep to increase following REM sleep deprivation.

Hypnosis

MODULE OVERVIEW

Module 9 explores whether hypnosis is a unique state of consciousness. Since the technique was first introduced, hypnosis has been surrounded by many unproven myths, such as the idea that a person under hypnosis will act in ways that he or she would not in the waking stage. In discussing theories to explain hypnosis, the text notes that psychologists are moving toward a unified theory of hypnosis.

NOTE: Answer guidelines for all Module 9 questions begin on page 79.

MODULE REVIEW

First, skim each section, noting headings and bold-face items. After you have read the section, review each objective by answering the fill-in and essay-type questions that follow it. Applications help you to know how well you understand the material. As you proceed, evaluate your performance by consulting the answers on page 79. Do not continue with the next section until you understand each answer. If you need to, review the section in the textbook before continuing.

Frequently Asked Questions About Hypnosis

Objective 9-1: Define *hypnosis,* and describe how a hypnotist can influence a hypnotized subject.

1. Hypnosis is a _____
   _____ in which a hypnotist suggests that a subject will experience certain feelings or thoughts, for example.

2. Most people are _____ (somewhat/ not at all) hypnotically suggestible.

Describe people who are the most susceptible to hypnosis.

3. Research studies show that "hypnotically refreshed" memories combine _____ with _____ .

4. To find out if hypnosis can get people to act against their will, Orne and Evans introduced a _____ group of people who pretended to be hypnotized.

5. Hypnotherapists have helped some people alleviate headaches, asthma, and stress-related skin disorders through the use of _____ suggestions. Hypnosis _____ (is/ is not) especially helpful for the treatment of obesity. It _____ (is/is not) useful in treating smoking, drug, and alcohol addictions.

6. Hypnosis _____ (can/cannot) relieve pain.

Explaining the Hypnotized State

Objective 9-2: Discuss whether hypnosis is an extension of normal consciousness or an altered state.

7. Skeptics believe that hypnosis may reflect the workings of _____
   _____ . These findings provide support for the _____ _____ theory of hypnosis.

8. An _____ person in a legitimate _____ can induce people—hypnotized or not—to perform some unlikely acts.

Summarize the argument that hypnosis is not an altered state of consciousness.

9. Hilgard has advanced the idea that during hypnosis there is a special _____ - _____ state of _____ , or split, between different levels of consciousness. For example, he believes that there is a split between the _____ and _____

aspects of pain. Hypnotic pain relief may also be due to selective _____ , that is, to the person's focusing on stimuli other than pain.

APPLICATIONS:

10. An attorney wants to know if the details and accuracy of an eyewitness's memory for a crime would be improved under hypnosis. Given the results of relevant research, what should you tell the attorney?
    a. Most hypnotically retrieved memories are either false or contaminated.
    b. Hypnotically retrieved memories are usually more accurate than conscious memories.
    c. Hypnotically retrieved memories are purely the product of the subject's imagination.
    d. Hypnosis only improves memory of anxiety-provoking childhood events.

11. Of the following individuals, who is likely to be the most hypnotically suggestible?
    a. Bill, a reality-oriented stockbroker
    b. Janice, an actress with a rich imagination
    c. Megan, a sixth-grader who has trouble focusing her attention on a task
    d. Darren, who has never been able to really "get involved" in movies or novels

12. Research studies of the effectiveness of hypnosis as a form of therapy have demonstrated that
    a. for problems of addiction, such as smoking, hypnosis has not been especially effective.
    b. posthypnotic suggestions have helped alleviate headaches, asthma, and stress-related skin disorders.
    c. as a form of therapy, hypnosis is no more effective than positive suggestions given without hypnosis.
    d. all of these statements are true.

13. Those who consider hypnosis a social phenomenon contend that
    a. hypnosis is an altered state of consciousness.
    b. hypnotic phenomena are unique to hypnosis.
    c. hypnotized subjects become unresponsive when they are no longer motivated to act as instructed.
    d. all of these statements are true.

PROGRESS TEST

Multiple-Choice Questions

Circle your answers to the following questions and check them with the answers beginning on page 79. If your answer is incorrect, read the explanation for why it is incorrect and then consult the text.

1. Which of the following statements concerning hypnosis is true?
   a. People will do anything under hypnosis.
   b. Hypnosis is the same as sleeping.
   c. Hypnosis is in part an extension of the division between conscious awareness and automatic behavior.
   d. Hypnosis improves memory recall.

2. Hypnotic responsiveness is
   a. the same in all people.
   b. generally greater in women than men.
   c. generally greater in men than women.
   d. greater when people are led to expect it.

3. According to Hilgard, hypnosis is
   a. no different from a state of heightened motivation.
   b. the same as dreaming.
   c. a dissociation between different levels of consciousness.
   d. a form of deep sleep.

4. As a form of therapy for relieving problems such as drug addiction, hypnosis is
    a. ineffective.
    b. no more effective than positive suggestions given without hypnosis.
    c. highly effective.
    d. more effective with adults than children.

5. Those who believe that hypnosis is a social phenomenon argue that "hypnotized" individuals are
    a. consciously faking their behavior.
    b. merely acting out a role.
    c. underachievers striving to please the hypnotist.
    d. doing all of these things.

TERMS AND CONCEPTS TO REMEMBER

Using your own words, on a separate piece of paper write a brief definition or explanation of each of the following terms.

1. hypnosis

2. posthypnotic suggestion

3. dissociation

ANSWERS
Module Review

Frequently Asked Questions About Hypnosis

1. social interaction

2. somewhat

Those who are most susceptible frequently become deeply absorbed in imaginative activities. Many researchers refer to this as hypnotic ability.

3. fact; fiction

4. control

5. posthypnotic; is; is not

6. can

Explaining the Hypontized State

7. normal consciousness; social influence

8. authoritative; context

The behavior of hypnotized subjects is not fundamentally different from that of other people. Therefore, hypnosis may be mainly a social phenomenon, with hypnotized subjects acting out the role of a "good hypnotic subject."

9. dual-processing; dissociation; sensory; emotional; attention

10. **a.** is the answer. Although people recall more under hypnosis, they "recall" a lot of fiction along with fact and appear unable to distinguish between the two.

    b. Hypnotically refreshed memories are usually no more accurate than conscious memories.

    c. Although the hypnotized subject's imagination may influence the memories retrieved, some actual memory retrieval also occurs.

    d. Hypnotically retrieved memories don't normally focus on anxiety-provoking events.

11. **b.** is the answer. People with the ability to become imaginatively absorbed have essentially the characteristics associated with hypnotic suggestibility. The fact that Janice is an actress also suggests she possesses such traits.

    a. Bill's reality orientation makes him an unlikely candidate for hypnosis.

    c. The hypnotically suggestible are generally able to focus on tasks or on imaginative activities.

    d. People who are hypnotically suggestible tend to become deeply engrossed in novels and movies.

12. **d.** is the answer.

13. **c.** is the answer.

Progress Test

Multiple-Choice Questions

1. **c.** is the answer.
    a. Hypnotized subjects usually perform only acts they might perform normally.
    b. The text does not suggest that sleeping and hypnosis are the same states. In fact, the brain waves of hypnotized subjects are not like those associated with sleeping.
    d. Hypnosis typically *disrupts*, or contaminates, memory.

2. **d.** is the answer.
    a. Hypnotic responsiveness varies greatly from person to person.
    b. & c. There is no evidence of a gender difference in hypnotic responsiveness.

3. **c.** is the answer. Hilgard believes that hypnosis reflects a dissociation, or split, in consciousness, as occurs normally, only to a much greater extent.

4. **a.** is the answer.

5. **b.** is the answer.
a. & c. There is no evidence that hypnotically responsive individuals fake their behaviors or that they are underachievers.

Terms and Concepts to Remember

1. **Hypnosis** is a social interaction in which one person (the hypnotist) suggests to another (the subject) that certain perceptions, feelings, thoughts, or behaviors will spontaneously occur.

2. A **posthypnotic suggestion** is a suggestion made during a hypnosis session that is to be carried out when the subject is no longer hypnotized.

3. **Dissociation** is a split between different levels of consciousness, allowing a person to divide attention between two or more thoughts or behaviors.

Drugs and Consciousness

MODULE OVERVIEW

Module 10 examines drug-altered states and near-death experiences. Although drug use and near-death experiences are very different, they often produce similar altered perceptions. Most of the terminology in this module is introduced in the section on Psychoactive Drugs. Doing the module review several times and rehearsing the material frequently will help you to memorize the names of the drugs and their effects on the nervous system. Also, pay particular attention to the section on the possible psychological and social-cultural roots of drug use.

NOTE: Answer guidelines for all Module 10 questions begin on page 87.

MODULE REVIEW

First, skim each section, noting headings and bold-face items. After you have read the section, review each objective by answering the fill-in and essay-type questions that follow it. In some cases, Study Tips explain how best to learn a difficult concept and Applications help you to know how well you understand the material. As you proceed, evaluate your performance by consulting the answers beginning on page 87. Do not continue with the next section until you understand each answer. If you need to, review or reread the section in the textbook before continuing.

Tolerance, Dependence, and Addiction

Objective 10-1: Discuss the nature of drug tolerance, dependence, and addiction, and identify some common misconceptions about addiction.

1. Drugs that alter moods and perceptions are called _____ drugs.

2. Drug users who require increasing doses to experience a drug's effects have developed _____ for the drug. With continued use, the user's brain counteracts the disruption to its normal functioning; thus, the user experiences _____ .

3. After ceasing to use a drug, a person who experiences _____ symptoms has developed a physical _____ . Regular use of a drug to relieve stress is an example of a _____ dependence. A person who has a compulsive craving for a substance despite adverse consequences is _____ to that substance.

(Thinking Critically) Briefly state three common misconceptions about addiction.

4. The three broad categories of drugs discussed in the text include _____ , which tend to slow body functions; _____ , which speed body functions; and _____ , which alter perception. These drugs all work by mimicking, stimulating, or inhibiting the activity of the brain's _____ .

APPLICATION:

5. Dan has recently begun using an addictive, euphoria-producing drug. Which of the following will probably occur if he repeatedly uses this drug?
    a. As tolerance to the drug develops, Dan will experience increasingly pleasurable "highs."
    b. The dosage needed to produce the desired effect will increase.
    c. After each use, he will become more and more elated.
    d. Dependence will become less of a problem.

Psychoactive Drugs

Objective 10-2: Identify the depressants, and describe their effects.

6. Depressants _____ nervous system activity and _____ body function. Low doses of alcohol, which is classified as a _____ , slow the activity of the _____ nervous system.

7. Alcohol is a _____ ; it may make a person more _____ or more _____ aggressive. Alcohol affects memory by interfering with the process of transferring experiences into _____- _____ memory. Also, blackouts after drinking result from alcohol's suppression of _____ _____ .

8. Excessive use of alcohol can also affect cognition by _____ the brain, especially in _____ (men/women). Alcohol use marked by tolerance and withdrawal symptoms when use is suspended indicates _____ _____ . Alcohol also reduces _____ and focuses one's attention on an _____ situation and away from _____ _____ and _____ consequences.
Describe how a person's expectations can influence the behavioral effects of alcohol.

9. Tranquilizers, which are also known as _____ , have effects similar to those of alcohol.

10. Opium, morphine, and heroin all _____ (excite/depress) neural functioning. Together, these drugs are called the _____ . When they are present, the brain eventually stops producing _____ .

Objective 10-3: Identify the stimulants, and describe their effects.

11. The most widely used stimulants are _____ , _____ , the _____ , _____ , _____ , and _____ . Stimulants _____ (are/are not) addictive.

12. Eliminating _____ would increase life expectancy more than any other preventive measure. Smoking usually begins during _____ _____ . Smokers _____ (do/do not) become dependent on _____ , and they _____ (do/do not) develop tolerance to the drug. Quitting causes _____- _____ symptoms that include _____ _____ .

13. Nicotine quickly triggers the release of _____ and _____ , two neurotransmitters that diminish _____ and boost _____ and _____ _____ . Nicotine also stimulates the _____ _____ system to release _____ and _____ , neurotransmitters that calm _____ and reduce sensitivity to _____ .

14. Cocaine and crack deplete the brain's supply of the neurotransmitters

_____ ,

_____ , and _

_____

and result in depression as the drugs' effects wear off. They do this by blocking the _____ of the neurotransmitters, which remain in the nerve cells' _____ .

15. Cocaine's psychological effects depend not only on dosage and form but also on the user's _____ and _____ and on the _____ .

16. Methamphetamine triggers the release of the neurotransmitter _____ , which stimulates brain cells that enhance _____ and _____ .

17. The drug _____ , or MDMA, is both a _____ and a _____ _____ . This drug triggers the release of the neurotransmitters _____ and _____ and blocks the reabsorption of _____ . Among the adverse effects of this drug are disruption of the body's _____ clock, suppression of the _____ _____ , impaired _____ , and slow _____ .

Objective 10-4: Identify the hallucinogens, and describe their effects.

18. Hallucinogens are also referred to as _____ . Two common synthetic hallucinogens are _____ and _____ .

19. The reports of people who have had _____-_____ _____ are very similar to the _____ reported by drug users. These experiences may be the result of a deficient supply of _____ or other insults to the brain.

20. The active ingredient in marijuana is abbreviated _____ .

Describe some of the physical and psychological effects of marijuana.

21. All psychoactive drugs trigger _____ _____ , which helps explain both _____ and _____ .

APPLICATIONS:

22. Roberto is moderately intoxicated by alcohol. Which of the following changes in his behavior is likely to occur?
    a. If angered, he is more likely to become aggressive than when he is sober.
    b. He will be less self-conscious about his behavior.
    c. If sexually aroused, he will be less inhibited about engaging in sexual activity.
    d. All of these changes are likely.

23. Which of the following statements concerning marijuana is true?
    a. The by-products of marijuana are cleared from the body more slowly than are the by-products of alcohol.
    b. Regular users may need a larger dose of the drug to achieve a high than occasional users would need to get the same effect.
    c. Marijuana is as addictive as nicotine or cocaine.
    d. Even small doses of marijuana hasten the loss of brain cells.

24. I am a synthetic stimulant and mild hallucinogen that produces euphoria and social intimacy by triggering the release of dopamine and serotonin. What am I? _____

25. Lyndall was in a car accident that required critical surgery to repair her damaged internal organs. During surgery, she had a sense of being outside her body, floating above the operating room. These _____-_____ experiences are similar to sensations of an LSD "trip."

26. Which of the following statements concerning alcohol dependence is NOT true?
    a. Adopted individuals are more susceptible to alcohol dependence if they had an adoptive parent with alcohol dependence.
    b. Having an identical twin with alcohol dependence puts a person at increased risk for alcohol problems.
    c. Geneticists have identified genes that are more common among people predisposed to alcohol dependence.
    d. Researchers have bred rats that prefer alcohol to water.

27. Which of the following statements concerning near-death experiences is true?
    a. Fewer than 1 percent of patients who come close to dying report having them.
    b. They typically consist of fantastic, mystical imagery.
    c. They are more commonly experienced by women than by men.
    d. They are more commonly experienced by men than by women.

Influences on Drug Use

Objective 10-5: Explain why some people become regular users of consciousness-altering drugs.

28. Drug use by North American youth _____ (increased/declined) during the 1970s, then declined until the early 1990s because of increased _____ _____ and efforts by the media to deglamorize drug use.

29. Adopted individuals are more susceptible to alcohol dependence if they had a(n) _____ (adoptive/biological) parent with a history of alcohol dependence. Boys who at age 6 are _____ (more/less) excitable are more likely as teens to smoke, drink, and use other drugs. Genes that are more common among people predisposed to alcohol dependence may cause deficiencies in the brain's _____ _____ system.

Identify some of the psychological and social-cultural roots of drug use.

30. Among teenagers, drug use _____ (varies/is about the same) across _____ and _____ groups.

31. Studies reveal that African-American teens have the _____ (highest/lowest) rates of drug use. A major social influence on drug use is the _____ culture.

32. State three possible channels of influence for drug prevention and treatment programs.

    a. _____

    b. _____

    c. _____

APPLICATIONS:

33. Which of the following was NOT suggested by the text as an important aspect of drug prevention and treatment programs?
    a. education about the long-term costs of a drug's temporary pleasures
    b. efforts to boost people's self-esteem and purpose in life
    c. attempts to modify peer associations
    d. "scare tactics" that frighten prepubescent children into avoiding drug experimentation

34. Which of the following statements concerning the roots of drug use is true?
    a. Heavy users of alcohol, marijuana, and cocaine often are always on a high.
    b. If an adolescent's friends use drugs, odds are that he or she will, too.
    c. Teenagers who are academically average students seldom use drugs.
    d. It is nearly impossible to predict whether a particular adolescent will experiment with drugs.

STUDY TIP: This chapter discusses three major categories of psychoactive drugs, drugs that when abused may lead to clinically significant impairment or distress. Information about their psychological effects and their actions on the nervous system is best organized in the form of a chart. To help you review this material, complete the missing information in the chart below. To get you started, the first drug category has already been filled in. In combination with text Table 10.2, you should have a useful summary of substance-related disorders.

35. Psychoactive Drug Category	Specific Drugs in This Category	Psychological Effects of These Drugs	How These Drugs Affect the Nervous System
Depressants	alcohol, barbiturates, opiates	disrupt judgment and inhibition, induce sleep, reduce anxiety	decrease neural activity, slow body functions
Stimulants			
Hallucinogens			

PROGRESS TEST

Multiple-Choice Questions

Circle your answers to the following questions and check them with the answers beginning on page 88. If your answer is incorrect, read the explanation for why it is incorrect and then consult the text.

1. Cocaine and crack produce a euphoric rush by
   a. blocking the actions of serotonin.
   b. depressing neural activity in the brain.
   c. blocking the reuptake of dopamine in brain cells.
   d. stimulating the brain's production of endorphins.

2. Which of the following is classified as a depressant?
   a. methamphetamine   c. marijuana
   b. LSD   d. alcohol

3. Which of the following preventive measures would have the greatest impact on average life expectancy?
   a. eliminating obesity
   b. eliminating smoking
   c. eliminating marijuana use, except for pain
   d. eliminating binge drinking

4. Psychoactive drugs affect behavior and perception through
   a. the power of suggestion.
   b. the placebo effect.
   c. alteration of neural activity in the brain.
   d. psychological, not physiological, influences.

5. All of the following are common misconceptions about addiction, EXCEPT the statement that
   a. to overcome an addiction a person almost always needs professional therapy.
   b. psychoactive and medicinal drugs very quickly lead to addiction.
   c. biological factors place some individuals at increased risk for addiction.
   d. many other repetitive, pleasure-seeking behaviors fit the drug-addiction-as-disease-needing-treatment model.

6. The lowest rates of drug use among high school seniors is reported by
   a. Asian-Americans.
   b. Hispanic-Americans.
   c. African-Americans.
   d. Native Americans.

7. Alcohol has the most profound effect on
   a. the transfer of experiences to long-term memory.
   b. immediate memory.
   c. previously established long-term memories.
   d. all of these factors.

8. A person who requires increasing amounts of a drug in order to feel its effect is said to have developed
   a. tolerance.
   b. physical dependency.
   c. psychological dependency.
   d. resistance.

9. Which of the following is NOT a stimulant?
   a. amphetamines
   c. nicotine
   b. caffeine
   d. alcohol

10. Which of the following was NOT cited in the text as evidence that heredity influences alcohol use?
    a. Children whose parents abuse alcohol have a lower tolerance for multiple alcoholic drinks taken over a short period of time.
    b. Boys who are impulsive and fearless at age 6 are more likely to drink as teenagers.
    c. Laboratory mice have been selectively bred to prefer alcohol to water.
    d. Adopted children are more susceptible if one or both of their biological parents have a history of alcohol dependence.

11. Which of the following is usually the most powerful determinant of whether teenagers begin using drugs?
    a. family strength
    c. school adjustment
    b. religiosity
    d. peer influence

12. THC is the major active ingredient in
    a. nicotine.
    c. marijuana.
    b. Ecstasy.
    d. cocaine.

13. I am a synthetic stimulant and mild hallucinogen that produces euphoria and social intimacy by triggering the release of dopamine and serotonin. What am I?
    a. LSD
    c. THC
    b. MDMA
    d. cocaine

14. How a particular psychoactive drug affects a person depends on
    a. the dosage and form in which the drug is taken.
    b. the user's expectations and personality.
    c. the situation in which the drug is taken.
    d. all of these conditions.

Matching Items

Match each term with its appropriate definition or description.

Definitions or Descriptions

_____ 1. depressant
_____ 2. hallucinogen
_____ 3. stimulant
_____ 4. drug that is both a stimulant and mild hallucinogen
_____ 5. drugs that increase energy and stimulate neural activity
_____ 6. drugs that reduce anxiety and depress central nervous system activity
_____ 7. natural painkillers produced by the brain
_____ 8. neurotransmitter that LSD resembles

Terms

a. marijuana
b. alcohol
c. cocaine
d. serotonin
e. Ecstasy
f. amphetamines
g. endorphins
h. barbiturates

Essay Question

You have just been assigned the task of writing an article tentatively titled "Alcohol and Alcohol Dependence: Roots, Effects, and Prevention." What information should you include in your article? (Use the space provided to list the points you want to make, and organize them. Then write the essay on a separate piece of paper.)

TERMS AND CONCEPTS TO REMEMBER

Using your own words, on a separate piece of paper write a brief definition or explanation of each of the following terms.

1. psychoactive drugs
2. tolerance
3. addiction
4. withdrawal
5. physical dependence
6. psychological dependence
7. depressants
8. alcohol dependence
9. barbiturates
10. opiates
11. stimulants
12. amphetamines
13. nicotine
14. methamphetamines
15. Ecstasy (MDMA)
16. hallucinogens
17. LSD
18. near-death experience
19. THC

ANSWERS

Module Review

Tolerance, Dependence, and Addiction

1. psychoactive
2. tolerance; neuroadaptation
3. withdrawal; dependence; psychological; addicted

The following are myths about addiction:

a. Taking a psychoactive drug automatically leads to addiction.
b. A person cannot overcome an addiction without professional help.
c. The addiction-as-disease-needing-treatment model is applicable to a broad spectrum of pleasure-seeking behaviors.
4. depressants; stimulants; hallucinogens; neurotransmitters

5. **b.** is the answer. Continued use of a drug produces a tolerance; to experience the same "high," Dan will have to use larger and larger doses.

Psychoactive Drugs

6. calm; slow; depressant; sympathetic
7. disinhibitor; helpful; sexually; long-term; REM sleep
8. shrinking; women; alcohol dependence; self-awareness; arousing; normal inhibitions; future

Studies have found that if people believe that alcohol affects social behavior in certain ways, then, when they drink alcohol (or even mistakenly think that they have been drinking alcohol), they will behave according to their expectations, which vary by culture. For example, if people believe alcohol promotes sexual feeling, on drinking they are likely to behave in a sexually aroused way.

9. barbiturates
10. depress; opiates; endorphins
11. caffeine; nicotine; amphetamines; cocaine; Ecstasy; methamphetamine; are
12. smoking; early adolescence; do; nicotine; do; nicotine-withdrawal; craving, insomnia, anxiety, irritability, and distractibility
13. epinephrine; norepinephrine; appetite; alertness; mental efficiency; central nervous; dopamine; opioids; anxiety; pain
14. dopamine; serotonin; norepinephrine; reuptake (reabsorption); synapses
15. expectations; personality; situation
16. dopamine; energy; mood
17. Ecstasy; stimulant; mild hallucinogen; dopamine; serotonin; serotonin; circadian; immune system; memory; thinking
18. psychedelics; Ecstasy (MDMA); LSD
19. near-death experiences; hallucinations; oxygen
20. THC

Like alcohol, marijuana relaxes, disinhibits, and may produce a euphoric feeling. Also like alcohol, marijuana impairs perceptual and motor skills. Marijuana is a mild hallucinogen; it can amplify sensitivity to colors, sounds, tastes, and smells. Marijuana also interrupts memory formation. Unlike alcohol, THC remains in the body for a week or more. Also, the users' experiences can vary with the situation.

21. negative aftereffects; tolerance; withdrawal

22. **d.** is the answer. Alcohol loosens inhibitions and reduces self-consciousness, making people more likely to act on their feelings of anger or sexual arousal. It also disrupts the processing of experience into long-term memory.

23. **a.** is the answer. THC, the active ingredient in marijuana, and its by-products linger in the body for a week or more.

24. Ecstasy (MDMA)

25. near-death

26. **a.** is the answer. Adopted individuals are more susceptible to alcohol dependence if they had a *biological* parent with alcohol dependence.

    b., c., & d. Each of these is true, which indicates that susceptibility to alcohol dependence is at least partially determined by heredity.

27. **b.** is the answer.
    a. Approximately 12 to 40 percent of people who have come close to death report some sort of near-death experience.
    c. & d. There is no gender difference in the prevalence of near-death experiences.

Influences on Drug Use

28. increased; drug education

29. biological; more; dopamine reward
A psychological factor in drug use is the feeling that one's life is meaningless and lacks direction. Regular users of psychoactive drugs often have experienced stress or failure and are somewhat depressed. Drug use often begins as a temporary way to relieve depression, anger, anxiety, or insomnia. A powerful social factor in drug use, especially among adolescents, is peer influence. Peers shape attitudes about drugs, provide drugs, and establish the social context for their use.

30. varies; cultural; ethnic

31. lowest; peer

32. **a.** education about the long-term costs of a drug's temporary pleasures
    b. efforts to boost people's self-esteem and purpose in life
    c. attempts to "inoculate" youths against peer pressures

33. **d.** is the answer.

34. **b.** is the answer.

35. Stimulants include caffeine, nicotine, amphetamines, cocaine, Ecstasy, and methamphetamines. They enhance energy and mood and can be addictive. They excite neural activity and speed up body functions.

Hallucinogens include Ecstasy, LSD, and marijuana. They distort perceptions and evoke sensory images in the absence of sensory input. They produce their effects by interfering with the serotonin neurotransmitter system.

Progress Test

Multiple-Choice Questions

1. **c.** is the answer. They also block the reuptake of serotonin and norepinephrine.
   a. This answer describes the effect of LSD.
   b. Depressants such as alcohol have this effect. Cocaine and crack are classified as stimulants.
   d. None of the psychoactive drugs has this effect. Opiates, however, *suppress* the brain's production of endorphins.

2. **d.** is the answer. Alcohol, which slows body functions and neural activity, is a depressant.
   a. Methamphetamine is a stimulant.
   b. & c. LSD and marijuana are hallucinogens.

3. **b.** is the answer.

4. **c.** is the answer. Such drugs work primarily at synapses, altering neural transmission.
   a. What people believe will happen after taking a drug will likely have some effect on their individual reactions, but psychoactive drugs actually work by altering neural transmission.
   b. Because a placebo is a substance without active properties, this answer is incorrect.
   d. This answer is incorrect because the effects of psychoactive drugs on behavior, perception, and so forth have a physiological basis.

5. **c.** is the answer. This is true. Heredity, for example, influences tendencies toward alcoholism.

6. **c.** is the answer.

7. **a.** is the answer. Alcohol disrupts the processing of experiences into long-term memory but has little effect on either immediate or previously established memories.

8. **a.** is the answer.
   b. Physical dependence may occur in the absence of tolerance. The hallmark of physical dependence is the presence of withdrawal symptoms when the person is off the drug.
   c. Psychological dependence refers to a felt, or psychological, need to use a drug, for example, a drug that relieves stress.
   d. There is no such thing as drug "resistance."

9. **d.** is the answer. Alcohol is a depressant.

10. **a.** is the answer. Compared with other children, children whose parents abuse alcohol have a

higher tolerance for multiple drinks, making it more likely that they will, in fact, consume more alcohol.

11. **d.** is the answer. If adolescents' friends use drugs, the odds are that they will, too.
    a., b., & c. These are also predictors of drug use but seem to operate mainly through their effects on peer association.

12. **c.** is the answer.

13. **b.** is the answer.
    a. & c. Unlike stimulants, LSD and THC do not speed up body functions.
    d. Unlike hallucinogens, cocaine is a stimulant and does not generally distort perceptions.

14. **d.** is the answer.

Matching Items

1.	b	5.	f
2.	a	6.	h
3.	c	7.	g
4.	e	8.	b

Essay Question

As a depressant, alcohol slows neural activity and body functions. Although low doses of alcohol may produce relaxation, with larger doses reactions slow, speech slurs, skilled performance deteriorates, and the processing of recent experiences into long-term memories is disrupted. Alcohol also reduces self-awareness and may facilitate sexual and aggressive urges the individual might otherwise resist.

Some people may be biologically vulnerable to alcoholism. This is indicated by the fact that individuals who have a biological parent with alcoholism, or people who have an identical twin with alcoholism, are more susceptible to alcoholism.

Stress, depression, and the feeling that life is meaningless and without direction are common feelings among heavy users of alcohol and may create a psychological vulnerability to alcoholism.

Especially for teenagers, peer group influence is strong. If an adolescent's friends use alcohol, odds are that he or she will too.

Research suggests three important channels of influence for drug prevention and treatment programs: (1) education about the long-term consequences of alcohol use; (2) efforts to boost people's self-esteem and purpose in life; and (3) attempts to counteract peer pressure that leads to experimentation with drugs.

Terms and Concepts to Remember

1. **Psychoactive drugs**—which include stimulants, depressants, and hallucinogens—are chemical substances that alter moods and perceptions. They work by affecting or mimicking the activity of neurotransmitters.

2. **Tolerance** is the diminishing of a psychoactive drug's effect that occurs with repeated use, requiring progressively larger doses to produce the same effect.

3. An **addiction** is a compulsive craving for a drug despite adverse consequences and withdrawal symptoms.

4. **Withdrawal** refers to the discomfort and distress that follow the discontinued use of an addictive drug.

5. **Physical dependence** is a physiological need for a drug that is indicated by the presence of unpleasant withdrawal symptoms when the drug is not taken.

6. The psychological need to use a drug is referred to as **psychological dependence**.

7. **Depressants** are psychoactive drugs, such as alcohol, opiates, and barbiturates, that reduce neural activity and slow body functions.

8. **Alcohol dependence** (popularly known as alcoholism) is alcohol use that is marked by tolerance, withdrawal if use is suspended, and a drive to continue use.

9. **Barbiturates** are depressants, sometimes used to induce sleep or reduce anxiety.

10. **Opiates** are depressants derived from the opium poppy, such as opium, morphine, and heroin; they reduce neural activity and temporarily lessen pain and anxiety.

11. **Stimulants** are psychoactive drugs, such as caffeine, nicotine, amphetamines, Ecstasy, methamphetamine, and cocaine, that excite neural activity and speed up body functions.

12. **Amphetamines** are a type of stimulant and, as such, speed up body functions and neural activity.

13. **Nicotine** is the stimulating and highly addictive psychoactive drug found in tobacco.

14. **Methamphetamine** is a powerfully addictive stimulant that speeds up body functions and is associated with energy and mood changes.

15. Classified as both a synthetic stimulant and a mild hallucinogen, **Ecstasy (MDMA)** produces short-term euphoria by increasing serotonin levels in the brain. Repeated use may permanently damage serotonin neurons, suppress immunity, and impair memory and other cognitive functions.

16. **Hallucinogens** are psychedelic drugs, such as LSD and marijuana, that distort perceptions and evoke sensory images in the absence of sensory input.

17. **LSD** (lysergic acid diethylamide) is a powerful hallucinogen capable of producing vivid false perceptions and disorganization of thought processes.

18. The **near-death experience** is an altered state of consciousness that has been reported by some people who have had a close brush with death.

19. The major active ingredient in marijuana, **THC** is classified as a mild hallucinogen.

Behavior Genetics and Evolutionary Psychology

MODULE OVERVIEW

Module 11 is concerned with the ways in which our biological heritage, or nature, interacts with our individual experiences, or nurture, to shape who we are. After a brief explanation of basic terminology, the module explores the field of behavior genetics, which studies twins and adopted children to weigh genetic and environmental influences on behaviors. The next section discusses psychology's use of evolutionary principles to answer universal questions about human behavior.

NOTE: Answer guidelines for all Module 11 questions begin on page 97.

MODULE REVIEW

First, skim each section, noting headings and bold-face items. After you have read the section, review each objective by answering the fill-in and essay-type questions that follow it. In some cases, Study Tips explain how best to learn a difficult concept and Think About It and Applications help you to know how well you understand the material. As you proceed, evaluate your performance by consulting the answers beginning on page 97. Do not continue with the next section until you understand each answer. If you need to, review the section in the textbook before continuing.

Introduction

1. Our differences as humans include our
   _____ , _____ , and
   _____ and _____
   backgrounds.

2. Our similarities as human beings include our
   common _____ _____ ,

our shared _____ architecture, and
our _____ behaviors.

3. A fundamental question in psychology deals with the extent to which we are shaped by our heredity, called our _____ , and by external influences, called our _____ .

Behavior Genetics: Predicting Individual Differences

Objective 11-1: Define *genes,* and describe how behavior geneticists explain our individual differences.

4. Researchers who specifically study genetic and environmental influences on behavior are called
   _____ _____ .

5. The term *environment* refers to every
   _____ influence.

6. The master plans for development are stored in the _____ . In number, each person inherits _____ of these structures, _____ from each parent. Each is composed of a coiled chain of the molecule _____ .

7. If chromosomes are the chapters of heredity, the words that make each of us a distinctive human being are called _____ .

8. Genes can either be _____ (active) or inactive. Genes are "turned on" by
   _____ _____ . When turned on, genes provide the code for creating _____ _____ , our body's building blocks.

9. The complete instructions for making an organism are referred to as the human

_____ .

STUDY TIP: To keep the relationship among genes, DNA, and chromosomes straight, try thinking about them visually. Chromosomes are the largest of the units. They are made of up genes, which are in turn made up of DNA. Test your understanding by identifying the elements of heredity in the drawing below. Note that c. is the unit that contains the code for proteins, and d. is the spiraling, complex molecule.

10. a. _____   c. _____
    b. _____   d. _____

11. To study the power and limits of genetic influences on behavior, researchers use _____ and _____ studies.

12. Twins who developed from a single (monozygotic) egg are genetically _____ . Twins who developed from different (dizygotic) fertilized eggs are no more genetically alike than siblings and are called _____ twins.

13. In terms of the personality traits of extraversion and neuroticism, identical twins are _____ (more/no more) alike than are fraternal twins.

14. Twin pairs reported _____ (being treated alike/being treated differently). However, their similarities _____ (could/could not) be attributed to how they were treated.

15. Through research on identical twins raised apart, psychologists are able to study the influence of the _____ .

16. Studies tend to show that the personalities of adopted children _____ (do/do not) closely resemble those of their adoptive parents.

However, adoption studies show that parenting _____ (does/does not) matter. For example, many adopted children score _____ (higher/lower) than their biological parents on intelligence tests.

17. The term that refers to the inborn personality, especially the child's emotional excitability, is _____ , which _____ (does/does not) endure over time.

18. From the first weeks of life, difficult babies are more _____ , _____ , and _____ . In contrast, easy babies are _____ , _____ , and _____ in feeding and sleeping. Slow-to-warm-up babies tend to resist or _____ from new people and situations. Faced with a new or strange situation, anxious infants become _____ (more/less) physiologically aroused than less excitable infants.

Objective 11-2: Identify the potential uses of molecular genetics research.

19. The subfield of biology that seeks to identify some of the many genes that influence normal human traits is _____

_____ .

Identify some results of research by these scientists.

Objective 11-3: Explain what is meant by heritability, and discuss how it relates to individuals and groups.

20. The extent to which variation among individuals can be attributed to differing genes is called _____ . This _____ (does/does not) mean that we can say what percentage of a person's personality or intelligence is inherited. Heritable individual differences _____ (imply/do not necessarily imply) heritable group differences.

STUDY TIP: Heritability is a difficult concept to grasp in part because it is often confused with genetic determination, which refers to what causes a characteristic to develop. The number of toes on your feet is genetically determined because your genes cause five toes to develop on each foot. Heritability, on the other hand, is what causes differences in a characteristic. As explained in the text, to say that the heritability of intelligence is 50 percent does not mean that half of an individual's intelligence is inherited. Rather, it means that we can attribute to heredity 50 percent of the variation of intelligence among those studied. A good way to keep the two concepts straight is to remember that while the concept of genetic determination makes sense in the case of a single person, heritability does not. Genetic determination is biological; heritability is a statistical measure. Heritability only makes sense relative to differences among groups of people. It doesn't make sense to ask, "What's the heritability of my intelligence?"

APPLICATIONS:

21. Despite growing up in the same home environment, Karen and her brother John have personalities as different from each other as two people selected randomly from the population.
    a. Personality is inherited. Because Karen and John are not identical twins, it is not surprising they have very different personalities.
    b. Gender is the most important factor in personality. If Karen had a sister, the two of them would probably be much more alike.
    c. The interaction of their individual genes and nonshared experiences accounts for the common finding that children in the same family are usually very different.
    d. Their case is unusual; children in the same family usually have similar personalities.

22. Dr. Gonzalez is conducting research on whether people who do well in school can thank their genes or their environment for their success. To distinguish how much genetic and environmental factors affect school success, Dr. Gonzalez should compare children with _____ (the same/different) genes and _____ (the same/different) environments.

23. My sibling and I developed from a single fertilized egg. Who are we?
    a. opposite-sex identical twins
    b. same-sex identical twins
    c. opposite-sex fraternal twins
    d. same-sex fraternal twins

24. Raoul and Fidel are identical twins separated at birth. Because they have similar heredity and different environments, heritability for their intelligence is likely to be _____ (high/low). Ramona was adopted by Francesa's parents when she was 2 months old. The heritability for their intelligence is likely to be _____ (high/low).

Objective 11-4: Discuss the interaction of heredity and environment.

25. Genes are self-_____; rather than acting as _____ that always lead to the same result, they _____ to the environmental context.

26. For _____ phenomena, human differences are nearly always the result of both _____ and _____ influences.

27. Throughout life, we are the product of the _____ of our _____ predispositions and our surrounding _____ .

28. Environments trigger activity in _____ , and our genetically influenced traits evoke _____ in other people. This may explain why _____ twins recall greater variations in their early family life than do _____ twins.

29. The new field of _____ studies the _____ mechanism by which _____ _____ trigger _____ expression.

APPLICATION:

30. Which of the following is an example of an interaction?
    a. Swimmers swim fastest during competition against other swimmers.
    b. Swimmers with certain personality traits swim fastest during competition, while those with other personality traits swim fastest during solo time trials.
    c. As the average daily temperature increases, sales of ice cream decrease.
    d. As the average daily temperature increases, sales of lemonade increase.

Evolutionary Psychology: Understanding Human Nature

Objective 11-5: Describe evolutionary psychologists' use of natural selection to explain behavior tendencies.

31. Researchers who study natural selection and the adaptive nature of human behavior are called _____ _____ .

32. Researchers in this field focus mostly on what makes people so _____ (much alike/different from one another).

33. According to the principle of _____ _____ , traits that lead to increased reproduction and survival will be most likely to be passed on to succeeding generations.

34. Genetic _____ are random errors in genetic replication that lead to _____ .

35. Genetic constraints on human behavior are generally _____ (tighter/looser) than those on animal behavior. The human species' ability to _____ and therefore to _____ in responding to different _____ contributes to our _____ , defined as our ability to _____ and _____ . Because of our genetic legacy, we love the tastes of sweets and _____ , which we tend to _____ , even though famine is unlikely in industrialized societies.

Objective 11-6: Discuss evolutionary explanations for gender differences in sexuality and mating preferences.

36. The characteristics by which people define *male* and *female* constitute _____ .

37. Compared with women, men are _____ (equally/more/less) likely to engage in casual, impulsive sex, and they are _____ (equally/more/less) likely to initiate sexual activity. This is an example of a _____ difference.

38. The _____ explanation of gender differences in attitudes toward sex is based on differences in the optimal strategy by which women and men pass on their _____ . According to this view, men and women _____ (are/are not) selected for different patterns of sexuality.

39. Cross-cultural research reveals that men judge women as more attractive if they have a _____ appearance, whereas women judge men who appear _____ , _____ , _____ , and _____ as more attractive.

Objective 11-7: Summarize the key criticisms of evolutionary psychology, and describe how evolutionary psychologists respond.

40. (Thinking Critically) Critics of the evolutionary explanation of the gender sexuality difference argue that it often works _____ (forward/backward) to propose a _____ explanation.

41. (Thinking Critically) Another critique is that gender differences in sexuality vary with _____ _____ tradition. Gender differences in mate preferences are largest in cultures characterized by greater gender _____ (equality/ inequality).

42. (Thinking Critically) Evolutionary psychologists counter the criticisms by noting that the sexes, having faced similar adaptive problems, are more _____ (alike/different) than they are _____ (alike/different). They also note that evolutionary principles offer testable _____ .

THINK ABOUT IT: A key concept closely related to the principle of natural selection is fitness. We've all heard about "survival of the fittest," but the phrase is often misunderstood. It is not always true that "only the strong survive." From the standpoint of evolutionary psychology, "fitness" most directly refers to reproductive success. Traits and behaviors that have a genetic basis obviously cannot be passed on to succeeding generations if individuals do not have offspring. As you think about gender issues and sexuality, it may be helpful to consider the question, "How might this trait or behavior have promoted reproductive success over evolutionary time?"

PROGRESS TEST

Multiple-Choice Questions

Circle your answers to the following questions and check them with the answers on page 98. If your answer is incorrect, read the explanation for why it is incorrect and then consult the text.

1. Dr. Ross believes that principles of natural selection help explain why infants come to fear strangers about the time they become mobile. Dr. Ross is most likely a(n)
   a. behavior geneticist.
   b. molecular geneticist.
   c. evolutionary psychologist.
   d. molecular biologist.

2. A pair of adopted children or identical twins reared in the same home are most likely to have similar
   a. temperaments.
   b. personalities.
   c. religious beliefs.
   d. emotional reactivity.

3. If a fraternal twin develops schizophrenia, the likelihood of the other twin developing serious mental illness is much lower than with identical twins. This suggests that
   a. schizophrenia is caused by genes.
   b. schizophrenia is influenced by genes.
   c. environment is unimportant in the development of schizophrenia.
   d. identical twins are especially vulnerable to mental disorders.

4. Of the following, the best way to separate the effects of genes and environment in research is to study
   a. fraternal twins.
   b. identical twins.
   c. adopted children and their adoptive parents.
   d. identical twins raised in different environments.

5. Through natural selection, the traits that are most likely to be passed on to succeeding generations are those that contribute to
   a. temperament.   c. aggressiveness.
   b. survival.   d. social power.

6. Which of the following is NOT true regarding gender and sexuality?
   a. Men more often than women attribute a woman's friendliness to sexual interest.
   b. Women are more likely than men to cite affection as a reason for first intercourse.
   c. Men are more likely than women to initiate sexual activity.
   d. Gender differences in sexuality are noticeably absent among gay men and lesbian women.

7. Evolutionary psychologists attribute gender differences in sexuality to the fact that women have
   a. greater reproductive potential than do men.
   b. lower reproductive potential than do men.
   c. weaker sex drives than men.
   d. stronger sex drives than men.

8. According to evolutionary psychology, men are drawn sexually to women who seem _____ , while women are attracted to men who seem

   _____ .
   a. nurturing; youthful
   b. youthful and fertile; mature and affluent
   c. slender; muscular
   d. exciting; dominant

9. Unlike _____ twins, who develop from a single fertilized egg, _____ twins develop from separate fertilized eggs.
   a. fraternal; identical
   b. identical; fraternal
   c. placental; nonplacental
   d. nonplacental; placental

10. Temperament refers to a person's characteristic
    a. emotional reactivity and intensity.
    b. attitudes.
    c. behaviors.
    d. role-related traits.

11. When evolutionary psychologists use the word *fitness*, they are specifically referring to
    a. an animal's ability to adapt to changing environments.
    b. the diversity of a species' gene pool.
    c. the total number of members of the species currently alive.
    d. our ability to survive and reproduce.

12. Physiological tests reveal that anxious, inhibited infants
    a. become less physiologically aroused when facing new situations.
    b. have slow, steady heart rates.
    c. have high and variable heart rates.
    d. have underreactive nervous systems.

13. Gender refers to
    a. the biological and social definition of male and female.
    b. the biological definition of male and female.
    c. one's sense of being male or female.
    d. the extent to which one exhibits traditionally male or female traits.

14. A molecular geneticist would be most interested in studying
    a. why most parents are so passionately devoted to their children.
    b. environmental influences on skin color.
    c. why certain diseases are more common among certain age groups.
    d. which genes influence extraversion.

15. Each cell of the human body has a total of
    a. 23 chromosomes.   c. 46 chromosomes.
    b. 23 genes.   d. 46 genes.

16. Genes direct our physical development by synthesizing
    a. hormones.   c. DNA.
    b. proteins.   d. chromosomes.

17. The *genome* is best defined as
    a. a complex molecule containing genetic information that makes up the chromosomes.
    b. a segment of DNA.
    c. the complete instructions for making an organism.
    d. the code for synthesizing protein.

18. Most human traits are
    a. learned.
    b. determined by a single gene.
    c. influenced by many genes acting together.
    d. unpredictable.

19. Mutations are random errors in _____ replication.
    a. gene   c. DNA
    b. chromosome   d. protein

20. Casual, impulsive sex is most frequent among
    a. males with high circulating levels of testosterone.
    b. males with traditional masculine attitudes.
    c. females and males who are weakly gender typed.
    d. females and males who are strongly gender typed.

21. Evolutionary explanations of gender differences in sexuality have been criticized because
    a. they offer "after-the-fact" explanations.
    b. standards of attractiveness vary with time and place.
    c. they underestimate cultural influences on sexuality.
    d. of all of these reasons.

22. Several studies of long-separated identical twins have found that these twins
    a. have little in common because of the different environments in which they were raised.
    b. have many similarities, in everything from medical histories to personalities.
    c. have similar personalities, but very different likes, dislikes, and lifestyles.
    d. are no more similar than are fraternal twins reared apart.

23. Adoption studies show that the personalities of adopted children
    a. closely match those of their adoptive parents.
    b. bear more similarities to their biological parents than to their adoptive parents.
    c. closely match those of the biological children of their adoptive parents.
    d. closely match those of other children reared in the same home, whether or not they are biologically related.

24. Chromosomes are composed of a coiled chain of
    a. DNA molecules that contain genes.
    b. DNA molecules that contain neurotransmitters.
    c. DNA molecules that contain endorphins.
    d. DNA molecules that contain enzymes.

25. When the effect of one factor (such as environment) depends on another (such as heredity), we say there is a(n) _____ between the two factors.
    a. norm
    b. positive correlation
    c. negative correlation
    d. interaction

26. An evolutionary psychologist would be most interested in studying
    a. why most parents are so passionately devoted to their children.
    b. hereditary influences on skin color.
    c. why certain diseases are more common among certain age groups.
    d. genetic differences in personality.

Matching Items

Match each term with its corresponding definition or description.

Terms

_____ **1.** fraternal
_____ **2.** genes
_____ **3.** DNA
_____ **4.** identical
_____ **5.** environment
_____ **6.** epigenetics

Functions or Descriptions

a. the biochemical units of heredity
b. twins that develop from a single egg
c. the study of influences on gene expression that occur without a change in DNA
d. twins that develop from separate eggs
e. nongenetic influences
f. a complex molecule containing the genetic information that makes up the chromosomes

10. molecular genetics

11. heritability

12. interaction

13. epigenetics

14. evolutionary psychology

15. natural selection

16. mutation

17. gender

True–False Items

Indicate whether each statement is true or false by placing *T* or *F* in the blank next to the item.

_____**1.** Gender differences in mate preferences vary widely from one culture to another.

_____**2.** The most emotionally reactive newborns tend to be the most restrained 9-month-olds.

_____**3.** Genes act as blueprints that lead to the same result no matter the context.

_____**4.** Nature selects behavioral tendencies that increase the likelihood of sending one's genes into the future.

_____**5.** Epigeneticists study the mechanisms by which gender identity is formed.

TERMS AND CONCEPTS TO REMEMBER

Using your own words, on a piece of paper write a brief definition or explanation of each of the following terms.

1. behavior genetics

2. environment

3. chromosomes

4. DNA

5. genes

6. genome

7. identical twins

8. fraternal twins

9. temperament

ANSWERS

Module Review

Introduction

1. personalities; interests; cultural; family

2. biological heritage; brain; social

3. nature; nurture

Behavior Genetics: Predicting Individual Differences

4. behavior geneticists

5. nongenetic

6. chromosomes; 46; 23; DNA

7. genes

8. expressed; environmental events; protein molecules

9. genome

10. **a.** cell nucleus   **b.** chromosome
    c. gene   **d.** DNA

11. twin; adoption

12. identical; fraternal

13. more

14. being treated alike; could not

15. environment

16. do not; does; higher

17. temperament; does

18. irritable; intense; unpredictable; cheerful; relaxed; predictable; withdraw; more

19. molecular genetics

Genetic tests can now reveal at-risk populations for at least a dozen diseases. Also, medical personnel are becoming able to give would-be parents a readout of how their fetus' genes differ from the normal pattern and what this might mean.

20. heritability; does not; do not necessarily imply

21. c. is the answer.
a. Although heredity does influence certain traits, such as outgoingness and emotional instability, it is the interaction of heredity and experience that ultimately molds personality
b. There is no single "most important factor" in personality. Moreover, for the same reason two sisters or brothers often have dissimilar personalities, a sister and brother may be very much alike.
d. Karen and John's case is not at all unusual.

22. the same; different

23. b. is the answer.
a. Because they are genetically the same, identical twins are always of the same sex.
c. & d. Fraternal twins develop from two fertilized eggs.

24. low; high

25. regulating; blueprints; react

26. psychological; genetic; environmental

27. interaction; genetic; environment

28. genes; responses; fraternal; identical

29. epigenetics; molecular; environmental events; genetic

30. b. is the answer.
a. An interaction requires at least two variables; in this example there is only one (competition).
c. This is an example of a negative correlation.
d. This is an example of a postive correlation.

Evolutionary Psychology: Understanding Human Nature

31. evolutionary psychologists

32. much alike

33. natural selection

34. mutations; change

35. looser; learn; adapt; environments; fitness; survive; reproduce; fats; store

36. gender; biological; social

37. more; more; gender

38. evolutionary; genes; are

39. youthful; mature; dominant; bold; affluent

40. backward; hindsight

41. social-cultural; inequality

42. alike; different; predictions

Progress Test

Multiple-Choice Questions

1. c. is the answer.
a., b., & d. Whereas evolutionary psychologists attempt to explain universal human tendencies, these researchers investigate genetic differences among individuals.

2. c. is the answer. Research has not shown a strong parental influence on personality, temperament, or emotional reactivity.

3. b. is the answer.
a. & c. Although an identical twin is at increased risk, the relationship is far from perfect. Mental disorders, like all psychological traits, are influenced by *both* nature and nurture.
d. This is not at all implied by the evidence from twin studies.

4. d. is the answer.
a., b., & c. To pinpoint the influence of one of the two factors (genes and environment), it is necessary to hold one of the factors constant.

5. b. is the answer.

6. d. is the answer. Such gender differences characterize both heterosexual and homosexual people.

7. b. is the answer. Women usually incubate only one infant at a time.
c. & d. The text does not suggest that there is a gender difference in the strength of the sex drive.

8. b. is the answer.
a. According to this perspective, women prefer mates with the potential for long-term nurturing investment in their joint offspring.
c. While men are drawn to women whose waists are roughly a third narrower than their hips, the text does not suggest that women equate muscularity with fertility.
d. Excitement was not mentioned as a criterion for mating.

9. b. is the answer.
c. & d. There are no such things as "placental" or "nonplacental" twins. All twins have a placenta during prenatal development.

10. **a.** is the answer.

11. **d.** is the answer.
    a. Survival ability is only one aspect of fitness.
    b. & c. Neither of these is related to fitness.

12. **c.** is the answer.
    a., b., & d. The reactions of these infants are the opposite of what these choices describe.

13. **a.** is the answer.
    b. This definition is incomplete.
    c. This defines gender identity.
    d. This defines gender typing.

14. **d.** is the answer.

15. **c.** is the answer.
    b. & d. Each cell of the human body contains hundreds of genes.

16. **b.** is the answer.
    a. Hormones are chemical messengers produced by the endocrine glands.
    c. & d. Genes are segments of DNA, which are the makeup of chromosomes.

17. **c.** is the answer.
    a. This defines DNA.
    b. This defines a gene.
    d. The genes provide the code for synthesizing proteins.

18. **c.** is the answer.

19. **a.** is the answer.

20. **b.** is the answer.
    a. Testosterone levels have not been linked to the frequency of casual sex.
    c. & d. Males are far more accepting of casual sex than are females.

21. **d.** is the answer.

22. **b.** is the answer.
    a., c., & d. Despite being raised in different environments, long-separated identical twins often have much in common, including likes, dislikes, and lifestyles. This indicates the significant heritability of many traits.

23. **b.** is the answer.
    a., c., & d. The personalities of adopted children do not much resemble those of their adoptive parents (therefore, not a.) or other children reared in the same home (therefore, not c. or d.).

24. **a.** is the answer.
    b. Neurotransmitters are the chemicals involved in synaptic transmission in the nervous system.
    d. Enzymes are chemicals that facilitate various chemical reactions throughout the body but are not involved in heredity.

25. **d.** is the answer.

a. A norm is a culturally determined set of expected behaviors for a particular role, such as a gender role.
b. & c. When two factors are correlated, it means either that increases in one factor are accompanied by increases in the other (positive correlation) or that increases in one factor are accompanied by decreases in the other (negative correlation).

26. **a.** is the answer. This is an example of a trait that contributes to survival of the human species and the perpetuation of one's genes.
    b., c., & d. These traits and issues would likely be of greater interest to a behavior geneticist because they concern the influence of specific genes on behavior.

Matching Items

1.	d	3.	f	5.	e
2.	a	4.	b	6.	c

True–False Items

1.	F	3.	F	5.	T
2.	F	4.	T		

Terms and Concepts to Remember

1. **Behavior genetics** is the study of the relative power and limits of genetic and environmental influences on behavior.

2. In behavior genetics, **environment** refers to every nongenetic, or external, influence on our traits and behaviors.

3. **Chromosomes** are threadlike structures made of DNA molecules that contain the genes. In conception, the 23 chromosomes in the egg are paired with the 23 chromosomes in the sperm.

4. **DNA** *(deoxyribonucleic acid)* is a complex molecule containing the genetic information that makes up the chromosomes.

5. **Genes** are the biochemical units of heredity that make up the chromosomes; they are segments of the DNA molecules capable of synthesizing a protein.

6. A **genome** is the complete genetic instructions for making an organism.

7. **Identical twins** develop from a single (monozygotic) fertilized egg that splits in two and therefore are genetically identical.

8. **Fraternal twins** develop from two separate (dizygotic) eggs fertilized by different sperm and therefore are no more genetically similar than ordinary siblings.

9. **Temperament** refers to a person's characteristic emotional reactivity and intensity.

10. **Molecular genetics** is the subfield of biology that studies the molecular structure and function of specific genes.

11. **Heritability** refers to the proportion of variation among individuals that can be attributed to genes.

12. An **interaction** occurs when the effects of one factor (such as environment) depend on another factor (such as heredity).

    Example: Because the way people react to us (an environmental factor) depends on our genetically influenced temperament (a genetic factor), there is an **interaction** between environment and heredity.

13. **Epigenetics** is the study of influences on gene expression that occur without a change in DNA.

14. **Evolutionary psychology** is the study of the evolution of behavior and the mind, using principles of natural selection.

15. **Natural selection** is the evolutionary principle that traits that lead to increased reproduction and survival are the most likely to be passed on to succeeding generations.

16. **Mutations** are random errors in gene replication that lead to change

17. In psychology, **gender** refers to the biological and social characteristics by which people define *male* and *female*.

Culture, Gender, and Other Environmental Influences

MODULE OVERVIEW

Module 12 focuses on environmental influences on behavior. The impact of the prenatal environment, parents, early experience, peers, and culture on the development of the brain and behavior are each discussed. The final section explores how genes and environment interact to shape both the biological and social aspects of our gender. In the end, the message is clear: our genes and our experience together form who we are.

NOTE: Answer guidelines for all Module 12 questions begin on page 107.

MODULE REVIEW

First, skim each section, noting headings and bold-face items. After you have read the section, review each objective by answering the fill-in and essay-type questions that follow it. In some cases, Applications help you to know how well you understand the material. As you proceed, evaluate your performance by consulting the answers beginning on page 107. Do not continue with the next section until you understand each answer. If you need to, review the section in the textbook before continuing.

How Does Experience Influence Development?

Objective 12-1: Describe how early experiences can modify the brain.

1. Environmental influences begin during the period of _____ development.

2. Rosenzweig and Krech discovered that rats raised from a young age in enriched environments had _____ (thicker/thinner) brain cortexes than animals raised in isolation.

Describe the effects of sensory stimulation on neural development.

3. Experience shapes the brain by preserving activated _____ connections and allowing unused connections to _____ . This process, called _____ , results in a massive loss of unused connections by _____ .

Objective 12-2: Describe the ways in which parents and peers shape children's development.

4. The idea that parents shape their children's futures came from _____ _____ and _____ .

5. Parents do influence some areas of their children's lives, such as their _____ _____ .

6. In areas such as _____ , the environment siblings share at home accounts for less than _____ percent of their differences.

7. Experiences with _____ have a powerful effect on how children develop, partly as a result of a _____ effect by which kids seek out others with similar attitudes and interests.

List the major influences of peers on children.

Cultural Influences

Objective 12-3: Describe how behavior is influenced by cultural norms.

8. The enduring behaviors, ideas, attitudes, values, and traditions of a group of people and transmitted from one generation to the next defines the group's _____ .

9. One landmark of human culture is the preservation of _____ , which is derived from our mastery of _____ , so that we can pass it on to future generations. Culture also enables an efficient division of _____ .

10. All cultural groups evolve their own rules for expected behavior, called _____ . When people don't understand what's expected, they may experience _____ _____ . After the language differences, the two greatest differences found by U.S. Peace Corps volunteers were in the _____ of life and sense of _____ .

11. The speed at which culture changes is much _____ (faster/slower) than the pace of evolutionary changes in the human _____ _____ .

Objective 12-4: Discuss how individualist and collectivist cultures influence people.

12. Cultures based on _____ give relatively greater priority to personal _____ and define their identity mostly in terms of personal _____ . Examples of such cultures occur in _____ _____ , _____ _____ , _____ , and _____ _____ .

13. In contrast, cultures based on _____ give priority to the goals of one's _____ and define their _____ accordingly. Examples of such cultures occur in _____ , _____ , and _____ .

14. (Table 4.1) In contrasting individualist and collectivist cultures, we say that in defining the self, individualists value _____ , while collectivists value _____ .

15. Whereas people in _____ cultures value freedom, they suffer more _____ , divorce, _____ and _____ -related disease.

16. Whereas most Western parents place more emphasis on _____ (emotional closeness/independence) in their children, many Asian and African parents focus on cultivating _____ (emotional closeness/independence). Children in collectivist cultures grow up with a strong sense of _____ _____ , a sense that what shames or honors the person also shames or honors the family.

17. In general, differences between groups are _____ (smaller/larger) than person-to-person differences within groups.

APPLICATION:

18. Chad, who grew up in the United States, is more likely to encourage _____ in his future children than Asian-born Hidiyaki, who is more likely to encourage _____ in his future children.

   a. obedience; independence
   b. independence; emotional closeness
   c. emotional closeness; obedience
   d. loyalty; emotional closeness

Gender Development

Objective 12-5: Discuss gender similarities and differences in psychological traits.

19. Compared with the average man, an average woman has more _____ , less _____ , and is a few inches _____ . Women are more likely than men to suffer from _____ , _____ , and _____ _____ .

20. Compared with women, men are more likely to commit _____ and to suffer _____ _____ . They are also more likely to be diagnosed with _____ , _____- _____ , _____- _____ _____ _____ , and _____ _____ _____ .

21. *Aggression* is defined as _____ or _____ behavior that is _____ to hurt someone.

22. The aggression gender gap pertains to _____ rather than _____ aggression.

23. Throughout the world, men are more likely than women to engage in _____ , _____ , and _____ .

24. Compared with women, men are perceived as being more _____ , _____ , and _____ . As leaders, they tend to be more _____ , while women are more _____ .

25. Compared with men, women are perceived as being more _____ , _____ , and _____ .

26. These perceived differences occur _____ (throughout the world/only in certain cultures).

27. This difference is noticeable in how children _____ , and it continues throughout the teen and adult years. Girls play in groups that are _____ and less _____ than boys' groups.

28. Asked difficult questions, men are more likely than women to hazard guesses rather than admit they don't know, a phenomenon called the _____ _____ _____ .

29. Because they are more _____ , women are likely to use conversation to _____ _____ , while men are likely to use conversation to _____ _____ .

30. Women tend and befriend—for example, they turn to others for _____ , especially when coping with _____ .

31. Gender differences in power, connectedness, and other traits peak in late _____ and early _____ . By age 50, the differences have _____ (decreased/increased).

APPLICATION:

32. Mackenzie and Zachary live next door to Ella and Michael. They've become good friends, and every Sunday they get together for dinner. Zachary and Michael discuss the best way to clean their roofs, demonstrating the male tendency to _____ _____ .. Mackenzie and Ella talk about how to make their new neighbors feel welcome, demonstrating the female tendency to _____ .

Objective 12-6: Explain how biological sex is determined, and describe the role of sex hormones in gender development.

33. Among your _____ (how many?) chromosomes, _____ (how many?) are unisex.

34. The twenty-third pair of chromosomes determines the developing person's _____ . The mother always contributes a(n) _____ chromosome. When the father contributes a(n) _____ chromosome, the testes begin producing the hormone _____ . In about the _____ (what week?), this hormone initiates the development of external male sex organs.

35. Sex chromosomes control _____ that influence the brain's wiring. In adulthood, part of the _____ lobe, an area involved in _____ fluency, is thicker in women. Part of the brain's _____ cortex, a key area for _____ perception, is thicker in men.

Objective 12-7: Discuss the importance of gender roles and gender typing in development.

36. Our expectations about the way men and women behave define our culture's _____ _____ .

37. Gender roles _____ (are/are not) rigidly fixed by evolution, as evidenced by the fact that they vary across _____ and over _____ . For instance, in _____ societies there tends to be minimal division of labor by sex; by contrast, in _____ societies, women remain close to home while men roam freely, herding cattle or sheep.

38. Our individual sense of being male or female is called our _____ _____ . The degree to which we exhibit traditionally male or female traits and interests is called _____ _____ .

39. According to _____ _____ theory, children learn gender-linked behaviors by observing and imitating others and being rewarded or punished. When their families discourage traditional gender typing, children _____ (do/do not) organize themselves into "boy worlds" and "girl worlds."

40. Children also learn from their _____ _____ what it means to be male or female and adjust their behavior accordingly, thereby demonstrating that _____ is important in the formation of gender identity.

41. People who are _____ have a sense of being male or female that differs from their birth sex.

APPLICATIONS:

42. Rod has always felt pressure to be the driver when traveling in a car with Sue because he learned that this was expected of men. Rod's feelings illustrate the influence of
    a. temperament.
    b. gender roles.
    c. the selection effect.
    d. natural selection.

43. Pat and Alex have been married for about 10 years. During that time, Alex is the one most likely to spend less time at work, more time with household chores, and more time caring for the very young and the very old. Alex is most likely _____ (male/female).

44. When his son cries because another child has taken his favorite toy, Brandon admonishes him by saying, "Big boys don't cry." Evidently, Brandon is an advocate of

    _____

    in accounting for the development of gender-linked behaviors.

45. Three-year-old Caleb shares a toy chest with his 18-month-old sister Elena. Caleb has put all cars, trucks, and superheros to his side of the chest and all the dolls, stuffed animals, and miniature furniture to Elena's side. Caleb has clearly formed a _____ _____ about gender-linked behaviors.

46. Four-year-old Sarah, who has very specific ideas about what it means to be female and frequently adjusts her behavior accordingly, is demonstrating the importance of _____ in the formation of gender identity.

a. gender schemas

b. norms

c. genes

d. behavior genetics

Reflections on Nature and Nurture

Objective 12-8: Describe the biopsychosocial approach to development.

47. As brute strength becomes _____ (more/less) relevant to power and status, gender roles are _____ (converging/diverging).

48. We are the product of both _____ and _____, but we are also a system that is _____. We know this because a _____ approach to development shows that no single factor is all-powerful.

49. The principle that we should prefer the simplest of competing explanations for a phenomenon is called _____ _____.

PROGRESS TEST

Multiple-Choice Questions

Circle your answers to the following questions and check them with the answers beginning on page 108. If your answer is incorrect, read the explanation for why it is incorrect and then consult the text.

1. Collectivist cultures

a. give priority to the goals of their groups.

b. value the maintenance of social harmony.

c. foster social interdependence.

d. are characterized by all of these values.

2. The traditions of a culture are passed from one generation to the next by means of

a. norms. c. genes.

b. testosterone. d. chromosomes.

3. Which of the following most accurately expresses the extent of parental influence on personality?

a. It is more extensive than most people believe.

b. It is weaker today than in the past.

c. It is more limited than popular psychology supposes.

d. It is almost completely unpredictable.

4. The fertilized egg will develop into a boy if, at conception,

a. the sperm contributes an X chromosome.

b. the sperm contributes a Y chromosome.

c. the egg contributes an X chromosome.

d. the egg contributes a Y chromosome.

5. The hormone testosterone

a. is found only in females.

b. determines the sex of the developing person.

c. stimulates growth of the female sex organs.

d. stimulates growth of the male sex organs.

6. Research studies have found that when infant rats and premature human babies are regularly touched or massaged, they

a. become attached to the person doing the massaging.

b. develop faster neurologically.

c. have more agreeable temperaments.

d. do none of these things.

7. Of the following, parents are most likely to influence their children's

a. temperament.

b. personality.

c. faith.

d. emotional reactivity.

8. Compared with Westerners, people in communal societies, such as Japan or China,

a. have a stronger sense of family.

b. exhibit greater shyness toward strangers.

c. exhibit greater concern for loyalty and social harmony.

d. have all of these characteristics.

9. The selection effect in peer influence refers to the tendency of children and youth to

a. naturally separate into same-sex playgroups.

b. establish large, fluid circles of friends.

c. seek out friends with similar interests and attitudes.

d. choose friends their parents like.

10. Which of the following is NOT true regarding cultural diversity?
    a. Culture influences how we raise our children.
    b. Culture influences how punctual we are.
    c. Culture does not have a strong influence on how strictly social roles are defined.
    d. All cultures evolve their own norms.

11. Women and men are most likely to be attracted to strongly gender-typed mates in cultures characterized by
    a. gender inequality.
    b. gender equality.
    c. flexible gender roles.
    d. few norms.

12. Children who are raised by parents who discourage traditional gender typing
    a. are less likely to display gender-typed behaviors themselves.
    b. often become confused and develop an ambiguous gender identity.
    c. nevertheless organize themselves into "girl worlds" and "boy worlds."
    d. display excessively masculine and feminine traits as adults.

13. Genetically male children who underwent sex-reassignment surgery and were raised as girls later
    a. all described themselves as female.
    b. all described themselves as male.
    c. all had an unclear sexual identity.
    d. described themselves either as female or male, or had an unclear sexual identity.

14. Providing a child with a stimulating educational environment during early childhood is likely to
    a. ensure the formation of a strong attachment with parents.
    b. foster the development of a calm, easygoing temperament.
    c. prevent neural connections from degenerating.
    d. do all of these things.

Matching Items

Match each term with its corresponding definition or description.

Terms

_____ 1. X chromosome
_____ 2. norm
_____ 3. Y chromosome
_____ 4. gender role
_____ 5. gender identity
_____ 6. gender typing
_____ 7. transgender

Functions or Descriptions

a. one's personal sense of being female or male
b. an understood rule for accepted and expected behavior
c. a term used to describe people whose gender identity doesn't match their birth sex
d. the acquisition of a traditional gender role
e. the sex chromosome found only in men
f. a set of expected behaviors for males and females
g. the sex chromosome found in both women and men

True–False Items

Indicate whether each statement is true or false by placing *T* or *F* in the blank next to the item.

_____ 1. Research on twins shows a substantial genetic influence on attitudes toward organized religion and many other issues.

_____ 2. Compared with identical twins reared in different families, fraternal twins recall their early family life more differently.

_____ 3. Parents have a stronger influence than do peers on whether a youth starts smoking.

_____4. People from individualist cultures avoid direct confrontation and blunt honesty.

_____5. Parental influence on personality is more limited than popular psychology supposes.

_____6. Lacking any exposure to language before adolescence, a person will never master any language.

Essay Question

Lakia's new boyfriend has been pressuring her to become more sexually intimate than she wants to at this early stage in their relationship. Strongly gender typed and "macho" in attitude, Jerome is becoming increasingly frustrated with Lakia's hesitation, while Lakia is starting to wonder if a long-term relationship with this type of man is what she really wants. In light of your understanding of the evolutionary explanation of gender differences in sexuality, explain why the tension between Lakia and Jerome would be considered understandable.

TERMS AND CONCEPTS TO REMEMBER

Using your own words, on a piece of paper write a brief definition or explanation of each of the following terms.

1. culture

2. norm

3. individualism

4. collectivism

5. gender

6. aggression

7. X chromosome

8. Y chromosome

9. testosterone

10. role

11. gender role

12. social learning theory

13. gender identity

14. gender typing

15. transgender

ANSWERS

Module Review

How Does Experience Influence Development?

1. prenatal

2. thicker

Research has shown that human and animal infants given extra sensory stimulation develop faster neurologically. Throughout life, sensory stimulation activates and strengthens particular neural connections, while other connections weaken with disuse. In this way, our experiences shape the very structure of the neural pathways that process those experiences.

3. neural; degenerate; pruning; puberty

4. Freudian psychiatry; psychology

5. attitudes, values, manners, faith, and politics

6. personality; 10

7. peers; selection

Peers are important for learning cooperation, for finding the road to popularity, and for inventing styles of interaction among people of the same age.

Cultural Influences

8. culture

9. innovation; language; labor

10. norms; culture shock; pace; punctuality

11. faster; gene pool

12. individualism; goals; attributes; North America; Western Europe; Australia; New Zealand

13. collectivism; group; identity; Korea; Japan; China

14. independence; interdependence

15. individualist; loneliness; homicide; stress

16. independence; emotional closeness; family self

17. smaller

18. **b.** is the answer. Although parental values differ from one time and place to another, studies reveal that Western parents today want their children to think for themselves, while Asian and African parents place greater value on emotional closeness.

   d.   Both of these values are more typical of Asian than Western cultures.

Gender Development

19. fat; muscle; shorter; depression; anxiety; eating disorders

20. suicide; alcohol dependence; autism; color-blindness; attention-deficit hyperactivity disorder; antisocial personality disorder

21. physical; verbal; relational; intended

22. physical; verbal; intended

23. hunting; fighting; warring

24. dominant; forceful; independent; directive (or autocratic); democratic

25. deferential; nurturant; affiliative

26. throughout the world

27. play; smaller; competitive

28. male answer syndrome

29. interdependent; explore relationships; communicate solutions

30. support; stress

31. adolescence; adulthood; decreased

32. communicate solutions; explore relationships

33. 46; 45

34. sex; X; Y; testosterone; seventh

35. hormones; frontal; verbal; parietal; space

36. gender roles

37. are not; cultures; time; nomadic; agricultural

38. gender identity; gender typing

39. social learning; do

40. gender schemas; cognition

41. transgender

42. **b.** is the answer.

43. female

44. gender typing

45. gender schema

46. **a.** is the answer.
   b. Norms are cultural standards of behavior unrelated to the person's gender.
   c. & d. Genes and behavior genetics apply to inherited characteristics. Here, we are talking about learned behavior.

Reflections on Nature and Nurture

47. less; converging

48. nature; nurture; open; biopsychosocial

49. Occam's razor

Progress Test

Multiple-Choice Questions

1. **d.** is the answer.

2. **a.** is the answer.

3. **c.** is the answer.

4. **b.** is the answer.
   a. In this case, a female would develop.
   c. & d. The egg can contribute only an X chromosome. Thus, the sex of the child is determined by which chromosome the sperm contributes.

5. **d.** is the answer.
   a. Although testosterone is the principal male hormone, it is present in both females and males.
   b. This is determined by the sex chromosomes.
   c. In the absence of testosterone, female sex organs will develop.

6. **d.** is the answer.

7. **c.** is the answer.
   a. & d. Temperament, which refers to a person's emotional reactivity, is determined primarily by genes.
   b. Genes limit parents' influence on their children's personalities.

8. **d.** is the answer.

9. **c.** is the answer.

10. **c.** is the answer.

11. **a.** is the answer.
   b. In such cultures, gender differences in mate preferences tend to be much smaller.
   c. Although flexibility in gender roles was not discussed per se, it is likely that greater flexibility would equate with greater equality in gender roles.
   d. All cultures develop norms.

12. **c.** is the answer.
   b. & d. There is no evidence that being raised in a "gender neutral" home confuses children or fosters a backlash of excessive gender typing.

13. **d.** is the answer. Some later described themselves as female, and some as male.

14. **c.** is the answer.
   a. Although early experiences are a factor in the development of attachment (discussed in Chapter 5), educational stimulation is probably less important than warmth and nurturance.
   b. Because temperament appears to be a strongly genetic trait, it is unlikely that early educational experiences would affect its nature.

Matching Items

1. g	**3.** e	**5.** a	**7.** c
2. b	**4.** f	**6.** d	

True–False Items

1. F	**3.** F	**5.** T
2. T	**4.** F	**6.** T

Essay Question

Evolutionary psychologists would not be surprised by the tension between Lakia and Jerome and would see it as a reflection of women's more relational and men's more recreational approach to sex. Since eggs are expensive, compared with sperm, women prefer mates with the potential for long-term investment in their joint offspring. According to this perspective, this may be why Lakia is not in a hurry to become sexually intimate with Jerome. Men, on the other hand, are selected for "pairing widely" but not necessarily wisely in order to maximize the spreading of their genes. This is especially true of men like Jerome, who have traditional masculine attitudes.

Terms and Concepts to Remember

1. A **culture** is the enduring behaviors, ideas, attitudes, values, and traditions shared by a group of people and transmitted from one generation to the next.

2. **Norms** are understood rules for accepted and expected behavior.

3. **Individualism** is giving priority to personal goals over group goals and defining one's identity in terms of personal attributes rather than group identification.

4. **Collectivism** is giving priority to the goals of one's group and defining one's identity accordingly.

5. In psychology, **gender** refers to the biological and social characteristics by which people define *male* and *female*.

6. **Aggression** is physical or verbal behavior intended to hurt someone.

7. The **X chromosome** is the sex chromosome found in both men and women. Females inherit an X chromosome from each parent.

8. The **Y chromosome** is the sex chromosome found only in men. Males inherit an X chromosome from their mothers and a Y chromosome from their fathers.

9. **Testosterone** is the most important male sex hormone. During prenatal development, testosterone stimulates the development of the external male sex organs. During puberty, it stimulates the development of the male sex characteristics.

10. A **role** is a cluster of prescribed behaviors expected of those who occupy a particular social position.

11. A **gender role** is a set of expected behaviors for males or for females.

12. According to **social learning theory,** people learn social behavior (such as gender roles) by observing and imitating and by being rewarded or punished.

13. **Gender identity** is one's sense of being male or female.

14. **Gender typing** is the acquisition of a traditional feminine or masculine role.

15. **Transgender** refers to people whose gender identity doesn't match their birth sex.

Developmental Issues, Prenatal Development, and the Newborn

MODULE OVERVIEW

Developmental psychologists study the life cycle, from conception to death, examining how we develop physically, mentally, and socially. Module 13 mentions again the relative impact of genes and experience on behavior and then introduces two other major issues in developmental psychology: (1) whether development is best described as gradual and continuous or as a discontinuous sequence of stages and (2) whether the individual's personality remains stable or changes over the life span.

Most of the module is devoted to describing prenatal development and birth, including the destructive effects of environmental toxins on the embryo and fetus. The final section explains how psychologists have uncovered the amazing abilities of the newborn.

NOTE: Answer guidelines for all Module 13 questions begin on page 113.

MODULE REVIEW

First, skim this section, noting headings and boldface items. After you have read the section, review each objective by completing the sentences and answering the questions that follow it. In some cases, Study Tips explain how best to learn a difficult concept and Think About It and Applications help you to know how well you understand the material. As you proceed, evaluate your performance by consulting the answers on page 113. Do not continue with the next section until you understand each answer. If you need to, review or reread the section in the textbook before continuing.

Developmental Psychology's Major Issues

Objective 13-1: Identify three issues that have engaged developmental psychologists.

1. Scientists who study physical, cognitive, and social changes throughout the life cycle are called
_____ _____ .

2. One of the major issues in developmental psychology concerns the relative importance of genetic inheritance and experience in determining behavior; this is called the issue of
_____ and_____ .

3. A second developmental issue concerns whether developmental changes are gradual or abrupt; this is called the issue of _____ and
_____ .

4. Stage theories that will be considered include the theory of cognitive development proposed by
_____ , the theory of moral development proposed by _____ ,
and the theory of psychosocial development proposed by _____ .

5. Although research casts doubt on the idea that life proceeds through age-linked
_____ , there are spurts of
_____ growth during childhood and puberty that correspond roughly to the stages proposed by _____ .

6. A third controversial issue concerns the consistency of personality and whether development is characterized more by _____
over time or by change.

7. The first two years of life _____ (do/do not) provide a good basis for predicting a person's eventual traits.

8. Research on the consistency of personality shows that some traits, such as those related to _____ , are more stable than others, such as social attitudes.

APPLICATION:

9. In thinking about stability and change over the life span, most developmental psychologists believe that
   a. development occurs in a series of sharply defined stages.
   b. the first two years are the most crucial in determining the individual's personality.
   c.. the consistency of personality in most people tends to increase over the life span.
   d. social and emotional style are among the characteristics that show the least stability over the life span.

Prenatal Development and the Newborn

Objective 13-2: Discuss the course of prenatal development, and explain how teratogens affect that development.

10. Conception begins when a woman's _____ releases a mature _____ .

11. The few _____ from the man that reach the egg release digestive _____ that eat away the egg's protective covering. As soon as one sperm penetrates the egg, the egg's surface _____ all other sperm.

12. The egg and sperm _____ fuse and become one.

13. Fertilized human eggs are called _____ . During the first week, the cells in this cluster begin to specialize in structure and function, that is, they begin to _____ . About 10 days after conception, the fertilized egg attaches to the mother's _____ wall.

14. From about 2 until 8 weeks of age the developing human, formed from the inner cells of the fertilized egg, is called a(n) _____ . The outer cells become the _____ , which transfers _____ and

_____ from mother to fetus. Along with nutrients, a range of harmful substances known as _____ can pass through the placenta.

15. During the final stage of prenatal development, the developing human is called a(n) _____ .

16. Moderate consumption of alcohol during pregnancy _____ (usually does not affect/can affect) the fetal brain. If a mother drinks heavily, her baby is at risk for the birth defects and mental retardation that accompany _____ _____ _____ .

APPLICATION:

17. Marissa has just learned that she is two months pregnant. She is concerned about her baby's health because in the last few months she has been drinking heavily. Marissa is afraid that her unborn child may be at risk for birth defects and for future behavior problems, _____ , and lower _____ .

Objective 13-3: Describe some abilities of the newborn, noting how researchers are able to identify their mental abilities.

18. When an infant's cheek is touched, it will vigorously _____ for a nipple. Other infant reflexes include _____ , _____ , _____ , and _____ .

19. American psychologist _____ believed that the newborn experiences a "blooming, buzzing confusion." This belief is _____ (correct/incorrect).

Give some evidence supporting the claim that a newborn's sensory equipment is biologically prewired to facilitate social responsiveness.

20. To study infants' thinking, developmental researchers have used _____ , which involves a _____ in responding with repeated stimulation. Using

_____

_____ , researchers have found that infants prefer sights, such as faces, that facilitate _____ responsiveness.

APPLICATION:

21. Leonardo is only 6 months old so he can't tell his Mom what he likes. However, by looking away from a mobile that now seems to bore him, he is saying that he sees and remembers the mobile. His behavior indicates that he has _____ to the mobile.

PROGRESS TEST

Multiple-Choice Questions

Circle your answers to the following questions and check them with the answers on page 114. If your answer is incorrect, read the explanation for why it is incorrect and then consult the text.

1. Dr. Joan Goodman is studying how memory changes as people get older. She is most likely a(n) _____ psychologist.
   a. social   c. developmental
   b. cognitive   d. experimental

2. Newborns vigorously root for a nipple when
   a. their foot is tickled.
   b. their cheek is touched.
   c. they hear a loud noise.
   d. they make eye contact with their caregiver.

3. A child can be born a drug addict because
   a. drugs used by the mother will pass into the child's bloodstream.
   b. addiction is an inherited personality trait.
   c. drugs used by the mother create genetic defects in her chromosomes.
   d. the fetus' blood has not yet developed a resistance to drugs.

4. A child whose mother drank heavily when she was pregnant is at heightened risk of
   a. being emotionally excitable during childhood.
   b. chromosomal abnormality.
   c. being born with the physical and cognitive abnormalities of fetal alcohol syndrome.
   d. addiction to a range of drugs throughout life.

5. Which is the correct order of stages of prenatal development?
   a. zygote, fetus, embryo
   b. zygote, embryo, fetus
   c. embryo, zygote, fetus
   d. embryo, fetus, zygote

6. Teratogens are
   a. physical abnormalities in the developing fetus.
   b. cognitive abnormalities in the developing fetus.
   c. chemicals and viruses that cross the placenta and may harm the developing fetus.
   d. fertilized eggs.

TERMS AND CONCEPTS TO REMEMBER

Using your own words, on a piece of paper write a brief definition or explanation of each of the following terms.

1. developmental psychology
2. zygote
3. embryo
4. fetus
5. teratogens
6. fetal alcohol syndrome (FAS)
7. habituation

ANSWERS

Module Review

Developmental Psychology's Major Issues

1. developmental psychologists
2. nature; nurture
3. continuity; stages
4. Piaget; Kohlberg; Erikson
5. stages; brain; Piaget
6. stability
7. do not
8. temperament

9. **c.** is the answer. Although some researchers emphasize stability and others emphasize potential for change, they all agree that stability increases over the life span.
a. One criticism of stage theories is that development does not occur in sharply defined stages.
b. Research has shown that individuals' adult personalities cannot be predicted from their first two years.
d. Social and emotional style are two of the most stable traits.

Prenatal Development and the Newborn

10. ovary; egg
11. sperm; enzymes; blocks
12. nuclei
13. zygotes; differentiate; uterine
14. embryo; placenta; nutrients; oxygen; teratogens
15. fetus
16. can affect; fetal alcohol syndrome
17. hyperactivity; intelligence
18. root; sucking; swallowing; tonguing; breathing
19. William James; incorrect

Newborns reflexively turn their heads in the direction of human voices. They gaze longer at a drawing of a facelike image. They focus best on objects about 8 to 12 inches away, which is about the distance between a nursing infant's eyes and the mother's. Within days, they recognize their mother's smell and voice.

20. habituation; decrease; visual preference; social
21. habituated

Progress Test

Multiple-Choice Questions

1. **c.** is the answer. Developmental psychologists study physical, cognitive (memory, in this example), and social change throughout the life span.
a. Social psychologists study how people influence and are influenced by others.
b. Cognitive psychologists *do* study memory; because Dr. Goodman is interested in life-span *changes* in memory, she is more likely a developmental psychologist.
d. Experimental psychologists study physiology, sensation, perception, learning, and other aspects of behavior. Only developmental psychologists focus on developmental changes in behavior and mental processes.

2. **b.** is the answer. The infant turns its head and begins sucking when its cheek is stroked.
a., c., & d. These stimuli produce other reflexes in the newborn.

3. **a.** is the answer. Any drug taken by the mother passes through the placenta and enters the child's bloodstream.
b. Addiction cannot be inherited; it requires exposure to an addictive drug.
c. Drugs may disrupt the mechanisms of heredity, but there is no evidence that such changes promote addiction.
d. This answer is incorrect because at no age does the blood "resist" drugs.

4. **c.** is the answer.
a., b., & d. A child's emotional temperament, attachment, and addiction have not been linked to the mother's drinking while pregnant.

5. **b.** is the answer.

6. **c.** is the answer.
a. & b. Physical and cognitive abnormalities usually result from teratogens, but that's not a definition of a teratogen.
d. A fertilized egg is a zygote.

Terms and Concepts to Remember

1. **Developmental psychology** is the branch of psychology concerned with physical, cognitive, and social change throughout the life span.

2. The **zygote** (a term derived from the Greek word for "joint") is the fertilized egg, that is, the cluster of cells formed during conception by the union of sperm and egg.

3. The **embryo** is the developing prenatal organism from about 2 weeks through 2 months after conception; formed from the inner cells of the zygote.

4. The **fetus** is the developing prenatal human from 9 weeks after conception to birth.

5. **Teratogens** (literally, "monster maker") are agents, such as chemicals and viruses, that cross the mother's placenta and can harm the developing embryo or fetus.

6. **Fetal alcohol syndrome (FAS)** refers to the physical and cognitive abnormalities that heavy drinking by a pregnant woman may cause in the developing child.

7. **Habituation** is decreasing responsiveness to a stimulus that is repeatedly presented. It is used by researchers to find out what infants see, hear, smell, and think.

Infancy and Childhood

MODULE OVERVIEW

Development continues at a fairly rapid pace in infancy and childhood, although physical growth begins to slow a bit in the middle years of childhood. Module 14 describes physical, cognitive, and social development through age 11, focusing on the stage theory of Piaget and the effects of attachment or lack of attachment on development. Although today's theorists see development as more continuous than Piaget did, his theory continues to provide a broad framework for studying development.

NOTE: Answer guidelines for all Module 14 questions begin on page 121.

MODULE REVIEW

First, skim this section, noting headings and boldface items. After you have read the section, review each objective by completing the sentences and answering the questions that follow it. In some cases, Study Tips explain how best to learn a difficult concept and Think About It and Applications help you to know how well you understand the material. As you proceed, evaluate your performance by consulting the answers beginning on page 121. Do not continue with the next section until you understand each answer. If you need to, review or reread the section in the textbook before continuing.

Physical Development

Objective 14-1: Describe some developmental changes in brain and motor abilities during infancy and childhood.

1. Biological growth processes that enable orderly changes in behavior are called

_____ .

2. The developing brain _____ (over/under) produces neurons. At birth, the human nervous system

_____ (is/is not) fully mature.

3. Between 3 and 6 years of age, the brain is developing most rapidly in the _____ lobes, which enable _____

_____ . The last areas of the brain to develop are the _____

_____ linked with _____ ,

_____ , and _____ .

4. After puberty, a process of _____ shuts down some neural connections and strengthens others.

5. Infants pass the milestones of _____ development at different rates, but the basic _____ of stages is fixed. Infants sit before they _____ and walk before they _____ .

6. Genes play a _____ (major/minor) role in motor development.

7. Until the necessary muscular and neural maturation is complete, including the rapid development of the brain's _____ , experience has a _____ (large/ small) effect on learning to walk, for example.

8. Our earliest memories generally do not occur before age _____ . This phenomenon has been called _____ .

9. Research has shown that babies _____ (are/are not) capable of learning.

APPLICATION:

10. Calvin, who is trying to impress his psychology professor with his knowledge of infant motor development, asks why some infants learn to roll over before they lift their heads from a prone position, while others develop these skills in the opposite order. What should Calvin's professor conclude from this question?
    a. Calvin clearly understands that the sequence of motor development is not the same for all infants.
    b. Calvin doesn't know what he's talking about. Although some infants reach these developmental milestones ahead of others, the order is the same for all infants.
    c. Calvin needs to be reminded that rolling over is an inherited reflex, not a learned skill.
    c. Calvin understands an important principle: Motor development is unpredictable.

Cognitive Development

Objective 14-2: Describe how a child's mind develops from the perspectives of Piaget, Vygotsky, and today's researchers.

11. *Cognition* refers to all the mental activities associated with _____ , _____ , _____ , and _____ .

12. The first researcher to show that the thought processes of adults and children are very different was _____ .

13. To organize and interpret his or her experiences, the developing child constructs cognitive concepts called _____ .

14. The interpretation of new experiences in terms of existing ideas is called _____ . The adaptation of existing ideas to fit new experiences is called _____ .

15. In Piaget's first stage of development, the _____ stage, children experience the world through their motor and sensory interactions with objects. This stage occurs between birth and nearly age _____ .

16. The awareness that things continue to exist even when they are removed from view is called _____ _____ . This awareness begins to develop at about _____ months of age.

17. Developmental researchers have found that Piaget and his followers _____ (overestimated/underestimated) young children's competence. For instance, babies have an intuitive grasp of simple laws of _____ , as seen in their reaction to a ball stopping in midair, and an understanding of _____ , as Karen Wynn demonstrated.

18. Preschoolers have difficulty perceiving things from another person's point of view. This inability is called _____ . Even adults may overestimate the extent to which others share their opinions and perspectives, a trait known as the _____ _____ _____ .

19. According to Piaget, during the preschool years and up to age _____ , children are in the _____ stage.

20. The principle that the quantity of a substance remains the same even when the shape of its container changes is called _____ . Piaget believed that preschoolers _____ (have/have not) developed this concept.

21. The child's growing ability to take another's perspective is evidence that the child is acquiring a _____ _____ _____ . Between about 3½ and 4½, children come to realize that others may hold _____ _____ .

22. (Close-Up) The disorder characterized by deficient _____ and _____ interaction and an impaired _____ _____ is _____ . This disorder is related to malfunctions of brain areas that allow us to take another's _____ .

23. (Close-Up) The term used to encompass a range of variations is _____ _____ _____ , one of which is the "high-functioning" form called _____ _____ .

24. (Close-Up) Baron-Cohen's theory proposes that autism represents an "extreme _____ brain." According to this theory, girls tend to be _____ , who are better than boys at reading facial expressions and gestures. Boys tend to be _____ , who understand things in terms of rules or laws.

25. Piaget believed that children acquire the mental abilities needed to comprehend mathematical transformations and conservation by about _____ years of age. At this time, they enter the _____ _____ stage.

26. In Piaget's final stage, the _____ _____ stage, reasoning expands from the purely concrete to encompass _____ thinking. Piaget believed most children begin to enter this stage by age _____ .

27. Russian psychologist _____ noted that by age _____ children stop thinking aloud and instead rely on _____ _____ . Talking to themselves helps children control their

_____ and _____ and master new skills.

28. Complementing Piaget's emphasis on interaction with the _____ environment is Vygotsky's emphasis on interaction with the _____ environment. To Vygotsky, children were young _____ mentored by parents and others who give them new words. Thus they provide a _____ upon which the child can build higher-level thinking.

Explain briefly how contemporary researchers view Piaget's theory.

STUDY TIP: Jean Piaget was the first major theorist to realize that each stage of life has its own characteristic way of thinking. To deepen your understanding of Jean Piaget's stages of cognitive development, fill in the blanks in the chart below. Do as much as you can without reviewing the text. To get you started, the first stage has been completed.

29. Typical Age Range	Stage	New Developments	Test to Determine if Someone Is in This Stage
Birth to nearly 2 years	Sensorimotor	Stranger anxiety Object permanence	Have the child's mother leave the room Hide a toy under a blanket
2 to _____	_____		
	Concrete _____		
About 12 through _____	_____		

APPLICATIONS:

30. Compared with when he was younger, 4-year-old Antonio is better able to empathize with his friend's feelings. This growing ability to take another's perspective indicates that Antonio is acquiring a _____ _____ _____ .

31. As 8-year-old Gabriella observes, liquid is transferred from a tall, thin tube into a short, wide jar. She is asked if there is now less liquid in order to determine if she has mastered the concept of _____ .

32. Caleb is 14 months old and he behaves as though "out of sight is out of existence." He is in Piaget's _____ stage of cognitive development.

33. Makayla is 3 years old, can use language, and has trouble taking another person's perspective. She is in Piaget's _____ _____ stage of cognitive development.

34. Four-year-old Jamail has a younger sister. When asked if he has a sister, he is likely to answer _____ (yes/no); when asked if his sister has a brother, Jamail is likely to answer _____ (yes/no).

35. In Piaget's theory, conservation is to egocentrism as the _____ stage is to the _____ stage.
    a. sensorimotor; formal operational
    b. formal operational; sensorimotor
    c. preoperational; sensorimotor
    d. concrete operational; preoperational

Social Development

Objective 14-3: Describe how parent-infant attachment bonds form.

36. Soon after _____ _____ emerges and children become mobile, a new fear, called _____ _____ , emerges.

37. This fear emerges at about age _____ .

38. The development of a strong emotional bond between infant and parent is called _____ .

39. The Harlows' studies of monkeys have shown that mother-infant attachment does not depend on the mother providing nourishment as much as it does on her providing the comfort of _____ . Another key to attachment is _____ .

40. Human attachment involves one person providing another with a _____ _____ when distressed and a _____ _____ from which to explore.

41. In some animals, attachment will occur only during a restricted time called a _____ _____ . Konrad Lorenz discovered that young birds would follow almost any object if it were the first moving thing they observed. This phenomenon is called _____ .

42. Human infants _____ (do/do not) have a precise critical period for becoming attached. However, because of _____ _____ , they attach to what they know.

APPLICATION:

43. In a 1998 movie, a young girl finds that a flock of geese follows her wherever she goes because she was the first "object" they saw after they were born. This is an example of
    a. conservation.   c. egocentrism.
    b. imprinting.   d. basic trust.

Objective 14-4: Describe how psychologists study attachment differences, and discuss their findings.

44. Placed in a research setting called the _____ _____ , children show one of two patterns of attachment: _____ attachment or _____ attachment.

Contrast the responses of securely and insecurely attached infants to strange situations.

Discuss the impact of responsive parenting on infant attachment.

45. A father's love and acceptance for his children are _____ (comparable to/less important than) a mother's love in predicting their children's health and well-being.

46. Separation anxiety peaks in infants around _____ months, then _____ (gradually declines/remains constant for about a year). This is true of children _____ (in North America/throughout the world).

47. According to Erikson, securely attached infants approach life with a sense of _____ _____ .

48. Most researchers now believe that early attachments _____ (do/do not) form the basis of adult attachments. Attachment style is also associated with _____ : Securely attached people exhibit greater drive to achieve.

APPLICATION:

49. Layla and Christian Bishop have a 13-month-old boy. According to Erikson, the Bishops' sensitive, loving care of their child contributes to the child's _____ _____ .

Objective 14-5: Describe how parental neglect, abuse, and family disruption affect children's attachment.

50. The Harlows found that when monkeys reared in social isolation were placed with other monkeys, they reacted with either fear or _____ .

51. Most abused children _____ (do/do not) later become abusive parents.

52. Although most children who grow up under adversity are _____ and become normal adults, early abuse and excessive exposure to _____ _____ may alter the development of the brain chemical _____ .

Objective 14-6: Describe the effect of day care on children.

53. Experts agree that child care per se _____ (does/does not) constitute a risk factor in children's development.

54. High-quality child care consists of warm, supportive interactions with adults in an environment that is _____ , _____ , and _____ .

55. More important than time spent in day care in influencing a child's aggression are _____ _____ .

Objective 14-7: Trace the onset and development of children's self-concept.

56. The primary social achievement of childhood is the development of a _____ , which occurs in most children by age _____ .

57. A child's self-image generally becomes stable between the ages of _____ and _____ , when children begin to describe themselves in terms of gender, group memberships, psychological _____ , and _____ and _____ compared with other children.

Identify several characteristics of children who have formed a positive self-concept.

Objective 14-8: Describe three parenting styles, and explain how children's traits relate to them.

58. Parents who impose rules and expect obedience are exhibiting a(n) _____ style of parenting.

59. Parents who make few demands of their children and tend to submit to their children's desires are identified as _____ parents.

60. Setting and enforcing standards after discussion with their children is the approach taken by _____ parents.

61. Studies have shown that children with the highest self-esteem, self-reliance, and social competence usually have _____ parents.

Explain why the correlation between authoritative parenting and social competence does not necessarily reveal cause and effect.

PROGRESS TEST

Multiple-Choice Questions

Circle your answers to the following questions and check them with the answers beginning on page 123. If your answer is incorrect, read the explanation for why it is incorrect and then consult the appropriate pages of the text (in parentheses following the correct answer).

1. In Piaget's stage of concrete operational intelligence, the child acquires an understanding of the principle of
   a. conservation.   c. attachment.
   b. deduction.   d. object permanence.

2. Piaget held that egocentrism is characteristic of the
   a. sensorimotor stage.
   b. preoperational stage.
   c. concrete operational stage.
   d. formal operational stage.

3. During which stage of cognitive development do children acquire object permanence?
   a. sensorimotor   c. concrete operational
   b. preoperational   d. formal operational

4. The Harlows' studies of attachment in monkeys showed that
   a. provision of nourishment was the single most important factor motivating attachment.
   b. a cloth mother produced the greatest attachment response.
   c. whether a cloth or wire mother was present mattered less than the presence or absence of other infants.
   d. attachment in monkeys is based on imprinting.

5. When psychologists discuss maturation, they are referring to stages of growth that are NOT influenced by
   a. conservation.   c. nurture.
   b. nature.   d. continuity.

6. The developmental theorist who suggested that securely attached children develop an attitude of basic trust is
   a. Piaget.   c. Vygotsky.
   b. Harlow.   d. Erikson.

7. Research findings on infant motor development are consistent with the idea that
   a. cognitive development lags significantly behind motor skills development.
   b. maturation of physical skills is relatively unaffected by experience.
   c. in the absence of relevant earlier learning experiences, the emergence of motor skills will be slowed.
   d. in humans, the process of maturation may be significantly altered by cultural factors.

8. Stranger anxiety develops soon after
   a. the concept of conservation.
   b. egocentrism.
   c. a theory of mind.
   d. the concept of object permanence.

9. Before Piaget, people were more likely to believe that
   a. the child's mind is a miniature model of the adult's.
   b. children think about the world in radically different ways from adults.
   c. the child's mind develops through a series of stages.
   d. children interpret their experiences in terms of their current understandings.

10. Which is the correct sequence of stages in Piaget's theory of cognitive development?
    a. sensorimotor, preoperational, concrete operational, formal operational
    b. sensorimotor, preoperational, formal operational, concrete operational
    c. preoperational, sensorimotor, concrete operational, formal operational
    d. preoperational, sensorimotor, formal operational, concrete operational

11. The term *critical period* refers to
    a. prenatal development.
    b. the initial 2 hours after a child's birth.
    c. the preoperational stage.
    d. a restricted time for learning.

12. Which of the following was NOT found by the Harlows in socially deprived monkeys?
    a. They had difficulty mating.
    b. They showed extreme fear or aggression when first seeing other monkeys.
    c. They showed abnormal physical development.
    d. The females were abusive mothers.

13. Most people's earliest memories do not predate _____ of age.
    a. 6 months   c. 2 years
    b. 1 year   d. 3 years

14. Insecurely attached infants who are left by their mothers in an unfamiliar setting often will
    a. hold fast to their mothers on their return.
    b. explore the new surroundings confidently.
    c. be indifferent toward their mothers on their return.
    d. display little emotion at any time.

True–False Items

Indicate whether each statement is true or false by placing *T* or *F* in the blank next to the item.

_____ 1. Most abused children later become abusive parents.

_____ 2. At birth, the brain and nervous system of a healthy child are fully developed.

_____ 3. The sequence in which children develop motor skills varies from one culture to another.

_____ 4. Current research shows that young children are more capable and development is more continuous than Piaget believed.

_____ 5. The impact of day care on child development, even if it is high quality, remains controversial.

TERMS AND CONCEPTS TO REMEMBER

Using your own words, on a piece of paper write a brief definition or explanation of each of the following terms.

1. maturation
2. cognition
3. schema
4. assimilation
5. accommodation
6. sensorimotor stage
7. object permanence
8. egocentrism
9. preoperational stage
10. conservation
11. theory of mind
12. autism
13. concrete operational stage
14. formal operational stage
15. stranger anxiety
16. attachment
17. critical period
18. imprinting
19. basic trust
20. self-concept

ANSWERS
Module Review

Physical Development

1. maturation
2. over; is not
3. frontal; rational planning; association areas; thinking; memory; language
4. pruning
5. motor; sequence; crawl; run
6. major
7. cerebellum; small
8. 3; infantile amnesia

9. are
10. **b.** is the answer.
    a. & d. Although the rate of motor development varies from child to child, the basic sequence is universal and, therefore, predictable.
    c. Rolling over and head lifting are both learned.

Cognitive Development

11. thinking; knowing; remembering; communicating
12. Jean Piaget
13. schemas
14. assimilation; accommodation
15. sensorimotor; 2
16. object permanence; 8
17. underestimated; physics; numbers
18. egocentrism; curse of knowledge
19. 6 or 7; preoperational
20. conservation; have not
21. theory of mind; false beliefs

22. communication; social; theory of mind; autism; viewpoint
23. Autism spectrum disorder; Asperger syndrome
24. male; empathizers; systemizers
25. 6 or 7; concrete operational
26. formal operational; abstract; 12
27. Lev Vygotsky; 7; inner speech; behavior; emotions
28. physical; social; apprentices; scaffold

Contemporary researchers see development as more continuous than did Piaget. By detecting the beginnings of each type of thinking at earlier ages, they have revealed conceptual abilities that Piaget missed. They also see formal logic as a smaller part of cognition than Piaget did. Despite these revisions to Piaget's theory, studies support the basic idea that cognitive development unfolds in the sequence Piaget described.

29. Piaget's stages are summarized below.

Typical Age Range	Stage	New Developments	Test to Determine If Someone Is in This Stage
Birth to nearly 2 years	Sensorimotor	Stranger anxiety Object permanence	Have the child's mother leave the room Hide a toy under a blanket
2 to 6 or 7 years	Preoperational	Egocentrism Not yet logical	Ask questions to determine child's ability to take another's perspective
6 or 7 to 11 years	Concrete operational	Conservation Simple math	Transfer liquid from a tall, thin glass into a short, wide glass
About 12 through adulthood	Formal operational	Abstract logic	Give child a hypothetical reasoning problem

30. theory of mind
31. conservation. This test is designed to determine if the child understands that the quantity of liquid is conserved, despite the shift to a container that is different in shape.
32. sensorimotor. The sensorimotor period is Piaget's first stage. Object permnence develops some time during this period.
33. preoperational. This child's age, ability to use language, and egocentrism clearly place her within Piaget's preoperational stage.
34. yes; no. Being 4 years old, Jamail would be in Piaget's preoperational stage. Preoperational thinking is egocentric, which means Jamail would find it difficult to "put himself in his sister's shoes" and perceive that she has a brother.

35. **d.** is the answer. Conservation is a hallmark of the concrete operational stage; egocentrism is a hallmark of the preoperational stage.

Social Development

36. object permanence; stranger anxiety
37. 8 months
38. attachment
39. body contact; familiarity
40. safe haven; secure base
41. critical period; imprinting
42. do not; mere exposure
43. **b.** is the answer.
    a. Conservation is the ability to realize that the amount of an object does not change even if its shape changes.

c. Egocentrism is having difficulty perceiving things from another's perspective.
d. According to Erikson, basic trust is feeling that the world is safe as a result of sensitive, loving caregivers.

44. strange situation; secure; insecure

Placed in a strange situation, securely attached infants play comfortably, happily exploring their new environment. In contrast, insecurely attached infants are less likely to explore their surroundings and may even cling to their mothers. When separated from their mothers, insecurely attached infants are much more distressed than securely attached infants. When reunited with their mothers, insecurely attached infants may be indifferent.

Research studies conducted by Mary Ainsworth have revealed that sensitive, responsive mothers tend to have securely attached infants, whereas insensitive, unresponsive mothers often have insecurely attached infants. Other studies have found that temperamentally difficult infants whose mothers receive training in responsive parenting are more likely to become securely attached than are control infants. This points to the importance of considering the infant's temperament in studying attachment.

45. comparable to

46. 13; gradually declines; throughout the world

47. basic trust

48. do; motivation

49. basic trust. Although loving parents will also produce securely attached children, Erikson's theory deals with trust or mistrust.

50. aggression

51. do not

52. resilient; stress hormones; serotonin

53. does not

54. safe; healthy; stimulating

55. the parents' sensitivity, the child's temperament, and the family's economic and educational level

56. self-concept; 12

57. 8; 10; traits; similarities; differences

Children who have formed a positive self-concept tend to be more confident, independent, optimistic, assertive, and sociable.

58. authoritarian

59. permissive

60. authoritative

61. authoritative

There are at least three possible explanations for the correlation between authoritative parenting and

social competence in children. (1) Parenting may foster children's competence. (2) Children's competence may promote authoritative parenting. (3) A third factor, such as heredity, may foster both authoritative parenting and child competence.

Progress Test

Multiple-Choice Questions

1. **a.** is the answer.
   b. Deduction, or deductive reasoning, is a formal operational ability.
   c. Piaget's theory is not concerned with attachment.
   d. Attaining object permanence is the hallmark of sensorimotor thought.

2. **b.** is the answer. The preoperational child sees the world from his or her own vantage point.
   a. As immature as egocentrism is, it represents a significant cognitive advance over the sensorimotor child, who knows the world only through senses and actions. Even simple self-awareness takes a while to develop.
   c. & d. As children attain the operational stages, they become more able to see the world through the eyes of others.

3. **a.** is the answer. Before object permanence is attained, "out of sight" is truly "out of mind."
   b., c., & d. Developments during the preoperational, concrete operational, and formal operational stages include the use of language, conservation, and abstract reasoning, respectively.

4. **b.** is the answer.
   a. When given the choice between a wire mother with a bottle and a cloth mother without, the monkeys preferred the cloth mother.
   c. The presence of other infants made no difference.
   d. Imprinting plays no role in the attachment of higher primates.

5. **c.** is the answer. Through maturation—an orderly sequence of biological growth processes that are relatively unaffected by experience—all humans develop.
   a. Conservation is the cognitive awareness that objects do not change with changes in shape.
   b. The forces of nature *are* those that direct maturation.
   d. The continuity/stages debate has to do with whether development is a gradual and continuous process or a discontinuous, stagelike process. Those who emphasize maturation see development as occurring in stages, not continuously.

6. **d.** is the answer. Erikson proposed that development occurs in a series of stages, in the first of which the child develops an attitude of either basic trust or mistrust.
   a. Piaget's theory is concerned with cognitive development.
   b. Harlow conducted research on attachment and deprivation.
   c. Vygotsky focused on the influence of social factors on cognitive development.

7. **b.** is the answer.

8. **d.** is the answer. With object permanence, a child develops schemas for familiar objects, including faces, and may become upset by a stranger who does not fit any of these schemas.
   a. The concept of conservation develops during the concrete operational stage, whereas stranger anxiety develops during the sensorimotor stage.
   b. & c. Egocentrism and a theory of mind both develop during the preoperational stage. This follows the sensorimotor stage, during which stranger anxiety develops.

9. **a.** is the answer.
   b., c., & d. Each of these is an understanding developed by Piaget.

10. **a.** is the answer.

11. **d.** is the answer. A critical period is a restricted time during which an organism must be exposed to certain influences or experiences for a particular kind of learning to occur.
   a. Critical periods refer to developmental periods after birth.
   b. Critical periods vary from behavior to behavior, but they are not confined to the hours following birth.
   c. Critical periods are not specifically associated with the preoperational period.

12. **c.** is the answer. Deprived monkeys were impaired in their social behaviors but not in their physical development.
   a., b., & d. Each of these was found in socially deprived monkeys.

13. **d.** is the answer. This is because of a lack of neural connections before that age.

14. **c.** is the answer.
   a. Insecurely attached infants often cling to their mothers when placed in a new situation; yet, when the mother returns after an absence, the infant's reaction tends to be one of indifference.
   b. These behaviors are characteristic of securely attached infants.
   d. Insecurely attached infants in unfamiliar surroundings will often exhibit a range of emotional behaviors.

True–False Items

1. F
2. F
3. F
4. T
5. F

Terms and Concepts to Remember

1. **Maturation** refers to the biological growth processes that enable orderly changes in behavior, relatively uninfluenced by experience or other environmental factors.

   Example: The ability to walk depends on a certain level of neural and muscular **maturation**. For this reason, until the toddler's body is physically ready to walk, practice "walking" has little effect.

2. **Cognition** refers to all the mental processes associated with thinking, knowing, remembering, and communicating.

3. In Piaget's theory of cognitive development, **schemas** are mental concepts or frameworks that organize and interpret information.

4. In Piaget's theory, **assimilation** refers to interpreting a new experience in terms of an existing schema.

5. In Piaget's theory, **accommodation** refers to changing an existing schema to incorporate new information that cannot be assimilated.

6. In Piaget's theory of cognitive stages, the **sensorimotor stage** lasts from birth to nearly age 2. During this stage, infants gain knowledge of the world through their senses and their actions.

7. **Object permanence,** which develops during the sensorimotor stage, is the awareness that things do not cease to exist when not perceived.

8. In Piaget's theory, **egocentrism** refers to the difficulty that preoperational children have in considering another's viewpoint. *Ego* means "self," and *centrism* indicates "in the center"; the preoperational child is "self-centered."

9. In Piaget's theory, the **preoperational stage** lasts from about 2 to 6 or 7 years of age. During this stage, language development is rapid, but the child is unable to understand the mental operations of concrete logic.

10. **Conservation** is the principle that properties such as number, volume, and mass remain constant despite changes in the forms of objects; it is acquired during the concrete operational stage.

11. Our ideas about our own and others' thoughts, feelings, and perceptions and the behaviors these might predict constitute our **theory of mind**.

12. **Autism** is a disorder that appears in childhood and is marked by deficient communication, social interaction, and understanding of others' states of mind.

13. During the **concrete operational stage,** lasting from about ages 6 or 7 to 11, children can think logically about concrete events and objects.

14. In Piaget's theory, the **formal operational stage** normally begins about age 12. During this stage people begin to think logically about abstract concepts.

    Memory aid: To help differentiate Piaget's stages remember that "operations" are mental transformations. *Pre*operational children, who lack the ability to perform transformations, are "before" this developmental milestone. Concrete operational children can operate on real, or concrete, objects. Formal operational children can perform logical transformations on abstract concepts.

15. **Stranger anxiety** is the fear of strangers that infants begin to display by about 8 months of age.

16. **Attachment** is an emotional tie with another person, shown in young children by their seeking closeness to a caregiver and showing distress on separation.

17. A **critical period** is a limited time shortly after birth during which an organism must be exposed to certain stimuli or experiences if it is to develop properly.

18. **Imprinting** is the process by which certain animals form attachments during a limited critical period early in life.

19. According to Erikson, **basic trust** is a sense that the world is predictable and trustworthy, a concept that infants form if their needs are met by responsive caregiving.

20. **Self-concept** is our understanding and evaluation of who we are.

Adolescence

MODULE OVERVIEW

Adolescence begins with the sexual maturity of puberty and ends with the social independence of emerging adulthood. Module 15 details the physical, cognitive, and social development of this period that has variously been referred to as a time of "storm and stress" and as a time of exciting discoveries and new possibilities. In discussing cognitive development, the module focuses on the moral thinking theories of Kohlberg and Haidt, and on Erikson's psychosocial stages of development.

Module 15 briefly discusses one of the major issues introduced in Module 13: whether development is best described as gradual and continuous or as a discontinuous sequence of stages.

NOTE: Answer guidelines for all Module 15 questions begin on page 131.

MODULE REVIEW

First, skim this section, noting headings and bold-face items. After you have read the section, review each objective by completing the sentences and answering the questions that follow it. In some cases, Applications help you to know how well you understand the material. As you proceed, evaluate your performance by consulting the answers beginning on page 131. Do not continue with the next section until you understand each answer. If you need to, review or reread the section in the textbook before continuing.

Physical Development

Objective 15-1: Define *adolescence,* and identify the major physical changes during this period.

1. *Adolescence* is defined as the transition period between _____ and

   _____ .

2. The "storm and stress" view of adolescence is credited to _____ , one of the first American psychologists to describe adolescence.

3. Adolescence begins with the time of developing sexual maturity known as _____ . A two-year period of rapid physical development begins in girls at about the age of _____ and in boys at about the age of _____ . This growth spurt is marked by the development of the reproductive organs and external genitalia, or _____ _____ characteristics, as well as by the development of traits such as pubic hair and enlarged breasts in females and facial hair in males. These nonreproductive traits are known as _____ characteristics.

4. The first menstrual period is called _____ . In boys, the first ejaculation is called _____ .

5. The _____ (timing/sequence) of pubertal changes is more predictable than their _____ (timing/sequence).

6. Boys who mature _____ (early/late) tend to be more popular, self-assured, and independent; they also are at increased risk for _____

_____ .

For girls, _____ (early/late) maturation can be stressful, especially when their bodies are out of sync with their _____

_____ . This reminds us that _____ and _____ interact.

7. The adolescent brain undergoes a selective _____ of unused neurons and connections. Also, teens' occasional impulsiveness and risky behaviors may be due, in part, to the fact that development in the brain's

_____ _____ lags

behind that of the _____

_____ .

APPLICATION:

8. Based on the text discussion of maturation and popularity, who among the following is probably the most popular sixth grader?

   a. Jessica, the most physically mature girl in the class
   b. Roger, the most intellectually mature boy in the class
   c. Rob, the tallest, most physically mature boy in the class
   d. Cindy, who is average in physical development and is on the school debating team

Cognitive Development

Objective 15-2: Describe adolescents cognitive and moral development, according to Piaget, Kohlberg, and later researchers.

9. Adolescents' developing cognitive ability enables them to think about what is _____ possible and _____ that with imperfect reality.

10. During the early teen years, reasoning is often _____ , as adolescents often feel their experiences are unique.

11. Piaget's final stage of cognitive development is the stage of _____

_____ . Adolescents in this stage are capable of thinking logically about

_____ as well as concrete propositions. This enables them to detect _____ in others' reasoning and to spot hypocrisy.

12. The theorist who proposed that moral thought progresses through stages is _____ . These stages are divided into three basic levels: _____ , _____ , and _____ .

13. In the preconventional stages of morality, characteristic of children, the emphasis is on obeying rules to avoid _____ or gain concrete _____ .

14. Conventional morality usually emerges by early _____ . The emphasis is on gaining social _____ or maintaining the social _____ .

15. Individuals who base moral judgments on their own perceptions of basic ethical principles are said by Kohlberg to employ _____ morality.

Explain why critics fault Kohlberg's theory of moral development.

16. The idea that moral feelings precede moral reasoning is expressed in the moral _____ view of morality. Research studies using

_____ _____ support the idea that moral judgment involves more than merely thinking; it is also gut-level feeling.

17. Morality involves doing the right thing, and what we do depends on _____ influences. Today's _____

_____ _____ focus on moral issues and doing the right thing. They teach children _____ for others' feelings.

18. Children who learn to delay _____ become more socially responsible, often engaging in responsible action through _____ learning. They also become more _____ successful and more productive.

19. Moral ideas grow _____ (stronger/weaker) when acted on.

APPLICATIONS:

20. Thirteen-year-old Irene has no trouble defeating her 11-year-old brother at a detective game that requires following clues in order to deduce the perpetrator of a crime. How might Piaget explain Irene's superiority at the game?
    a. Being older, Irene has had more years of schooling.
    b. Girls develop intellectually at a faster rate than boys.
    c. Being an adolescent, Irene is beginning to develop abstract reasoning skills.
    d. Girls typically have more experience than boys at playing games.

21. Jake, a junior in high school, regularly attends church because his family and friends think he should. Jake is in Kohlberg's _____ stage of moral reasoning.

22. In Jada's country, people believe in family togetherness above all else. Because her culture does not give priority to _____ , Kohlberg would say that she is not at his highest level of moral reasoning, the _____ level.

Social Development

Objective 15-3: Describe the social tasks and challenges of adolescence.

Complete the missing information in the following table of Erikson's stages of psychosocial development.

Group Age	Psychosocial Stage
Infancy	_____
_____	Autonomy vs. shame and doubt
Preschooler	_____
_____	Competence vs. inferiority
Adolescence	_____
_____	

Group Age	Psychosocial Stage
_____	Intimacy vs. isolation
Middle adulthood	_____
_____	Integrity vs. despair

23. To refine their sense of identity, adolescents in individualistic cultures experiment with different "_____" in different situations. The result may be role _____ , which is resolved by forming a self-definition, or _____ _____ . The aspect of peoples self-concept that forms around their group membership is their _____ _____ .

24. Some adolescents forge their identity early, simply by _____ their parents' values and expectations. Others may adopt the identity of a particular _____ _____ .

25. During the early to mid-teen years, self-esteem generally _____ (rises/falls/remains stable). During the late teens and twenties, self-esteem generally _____ (rises/falls/remains stable) and agreeableness and emotional stability scores _____ (increase/decrease).

26. Erikson saw the formation of identity as a prerequisite for the development of _____ in young adulthood.

Objective 15-4: Contrast parental and peer influences during adolescence.

27. Adolescence is typically a time of increasing influence from one's _____ and decreasing influence from _____ .

28. Most adolescents report that they _____ (do/do not) get along with their parents. They see their parents as having the most influence in shaping their _____ _____ , for example.

29. Research on social relationships between parents and their adolescent children shows that high school girls who have the most _____ relationships with their mothers tend to enjoy the most _____ friendships with girlfriends.

30. When rejected adolescents withdraw, they are vulnerable to _____ , low _____ , and _____ .

APPLICATION:

31. Fourteen-year-old Cassandra feels freer and more open with her friends than with her family. Knowing this is the case, Cassandra's parents should
    a. be concerned, because deteriorating parent-teen relationships, such as this one, are often followed by a range of problem behaviors.
    b. encourage Cassandra to find new friends.
    c. seek family counseling.
    d. not worry, since adolescence is typically a time of growing peer influence and diminishing parental influence.

Objective 15-5: Discuss the characteristics of emerging adulthood.

32. As a result of increased _____ . _____ and weakened _____-_____ bonds, sexual maturity is beginning _____ (earlier/later) than in the past.

33. Because the time from 18 to the mid-twenties is increasingly a not-yet-settled phase of life, some psychologists refer to this period as a time of _____ _____ .

PROGRESS TEST

Multiple-Choice Questions

Circle your answers to the following questions and check them with the answers beginning on page 132. If your answer is incorrect, read the explanation for why it is incorrect and then consult the text.

1. According to Erikson, the central psychological challenges pertaining to adolescence, young adulthood, and middle age, respectively, are
   a. identity formation; intimacy; generativity.
   b. intimacy; identity formation; generativity.
   c. generativity; intimacy; identity formation.
   d. intimacy; generativity; identity formation.

2. In preconventional morality, the person
   a. obeys out of a sense of social duty.
   b. conforms to gain social approval.
   c. obeys to avoid punishment or to gain concrete rewards.
   d. follows the dictates of his or her conscience.

3. Which of the following is correct?
   a. Early maturation places both boys and girls at a distinct social advantage.
   b. Early maturing girls are more popular and self-assured than girls who mature late.
   c. Early maturation places both boys and girls at a distinct social disadvantage.
   d. Early maturing boys are more popular and self-assured than boys who mature late.

4. Among the hallmarks of growing up are a boy's first ejaculation and a girl's first menstrual period, which also is called
   a. puberty.   c. menarche.
   b. maturation.   d. generativity.

5. According to Piaget, the ability to think logically about abstract propositions is indicative of the stage of
   a. preoperational thought.
   b. concrete operations.
   c. formal operations.
   d. postconventional thought.

6. The average age at which puberty begins is _____ in boys; in girls, it is _____ .
   a. 14; 13   c. 11; 10
   b. 13; 11   d. 10; 9

7. After puberty, the self-concept usually becomes
   a. more positive in boys.
   b. more positive in girls.
   c. more positive in both boys and girls.
   d. more negative in both boys and girls.

8. Adolescence is marked by the onset of
   a. an identity crisis.
   b. parent-child conflict.
   c. the concrete operational stage.
   d. puberty.

9. Whose stage theory of moral development was based on how people reasoned about ethical dilemmas?
   a. Erikson   c. Harlow
   b. Piaget   d. Kohlberg

10. To which of Kohlberg's levels would moral reasoning based on the existence of fundamental human rights pertain?
    a. preconventional morality
    b. conventional morality
    c. postconventional morality
    d. generative morality

11. In Erikson's theory, individuals generally focus on developing _____ during adolescence and then _____ during young adulthood.
    a. identity; intimacy
    b. intimacy; identity
    c. basic trust; identity
    d. identity; basic trust

12. The idea that morality is rooted in moral intuitions rather than moral reasoning is the basis for
    a. Lawrence Kohlberg's theory.
    b. Jean Piaget's theory.
    c. Jonathan Haidt's theory.
    d. Erik Erikson's theory.

Essay

Sheryl is a 12-year-old living in the United States. She is in the sixth grade. Describe the developmental changes she is likely to be experiencing according to Piaget, Kohlberg, and Erikson. (Use the space below to list the points you want to make, and organize them. Then write the essay on a separate sheet of paper.)

TERMS AND CONCEPTS TO REMEMBER

Using your own words, on a piece of paper write a brief definition or explanation of each of the following terms.

1. adolescence

2. puberty

3. primary sex characteristics

4. secondary sex characteristics

5. menarche

6. identity

7. social identity

8. intimacy

9. emerging adulthood

ANSWERS
Module Review

Physical Development

1. childhood; adulthood

2. G. Stanley Hall

3. puberty; 11; 13; primary sex; secondary sex

4. menarche; spermarche

5. sequence; timing

6. early; alcohol use, delinquency, and premature sexual activity; early; emotional maturity; heredity; environment

7. pruning; frontal lobe; limbic system

8. c. is the answer. Early maturing boys tend to be more popular.
   a. Early maturing girls may temporarily suffer embarrassment and be the objects of teasing.
   b. & d. The social benefits of early or late maturation are based on physical development, not on cognitive skills.

Cognitive Development

9. ideally; compare

10. self-focused

11. formal operations; abstract; inconsistencies

12. Lawrence Kohlberg; preconventional; conventional; postconventional

13. punishment; rewards

14. adolescence; approval; order

15. postconventional

Kohlberg's critics note that his postconventional stage is culturally limited, appearing mostly among people who prize individualism.

16. intuitionist; moral paradoxes

17. social; character education programs; empathy

18. gratification; service; academically

19. stronger

20. c. is the answer.
    a., b., & d. Piaget did not link cognitive ability to amount of schooling, gender, or differences in how boys and girls are socialized.

21. conventional. Conventional morality is based in part on a desire to gain others' approval.

22. individualism; postconventional

Social Development

Erikson's stages of psychosocial development

Group Age	Psychosocial Stage
Infancy	Trust vs. mistrust
Toddlerhood	Autonomy vs. shame and doubt
Preschooler	Initiative vs. guilt
Elementary school	Competence vs. inferiority
Adolescence	Identity vs. role confusion
Young adulthood	Intimacy vs. isolation
Middle adulthood	Generativity vs. stagnation
Late adulthood	Integrity vs. despair

23. selves; confusion; identity; social identity

24. adopting; peer group

25. falls; rises; increase

26. intimacy

27. peers; parents

28. do; religious faith

29. affectionate; intimate

30. loneliness; self-esteem; depression

31. **d.** is the answer.
    a. This description of Cassandra's feelings does not suggest that her relationship with her parents is deteriorating. Cassandra's social development, like that of most adolescents, is coming under increasing peer influence and diminishing parental influence.
    b. & c. Because Cassandra's feelings are normal, there is no reason for her to change her circle of friends or for her parents to seek counseling.

32. body fat; parent-child; earlier

33. emerging adulthood

Progress Test

Multiple-Choice Questions

1. **a.** is the answer.

2. **c.** is the answer. At the preconventional level, moral reasoning centers on self-interest, whether this means obtaining rewards or avoiding punishment.

a. & b. Moral reasoning based on a sense of social duty or a desire to gain social approval is associated with the conventional level of moral development.
d. Reasoning based on ethical principles is characteristic of the postconventional level of moral development.

3. **d.** is the answer. Boys who show early physical maturation are generally stronger and more athletic than boys who mature late; these qualities may lead to greater popularity and self-assurance.
   a. & c. Early maturation tends to be socially advantageous for boys but not for girls.
   b. Early maturing girls often suffer embarrassment and are objects of teasing.

4. **c.** is the answer.
   a. Puberty refers to the early adolescent period during which accelerated growth and sexual maturation occur, not to the first menstrual period.
   b. Maturation refers to biological changes relatively uninfluenced by experience.
   d. In Erikson's theory, generativity, or the sense of contributing and being productive, is the task of middle adulthood.

5. **c.** is the answer. Once formal operational thought has been attained, thinking is no longer limited to concrete propositions.
   a. & b. Preoperational thought and concrete operational thought emerge before, and do not include, the ability to think logically about abstract propositions.
   d. Postconventional thought is Kohlberg's final stage of moral development.

6. **b.** is the answer.

7. **c.** is the answer. Because the late teen years provide many new opportunities for trying out possible roles, adolescents' identities typically incorporate an increasingly positive self-concept.

8. **d.** is the answer. The physical changes of puberty mark the onset of adolescence.
   a. & b. An identity crisis or parent-child conflict may or may not occur during adolescence; neither of these formally marks its onset.
   c. Formal operational thought, rather than concrete reasoning, typically develops in adolescence.

9. **d.** is the answer.
   a. Erikson is known for his theory of psychosocial development.
   b. Piaget is known for his theory of cognitive development.
   c. Harlow is known for his studies of attachment in infant monkeys.

10. **c.** is the answer.
    a. Preconventional morality is based on avoiding punishment and obtaining rewards.
    b. Conventional morality is based on gaining the approval of others and/or on following the law and social convention.
    d. There is no such thing as generative morality.

11. **a.** is the answer.
    b. According to Erikson, identity develops before intimacy.
    c. & d. The formation of basic trust is the task of infancy.

12. **c.** is the answer.
    a. Kohlberg focused on moral reasoning.
    b. Piaget studied cognitive development in children.
    d. Erikson proposed eight stages of social development throughout the life span.

Essay Question

Sheryl's age would place her at the threshold of Piaget's stage of formal operations. Although her thinking is probably still somewhat self-focused, Sheryl is becoming capable of abstract, logical thought. This will increasingly allow her to reason hypothetically and deductively. Because her logical thinking also enables her to detect inconsistencies in others' reasoning and between their ideals and actions, Sheryl and her parents may be having some heated debates about now.

According to Kohlberg, Sheryl is probably at the threshold of postconventional morality. When she was younger, Sheryl probably abided by rules in order to gain social approval, or simply because "rules are rules" (conventional morality). Now that she is older, Sheryl's moral reasoning will increasingly be based on her own personal code of ethics and an affirmation of people's agreed-upon rights.

According to Erikson, psychosocial development occurs in eight stages, each of which focuses on a particular task. As an adolescent, Sheryl's psychosocial task is to develop a sense of self by testing roles, then integrating them to form a single identity. Erikson called this stage *identity versus role confusion.*

Terms and Concepts to Remember

1. **Adolescence** refers to the life stage from puberty to independent adulthood, denoted physically by a growth spurt and maturation of primary and secondary sex characteristics, cognitively by the onset of formal operational thought, and socially by the formation of identity.

2. **Puberty** is the early adolescent period of sexual maturation, during which a person becomes capable of reproducing.

3. The **primary sex characteristics** are the body structures (ovaries, testes, and external genitalia) that enable reproduction.

4. The **secondary sex characteristics** are the non-reproductive sexual characteristics, for example, female breasts, male voice quality, and body hair.

5. **Menarche** is the first menstrual period.

6. In Erikson's theory, establishing an **identity**, or one's sense of self, is the primary task of adolescence.

7. **Social identity** refers to person's self-concept as defined by the groups to which he or she belongs.

8. In Erikson's theory, **intimacy**, or the ability to establish close, loving relationships, is the primary task of late adolescence and early adulthood.

9. For some people in modern cultures, **emerging adulthood** is the period from age 18 to the mid-twenties, when many young people are not yet fully independent.

Adulthood

MODULE OVERVIEW

Module 16 takes us from middle adulthood through old age and dying and death. It describes the physical, cognitive, and social development that occur in each group. At one time, psychologists believed that adolescence marked the end of developmental growth; today, they know that development occurs throughout the life span and that how we age depends on how we live.

Module 16 briefly discusses one of the major issues introduced in Module 13: whether the individual's personality remains stable or changes over the life span.

NOTE: Answer guidelines for all Module 16 questions begin on page 139.

MODULE REVIEW

First, skim this section, noting headings and boldface items. After you have read the section, review each objective by completing the sentences and answering the questions that follow it. In some cases, Applications help you to know how well you understand the material. As you proceed, evaluate your performance by consulting the answers beginning on page 139. Do not continue with the next section until you understand each answer. If you need to, review or reread the section in the textbook before continuing.

Physical Development

Objective 16-1: Identify the physical changes that occur during middle and late adulthood.

1. During adulthood, age _____ (is/is not) a very good predictor of people's traits.

2. The mid-twenties are the peak years for

   _____ _____ ,
   _____ _____ ,
   _____ _____ , and
   _____ _____ . Because
   they mature earlier, _____
   (women/men) also peak earlier.

3. During early and middle adulthood, physical vigor has less to do with _____ than with a person's _____ and _____ habits.

4. The cessation of the menstrual cycle, known as _____ , occurs within a few years of _____ . A woman's experience during this time depends largely on her _____ and _____ .

5. Although men experience no equivalent to menopause, they do experience a more gradual decline in _____ count, level of the hormone _____ , and speed of erection and ejaculation during later life.

6. Worldwide, life expectancy at birth has increased from 49 years in 1950 to _____ years and beyond in 2010 in some developed countries. Women outlive men by nearly _____ years worldwide.

7. With age, the tips of our chromosomes, called _____ , shorten.

8. The human spirit also affects life expectancy. The death rate increases when people reach their birthdays, a finding referred to as the

   _____ - _____

   phenomenon.

9. With age, the eye's pupil _____ (shrinks/enlarges) and its lens becomes _____ (more/less) transparent. As a result, the amount of light that reaches the retina is _____ (increased/reduced).

10. Although older adults are _____ (more/less) susceptible to life-threatening ailments, they suffer from short-term ailments such as flu _____ (more/less) often than younger adults.

11. Aging _____ (slows/speeds/has no effect on) neural processing and causes a gradual loss of _____ _____ .

12. Physical exercise stimulates _____ _____ development and _____ connections, thanks perhaps to increased _____ and nutrient flow.

13. The mental erosion that results from progressive damage to the brain is called _____ .

14. The irreversible disorder that causes progressive brain deterioration is _____ disease. This disease has been linked to a deterioration of neurons that produce the neurotransmitter _____ .

Cognitive Development

Objective 16-2: Assess the impact of aging on memory.

15. Studies of developmental changes in learning and memory show that during adulthood there is a decline in the ability to _____ (recall/recognize) new information but not in the ability to _____ (recall/recognize) such information. One factor that influences memory in older people is the _____ of material.

16. Adults' _____ memory remains strong when events help trigger recall.

17. Cognitive abilities among 70-year-olds are _____ (less/more) varied than among 20-year-olds.

18. A research study in which people of various ages are compared with one another is called a _____-_____ study.

19. A research study in which the same people are retested over a period of years is called a _____ study.

20. Especially in the last three or four years of life, cognitive decline typically accelerates. Researchers call this near-death drop _____ _____ .

APPLICATION:

21. Which statement illustrates cognitive development during the course of adult life?
    a. Forty-three-year-old Sophia has better recognition memory than 72-year-old Kylie.
    b. Both Sophia and Kylie have strong recall and recognition memory.
    c. Kylie's recognition memory decreased sharply at age 50.
    d. Forty-three-year-old Sophia has better recall memory than 72-year-old Kylie.

Social Development

Objective 16-3: Discuss the themes and influences that mark the social journey from early adulthood to death.

22. Contrary to popular opinion, job and marital dissatisfaction do not surge during the forties, thus suggesting that a midlife _____ need not occur.

23. The term used to refer to the culturally preferred timing for leaving home, getting a job, marrying, and so on is the _____ _____ . Today, the timing of such life events is becoming _____ (more/less) predictable. More important than age are _____ _____ and chance encounters.

24. According to Erikson, the two basic tasks of adulthood are achieving _____ and _____ . According to Freud, the healthy adult is one who can _____ and _____ .

25. Human societies have nearly always included a relatively _____ bond. Marriage bonds are usually lasting when couples marry after age _____ and are

_____ _____ .

26. Marriages today are _____ (half/twice) as likely to end in divorce as they were in the 1960s. Couples who live together before marrying have a _____ (higher/ lower) divorce rate than those who do not.

27. Marriage is a predictor of _____ ,

_____ _____ ,

_____ , and physical and mental _____ . Lesbian couples report _____ (greater/less) well-being than those who are alone.

28. As children begin to absorb time and energy, satisfaction with the marriage itself _____ (increases/decreases). This is particularly true among _____ women, who shoulder most of the burden.

29. For most couples, the children's leaving home produces a(n) _____ (increase/ decrease) in marital satisfaction.

30. During the first two years of college or university, most students _____ (can/cannot) predict their later careers.

APPLICATION:

31. After a series of unfulfilling relationships, 30-year-old Carlos tells a friend that he doesn't want to marry because he is afraid of losing his freedom and independence. Erikson would say that Carlos is having difficulty with the psychosocial task of
   a. trust versus mistrust.
   b. autonomy versus doubt.
   c. intimacy versus isolation.
   d. identity versus role confusion.

Objective 16-4: Describe trends in people's self-confidence and life satisfaction across the life span.

32. From early adulthood to midlife, people typically experience a strengthening sense of

_____ , _____ , and

_____ .

33. According to studies, older people _____ (do/do not) report as much happiness and satisfaction with life as younger people do. In addition, their feelings _____ (do/do not) mellow.

34. As we age, the brain area called the _____ shows _____ (increased/decreased) activity in response to negative events.

35. More and more people flourish into later life, thanks to _____ influences.

APPLICATION:

36. The text discusses well-being across the life span. Which of the following people is likely to report the greatest life satisfaction?
   a. Billy, a 7-year-old second-grader
   b. Kathy, a 17-year-old high-school senior
   c. Mildred, a 70-year-old retired teacher
   d. too little information to tell

Objective 16-5: Describe the range of reactions to the death of a loved one.

37. Grief over a loved one's death is especially severe when it comes _____

_____ .

38. Reactions to a loved one's death _____ (do/do not) vary according to cultural norms. Those who express the strongest grief immediately _____ (do/do not) purge their grief more quickly.

39. Terminally ill and bereaved people _____ (do/do not) go through predictable stages.

40. According to Erikson, the final task of adulthood is to achieve a sense of _____ .

PROGRESS TEST

Multiple-Choice Questions

Circle your answers to the following questions and check them with the answers on page 140. If your answer is incorrect, read the explanation for why it is incorrect and then consult the text.

1. An older person who can look back on life with satisfaction and reminisce with a sense of completion has attained Erikson's stage of
   a. generativity.
   b. intimacy.
   c. isolation.
   d. integrity.

2. The cognitive ability that has been shown to decline during adulthood is the ability to
   a. recall new information.
   b. recognize new information.
   c. learn meaningful new material.
   d. use judgment in dealing with daily life problems.

3. Which of the following statements concerning the effects of aging is true?
   a. Aging almost inevitably leads to total memory failure if the individual lives long enough.
   b. Aging increases susceptibility to short-term ailments such as the flu.
   c. Significant increases in life satisfaction are associated with aging.
   d. The aging process can be significantly affected by the individual's activity patterns.

4. Longitudinal research
   a. compares people of different ages.
   b. studies the same people at different times.
   c. usually involves a larger sample than does cross-sectional research.
   d. usually involves a smaller sample than does cross-sectional research.

5. Of the following, which is a possible cause of dementia?
   a. stroke
   b. brain tumor
   c. alcohol dependence
   d. All of these are possible causes.

6. The end of menstruation is called
   a. the social clock.
   b. menopause.
   c. the midlife crisis.
   d. generativity.

7. Cross-sectional research
   a. compares people of different ages with one another.
   b. studies the same group of people at different times.
   c. is used for studying cognitive development during infancy.
   d. is used for studying social development during infancy.

8. The social clock refers to
   a. an individual or society's distribution of work and leisure time.
   b. adulthood responsibilities.
   c. typical ages for starting a career, marrying, and so on.
   d. age-related changes in one's circle of friends.

9. After their grown children have left home, most couples experience
   a. the distress of the empty nest syndrome.
   b. increased strain in their marital relationship.
   c. the need to have their children visit often.
   d. greater happiness and enjoyment in their relationship.

10. Underlying Alzheimer's disease is a deterioration in neurons that produce
    a. epinephrine.
    b. norepinephrine.
    c. serotonin.
    d. acetylcholine.

11. In terms of incidence, susceptibility to short-term illnesses _____ with age and susceptibility to long-term ailments _____ with age.
    a. decreases; increases
    b. increases; decreases
    c. increases; increases
    d. decreases; decreases

12. Research on the American family indicates that
    a. fewer than 23 percent of unmarried adults, but nearly 40 percent of married adults, report being "very happy" with life.
    b. the divorce rate is now one-half the marriage rate.
    c. children born to cohabiting parents are five times more likely to experience their parents' separation.
    d. all of these statements are true.

13. The popular idea that terminally ill and bereaved people go through predictable stages, such as denial, anger, and so forth
    a. is widely supported by research.
    b. more accurately describes grieving in some cultures than others.
    c. is true of women but not men.
    d. is not supported by research studies.

True–False Items

Indicate whether each statement is true or false by placing *T* or *F* in the blank next to the item.

_____ 1. The process of grieving is much the same throughout the world.

_____ 2. During adulthood, age only moderately correlates with people's traits.

_____ 3. By the age of 50, most adults have experienced a "midlife crisis."

_____ 4. Compared with those who are younger, older people are more susceptible to short-term ailments such as flu and cold viruses.

_____ 5. The symptoms of Alzheimer's disease are simply an intensified version of normal aging.

TERMS AND CONCEPTS TO REMEMBER

Using your own words, on a piece of paper write a brief definition or explanation of each of the following terms.

1. menopause

2. cross-sectional study

3. longitudinal study

4. social clock

ANSWERS

Module Review

Physical Develolpment

1. is not

2. muscular strength, reaction time, sensory keenness, cardiac output; women

3. age; health; exercise

4. menopause; 50; expectations; attitude

5. sperm; testosterone

6. 80; 4

7. telomeres

8. death-deferral

9. shrinks; less; reduced

10. more; less

11. slows; brain cells

12. brain cell; neural; oxygen

13. dementia

14. Alzheimer's; acetylcholine

15. recall; recognize; meaningfulness

16. prospective

17. more

18. cross-sectional

19. longitudinal

20. terminal decline

21. **d.** is the answer.
    a. & c. In tests of recognition memory, the performance of older persons shows little decline.
    b. The ability to recall material, especially meaningless material, declines with age.

Social Development

22. transition (crisis)

23. social clock; less; life events

24. intimacy; generativity; love; work

25. monogamous; 20; well educated

26. twice; higher

27. happiness; sexual satisfaction; health; income; greater

28. decreases; employed

29. increase

30. cannot

31. **c.** is the answer. Carlos' age and struggle to form a close relationship place him squarely in this stage.
    a. Trust versus mistrust is the psychosocial task of infancy.
    b. Autonomy versus doubt is the psychosocial task of toddlerhood.
    d. Identity versus role confusion is the psychosocial task of adolescence.

32. identity; confidence; self-esteem

33. do; do

34. amygdala; decreased

35. biopsychosocial

36. **d.** is the answer. Research has not uncovered a tendency for people of any particular age group to report greater feelings of satisfaction or well-being.

37. suddenly and before its expected time on the social clock

38. do; do not

39. do not

40. integrity

Progress Test

Multiple-Choice Questions

1. **d.** is the answer.
   a. Generativity is associated with middle adulthood.
   b. & c. Intimacy and isolation are associated with young adulthood.

2. **a.** is the answer.
   b., c., & d. These cognitive abilities remain essentially unchanged as the person ages.

3. **d.** is the answer. "Use it or lose it" seems to be the rule: Often, changes in activity patterns contribute significantly to problems regarded as being part of usual aging.
   a. Most older people suffer some memory loss but remember some events very well.
   b. Although older people are more subject to long-term ailments than younger adults, they actually suffer fewer short-term ailments.
   c. People of all ages report equal happiness or satisfaction with life.

4. **b.** is the answer.

5. **d.** is the answer.

6. **b.** is the answer.
   a. The social clock refers to the appropriate time for significant events.
   c. When it does occur, the midlife crisis is a psychological, rather than biological, phenomenon.
   d. Generativity is Erikson's term for productivity during middle adulthood.

7. **a.** is the answer.
   b. This answer describes the longitudinal research method.
   c. Cross-sectional studies compare people of different ages throughout the life span, generally beginning after the person is able to verbalize.

   d. Cross-sectional studies do not deal with social development.

8. **c.** is the answer. Different societies and eras have somewhat different ideas about the age at which major life events should ideally occur.

9. **d.** is the answer.
   a., b., & c. Most couples do not feel a loss of purpose or marital strain following the departure of grown children.

10. **d.** is the answer. Significantly, drugs that block the activity of the neurotransmitter acetylcholine produce Alzheimer's-like symptoms.
    a. & b. Epinephrine and norepinephrine are hormones produced by the adrenal glands of the endocrine system.
    c. Serotonin is a neurotransmitter and hence is produced by neurons, but it has not been implicated in Alzheimer's disease.

11. **a.** is the answer.

12. **d.** is the answer.

13. **d.** is the answer.

True–False Items

1. F
2. T
3. F
4. F
5. F

Terms and Concepts to Remember

1. **Menopause** is the cessation of menstruation and typically occurs within a few years of age 50. It also refers to the biological changes experienced during a woman's years of declining ability to reproduce.

2. In a **cross-sectional study,** people of different ages are compared with one another.

3. In a **longitudinal study,** the same people are tested and retested over a period of years.

4. The **social clock** refers to the culturally preferred timing of social events, such as leaving home, marrying, having children, and retiring.

Basic Principles of Sensation and Perception

MODULE OVERVIEW

Sensation refers to the process by which we detect physical energy from the environment and encode it as neural signals. Perception refers to the processes by which we select, organize, and interpret that energy. This module describes the basic principles underlying sensation and perception. For example, sensory adaptation enables us to ignore many of the stimuli constantly bombarding us while focusing on important stimuli. Similarly, our perceptions are strongly influenced by our expectations and context effects.

NOTE: Answer guidelines for all Module 17 questions begin on page 144.

MODULE REVIEW

First, skim each section, noting headings and bold-face items. After you have read the section, review each objective by answering the fill-in and essay-type questions that follow it. In some cases, Study Tips explain how best to learn a difficult concept and Applications help you to know how well you understand the material. As you proceed, evaluate your performance by consulting the answers beginning on page 144. Do not continue with the next section until you understand each answer. If you need to, review or reread the section in the textbook before continuing.

Introduction

Objective 17-1: Contrast sensation and perception, and explain the difference between bottom-up and top-down processing.

1. The perceptual disorder in which a person has lost the ability to recognize familiar faces is

   _____ .

2. The process by which we detect physical energy from the environment and encode it as neural signals is _____ . The process by which sensations are organized and interpreted is

   _____ .

3. Sensory analysis, which starts at the entry level and works up, is called _____ -

   _____ _____ .

   Perceptual analysis, which works from our experience and expectations, is called

   _____ - _____

   _____ .

APPLICATIONS:

4. Sensation is to _____ as perception is to _____ .
   a. recognizing a stimulus; interpreting a stimulus
   b. detecting a stimulus; recognizing a stimulus
   c. interpreting a stimulus; detecting a stimulus
   d. seeing; hearing

5. Superman's eyes used _____ ,
   while his brain used _____ .
   a. perception; sensation
   b. top-down processing; bottom-up processing
   c. bottom-up processing; top-down processing

6. Concluding her presentation on sensation and perception, Kelly notes that
   a. perception is bottom-up processing.
   b. sensation is top-down processing.
   c. without sensation there is no perception.
   d. sensation and perception blend into one continuous process.

Transduction

Objective 17-2: Identify the three steps that are basic to all our sensory systems.

7. All our senses perform three basic steps; they _____ sensory information, transform (or_____) that stimulation into neural impulses that our brain can use, and _____ that neural information to our brain.

8. The study of relationships between the physical characteristics of stimuli and our psychological experience of them is _____ .

Thresholds

Objective 17-3: Distinguish between absolute and difference thresholds, and discuss whether we can sense and be affected by stimuli below the absolute threshold.

9. The _____ _____ refers to the minimum stimulation necessary for a stimulus to be detected _____ percent of the time.

10. According to _____ _____ theory, a person's experience, expectations, motivation, and alertness all influence the detection of a stimulus.

11. Some entrepreneurs claim that exposure to "below threshold," or _____ , stimuli can be persuasive, but their claims are probably unwarranted. Some weak stimuli may trigger in our sensory receptors a response that is processed by the brain, even though the response doesn't cross the threshold into _____ awareness.

12. Under certain conditions, an invisible image or word can _____ a person's response to a later question. This illustrates that much of our information processing occurs _____ .

13. The minimum difference required to distinguish two stimuli 50 percent of the time is called the _____ _____ .

    Another term for this value is the _____ _____

    _____ .

14. The principle that the difference threshold is not a constant amount, but a constant proportion, is known as _____ _____ . The proportion depends on the _____ .

STUDY TIP: The concept of threshold can be confusing. Since you can count on at least one exam question on this topic, be sure you understand the concept: "Below threshold" means the stimulus is undetectable; "above threshold" means the stimulus is strong enough to be detected.

APPLICATION:

15. In shopping for a new stereo, you discover that you cannot differentiate between the sounds of models X and Y. The difference between X and Y is below your
    a. absolute threshold.
    b. subliminal threshold.
    c. receptor threshold.
    d. difference threshold.

Sensory Adaptation

Objective 17-4: Explain the function of sensory adaptation.

16. After constant exposure to an unchanging stimulus, the receptor cells of our senses begin to fire less vigorously; this phenomenon is called _____ _____ .

17. This phenomenon illustrates that sensation is designed to focus on _____ changes in the environment.

APPLICATION:

18. Calvin usually runs his fingertips over a cloth's surface when trying to decide whether the texture is right for what he wants. By moving his fingers over the cloth, he prevents the occurrence of _____ _____ to the feel.

Perceptual Set, Context Effects, and Emotion and Motivation

Objective 17-5: Explain how our expectations, contexts, emotions, and motivation influence our perceptions.

19. A mental predisposition that influences perception is called a _____

    _____ .

20. How a stimulus is perceived depends on our perceptual _____ and the _____ in which it is experienced.

21. The context of a stimulus creates a _____ (top-down/bottom-up) expectation that influences our perception as we match our _____ (top-down/bottom-up) signal against it.

22. Our perception is also influenced by _____ about gender and the _____ context of our experiences.

23. Our perceptions are also directed by our _____ , as when a water bottle appears closer if we are thirsty.

APPLICATION:

24. Although carpenter Smith perceived a briefly viewed object as a screwdriver, police officer Wesson perceived the same object as a knife. This illustrates that perception is guided by
    a. bottom-up processing.
    b. sensory adaptation.
    c. transduction.
    d. perceptual set.

PROGRESS TEST

Multiple-Choice Questions

Circle your answers to the following questions and check them with the answers on page 145. If your answer is incorrect, read the explanation for why it is incorrect and then consult the text.

1. Which of the following is true?
   a. The absolute threshold for any stimulus is a constant.
   b. The absolute threshold for any stimulus varies somewhat.
   c. The absolute threshold is defined as the minimum amount of stimulation necessary for a stimulus to be detected 75 percent of the time.
   d. The absolute threshold is defined as the minimum amount of stimulation necessary for a stimulus to be detected 60 percent of the time.

2. If you can just notice the difference between 10- and 11-pound weights, which of the following weights could you differentiate from a 100-pound weight?
   a. 101-pound weight
   b. 105-pound weight
   c. 110-pound weight
   d. There is no basis for prediction.

3. A decrease in sensory responsiveness accompanying an unchanging stimulus is called
   a. sensory fatigue.
   b. bottom-up processing.
   c. sensory adaptation.
   d. transduction.

4. Which of the following is an example of sensory adaptation?
   a. finding the cold water of a swimming pool warmer after you have been in it for a while
   b. developing an increased sensitivity to salt the more you use it in foods
   c. becoming very irritated at the continuing sound of a dripping faucet
   d. All of these are examples.

5. _____ processing refers to how the physical characteristics of stimuli influence their interpretation.
   a. Top-down   c. Signal detection
   b. Bottom-up   d. Psychophysical

6. The study of perception is primarily concerned with how we
   a. detect sights, sounds, and other stimuli.
   b. sense environmental stimuli.
   c. develop sensitivity to illusions.
   d. interpret sensory stimuli.

7. Which of the following influences perception?
   a. biological maturation
   b. the context in which stimuli are perceived
   c. expectations
   d. all of these factors

8. The process by which sensory information is converted into neural energy is
   a. sensory adaptation.   c. psychophysics.
   b. top-down processing.   d. transduction.

9. Weber's law states that
   a. the absolute threshold for any stimulus is a constant.
   b. the jnd for any stimulus is a constant.
   c. the absolute threshold for any stimulus is a constant proportion.
   d. the jnd for any stimulus is a constant proportion.

10. Concerning the evidence for subliminal stimulation, which of the following is the best answer?
    a. The brain processes some information without our awareness.
    b. Stimuli too weak to cross our thresholds for awareness may trigger a response in our sense receptors.
    c. Because the absolute threshold is a statistical average, we are able to detect weaker stimuli some of the time.
    d. All of these statements are true.

11. Given normal sensory ability, a person standing atop a mountain on a dark, clear night can see a candle flame atop a mountain 30 miles away. This is a description of vision's
    a. difference threshold.   c. absolute threshold.
    b. jnd.   d. feature detection.

12. The phenomenon that refers to the ways in which an individual's expectations influence perception is called
    a. perceptual set.
    b. signal detection.
    c. bottom-up processing.
    d. psychophysics.

13. _____ processing refers to how our knowledge and expectations influence perception.
    a. Top-down   c. Signal detection
    b. Bottom-up   d. Psychophysical

TERMS AND CONCEPTS TO REMEMBER

Using your own words, on a piece of paper write a brief definition or explanation of each of the following terms.

1. sensation
2. perception
3. bottom-up processing
4. top-down processing
5. transduction

6. psychophysics
7. absolute threshold
8. signal detection theory
9. subliminal
10. priming
11. difference threshold
12. Weber's law
13. sensory adaptation
14. perceptual set

ANSWERS
Module Review

Introduction

1. prosopagnosia
2. sensation; perception
3. bottom-up processing; top-down processing
4. **b.** is the answer.
   a. Both recognition and interpretation are examples of perception.
   c. This answer would have been correct if the question had read, "Perception is to sensation as _____ is to _____ ."
   d. Sensation and perception are important processes in both hearing and seeing.
5. **c.** is the answer.
6. **d.** is the answer.

Transduction

7. receive; transduce; deliver
8. psychophysics

Thresholds

9. absolute threshold; 50
10. signal detection
11. subliminal; conscious
12. prime; automatically
13. difference threshold; just noticeable difference (jnd)
14. Weber's law; stimulus
15. **d.** is the answer.

    a. The absolute threshold refers to whether a single stimulus can be detected, not to whether two stimuli can be differentiated.

    b. Subliminal refers to stimuli below the absolute threshold.

c. A receptor threshold is a minimum amount of energy that will elicit a neural impulse in a receptor cell.

Sensory Adaptation

16. sensory adaptation
17. informative
18. sensory adaptation. This occurs when we remain fixed on a stimulus. Moving his fingers prevents his sense of touch from adapting.

Perceptual Set, Context Effects, and Emotion and Motivation

19. perceptual set
20. set; context
21. top-down; bottom-up
22. stereotypes; emotional
23. motives
24. **d.** is the answer. The two people interpreted a briefly perceived object in terms of their perceptual sets, or mental predispositions, in this case conditioned by their work experiences.
    a. Their different interpretations reflect top-down processing.
    b. Sensory adaptation refers to the decreased sensitivity that occurs with continued exposure to an unchanging stimulus.
    c. Transduction is the transformation of one form of energy into another.

Progress Test

Multiple-Choice Questions

1. **b.** is the answer. Psychological factors can affect the absolute threshold for a stimulus.
   a. The absolute threshold for detecting a stimulus depends not only on the strength of the stimulus but also on psychological factors such as experience, expectations, motivation, and fatigue. Thus, the threshold cannot be a constant.
   c. & d. The absolute threshold is defined as the minimum stimulus that is detected 50 percent of the time.

2. **c.** is the answer. According to Weber's law, the difference threshold is a constant proportion of the stimulus. There is a 10 percent difference between 10 and 11 pounds; since the difference threshold is a constant proportion, the weight closest to 100 pounds that can nonetheless be differentiated from it is 110 pounds (or 100 pounds plus 10 percent).

3. **c.** is the answer.
   a. "Sensory fatigue" is not a term in psychology.
   b. Bottom-up processing is analysis that begins with the sensory receptors and works up to the brain's integration of sensory information.
   d. Transduction refers to the conversion of one form of energy into another.

4. **a.** is the answer. Sensory adaptation means a diminishing sensitivity to an unchanging stimulus. Only the adjustment to cold water involves a decrease in sensitivity; the other examples involve an increase.

5. **b.** is the answer.
   a. Top-down processing refers to how our knowledge and expectations influence perception.
   c. Signal detection explains precisely how and when we detect the presence of a faint stimulus (*signal*) amid background stimulation (*noise*).
   d. Psychophysics is the study of the relationship between the physical characteristics of objects and our psychological experience of them.

6. **d.** is the answer.
   a. & b. The study of sensation is concerned with these processes.
   c. Although studying illusions has helped psychologists understand ordinary perceptual mechanisms, it is not the primary focus of the field of perception.

7. **d.** is the answer.

8. **d.** is the answer.
   a. Sensory adaptation refers to the diminished sensitivity that occurs with unchanging stimulation.
   b. Top-down processing is information processing guided by higher-level mental processes..
   c. Psychophysics is the study of the relationship between the physical characteristics of objects and our psychological experience of them.

9. **d.** is the answer. Weber's law concerns difference thresholds (jnd's), not absolute thresholds, and states that these are constant proportions of the stimuli, not that they remain constant.

10. **d.** is the answer.

11. **c.** is the answer. The absolute threshold is the minimum stimulation needed to detect a stimulus.
    a. & b. The difference threshold, which is also known as the jnd, is the minimum difference between two stimuli that a person can detect. In this example, there is only one stimulus—the sight of the flame.
    d. Feature detection refers to nerve cells in the brain responding to specific features of a stimulus.

12. **a.** is the answer.
   b. Signal detection explains precisely how and when we detect the presence of a faint stimulus *(signal)* amid background stimulation *(noise)*.
   c. Bottom-up processing is analysis that begins with the sensory receptors and works up to the brain's integration of sensory information.
   d. Psychophysics is the study of relationships between the physical characteristics of stimuli and our psychological experience of them.

13. **a.** is the answer.
   b. Bottom-up processing refers to the physical characteristics of stimuli rather than their perceptual interpretation.
   c. Signal detection explains precisely how and when we detect the presence of a faint stimulus *(signal)* amid background stimulation *(noise)*.
   d. Psychophysics is the study of the relationship between the physical characteristics of objects and our psychological experience of them.

Terms and Concepts to Remember

1. **Sensation** is the process by which our sensory receptors and nervous system receive and represent physical energy from the environment.

2. **Perception** is the process by which we organize and interpret sensory information, enabling us to recognize meaningful objects and events.

3. **Bottom-up processing** is analysis that begins with the sensory receptors and works up to the brain's integration of sensory information.

4. **Top-down processing** is information processing guided by higher-level mental processes.

5. **Transduction** refers to the conversion of one form of energy into another. In sensation, it is the process by which receptor cells in the eyes, ears, skin, and nose convert stimulus energies into neural impulses our brain can interpret.

6. **Psychophysics** is the study of relationships between the physical characteristics of stimuli and our psychological experience of them.

7. The **absolute threshold** is the minimum stimulation needed to detect a stimulus 50 percent of the time.

8. **Signal detection theory** explains precisely how and when we detect the presence of a faint stimulus *(signal)* amid background stimulation *(noise)*. Detection depends partly on experience, expectations, motivation, and alertness.

9. A stimulus that is **subliminal** is one that is below the absolute threshold for conscious awareness.
   Memory aid: Limen is the Latin word for "threshold." A stimulus that is **subliminal** is one that is *sub-* ("below") the *limen*, or threshold.

10. **Priming** is the activation, often unconsciously, of an association by an imperceptible stimulus, the effect of which is to predispose a perception, memory, or response.

11. The **difference threshold** (also called the *just noticeable difference*, or *jnd*), is the minimum difference between two stimuli required for detection 50 percent of the time.

12. **Weber's law** states that, to be perceived as different, the just noticeable difference between two stimuli must differ by a constant minimum percentage.
   Example: If a difference of 10 percent in weight is noticeable, **Weber's law** predicts that a person could discriminate 10- and 11-pound weights or 50- and 55-pound weights.

13. **Sensory adaptation** refers to the decreased sensitivity that occurs with continued exposure to an unchanging stimulus.

14. **Perceptual set** is a mental predisposition to perceive one thing and not another.

Vision and Perceptual Organization and Interpretation

MODULE OVERVIEW

Module 18 describes the sense of vision, including the structure of the eye, the process through which the stimulus energy is transmitted through the eye and interpreted in the brain, and how we perceive color. The module concludes with a discussion of the major theories proposed to explain color vision.

Module 18 further explores how we select, organize, and interpret our visual sensations as meaningful perceptions. It deals with two important issues. The first issue is the role of experience in perception. Make sure you understand the results of studies of recovery from blindness, early sensory restriction, and adaptation to distorted environments. The second is the possible existence of ESP, or perception without sensation. You should be able to discuss both the claims made for ESP and the criticisms of these claims.

In this module there are many terms to learn. Many of the terms are related to the structure of the eye. Doing the module review several times, labeling the diagram of the eye, and rehearsing the material frequently will help you to memorize the parts of the eye and their functions. As you study the Young-Helmholtz three-color and opponent-process theories of color vision, concentrate on understanding the strengths and weaknesses of each.

NOTE: Answer guidelines for all Module 18 questions begin on page 158.

MODULE REVIEW

First, skim each section, noting headings and bold-face items. After you have read the section, review each objective by answering the fill-in and essay-type questions that follow it. In some cases, Study Tips explain how best to learn a difficult concept and Applications help you to know how well you under-stand the material. As you proceed, evaluate your performance by consulting the answers beginning on page 158. Do not continue with the next section until you understand each answer. If you need to, review or reread the section in the textbook before continuing.

The Stimulus Input and The Eye

Objective 18-1: Describe the characteristics of visible light, and explain the process by which the eye transforms light energy into neural messages.

1. The visible spectrum of light is a small portion of the larger spectrum of _____ energy.

2. The distance from one light wave peak to the next is called _____ . This value determines the wave's color, or

   _____ .

3. The amount of energy in light waves, or _____ , determined by a wave's _____ , or height, influences the _____ of a light.

STUDY TIP: The stimulus energy for vision can be described as a traveling wave that varies in wavelength and amplitude. The wavelength of a visual stimulus is measured as the distance from the peak of one wave to the next—the shorter the distance, the greater the frequency of the waves. Short, high frequency waves produce "cool" or bluish colors for visual stimuli. Long, low frequency waves produce "warm" or reddish colors

The wave's amplitude is measured as the distance from the top of its peak to the bottom. High amplitude waves produce bright colors, while low amplitude waves produce dull colors.

To test your understanding, take a look at the two waves on the next page.

4. Assuming that these two waves were light energy, would they differ in appearance? How so?

5. Light enters the eye through the _____ , then passes through a small opening called the _____ ; the size of this opening is controlled by the colored _____ .

6. By changing its curvature, the _____ can focus the image of an object onto the _____ , the light-sensitive inner surface of the eye. The process by which the lens changes shape to focus images is called _____ .

7. The retina's receptor cells are the _____ and _____ .

8. The neural signals produced in the rods and cones activate the neighboring _____ cells, which then activate a network of _____ cells.

9. The axons of ganglion cells converge to form the _____ _____ , which carries the visual information to the _____ .

10. Where this nerve leaves the eye, there are no receptors; thus, the area is called the _____ _____ .

11. Most cones are clustered around the retina's point of central focus, called the _____ , whereas the rods are concentrated in more _____ regions of the retina. Many cones have their own _____ cells to communicate with the visual cortex. Rods _____ (do/do not) have direct links.

12. It is the _____ (rods/cones) of the eye that permit the perception of color, whereas _____ (rods/cones) enable black-and-white vision.

13. Unlike cones, in dim light the rods are _____ (sensitive/insensitive). Adapting to a darkened room will take the retina approximately _____ minutes.

APPLICATIONS:

14. To maximize your sensitivity to fine visual detail you should
   a. stare off to one side of the object you are attempting to see.
   b. close one eye.
   c. decrease the intensity of the light falling upon the object.
   d. stare directly at the object.

15. In comparing the human eye to a camera, the film would be located in the eye's
   a. pupil.   c. cornea.
   b. lens.   d. retina.

16. Which of the following is true of cones?
   a. Cones enable color vision.
   b. Cones are highly concentrated in the foveal region of the retina.
   c. Cones have a higher absolute threshold for brightness than rods.
   d. All of these statements are true.

17. Assuming that the visual systems of humans and other mammals function similarly, you would expect that the retina of a nocturnal mammal (one active only at night) would contain
   a. mostly cones.
   b. mostly rods.
   c. an equal number of rods and cones.
   d. more bipolar cells than an animal active only during the day.

18. As the football game continued into the night, LeVar noticed that he was having difficulty distinguishing the colors of the players' uniforms. This is because the _____ , which enable color vision, have a _____ absolute threshold for brightness than the available light intensity.
   a. rods; higher   c. rods; lower
   b. cones; higher   d. cones; lower

Visual Information Processing

Objective 18-2: Describe how the eye and brain process visual information.

19. Visual information percolates through progressively more _____ levels. In the brain, it is routed by the _____ to higher-level brain areas. Hubel and Wiesel discovered that certain neurons in the _____ _____ of the brain respond only to specific features of what is viewed. They called these neurons _____ _____ .

20. Feature detectors pass their information to higher-level cells in the brain, which respond to specific visual scenes. Research has shown that in monkey brains such cells specialize in responding to a specific _____ , _____ _____ , _____ , or _____ _____ . In many cortical areas, teams of cells (_____ _____) respond to complex patterns.

21. The brain achieves its remarkable speed in visual perception by processing several subdivisions of a stimulus _____ (simultaneously/sequentially). This procedure, called _____ _____ , may explain why people who have suffered a stroke may lose just one aspect of vision.

22. Other brain-damaged people may demonstrate _____ by responding to a stimulus that is not consciously perceived.

Color Vision

Objective 18-3: Discuss the theories that help us understand color vision.

23. An object appears to be red in color because it _____ the long wavelengths of red and because of our mental _____ of the color.

24. One out of every 50 people is color deficient; this is usually a male because the defect is genetically _____ _____ .

25. According to the _____-_____ _____ theory, the eyes have three types of color receptors: one reacts most strongly to _____ , one to _____ , and one to _____ .

26. After staring at a green square for a while, you will see the color red, its _____ color, as an _____ .

27. Hering's theory of color vision is called the _____-_____ theory. According to this theory, after visual information leaves the receptors it is analyzed in terms of pairs of opposing colors: _____ versus _____ , _____ versus _____ , and _____ versus _____ .

Summarize the two stages of color processing.

APPLICATIONS:

28. I am a cell in the thalamus that is excited by red and inhibited by green. I am a(n)
    a. feature detector.
    b. cone.
    c. bipolar cell.
    d. opponent-process cell.

29. After staring at a very intense red stimulus for a few minutes, Carrie shifted her gaze to a beige wall and "saw" the color _____ . Carrie's experience provides support for the _____ theory.
    a. green; trichromatic
    b. blue; opponent-process
    c. green; opponent-process
    d. blue; trichromatic

Visual Organization

Objective 18-4: Describe Gestalt psychologists' understanding of perception, and explain how figure-ground and grouping principles contribute to our perceptions.

30. According to the _____ school of psychology, we tend to organize a cluster of sensations into a _____ , or form.

31. When we view a scene, we see the central object, or _____ , as distinct from surrounding stimuli, or the _____ .

32. Proximity, continuity, and closure are examples of Gestalt rules of_____ .

33. The principle that we organize stimuli into smooth, continuous patterns is called _____ . The principle that we fill in gaps to create a complete, whole object is _____ . The grouping of items that are close to each other is the principle of _____ .

APPLICATION:

34. Studying the road map before her trip, Colleen had no trouble following the route of the highway she planned to travel. Colleen's ability illustrates the principle of
   a. closure.
   b. relative size.
   c. continuity.
   d. proximity.

Objective 18-5: Explain how we use binocular and monocular cues to perceive the world in three dimensions and perceive motion.

35. The ability to see objects in three dimensions despite their two-dimensional representations on our retinas is called _____ _____ . It enables us to estimate _____ .

36. Gibson and Walk developed the _____ _____ to test depth perception in infants. They found that each species, by the time it is _____ , has the perceptual abilities it needs.

Summarize the results of Gibson and Walk's studies of depth perception.

For questions 37-45, identify the depth perception cue that is defined.

37. Any cue that requires both eyes: _____ .

38. The greater the difference between the images received by the two eyes, the nearer the object: _____ _____ . 3-D movies simulate this cue by photographing each scene with two cameras.

39. Any cue that requires either eye alone: _____ .

40. If two objects are presumed to be the same size, the one that casts a smaller retinal image is perceived as farther away: _____ _____ .

41. An object partially covered by another is seen as farther away: _____ .

42. Objects lower in the visual field are seen as nearer: _____ _____ .

43. As we move, objects at different distances appear to move at different rates: _____ _____ .

44. Parallel lines appear to converge in the distance: _____ _____ .

45. The dimmer of two objects seems farther away: _____ _____ _____ .

46. Our brain normally computes motion based partly on the assumption that shrinking objects are _____ (approaching/retreating) and enlarging objects are _____ (approaching/retreating). Sometimes, we are fooled because larger objects seem to move _____ (faster/more slowly) than smaller objects.

47. The brain interprets a rapid series of slightly varying images as _____ . This phenomenon is called _____

_____ .

48. The illusion of movement that results when two adjacent stationary spots of light blink on and off in quick succession is called the

_____ _____ .

STUDY TIP: Monocular depth cues are used by either eye alone to determine the distance of objects. They include relative height and size, interposition, linear perspective, and light and shadow.

49. Test your understanding of these cues by drawing a picture (in the box below) of a person on a bus or train, a fence, a house, and trees. Use each cue at least once, and in your drawing place the objects in the following order (closest to most distant): person, fence, house, and trees.

APPLICATIONS:

50. When two familiar objects of equal size cast unequal retinal images, the object that casts the smaller retinal image will be perceived as being
    a. closer than the other object.
    b. more distant than the other object.
    c. larger than the other object.
    d. smaller than the other object.

51. As her friend Milo walks toward her, Noriko perceives his size as remaining constant because his perceived distance _____ at the same time that her retinal image of him

_____ .

    a. increases; decreases
    b. increases; increases
    c. decreases; decreases
    d. decreases; increases

52. How do we perceive a pole that partially covers a wall?
    a. as farther away
    b. as nearer
    c. as larger
    d. There is not enough information to determine the object's size or distance.

53. An artist paints a tree orchard so that the parallel rows of trees converge at the top of the canvas. Which cue has the artist used to convey distance?
    a. interposition
    b. retinal disparity
    c. linear perspective
    d. figure-ground

54. Objects higher in our field of vision are perceived as _____ due to the principle of _____ .
    a. nearer; relative height
    b. nearer; linear perspective
    c. farther away; relative height
    d. farther away; linear perspective

Objective 18-6: Explain how perceptual constancies help us organize our sensations into meaningful patterns.

55. Our tendency to see objects as unchanging while the stimuli from them change in size, shape, and brightness is called _____

_____ .

56. The brain computes an object's brightness _____ (relative to/independent of) surrounding objects.

57. The amount of light an object reflects relative to its surroundings is called

_____ _____ .

58. The experience of color depends on the surrounding _____ in which an object is seen. In an unvarying context, a familiar object will be perceived as having consistent color, even as the light changes. This phenomenon is called

_____ _____ .

59. We see color as a result of our brains' computations of the light _____ by any object relative to its _____

_____ .

60. Due to shape and size constancy, familiar objects _____ (do/do not) appear to change shape or size despite changes in our _____ images of them.

61. Several illusions, including the _____ illusion, are explained by the interplay between perceived _____ and perceived _____ . When distance cues are removed, these illusions are _____ (diminished/strengthened).

APPLICATIONS:

62. The fact that a white object under dim illumination appears lighter than a gray object under bright illumination is called
    a. relative luminance.
    b. perceptual adaptation.
    c. color contrast.
    d. lightness constancy.

63. In the absence of perceptual constancy
    a. objects would appear to change size as their distance from us changed.
    b. depth perception would be based exclusively on monocular cues.
    c. depth perception would be based exclusively on binocular cues.
    d. depth perception would be impossible.

64. Your friend tosses you a frisbee. You know that it is getting closer instead of larger because of
    a. shape constancy.
    b. relative motion.
    c. size constancy.
    d. all of these factors.

Visual Interpretation

Objective 18-7: Describe what research on restored vision, sensory restriction, and perceptual adaptation reveals about the effects of experience on perception.

65. The idea that knowledge comes from inborn ways of organizing sensory experiences was proposed by the philosopher _____ .

66. On the other side were philosophers who maintained that we learn to perceive the world by experiencing it. One philosopher of this school was _____ .

67. Studies of cases in which vision has been restored to a person who was blind from birth show that, upon seeing tactilely familiar objects for the first

time, the person _____ (can/cannot) recognize them.

68. Studies of sensory restriction demonstrate that visual experiences during _____ are crucial for perceptual development. Such experiences suggest that there is a _____ _____ for normal sensory and perceptual development.

69. Humans given glasses that shift or invert the visual field _____ (will/will not) adapt to the distorted perception. This is called _____ _____ .

    Animals such as chicks _____ (adapt/do not adapt) to distorting lenses.

(Thinking Critically) ESP—Perception Without Sensation?

Objective 18-8: List the claims of ESP, and discuss the conclusions of most research psychologists after putting these claims to the test.

70. Perception outside the range of normal sensation is called _____ .

71. Psychologists who study ESP are called _____ .

72. The form of ESP in which people claim to be capable of reading others' minds is called _____ . A person who "senses" that a friend is in danger might claim to have the ESP ability of _____ .
    An ability to "see" into the future is called _____ . A person who claims to be able to levitate and move objects is claiming the power of _____ .

73. Analyses of psychic visions and premonitions reveal _____ (high/chance-level) accuracy. Nevertheless, some people continue to believe in their accuracy because vague predictions often are later _____ to match events that have already occurred. In addition, people are more likely to recall or _____ dreams that seem to have come true.

74. Critics point out that a major difficulty for parapsychology is that ESP phenomena are not consistently _____ .

75. Daryl Bem, who has been skeptical of stage psychics, conducted research in which Cornell University participants _____ (did/did not) accurately guess the position of an erotic scene.

APPLICATIONS:

76. Regina claims that she can bend spoons, levitate furniture, and perform many other "mind over matter" feats. Regina apparently believes she has the power of
   a. telepathy.
   b. clairvoyance.
   c. precognition.
   d. psychokinesis.

77. Which of the following is true of the predictions of leading psychics?
   a. They are often ambiguous prophecies later interpreted to match actual events.
   b. They are no more accurate than guesses made by others.
   c. They are nearly always inaccurate.
   d. All of these statements are true.

PROGRESS TEST

Multiple-Choice Questions

Circle your answers to the following questions and check them with the answers beginning on page 160. If your answer is incorrect, read the explanation for why it is incorrect and then consult the text.

1. The size of the pupil is controlled by the
   a. lens.   **c.** cornea.
   b. retina.   **d.** iris.

2. The process by which the lens changes its curvature is
   a. accommodation.   **c.** feature detection.
   b. parallel processing.   **d.** transduction.

3. The receptor of the eye that functions best in dim light is the
   a. fovea.   **c.** bipolar cell.
   b. cone.   **d.** rod.

4. The Young-Helmholtz theory proposes that
   a. there are three different types of color-sensitive cones.
   b. retinal cells are excited by one color and inhibited by its complementary color.
   c. there are four different types of cones.
   d. rod, not cone, vision accounts for our ability to detect fine visual detail.

5. The transduction of light energy into nerve impulses takes place in the
   a. iris.   **c.** lens.
   b. retina.   **d.** optic nerve.

6. The brain breaks vision into separate dimensions such as color, depth, movement, and form, and works on each aspect simultaneously. This is called
   a. feature detection.
   b. parallel processing.
   c. accommodation.
   d. opponent processing.

7. One light may appear reddish and another greenish if they differ in
   a. wavelength.   **c.** opponent processes.
   b. amplitude.   **d.** brightness.

8. Which of the following explains why a rose appears equally red in bright and dim light?
   a. the Young-Helmholtz theory
   b. the opponent-process theory
   c. feature detection
   d. color constancy

9. Most color-deficient people will probably
   a. lack functioning red- or green-sensitive cones.
   b. see the world in only black and white.
   c. also suffer from poor vision.
   d. have above-average vision to compensate for the deficit.

10. The historical movement associated with the statement "The whole may exceed the sum of its parts" is
   a. parapsychology.
   b. behavioral psychology.
   c. functional psychology.
   d. Gestalt psychology.

11. Figures tend to be perceived as whole, complete objects, even if spaces or gaps exist in the representation, thus demonstrating the principle of
   a. interposition.   **c.** continuity.
   b. linear perspective. **d.** closure.

12. The figure-ground relationship has demonstrated that
   a. perception is largely innate.
   b. perception is simply a point-for-point representation of sensation.
   c. the same stimulus can trigger more than one perception.
   d. different people see different things when viewing a scene.

13. When we stare at an object, each eye receives a slightly different image, providing a depth cue known as
    a. interposition.
    c. relative motion.
    b. linear perspective.
    d. retinal disparity.

14. As we move, viewed objects cast changing shapes on our retinas, although we do not perceive the objects as changing. This is part of the phenomenon of
    a. perceptual constancy.
    b. relative motion.
    c. linear perspective.
    d. continuity.

15. A person claiming to be able to read another's mind is claiming to have the ESP ability of
    a. psychokinesis.
    c. clairvoyance.
    b. precognition.
    d. telepathy.

16. Which philosopher maintained that knowledge comes from inborn ways of organizing our sensory experiences?
    a. Locke
    c. Gibson
    b. Kant
    d. Walk

17. Kittens and monkeys reared seeing only diffuse, unpatterned light
    a. later had difficulty distinguishing color and brightness.
    b. later had difficulty perceiving color and brightness, but eventually regained normal sensitivity.
    c. later had difficulty perceiving the shape of objects.
    d. showed no impairment in perception, indicating that neural feature detectors develop even in the absence of normal sensory experiences.

18. Adults who are born blind but later have their vision restored
    a. are almost immediately able to recognize familiar objects.
    b. typically fail to recognize familiar objects.
    c. are unable to follow moving objects with their eyes.
    d. have excellent eye-hand coordination.

19. Which of the following is NOT a monocular depth cue?
    a. light and shadow
    c. retinal disparity
    b. relative height
    d. interposition

20. The Moon illusion occurs in part because distance cues at the horizon make the Moon seem
    a. farther away and therefore larger.
    b. closer and therefore larger.
    c. farther away and therefore smaller.
    d. closer and therefore smaller.

21. Figure is to ground as _____ is to _____ .
    a. night; day
    b. top; bottom
    c. cloud; sky
    d. sensation; perception

22. Jack claims that he often has dreams that predict future events. He claims to have the power of
    a. telepathy.
    c. precognition.
    b. clairvoyance.
    d. psychokinesis.

23. Which of the following is true regarding scientific investigations of precognition?
    a. A growing body of research demonstrates that some people are truly "psychic."
    b. Studies that seem to provide evidence of precognitive ability have been criticized for being badly flawed.
    c. The search for a valid test of ESP has resulted in only a handful of studies.
    d. All of these statements are true.

24. According to the opponent-process theory
    a. there are three types of color-sensitive cones.
    b. the process of color vision begins in the cortex.
    c. neurons involved in color vision are stimulated by one color's wavelength and inhibited by another's.
    d. all of these statements are true.

25. Hubel and Wiesel discovered feature detectors in the visual
    a. fovea.
    c. iris.
    b. optic nerve.
    d. cortex.

26. Which of the following is the correct order of the structures through which light passes after entering the eye?
    a. lens, pupil, cornea, retina
    b. pupil, cornea, lens, retina
    c. pupil, lens, cornea, retina
    d. cornea, pupil, lens, retina

27. In the opponent-process theory, the three pairs of processes are
    a. red-green, blue-yellow, black-white.
    b. red-blue, green-yellow, black-white.
    c. red-yellow, blue-green, black-white.
    d. dependent upon the individual's experience.

28. Wavelength is to _____ as _____ is to brightness.
    a. hue; intensity
    b. intensity; hue
    c. frequency; amplitude
    d. brightness; hue

29. Which of the following is the most accurate description of how we process color?
    a. Throughout the visual system, color processing is divided into separate red, green, and blue systems.
    b. Red-green, blue-yellow, and black-white opponent processes operate throughout the visual system.
    c. Color processing occurs in two stages: (1) a three-color system in the retina and (2) opponent-process cells en route to the visual cortex.
    d. Color processing occurs in two stages: (1) an opponent-process system in the retina and (2) a three-color system en route to the visual cortex.

30. One reason that your ability to detect fine visual details is greatest when scenes are focused on the fovea of your retina is that
    a. there are more feature detectors in the fovea than in the peripheral regions of the retina.
    b. cones in the fovea are nearer to the optic nerve than those in peripheral regions of the retina.
    c. many rods, which are clustered in the fovea, have individual bipolar cells to relay their information to the cortex.
    d. many cones, which are clustered in the fovea, have individual bipolar cells to relay their information to the cortex.

31. The tendency to organize stimuli into smooth, uninterrupted patterns is called
    a. closure.   c. interposition.
    b. continuity.   d. proximity.

32. Which of the following statements is consistent with the Gestalt theory of perception?
    a. Perception develops largely through learning.
    b. Perception is the product of heredity.

    c. The mind organizes sensations into meaningful perceptions.
    d. Perception results directly from sensation.

33. Experiments with distorted visual environments demonstrate that
    a. adaptation rarely takes place.
    b. animals adapt readily, but humans do not.
    c. humans adapt readily, while lower animals typically do not.
    d. adaptation is possible during a critical period in infancy but not thereafter.

34. According to the philosopher _____ , we learn to perceive the world.
    a. Locke   c. Gibson
    b. Kant   d. Walk

35. The phenomenon of size constancy is based on the close connection between an object's perceived _____ and its perceived _____ .
    a. size; shape   c. size; brightness
    b. size; distance   d. shape; distance

36. Which of the following statements best describes the effects of sensory restriction?
    a. It produces functional blindness when experienced for any length of time at any age.
    b. It has greater effects on humans than on animals.
    c. It has more damaging effects when experienced during infancy.
    d. It has greater effects on adults than on children.

37. Psychologists who study ESP are called
    a. clairvoyants.   c. parapsychologists.
    b. telepaths.   d. levitators.

38. The depth cue that occurs when we watch stable objects at different distances as we are moving is
    a. linear perspective.   c. light and shadow.
    b. interposition.   d. relative motion.

39. Which of the following statements concerning ESP is true?
    a. Most ESP researchers are quacks.
    b. There have been a large number of reliable demonstrations of ESP.
    c. Most research psychologists are skeptical of the claims of defenders of ESP.
    d. There have been reliable laboratory demonstrations of ESP, but the results are no different from those that would occur by chance.

40. Each time you see your car, it projects a different image on the retinas of your eyes, yet you do not perceive it as changing. This is because of

a. closure.
b. retinal disparity.
c. perceptual constancy.
d. figure-ground.

41. The term *gestalt* means

a. grouping.   c. perception.
b. sensation.   d. whole.

42. Studies of the visual cliff have provided evidence that much of depth perception is

a. innate.
b. learned.
c. innate in lower animals, learned in humans.
d. innate in humans, learned in lower animals.

43. All of the following are laws of perceptual organization EXCEPT

a. proximity.   c. continuity.
b. closure.   d. retinal disparity.

44. You probably perceive the diagram above as three separate objects due to the principle of

a. proximity.   c. closure.
b. continuity.   d. linear perspective.

Matching Items

Match each of the structures with its function or description.

Structures or Conditions

_____ **1.** lens
_____ **2.** iris
_____ **3.** pupil
_____ **4.** rods
_____ **5.** cones

Functions or Descriptions

a. controls pupil
b. accommodation
c. admits light
d. vision in dim light
e. color vision

True–False Items

Indicate whether each statement is true or false by placing *T* or *F* in the blank next to the item.

_____ **1.** Once we perceive an item as a figure, it is impossible to see it as ground.
_____ **2.** Laboratory experiments have laid to rest all criticisms of ESP.
_____ **3.** Six-month-old infants will cross a visual cliff if their mother calls.
_____ **4.** Unlike other animals, humans have no critical period for visual stimulation.
_____ **5.** Immanuel Kant argued that experience determined how we perceive the world.

_____ **6.** It is just as easy to touch two pencil tips together with only one eye open as it is with both eyes open.
_____ **7.** After some time, humans are able to adjust to living in a world made upside down by distorting goggles.
_____ **8.** As our distance from an object changes, the object's size seems to change.
_____ **9.** John Locke argued that perception is inborn.

Essay Question

In many movies from the 1930s, dancers performed seemingly meaningless movements which, when viewed from above, were transformed into intricate patterns and designs. Similarly, the formations of marching bands often create pictures and spell words. Identify and describe at least four Gestalt principles of grouping that explain the audience's perception of the images created by these types of formations. (Use the space below to list the points you want to make, and organize them. Then write the essay on a separate piece of paper.)

Summing Up

Use the diagram at the top of the right-hand column to identify the parts of the eye, then describe how each contributes to vision.

1. _____
_____

2. _____
_____

3. _____
_____

4. _____
_____

5. _____
_____

6. _____
_____

7. _____
_____

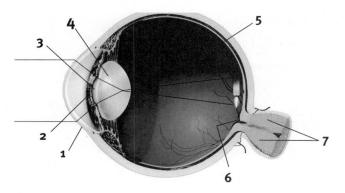

TERMS AND CONCEPTS TO REMEMBER

Using your own words, on a piece of paper write a brief definition or explanation of each of the following terms.

1. wavelength and hue
2. intensity
3. pupil
4. iris
5. lens
6. retina
7. accommodation
8. rods and cones
9. optic nerve
10. blind spot
11. fovea
12. feature detectors
13. parallel processing
14. Young-Helmholtz trichromatic (three-color) theory
15. opponent-process theory
16. gestalt
17. figure-ground
18. grouping
19. depth perception
20. visual cliff
21. binocular cue
22. retinal disparity
23. monocular cue
24. phi phenomenon
25. perceptual constancy

26. color constancy

27. perceptual adaptation

28. extrasensory perception (ESP)

29. parapsychology

ANSWERS

Module Review

The Stimulus Input and *The Eye*

1. electromagnetic

2. wavelength; hue

3. intensity; amplitude; brightness

4. yes. The left-hand wave has lower amplitude and the colors would be duller. The right-hand wave has similar frequency (and therefore hue) but a higher amplitude, making it brighter.

5. cornea; pupil; iris

6. lens; retina; accommodation

7. rods; cones

8. bipolar; ganglion

9. optic nerve; brain

10. blind spot

11. fovea; peripheral; bipolar; do not

12. cones; rods

13. sensitive; 20

14. **d.** is the answer. Greater sensitivity to fine visual detail is associated with the cones, which have their own bipolar cells to relay information to the cortex. The cones are concentrated in the fovea, the retina's point of central focus. For this reason, staring directly at an object maximizes sensitivity to fine detail.

    a. If you stare off to one side, the image falls onto peripheral regions of the retina, where rods are concentrated and sensitivity to fine visual detail is poor.

    b. Sensitivity to detail is not directly influenced by whether one or both eyes are stimulated.

    c. Decreasing the intensity of light would only impair the functioning of the cones, which are sensitive to visual detail but have a high threshold for light intensity.

15. **d.** is the answer. Just as light strikes the film of a camera, visual images entering the eye are projected onto the retina.

    a. The pupil would be analogous to the aperture of a camera, since both control the amount of light permitted to enter.

    b. The lens of the eye performs a focusing function similar to the lens of the camera.

    c. The cornea would be analogous to a camera's lens cap in that both protect delicate inner structures.

16. **d.** is the answer.

17. **b.** is the answer. Rods and cones enable vision in dim and bright light, respectively. If an animal is active only at night, it is likely to have more rods than cones in its retinas.

    d. Bipolar cells link both cones and rods to ganglion cells. There is no reason to expect that a nocturnal mammal would have more bipolar cells than a mammal active both during the day and at night. If anything, because several rods share a single bipolar cell, whereas many cones have their own, a nocturnal animal (with a visual system consisting mostly of rods) might be expected to have fewer bipolar cells than an animal active during the day (with a visual system consisting mostly of cones).

18. **b.** is the answer.

    a. & c. It is the cones, rather than the rods, that enable color vision.

    d. If the cones' threshold were lower than the available light intensity, they would be able to function and therefore detect the colors of the players' uniforms.

Visual Information Processing

19. abstract; thalamus; visual cortex; feature detectors

20. gaze; head angle; posture; body movement; supercell clusters

21. simultaneously; parallel processing

22. blindsight

Color Vision

23. reflects (rejects); construction

24. sex linked

25. Young-Helmholtz trichromatic; red; green; blue

26. opponent; afterimage

27. opponent-process; red; green; yellow; blue; black; white

In the first stage of color processing, the retina's red, green, and blue cones respond in varying degrees to different color stimuli, as suggested by the three-color theory. The resulting signals are then processed in the thalamus by red-green, blue-yellow, and black-white opponent-process cells, which are turned "on" by one wavelength and turned "off" by its opponent.

28. d. is the answer.
a. Feature detectors are located in the visual cortex and respond to features such as movement, shape, and angle.
b. & c. Cones and bipolar cells are located in the retina. Moreover, neither are excited by some colors and inhibited by others.

29. c. is the answer.
a. The trichromatic theory cannot account for the experience of afterimages.
b. & d. Afterimages are experienced as the complementary color of a stimulus. Green, not blue, is red's complement.

Visual Organization

30. Gestalt; whole

31. figure; ground

32. grouping

33. continuity; closure; proximity

34. c. is the answer. She perceives the line for the road as continuous, even though it is interrupted by lines indicating other roads.

a. Closure refers to the perceptual filling in of gaps in a stimulus to create a complete, whole object.

d. Proximity is the tendency to group objects near to one another as a single unit.

35. depth perception; distance

36. visual cliff; mobile

Research on the visual cliff suggests that in many species the ability to perceive depth is present at, or very shortly after, birth.

37. binocular

38. retinal disparity

39. monocular

40. relative size

41. interposition

42. relative height

43. relative motion

44. linear perspective

45. light and shadow

46. retreating; approaching; more slowly

47. movement; stroboscopic movement

48. phi phenomenon

49. See top of next column.

50. b. is the answer. The phenomenon described is the basis for the monocular cue of relative size.

a. The object casting the *larger* retinal image would be perceived as closer.
c. & d. Because of size constancy, the perceived size of familiar objects remains constant, despite changes in their retinal image size.

51. d. is the answer.

52. b. is the answer. This is an example of the principle of interposition in depth perception.
a. The partially obscured object is perceived as farther away.
c. The perceived size of an object is not altered when that object overlaps another.

53. c. is the answer.
a. Interposition is a monocular depth cue in which an object that partially covers another is perceived as closer.
b. Retinal disparity refers to the difference between the two images received by our eyes that allows us to perceive depth. It has nothing to do with the way the artist placed the trees.
d. Figure-ground refers to the organization of the field into objects that stand out from their surroundings.

54. c. is the answer.
b. & d. Linear perspective is the apparent convergence of parallel lines as a cue to distance.

55. perceptual constancy

56. relative to

57. relative luminance

58. context; color constancy

59. reflected; surrounding objects

60. do not; retinal

61. Moon; size; distance; diminished

62. d. is the answer. Although the amount of light reflected from a white object is less in dim light than in bright light—and may be less than the amount of light reflected from a brightly lit gray object—the brightness of the white object is perceived as remaining constant. Because a white object reflects a higher percentage of the light fall-

ing on it than does a gray object, and the brightness of objects is perceived as constant despite variations in illumination, white is perceived as brighter than gray even under dim illumination.
a. Relative luminance refers to the relative intensity of light falling on surfaces that are in proximity. Lightness constancy is perceived despite variations in illumination.
b. Perceptual adaptation refers to the ability to adjust to an artificially modified perceptual environment, such as an inverted visual field.
c. Color contrast is not discussed in this text.

63. **a.** is the answer. Because we perceive the size of a familiar object as constant even as its retinal image grows smaller, we perceive the object as being farther away.
b. & c. Perceptual constancy is a cognitive, rather than sensory, phenomenon. Therefore, the absence of perceptual constancy would not alter sensitivity to monocular or binocular cues.
d. Although the absence of perceptual constancy would impair depth perception based on the size-distance relationship, other cues to depth, such as texture gradient, could still be used.

64. **a.** is the answer.

Visual Interpretation

65. Immanuel Kant
66. John Locke
67. cannot
68. infancy; critical period
69. will; perceptual adaptation; do not adapt

(Thinking Critically) ESP—Perception Without Sensation?

70. extrasensory perception
71. parapsychologists
72. telepathy; clairvoyance; precognition; psychokinesis
73. chance-level; interpreted (retrofitted); reconstruct
74. reproducible
75. did
76. **d.** is the answer.
a. Telepathy is the claimed ability to "read" minds.
b. Clairvoyance refers to the claimed ability to perceive remote events.
c. Precognition refers to the claimed ability to perceive future events.
77. **d.** is the answer.

Progress Test

Multiple-Choice Questions

1. **d.** is the answer.
a. The lens lies behind the pupil and focuses light on the retina.
b. The retina is the inner surface of the eyeball and contains the rods and cones.
c. The cornea lies in front of the pupil and is the first structure that light passes through as it enters the eye.

2. **a.** is the answer.
b. Parallel processing is information processing in which several aspects of a stimulus, such as light or sound, are processed simultaneously.
c. Feature detection is the process by which neural cells in the brain respond to specific visual features.
d. Transduction refers to the conversion of an environmental stimulus, such as light, into a neural impulse by a receptor—a rod or a cone.

3. **d.** is the answer.
a. The fovea is not a receptor; it is a region of the retina that contains only cones.
b. Cones have a higher threshold for brightness than rods and therefore do not function as well in dim light.
c. Bipolar cells are not receptors; they are neurons in the retina that link rods and cones with ganglion cells, which make up the optic nerve.

4. **a.** is the answer. The Young-Helmholtz theory proposes that there are red-, green-, and blue-sensitive cones.
b. This answer describes Hering's opponent-process theory.
c. The Young-Helmholtz theory proposes that there are three types of cones, not four.
d. The Young-Helmholtz theory concerns only color vision, not the detection of visual detail.

5. **b.** is the answer.
a. The iris controls the diameter of the pupil.
c. The lens accommodates its shape to focus images on the retina.
d. The optic nerve carries nerve impulses from the retina to the visual cortex.

6. **b.** is the answer.
a. Feature detection is the process by which nerve cells in the brain respond to specific visual features of a stimulus, such as movement or shape.
c. Accommodation is the process by which the lens changes its curvature to focus images on the retina.
d. The opponent-process theory suggests that color vision depends on the response of brain

cells to red-green, yellow-blue, and black-white opposing colors.

7. **a.** is the answer. Wavelength determines hue, or color.

   b. & d. The amplitude of light determines its brightness.

   c. Opponent processes are neural systems involved in color vision, not properties of light.

8. **d.** is the answer. Color constancy is the perception that a familiar object has consistent color, even if changing illumination alters the wavelengths reflected by that object.

   a. & b. These theories explain how the visual system detects color; they do not explain why colors do not seem to change when lighting does.

   c. Feature detection explains how the brain recognizes visual images by analyzing their distinctive features of shape, movement, and angle.

9. **a.** is the answer. Thus, they have difficulty discriminating these two colors.

   b. Those who are color deficient are usually not "color blind" in a literal sense. Instead, they are unable to distinguish certain hues, such as red from green.

   c. Failure to distinguish red and green is separate from, and does not usually affect, general visual ability.

   d. Color deficiency does not enhance vision. A deficit in one sense often is compensated for by overdevelopment of another sense—for example, hearing in blind people.

10. **d.** is the answer. Gestalt psychology, which developed in Germany early in the twentieth century, was interested in how clusters of sensations are organized into "whole" perceptions.

    a. Parapsychology is the study of ESP and other paranormal phenomena.

    b. & c. Behavioral and functional psychology developed later in the United States.

11. **d.** is the answer.

    a. Interposition is the tendency to perceive objects that partially block our view of another object as closer.

    b. Linear perspective involves the appearance of parallel lines meeting in the distance.

    c. Continuity refers to the tendency to group stimuli into smooth, continuous patterns.

12. **c.** is the answer. Although we always differentiate a stimulus into figure and ground, those elements of the stimulus we perceive as figure and those as ground may change. In this way, the same stimulus can trigger more than one perception.

a. The idea of a figure-ground relationship has no bearing on the issue of whether perception is innate.

b. Perception cannot be simply a point-for-point representation of sensation, since in figure-ground relationships a single stimulus can trigger more than one perception.

d. Figure-ground relationships demonstrate the existence of general, rather than individual, principles of perceptual organization. Significantly, even the same person can see different figure-ground relationships when viewing a scene.

13. **d.** is the answer. The greater the retinal disparity, or difference between the images, the less the distance.

    a. Interposition is the monocular distance cue in which an object that partially blocks another object is seen as closer.

    b. Linear perspective is the monocular distance cue in which parallel lines appear to converge in the distance.

    c. Relative motion is the monocular distance cue in which objects at different distances change their relative positions in our visual image, with those closest moving most.

14. **a.** is the answer. Perception of constant shape, like perception of constant size, is part of the phenomenon of perceptual constancy.

    b. Relative motion is a monocular distance cue in which objects at different distances appear to move at different rates.

    c. Linear perspective is a monocular distance cue in which lines we know to be parallel converge in the distance, thus indicating depth.

    d. Continuity is the perceptual tendency to group items into continuous patterns.

15. **d.** is the answer.

    a. Psychokinesis refers to the claimed ability to perform acts of "mind over matter."

    b. Precognition refers to the claimed ability to perceive future events.

    c. Clairvoyance refers to the claimed ability to perceive remote events.

16. **b.** is the answer.

    a. Locke argued that knowledge is not inborn but comes through learning.

    c. & d. Gibson and Walk studied depth perception using the visual cliff; they made no claims about the source of knowledge.

17. **c.** is the answer.

    a. & b. The kittens had difficulty only with lines they had never experienced, and never regained normal sensitivity.

d. Both perceptual and feature-detector impairment resulted from visual restriction.

18. **b.** is the answer. Because they have not had early visual experiences, these adults typically have difficulty learning to perceive objects.
    a. Such patients typically could not visually recognize objects with which they were familiar by touch, and in some cases this inability persisted.
    c. Being able to perceive figure-ground relationships, patients are able to follow moving objects with their eyes.
    d. This answer is incorrect because eye-hand coordination is an acquired skill and requires much practice.

19. **c.** is the answer. Retinal disparity is a *binocular* cue; all the other cues mentioned are monocular.

20. **a.** is the answer. The Moon appears larger at the horizon than overhead in the sky because objects at the horizon provide distance cues that make the Moon seem farther away and therefore larger. In the open sky, of course, there are no such cues.

21. **c.** is the answer. We see a cloud as a figure against the background of sky.
    a., b., & d. The figure-ground relationship refers to the organization of the visual field into objects (figures) that stand out from their surroundings (ground).

22. **c.** is the answer.
    a. This answer would be correct had Jack claimed to be able to read someone else's mind.
    b. This answer would be correct had Jack claimed to be able to sense remote events, such as a friend in distress.
    d. This answer would be correct had Jack claimed to be able to levitate objects or bend spoons without applying any physical force.

23. **b.** is the answer.

24. **c.** is the answer. After leaving the receptor cells, visual information is analyzed in terms of pairs of opponent colors; neurons stimulated by one member of a pair are inhibited by the other.
    a. The idea that there are three types of color-sensitive cones is the basis of the Young-Helmholtz three-color theory.
    b. According to the opponent-process theory, and all other theories of color vision, the process of color vision begins in the retina.

25. **d.** is the answer. Feature detectors are cortical neurons and hence are located in the visual cortex.
    a. The fovea contains cones.
    b. The optic nerve contains neurons that relay nerve impulses from the retina to higher centers in the visual system.
    c. The iris is simply a ring of muscle tissue, which controls the diameter of the pupil.

26. **d.** is the answer.

27. **a.** is the answer.

28. **a.** is the answer. Wavelength determines hue, and intensity determines brightness.

29. **c.** is the answer.
    a. This answer is incorrect because separate red, green, and blue systems operate only in the retina.
    b. This answer is incorrect because opponent-process systems operate en route to the brain, after visual processing in the receptors is completed.
    d. This answer is incorrect because it reverses the correct order of the two stages of processing.

30. **d.** is the answer.
    a. Feature detectors are nerve cells located in the visual cortex, not in the fovea of the retina.
    b. The proximity of rods and cones to the optic nerve does not influence their ability to resolve fine details.
    c. Rods are concentrated in the peripheral regions of the retina, not in the fovea; moreover, several rods share a single bipolar cell.

31. **b.** is the answer.
    a. Closure refers to the tendency to perceptually fill in gaps in recognizable objects in the visual field.
    c. Interposition is the tendency to perceive objects that partially block our view of another object as closer.
    d. Proximity refers to the tendency to group items that are near one another.

32. **c.** is the answer.
    a. & b. The Gestalt psychologists did not deal with the origins of perception; they were more concerned with its form.
    d. In fact, they argued just the opposite: Perception is more than mere sensory experience.

33. **c.** is the answer. Humans are able to adjust to upside-down worlds and other visual distortions, figuring out the relationship between the perceived and the actual reality; lower animals, such as chicks, are typically unable to adapt.
    a. Humans are able to adapt quite well to distorted visual environments (and then to readapt).
    b. This answer is incorrect because humans are the most adaptable of creatures.
    d. Humans are able to adapt at any age to distorted visual environments.

34. **a.** is the answer.
    b. Kant claimed that knowledge is inborn.

c. & d. Gibson and Walk make no claims about the origins of perception.

36. b. is the answer.

37. c. is the answer. There appears to be a critical period for perceptual development, in that sensory restriction has severe, even permanent, disruptive effects when it occurs in infancy but not when it occurs later in life.
a. & d. Sensory restriction does not have the same effects at all ages, and it is more damaging to children than to adults. This is because there is a critical period for perceptual development; whether functional blindness will result depends in part on the nature of the sensory restriction.
b. Research studies have not indicated that sensory restriction is more damaging to humans than to animals.

37. c. is the answer.
a., b., & d. These psychics claim to exhibit the phenomena studied by parapsychologists.

38. d. is the answer. When we move, stable objects we see also appear to move, and the distance and speed of the apparent motion cue us to the objects' relative distances.
a., b., & c. These depth cues are unrelated to movement and thus work even when we are stationary.

39. c. is the answer.
a. Many ESP researchers are sincere, reputable researchers.
b. & d. There have been no reliable demonstrations of ESP.

40. c. is the answer. Because of perceptual constancy, we see the car's shape and size as always the same.
a. Closure refers to the tendency to perceptually fill in gaps in recognizable objects in the visual field.
b. Retinal disparity means that our right and left eyes each receive slightly different images.
d. Figure-ground refers to the organization of the visual field into two parts.

41. d. is the answer. Gestalt means a "form" or "organized whole."

42. a. is the answer. Most infants refused to crawl out over the "cliff" even when coaxed, suggesting that much of depth perception is innate. Studies with the young of "lower" animals show the same thing.

43. d. is the answer.

44. a. is the answer. Proximity is the tendency to group objects near to one another. The diagram is

perceived as three distinct units, even though the lines are evenly spaced.
b. Continuity is the tendency to group stimuli into smooth, uninterrupted patterns. There is no such continuity in the diagram.
c. Closure is the perceptual tendency to fill in gaps in a form. In the diagram, three disconnected units are perceived rather than a single whole.
d. Linear perspective is when parallel lines appear to meet in the distance.

Matching Items

1. b   4. d
2. a   5. e
3. c

True–False Items

1. F   5. F   9. F
2. F   6. F
3. F   7. T
4. F   8. F

Essay Question

1. *Proximity.* We tend to perceive items that are near each other as belonging together. Thus, a small section of dancers or members of a marching band may separate themselves from the larger group in order to form part of a particular image.

2. *Similarity.* Because we perceive similar figures as belonging together, choreographers and band directors often create distinct visual groupings within the larger band or dance troupe by having the members of each group wear a distinctive costume or uniform.

3. *Continuity.* Because we perceive smooth, continuous patterns rather than discontinuous ones, dancers or marching musicians moving together (as in a column, for example) are perceived as a separate unit.

4. *Closure.* If a figure has gaps, we complete it, filling in the gaps to create a whole image. Thus, we perceptually fill in the relatively wide spacing between dancers or marching musicians in order to perceive the complete words or forms they are creating.

Summing Up

1. Cornea. Light enters the eye through this transparent membrane, which protects the inner structures from the environment.

2. Iris. The colored part of the eye, the iris functions like the aperture of a camera, controlling the size

of the pupil to optimize the amount of light that enters the eye.

3. Pupil. The adjustable opening in the iris, the pupil allows light to enter.

4. Lens. This transparent structure behind the pupil changes shape to focus images on the retina.

5. Retina. The light-sensitive inner surface of the eye, the retina contains the rods and cones, which transduce light energy into neural impulses.

6. Blind spot. The region of the retina where the optic nerve leaves the eye, the blind spot contains no rods or cones and so there is no vision here.

7. Optic nerve. This bundle of nerve fibers carries neural impulses from the retina to the brain.

Terms and Concepts to Remember

1. **Wavelength**, which refers to the distance from the peak of one light wave to the next, gives rise to the perceptual experiences of **hue**, or color, in vision.

2. The **intensity** of light is determined by the amplitude of the waves and is experienced as brightness.

3. The **pupil** is the adjustable opening in the eye through which light enters.

4. The **iris** is a ring of muscle tissue that forms the colored part of the eye that controls the diameter of the pupil.

5. The **lens** is the transparent structure of the eye behind the pupil that changes shape to focus images on the retina.

6. The **retina** is the light-sensitive, multilayered inner surface of the eye that contains the rods and cones as well as neurons that form the beginning of the optic nerve.

7. **Accommodation** is the process by which the lens of the eye changes shape to focus near objects on the retina.

8. The **rods** and **cones** are visual receptors that convert light energy into neural impulses. The rods are concentrated in the periphery of the retina, the cones in the fovea. The rods have poor sensitivity; detect black, white, and gray; function well in dim light; and are needed for peripheral vision. The cones have excellent sensitivity, enable color vision, and function best in daylight or bright light.

9. Comprised of the axons of retinal ganglion cells, the **optic nerve** carries neural impulses from the eye to the brain.

10. The **blind spot** is the region of the retina where the optic nerve leaves the eye. Because there are no rods or cones in this area, there is no vision here.

11. The **fovea** is the retina's point of central focus. It contains only cones; therefore, images focused on the fovea are the clearest.

12. **Feature detectors**, located in the visual cortex of the brain, are nerve cells that selectively respond to specific visual features, such as movement, shape, or angle. Feature detectors are evidently the basis of visual information processing.

13. **Parallel processing** is information processing in which several aspects of a stimulus, such as light, are processed simultaneously.

14. The **Young-Helmholtz trichromatic (three-color) theory** maintains that the retina contains red-, green-, and blue-sensitive color receptors that in combination can produce the perception of any color. This theory explains the first stage of color processing.

15. The **opponent-process theory** maintains that color vision depends on pairs of opposing retinal processes (red-green, yellow-blue, and white-black). This theory explains the second stage of color processing.

16. **Gestalt** means "organized whole." The Gestalt psychologists emphasized our tendency to integrate pieces of information into meaningful wholes.

17. **Figure-ground** refers to the organization of the visual field into two parts: the figure, which stands out from its surroundings, and the surroundings, or background.

18. **Grouping** is the perceptual tendency to organize stimuli into coherent groups. Gestalt psychologists identified various principles of grouping.

19. **Depth perception** is the ability to see objects in three dimensions although the images that strike the retina are two-dimensional; it allows us to judge distance.

20. The **visual cliff** is a laboratory device for testing depth perception, especially in infants and young animals. In their experiments with the visual cliff, Gibson and Walk found strong evidence that depth perception is at least in part innate.

21. **Binocular cues** are depth cues that depend on information from both eyes.

    Memory aid: *Bi-* indicates "two"; *ocular* means something pertaining to the eye. **Binocular cues** are cues for the "two eyes."

22. **Retinal disparity** refers to the differences between the images received by the left eye and the right eye as a result of viewing the world from slightly different angles. It is a binocular depth cue, since the greater the difference between the two images, the nearer the object.

23. **Monocular cues** are depth cues that depend on information from either eye alone.

    Memory aid: *Mono-* means one; a monocle is an eyeglass for one eye. A **monocular cue** is one that is available to either the left or the right eye.

24. The **phi phenomenon** is an illusion of movement created when two or more adjacent lights blink on and off in succession.

25. **Perceptual constancy** is the perception that objects have consistent lightness, color, shape, and size, even as illumination and retinal images change.

26. **Color constancy** is the perception that familiar objects have consistent color despite changes in illumination that shift the wavelengths they reflect.

27. **Perceptual adaptation** refers to our ability to adjust to an artificially displaced or even inverted visual field. Given distorting lenses, we perceive things accordingly but soon adjust by learning the relationship between our distorted perceptions and the reality.

28. **Extrasensory perception (ESP)** refers to the controversial claim that perception can occur without sensory input. Supposed ESP powers include telepathy, clairvoyance, and precognition.

    Memory aid: *Extra-* means "beyond" or "in addition to"; **extrasensory perception** is perception outside or beyond the normal senses.

29. **Parapsychology** is the study of ESP, psychokinesis, and other paranormal forms of interaction between the individual and the environment.

    Memory aid: *Para-*, like *extra-*, indicates "beyond"; thus, paranormal is beyond the normal and **parapsychology** is the study of phenomena beyond the realm of psychology and known natural laws.

The Nonvisual Senses

MODULE OVERVIEW

This module describes all the nonvisual senses: hearing, touch, taste, smell, and body position and movement. The discussion of hearing includes the structure of the ear and the process through which the stimulus energy is transmitted through the ear and interpreted in the brain. Following a description of the sense of touch, the module explores the meaning and treatment of pain. Although vision and hearing are the most important human senses, the other senses are also vital to our ability to function. Without pain, for example, we might not realize when we cut ourselves or when some internal organ is not functioning properly.

NOTE: Answer guidelines for all Module 19 questions begin on page 173.

STUDY TIP: An excellent way to study all the technical material in this module is to organize it into a chart. For each sense you need to know several facts, including the nature of the stimulus input, the type of receptor that transmits the stimulus energy, and how the information is processed in the brain. To help you review your understanding of the nonvisual senses, refer often to the summary chart below.

Sense	Stimulus Input	Receptors	Notes
Hearing	Sound waves of moving air molecules	Hair cells in the cochlea	wavelength = pitch; amplitude = loudness
Touch	Pressure, warmth, cold, pain	Specialized nerve endings	Cold + pressure = wetness; side-by-side pressure = tickle
Pain	No one type of stimulus	No special receptors	Natural endorphins relieve pain; hypnosis used for treating pain
Taste	Chemical molecules corresponding to sweet, salty, sour, bitter, and umami	Hair cells in the taste pores	Sensory interaction: smell influences; taste; smell + texture = taste = flavor
Smell	Airborne chemical molecules	Olfactory receptor cells in the nasal cavity	The brain's circuitry for smell connects with areas involved in memory storage
Body position and movement	Changes in body's position (kinesthesis) Changes in head position (vestibular sense)	Sensors in muscles, tendons, and joints Hairlike receptors in the ear's semicircular canals and vestibular sacs of the inner ear	Millions of position and motion sensors Messages sent to the brain's cerebellum

MODULE REVIEW

First, skim each section, noting headings and boldface items. After you have read the section, review each objective by answering the fill-in and essay-type questions that follow it. In some cases, Study Tips explain how best to learn a difficult concept and Applications help you to know how well you understand the material. As you proceed, evaluate your performance by consulting the answers beginning on page 173. Do not continue with the next section until you understand each answer. If you need to, review or reread the section in the textbook before continuing.

Hearing

Objective 19-1: Describe the characteristics of air pressure waves, and explain the process by which the ear transforms sound energy into neural messages.

1. The stimulus for hearing, or
_____ , is sound waves, created by the compression and expansion of
_____ _____ .

2. The amplitude of a sound wave determines the sound's _____ .

3. The frequency of a sound wave determines the _____ we perceive.

4. Sound energy is measured in units called
_____ . The absolute threshold for hearing is arbitrarily defined as
_____ such units.

STUDY TIP: The stimulus energy for hearing can be described as a traveling wave that varies in wavelength and amplitude. The wavelength of an auditory stimulus is measured as the distance from the peak of one wave to the next—the shorter the distance, the greater the frequency of the waves. Short, high frequency waves produce high-pitched sounds. Long, low frequency waves produce low-pitched sounds.

The wave's amplitude is measured as the distance from the top of its peak to the bottom. High amplitude waves produce bright colors and loud sounds, while low amplitude waves produce dull colors and soft sounds.

To test your understanding, take a look at these two waves.

5. Assuming that these two waves were sound energy, would they sound the same? If not, how would they differ?

---

6. The ear is divided into three main parts: the
_____ ear, the
_____ ear, and the
_____ ear.

7. The outer ear channels sound waves toward the
_____ , a tight membrane that then vibrates.

8. The middle ear transmits the vibrations through a piston made of three small bones: the
_____ , _____ ,
and _____ .

9. In the inner ear, a coiled, bony, fluid-filled tube called the _____ contains the receptor cells for hearing. The incoming vibrations cause the _____
_____ to vibrate the fluid that fills the tube, which causes ripples in the
_____ _____ ,
bending the _____
_____
that line its surface. This movement triggers impulses in the adjacent nerve fibers that converge to form the auditory nerve, which carries the neural messages (via the _____)
to the _____ lobe's auditory cortex.

10. Damage to the cochlea's hair cell receptors or their associated auditory nerves can cause
_____ hearing loss. It may be caused by disease, but more often it results from the biological changes linked with heredity,
_____ , and prolonged exposure to ear-splitting noise or music.

11. Problems in the mechanical system that conducts sound waves to the cochlea may cause
_____ _____
_____ .

12. An electronic device that restores hearing among nerve-deafened people is a
_____ _____ .

13. The brain interprets loudness from the
_____ of hair cells a sound activates.

APPLICATIONS:

14. Which of the following correctly lists the order of structures through which sound travels after entering the ear?

    a. auditory canal, eardrum, middle ear, cochlea
    b. eardrum, auditory canal, middle ear, cochlea
    c. eardrum, middle ear, cochlea, auditory canal
    d. cochlea, eardrum, middle ear, auditory canal

15. Dr. Frankenstein has forgotten to give his monster an important part; as a result, the monster cannot transduce sound. Dr. Frankenstein omitted the

    a. eardrum.
    b. middle ear.
    c. semicircular canals.
    d. basilar membrane.

Objective 19-2: Discuss the theories that help us understand pitch perception.

16. One theory of pitch perception proposes that different pitches activate different places on the cochlea's basilar membrane; this is the _____ theory. This theory has difficulty accounting for how we hear _____-pitched sounds, which do not have such localized effects.

17. A second theory proposes that the frequency of neural impulses, sent to the brain at the same frequency as sound waves, allows the perception of different pitches. This is the _____ theory. This theory fails to account for the perception of _____-pitched sounds because individual neurons cannot fire faster than _____ times per second.

18. For the higher pitches, cells may alternate their firing to match the sound's frequency, according to the _____ principle.

Objective 19-3: Describe how we locate sounds.

19. We locate a sound by sensing differences in the _____ and _____ with which it reaches our ears.

20. A sound that comes from directly ahead will be _____ (easier/harder) to locate than a sound that comes from off to one side.

The Other Senses

Objective 19-4: Describe the sense of touch.

21. The sense of touch is a mixture of at least four senses: _____ , _____ , _____ , and _____ . Other skin sensations, such as tickle, itch, hot, and wetness, are _____ of the basic ones.

22. The _____-_____ influence on touch is illustrated by the fact that a self-produced tickle produces less activation in the _____ _____ than someone else's tickle.

Objective 19-5: Discuss how we best understand and control pain.

23. People born without the ability to feel pain may be unaware of experiencing severe _____ . More numerous are those who live with _____ pain in the form of persistent headaches and backaches, for example.

24. Pain is a property of our _____ as well as our _____ and _____ , and our surrounding _____ .

25. The pain system _____ (is/is not) triggered by one specific type of physical energy. The body has specialized _____ , sensory receptors that detect hurtful stimuli.

26. Melzack and Wall have proposed a theory of pain called the _____-_____ theory, which proposes that there is a neurological _____ in the _____ _____ that blocks pain signals or lets them through. It may be opened by activation of _____ (small/large) nerve fibers and closed by activation of _____ (small/large) fibers or by information from the _____ .

27. Pain-producing brain activity may be triggered with or without _____ .

28. A sensation of pain in an amputated leg is referred to as a _____ _____ sensation. Another example is _____ , experienced by people who have a ringing-in-the-ears sensation.

29. Because our experience of pain is also influenced by psychological factors as well as our social situation and our _____ traditions, we can say our perception of pain is a(n) _____ phenomenon.

List some pain control techniques used in health care situations.

APPLICATIONS:

30. The phantom limb sensation indicates that
    a. pain is a purely sensory phenomenon.
    b. the central nervous system plays only a minor role in the experience of pain.
    c. pain involves the brain's interpretation of neural activity.
    d. all of these are true.

31. While competing in the Olympic trials, marathoner Kirsten O'Brien suffered a stress fracture in her left leg. That she did not experience significant pain until the race was over is probably attributable to the fact that during the race
    a. the pain gate in her spinal cord was closed by information coming from her brain.
    b. her body's production of endorphins decreased.
    c. an increase in the activity of small pain fibers closed the pain gate.
    d. a decrease in the activity of large pain fibers closed the pain gate.

32. How does pain differ from other senses?
    a. It has no special receptors.
    b. It has no single stimulus.
    c. It is influenced by both physical and psychological phenomena.
    d. All of these statements are true.

Objective 19-5: Describe the senses of taste and smell, and comment on their interaction.

33. The basic taste sensations are _____ , _____ , _____ , _____ , and a meaty taste called _____ .

34. Taste, which is a _____ sense, is enabled by the 200 or more _____ _____ on the top and sides of the tongue. Each contains a _____ that catches food chemicals.

35. Taste receptors reproduce themselves every _____ . As we age, the number of taste buds _____ (increases/decreases/remains unchanged) and our taste sensitivity _____ (increases/decreases/remains unchanged). Taste is also affected by _____ and by _____ use.

36. When the sense of smell is blocked, as when we have a cold, foods do not taste the same; this illustrates the principle of _____ _____ . The _____ effect occurs when we _____ a speaker saying one syllable while _____ another.

37. The influence of bodily sensations, gestures, and other states on our cognitive preferences and judgments is called _____ _____ .

38. Like taste, smell, or _____ , is a _____ sense. There _____ (is/is not) a distinct receptor for each detectable odor.

39. Odors are able to evoke memories and feelings because there is a direct link between the brain area that gets information from the nose and the ancient _____ centers associated with memory and emotion.

APPLICATIONS:

40. Which of the following is an example of sensory interaction?
  a. finding that despite its delicious aroma, a weird-looking meal tastes awful
  b. finding that food tastes bland when you have a bad cold
  c. finding it difficult to maintain your balance when you have an ear infection
  d. All of these are examples.

41. Seventy-year-old Mrs. Martinez finds that she must spice her food heavily or she cannot taste it. Unfortunately, her son often finds her cooking inedible because it is so spicy. What is the likely explanation for their taste differences?
  a. Women have higher taste thresholds than men.
  b. Men have higher taste thresholds than women.
  c. Being 70 years old, Mrs. Martinez probably has fewer taste buds than her son.
  d. All of these are likely explanations.

42. Tamiko hates the bitter taste of her cough syrup. Which of the following would she find most helpful in minimizing the syrup's bad taste?
  a. tasting something very sweet before taking the cough syrup
  b. keeping the syrup in her mouth for several seconds before swallowing it
  c. holding her nose while taking the cough syrup
  d. gulping the cough syrup so that it misses her tongue

Objective 19-6: Explain how we sense our body's position and movement.

43. The system for sensing the position and movement of body parts is called _____ . The receptors for this sense are located in the _____ , _____ , _____ , and _____ .

44. The sense that monitors the position and movement of the head (and thus the body) is the _____ _____ . The receptors for this sense are located in the _____ _____ and _____ _____ of the inner ear.

PROGRESS TEST

Multiple-Choice Questions

Circle your answers to the following questions and check them with the answers beginning on page 174. If your answer is incorrect, read the explanation for why it is incorrect and then consult the text.

1. Frequency is to pitch as _____ is to _____ .
  a. wavelength; loudness
  b. amplitude; loudness
  c. wavelength; intensity
  d. amplitude; intensity

2. Our experience of pain when we are injured depends on
  a. our biological makeup and the type of injury we have sustained.
  b. how well medical personnel deal with our injury.
  c. our physiology, experiences and attention, and surrounding culture.
  d. what our culture allows us to express in terms of feelings of pain.

3. According to the gate-control theory, a way to alleviate chronic pain would be to stimulate the _____ nerve fibers that _____ the spinal gate.
  a. small; open   **c.** large; open
  b. small; close   **d.** large; close

4. Kinesthesis involves
  a. the bones of the middle ear.
  b. information from the bones, ears, tendons, joints, and ears.
  c. membranes within the cochlea.
  d. the body's sense of balance.

5. The frequency theory of hearing is better than place theory at explaining our sensation of
  a. the lowest pitches.
  b. pitches of intermediate range.
  c. the highest pitches.
  d. all of these pitches.

6. Which of the following is NOT one of the basic tastes?
  a. sweet   **c.** umami
  b. salty   **d.** bland

7. Of the four distinct skin senses, the only one that has definable receptors is
  a. warmth.   **c.** pressure.
  b. cold.   **d.** pain.

8. The receptors for taste are located in the
   a. taste buds.
   b. cochlea.
   c. fovea.
   d. cortex.

9. The inner ear contains receptors for
   a. audition and kinesthesis.
   b. kinesthesis and the vestibular sense.
   c. audition and the vestibular sense.
   d. audition, kinesthesis, and the vestibular sense.

10. What enables you to feel yourself wiggling your toes even with your eyes closed?
    a. vestibular sense
    b. kinesthesis
    c. the skin senses
    d. sensory interaction

11. The principle that one sense may influence another is
    a. transduction.
    b. gate-control theory.
    c. kinesthesis.
    d. sensory interaction.

12. The place theory of pitch perception cannot account for how we hear
    a. low-pitched sounds.
    b. middle-pitched sounds.
    c. high-pitched sounds.
    d. chords (three or more pitches simultaneously).

13. Sensorineural hearing loss is caused by
    a. wax buildup in the outer ear.
    b. damage to the eardrum.
    c. blockage in the middle ear because of infection.
    d. damage to the cochlea.

Matching Items

Match each of the structures with its function or description.

Structures or Conditions

_____ 1. middle ear
_____ 2. inner ear
_____ 3. large nerve fiber
_____ 4. small nerve fiber
_____ 5. semicircular canals
_____ 6. sensors in joints

Functions or Descriptions

a. amplifies sounds
b. closes pain gate
c. vestibular sense
d. opens pain gate
e. transduction of sound
f. kinesthesis

Summing Up

Use the diagram to identify the parts of the ear, then describe how each contributes to hearing. Also, briefly explain the role of each structure.

1. _____
   _____

2. _____
   _____

3. _____
   _____

4. _____
   _____

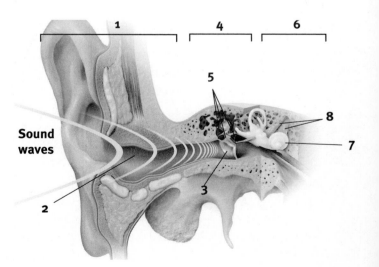

Sound waves

5. _____

_____

6. _____

_____

7. _____

_____

8. _____

_____

TERMS AND CONCEPTS TO REMEMBER

Using your own words, on a piece of paper write a brief definition or explanation of each of the following terms.

1. audition

2. frequency and pitch

3. middle ear

4. cochlea

5. inner ear

6. sensorineural hearing loss

7. conduction hearing loss

8. cochlear implant

9. place theory

10. frequency theory

11. gate-control theory

12. sensory interaction

13. embodied cognition

14. kinesthesis

15. vestibular sense

ANSWERS

Module Review

Hearing

1. audition; air molecules

2. loudness

3. pitch

4. decibels; zero

5. yes. The sounds have similar frequency (and therefore pitch), but the right-hand sound has higher amplitude and would therefore be louder.

6. outer; middle; inner

7. eardrum

8. hammer; anvil; stirrup

9. cochlea; oval window; basilar membrane; hair cells; thalamus; temporal

10. sensorineural; aging

11. conduction hearing loss

12. cochlear implant

13. number

14. **a.** is the answer.

15. **d.** is the answer. The hair cells, which transduce sound energy, are located on the basilar membrane.
    a. & b. The eardrum and bones of the middle ear merely conduct sound waves to the inner ear, where they are transduced.
    c. The semicircular canals are involved in the vestibular sense, not hearing.

16. place; low

17. frequency; high; 1000

18. volley

19. speed (timing); intensity

20. harder

The Other Senses

21. pressure; warmth; cold; pain; variations

22. top-down; somatosensory cortex

23. injury; chronic

24. physiology; experience; attention; culture

25. is not; nociceptors

26. gate-control; gate; spinal cord; small; large; brain

27. sensory input

28. phantom limb; tinnitus

29. cultural; biopsychosocial

Pain control techniques include drugs, surgery, acupuncture, thought distraction, exercise, hypnosis, relaxation training, electrical stimulation, and massage. Similarly, for burn victims, distraction during painful wound care can be created by immersion in a computer-generated 3-D world.

30. **c.** is the answer. Since pain is felt in the limb that does not exist, the pain is simply the brain's (mis)interpretation of neural activity.
    a. If pain were a purely sensory phenomenon, phantom limb pain would not occur, since the receptors are no longer present.

b. That pain is experienced when a limb is missing indicates that the central nervous system, especially the brain, is where pain is sensed.

31. **a.** is the answer.
    b. Since endorphins relieve pain, a decrease in their production would have made Kirsten more likely to experience pain. Moreover, because endorphins are released in response to pain, their production probably would have increased.
    c. Neural activity in small fibers tends to open the pain gate.
    d. An increase in large-fiber activity would tend to close the pain gate.

32. **d.** is the answer.

33. sweet; sour; salty; bitter; umami

34. chemical; taste buds; pore

35. week or two; decreases; decreases; smoking; alcohol

36. sensory interaction; McGurk; see; hearing

37. embodied cognition

38. olfaction; chemical; is not

39. limbic

40. **d.** is the answer. Each of these is an example of the interaction of two senses—smell and taste in the case of (a.), taste and smell in the case of (b.), and hearing and the vestibular sense in the case of (c.).

41. **c.** is the answer. As people age they lose taste buds and their taste thresholds increase. For this reason, Mrs. Martinez needs more concentrated tastes than her son to find food palatable.
    a. & b. There is no evidence that women and men differ in their absolute thresholds for taste.

42. **c.** is the answer. Because of the powerful sensory interaction between taste and smell, eliminating the odor of the cough syrup should make its taste more pleasant.
    a. If anything, the contrasting tastes might make the bitter syrup even less palatable.
    b. If Tamiko keeps the syrup in her mouth for several seconds, it will ensure that her taste pores fully "catch" the stimulus, thus intensifying the bitter taste.
    d. It's probably impossible to miss the tongue completely.

43. kinesthesis; tendons; joints; bones; ears

44. vestibular sense; semicircular canals; vestibular sacs

Progress Test

Multiple-Choice Questions

1. **b.** is the answer. Just as wave frequency determines pitch, so wave amplitude determines loudness.
    a. Amplitude is the physical basis of loudness; wavelength determines frequency and thereby pitch.
    c. & d. Wavelength, amplitude, and intensity are physical aspects of sound. Because the question is based on a relationship between a physical property (frequency) of a stimulus and its psychological attribute (pitch), these answers are incorrect.

2. **c.** is the answer. The biopsychosocial approach tells us that our experience of pain depends on biological, psychological, and social-cultural factors.

3. **d.** is the answer. The small fibers conduct most pain signals; the large fibers conduct most other sensory signals from the skin. The gate either allows pain signals to pass on to the brain or blocks them from passing. When the large fibers are stimulated, the pain gate is closed and other sensations are felt in place of pain.

4. **b.** is the answer. Kinesthesis, or the sense of the position and movement of body parts, is based on information from the tendons, joints, bones, and ears.
    a. & c. The ear alone plays no role in kinesthesis.
    d. Equilibrium, or the vestibular sense, is not involved in kinesthesis but is, rather, a companion sense.

5. **a.** is the answer. Frequency theory best explains the lowest pitches. Place theory best explains the highest pitches, and some combination of the two theories probably accounts for our sensation of intermediate-range pitches.

6. **d.** is the answer.

7. **c.** is the answer. Researchers have identified receptors for pressure but have been unable to do so for the other skin senses.

8. **a.** is the answer.
    b. The cochlea contains receptors for hearing.
    c. The fovea contains receptors for vision (the cones).
    d. The cortex is the outer layer of the brain, where information detected by the receptors is processed.

9. **c.** is the answer. The inner ear contains the receptors for audition (hearing) and the vestibular sense; those for kinesthesis are located in the tendons, joints, bones, and ears.

10. **b.** is the answer. Kinesthesis, the sense of movement of body parts, would enable you to feel your toes wiggling.

    a. The vestibular sense is concerned with movement and position, or balance, of the whole body, not of its parts.

    c. The skin, or tactile, senses are pressure, pain, warmth, and cold; they have nothing to do with movement of body parts.

    d. Sensory interaction, the principle that the senses influence each other, does not play a role in this example, which involves only the sense of kinesthesis.

11. **d.** is the answer.

    a. Transduction is the process by which stimulus energy is converted into nerve impulses.

    b. Gate-control theory maintains that a "gate" in the spinal cord determines whether pain signals are permitted to reach the brain.

    c. Kinesthesis is the sense of the position and movement of the parts of the body.

12. **a.** is the answer.

    b. & c. Although the localization of low-pitched sounds along the basilar membrane is poor, that for sounds of middle and, especially, high pitch is good. Therefore, place theory accounts well for high-pitched sounds and, together with frequency theory, can account for middle-pitched sounds.

    d. As long as the notes of a chord are within the range of responsiveness of the basilar membrane, place theory can account for chord perception.

13. **d.** is the answer. Sensorineural hearing loss is caused by destruction of neural tissue as a result of problems with the cochlea's receptors or the auditory nerve.

    a. & c. Wax buildup and blockage because of infection are temporary states; sensorineural hearing loss is permanent. Moreover, sensorineural hearing loss involves the inner ear rather than the outer or middle ear.

    b. Damage to the eardrum impairs the mechanical system that conducts sound waves; it could therefore cause conduction hearing loss, not sensorineural hearing loss.

Matching Items

1.	a	**4.**	d
2.	e	**5.**	c
3.	b	**6.**	f

Summing Up

1. Outer ear. Hearing begins as sound waves enter the auditory canal of the outer ear.
2. Auditory canal. Sound waves passing through the auditory canal are brought to a point of focus at the eardrum.
3. Eardrum. Lying between the outer and middle ear, this membrane vibrates in response to sound waves.
4. Middle ear. Lying between the outer and inner ear, this air-filled chamber contains the hammer, anvil, and stirrup.
5. Hammer, anvil, and stirrup. These tiny bones of the middle ear concentrate the eardrum's vibrations on the cochlea's oval window.
6. Inner ear. This region of the ear contains the cochlea and the semicircular canals, which play an important role in balance.
7. Cochlea. This fluid-filled multichambered structure contains the hair cell receptors that transduce sound waves into neural impulses.
8. Auditory nerve. This bundle of fibers carries nerve impulses from the inner ear to the brain.

Terms and Concepts to Remember

1. **Audition** refers to the sense of hearing.
2. **Frequency** is directly related to wavelength: longer waves produce lower pitch; shorter waves produce higher pitch. The **pitch** of a sound is determined by its frequency, that is, the number of complete wavelengths that can pass a point in a given time.
3. The **middle ear** is the chamber between the eardrum and cochlea containing the three bones (hammer, anvil, and stirrup) that concentrate the eardrum's vibrations on the cochlea's oval window.
4. The **cochlea** is the coiled, bony, fluid-filled tube of the inner ear through which sound waves trigger neural impulses.
5. The **inner ear** contains the semicircular canals and the cochlea, which includes the receptors that transform sound energy into neural impulses. Because it also contains the vestibular sac, the inner ear plays an important role in balance, as well as in audition.
6. **Sensorineural hearing loss** (nerve deafness) is hearing loss caused by damage to the auditory receptors of the cochlea or to the auditory nerve due to disease, aging, or prolonged exposure to ear-splitting noise.

7. **Conduction hearing loss** refers to the hearing loss that results from damage in the mechanics of the outer or middle ear, which impairs the conduction of sound waves to the cochlea.

8. A **cochlear implant** is an electronic device that converts sounds into electrical signals that stimulate the auditory nerve.

9. The **place theory** of hearing states that we hear different pitches because sound waves of various frequencies trigger activity at different places on the cochlea's basilar membrane.

   Memory aid: **Place theory** maintains that the *place* of maximum vibration along the cochlea's membrane is the basis of pitch discrimination.

10. The **frequency theory** of hearing presumes that the rate, or frequency, of nerve impulses in the auditory nerve matches the frequency of a tone, thus enabling us to sense its pitch.

11. Melzack and Wall's **gate-control theory** maintains that a "gate" in the spinal cord determines whether pain signals are permitted to reach the brain. Neural activity in small nerve fibers opens the gates; activity in large fibers or information from the brain closes the gate.

   Example: The **gate-control theory** gained support with the discovery of endorphins. Production of these opiatelike chemicals may be the brain's mechanism for closing the spinal gate.

12. **Sensory interaction** is the principle that one sense may influence another.

13. **Embodied cognition** refers to the influence of bodily sensations, gestures, and other states on cognitive preferences and judgments.

14. **Kinesthesis** is the sense of the position and movement of the parts of the body.

15. The sense of body movement and position, including the sense of balance, is called the **vestibular sense**.

Basic Learning Concepts and Classical Conditioning

MODULE OVERVIEW

"No topic is closer to the heart of psychology than learning, a relatively permanent change in an organism's behavior due to experience." Module 20 covers the basic principles of classical, or respondent, conditioning, in which we learn associations between events. The module concludes with a discussion of the importance of classical conditioning in everyday life.

NOTE: Answer guidelines for all Module 20 questions begin on page 181.

MODULE REVIEW

First, skim each section, noting headings and bold-face items. After you have read the section, review each objective by answering the fill-in and essay-type questions that follow it. In some cases, Study Tips explain how best to learn a difficult concept and Applications help you to know how well you understand the material. As you proceed, evaluate your performance by consulting the answers beginning on page 181. Do not continue with the next section until you understand each answer. If you need to, review or reread the section in the textbook before continuing.

How Do We Learn?

Objective 20-1: Define *learning*, and identify some basic forms of learning.

1. The process of acquiring new and relatively enduring information or behaviors is called
   _____ .

2. More than 200 years ago, philosophers such as John Locke and David Hume argued that an important factor in learning is our tendency to _____ events that occur in

sequence. Even simple animals, such as the sea slug *Aplysia*, can learn simple _____ between stimuli. This type of learning is called _____ _____ .

3. The type of learning in which the organism learns to associate two stimuli is _____ conditioning. A situation or event that evokes a response is a _____ .

4. The tendency of organisms to associate a response and its consequence forms the basis of _____ conditioning.

5. We acquire mental information that guides our behavior through _____ _____ . Complex animals often learn behaviors merely by _____ others perform them. This is called _____ _____ .

Classical Conditioning

Objective 20-2: Define *classical conditioning* and *behaviorism*, and describe the basic components of classical conditioning.

6. Classical conditioning was first explored by the Russian physiologist _____ . Early in the twentieth century, psychologist _____ urged psychologists to discard references to mental concepts in favor of studying observable behavior. This view, called _____ , influenced American psychology during the first half of that century.

7. The reflexive responses of classical conditioning involve _____ behavior.

8. In Pavlov's classic experiment, a tone, or

_____ _____ ,

is sounded just before food, the

_____ _____ ,

is placed in the animal's mouth.

9. An animal will salivate when food is placed in its mouth. This salivation is called the

_____ _____ .

10. Eventually, the dogs in Pavlov's experiment would salivate on hearing the tone, now called the_____ _____ .

This salivation is called the _____

_____ .

STUDY TIP: Students often confuse "stimulus" with "response" and "conditioned" with "unconditioned." The stimulus is the event that causes something else, the response, to happen. Unconditioned means "unlearned"; conditioned means "learned." Thus, an unconditioned response (UR) is an event that occurs naturally in response to some stimulus. An unconditioned stimulus (US) is something that naturally and automatically triggers the unlearned response. A conditioned stimulus (CS) is an originally neutral stimulus (NS) that, through learning, comes to be associated with some unlearned response. A conditioned response (CR) is the learned response to the originally neutral but now conditioned stimulus.

    Stimulus (event or other trigger) → Response
            Unconditioned = unlearned
            Conditioned = learned
So, unconditioned stimulus + conditioned stimulus
            ↓   ↓
    unconditioned response   conditioned response

APPLICATIONS:

Classical conditioning is all around us. It is especially common in the realm of emotional behavior. Test your understanding of the basic elements of classical conditioning in the following example. Then, consider whether there are emotions of your own that might have developed as the product of classical conditioning.

    As a child, you were playing in the yard one day when a neighbor's cat wandered over. Your mother (who has a terrible fear of animals) screamed and snatched you into her arms. Her behavior caused you to cry. You now have a fear of cats.

11. The NS, then CS is _____ .

12. The US is _____ .

13. The CR is _____ .

14. The UR is _____ .

15. You always rattle the box of dog biscuits before giving your dog a treat. As you do so, your dog salivates. At first, rattling the box is a _____ , which eventually becomes a _____ . Your dog's salivation is a _____ .
    a. NS; CS; CR   c. NS; US; CR
    b. CS; NS; UR   d. US; NS; UR

Objective 20-3: Summarize the processes of acquisition, extinction, spontaneous recovery, generalization, and discrimination.

Use the following graph as a reference for the answers to 16(a), 20(b), and 21(c).

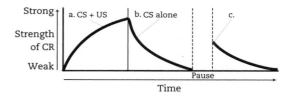

16. The initial learning of a conditioned response is called (a) _____ . For many conditioning situations, the optimal interval between a neutral stimulus and the US is

    _____ _____ .

17. When the US is presented prior to a neutral stimulus, conditioning _____ (does/does not) occur.

18. Sexual conditioning studies with quail demonstrate that classical conditioning is highly adaptive because it helps animals

    _____ and _____ .

19. The procedure in which an established conditioned stimulus is paired with a different _____ stimulus, thereby establishing the latter as a _____ stimulus, is called _____-_____ .

20. If a CS is repeatedly presented without the US, (b) _____ soon occurs; that is, the CR diminishes.

21. Following a pause, however, the CR reappears in response to the CS; this phenomenon is called (c) _____ _____ .

22. Subjects often respond to a similar stimulus as they would to the original CS. This phenomenon is called _____ .

23. Humans and other animals can also be trained not to respond to _____ stimuli. This learned ability is called _____ . Being able to recognize differences among stimuli has _____ value because it lets us limit our learned responses to appropriate stimuli.

STUDY TIP: Some students find the terms *discrimination* and *generalization* confusing because of their negative social connotations. In the context of classical conditioning, discrimination is a healthy sign that the subject of conditioning has learned the difference between two stimuli, much as a "discriminating coffee lover" can taste subtle variations between two coffee blends. Generalization is apparent when discrimination does not occur.

APPLICATION:

Bill had an American-made car that was in the shop more than it was out. Since then he will not even consider owning an American-made car.

24. Bill's attitude is an example of _____ . Bill's friend Andy also had an American-made car with similar problems. Deciding that it was just that brand, Andy decided to try another brand. Rather than bunch all American-made cars together, he was a _____ buyer of cars.

Objective 20-4: Explain why Pavlov's work remains so important, and describe some applications of his work to human health and well-being.

25. Classical conditioning is one way that virtually all organisms learn to _____ to their environment.

26. Another aspect of Pavlov's legacy is that he showed how a process such as learning could be studied _____ .

Explain why the study of classical conditioning is important.

27. Through classical conditioning, former drug users often feel a _____ when they are in the _____ associated with previous highs.

28. Research studies demonstrate that the body's immune system _____ (can/cannot) be classically conditioned.

Describe the Watson and Rayner experiment.

PROGRESS TEST

Multiple-Choice Questions

Circle your answers to the following questions and check them with the answers on page 182. If your answer is incorrect, read the explanation for why it is incorrect and then consult the text.

1. *Learning* is best defined as
   a. any behavior produced by an organism without being provoked.
   b. a change in the behavior of an organism.
   c. a relatively permanent change in the behavior of an organism due to experience.
   d. behavior based on operant rather than respondent conditioning.

2. In Pavlov's original experiment with dogs, the meat served as a
   a. CS.   c. US.
   b. CR.   d. UR.

3. In Pavlov's original experiment with dogs, the tone was initially a(n) _____ stimulus; after it was paired with meat, it became a(n) _____ stimulus.
   a. conditioned; neutral
   b. neutral; conditioned
   c. conditioned; unconditioned
   d. unconditioned; conditioned

4. To obtain a reward, a monkey learns to press a lever when a 1000-Hz tone is on but not when a 1200-Hz tone is on. What kind of training is this?
   a. extinction
   b. generalization
   c. classical conditioning
   d. discrimination

5. When a conditioned stimulus is presented without an accompanying unconditioned stimulus, _____ will soon take place.
   a. generalization   c. extinction
   b. discrimination   d. aversion

6. In Pavlov's original experiment with dogs, salivation to meat was the
   a. CS.   c. US.
   b. CR.   d. UR.

7. Which of the following is a form of associative learning?
   a. classical conditioning
   b. cognitive learning
   c. observational learning
   d. all of these types of learning

8. For the most rapid conditioning, a CS should be presented
   a. about 1 second after the US.
   b. about one-half second before the US.
   c. about 15 seconds before the US.
   d. at the same time as the US.

9. During extinction, the _____ is omitted; as a result, the _____ seems to disappear.
   a. US; UR   c. US; CR
   b. CS; CR   d. CS; UR

10. In Watson and Rayner's experiment, the loud noise was the _____ and the white rat was the _____ .
    a. CS; CR   c. CS; US
    b. US; CS   d. US; CR

11. In which of the following may classical conditioning play a role?
    a. emotional problems
    b. the body's immune response
    c. helping drug addicts
    d. in all of these cases

12. In Pavlov's studies of classical conditioning of a dog's salivary responses, spontaneous recovery occurred
    a. during acquisition, when the CS was first paired with the US.
    b. during extinction, when the CS was first presented by itself.
    c. when the CS was reintroduced following extinction of the CR and a rest period.
    d. during discrimination training, when several conditioned stimuli were introduced.

Matching Items

Match each definition or description with the appropriate term.

Definitions or Descriptions

_____ 1. tendency for similar stimuli to evoke a CR
_____ 2. the reappearance of a weakened CR
_____ 3. the ability to differentiate between similar stimuli
_____ 4. the weakening of the CR when the CS is no longer followed by the US
_____ 5. the initial stage of conditioning

Terms

a. spontaneous recovery
b. generalization
c. extinction
d. discrimination
e. acquisition

True–False Items

Indicate whether each statement is true or false by placing *T* or *F* in the blank next to the item.

_____ 1. The optimal interval between CS and US is about 15 seconds.

_____ 2. Whether the CS or US is presented first seems not to matter in terms of the ease of classical conditioning.

_____ 3. Spontaneous recovery refers to the tendency of extinguished behaviors to reappear suddenly.

TERMS AND CONCEPTS TO REMEMBER

Using your own words, on a piece of paper write a brief definition or explanation of each of the following terms.

1. learning
2. associative learning
3. stimulus
4. cognitive learning
5. classical conditioning
6. behaviorism
7. respondent behavior
8. neutral stimulus
9. unconditioned response (UR)
10. unconditioned stimulus (US)
11. conditioned response (CR)
12. conditioned stimulus (CS)
13. acquisition
14. higher-order conditioning
15. extinction
16. spontaneous recovery
17. generalization
18. discrimination

ANSWERS
Module Review

How Do We Learn?

1. learning
2. associate; associations; associative learning
3. classical; stimulus
4. operant
5. cognitive learning; observing; observational learning

Classical Conditioning

6. Ivan Pavlov; John Watson; behaviorism
7. respondent
8. neutral stimulus; unconditioned stimulus
9. unconditioned response
10. conditioned stimulus; conditioned response
11. the cat
12. your mother's behavior
13. your fear today
14. your crying
15. **a.** is the answer. Your dog had to learn to associate the rattling sound with the food. Rattling is therefore a conditioned, or learned, stimulus, and salivation in response to this rattling is a learned, or conditioned, response.
16. acquisition; one-half second
17. does not
18. survive; reproduce
19. neutral; conditioned; higher-order conditioning
20. extinction
21. spontaneous recovery
22. generalization
23. similar; discrimination; adaptive
24. generalization; discriminating
25. adapt
26. objectively

Classical conditioning is one way that virtually all organisms learn to adapt to their environment. Classical conditioning also provided an example to the young field of psychology of how complex, internal processes could be studied objectively. In addition, classical conditioning has proven to have many helpful applications to human health and well-being.

27. craving; context
28. can

In Watson and Rayner's experiment, classical conditioning was used to condition fear of a rat in Albert, an 11-month-old infant. When Albert touched the white rat (neutral stimulus), a loud noise (unconditioned stimulus) was sounded. After several pairings of the rat with the noise, Albert began crying at the mere sight of the rat. The rat had become a conditioned stimulus, triggering a conditioned response of fear. This showed that human emotions and behaviors, though biologically influenced, are a bundle of conditioned responses.

Progress Test

Multiple-Choice Questions

1. **c.** is the answer.
   a. This answer is incorrect because it simply describes any behavior that is automatic rather than being triggered by a specific stimulus.
   b. This answer is too general, since behaviors can change for reasons other than learning.
   d. Respondently conditioned behavior also satisfies the criteria of our definition of learning.

2. **c.** is the answer. Meat automatically triggers the response of salivation and is therefore an unconditioned stimulus.
   a. A conditioned stimulus acquires its response-triggering powers through learning. A dog does not learn to salivate to meat.
   b. & d. Responses are behaviors triggered in the organism, in this case the dog's salivation. The meat is a stimulus.

3. **b.** is the answer. Prior to its pairing with meat (the US), the tone did not trigger salivation and was therefore a neutral stimulus. Afterward, the tone triggered salivation (the CR) and was therefore a conditioned stimulus (CS).
   c. & d. Unconditioned stimuli, such as meat, innately trigger responding. Pavlov's dogs had to learn to associate the tone with the food.

4. **d.** is the answer. In learning to distinguish between the conditioned stimulus and another, similar stimulus, the monkey has received training in discrimination.
   a. In extinction training, a stimulus and/or response is allowed to go unreinforced.
   b. Generalization training involves responding to stimuli similar to the conditioned stimulus; here the monkey is being trained not to respond to a similar stimulus.
   c. This cannot be classical conditioning since the monkey is acting in order to obtain a reward. Thus, this is an example of operant conditioning.

5. **c.** is the answer. In this situation, the CR will decline, a phenomenon known as extinction.
   a. Generalization occurs when the subject makes a CR to stimuli similar to the original CS.

   b. Discrimination is when the subject does not make a CR to stimuli other than the original CS.
   d. An aversion is a CR to a CS that has been associated with an unpleasant US, such as shock or a nausea-producing drug.

6. **d.** is the answer. A dog does not have to learn to salivate to food; therefore, this response is unconditioned.
   a. & c. Salivation is a response, not a stimulus.

7. **a.** is the answer.

8. **b.** is the answer.
   a. Backward conditioning, in which the US precedes the CS, is ineffective.
   c. This interval is longer than is optimum for the most rapid acquisition of a CS-US association.
   d. Simultaneous presentation of CS and US is ineffective because it does not permit the subject to anticipate the US.

9. **c.** is the answer.

10. **b.** is the answer. The loud noise automatically triggered Albert's fear and therefore functioned as a US. After being associated with the US, the white rat acquired the power to trigger fear and thus became a CS.

11. **d.** is the answer.

12. **c.** is the answer.
    a., b., & d. Spontaneous recovery occurs after a CR has been extinguished, and in the absence of the US. The situations described here all involve the continued presentation of the US and, therefore, the further strengthening of the CR.

Matching Items

1. b   4. c
2. a   5. e
3. d

True–False Items

1. F   3. T
2. F

Terms and Concepts to Remember

1. **Learning** is the process of acquiring new and relatively enduring information or behaviors.

2. In **associative learning**, organisms learn that certain events occur together. Two variations of associative learning are classical conditioning and operant conditioning.

3. A **stimulus** is any situation or event that evokes a response.

4. **Cognitive learning** is the acquisition of mental information that guides our behavior.

5. **Classical conditioning** is a type of learning in which one learns to link two or more stimuli and anticipate events; specifically, a neutral stimulus becomes capable of triggering a conditioned response after having become associated with an unconditioned stimulus.

6. **Behaviorism** is the view that psychology should be an objective science that studies only observable behaviors without reference to mental processes.

   Example: Because he was an early advocate of the study of observable behavior, John Watson is often called the father of behaviorism.

7. **Respondent behavior** is that which occurs as an automatic response to some stimulus.

   Example: In classical conditioning, conditioned and unconditioned responses are examples of **respondent behavior** in that they are automatic responses triggered by specific stimuli.

8. In classical conditioning, a **neutral stimulus (NS)** is one that elicits no response before conditioning.

9. In classical conditioning, the **unconditioned response (UR)** is an unlearned, naturally occurring response to an unconditioned stimulus.

10. In classical conditioning, the **unconditioned stimulus (US)** is a stimulus that naturally and automatically triggers a reflexive unconditioned response.

11. In classical conditioning, the **conditioned response (CR)** is a learned response to a previously neutral (but now conditioned) stimulus, which results from the acquired association between the CS and US.

12. In classical conditioning, the **conditioned stimulus (CS)** is an originally neutral stimulus that comes to trigger a CR after association with an unconditioned stimulus.

13. In a learning experiment, **acquisition** refers to the initial stage of conditioning in which the new response is established and gradually strengthened.

14. In **higher-order conditioning,** pairing an established conditioned stimulus (CS) with a neutral stimulus may cause the latter to become a weak CS itself.

15. **Extinction** refers to the diminishing of a CR when the CS is no longer followed by the US.

16. **Spontaneous recovery** is the reappearance of an extinguished CR after a pause.

17. **Generalization** refers to the tendency, once a response has been conditioned, for stimuli similar to the original CS to elicit similar responses.

18. **Discrimination** in classical conditioning refers to the ability to distinguish the CS from similar stimuli that do not signal a US.

Operant Conditioning

MODULE OVERVIEW

Module 21 covers the basic principles of operant conditioning, in which we learn to engage in behaviors that are rewarded and to avoid behaviors that are punished. The module also includes a discussion of how operant conditioning principles are applied in everyday life. The module begins and concludes by contrasting classical and operant conditioning techniques.

NOTE: Answer guidelines for all Module 21 questions begin on page 192.

MODULE REVIEW

First, skim each section, noting headings and bold-face items. After you have read the section, review each objective by answering the fill-in and essay-type questions that follow it. In some cases, Study Tips explain how best to learn a difficult concept and Applications help you to know how well you understand the material. As you proceed, evaluate your performance by consulting the answers beginning on page 192. Do not continue with the next section until you understand each answer. If you need to, review or reread the section in the textbook before continuing.

Objective 21-1: Define *operant conditioning,* and describe how operant behavior is reinforced and shaped.

1. Like classical conditioning, operant conditioning is a form of _____ learning in which the organism's response to a _____ is strengthened when it is rewarded.

Skinner's Experiments

2. B. F. Skinner used Thorndike's _____ _____ _____ as a starting point in developing a behavioral technology. This principle states that _____ behavior is likely to _____ .

3. In operant conditioning, organisms associate their own actions with _____ . Actions followed by _____ increase; actions followed by _____ decrease.

4. Skinner designed an apparatus, called the _____ _____ , to investigate _____ in animals. This design creates a stage on which organisms act out Skinner's concept of _____ , any event that increases the frequency of a preceding response.

5. The procedure in which a person teaches an animal to perform an intricate behavior by building up to it in small steps is called _____ . This method involves reinforcing successive _____ of the desired behavior.

6. In experiments to determine what an animal can perceive, researchers have found that animals are capable of forming _____ and _____ between stimuli.

Similar experiments have been conducted with babies, who also can't verbalize their responses.

7. A situation, event, or signal that a certain response will be reinforced is a

_____ _____ .

APPLICATION:

8. Which of the following is an example of shaping?
   a. A dog learns to salivate at the sight of a box of dog biscuits.
   b. A new driver learns to stop at an intersection when the light changes to red.
   c. A parrot is rewarded first for making any sound, then for making a sound similar to "Laura," and then for "speaking" its owner's name.

Objective 21-2 Discuss the differences between positive and negative reinforcement, and identify the basic types of reinforcers.

9. A stimulus that strengthens a response by presenting a typically pleasurable stimulus after a response is a _____

_____ .

10. A stimulus that strengthens a response by reducing or removing an aversive (unpleasant) stimulus is a _____ _____ .

11. Reinforcers, such as food and shock, that are related to basic needs and therefore do not rely on learning are called _____

_____ .

12. Reinforcers that must be conditioned and therefore derive their power through association are called _____ _____ .

13. Children who are able to delay gratification tend to become _____ (more/less) socially competent and high achieving as they mature.

14. Immediate reinforcement _____ (is/is not) more effective than its alternative, _____ reinforcement. This explains in part the difficulty that _____ users have in quitting their habits, as well as the tendency of some teens to engage in risky, _____ _____ .

STUDY TIP: Some students have a problem differentiating positive and negative reinforcers because they naturally think "positive" indicates a "good," or desirable, outcome, while "negative" connotes a "bad," or undesirable, outcome. Remember that from the organism's point of view, reinforcement is always a desirable outcome. You may find it useful to think of a photography analogy. A "negative" is a reverse image in which the "positive" photographic image is not present. So too, negative reinforcement involves taking away an event—in this case, one that is undesirable.

Objective 21-3: Explain how the different reinforcement schedules affect behavior.

15. A _____ _____ is a pattern specifying how often a _____ _____ is reinforced.

16. The procedure involving reinforcement of each and every response is called

_____ _____ .

Under these conditions, learning is _____ (rapid/slow). When this type of reinforcement is discontinued, extinction is _____ (rapid/slow).

17. The procedure in which responses are reinforced only part of the time is called _____ reinforcement. Under these conditions, learning is generally _____ (faster/ slower) than it is with continuous reinforcement. Behavior reinforced in this manner is _____ (very/not very) resistant to extinction.

18. When behavior is reinforced after a set number of responses, a _____- _____ schedule is in effect.

19. Three-year-old Yusef knows that if he cries when he wants a treat, his mother will sometimes give in. When, as in this case, reinforcement occurs after an unpredictable number of responses, a

_____-_____ schedule is being used.

20. Reinforcement of the first response after a set interval of time defines the

    _____-_____ sched-

    ule. An example of this schedule is

    _____ .

21. When the first response after varying amounts of time is reinforced, a _____-

    _____ schedule is in effect.

Describe the typical patterns of response under fixed-interval, fixed-ratio, variable-interval, and variable-ratio schedules of reinforcement.

APPLICATIONS:

22. You are expecting an important letter in the mail. As the regular delivery time approaches you glance more and more frequently out the window, searching for the letter carrier. Your behavior in this situation typifies that associated with which schedule of reinforcement?

    a. fixed-ratio   **c.** fixed-interval
    b. variable-ratio   **d.** variable-interval

23. From a casino owner's viewpoint, which of the following jackpot-payout schedules would be the most desirable for reinforcing customer use of a slot machine?

    a. variable-ratio   c. variable-interval
    b. fixed-ratio   **d.** fixed-interval

24. Lars, a shoe salesman, is paid every two weeks, whereas Tom receives a commission for each pair of shoes he sells. Evidently, Lars is paid on a _____ schedule of reinforcement, and Tom on a _____ schedule of reinforcement.

    a. fixed-ratio; fixed-interval
    b. continuous; intermittent
    c. fixed-interval; fixed-ratio
    d. variable-interval; variable-ratio

25. Jack finally takes out the garbage in order to get his father to stop pestering him. Jack's behavior is being influenced by _____

    _____ .

26. Your instructor invites you to her home as part of a select group of students to discuss possible careers in psychology. The invitation is an example of a _____

    _____ .

Objective 21-4: Discuss how punishment and negative reinforcement differ, and explain how punishment affects behavior.

27. Negative reinforcement _____ (increases/decreases) a response by

    _____ an aversive stimulus after that response. Punishment _____ (increases/decreases) a response by

    _____ an aversive stimulus after that response.

28. An aversive consequence that decreases the likelihood of the behavior that preceded it is called

    _____ . If an aversive stimulus is administered, it is called _____

    _____ . If a desirable stimulus is withdrawn, it is called _____

    _____ .

29. Because punished behavior is merely

    _____ , it may reappear. Also, punishment teaches _____ , that behavior that is unacceptable in one context may be acceptable in another. Punishment can also lead to _____ and a sense of helplessness, as well as to the association of the aversive event with _____

    _____ .

30. Punishment also often increases _____ and does not guide the individual toward more desirable behavior.

STUDY TIP/APPLICATION: To avoid the natural tendency to confuse punishment and negative reinforcement, remember that positive reinforcement and negative reinforcement both lead to an *increase* in behavior, while punishment *decreases* behavior. In punishment, something bad occurs following an undesirable behavior; in negative reinforcement, something bad is removed. Complete the chart below of examples of punishment and negative reinforcement. The first example has been filled in for you.

31.

Behavior	Consequence	Which Is Taken Away, Something Good or Bad?	Is This Punishment or Negative Reinforcement?
Driving while intoxicated	Lose driver's license	Good	Punishment
a. Forgetting to give your roommate a phone message			
b. Putting on your coat so that you are no longer cold			
c. Getting a drink when you are thirsty			
d. Using your laptop until the battery dies			
e. Your brother nagging you until you help him with his homework			

Skinner's Legacy

Objective 21-5: Describe the controversy over Skinner's views of human behavior, and identify some ways to apply operant conditioning principles at school, in sports, at work, and at home.

32. Skinner's views were controversial because he insisted that _____ influences, rather than _____ _____ and _____ , shape behavior.

33. Skinner also advocated the use of _____ principles to influence people in ways that promote more desirable _____ .

34. Skinner's critics argued that he _____ people by neglecting their personal _____ and by seeking to _____ their actions.

35. The use of teaching machines and programmed textbooks was an early application of the operant conditioning procedure of _____ to education. Online _____ systems, software that is _____ , and _____-based learning are newer examples of this application of operant principles. Reinforcement principles can also be used to enhance _____ abilities by shaping successive approximations of new skills.

36. In boosting productivity in the workplace, positive reinforcement is _____ (more/less) effective when applied to specific behaviors than when given to reward general merit and when the desired performance is well defined and _____ . For such behaviors, immediate reinforcement is _____ (more/no more) effective than delayed reinforcement.

37. In using operant conditioning to change your own behavior, you would follow these four steps
    a. _____
    b. _____
    c. _____
    d. _____

APPLICATIONS:

38. The manager of a manufacturing plant wishes to use positive reinforcement to increase the productivity of workers. Which of the following procedures would probably be the most effective?
    a. Deserving employees are given a general merit bonus at the end of each fiscal year.
    b. A productivity goal that seems attainable, yet is unrealistic, is set for each employee.
    c. Employees are given immediate bonuses for specific behaviors related to productivity.
    d. Employees who fail to meet standards of productivity receive pay cuts.

39. Reggie's mother tells him that he can watch TV after he cleans his room. Evidently, Reggie's mother is attempting to use _____ to increase room cleaning.
    a. operant conditioning
    b. secondary reinforcement
    c. positive reinforcement
    d. all of these procedures

Contrasting Classical and Operant Conditioning

Objective 21-6: Identify the characteristics that distinguish operant conditioning from classical conditioning.

40. Classical conditioning and operant conditioning are both forms of _____
_____ .

41. Both types of conditioning involve similar processes of _____ ,
_____ , _____
_____ , _____ ,
and _____ .

42. Classical conditioning associates _____ stimuli with stimuli that trigger responses that are _____ . Thus, in this form of conditioning, the organism _____ (does/does not) control the responses.

43. The reflexive responses of classical conditioning involve _____ behavior.

44. In contrast, behavior that is more spontaneous and that is influenced by its consequences is called _____ behavior.

45. Classical and operant conditioning are both subject to the influences of _____ processes and _____ predispositions.

STUDY TIP/APPLICATION: If you still find yourself confusing classical conditioning and operant conditioning, try the following. Ask yourself two questions: (1) Is the behavior voluntary (operant conditioning) or involuntary (classical conditioning)? (2) Does the learning involve an association between two stimuli (classical conditioning) or between a response and an outcome (operant conditioning)? Test your understanding with the following examples.

46. Behavior	Is the Behavior Voluntary or Involuntary?	Type of Conditioning
a. After receiving a mild shock from the "invisible fence" surrounding his yard, a dog no longer crosses the boundary.		
b. You flinch when someone yells, "Duck!"		
c. You ask more questions in class after the professor praises you for a good question.		
d. The pupil of your eye dilates (opens wider) after you enter a darkened theater.		

PROGRESS TEST

Multiple-Choice Questions

Circle your answers to the following questions and check them with the answers beginning on page 193. If your answer is incorrect, read the explanation for why it is incorrect and then consult the text.

1. *Learning* is best defined as
   a. any behavior produced by an organism without being provoked.
   b. a change in the behavior of an organism.
   c. a relatively permanent change in the behavior of an organism due to experience.
   d. behavior based on operant rather than respondent conditioning.

2. Which of the following statements concerning reinforcement is correct?
   a. Learning is most rapid with intermittent reinforcement, but continuous reinforcement produces the greatest resistance to extinction.
   b. Learning is most rapid with continuous reinforcement, but intermittent reinforcement produces the greatest resistance to extinction.
   c. Learning is fastest and resistance to extinction is greatest after continuous reinforcement.
   d. Learning is fastest and resistance to extinction is greatest following intermittent reinforcement.

3. The highest and most consistent rate of response is produced by a _____ schedule.
   a. fixed-ratio   c. fixed-interval
   b. variable-ratio   d. variable-interval

4. A response that leads to the removal of an unpleasant stimulus is one being
   a. positively reinforced.
   b. negatively reinforced.
   c. punished.
   d. extinguished.

5. One difference between classical and operant conditioning is that
   a. in classical conditioning the responses operate on the environment to produce rewarding or punishing stimuli.
   b. in operant conditioning the responses are triggered by preceding stimuli.
   c. in classical conditioning the responses are automatically triggered by stimuli.
   d. in operant conditioning the responses are reflexive.

6. Punishment is a controversial way of controlling behavior because
   a. behavior is not forgotten and may return.
   b. punishing stimuli often create fear.
   c. punishment often increases aggressiveness.
   d. of all of these reasons.

7. Which of the following is an example of reinforcement?
   a. presenting a positive stimulus after a response
   b. removing an unpleasant stimulus after a response
   c. being told that you have done a good job
   d. All of these are examples.

8. Shaping is a(n) _____ technique for _____ a behavior.
   a. operant; establishing
   b. operant; suppressing
   c. respondent; establishing
   d. respondent; suppressing

9. For operant conditioning to be most effective, when should the reinforcers be presented in relation to the desired response?
   a. immediately before
   b. immediately after
   c. at the same time as
   d. at least a half-hour before

10. In distinguishing between negative reinforcers and punishment, we note that
    a. punishment, but not negative reinforcement, involves use of an aversive stimulus.
    b. in contrast to punishment, negative reinforcement decreases the likelihood of a response by the presentation of an aversive stimulus.
    c. in contrast to punishment, negative reinforcement increases the likelihood of a response by the presentation of an aversive stimulus.
    d. in contrast to punishment, negative reinforcement increases the likelihood of a response by the termination of an aversive stimulus.

11. The "piecework," or commission, method of payment is an example of which reinforcement schedule?
    a. fixed-interval   c. fixed-ratio
    b. variable-interval   d. variable-ratio

12. Putting on your coat when it is cold outside is a behavior that is maintained by
    a. discrimination learning.
    b. punishment.
    c. negative reinforcement.
    d. classical conditioning.

13. On an intermittent reinforcement schedule, reinforcement is given
   a. in very small amounts.
   b. randomly.
   c. for successive approximations of a desired behavior.
   d. only some of the time.

14. You teach your dog to fetch the paper by giving him a cookie each time he does so. This is an example of
   a. operant conditioning.
   b. classical conditioning.
   c. conditioned reinforcement.
   d. partial reinforcement.

15. Leon's psychology instructor has scheduled an exam every third week of the term. Leon will probably study the most just before an exam and the least just after an exam. This is because the schedule of exams is reinforcing studying according to which schedule?
   a. fixed-ratio   **c.** fixed-interval
   b. variable-ratio   **d.** variable-interval

16. Operant conditioning is to _____ as classical conditioning is to _____ .
   a. Pavlov; Watson   **c.** Pavlov; Skinner
   b. Skinner; Bandura   **d.** Skinner; Pavlov

17. Online testing systems and interactive software are applications of the operant conditioning principles of
   a. shaping and immediate reinforcement.
   b. immediate reinforcement and punishment.
   c. shaping and primary reinforcement.
   d. continuous reinforcement and punishment.

18. Which of the following is the best example of a conditioned reinforcer?
   a. putting on a coat on a cold day
   b. relief from pain after the dentist stops drilling your teeth
   c. receiving a cool drink after washing your mother's car on a hot day
   d. receiving an approving nod from the boss for a job well done

Matching Items

Match each definition or description with the appropriate term.

Definitions or Descriptions

_____ **1.** presentation of a desired stimulus
_____ **2.** removal of an aversive stimulus
_____ **3.** an innately reinforcing stimulus
_____ **4.** an acquired reinforcer
_____ **5.** responses are reinforced after an unpredictable amount of time
_____ **6.** reinforcing closer and closer approximations of a behavior
_____ **7.** presentation of an aversive stimulus
_____ **8.** each and every response is reinforced

Terms

   a. shaping
   b. punishment
   c. positive reinforcement
   d. negative reinforcement
   e. primary reinforcer
   f. conditioned reinforcer
   g. continuous reinforcement
   h. variable-interval schedule

True–False Items

Indicate whether each statement is true or false by placing *T* or *F* in the blank next to the item.

_____ **1.** Operant conditioning involves behavior that is primarily reflexive.
_____ **2.** Negative reinforcement decreases the likelihood that a response will recur.
_____ **3.** The learning of a new behavior proceeds most rapidly with continuous reinforcement.
_____ **4.** As a rule, variable schedules of reinforcement produce more consistent rates of responding than fixed schedules.
_____ **5.** Although punishment may be effective in suppressing behavior, it can have several undesirable side effects.

Essay Question

Describe the best way for a pet owner to condition her dog to roll over. (Use the space below to list the points you want to make, and organize them. Then write the essay on a separate piece of paper.)

TERMS AND CONCEPTS TO REMEMBER

Using your own words, on a piece of paper write a brief definition or explanation of each of the following terms.

1. learning

2. associative learning

3. stimulus

4. operant conditioning

5. law of effect

6. operant chamber (Skinner box)

7. reinforcement

8. shaping

9. positive reinforcement

10. negative reinforcement

11. primary reinforcer

12. conditioned reinforcer

13. reinforcement schedule

14. continuous reinforcement

15. partial (intermittent) reinforcement

16. fixed-ratio schedule

17. variable-ratio schedule

18. fixed-interval schedule

19. variable-interval schedule

20. punishment

21. respondent behavior

22. operant behavior

ANSWERS
Module Review

Skinner's Experiments

1. associative; stimulus

2. law of effect; rewarded; recur

3. consequences; reinforcers; punishers

4. Skinner box (operant chamber); learning; reinforcement

5. shaping; approximations

6. concepts; discriminating

7. discriminative stimulus

8. **c.** is the answer. The parrot is reinforced for making successive approximations of a goal behavior. This defines shaping.
   a. Shaping is an operant conditioning procedure; salivation at the sight of dog biscuits is a classically conditioned response.
   b. Shaping involves the systematic reinforcement of successive approximations of a more complex behavior. In this example there is no indication that the response of stopping at the intersection involved the gradual acquisition of simpler behaviors.

9. positive reinforcer

10. negative reinforcer

11. primary reinforcers

12. conditioned (secondary) reinforcers

13. more

14. is; delayed; drug; unprotected sex

15. reinforcement schedule; desired response

16. continuous reinforcement; rapid; rapid

17. partial (intermittent); slower; very

18. fixed-ratio

19. variable-ratio

20. fixed-interval; checking the mail as delivery time approaches

21. variable-interval

Following reinforcement on a fixed-interval schedule, there is a pause in responding and then an increasing rate of response as time for the next reinforcement draws near. On a fixed-ratio schedule there also is a post-reinforcement pause, followed, however, by a return to a consistent, high rate of response. Both kinds of variable schedules produce steadier rates of response, without the pauses associated with fixed schedules. In general, schedules linked to responses produce higher response rates and variable schedules produce more consistent responding than the related fixed schedules.

22. **c.** is the answer. Reinforcement (the letter) comes after a fixed interval, and as the likely end of the interval approaches, your behavior (glancing out the window) becomes more frequent.

a. & b. These answers are incorrect because with ratio schedules, reinforcement is contingent upon the number of responses rather than on the passage of time.

d. Assuming that the mail is delivered at about the same time each day, the interval is fixed rather than variable. Your behavior reflects this, since you glance out the window more often as the delivery time approaches.

23. **a.** is the answer. Ratio schedules maintain higher rates of responding—gambling in this example— than do interval schedules. Furthermore, variable schedules are not associated with the pause in responding following reinforcement that is typical of fixed schedules. The slot machine would therefore be used more often, and more consistently, if jackpots were scheduled according to a variable-ratio schedule.

24. **c.** is the answer. Whereas Lars is paid (reinforced) after a fixed period of time (fixed-interval), Tom is reinforced for each sale (fixed-ratio) he makes.

25. negative reinforcement. By taking out the garbage, Jack terminates a negative stimulus—his father's nagging.

26. conditioned reinforcer. Being invited to your instructor's home as part of a select group is a conditioned reinforcer in that it doesn't satisfy an innate need but has become linked with desirable consequences.

27. increases; removing; decreases; presenting

28. punishment; positive punishment; negative punishment

29. suppressed; discrimination; fear; the person who administered it

30. aggressiveness

31. **a.** Punishment. You lose something good— conversation with your roommate.
b. Negative reinforcement. You are no longer cold, which means something bad has been removed.
c. Negative reinforcement. You are no longer thirsty, so something bad has been removed.
d. Punishment. You can't use your laptop; certainly, something good has been taken away.
e. Negative reinforcement. Your brother stops

nagging you, so something bad has been removed.

Skinner's Legacy

32. external; internal thoughts; feelings

33. operant; behavior

34. dehumanized; freedom; control

35. shaping; testing; interactive; web; athletic

36. more; achievable; more

37. **a.** State your goal in measurable terms.

b. Monitor the behavior (when and where it occurs).
c. Reinforce the desired behavior.
d. Reduce the rewards gradually.

38. **c.** is the answer.
a. Positive reinforcement is most effective in boosting productivity in the workplace when specific behavior, rather than vaguely defined general merit, is rewarded. Also, immediate reinforcement is much more effective than the delayed reinforcement described in a.
b. Positive reinforcement is most effective in boosting productivity when performance goals are achievable, rather than unrealistic.
d. The text does not specifically discuss the use of punishment in the workplace. However, it makes the general point that although punishment may temporarily suppress unwanted behavior, it does not guide one toward more desirable behavior. Therefore, workers who receive pay cuts for poor performance may learn nothing about how to improve their productivity.

39. **d.** is the answer. By making a more preferred activity (watching TV) contingent on a less preferred activity (room cleaning), Reggie's mother is employing the operant conditioning technique of positive reinforcement.

Contrasting Classical and Operant Conditioning

40. associative learning

41. acquisition; extinction; spontaneous recovery; generalization; discrimination

42. neutral; automatic; does not

43. respondent

44. operant

45. cognitive; biological

46. **a.** voluntary; operant conditioning
b. involuntary; classical conditioning
c. voluntary; operant conditioning
d. involuntary; classical conditioning

Progress Test

Multiple-Choice Questions

1. **c.** is the answer.
   a. This answer is incorrect because it simply describes any behavior that is automatic rather than being triggered by a specific stimulus.
   b. This answer is too general, since behaviors can change for reasons other than learning.
   d. Respondently conditioned behavior also satisfies the criteria of our definition of learning.

2. **b.** is the answer. A continuous association will naturally be easier to learn than one that occurs on only some occasions, so learning is most rapid with continuous reinforcement. Yet, once the continuous association is no longer there, as in extinction training, extinction will occur more rapidly than it would have had the organism not always experienced reinforcement.

3. **b.** is the answer.
   a. With fixed-ratio schedules, there is a pause following each reinforcement.
   c. & d. Because reinforcement is not contingent on the rate of response, interval schedules, especially fixed-interval schedules, produce lower response rates than ratio schedules.

4. **b.** is the answer.
   a. Positive reinforcement involves presenting a favorable stimulus following a response.
   c. Punishment involves presenting an unpleasant stimulus following a response.
   d. In extinction, a previously reinforced response is no longer followed by reinforcement. In this situation, a response causes a stimulus to be terminated or removed.

5. **c.** is the answer.
   a. In *operant* conditioning the responses operate on the environment.
   b. In *classical* conditioning responses are triggered by preceding stimuli.
   d. In *classical* conditioning responses are reflexive.

6. **d.** is the answer.

7. **d.** is the answer. a. is an example of positive reinforcement, b. is an example of negative reinforcement, and c. is an example of conditioned reinforcement.

8. **a.** is the answer. Shaping works on operant behaviors by reinforcing successive approximations to a desired goal.

9. **b.** is the answer.
   a., c., & d. Reinforcement that is delayed, presented before a response, or at the same time as a

response does not always increase the response's frequency of occurrence.

10. **d.** is the answer.
    a. Both involve an aversive stimulus.
    b. All reinforcers, including negative reinforcers, increase the likelihood of a response.
    c. In negative reinforcement, an aversive stimulus is withdrawn following a desirable response.

11. **c.** is the answer. Payment is given after a fixed number of pieces have been completed.
    a. & b. Interval schedules reinforce according to the passage of time, not the amount of work accomplished.
    d. Fortunately for those working on commission, the work ratio is fixed and therefore predictable.

12. **c.** is the answer. By learning to put on your coat before going outside, you have learned to reduce the aversive stimulus of the cold.
    a. Discrimination learning involves learning to make a response in the presence of the appropriate stimulus and not other stimuli.
    b. Punishment is the suppression of an undesirable response by the presentation of an aversive stimulus.
    d. Putting on a coat is a response that operates on the environment. Therefore, this is an example of operant, not classical, conditioning.

13. **d.** is the answer.
    a. Intermittent reinforcement refers to the ratio of responses to reinforcers, not the overall quantity of reinforcement delivered.
    b. Unlike intermittent reinforcement, in which the delivery of reinforcement is contingent on responding, random reinforcement is delivered independently of the subject's behavior.
    c. This defines the technique of shaping, not intermittent reinforcement.

14. **a.** is the answer. You are teaching your dog by rewarding him when he produces the desired behavior.
    b. This is not classical conditioning because the cookie is a primary reinforcer presented after the operant behavior of the dog fetching the paper.
    c. Food is a primary reinforcer; it satisfies an innate need.
    d. Rewarding your dog each time he fetches the paper is continuous reinforcement.

15. **c.** is the answer. Because reinforcement (earning a good grade on the exam) is available according to the passage of time, studying is reinforced on an interval schedule. Because the interval between exams is constant, this is an example of a fixed-interval schedule.

16. **d.** is the answer.
   a. Pavlov and Watson are both associated with classical conditioning.
   b. Skinner is associated with operant conditioning, and Bandura is associated with observational learning.

17. **a.** is the answer. Online testing systems apply operant principles such as reinforcement, immediate feedback, and shaping to the teaching of new skills.
   b. & d. Online testing systems provide immediate, and continuous, reinforcement for correct responses, but do not use aversive control procedures such as punishment.
   c. Online testing systems are based on feedback for correct responses; this feedback constitutes conditioned, rather than primary, reinforcement.

18. **d.** is the answer. An approving nod from the boss is a conditioned reinforcer in that it doesn't satisfy an innate need but has become linked with desirable consequences. Cessation of cold, cessation of pain, and a drink are all primary reinforcers, which meet innate needs.

Matching Items

1.	c	5.	h
2.	d	6.	a
3.	e	7.	b
4.	f	8.	g

True–False Items

1.	F	4.	T
2.	F	5.	T
3.	T		

Essay Question

The first step in shaping an operant response, such as rolling over, is to find an effective reinforcer. Some sort of biscuit or dog treat is favored by animal trainers. This primary reinforcement should be accompanied by effusive praise (secondary reinforcement) whenever the dog makes a successful response.

Rolling over (the goal response) should be divided into a series of simple approximations, the first of which is a response, such as lying down on command, that is already in the dog's repertoire. This response should be reinforced several times. The next step is to issue a command, such as "Roll over," and withhold reinforcement until the dog (usually out of frustration) makes a closer approximation (such as rotating slightly in one direction). Following this example, the trainer should gradually require closer and closer approximations until the goal response is attained. When the new response has been estab-

lished, the trainer should switch from continuous to partial reinforcement, in order to strengthen the skill.

Terms and Concepts to Remember

1. **Learning** is the process of acquiring new and relatively enduring information or behaviors.

2. In **associative learning**, organisms learn that certain events occur together. Two variations of associative learning are classical conditioning and operant conditioning.

3. A **stimulus** is any situation or event that evokes a response.

4. **Operant conditioning** is a type of learning in which behavior is strengthened if followed by a reinforcer or diminished if followed by a punisher.

   Example: Unlike classical conditioning, which works on automatic behaviors, **operant conditioning** works on behaviors that operate on the environment.

5. E. L. Thorndike proposed the **law of effect**, which states that behaviors followed by favorable consequences are likely to recur, and that behaviors followed by unfavorable consequences become less likely.

6. An **operant chamber** (*Skinner box*) is an experimental chamber for the operant conditioning of an animal such as a pigeon or rat. The controlled environment enables the investigator to present visual or auditory stimuli, deliver reinforcement or punishment, and precisely measure simple responses such as bar presses or key pecking.

7. In operant conditioning, **reinforcement** is any event that strengthens the behavior it follows.

8. **Shaping** is the operant conditioning procedure for establishing a new response by reinforcing successive approximations of the desired behavior.

9. In operant conditioning, **positive reinforcement** strengthens a response by *presenting* a typically pleasurable stimulus after that response.

10. In operant conditioning, **negative reinforcement** strengthens a response by *removing* an aversive stimulus after that response.

11. The powers of **primary reinforcers** are inborn and do not depend on learning.

12. **Conditioned reinforcers** are stimuli that acquire their reinforcing power through their association with primary reinforcers; also called *secondary reinforcers*.

13. In operant conditioning, a **reinforcement schedule** is a pattern that defines how often a desired response will be reinforced.

14. **Continuous reinforcement** is the operant procedure of reinforcing the desired response every time it occurs. In promoting the acquisition of a new response it is best to use continuous reinforcement.

15. **Partial (intermittent) reinforcement** is the operant procedure of reinforcing a response intermittently. A response that has been partially reinforced is much more resistant to extinction than one that has been continuously reinforced.

16. In operant conditioning, a **fixed-ratio schedule** is one in which reinforcement is presented after a set number of responses.

    Example: Continuous reinforcement is a special kind of **fixed-ratio schedule**: Reinforcement is presented after *each* response, so the ratio of reinforcements to responses is one to one.

17. In operant conditioning, a **variable-ratio schedule** is one in which reinforcement is presented after a varying number of responses.

18. In operant conditioning, a **fixed-interval schedule** is one in which a response is reinforced after a specified time has elapsed.

19. In operant conditioning, a **variable-interval schedule** is one in which responses are reinforced after varying intervals of time.

20. In operant conditioning, **punishment** is the presentation of an aversive stimulus, such as shock, which decreases the behavior it follows.

    Memory aid: People often confuse negative reinforcement and **punishment**. The former strengthens behavior, while the latter weakens it.

21. **Respondent behavior** is that which occurs as an automatic response to some stimulus.

    Example: In classical conditioning, conditioned and unconditioned responses are examples of **respondent behavior** in that they are automatic responses triggered by specific stimuli.

22. **Operant behavior** is behavior that operates on the environment, producing consequences.

Effects of Biology and Cognition, and Learning by Observation

MODULE OVERVIEW

Module 22 begins with a discussion of two important issues relevant to an organism's ability to learn. These include the ways in which learning is constrained by a species' biological predispositions and the role of cognitive processes in conditioning.

The module then covers observational learning, in which we learn by observing and imitating others. Although the basic forms of learning—classical and operant conditioning—account for much of human behavior, we also learn indirectly, by observing other people.

NOTE: Answer guidelines for all Module 22 questions begin on page 201.

MODULE REVIEW

First, skim each section, noting headings and bold-face items. After you have read the section, review each objective by answering the fill-in and essay-type questions that follow it. In some cases, Study Tips explain how best to learn a difficult concept and Applications help you to know how well you understand the material. As you proceed, evaluate your performance by consulting the answers beginning on page 201. Do not continue with the next section until you understand each answer. If you need to, review or reread the section in the textbook before continuing.

Biological Constraints on Conditioning

Objective 22-1: Explain how biological constraints affect classical and operant conditioning.

1. Some psychologists once believed that any natural _____ could be conditioned to any neutral _____ .

2. Garcia discovered that rats would associate _____ with taste but not with other stimuli.

3. Garcia found that taste-aversion conditioning _____ (would/would not) occur when the delay between the CS and the US was more than an hour. Conditioning is speedier, stronger, and more durable when the CS is _____ relevant.

4. Results such as these demonstrate that the principles of learning are constrained by the _____ predispositions of each animal species and that they help each species _____ to its environment. They also demonstrate the importance of different _____ _____ _____ in understanding complex phenomena.

5. Operant conditioning _____ (is/is not) constrained by an animal's biological predispositions.

6. For instance, with animals it is difficult to use food as a _____ to _____ behaviors that are not naturally associated with _____ .

7. Biological constraints predispose organisms to learn associations that are naturally _____ . When animals revert to their biologically predisposed patterns, they are exhibiting what is called _____ _____ .

APPLICATIONS:

8. A pigeon can easily be taught to flap its wings to avoid shock but not for food reinforcement. According to the text, this is most likely so because
   a. pigeons are biologically predisposed to flap their wings to escape aversive events and to use their beaks to obtain food.
   b. shock is a more motivating stimulus for birds than food is.
   c. hungry animals have difficulty delaying their eating long enough to learn any new skill.
   d. of all of these reasons.

9. Last evening May-Ling ate her first cheeseburger and french fries at an American fast-food restaurant. A few hours later she became ill. It can be expected that May-Ling will
   a. develop an aversion to the sight of a cheeseburger and french fries.
   b. develop an aversion to the taste of a cheeseburger and french fries.
   c. not associate her illness with the food she ate.
   d. associate her sickness with something she experienced immediately before she became ill.

Cognition's Influences on Conditioning

Objective 22-2: Explain how cognitive processes affect classical and operant conditioning.

10. The early behaviorists believed that to understand behavior in various organisms, any presumption of _____ was unnecessary.

11. We now know that we can acquire mental information that guides our behavior through
    _____ .

12. Experiments by Rescorla and Wagner demonstrate that a CS must reliably
    _____ the US for an association to develop and, more generally, that
    _____ processes play a role in conditioning. It is as if the animal learns to
    _____ that the US will occur.

13. The importance of cognitive processes in human conditioning is demonstrated by the failure of classical conditioning as a treatment for
    _____ _____ .

14. Skinner and other behaviorists resisted the growing belief that expectations, perceptions, and other _____ processes have a valid place in the science of psychology.

15. When a well-learned route in a maze is blocked, rats sometimes choose an alternative route, acting as if they were consulting a _____
    _____ .

16. Animals may learn from experience even when reinforcement is not available. When learning is not apparent until reinforcement has been provided, _____
    _____ is said to have occurred.

17. Excessive rewards may undermine
    _____ _____ ,
    which is the desire to perform a behavior for its own sake. The motivation to seek external rewards and avoid punishment is called
    _____ _____ .

APPLICATIONS:

18. After discovering that her usual route home was closed due to road repairs, Sharetta used her knowledge of the city and sense of direction to find an alternative route. This is an example of
    a. latent learning.
    b. observational learning.
    c. shaping.
    d. using a cognitive map.

19. Two rats are independently placed in a maze. One rat is rewarded with food in the goal box. The other receives no food reward. On a later trial, food is placed in the goal box for the "unrewarded" rat. What can you say about the rat's behavior on that trial?
    a. The "unrewarded" rat will run to the goal box just as quickly as the rewarded rat.
    b. The rat will wander around the maze and never find the food reward.
    c. The rat will find the food reward, but it will take much longer than the rewarded rat.
    d. The rat will not even try to find the food reward.

20. Nancy decided to take introductory psychology because she has always been interested in human behavior. Jack enrolled in the same course because he thought it would be easy. Nancy's behavior was motivated by
    _____ , Jack's by _____ .
    a. extrinsic motivation; intrinsic motivation
    b. intrinsic motivation; extrinsic motivation
    c. drives; incentives
    d. incentives; drives

Learning by Observation

Objective 22-3: Describe the process of observational learning, and explain how some scientists believe it is enabled by mirror neurons.

21. Learning by observing and imitating others is called _____ , or _____ _____ . This form of learning _____ (occurs/ does not occur) in species other than our own.

22. The psychologist best known for research on observational learning is _____ .

23. In one experiment, the child who viewed an adult punch an inflatable doll played _____ (more/less) aggressively than the child who had not observed the adult.

24. Bandura believes people imitate a model because of _____ and _____ , those received by the model as well as by imitators.

25. Models are most effective when they are perceived as _____ , _____ , or _____ . Models are also most effective when their words and actions are _____ .

26. Neuroscientists have found _____ neurons in the brain's_____ lobe that provide a neural basis for _____ learning. These neurons have been observed to fire when monkeys perform a simple task and when they _____ . This type of neuron _____ (has/has not) been found in human brains.

27. By age _____ , infants will imitate novel various novel gestures. By age _____ , they will imitate acts modeled on television. Children's brains enable their _____ and their _____ _____ .

APPLICATIONS: Children—and, of course, adults— learn a great deal by watching other people. Depending on the models, the behavior they learn may be good or bad.

28. During holiday breaks Lionel watches wrestling, which _____ his aggressive tendencies. His brother Michael won't watch the wrestling because he feels the pain of the choke hold, for example, as reflected in his brain's

_____ _____ .

Instead, Michael spends time with Grandma, who cooks for the poor during the holiday season, helping Michael to learn _____ behavior.

29. Mrs. Ramirez often tells her children that it is important to buckle their seat belts while riding in the car, but she rarely does so herself. Her children will probably learn to
    a. use their seat belts and tell others it is important to do so.
    b. use their seat belts but not tell others it is important to do so.
    c. tell others it is important to use seat belts but rarely use them themselves.
    d. neither tell others that seat belts are important nor use them.

30. After watching coverage of the Olympics on television recently, Lynn and Susan have been staging their own "summer games." Which of the following best accounts for their behavior?
    a. classical conditioning
    b. observational learning
    c. latent learning
    d. shaping

Objective 22-4: Discuss the impact of prosocial modeling and of antisocial modeling.

31. Children will model positive, or _____ , behaviors.

32. Children will also model negative, or _____ , behaviors. This may help explain why _____ parents might have _____ children. However, _____ factors may also be involved.

33. Children in developed countries spend more time _____ _____ than they spend in school.

34. Compared with the real world, television depicts a much higher percentage of crimes as being _____ in nature.

35. (Thinking Critically) Correlational studies _____ (link/do not link) watching television violence with violent behavior.

36. (Thinking Critically) The more hours children spend watching violent programs, the more at risk they are for _____ and _____ as teens and adults.

37. (Thinking Critically) Correlation does not prove _____ . Most researchers believe that watching violence on television _____ (does/does not) lead to aggressive behavior.

38. (Thinking Critically) The violence-viewing effect stems from several factors, including _____ of observed aggression and the tendency of prolonged exposure to violence to _____ viewers.

PROGRESS TEST

Multiple-Choice Questions

Circle your answers to the following questions and check them with the answers beginning on page 202. If your answer is incorrect, read the explanation for why it is incorrect and then consult the text.

1. *Learning* is best defined as
   a. any behavior produced by an organism without being provoked.
   b. a change in the behavior of an organism.
   c. a relatively permanent change in the behavior of an organism due to experience.
   d. behavior based on operant rather than respondent conditioning.

2. Cognitive processes are
   a. unimportant in classical and operant conditioning.
   b. important in both classical and operant conditioning.
   c. more important in classical than in operant conditioning.
   d. more important in operant than in classical conditioning.

3. In Garcia and Koelling's studies of taste-aversion learning, rats learned to associate
   a. taste with electric shock.
   b. sights and sounds with sickness.
   c. taste with sickness.
   d. taste and sounds with electric shock.

4. Learning by imitating others' behaviors is called _____ learning. The researcher best known for studying this type of learning is _____ .
   a. secondary; Skinner
   b. observational; Bandura
   c. secondary; Pavlov
   d. observational; Watson

5. Classical conditioning experiments by Rescorla and Wagner demonstrate that an important factor in conditioning is
   a. the research participant's age.
   b. the strength of the stimuli.
   c. the predictability of an association.
   d. the similarity of stimuli.

6. Mirror neurons are found in the brain's _____ and are believed by some scientists to be the neural basis for _____ .
   a. frontal lobe; observational learning
   b. frontal lobe; classical conditioning
   c. temporal lobe; operant conditioning
   d. temporal lobe; observational learning

7. In promoting observational learning, the most effective models are those that we perceive as
   a. similar to ourselves.
   b. respected and admired.
   c. successful.
   d. having any of these characteristics.

8. A cognitive map is a
   a. mental representation of one's environment.
   b. sequence of thought processes leading from one idea to another.
   c. set of instructions detailing the most effective means of teaching a particular concept.
   d. biological predisposition to learn a particular skill.

9. After exploring a complicated maze for several days, a rat subsequently ran the maze with very few errors when food was placed in the goal box for the first time. This performance illustrates
   a. classical conditioning.
   b. discrimination learning.
   c. observational learning.
   d. latent learning.

10. Experiments on taste-aversion learning demonstrate that
   a. for the conditioning of certain stimuli, the US need not immediately follow the CS.
   b. any perceivable stimulus can become a CS.
   c. all animals are biologically primed to associate illness with the taste of a tainted food.
   d. all of these statements are true.

11. Regarding the impact of watching television violence on children, most researchers believe that

    a. aggressive children simply prefer violent programs.

    b. television simply reflects, rather than contributes to, violent social trends.

    c. watching violence on television leads to aggressive behavior.

    d. there is only a weak correlation between exposure to violence and aggressive behavior.

Matching Items

Match each definition or description with the appropriate term.

Definitions or Descriptions

_____ **1.** the motivation to perform a behavior for its own sake

_____ **2.** learning that becomes apparent only after reinforcement is provided

_____ **3.** a desire to perform a behavior because of promised rewards

Terms

    a. latent learning

    b. extrinsic motivation

    c. intrinsic motivation

True–False Items

Indicate whether each statement is true or false by placing *T* or *F* in the blank next to the item.

_____ **1.** Cognitive processes are of relatively little importance in learning.

_____ **2.** All animals, including rats and birds, are biologically predisposed to associate taste cues with sickness.

_____ **3.** Researchers have discovered brain neurons that fire when a person performs a task *or* when another person is observed performing the same task.

TERMS AND CONCEPTS TO REMEMBER

Using your own words, on a piece of paper write a brief definition or explanation of each of the following terms.

1. learning
2. cognitive learning
3. cognitive map
4. latent learning
5. intrinsic motivation
6. extrinsic motivation
7. observational learning
8. modeling
9. mirror neurons
10. prosocial behavior

ANSWERS
Module Review

Biological Constraints on Conditioning

1. response; stimulus

2. sickness

3. would; ecologically

4. biological; adapt; levels of analysis

5. is

6. reinforcer; shape; food

7. adaptive; instinctive drift

8. **a.** is the answer. As in this example, conditioning must be consistent with the particular organism's biological predispositions.
   b. Some behaviors, but certainly not all, are acquired more rapidly than others when shock is used as negative reinforcement.
   c. Pigeons are able to acquire many new behaviors when food is used as reinforcement.

9. **b.** is the answer.
   a., c., & d. Taste-aversion research demonstrates that humans and some other animals, such as rats, are biologically primed to associate illness with the taste of tainted food, rather than with other cues, such as the food's appearance. Moreover, taste aversions can be acquired even when the interval between the CS and the illness is several hours.

10. cognition

11. cognitive learning

12. predict; cognitive; expect

13. alcohol dependence

14. cognitive

15. cognitive map

16. latent learning

17. intrinsic motivation; extrinsic motivation

18. **d.** is the answer. Sharetta is guided by her mental representation of the city, or cognitive map.
    a. Latent learning, or learning in the absence of reinforcement that is demonstrated when reinforcement becomes available, has no direct relevance to the example.
    b. Observational learning refers to learning from watching others.
    c. Shaping is the technique of reinforcing successive approximations of a desired behavior.

19. **a.** is the answer. The unrewarded rat is demonstrating latent learning. It has developed a cognitive map of the maze.

20. **b.** is the answer. Wanting to do something for its own sake is intrinsic motivation; wanting to do something for a reward (in this case, presumably, a high grade) is extrinsic motivation.
    a. The opposite is true. Nancy was motivated to take the course for its own sake, whereas Jack was evidently motivated by the likelihood of a reward in the form of a good grade.
    c. & d. A good grade, such as the one Jack is expecting, is an incentive. Drives, however, are aroused states that result from physical deprivation; they are not involved in this example.

21. modeling; observational learning; occurs

22. Bandura

23. more

24. rewards; punishments

25. similar; successful; admirable; consistent

26. mirror; frontal; observational; observe other monkeys performing the same task; has

27. 8 to 16 months; 14 months; empathy; theory of mind

28. increases; mirror neurons; prosocial

29. **c.** is the answer. Studies indicate that when a model says one thing but does another, subjects do the same and learn not to practice what they preach.

30. **b.** is the answer. The girls are imitating behavior they have observed and admired.

a. Because these behaviors are clearly willful rather than involuntary, classical conditioning plays no role.
c. Latent learning plays no role in this example.
d. Shaping is a procedure for teaching the acquisition of a new response by reinforcing successive approximations of the behavior.

31. prosocial

32. antisocial; abusive; aggressive; genetic

33. watching television

34. violent

35. link

36. aggression; crime

37. causation; does

38. imitation; desensitize

Progress Test

Multiple-Choice Questions

1. **c.** is the answer.
   a. This answer is incorrect because it simply describes any behavior that is automatic rather than being triggered by a specific stimulus.
   b. This answer is too general, since behaviors can change for reasons other than learning.
   d. Respondently conditioned behavior also satisfies the criteria of our definition of learning.

2. **b.** is the answer.
   c. & d. The text does not present evidence regarding the relative importance of cognitive processes in classical and operant conditioning.

3. **c.** is the answer.
   a. & d. These studies also indicated that rats are biologically predisposed to associate visual and auditory stimuli, but not taste, with shock.
   b. Rats are biologically predisposed to associate taste with sickness.

4. **b.** is the answer.
   a. Skinner is best known for studies of *operant* learning. Moreover, there is no such thing as secondary learning.
   c. Pavlov is best known for classical conditioning.
   d. Watson is best known as an early proponent of behaviorism.

5. **c.** is the answer.
   a., b., & d. Rescorla and Wagner's research did not address the importance of these factors in classical conditioning.

6. **a.** is the answer.

7. **d.** is the answer.

8. **a.** is the answer.

9. **d.** is the answer. The rat had learned the maze but did not display this learning until reinforcement became available.
   a. Negotiating a maze is clearly operant behavior.
   b. This example does not involve learning to distinguish between stimuli.
   c. This is not observational learning because the rat has no one to observe!

10. **a.** is the answer. Taste-aversion experiments demonstrate conditioning even with CS-US intervals as long as several hours.
    b. Despite being perceivable, a visual or auditory stimulus cannot become a CS for illness in some animals, such as rats.
    c. Some animals, such as birds, are biologically primed to associate the *appearance* of food with illness.

11. **c.** is the answer.

Matching Items

1. c   3. b
2. a

True–False Items

1. F   3. T
2. F

Terms and Concepts to Remember

1. **Learning** is the process of acquiring new and relatively enduring information or behaviors.

2. **Cognitive learning** is the acquisition of mental information that guides our behavior.

3. A **cognitive map** is a mental representation of the layout of one's environment.

4. **Latent learning** is learning that occurs in the absence of reinforcement but only becomes apparent when there is an incentive to demonstrate it.

5. **Intrinsic motivation** is the desire to perform a behavior effectively for its own sake, rather than for some external reason.
   Memory aid: Intrinsic means "internal": A person who is **intrinsically motivated** is motivated from within.

6. **Extrinsic motivation** is the desire to perform a behavior to receive promised rewards or avoid threatened punishment.
   Memory aid: Extrinsic means "external": A person who is extrinsically motivated is motivated by some outside factor.

7. **Observational learning** is learning by watching and imitating the behavior of others.

8. **Modeling** is the process of watching and then imitating a specific behavior and is thus an important means through which observational learning occurs.

9. Found in the brain's frontal lobe, **mirror neurons** may be the neural basis for observational learning. These neurons generate impulses when certain actions are performed or when another individual who performs those actions is observed.

10. The opposite of antisocial behavior, **prosocial behavior** is positive, helpful, and constructive and is subject to the same principles of observational learning as is undesirable behavior, such as aggression.

Studying and Building Memories

MODULE OVERVIEW

Module 23 explores human memory as a system that processes information in three steps. Encoding refers to the process of putting information into the memory system. Storage is the mechanism by which information is maintained in memory. Retrieval is the process by which information is accessed from memory through recall or recognition. This module introduces the Atkinson-Shiffrin classic-three stage model and the more current revision of the model that includes working memory.

Although we encode some information automatically, such as for time, frequency, and space, most encoding requires effort. We use a variety of strategies to encode this information—including chunking and the peg-word system.

NOTE: Answer guidelines for all Module 23 questions begin on page 209.

MODULE REVIEW

First, skim this section, noting headings and boldface items. After you have read the section, review each objective by completing the sentences and answering the questions that follow it. In some cases, Study Tips explain how best to learn a difficult concept and Applications help you to know how well you understand the material. As you proceed, evaluate your performance by consulting the answers beginning on page 209. Do not continue with the next section until you understand each answer. If you need to, review or reread the section in the textbook before continuing.

Studying Memory

Objective 23-1: Define *memory*.

1. Learning that persists over time indicates the existence of _____ for that learning.

2. The ability to retrieve information not in conscious awareness but that was learned at an earlier time is called _____ . The ability to identify previously learned items is called _____ .

3. If you have learned something and then forgotten it, you will probably be able to _____ it _____ (more/less) quickly than you did originally.

Objective 23-2: Explain how psychologists describe the human memory system.

4. Both human memory and computer memory can be viewed as _____- _____ systems that perform three tasks: _____ , _____ , and _____ . Unlike the computer, which processes _____ (sequentially/simultaneously), our brain processes many things _____ (sequentially/simultaneously). The model called _____ views memory as emerging from interconnected _____ _____ .

5. The classic model of memory has been Atkinson and Shiffrin's _____- _____ _____ model. According to this model, we first record information as a fleeting _____- _____ , from which it is processed into _____-_____ memory, where the information is _____ through rehearsal into _____-_____ memory for later retrieval.

6. The phenomenon of short-term memory has been clarified by the concept of _____ memory, which focuses more on the _____ processing of briefly stored information. This form of memory is sometimes called the _____ _____ .

Objective 23-3: Distinguish between explicit and implicit memories.

7. Facts and experiences that we can consciously declare make up _____ memory, which is also called _____ memory. Such memories are processed through conscious, _____ processing. Processing that happens without our awareness, called _____ , produces _____

memories, which are also called _____ _____ .

STUDY TIP: To remember the material in the first half of this chapter, you might find it helpful to use the concept of a *three-part model* as a retrieval cue. In this section, the modified three-stage information-processing model proposes that external events are processed through separate stages of sensory memory, short-term/working memory, and long-term memory. In the next section, the three processes of (1) getting information into the memory system (encoding), (2) retaining information over time (storage), and (3) getting information out of memory storage (retrieval) are described. Each process (encoding, storage, and retrieval) can occur at each memory stage (sensory memory, short-term memory, long-term memory). The chart below applies what can happen at each stage to the example of getting the written words of a memorable poem in and out of memory. To bolster your understanding of these important concepts, you might try using this type of chart as the basis for an example you create.

Sensory Memory	Short-Term/Working Memory	Long-Term Memory
Encoding: light reflecting from printed words in the poem automatically triggers a response in the eye's receptor cells	*Encoding:* automatic processing of location of words on the page; effortful processing of meaning	*Encoding:* Memorable passage triggers deep processing of material from STM to LTM
Storage: image of each word persists in the visual system for about 1/2 sec.	*Storage:* limited capacity and duration of storing words on the page	*Storage:* relatively permanent and limitless; meaningful passage stays with you
Retrieval: visual image is attended to as it passes into STM/Working memory	*Retrieval:* conscious working memory allows reader to process the meaning of the poem's words	*Retrieval:* recall, recognition, or relearning of memorized passage from the poem

APPLICATION:

8. Elderly Mr. Flanagan, a retired electrician, can easily remember how to wire a light switch, but he cannot remember the name of the president of the United States. Evidently, Mr. Flanagan's _____ memory is better than his _____ memory.
   a. implicit; explicit
   b. explicit; implicit
   c. declarative; nondeclarative
   d. explicit; declarative

Building Memories

Objective 23-4: Identify the information we process automatically.

9. Implicit memories include _____ memory for skills and associations among stimuli formed by _____ .

Give examples of material that is typically encoded with little or no effort.

APPLICATION:

10. The first thing Karen did when she discovered that she had misplaced her keys was to re-create in her mind the day's events. That she had little difficulty in doing so illustrates _____ processing.

Objective 23-5: Explain how sensory memory works.

11. Stimuli from the environment are first recorded in _____ memory.

12. George Sperling found that when people were briefly shown three rows of letters, they could recall _____ (virtually all/about half) of them. When Sperling sounded a tone immediately after a row of letters was flashed to indicate which letters were to be recalled, the participants were much _____ (more/ less) accurate. This suggests that people have a brief photographic, or _____ , memory lasting about a few tenths of a second.

13. Sensory memory for sounds is called _____ memory. This memory fades _____ (more/less) rapidly than photographic memory, lasting for as long as _____ .

Objective 23-6: Describe the capacity of our short-term and working memory.

14. Our short-term memory capacity is about _____ chunks of information. This capacity was discovered by_____ .

15. Peterson and Peterson found that when _____ was prevented by asking people to count backward, memory for letters was gone after 12 seconds. Without _____ processing, short-term memories have a limited life.

16. The capacity of working memory _____ (reflects/does not reflect) a person's intelligence level.

APPLICATION:

17. Brenda has trouble remembering her new five-digit ZIP plus four-digit address code. What is the most likely explanation for the difficulty Brenda is having?
    a. Nine digits are at or above the upper limit of most people's short-term memory capacity.
    b. Nine digits are at or above the upper limit of most people's iconic memory capacity.
    c. The extra four digits cannot be organized into easily remembered chunks.
    d. Brenda evidently has an impaired implicit memory.

Objective 23-7: Describe the effortful processing methods that help us remember new information.

18. Memory may be aided by grouping information into meaningful units called _____ .

19. Memory aids are known as _____ devices.

20. Using a jingle, such as the one that begins "one is a bun," is an example of the _____-_____ system.

21. Another memory aid involves forming words from the first letters of to-be-remembered words; the resulting word is called an _____ .

22. When people develop expertise in an area, they process information into _____ .

23. A pioneering researcher in verbal memory was _____ . In one experiment, he found that distributed rehearsal is more effective for retention; this is called the _____ _____ .

24. Repeated self-testing is a good way to _____ practice. Henry Roediger and Jeffrey Karpicke called this the _____ _____ .

Objective 23-8: Describe the levels of processing and their effect on encoding.

25. Encoding material on a basic level based on _____ or the _____ of words is called _____ _____ . Encoding material _____ , based on the meaning of words, is called _____ _____ . _____ (Shallow/Deep) processing tends to yield the best retention.

26. Material that is not _____ is difficult to process. We have especially good recall for information we can meaningfully relate to ourselves, called the _____-_____ effect.

PROGRESS TEST

Multiple-Choice Questions

Circle your answers to the following questions and check them with the answers beginning on page 210. If your answer is incorrect, read the explanation for why it is incorrect and then consult the text.

1. The three steps in memory information processing are
   a. input, processing, output.
   b. input, storage, output.
   c. input, storage, retrieval.
   d. encoding, storage, retrieval.

2. Visual sensory memory is referred to as
   a. iconic memory.   c. photomemory.
   b. echoic memory.   d. semantic memory.

3. Echoic memories fade after approximately
   a. 1 hour.   c. 1 second.
   b. 1 minute.   d. 3 to 4 seconds.

4. Which of the following is NOT a measure of retention?
   a. recall   c. relearning
   b. recognition   d. retrieval

5. Our short-term memory span is approximately _____ items.
   a. 2   c. 7
   b. 5   d. 10

6. Memory techniques such as acronyms and the peg-word system are called
   a. consolidation devices.
   b. imagery techniques.
   c. encoding strategies.
   d. mnemonic devices.

7. One way to increase the amount of information in memory is to group it into larger, familiar units. This process is referred to as
   a. consolidating.   c. encoding.
   b. organization.   d. chunking.

8. The spacing effect means that
   a. distributed study yields better retention than cramming.
   b. retention is improved when encoding and retrieval are separated by no more than 1 hour.
   c. learning causes a reduction in the size of the synaptic gap between certain neurons.
   d. delaying retrieval until memory has consolidated improves recall.

9. In Sperling's memory experiment, research participants were shown three rows of three letters, followed immediately by a low, medium, or high tone. The participants were able to report
   a. all three rows with perfect accuracy.
   b. only the top row of letters.
   c. only the middle row of letters.
   d. any one of the three rows of letters.

10. Memory for skills is called
    a. explicit memory.   c. prime memory.
    b. declarative memory.   d. implicit memory.

11. When Gordon Bower presented words grouped by category or in random order, recall was
    a. the same for all words.
    b. better for the categorized words.
    c. better for the random words.
    d. improved when participants developed their own mnemonic devices.

12. The three-stage processing model of memory was proposed by
    a. Atkinson and Shiffrin.
    b. Herman Ebbinghaus.
    c. Loftus and Palmer.
    d. George Sperling.

13. Which type of word processing results in the greatest retention?
    a. shallow
    b. deep
    c. visual
    d. auditory

14. The process of getting information out of memory storage is called
    a. encoding.   c. rehearsal.
    b. retrieval.   d. storage.

15. Information is maintained in short-term memory only briefly unless it is
    a. encoded.   c. iconic or echoic.
    b. rehearsed.   d. retrieved.

16. Textbook chapters are often organized into _____ to facilitate information processing.
    a. mnemonic devices   c. hierarchies
    b. chunks   d. recognizable units

17. Semantic encoding is a type of
    a. mnemonic.
    b. shallow processing.
    c. deep processing.
    d. echoic memory.

Matching Items

Match each definition or description with the appropriate term.

Definitions or Descriptions

_____ 1. sensory memory that decays more slowly than visual sensory memory
_____ 2. the process by which information gets into the memory system
_____ 3. "one is a bun, two is a shoe" mnemonic device
_____ 4. word that chunks to-be-remembered information into a more familiar form
_____ 5. encoding the meaning of words

Terms

a. peg-word system
b. acronym
c. deep processing
d. echoic memory
e. encoding

TERMS AND CONCEPTS TO REMEMBER

Writing Definitions

Using your own words, on a separate piece of paper write a brief definition or explanation of each of the following terms.

1. memory
2. recall
3. recognition
4. relearning
5. encoding
6. storage
7. retrieval
8. sensory memory
9. short-term memory
10. long-term memory
11. working memory
12. explicit memory
13. effortful processing
14. automatic processing
15. implicit memory
16. iconic memory
17. echoic memory
18. chunking
19. mnemonics
20. spacing effect
21. testing effect
22. shallow processing
23. deep processing

ANSWERS
Module Review

Studying Memory

1. memory
2. recall; recognition
3. relearn; more
4. information-processing; encoding; storage; retrieval; sequentially; simultaneously; connectionism; neural networks
5. three-stage processing; sensory memory; short-term; encoded; long-term
6. working; active; central executive
7. explicit; declarative; effortful; automatic processing; implicit; nondeclarative memory
8. **a.** is the answer.
   b., c., & d. Explicit memory, also called declarative memory, is the memory of facts that one can consciously "declare." Nondeclarative memory is what Mr. Flanagan has retained.

Building Memories

9. procedural; classical conditioning

Automatic processing includes the encoding of information about space, time, and frequency. It also includes well-learned information, such as words in your native language.

10. automatic

11. sensory

12. about half; more; iconic

13. echoic; less; 3 or 4 seconds

14. 7; George Miller

15. rehearsal; active

16. reflects

17. **a.** is the answer. Short-term memory capacity is approximately seven digits.
b. Because iconic memory lasts no more than a few tenths of a second, regardless of how much material is experienced, this cannot be the explanation for Brenda's difficulty.
c. The final four digits should be no more difficult to organize into chunks than the first five digits of the address code.
d. Memory for digits is an example of explicit, rather than implicit, memory.

18. chunks

19. mnemonic

20. peg-word

21. acronym

22. hierarchies

23. Hermann Ebbinghaus; spacing effect

24. distribute; testing effect

25. structure; appearance; shallow processing; semantically; deep processing; Deep

26. meaningful; self-reference

Progress Test

Multiple-Choice Questions

1. **d.** is the answer. Information must be encoded, or put into appropriate form; stored, or retained over time; and retrieved, or located and gotten out when needed.

2. **a.** is the answer. Iconic memory is our fleeting memory of visual stimuli.
b. Echoic memory is auditory sensory memory.
c. There is no such thing as photomemory.

d. Semantic memory is memory for meaning, not a form of sensory memory.

3. **d.** is the answer. Echoic memories last 3 to 4 seconds.

4. **d.** is the answer. Retrieval refers to the *process* of remembering.

5. **c.** is the answer.

6. **d.** is the answer.
a. There is no such term as "consolidation techniques."
b. & c. Imagery and encoding strategies are important in storing new memories, but *mnemonic device* is the general designation of techniques that facilitate memory, such as acronyms and the peg-word system.

7. **d.** is the answer.
a. There is no such process of "consolidating."
b. Organization *does* enhance memory, but it does so through hierarchies, not grouping.
c. Encoding refers to the processing of information into the memory system.

8. **a.** is the answer.
b. & d. The text does not suggest that there is an optimal interval between encoding and retrieval.
c. Learning increases the efficiency of synaptic transmission in certain neurons, but not by altering the size of the synapse.

9. **d.** is the answer. When asked to recall all the letters, participants could recall only about half; however, if immediately after the presentation they were signaled to recall a particular row, their recall was near perfect. This showed that they had a brief photographic memory—so brief that it faded in less time than it would have taken to say all nine letters.

10. **d.** is the answer.
a. & b. Explicit memory (also called declarative memory) is memory of facts and experiences that one can consciously know and declare.
c. There is no such thing as prime memory.

11. **b.** is the answer. When the words were organized into categories, recall was two to three times better, indicating the benefits of hierarchical organization in memory.
d. This study did not examine the use of mnemonic devices.

12. **a.** is the answer.
b. Herman Ebbinghaus conducted pioneering studies of verbal learning and memory.
c. Loftus and Palmer conducted influential research studies of eyewitness memory.

d. George Sperling is known for his research studies of iconic memory.

13. **b.** is the answer.

a., c., & d. Visual and auditory processing, both of which are examples of shallow processing, are not as effective in enhancing memory formation as deep processing.

14. **b.** is the answer.

a. Encoding is the process of getting information *into* memory.

c. Rehearsal is the conscious repetition of information in order to maintain it in memory.

d. Storage is the maintenance of encoded material over time.

15. **b.** is the answer.

a. Information in short-term memory has *already* been encoded.

c. Iconic and echoic are types of *sensory* memory.

d. Retrieval is the process of getting material out of storage and into conscious, short-term memory. Thus, all material in short-term memory has either already been retrieved or is about to be placed in storage.

16. **c.** is the answer. By breaking concepts down into subconcepts and yet smaller divisions and showing the relationships among these, hierarchies facilitate information processing. Use of main heads and subheads is an example of the organization of textbook chapters into hierarchies.

a. Mnemonic devices are the method of loci, acronyms, and other memory *techniques* that facilitate retention.

b. Chunks are organizations of knowledge into familiar, manageable units.

d. Recognition is a measure of retention.

17. **c.** is the answer.

a. Mnemonics are memory aids such as acronyms and peg-words.

b. Shallow processing is encoding words on a basic level based on their appearance or some other superficial characteristic.

d. Echoic memory is the momentary sensory memory of auditory stimuli.

Matching Items

1. d
2. e
3. a
4. b
5. c

Terms and Concepts to Remember

1. **Memory** is the persistence of learning over time through the storage and retrieval of information.

2. **Recall** is a measure of memory in which the person must retrieve information learned earlier, with few retrieval cues.

3. **Recognition** is a measure of memory in which one need only identify, rather than recall, previously learned information.

4. **Relearning** is a measure of memory that assesses the amount of time saved when learning material again.

5. **Encoding** is the first step in memory; information is translated into some form that enables it to enter our memory system.

6. **Storage** is the process by which encoded information is maintained over time.

7. **Retrieval** is the process of getting information out of memory storage.

8. **Sensory memory** is the immediate, very brief recording of sensory information in the memory system.

9. **Short-term memory** is activated memory, which can hold about seven items for a short time.

10. **Long-term memory** is the relatively permanent and unlimited capacity memory system into which information from short-term memory may pass. It includes knowledge, skills, and experiences.

11. **Working memory** is the newer way of conceptualizing short-term memory as a work site for the active processing of incoming auditory and visual-spatial information, and of information retrieved from long-term memory.

12. **Explicit memory** is memory of facts, including names, images, and events. It is also called *declarative memory*.

13. **Effortful processing** is encoding that requires attention and conscious effort.

14. **Automatic processing** refers to our unconscious encoding of incidental information such as space, time, and frequency and of well-learned information.

15. **Implicit memory** is procedural memory for automatic skills and classically conditioned associations among stimuli. These memories are evidently processed, not by the hippocampus, but by the cerebellum and basal ganglia. They are also called *nondeclarative memories*.

16. **Iconic memory** is the visual sensory memory consisting of a perfect photographic memory, which lasts no more than a few tenths of a second.

Memory aid: Icon means "image" or "representation." **Iconic memory** consists of brief visual images.

17. **Echoic memory** is the momentary sensory memory of auditory stimuli, lasting about 3 or 4 seconds.

18. **Chunking** is the memory technique of organizing material into familiar, manageable units.

19. **Mnemonics** are memory aids (acronyms, pegwords, etc.), which often use vivid imagery and organizational devices.

20. The **spacing effect** is the tendency for distributed study or practice to yield better long-term retention than massed study or practice.

21. The **testing effect** is the phenomenon in which memory is enhanced more by retrieval of the information than simply reading it.

22. **Shallow processing** is encoding words on a basic level based on their appearance or some other superficial characteristic.

23. **Deep processing** is encoding words based on their meaning (semantic encoding).

Storage: Retaining Information in the Brain

MODULE OVERVIEW

Module 24 explores the second of the three steps in the memory process—storage. Storage is the purely passive mechanism by which information is maintained in memory. This module also discusses how memory is represented physically in the brain, noting that we actually have two memory systems operating in tandem.

NOTE: Answer guidelines for all Module 24 questions begin on page 215.

MODULE REVIEW

First, skim this section, noting headings and boldface items. After you have read the section, review each objective by completing the sentences and answering the questions that follow it. In some cases, Study Tips explain how best to learn a difficult concept and Applications help you to know how well you understand the material. As you proceed, evaluate your performance by consulting the answers beginning on page 215. Do not continue with the next section until you understand each answer. If you need to, review or reread the section in the textbook before continuing.

Retaining Information in the Brain

Objective 24-1: Describe the capacity and location of our long-term memories.

1. In contrast to short-term memory—and contrary to popular belief—the capacity of permanent memory is essentially_____ .

2. Psychologist _____ attempted to locate memory by cutting out pieces of rats' _____ after they had learned a maze. He found that no matter where he cut, the rats _____ (remembered/forgot) the maze.

Objective 24-2: Describe the role of the frontal lobes and hippocampus in memory storage.

3. Many brain regions send input to your _____ lobes for working memory processing.

4. Amnesia patients typically have suffered damage to the _____ of their limbic system. This brain structure is important in the processing and storage of _____ memories. Damage on the left side of this structure impairs _____ memory; damage on the right side impairs memory for _____ designs and locations. The rear part of this structure processes _____ memory.

5. The hippocampus seems to function as a zone where the brain _____ (temporarily/permanently) stores the elements of a memory. However, memories _____ (do/do not) migrate for storage elsewhere. The hippocampus is active during _____ sleep, as memories are processed and filed for later retrieval. Sensory cortex areas also receive information from the outside

world and send it to the _____ and to other parts of the _____ lobes.

APPLICATIONS:

6. Brad, who suffered accidental damage to the left side of his hippocampus, has trouble remembering
   a. visual designs.
   b. locations.
   c. all nonverbal information.
   d. verbal information.

7. After suffering damage to the hippocampus, a person would probably
   a. lose memory for skills such as bicycle riding.
   b. be incapable of being classically conditioned.
   c. lose the ability to store new facts.
   d. experience all of these changes.

Objective 24-3: Describe the role of the cerebellum and basal ganglia in our memory processing.

8. The cerebellum is important in the processing of _____ memories. Humans and laboratory animals with a damaged cerebellum are incapable of simple _____ conditioning.

9. Deep brain structures called the _____ _____ , which are also involved in _____ movement, facilitate formation of _____ memories for skills.

10. The dual explicit-implicit memory system helps explain _____ amnesia. We do not have explicit memories of our first three years for two reasons: explicit memory requires the use of words that nonspeaking children _____ (have/have not) learned and the _____ is one of the last brain structures to mature.

The Amygdala, Emotions, and Memory

Objective 24-4: Discuss how emotions affect our memory processing.

11. Emotions trigger _____ hormones that _____ (influence/do not influence) memory formation by making more _____ available to fuel brain activity.

12. Stress hormones provoke the _____ to initiate a memory trace in the _____ _____ and _____ _____ to boost activity in the brain's memory-forming areas.

13. Memories for surprising, significant moments that are especially clear are called _____ memories. Like other memories, these memories _____ (can/cannot) err.

APPLICATION:

14. Which of the following is the best example of a flashbulb memory?
    a. suddenly remembering to buy bread while standing in the checkout line at the grocery store
    b. recalling the name of someone from high school while looking at his or her yearbook snapshot
    c. remembering to make an important phone call
    d. remembering what you were doing on September 11, 2001, when terrorists crashed planes into the World Trade Center towers

Synaptic Changes

Objective 24-5: Explain how changes at the synapse level affect our memory processing.

15. Eric Kandel and James Schwartz have found that when learning occurs in the sea slug *Aplysia*, the neurotransmitter _____ is released in greater amounts, making synapses more efficient.

16. After learning has occurred, a sending neuron needs _____ (more/less) prompting to release its neurotransmitter, and the number of _____ _____ it stimulates may increase. This phenomenon, called _____-_____ _____ , may be the neural basis for learning and memory. Blocking this process with a specific _____ , or by genetic engineering that causes the absence of an _____ , interferes with learning. Rats given a drug that enhances _____ will learn a maze _____ (faster/more slowly).

17. After LTP has occurred, an electric current passed through the brain _____ (will/will not) disrupt old memories and _____ (will/will not) wipe out recent experiences.

18. To enhance memory, one approach focuses on drugs that boost the LTP-enhancing neurotransmitter _____ . Another approach involves developing drugs that boost production of _____ , a protein that also enhances the LTP process.

PROGRESS TEST

Multiple-Choice Questions

Circle your answers to the following questions and check them with the answers on page 216. If your answer is incorrect, read the explanation for why it is incorrect and then consult the text.

1. Kandel and Schwartz have found that when learning occurs, more of the neurotransmitter _____ is released into synapses.
   a. ACh
   b. dopamine
   c. serotonin
   d. noradrenaline

2. Studies demonstrate that learning causes permanent neural changes in the _____ of animals' neurons.
   a. myelin
   b. cell bodies
   c. synapses
   d. all of these parts

3. The basal ganglia of the brain play a critical role in the formation of
   a. iconic memory.
   b. echoic memory.
   c. procedural memory.
   d. explicit memory.

4. Which area of the brain is most important in the processing of implicit memories?
   a. hippocampus
   b. cerebellum
   c. hypothalamus
   d. amygdala

5. Lashley's studies, in which rats learned a maze and then had various parts of their brains surgically removed, showed that the memory
   a. was lost when surgery took place within 1 hour of learning.
   b. was lost when surgery took place within 24 hours of learning.
   c. was lost when any region of the brain was removed.
   d. remained no matter which area of the brain was tampered with.

6. *Long-term potentiation* refers to
   a. the disruptive influence of old memories on the formation of new memories.
   b. the disruptive influence of recent memories on the retrieval of old memories.
   c. our tendency to recall experiences that are consistent with our current mood.
   d. the increased efficiency of synaptic transmission between certain neurons following learning.

TERMS AND CONCEPTS TO REMEMBER

Using your own words, on a separate piece of paper write a brief definition or explanation of each of the following terms.

1. explicit memory

2. hippocampus

3. implicit memory

4. flashbulb memory

5. long-term potentiation

ANSWERS
Module Review

Retaining Information in the Brain

1. unlimited (limitless)

2. Karl Lashley; cortexes; remembered

3. frontal

4. hippocampus; explicit; verbal; visual; spatial

5. temporarily; do; deep; hippocampus; temporal

6. **d.** is the answer.
   a., b., & c. Damage to the right side, not the left side, of the hippocampus would cause these types of memory deficits.

7. **c.** is the answer. The hippocampus is involved in processing new facts for storage.
   a., b., & d. Studies of amnesia victims with hippocampal damage show that neither classical conditioning nor skill memory are impaired, indicating that these aspects of memory are controlled by other regions of the brain.

8. implicit; eyeblink
9. basal ganglia; motor; procedural
10. infantile; have not; hippocampus

The Amygdala, Emotions, and Memory

11. stress; influence; glucose
12. amygdala; frontal lobes; basal ganglia
13. flashbulb; can
14. **d.** is the answer. Flashbulb memories are unusually clear memories of emotionally significant moments in life.

Synaptic Changes

15. serotonin
16. less; receptor sites; long-term potentiation; drug; enzyme; LTP; faster
17. will not; will
18. glutamate; CREB

Progress Test

Multiple-Choice Questions

1. **c.** is the answer. Kandel and Schwartz found that when learning occurred in the sea slug *Aplysia*, serotonin was released at certain synapses, which then became more efficient at signal transmission.
2. **c.** is the answer.
3. **c.** is the answer.
   a & b. The basal ganglia are involved in motor movement, not visual or auditory sensory memory.
   d. The basal ganglia are involved in the formation of implicit memories, not explicit memories.

4. **b.** is the answer.
   a. The hippocampus is a temporary processing site for *explicit memories.*
   c. & d. These areas of the brain are not directly involved in the memory system.
5. **d.** is the answer. Surprisingly, Lashley found that no matter where he cut, the rats had at least a partial memory of how to solve the maze.
   a. & b. Lashley's studies did not investigate the significance of the interval between learning and cortical lesioning.
6. **d.** is the answer.

Terms and Concepts to Remember

1. **Explicit memories** are memories of facts, including names, images, and events. They are also called *declarative memories.*
2. The **hippocampus** is a temporal lobe neural center located in the limbic system that is important in the processing of explicit memories for storage.
3. **Implicit memories** are procedural memories for automatic skills and classically conditioned associations among stimuli. These memories are evidently processed, not by the hippocampus, but by the cerebellum and basal ganglia. They are also called *nondeclarative memories.*
4. A **flashbulb memory** is an unusually vivid memory of an emotionally important moment or event.
5. **Long-term potentiation (LTP)** is an increase in a synapse's firing potential following brief, rapid stimulation. LTP is believed to be the neural basis for learning and memory.

Retrieval

MODULE OVERVIEW

Module 25 explores the third stage of the memory process—retrieval. Retrieval is the process by which information is accessed from memory through recall or recognition. The module also discusses the factors that affect what we remember.

NOTE: Answer guidelines for all Module 25 questions begin on page 219.

MODULE REVIEW

First, skim this section, noting headings and boldface items. After you have read the section, review each objective by completing the sentences and answering the questions that follow it. In some cases, Study Tips explain how best to learn a difficult concept and Applications help you to know how well you understand the material. As you proceed, evaluate your performance by consulting the answers beginning on page 219. Do not continue with the next section until you understand each answer. If you need to, review or reread the section in the textbook before continuing.

Measures of Retention

Objective 25-1: Identify three measures of retention.

1. The ability to retrieve information not in conscious awareness but that was learned at an earlier time is called _____ . The ability to identify previously learned items is called _____ .

2. If you have learned something and then forgotten it, you will probably be able to _____ it _____ (more/less) quickly than you did originally.

3. Researchers found that 25 years after graduation, people were not able to _____ (recall/recognize) the names of their classmates but were able to _____ (recall/recognize) 90 percent of their names and their yearbook pictures.

4. If you have learned something and then forgotten it, you will probably be able to _____ it _____ (more/less) quickly than you did originally. Additional rehearsal of learned material, called _____ , _____ (increases/does not increase) retention.

APPLICATION:

5. Complete this analogy: Fill-in-the-blank test questions are to multiple-choice questions as
   a. encoding is to storage.
   b. storage is to encoding.
   c. recognition is to recall.
   d. recall is to recognition.

Retrieval Cues

Objective 25-2: Describe how external cues, internal emotions, and order of appearance influence memory retrieval.

6. The best retrieval cues come from the associations formed at the time we _____ a memory.

7. The process by which associations can lead to retrieval is called _____ .

8. Studies have shown that retention is best when learning and testing are done in _____ (the same/different) contexts.

9. What we learn in one condition is best remembered in that condition, called

_____-_____

memory. For example, we tend to recall experiences that are consistent with our current emotional state, which is called _____-_____ memory.

Describe the effects of mood on memory.

10. People who are currently depressed may recall their parents as _____ _____ . People who have recovered from depression typically recall their parents about the same as do people who _____ _____ .

11. The tendency to remember the first and last items in a list best is called the _____ _____ _____ .

12. People briefly recall the last items in a list quickly and well, called the _____ effect. Following a delay, first items are remembered _____ (better/less well) than last items, called the _____ effect.

APPLICATIONS:

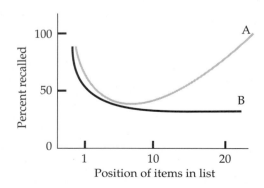

13. The figure in the left-hand column depicts the recall of a list of words under two conditions. Which of the following best describes the difference between the conditions?

a. In A, the words were studied and retrieved in the same context; in B, the contexts were different.

b. In B, the words were studied and retrieved in the same context; in A, the contexts were different.

c. The delay between presentation of the last word and the test of recall was longer for A than for B.

d. The delay between presentation of the last word and the test of recall was longer for B than for A.

14. Being in a bad mood after a hard day of work, Susan could think of nothing positive in her life. This is best explained as an example of

a. priming.
b. the spacing effect.
c. mood-congruent memory.
d. shallow processing.

15. In an effort to remember the name of the classmate who sat behind her in fifth grade, Martina mentally recited the names of other classmates who sat near her. Martina's effort to refresh her memory by activating related associations is an example of

a. priming.   c. encoding.
b. mnemonics.   d. relearning.

16. Walking through the halls of his high school 10 years after graduation, Tom experienced a flood of old memories. Tom's experience showed the role of

a. state-dependent memory.
b. context effects.
c. implicit memory.
d. echoic memory.

PROGRESS TEST

Multiple-Choice Questions

Circle your answers to the following questions and check them with the answers on page 220. If your answer is incorrect, read the explanation for why it is incorrect and then consult the text.

1. Which of the following is NOT a measure of retention?

a. recall   c. relearning
b. recognition   d. retrieval

2. In a study on context cues, people learned words while on land or when they were underwater. In a later test of recall, those with the best retention had

a. learned the words on land, that is, in the more familiar context.

b. learned the words underwater, that is, in the more exotic context.

c. learned the words and been tested on them in different contexts.

d. learned the words and been tested on them in the same context.

3. Which of the following measures of retention is the least sensitive in triggering retrieval?

a. recall   c. relearning
b. recognition   d. They are equally sensitive.

4. According to the serial position effect, when recalling a list of words you should have the greatest difficulty with those

a. at the beginning of the list.
b. at the end of the list.
c. at the end and in the middle of the list.
d. in the middle of the list.

5. Experimenters gave people a list of words to be recalled. When the participants were tested after a delay, the items that were best recalled were those

a. at the beginning of the list.
b. in the middle of the list.
c. at the end of the list.
d. at the beginning and the end of the list.

6. The process of getting information out of memory storage is called

a. encoding.   c. rehearsal.
b. retrieval.   d. storage.

Matching Items

Match each definition or description with the appropriate term.

Definitions or Descriptions

_____ 1. the phenomenon in which one's mood can influence retrieval

_____ 2. memory for a list of words is affected by word order

_____ 3. a measure of memory

Terms

a. relearning
b. serial position effect
c. mood-congruent memory

TERMS AND CONCEPTS TO REMEMBER

Using your own words, on a separate piece of paper write a brief definition or explanation of each of the following terms.

1. recall

2. recognition

3. relearning

4. priming

5. mood-congruent memory

6. serial position effect

ANSWERS
Module Review

Measures of Retention

1. recall; recognition

2. relearn; more

3. recall; recognize

4. relearn; more; overlearning; increasees

5. **d.** is the answer.
   a. & b. To correctly answer either type of question, the knowledge must have been encoded and stored.
   c. With fill-in-the-blank questions, the answer must be recalled with no retrieval cues other than the question. With multiple-choice questions, the correct answer merely has to be recognized from among several alternatives.

6. encode

7. priming

8. the same

9. state-dependent; mood-congruent

When happy, for example, we perceive things in a positive light and recall happy events; these perceptions and memories, in turn, prolong our good mood.

10. rejecting, punitive, and guilt-promoting; have never suffered depression

11. serial position effect

12. recency; better; primacy

13. **d.** is the answer.
    a. & b. A serial position effect would presumably occur whether the study and retrieval contexts were the same or different.
    c. As researchers found, when recall is delayed, only the first items in a list are recalled more accurately than the others. With immediate recall, both the first and last items are recalled more accurately.

14. **c.** is the answer. Susan's memories are affected by her bad mood.
    a. Priming refers to the conscious or unconscious activation of particular associations in memory.
    b. Priming is the activation of a web of associations in order to retrieve a memory.
    d. Shallow processing refers only to the idea that words are encoded on a basic level.

15. **a.** is the answer. Priming is the conscious or unconscious activation of particular associations in memory.
    b. Mnemonics are memory aids.
    c. That Martina is able to retrieve her former classmates' names implies that they already have been encoded.
    d. Relearning is a measure of retention based on how long it takes to relearn something already mastered. Martina is recalling her former classmates' names, not relearning them.

16. **b.** is the answer. Being back in the context in which the original experiences occurred triggered memories of these experiences.
    a. The memories were triggered by similarity of place, not mood.
    c. Implicit memories are procedural memories for automatic skills and classically conditioned associations.
    d. Echoic memory refers to momentary memory of auditory stimuli.

Progress Test

Multiple-Choice Questions

1. **d.** is the answer. Retrieval refers to the *process* of remembering.

2. **d.** is the answer. In general, being in a context similar to that in which you experienced something will tend to help you recall the experience.

a. & b. The learning environment per se—and its familiarity or exoticness—did not affect retention.

3. **a.** is the answer. A test of recall presents the fewest retrieval cues and usually produces the most limited retrieval.

4. **d.** is the answer. According to the serial position effect, items at the beginning and end of a list tend to be remembered best.

5. **a.** is the answer.
   b. In the serial position effect, the items in the middle of the list always show the *poorest* retention.
   c. & d. Delayed recall erases the memory facilitation for items at the end of the list.

6. **b.** is the answer.
   a. Encoding is the process of getting information *into* memory.
   c. Rehearsal is the conscious repetition of information in order to maintain it in memory.
   d. Storage is the maintenance of encoded material over time.

Matching Items

1. c
2. b
3. a

Terms and Concepts to Remember

1. **Recall** is a measure of memory in which the person must retrieve information learned earlier, with few retrieval cues.

2. **Recognition** is a measure of memory in which one need only identify, rather than recall, previously learned information.

3. **Relearning** is a measure of memory that assesses the amount of time saved when learning material again.

4. **Priming** is the activation, often unconsciously, of a web of associations in memory in order to retrieve a specific memory.

5. **Mood-congruent memory** is the tendency to recall experiences that are consistent with our current mood.

6. The **serial position effect** is the tendency for items at the beginning and end of a list to be more easily retained than those in the middle.

Forgetting, Memory Construction, and Improving Memory

MODULE OVERVIEW

Module 26 first explains how forgetting may result from failure to encode or store information or to find appropriate retrieval cues. The next section discusses the issue of memory construction. How "true" are our memories of events? A particularly controversial issue in this area involves suspicious claims of long-repressed memories of sexual abuse and other traumas that are "recovered" with the aid of hypnosis and other techniques.

This module also provides a number of helpful study hints, which form the basis for the SQ3R (survey, question, read, retrieve, review) study technique.

NOTE: Answer guidelines for all Module 26 questions begin on page 225.

MODULE REVIEW

First, skim this section, noting headings and boldface items. After you have read the section, review each objective by completing the sentences and answering the questions that follow it. In some cases, Study Tips explain how best to learn a difficult concept and Applications help you to know how well you understand the material. As you proceed, evaluate your performance by consulting the answers beginning on page 225. Do not continue with the next section until you understand each answer. If you need to, review or reread the section in the textbook before continuing.

Forgetting

Objective 26-1: Explain why we forget.

1. Without the ability to _____ , we would constantly be overwhelmed by information.

2. The disorder called _____ _____ involves an inability to form new memories. The disorder called _____ _____ involves an inability to retrieve old memories.

3. People who cannot form new memories can learn _____ _____ and can be _____ _____ . However, they have no _____ memory of having learned these things.

4. The first type of forgetting is caused by _____ failure. This type of forgetting occurs because some of the information that we sense never actually _____ .

5. One reason for age-related memory decline is that the brain areas responsible for _____ new information are _____ (more/less) responsive in older adults.

6. Studies by Hermann Ebbinghaus and by Harry Bahrick indicate that most forgetting occurs _____ (soon/a long time) after the material is learned.

7. This type of forgetting is known as _____ _____ , which may be caused by a gradual fading of the physical _____ _____ .

8. When information that is stored in memory temporarily cannot be found, _____ failure has occurred.

9. Research suggests that memories are also lost as a result of _____ , which is especially possible if we simultaneously learn similar, new material.

10. The disruptive effect of previous learning on current learning is called _____ _____ . The disruptive effect of learning new material on efforts to recall material previously learned is called _____ _____ .

11. John Jenkins and Karl Dallenbach found that if people went to sleep after learning, their memory for a list of nonsense syllables was _____ (better/worse) than it was if they stayed awake.

12. In some cases, old information facilitates our learning of new information. This is called _____ _____ .

13. Freud proposed that motivated forgetting, or _____ , may protect a person from painful memories.

14. Increasing numbers of memory researchers think that motivated forgetting is _____ (less/more) common than Freud believed.

When Do We Forget?

Sensory memory
The senses momentarily register amazing detail.

Working (short-term) memory
A few items are both noticed and encoded.

Long-term storage
Some items are altered or lost.

Retrieval from long-term memory
Depending on interference, retrieval cues, moods, and motives, some things get retrieved, some don't.

Information bits

APPLICATIONS:

15. At your high school reunion you cannot remember the last name of your homeroom teacher. Your failure to remember is most likely the result of _____ failure.

16. Which of the following sequences would be best to follow if you wanted to minimize interference-induced forgetting in order to improve your recall on the psychology midterm?
   a. study, eat, test
   b. study, sleep, test
   c. study, listen to music, test
   d. study, exercise, test

17. When Carlos was promoted, he moved into a new office with a new phone extension. Every time he is asked for his phone number, Carlos first thinks of his old extension, illustrating the effects of
   a. proactive interference.
   b. retroactive interference.
   c. encoding failure.
   d. storage failure.

18. Lewis cannot remember the details of the torture he experienced as a prisoner of war. According to Freud, Lewis' failure to remember these painful memories is an example of
   a. repression.
   b. retrieval failure.
   c. state-dependent memory.
   d. flashbulb memory.

19. After finding her old combination lock, Janice can't remember its combination because she keeps confusing it with the combination of her new lock. She is experiencing
   a. proactive interference.
   b. retroactive interference.
   c. encoding failure.
   d. storage failure.

Memory Construction Errors

Objective 26-2: Explain how misinformation, imagination, and source amnesia influence our memory construction, and describe how we decide whether a memory is real or false.

20. As memories are replayed, they are often modified. This process is called _____ .

21. When witnesses to an event receive misleading information about it, they may experience a _____ _____ and misremember the event. A number of

experiments have demonstrated that false memories _____ (can/cannot) be created when people are induced to imagine nonexistent events; that is, these people later experience _____ _____ . This occurs in part because visualizing something and actually perceiving it _____ .

Describe what Loftus' studies have shown about the effects of misleading postevent information.

22. At the heart of many false memories is _____ _____ , which occurs when we _____ an event to the wrong source. This phenomenon helps explain _____ _____ , which is the sense that a current situation has already been experienced.

23. Because memory is reconstruction as well as reproduction, we _____ (can/cannot) be sure whether a memory is real by how real it feels.

24. Memory construction explains why memories "refreshed" under _____ are often inaccurate.

APPLICATION

25. Which of the following illustrates the constructive nature of memory?
   a. Janice keeps calling her new boyfriend by her old boyfriend's name.
   b. After studying all afternoon and then getting drunk in the evening, Don can't remember the material he studied.
   c. After getting some good news, elated Kareem has a flood of good memories from his younger years.

   d. Although Mrs. Harvey, who has Alzheimer's disease, has many gaps in her memory, she invents sensible accounts of her activities so that her family will not worry.

Objective 26-3: Describe the reliability of young children's eyewitness descriptions, and discuss the controversy related to claims of repressed and recovered memories.

26. Whether a child produces an accurate eyewitness memory depends heavily on how he or she is _____ . Children are most accurate when it is a first interview with a _____ person who asks _____ questions.

27. Researchers increasingly agree that memories obtained under the influence of hypnosis or using other "memory work" techniques _____ (are/are not) reliable.

28. Memories of events that happened before age _____ are unreliable. As noted earlier, this phenomenon is called _____ .

Improving Memory

Objective 26-4: Describe how you can use memory research findings to do better in this and other courses.

29. The SQ3R study technique identifies five strategies for boosting memory: _____ , _____ , _____ , _____ , and _____ .

Discuss several specific strategies for improving memory.

PROGRESS TEST

Multiple-Choice Questions

Circle your answers to the following questions and check them with the answers beginning on page 226. If your answer is incorrect, read the explanation for why it is incorrect and then consult the text.

1. Research on memory construction reveals that memories
   a. are stored as exact copies of experience.
   b. reflect a person's biases and assumptions.
   c. may be chemically transferred from one organism to another.
   d. even if long term, usually decay within about five years.

2. The eerie feeling of having been somewhere before is an example of
   a. state dependency.   c. priming.
   b. encoding failure.   d. déjà vu.

3. Hypnotically "refreshed" memories may prove inaccurate—especially if the hypnotist asks leading questions—because of
   a. encoding failure.
   b. state-dependent memory.
   c. proactive interference.
   d. memory construction.

4. Which of the following best describes the typical forgetting curve?
   a. a steady, slow decline in retention over time
   b. a steady, rapid decline in retention over time
   c. a rapid initial decline in retention becoming stable thereafter
   d. a slow initial decline in retention becoming rapid thereafter

5. Jenkins and Dallenbach found that memory was better in people who were
   a. awake during the retention interval, presumably because decay was reduced.
   b. asleep during the retention interval, presumably because decay was reduced.
   c. awake during the retention interval, presumably because interference was reduced.
   d. asleep during the retention interval, presumably because interference was reduced.

6. Amnesia victims typically have experienced damage to the _____ of the brain.
   a. frontal lobes   c. thalamus
   b. cerebellum   d. hippocampus

7. Anterograde amnesia is the inability to
   a. retrieve old memories.
   b. remember where information came from.
   c. form new memories.
   d. hold more than 7 items in working memory.

8. Repression is an example of
   a. encoding failure.   c. motivated forgetting.
   b. memory decay.   d. all of these things.

9. Studies by Loftus and Palmer, in which people were quizzed about a film of an accident, indicate that
   a. when quizzed immediately, people can recall very little because of the stress of witnessing an accident.
   b. when questioned as little as one day later, their memory was very inaccurate.
   c. most people had very accurate memories as much as 6 months later.
   d. people's recall may easily be affected by misleading information.

10. Which of the following was NOT recommended as a strategy for improving memory?
    a. active rehearsal
    b. distributed study
    c. speed reading
    d. encoding meaningful associations

11. Amnesia patients typically experience disruption of
    a. implicit memories.   c. iconic memories.
    b. explicit memories.   d. echoic memories.

12. Memory researchers are suspicious of long-repressed memories of traumatic events that are "recovered" with the aid of drugs or hypnosis because
    a. such experiences usually are vividly remembered.
    b. such memories are unreliable and easily influenced by misinformation.
    c. memories of events happening before about age 3 are especially unreliable.
    d. of all of these reasons.

13. The misinformation effect provides evidence that memory
    a. is constructed during encoding.
    b. is unchanging once established.
    c. may be reconstructed during recall according to how questions are framed.
    d. is highly resistant to misleading information.

Matching Items

Match each definition or description with the appropriate term.

Definitions or Descriptions

_____ 1. the blocking of painful memories
_____ 2. new learning interferes with previous knowledge
_____ 3. old knowledge interferes with new learning
_____ 4. misattributing the origin of an event
_____ 5. inability to form new memories
_____ 6. inability to retrieve old memories

Terms

a. repression
b. anterograde amnesia
c. proactive interference
d. retroactive interference
e. source amnesia
f. retrograde amnesia

True–False Items

Indicate whether each statement is true or false by placing *T* or *F* in the blank next to the item.

_____ 1. Studying that is distributed over time produces better retention than cramming.
_____ 2. Preschool children can be induced to report false events through the use of suggestive interview techniques.
_____ 3. Most people do not have memories of events that occurred before the age of 3.
_____ 4. Studies by Ebbinghaus show that most forgetting takes place soon after learning.
_____ 5. The persistence of a memory is a good clue as to whether it derives from an actual experience.
_____ 6. Recall of newly acquired knowledge is no better after sleeping than after being awake for the same period of time.
_____ 7. Although repression has not been confirmed experimentally, most psychologists believe it happens.
_____ 8. Overlearning material by continuing to restudy it beyond mastery often disrupts recall.

Essay Question

Discuss the points of agreement among experts regarding the validity of recovered memories of child abuse. (Use the space below to list the points you want to make, and organize them. Then write the essay on a separate piece of paper.)

TERMS AND CONCEPTS TO REMEMBER

Using your own words, on a separate piece of paper write a brief definition or explanation of each of the following terms.

1. anterograde amnesia
2. retrograde amnesia
3. proactive interference
4. retroactive interference
5. repression
6. misinformation effect
7. source amnesia
8. déjà vu

ANSWERS
Module Review

Forgetting

1. forget
2. anterograde amnesia; retrograde amnesia
3. nonverbal tasks; classically conditioned; explicit
4. encoding; enters the memory system
5. encoding; less
6. soon
7. storage decay; memory trace
8. retrieval
9. interference
10. proactive interference; retroactive interference
11. better

12. positive transfer

13. repression

14. less

15. retrieval

16. **b.** is the answer.
    a., c., & d. Involvement in other activities, even just eating or listening to music, is more disruptive than sleeping.

17. **a.** is the answer. Proactive interference occurs when old information makes it difficult to recall new information.
    b. If Carlos were having trouble remembering the old extension, this answer would be correct.
    c. & d. Carlos has successfully encoded and stored the extension; he's just having problems retrieving it.

18. **a.** is the answer.
    b. Although Lewis' difficulty in recalling these memories could be considered retrieval failure, it is caused by repression, which is therefore the best explanation.
    c. This answer is incorrect because it is clear that Lewis fails to remember these experiences because they are painful memories and not because he is in a different emotional or physiological state.
    d. Flashbulb memories are especially vivid memories for emotionally significant events. Lewis has no memory at all.

19. **b.** is the answer. Retroactive interference is the disruption of something you once learned by new information.
    a. Proactive interference occurs when old information makes it difficult to correctly remember new information.
    c. & d. Interference produces forgetting even when the forgotten material was effectively encoded and stored. Janice's problem is at the level of retrieval.

Memory Construction Errors

20. reconsolidation

21. misinformation effect; can; imagination inflation; activate similar brain areas

When people viewed a film of a traffic accident and were quizzed a week later, phrasing of questions affected answers; the word "smashed," for instance, made viewers mistakenly think they had seen broken glass.

22. source amnesia; misattribute; déjà vu

23. cannot

24. hypnosis

25. **d.** is the answer.
    a. This is an example of proactive interference.
    b. This is an example of the disruptive effects of depressant drugs, such as alcohol, on the formation of new memories.
    c. This is mood-congruent memory.

26. questioned; neutral; nonleading

27. are not

28. 3; infantile amnesia

Improving Memory

29. Survey; Question; Read; Retrieve; Review

Suggestions for improving memory include rehearsing material over many separate and distributed study sessions with the objective of overlearning material. Studying should also involve making the material meaningful rather than mindlessly repeating information. Using mnemonic devices that incorporate vivid imagery is helpful, too. Frequent activation of retrieval cues, such as the context and mood in which the original learning occurred, can also help strengthen memory. Studying should also be arranged to minimize potential sources of interference. And, of course, sleep more, so the brain has a chance to organize and consolidate information. Finally, self-tests in the same format (recall or recognition) that will later be used on the actual test are useful.

Progress Test

Multiple-Choice Questions

1. **b.** is the answer. In essence, we construct our memories, bringing them into line with our biases and assumptions, as well as with our subsequent experiences.
   a. If this were true, it would mean that memory construction does not occur. Through memory construction, memories may deviate significantly from the original experiences.
   c. There is no evidence that such chemical transfers occur.
   d. Many long-term memories are apparently unlimited in duration.

2. **d.** is the answer.
   a. State-dependent memory is the phenomenon in which information is best retrieved when the

person is in the same emotional or physiological state he or she was in when the material was learned.

b. Encoding failure occurs when a person has not processed information sufficiently for it to enter the memory system.

c. Priming is the process by which a memory is activated through retrieval of an associated memory.

3. **d.** is the answer. It is in both encoding and retrieval that we construct our memories, and as Loftus' studies showed, leading questions affect people's memory construction.

a. The memory encoding occurred at the time of the event in question, not during questioning by the hypnotist.

b. State-dependent memory refers to the influence of one's own emotional or physiological state on encoding and retrieval, and would not apply here.

c. Proactive interference is the interfering effect of prior learning on the recall of new information.

4. **c.** is the answer. As Ebbinghaus and Bahrick both showed, most of the forgetting that is going to occur happens soon after learning.

5. **d.** is the answer.

a. & b. This study did not find evidence that memories fade (decay) with time.

c. When one is awake, there are many *more* potential sources of memory interference than when one is asleep.

6. **d.** is the answer.

7. **c.** is the answer.

a. This is retrograde amnesia.

b. This is source amnesia.

d. The capacity of working memory *averages 7* items.

8. **c.** is the answer. According to Freud, we repress painful memories to preserve our self-concepts.

a. & b. The fact that repressed memories can sometimes be retrieved suggests that they were encoded and have not decayed with time.

9. **d.** is the answer. When misled by the phrasings of questions, subjects incorrectly recalled details of the film and even "remembered" objects that weren't there.

10. **c.** is the answer. Speed reading, which entails little active rehearsal, yields poor retention.

11. **b.** is the answer. Amnesia patients typically have suffered damage to the hippocampus, a brain structure involved in processing explicit memories for facts.

a. Amnesia patients do retain implicit memories for how to do things; these are processed in the cerebellum.

c. & d. Amnesia patients generally do not experience impairment in their iconic and echoic sensory memories.

12. **d.** is the answer.

13. **c.** is the answer. Loftus and Palmer found that eyewitness testimony could easily be altered when questions were phrased to imply misleading information.

a. Although memories *are* constructed during encoding, the misinformation effect is a retrieval, rather than an encoding, phenomenon.

b. & d. In fact, just the opposite is true.

Matching Items

1.	a	**4.**	e
2.	d	**5.**	b
3.	c	**6.**	f

True–False Items

1.	T	**5.**	F
2.	T	**6.**	F
3.	T	**7.**	F
4.	T	**8.**	F

Essay Question

Experts agree that child abuse is a real problem that can have long-term adverse effects on individuals. They also acknowledge that forgetting of isolated events, both good and bad, is an ordinary part of life. Although experts all accept the fact that recovered memories are commonplace, they warn that memories "recovered" under hypnosis or with the use of drugs are unreliable, as are memories of events before age 3. Finally, they agree that memories can be traumatic, whether real or false.

Terms and Concepts to Remember

1. **Anterograde amnesia** is an inability to form new memories.

2. **Retrograde amnesia** is an inability to retrieve old memories.

3. **Proactive interference** is the disruptive effect of something you already have learned on your efforts to learn or recall new information.

4. **Retroactive interference** is the disruptive effect of new learning on the recall of old knowledge.

Memory aid: Retro means "backward." **Retroactive interference** is "backward-acting" interference.

5. **Repression** is an example of motivated forgetting in that anxiety-arousing thoughts, feelings, and memories are prevented from entering consciousness. In psychoanalytic theory, it is the basic defense mechanism.

6. The **misinformation effect** is the tendency of eyewitnesses to an event to incorporate misleading information into their memories of the event.

7. At the heart of many false memories, **source amnesia** refers to attributing an event to the wrong source. (Also called *source misattribution*.)

8. **Déjà vu** is the false sense that you have already experienced a current situation.

Thinking

MODULE OVERVIEW

Module 27 deals with thinking, with emphasis on how people logically—or at times illogically—use tools such as algorithms and heuristics when making decisions and solving problems. Also discussed are several common obstacles to problem solving, including fixations that prevent us from taking a fresh perspective on a problem and our bias to search for information that confirms rather than challenges existing hypotheses. The section also discusses the power and perils of intuition. It concludes with an exploration of animal cognitive skills.

NOTE: Answer guidelines for all Module 27 questions begin on page 234.

MODULE REVIEW

First, skim each section, noting headings and bold-face items. After you have read the section, review each objective by answering the fill-in and essay-type questions that follow it. In some cases, Study Tips explain how best to learn a difficult concept and Applications help you to know how well you understand the material. As you proceed, evaluate your performance by consulting the answers beginning on page 234. Do not continue with the next section until you understand each answer. If you need to, review or reread the section in the textbook before continuing.

Concepts

Objective 27-1: Define *cognition*, and describe the functions of concepts.

1. Cognition, or _____ , can be defined as _____
   _____ .

2. People tend to organize specific items into mental groupings called_____ .

3. Concepts are typically formed through the development of a best example, or
   _____ , of a category. People more easily detect _____
   (male/female) prejudice against
   _____ (males/females) than vice versa.

APPLICATION:

4. Complete the following analogy: Rose is to flower as
   a. concept is to prototype.
   b. prototype is to concept.
   c. concept is to cognition.
   d. cognition is to concept.

Problem Solving: Strategies and Obstacles

Objective 27-2: Describe the cognitive strategies that assist our problem solving, and identify the obstacles that hinder it.

5. Humans are especially capable of using their reasoning powers for coping with new situations, and thus for _____
   _____ .

6. When we try each possible solution to a problem, we are using _____
   _____ _____ .

7. Logical, methodical, step-by-step procedures for solving problems are called

_____ .

8. Simple thinking strategies that provide us with problem-solving shortcuts are referred to as

_____ .

9. When you suddenly realize a problem's solution, _____ has occurred. Research studies show that such moments are preceded by

_____ _____ activity involved in focusing attention and accompanied by a burst of activity in the _____

_____ _____ .

10. The tendency of people to look for information that supports their preconceptions is called

_____ _____ .

11. It is human nature to seek evidence that _____ our ideas more eagerly than to seek evidence that might _____ them.

12. Not being able to take a new perspective when attempting to solve a problem is referred to as _____ . One example of this obstacle to problem solving is the tendency to repeat solutions that have worked previously; this phenomenon is known as the development of a

_____ _____ .

STUDY TIP/APPLICATION: We all use any of four techniques for solving problems: trial and error, algorithms, heuristics, and insight. To test your understanding of these approaches, apply them to a problem you might actually face, such as finding a misplaced set of car keys. Using the chart below, see if you can come up with an example of how you could find your keys using each of the four problem-solving approaches.

13. Problem-Solving Approach	How You Would Find Car Keys Using Each Method
a. Trial and error	
b. Algorithm	
c. Heuristics	
d. Insight	

APPLICATIONS:

14. A dessert recipe that gives you the ingredients, their amounts, and the steps to follow is an example of a(n)

   a. prototype.   **c.** heuristic.
   b. algorithm.   **d.** mental set.

15. Boris the chess master selects his next move by considering moves that would threaten his opponent's queen. His opponent, a chess-playing computer, selects its next move by considering *all* possible moves. Boris is using a(n) _____ and the computer is using a(n) _____ .

   a. algorithm; heuristic
   b. prototype; mental set
   c. mental set; prototype
   d. heuristic; algorithm

16. Experts in a field prefer heuristics to algorithms because heuristics
    a. guarantee solutions to problems.
    b. prevent mental sets.
    c. often save time.
    d. prevent fixation.

Forming Good and Bad Decisions and Judgments

Objective 27-3: Explain what is meant by intuition, and describe how the availability heuristic, overconfidence, belief perseverance, and framing influence our decisions and judgments.

17. Effortless, immediate, and automatic feelings or thoughts characterize our _____ .

18. When we judge the likelihood of something occurring in terms of how readily it comes to mind, we are using the _____ _____ .

Explain how this heuristic may lead us to make judgmental errors.

19. (Thinking Critically) Many people fear _____ more than _____ , despite the fact that these fears are not supported by death and injury statistics. This type of faulty thinking occurs because we fear
    a. _____
    b. _____
    c. _____
    d. _____

20. The tendency of people to overestimate the accuracy of their knowledge results in _____ .

21. Overconfidence has _____ value because self-confident people tend to live _____ (more/less) happily, find it

_____ (easier/harder) to make tough decisions, and seem _____ (more/less) credible.

22. When research participants are given feedback on the accuracy of their judgments, such feedback generally _____ (does/does not) help them become more realistic about how much they know.

23. Research has shown that once we form a belief or a concept, it may take more convincing evidence for us to change the concept than it did to create it; this is because of _____ _____ .

24. A cure for this is to _____ _____ .

25. The way an issue is posed is called _____ . This effect influences political and business decisions, suggesting that our judgments _____ (may/may not) always be well reasoned.

APPLICATIONS:

26. During a televised political debate, the Republican and Democratic candidates each argued that the results of a recent public opinion poll supported their party's platform regarding sexual harassment. Because both candidates saw the information as supporting their belief, it is clear that both were victims of
    a. fixation.
    b. mental set.
    c. belief perseverance.
    d. confirmation bias.

27. In relation to ground beef, consumers respond more positively to an ad describing it as "75 percent lean" than to one referring to its "25 percent fat" content. This is an example of
    a. the framing effect.   c. mental set.
    b. confirmation bias.   d. overconfidence.

28. Most people tend to
    a. accurately estimate the accuracy of their knowledge and judgments.
    b. underestimate the accuracy of their knowledge and judgments.
    c. overestimate the accuracy of their knowledge and judgments.
    d. lack confidence in their decision-making strategies.

29. Dominic is certain that he will be able to finish reading the assigned text chapter over the weekend even though he also has to write a five-page essay on the U.S. political process and will be going to a party on Saturday night. If he's like most people, Dominic
    a. is accurate in knowing how much he can do over the weekend.
    b. underestimates how much he'll get done over the weekend.
    c. overestimates how much he can get done over the weekend.

30. Which of the following illustrates belief perseverance?
    a. Your belief remains intact even in the face of evidence to the contrary.
    b. You refuse to listen to arguments counter to your beliefs.
    c. You tend to become flustered and angered when your beliefs are refuted.
    d. You tend to search for information that supports your beliefs.

31. Marilyn was asked to solve a series of five math problems. The first four problems could only be solved by a particular sequence of operations. The fifth problem could also be solved following this sequence; however, a much simpler solution was possible. Marilyn did not realize this simpler solution and solved the problem in the way she had solved the first four. Her problem-solving strategy was hampered by
    a. fixation.
    b. the overconfidence phenomenon.
    c. mental set.
    d. her lack of a prototype for the solution.

32. Airline reservations typically decline after a highly publicized airplane crash because people overestimate the incidence of such disasters. In such instances, their decisions are being influenced by
    a. belief perseverance.
    b. the availability heuristic.
    c. the representativeness heuristic.
    d. fixation.

Objective 27-4: Describe how smart thinkers use intuition.

33. Researchers have shown that in making complex decisions, we benefit from using _____ (rational/intuitive) thinking. Although critics disagree, letting a problem "_____" while we attend to other things can pay dividends.

34. Another advantage of intuition is that it enables us to react quickly, which is _____ .

35. Finally, intuition is _____ knowledge, resulting from experience.

Do Other Species Share Our Cognitive Abilities?

Objective 27-5: Describe what is known about animal thinking.

36. Animals are capable of forming _____ . Wolfgang Köhler demonstrated that chimpanzees also exhibit the "Aha!" reaction that characterizes reasoning by _____ .

37. Forest-dwelling chimpanzees learn to use different sticks as _____ . These behaviors, along with behaviors related to grooming and courtship, _____ (vary/do not vary) from one group of chimpanzees to another, suggesting the transmission of _____ customs.

38. Animals _____ (do/do not) have many other cognitive skills. For example, chimpanzees have demonstrated _ _____ , _____ , and group aggression.

PROGRESS TEST

Multiple-Choice Questions

Circle your answers to the following questions and check them with the answers beginning on page 236. If your answer is incorrect, read the explanation for why it is incorrect and then consult the text.

1. The text defines *cognition* as
   a. silent speech.
   b. all mental activity.
   c. the mental activities associated with thinking, knowing, remembering, and communicating information.
   d. logical reasoning.

2. A mental grouping of similar things, events, or people is called a(n)
   a. prototype.   c. algorithm.
   b. concept.   d. heuristic.

3. When forming a concept, people often develop a best example, or _____ , of a category.
   a. denoter
   b. heuristic
   c. prototype
   d. algorithm

4. Confirmation bias refers to the tendency to
   a. allow preexisting beliefs to distort logical reasoning.
   b. cling to one's initial conceptions after the basis on which they were formed has been discredited.
   c. search randomly through alternative solutions when problem solving.
   d. look for information that is consistent with one's beliefs.

5. Mental set is an example of a(n)
   a. algorithm.
   b. heuristic.
   c. fixation.
   d. insight.

6. Thoughts and feelings that are automatic, effortless, immediate, and unreasoned are examples of
   a. mental set.
   b. confirmation bias.
   c. heuristics.
   d. intuition.

7. Which of the following is an example of the use of heuristics?
   a. trying every possible letter ordering when unscrambling a word
   b. considering each possible move when playing chess
   c. using the formula "area = length × width" to find the area of a rectangle
   d. playing chess using a defensive strategy that has often been successful for you

8. The chimpanzee Sultan used a short stick to pull a longer stick that was out of reach into his cage. He then used the longer stick to reach a piece of fruit. Researchers hypothesized that Sultan's discovery of the solution to his problem was the result of:
   a. trial and error.
   b. heuristics.
   c. fixation.
   d. insight.

9. Researchers who are convinced that animals can think point to evidence that
   a. chimpanzees demonstrate the ability to "count" by learning to touch pictures of objects in ascending numerical order.
   b. chimpanzees regularly use sticks as tools in their natural habitats.

   c. chimps invent grooming and courtship customs and pass them on to their peers.
   d. they exhibit all of these skills.

10. A common problem in everyday reasoning is our tendency to
    a. accept as logical those conclusions that agree with our own opinions.
    b. accept as logical those conclusions that disagree with our own opinions.
    c. underestimate the accuracy of our knowledge.
    d. accept as logical conclusions that involve unfamiliar concepts.

11. Availability an example of a(n)
    a. mental set.
    b. belief bias.
    c. algorithm.
    d. heuristic.

12. The basic units of cognition are
    a. algorithms.
    b. concepts.
    c. prototypes.
    d. heuristics.

13. Researchers who believe that some primates can read intent point to evidence that
    a. chimpanzees show more interest in a food container you have deliberately grasped.
    b. great apes have recognized themselves in a mirror.
    c. chimpanzees in the wild use sticks as tools.
    d. sheep can recognize and remember individual faces.

14. Assume that Congress is considering revising its approach to welfare and to this end is hearing a range of testimony. A member of Congress who uses the availability heuristic would be most likely to
    a. want to experiment with numerous possible approaches to see which of these seems to work best.
    b. want to cling to approaches to welfare that seem to have had some success in the past.
    c. refuse to be budged from his or her beliefs despite persuasive testimony to the contrary.
    d. base his or her ideas on the most vivid, memorable testimony given, even though many of the statistics presented run counter to this testimony.

15. If you want to be absolutely certain that you will find the solution to a problem you know *is* solvable, you should use
    a. a heuristic.
    b. an algorithm.
    c. insight.
    d. trial and error.

Matching Items

Match each definition or description with the appropriate term.

Definitions or Descriptions

_____ 1. the way an issue or question is posed

_____ 2. presuming that something is likely if it comes readily to mind

_____ 3. the tendency to overestimate the accuracy of one's judgments

_____ 4. being unable to see a problem from a different angle

_____ 5. haphazard problem solving by trying one solution after another

_____ 6. the sudden realization of the solution to a problem

_____ 7. the tendency to repeat problem-solving techniques that worked in the past even though a fresh approach may be more appropriate

Terms

a. mental set
b. trial and error
c. availability heuristic
d. insight
e. framing
f. overconfidence
g. fixation

True–False Items

Indicate whether each statement is true or false by placing *T* or *F* in the blank next to the item.

_____ 1. According to the confirmation bias, people often interpret ambiguous evidence as support for their beliefs.

_____ 2. Most human problem solving involves the use of heuristics rather than reasoning that systematically considers every possible solution.

_____ 3. When asked, most people underestimate the accuracy of their judgments.

_____ 4. Studies have shown that even animals may sometimes have insight reactions.

_____ 5. Mental set is the tendency to repeat problem-solving solutions that have worked in the past.

TERMS AND CONCEPTS TO REMEMBER

Using your own words, on a piece of paper write a brief definition or explanation of each of the following terms.

1. cognition

2. concept

3. prototype

4. algorithm

5. heuristic

6. insight

7. confirmation bias

8. mental set

9. intuition

10. availability heuristic

11. overconfidence

12. belief perseverance

13. framing

ANSWERS
Module Review

Concepts

1. thinking; the mental activities associated with thinking, knowing, remembering, and communicating

2. concepts

3. prototype; male; females

4. **b.** is the answer. A rose is a prototypical example of the concept *flower.*
   c. & d. The concept is *flower; cognition* refers to all the mental activities associated with thinking, knowing, remembering, and communicating information.

Problem Solving: Strategies and Obstacles

5. problem solving

6. trial and error

7. algorithms

8. heuristics

9. insight; frontal lobe; right temporal lobe

10. confirmation bias

11. verifies; refute

12. fixation; mental set

13. **a.** Trial and error: randomly looking everywhere in the house

    b. Algorithm: Methodically checking every possible location in the house as well as all the pockets in your clothes

    c. Heuristics: Thinking about the most logical place for you to have left your keys

    d. Insight: Suddenly realizing that you left your keys in the car when you took the groceries out

14. **b.** is the answer. Follow the directions precisely and you can't miss!
    a. A prototype is the best example of a concept.
    c. Heuristics are simple thinking strategies that help solve problems but, in contrast to a recipe that is followed precisely, do not guarantee success.
    d. A mental set is a tendency to approach a problem in a way that has been successful in the past.

15. **d.** is the answer.
    b. & c. If Boris always attacks his opponent's queen when playing chess, he is a victim of mental set; prototypes, however, have nothing to do with chess playing.

16. **c.** is the answer.
    a., b., & d. Heuristics do not guarantee solutions or prevent mental sets.

Forming Good and Bad Decisions and Judgments

17. intuition

18. availability heuristic

The availability heuristic leads us to estimate the likelihood of events based on how readily they come to mind. Thus, we are likely to think certain ethnic groups are more likely to be terrorists because of the vividness of the events of September 11, 2001.

19. flying; driving

    a. what our ancestral history has prepared us to fear.

    b. what we cannot control.

    c. what is immediate.

    d. what is most readily available in memory.

20. overconfidence

21. adaptive; more; easier; more

22. does

23. belief perseverance

24. consider the opposite

25. framing; may not

26. **d.** is the answer. The confirmation bias is the tendency to search for information that confirms one's preconceptions. In this example, the politicians' preconceptions are biasing their interpretation of the survey results.
    a. Fixation is the inability to see a problem from a fresh perspective
    b. Mental set is the tendency to approach a problem in a particular way. There is no problem per se in this example.
    c. Belief perseverance is the tendency to cling to one's beliefs despite evidence to the contrary.

27. **a.** is the answer. In this example, the way the issue is posed, or framed, has evidently influenced consumers' judgments.
    b. Confirmation bias is the tendency to search for information that confirms one's preconceptions.
    c. Mental set is the tendency to approach a problem in a particular way.
    d. Overconfidence is the tendency to be more confident than correct.

28. **c.** is the answer. This is referred to as overconfidence.

29. **c.** is the answer. Most people are more confident than correct in estimating their knowledge and the amount of time a task will take.

30. **a.** is the answer. Although b. and c. may be true, they do not describe belief perseverance. The d. answer is the confirmation bias.

31. **c.** is the answer. By simply following a strategy that has worked well in the past, Marilyn is hampered by the type of fixation called mental set.
    a. Fixation is the inability to see a problem from a fresh perspective.
    b. Overconfidence is exhibited by the person who overestimates the accuracy of his or her judgments.
    d. Prototypes are best examples of categories, not strategies for solving problems.

32. **b.** is the answer. The publicity surrounding disasters makes such events vivid and seemingly more probable than they actually are.
    a. Belief perseverance is the tendency to cling to one's beliefs despite evidence to the contrary.
    c. The representativeness heuristic operates when we judge the likelihood of things in terms of how

well they represent particular prototypes. This example does not involve such a situation.

d. Fixation is the inability to see a problem from a fresh perspective.

33. intuitive; incubate

34. adaptive

35. implicit

Do Other Species Share Our Cognitive Abilities

36. concepts; insight

37. tools; vary; culture

38. do; altruism; cooperation

Progress Test

Multiple-Choice Questions

1. **c.** is the answer.

2. **b.** is the answer.
   a. A prototype is the best example of a particular category, or concept.
   c. & d. Algorithms and heuristics are problem-solving strategies.

3. **c.** is the answer.
   a. There is no such thing as a "denoter."
   b. & d. Heuristics and algorithms are problem-solving strategies.

4. **d.** is the answer. It is a major obstacle to problem solving.
   a. & b. These refer to belief bias and belief perseverance, respectively.
   c. This is trial-and-error problem solving.

5. **c.** is the answer. Both involve failing to see a problem from a new perspective.
   a. & b. Algorithms and heuristics are problem-solving strategies.
   d. Insight is the sudden realization of a problem's solution.

6. **d.** is the answer.
   a. Mental set is the tendency to approach a problem in a particular way that worked previously.
   b. Confirmation bias is the tendency to search for information that supports our preconceptions.
   c. Heuristics are simple thinking strategies that are based on past successes in similar situations.

7. **d.** is the answer. Heuristics are simple thinking strategies—such as playing chess defensively—that are based on past successes in similar situations.
   a., b., & c. These are all algorithms.

8. **d.** is the answer. Sultan suddenly arrived at a

novel solution to his problem, thus displaying apparent insight.
   a. Sultan did not randomly try various strategies of reaching the fruit; he demonstrated the "light bulb" reaction that is the hallmark of insight.
   b. Heuristics are simple thinking strategies.
   c. Fixation is an impediment to problem solving. Sultan obviously solved his problem.

9. **d.** is the answer.

10. **a.** is the answer. Reasoning in daily life is often distorted by our beliefs, which may lead us, for example, to accept conclusions that haven't been arrived at logically.
    b., c., & d. These are just the opposite of what we tend to do.

11. **d.** is the answer. This is a simple thinking strategy that allows us to make quick judgments.
    a. Mental sets are obstacles to problem solving, in which the person tends to repeat solutions that have worked in the past and is unable to conceive of other possible solutions.
    b. Belief perseverance is the tendency to cling to a belief even after the information that led to the formation of the belief is discredited.
    c. Algorithms are methodical strategies that guarantee a solution to a particular problem.

12. **b.** is the answer.
    a. & d. Algorithms and heuristics are problem-solving strategies.

13. **a.** is the answer.
    b., c., & d. Self-awareness and tool use are clear indicators of animal thinking. However, they reveal nothing about the ability to read intent in another. Facial recognition also doesn't reveal an ability to read intent.

14. **d.** is the answer. If we use the availability heuristic, we base judgments on the availability of information in our memories, and more vivid information is often the most readily available.
    a. This would exemplify use of the trial-and-error approach to problem solving.
    b. This would exemplify a mental set.
    c. This would exemplify belief perseverance.

15. **b.** is the answer. Because they involve the systematic examination of all possible solutions to a problem, algorithms guarantee that a solution will be found.
    a., c., & d. None of these methods guarantees that a problem's solution will be found.

Matching Items

1. e   4. g   7. a
2. c   5. b
3. f   6. d

True–False Items

1. T   4. T
2. T   5. T
3. F

Terms and Concepts to Remember

1. **Cognition** refers to all the mental activities associated with thinking, knowing, remembering, and communicating information.

2. A **concept** is a mental grouping of similar objects, events, ideas, or people.

3. A **prototype** is a mental image or best example of a particular category.

4. An **algorithm** is a methodical, logical rule or procedure that, while sometimes slow, guarantees success.

5. A **heuristic** is a simple thinking strategy that often allows us to make judgments and solve problems efficiently. Although heuristics are more efficient than algorithms, they do not guarantee success and sometimes even impede problem solving.

6. **Insight** is a sudden and often novel realization of the solution to a problem. Insight contrasts with trial and error and, indeed, may often follow an unsuccessful episode of trial and error.

7. The **confirmation bias** is an obstacle to problem solving in which people tend to search for information that supports their preconceptions.

8. **Mental set** refers to the tendency to continue applying a particular problem-solving strategy even when it is no longer helpful.

9. **Intuition** is an immediate, automatic, and effortless feeling or thought.

10. The **availability heuristic** is based on estimating the probability of certain events in terms of how readily they come to mind.

11. Another obstacle to problem solving, **overconfidence** refers to the tendency to overestimate the accuracy of our beliefs and judgments.

12. **Belief perseverance** is the tendency for people to cling to a particular belief even after the information that led to the formation of the belief is discredited.

13. **Framing** refers to the way an issue or question is posed. It can affect people's perception of the issue or answer to the question.

Language and Thought

MODULE OVERVIEW

The first section of Module 28 is concerned with language, including its structure and development in children, and use by animals. Chomsky's theory that humans have a biological predisposition to acquire language introduces the section on language development. The section also describes the brain's role in language processing and speech. The module concludes with a discussion of the relationship between language and thinking.

NOTE: Answer guidelines for all Module 28 questions begin on page 245.

MODULE REVIEW

First, skim each section, noting headings and bold-face items. After you have read the section, review each objective by answering the fill-in and essay-type questions that follow it. In some cases, Study Tips explain how best to learn a difficult concept and Applications help you to know how well you understand the material. As you proceed, evaluate your performance by consulting the answers beginning on page 245. Do not continue with the next section until you understand each answer. If you need to, review or reread the section in the textbook before continuing.

Language Structure

Objective 28-1: Describe the structural components of language.

1. Language is defined as _____ _____ .

2. The basic sound units of language are its _____ . English has approximately _____ of these units.

3. Phonemes are grouped into units of meaning called _____ .

4. The system of rules that enables us to use our language to speak to and understand others is called _____ .

APPLICATIONS:

5. The word "predates" contains _____ phonemes and _____ morphemes.
   a. 7; 3   c. 7; 2
   b. 3; 7   d. 3; 2

6. The sentence "Blue jeans wear false smiles" has correct _____ but incorrect _____ .
   a. morphemes; phonemes
   b. phonemes; morphemes
   c. semantics; syntax
   d. syntax; semantics

Language Development

Objective 28-2: Identify the milestones in language development.

7. By _____ months of age, babies can read lips and discriminate speech sounds. This marks the beginning of their _____ _____ , their ability to comprehend speech. This ability begins to mature before their _____ _____ , or ability to produce words.

8. The first stage of language development, in which children spontaneously utter different sounds, is the _____ stage. This stage typically begins at about _____ months of age. The sounds children make

239

during this stage _____ (do/do not) include only the sounds of the language they hear.

9. Deaf infants _____ (do/do not) babble. Many natural babbling sounds are _____-_____ pairs formed by _____ _____ .

10. By about _____ months of age, infant babbling begins to resemble the household language. At about the same time, the ability to perceive speech sounds outside their native language is _____ (lost/acquired).

11. During the second stage, called the _____-_____ stage, children convey complete thoughts using single words. This stage begins at about _____ year(s) of age.

12. During the _____-_____ stage, children speak in sentences containing mostly nouns and verbs. This type of speech is called _____ speech. It _____ (does/does not) follow the rules of syntax.

APPLICATIONS:

13. A listener hearing a recording of Japanese, Spanish, and North American children babbling would
    a. not be able to tell them apart.
    b. be able to tell them apart if they were older than 6 months.
    c. be able to tell them apart if they were older than 8 to 10 months.
    d. be able to tell them apart at any age.

14. The child who says "Milk gone" is engaging in _____ . This type of utterance demonstrates that children are actively experimenting with the rules of _____ .
    a. babbling; syntax
    b. telegraphic speech; syntax
    c. babbling; semantics
    d. telegraphic speech; semantics

Objective 28-3: Describe how we acquire language.

15. According to linguist _____ , all human languages have the same grammatical building blocks, which suggests that there is a _____ _____ .

16. Research has demonstrated that human infants are able to discern _____ _____ and to _____ analyze which syllables most often go together.

17. Research studies of infants' knack for soaking up language suggest that babies come with a built-in readiness to learn _____ _____ .

18. Childhood seems to represent a _____ _____ for mastering certain aspects of language. Those who learn a second language as adults usually speak it with the _____ of their first language. Moreover, they typically show _____ (poorer/better) mastery of the _____ of the second language.

19. The window for learning language gradually begins to close after age _____ . When a young brain doesn't learn any language, its language-learning capacity _____ (never/may still) fully develop(s).

20. People who learn sign language as teens or adults _____ (eventually do/do not) learn to sign as fluently as those who learned sign as infants.

21. Some deaf children receive _____ _____ that convert sounds into electrical signals which stimulate the _____ _____ .

22. People who lose one channel of sensation _____ (do/do not) seem to compensate with an enhancement of other sensory abilities.

APPLICATION:

23. In preparing her class presentation, "Updating Chomsky's Understanding of Language Development," Britney's outline includes all of the following evidence, EXCEPT that
    a. computers programmed to learn to form the past tense of irregular verbs can learn to do so, even without "inborn" linguistic rules.
    b. infants rapidly learn to detect subtle differences between simple sequences of syllables.
    c. infants can recognize color differences even before they can name different colors.
    d. children isolated from language during the first seven years of life never fully develop language.

The Brain and Language

Objective 28-4: Identify the brain areas involved in language processing and speech.

24. Brain injuries may produce an impairment in language use called
_____ . Studies of people with such impairments have shown that
(a) _____ _____ is involved in producing speech and (b) _____ _____ is involved in understanding speech.

**(a)
Speaking words
(_____ and
the motor cortex)**

25. Although our conscious experience of language seems indivisible, functional MRI scans show that different _____ are activated by nouns and verbs, or objects and actions, for example.

**(b)
Hearing words
(auditory cortex and
_____)**

26. As in other forms of information processing, the brain operates by dividing its mental functions into _____ .

APPLICATION:

27. In a soccer game, Laura suffered damage to her left temporal lobe. As a result, she is unable to speak in meaningful sentences. The damage affected
   a. Wernicke's area.
   b. Broca's area.
   c. the hypothalamus.
   d. the hippocampus.

Do Other Species Have Language?

Objective 28-5: Discuss whether other species share our capacity for language.

28. Animals definitely _____ (do/do not) communicate.

29. The Gardners attempted to communicate with the chimpanzee Washoe by teaching her
_____ _____ .

30. Most now agree that humans _____ (alone/along with primates) possess language that involves complex grammar.

Summarize some of the arguments of skeptics of the "talking apes" research and some responses of believers.

Thinking and Language

Objective 28-6: Describe the relationship between language and thinking, and discuss the value of thinking in images.

31. According to the _____ _____ hypothesis, language shapes our thinking. The linguist who proposed this hypothesis is _____ .

32. Although this hypothesis is too extreme, many people who are bilingual report feeling a different sense of _____ , depending on which language they are using.

33. In several studies, researchers have found that using the pronoun "he" (instead of "he or she") _____ (does/does not) influence people's thoughts concerning gender.

34. Bilingual children, who learn to inhibit one language while using their other language, are better able to inhibit their _____ to irrelevant information. This has been called the
_____ _____ .

35. One study of Canadian children found that English-speaking children who were _____ in French had higher _____ scores and math scores than control children.

36. It appears that thinking _____ (can/cannot) occur without the use of language. Thinking in terms of mental pictures is called
_____ _____ .

Athletes often supplement physical training with _____ practice.

37. In one study of psychology students preparing for a midterm exam, the greatest benefits were achieved by those who visualized themselves _____ (receiving a high grade/ studying effectively).

Summarize the probable relationship between thinking and language.

APPLICATION:

38. Luke is the backup quarterback for his high school football team. The starting quarterback has been injured, so Luke will play on Saturday. In addition to physical practice, Luke should visualize throwing the ball, a process called

_____ _____ ,

rather than seeing a touchdown noted on the scoreboard, called _____

_____ .

PROGRESS TEST

Multiple-Choice Questions

Circle your answers to the following questions and check them with the answers beginning on page 246. If your answer is incorrect, read the explanation for why it is incorrect and then consult the text.

1. The English language has approximately _____ phonemes.
   - **a.** 25
   - **b.** 30
   - **c.** 40
   - **d.** 45

2. Which of the following is NOT true of babbling?
   - **a.** It is imitation of adult speech.
   - **b.** It is the same in all cultures.
   - **c.** It typically occurs from about age 4 months to 1 year.
   - **d.** Babbling increasingly comes to resemble a particular language.

3. Which of the following has been argued by critics of ape language research?
   - **a.** Ape language is merely imitation of the trainer's behavior.
   - **b.** There is little evidence that apes can equal even a 3-year-old's ability to order words with proper syntax.
   - **c.** By seeing what they wish to see, trainers attribute greater linguistic ability to apes than actually exists.
   - **d.** All of these are arguments by critics.

4. Whorf's linguistic determinism hypothesis states that
   - **a.** language is primarily a learned ability.
   - **b.** language is partially an innate ability.
   - **c.** the size of a person's vocabulary reflects his or her intelligence.
   - **d.** our language shapes our thinking.

5. Which of the following BEST describes Chomsky's view of language development?
   - **a.** Language is an entirely learned ability.
   - **b.** Language is an innate ability.
   - **c.** Humans have a biological predisposition to acquire language.
   - **d.** There are no cultural influences on the development of language.

6. Damage to _____ will usually cause a person to lose the ability to comprehend language.
   - **a.** any area of the brain
   - **b.** Broca's area
   - **c.** Wernicke's area
   - **d.** frontal lobe association areas

7. Deaf children who are not exposed to sign language until they are teenagers
   - **a.** are unable to master the basic words of sign language.
   - **b.** learn the basic words but not how to order them.
   - **c.** are unable to master either the basic words or syntax of sign language.
   - **d.** never become as fluent as those who learned to sign at a younger age.

8. According to the text, language acquisition is best described as
   - **a.** the result of conditioning and reinforcement.
   - **b.** a biological process of maturation.
   - **c.** an interaction between biology and experience.
   - **d.** a mystery of which researchers have no real understanding.

9. Human infants display a remarkable ability to learn statistical aspects of speech. Specifically, research studies have shown that they
   a. are quickly able to recognize syllable sequences that appear repeatedly.
   b. respond to changes in the pitch of a speaker's voice.
   c. pay less attention to a same-gender voice.
   d. do all of these things.

10. The linguistic determinism hypothesis is challenged by the finding that
   a. chimps can learn to communicate spontaneously by using sign language.
   b. people with no word for a certain color can still perceive that color accurately.
   c. the Eskimo language contains a number of words for snow, whereas English has only one.
   d. infants' babbling contains many phonemes that do not occur in their own language and that they therefore cannot have heard.

11. Several studies have indicated that the generic pronoun "he"
   a. tends for children and adults alike to trigger images of both males and females.
   b. tends for adults to trigger images of both males and females, but for children to trigger images of males.
   c. tends for both children and adults to trigger images of males but not females.
   d. for both children and adults triggers images of females about one-fourth of the time it is used.

12. Phonemes are the basic units of _____ in language.
   a. sound   c. grammar
   b. meaning   d. semantics

13. Syntax refers to the
   a. sounds in a word.
   b. rules for ordering words into sentences.
   c. rules by which meaning is derived from sentences.
   d. overall rules of a language.

14. Our ability to learn a new language
   a. diminishes with age.
   b. is limited by a sharply defined critical period.
   c. remains constant throughout our lives.
   d. depends on the language.

15. Many psychologists are skeptical of claims that chimpanzees can acquire language because the chimps have not shown the ability to
   a. use symbols meaningfully.
   b. acquire speech.
   c. acquire even a limited vocabulary.
   d. use syntax in communicating.

16. Complete the following: -ed is to sh as _____ is to _____.
   a. phoneme; morpheme   c. grammar; syntax
   b. morpheme; phoneme   d. syntax; grammar

17. Which of the following is cited by Chomsky as evidence that humans are born with a predisposition to learn language?
   a. Children master the complicated rules of grammar with ease.
   b. Different languages do not have the same grammatical building blocks.
   c. Children make unpredictable mistakes as they acquire grammar.
   d. Children raised in isolation from language spontaneously begin speaking words.

18. Telegraphic speech is typical of the _____ stage.
   a. babbling   c. two-word
   b. one-word   d. three-word

19. Children first demonstrate a rudimentary understanding of syntax during the _____ stage.
   a. babbling   c. two-word
   b. one-word   d. three-word

20. The study in which people who immigrated to the United States at various ages were compared in terms of their ability to understand English grammar found that
   a. age of arrival had no effect on mastery of grammar.
   b. those who immigrated as children understood grammar as well as native speakers.
   c. those who immigrated as adults understood grammar as well as native speakers.
   d. whether English was spoken in the home was the most important factor in mastering the rules of grammar.

21. Researchers taught the chimpanzee Washoe and the gorilla Koko to communicate by using
   a. various sounds.
   b. plastic symbols of various shapes and colors.
   c. sign language.
   d. all of these methods.

22. Regarding the relationship between thinking and language, which of the following most accurately reflects the position taken in the text?
    a. Language determines everything about our thinking.
    b. Language determines the way we think.
    c. Thinking without language is not possible.
    d. Thinking affects our language, which then affects our thought.

23. The bilingual advantage refers to the fact that people who are fluent in two languages are better at
    a. inhibiting their attention to irrelevant information.
    b. acquiring large vocabularies in both languages.
    c. thinking in images.
    d. all of these abilities.

24. Which of the following is true regarding the relationship between thinking and language?
    a. "Real" thinking requires the use of language.
    b. People sometimes think in images rather than in words.

c. A thought that cannot be expressed in a particular language cannot occur to speakers of that language.
    d. All of these statements are true.

25. One reason an English-speaking adult may have difficulty pronouncing Russian words is that
    a. the vocal tracts of English- and Russian-speaking people develop differently in response to the demands of the two languages.
    b. although English and Russian have very similar morphemes, their phonemic inventories are very different.
    c. although English and Russian have very similar phonemes, their morphemic inventories are very different.
    d. after the babbling stage, a child who hears only English stops uttering other phonemes.

Matching Items

Match each definition or description with the appropriate term.

Definitions or Descriptions

_____ 1. the basic units of sound in a language
_____ 2. rules for combining words into sentences
_____ 3. the rules by which meaning is derived from sounds
_____ 4. the basic units of meaning in a language
_____ 5. controls speech production
_____ 6. responsible for language comprehension
_____ 7. language disorder

Terms

a. syntax
b. morphemes
c. phonemes
d. semantics
e. aphasia
f. Broca's area
g. Wernicke's area

True–False Items

Indicate whether each statement is true or false by placing *T* or *F* in the blank next to the item.

_____ 1. The order in which children acquire an understanding of various morphemes is unpredictable.
_____ 2. Although the morphemes differ from language to language, the phonemes for all languages are the same.

_____ 3. Children of all cultures babble using the same phonemes.
_____ 4. Thinking without using language is not possible.
_____ 5. Most researchers believe that we can perform statistical analyses of language throughout our lives.

Essay Question

The lectures of your linguistics professor, who happens to be a staunch behaviorist, clearly imply that she believes language development can be explained according to principles of conditioning. What evidence should you present to convince her that she is wrong? (Use the space below to list the points you want to make, and organize them. Then write the essay on a separate piece of paper.)

TERMS AND CONCEPTS TO REMEMBER

Using your own words, on a piece of paper write a brief definition or explanation of each of the following terms.

1. language

2. phoneme

3. morpheme

4. grammar

5. babbling stage

6. one-word stage

7. two-word stage

8. telegraphic speech

9. aphasia

10. Broca's area

11. Wernicke's area

12. linguistic determinism

ANSWERS
Module Review
Language Structure

1. our spoken, written, or signed words and the ways we combine them to communicate meaning.

2. phonemes; 40

3. morphemes

4. grammar

5. **a.** is the answer. Each sound of the word is a phoneme (note that the second letter "e" does not itself represent a sound); the morphemes are "pre," which means before; "date"; and "s," which indicates the plural.

6. **d.** is the answer. This sentence, although semantically meaningless, nevertheless follows the grammatical rules of English syntax for combining words into sentences.

   a. & b. The phonemes (smallest units of sound) and morphemes (smallest units of meaning) of this sentence are equally correct.

Language Development

7. 4; receptive language; productive language

8. babbling; 4; do not

9. do; consonant-vowel; bunching the tongue in the front of the mouth

10. 10; lost

11. one-word; 1

12. two-word; telegraphic; does

13. **a.** is the answer.

14. **b.** is the answer. Such utterances, characteristic of a child of about 2 years, are like telegrams, in that they consist mainly of nouns and verbs and show use of syntax.

   a. & c. Babbling consists of phonemes, not words.

   d. Semantics refers to the rules by which meaning is derived from sounds; this speech example indicates nothing in particular about the child's understanding of semantics.

15. Noam Chomsky; universal grammar

16. word breaks; statistically

17. grammatical rules

18. critical period; accent; poorer; grammar

19. 7; never

20. do not

21. cochlear implants; auditory nerve

22. do

23. **c.** is the answer. This fact challenges the linguistic determinism hypothesis; it neither supports nor refutes Chomsky's concept of an inborn universal grammar.

The Brain and Language

24. aphasia; Broca's area; Wernicke's area

25. neural networks

26. subfunctions

27. **a.** is the answer.

   b. Broca's area is involved in speech production.

   c. & d. The hypothalamus and the hippocampus have nothing to do with language.

28. do

29. sign language

30. alone

Chimps have acquired only limited vocabularies and—in contrast to children—have acquired these vocabularies only with great difficulty. Also in contrast to children, it's unclear that chimps can use syntax to express meaning. The signing of chimps is often nothing more than imitation of the trainer's actions. People tend to interpret such ambiguous behavior in terms of what they want to see. Believers contend that although animals do not have our facility for language, they have the abilities to communicate. For example, Washoe and Loulis sign spontaneously. Also, pygmy chimps can learn to comprehend the nuances of spoken English.

Thinking and Language

31. linguistic determinism; Benjamin Whorf

32. self

33. does

34. attention; bilingual advantage

35. immersed; aptitude

36. can; nondeclarative (procedural) memory; mental

37. studying effectively

The relationship is probably a two-way one: the linguistic determinism hypothesis suggests that language helps shape thought; that words come into the language to express new ideas indicates that thought also shapes language.

38. process simulation; outcome simulation. Process simulation produces better results than outcome simulation because imagining the procedure activates the brain areas involved in actually performing the activity.

Progress Test

Multiple-Choice Questions

1. **c.** is the answer.

2. **a.** is the answer. Babbling is not the imitation of adult speech since babbling infants produce phonemes from languages they have not heard and could not be imitating.

3. **d.** is the answer.

4. **d.** is the answer.
   a. This is Skinner's position regarding language development.
   b. This is Chomsky's position regarding language development.
   c. The linguistic determinism hypothesis is concerned with the content of thought, not intelligence.

5. **c.** is the answer.
   a. This is Skinner's position.
   b. According to Chomsky, although the *ability* to acquire language is innate, the child can only acquire language in association with others.
   d. Cultural influences are an important example of the influence of learning on language development, an influence Chomsky fully accepts.

6. **c.** is the answer.
   b. Broca's area is involved in speech production.
   d. The association areas are involved in higher-order activities such as planning.

7. **d.** is the answer. Compared with deaf children exposed to sign language from birth, those who learn to sign as teens have the same grammatical difficulties as do hearing adults trying to learn a second spoken language.

8. **c.** is the answer. Children are biologically prepared to learn language as they and their caregivers interact.
   a. This would be the view of a behaviorist.
   b. No psychologist, including Chomsky, believes that language is entirely a product of biological maturation.
   d. Although language acquisition is not completely understood, research has shed sufficient light on it to render it less than a complete mystery.

9. **a.** is the answer.
   b. & c. This research is unrelated to infants' ability to detect different pitches of voices or distinguish between male and female voices.

10. **b.** is the answer. The evidence that absence of a term for a color does not affect ability to perceive the color challenges the idea that language always shapes thought.

a. & d. These findings are not relevant to the linguistic determinism hypothesis, which addresses the relationship between language and thought.

c. This finding is in keeping with the linguistic determinism hypothesis.

11. **c.** is the answer. The generic pronoun *he* evidently tends, for both adults and children, to conjure up images of males.

12. **a.** is the answer.

b. Morphemes are the basic units of meaning.

c. & d. The text does not refer to basic units of grammar or semantics.

13. **b.** is the answer.

a. Phonemes are the sounds in a word.

c. Such rules are known as semantics.

d. Such rules are the language's grammar, which would include its syntax as well as its semantics.

14. **a.** is the answer.

15. **d.** is the answer. Syntax is one of the fundamental aspects of language, and chimps seem unable, for example, to use word order to convey differences in meaning.

a. & c. Chimps' use of sign language demonstrates both the use of symbols and the acquisition of fairly sizable vocabularies.

b. No psychologist would require the use of speech as evidence of language; significantly, all the research and arguments focus on what chimps are and are not able to do in acquiring other facets of language.

16. **b.** is the answer. The morpheme *-ed* changes the *meaning* of a regular verb to form its past tense; the phoneme *sh* is a unique *sound* in the English language.

c. & d. Syntax, which specifies rules for combining words into grammatical sentences, is one aspect of the grammar of a language.

17. **a.** is the answer.

18. **c.** is the answer.

19. **c.** is the answer. Although the child's utterances are only two words long, the words are placed in a sensible order. In English, for example, adjectives are placed before nouns.

a. & b. Syntax specifies rules for *combining* two or more units in speech.

d. There is no three-word stage.

20. **b.** is the answer.

21. **c.** is the answer.

22. **d.** is the answer.

23. **a.** is the answer.

24. **b.** is the answer.

a. Researchers do not make a distinction between "real" and other thinking, nor do they consider nonlinguistic thinking less valid than linguistic thinking.

c. As indicated by several studies cited in the text, this is not true.

25. **d.** is the answer. Following the babbling stage, the child's ability to produce all phonemes becomes in a sense shaped and limited to the ability to produce those phonemes he or she hears.

a. The vocal tract of *Homo sapiens* does not develop in specialized ways for different languages.

b. & c. English and Russian differ significantly in both their phonemes and their morphemes. Nor is there any reason why differences in morphemes would in and of themselves cause pronunciation difficulties.

Matching Items

1. c	4. b	7. e
2. a	5. f	
3. d	6. g	

True–False Items

1. F	4. F
2. F	5. F
3. T	

Essay Question

You should point out that the rate at which children acquire words and grammar is too extraordinary to be explained solely according to principles of learning. Children also utter all sorts of word forms they have never heard and could not, therefore, be imitating. Furthermore, children begin using morphemes in a predictable order, which learning theorists would not expect since each child experiences a unique linguistic environment. It therefore seems clear that children are biologically prepared to acquire language and that the behaviorist position is incorrect.

Terms and Concepts to Remember

1. **Language** refers to spoken, written, or signed words and how we combine them to communicate meaning.

2. **Phonemes** are the smallest units of sound in a language that are distinctive for speakers of the language.

3. **Morphemes** are the smallest units of language that carry meaning.

Example: The word "dogs," which contains four phonemes, contains only two **morphemes**—"dog" and "-s." Although most morphemes are combinations of two or more phonemes, the plural "-s" conveys a distinctive meaning of "more than one."

4. **Grammar** is a system of rules that enables us to communicate with and understand others.

5. The **babbling stage** of speech development, which begins around 4 months, is characterized by the spontaneous utterance of speech sounds. During the babbling stage, children the world over sound alike.

6. Between 1 and 2 years of age, children speak mostly in single words; they are therefore in the **one-word stage** of linguistic development.

7. Beginning about age 2, children are in the **two-word stage** and speak mostly in two-word sentences.

8. **Telegraphic speech** is the economical, telegram-like speech of children in the two-word stage. Utterances consist mostly of nouns and verbs; however, words occur in the correct order, showing that the child has learned some of the language's syntactic rules.

9. **Aphasia** is an impairment of language, usually caused by left-hemisphere damage either to Broca's area or to Wernicke's area.

10. **Broca's area,** located in the left frontal lobe, is involved in controlling the motor ability to produce speech.

11. **Wernicke's area,** located in the left temporal lobe, is involved in language comprehension and expression.

12. **Linguistic determinism** is Benjamin Whorf's hypothesis that language determines the way we think.

Introduction to Intelligence

MODULE OVERVIEW

An enduring controversy in psychology involves attempts to define and measure intelligence. Module 29 discusses whether intelligence is a single general ability or several specific ones, as well as research that attempts to assess the neurological basis of intelligence.

NOTE: Answer guidelines for all Module 29 questions begin on page 253.

MODULE REVIEW

First, skim each section, noting headings and bold-face items. After you have read the section, review each objective by answering the fill-in and essay-type questions that follow it. In some cases, Study Tips explain how best to learn a difficult concept and Applications help you to know how well you understand the material. As you proceed, evaluate your performance by consulting the answers beginning on page 253. Do not continue with the next section until you understand each answer. If you need to, review or reread the section in the textbook before continuing.

Introducing Intelligence

Objective 29-1: Discuss the difficulty of defining *intelligence*.

1. Psychologists _____ (do/do not) agree on a definition of intelligence.

2. Psychologists agree that intelligence is a _____ and not a "thing." It has been defined as whatever _____ _____ measure, but that _____ (does/does not) take into account the different qualities that enable success in different cultures.

3. In any context, intelligence can be defined as _____ _____ .

4. An intelligence test assesses _____ _____ .

Is Intelligence One General Ability or Several Specific Abilities?

Objective 29-2: Present arguments for and against considering intelligence as one general mental ability.

5. One controversy regarding the nature of intelligence centers on whether intelligence is one _____ ability or several _____ abilities.

6. The statistical procedure used to identify clusters of items that appear to measure a common ability is called _____ _____ .

7. Charles Spearman, one of the developers of this technique, believed that a factor called *g*, or _____ _____ , runs through the more specific aspects of intelligence.

8. Opposing Spearman, _____ identified seven clusters of _____ _____ .

9. Satoshi Kanazawa believes that general intelligence evolved as a means of helping people solve _____ _____ .

Objective 29-3: Compare Gardner's and Sternberg's theories of intelligence.

10. People with _____ _____ score at the low end of intelligence tests but possess extraordinary specific skills.

11. Howard Gardner proposes that there are

_____ _____ , each independent of the others. However, critics point out that the world is not so just: General intelligence scores _ _____ (do/do not) predict performance on various complex tasks and in various jobs. Even so, success requires a combination of talent and _____ .

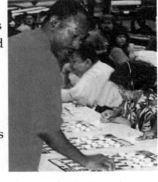

12. Sternberg's _____ theory distinguishes three types of intelligence: _____ intelligence, _____ intelligence, and _____ intelligence.

APPLICATIONS:

13. Melvin is limited in mental ability but has an exceptional ability to play complex music on the piano after hearing it only once. He has been diagnosed as having

_____ _____ .

14. Don's intelligence scores were only average, but he has been enormously successful as a corporate manager. Psychologists Sternberg and Wagner would probably suggest that
   a. Don's verbal intelligence exceeds his performance intelligence.
   b. Don's performance intelligence exceeds his verbal intelligence.
   c. Don's academic intelligence exceeds his practical intelligence.
   d. Don's practical intelligence exceeds his academic intelligence.

Intelligence and Creativity

Objective 29-4: Identify the factors associated with creativity, and describe ways of promoting creativity.

15. The ability to produce ideas that are both novel and valuable is called _____ . The relationship between intelligence and creativity holds only up to a certain point—an intelligence score of about _____ .

16. Standard intelligence tests, which demand single correct answers to questions, measure _____ thinking. Tests that allow multiple possible answers to problems measure _____ thinking.

Describe five components of creativity other than intelligence.

Describe research findings on how to foster creativity.

APPLICATION:

17. Vanessa is a very creative sculptress. We would expect that Vanessa also
   a. has an exceptionally high intelligence score.
   b. tries to solve problems in ways that worked before.
   c. has a venturesome personality and is intrinsically motivated.
   d. lacks expertise in most other skills.

Emotional Intelligence

Objective 29-5: Describe the four components of emotional intelligence.

18. The know-how involved in comprehending social situations and managing oneself successfully differs from _____ intelligence and is referred to as _____ intelligence.

19. A critical part of social intelligence is _____ _____ —the ability to _____ , _____ , _____ , and _____ _____ emotions.

20. More specifically, the four components of emotional intelligence are as follows: the ability to _____ emotions in faces, the ability to _____ them and how they change and blend, the ability to _____ them correctly in varied situations, and the ability to use them to enable _____ or creative thinking.
Briefly describe emotionally intelligent people.

21. Some scholars believe that the concept of _____ intelligence stretches the idea of multiple intelligences too far.

APPLICATION:

22. Gerardeen has superb social skills, manages conflicts well, and has great empathy for her friends and co-workers. Researchers would probably say that Gerardeen possesses a high degree of _____ .

Is Intelligence Neurologically Measurable?

Objective 29-6: Describe the relationship between intelligence and brain anatomy.

23. Studies that measure brain _____ using _____ scans reveal a correlation of about _____ between brain size (adjusted for body size) and intelligence score.

24. A review of 37 brain-imaging studies revealed associations between intelligence and brain size and activity in specific areas, especially within the _____ and _____ lobes.

25. Intelligence is having ample _____ _____ (mostly neural cell bodies) and ample _____ _____ (axons) that enable _____ .

26. A study of Einstein's brain revealed that it was 15 percent larger in the lower _____ lobe—known to be an important neural center for processing _____ and _____ information.

Objective 29-7: Describe the relationship between intelligence and neural processing speed.

27. When people ponder intelligence test questions, for example, an area in the brain's _____ _____ becomes especially active in the _____ (left/right) brain for verbal questions and _____ (in the right brain/in the left brain/on both sides of the brain) for spatial questions. People who are able to more quickly retrieve information from memory tend to score high in _____ ability.

28. Across many studies, the correlation between intelligence score and speed of taking in perceptual information tends to be about _____ . In a typical experiment, the researcher flashes an incomplete stimulus, then a _____ _____ . Participants are asked whether the long side of the stimulus appeared on the left or right. Those who require the least _____ time to register the information score somewhat higher on intelligence tests.

29. One research team believes that processing speed and intelligence correlate because they share an underlying _____ _____ .

PROGRESS TEST

Multiple-Choice Questions

Circle your answers to the following questions and check them with the answers on page 254. If your answer is incorrect, read the explanation for why it is incorrect and then consult the text.

1. Which of the following best describes the relationship between creativity and intelligence?
   a. Creativity appears to depend on the ability to think imaginatively and has little if any relationship to intelligence.
   b. Creativity is best understood as a certain kind of intelligence.
   c. The more intelligent a person is, the greater his or her creativity.
   d. A certain level of intelligence is necessary but not sufficient for creativity.

2. The existence of _____ reinforces the generally accepted notion that intelligence is a multidimensional quality.
   a. adaptive skills
   b. the *g* factor
   c. general intelligence
   d. savant syndrome

3. The concept of a *g* factor implies that intelligence
   a. is a single overall ability.
   b. is several specific abilities.
   c. cannot be defined or measured.
   d. is a socially constructed concept.

4. When highly skilled people are performing a task, their brains
   a. retrieve information from memory more quickly.
   b. register simple stimuli more quickly.
   c. use less energy to solve problems.
   d. do all of these things.

5. Most experts view intelligence as a person's
   a. ability to perform well on intelligence tests.
   b. innate mental capacity.
   c. ability to learn from experience, solve problems, and adapt to new situations.
   d. diverse skills acquired throughout life.

6. In recent years, researchers are more likely than before to consider intelligence as
   a. a single entity.
   b. primarily determined by heredity.
   c. entirely the product of learning.
   d. made up of several abilities.

7. The psychologist who has proposed that intelligence is composed of analytic, creative, and practical aspects is
   a. Charles Spearman.
   b. Howard Gardner.
   c. Robert Sternberg.
   d. Sandra Scarr.

Matching Items

Match each term with its definition or description.

Terms

_____ 1. *g*
_____ 2. savant syndrome
_____ 3. factor analysis
_____ 4. analytic intelligence
_____ 5. creative intelligence
_____ 6. practical intelligence

Definitions or Descriptions

a. an underlying, general intelligence factor
b. a very low intelligence score accompanied by one extraordinary skill
c. a statistical technique that identifies related items on a test
d. intellectual skills used in everyday problem solving
e. the ability to generate novel ideas
f. academic problem-solving

True–False Items

Indicate whether each statement is true or false by placing *T* or *F* in the blank next to the item.

_____ 1. People with high intelligence scores tend to process sensory information more quickly.

_____ 2. Historically, most psychologists have considered intelligence to be comprised of several distinct abilities.

_____ 3. Today, most researchers studying cognitive abilities believe that intelligence is multidimensional.

TERMS AND CONCEPTS TO REMEMBER

Using your own words, write on a separate piece of paper a brief definition or explanation of each of the following terms.

1. intelligence

2. intelligence test

3. general intelligence (*g*)

4. factor analysis

5. savant syndrome

6. creativity

7. emotional intelligence

ANSWERS

Module Review

What Is Intelligence?

1. do not

2. concept; intelligence tests; does not

3. a mental quality consisting of the ability to learn from experience, solve problems, and use knowledge to adapt to new situations

4. people's mental abilities and compares them with others, using numerical scores.

Is Intelligence One General Ability or Several Specific Abilities?

5. overall (general); specific

6. factor analysis

7. general intelligence

8. Thurstone; primary mental abilities

9. novel problems

10. savant syndrome

11. multiple intelligences; do; grit

12. triarchic; analytical (academic problem-solving); practical; creative

13. savant syndrome

14. **d.** is the answer. Sternberg and Wagner distinguish among *academic* intelligence, as measured by intelligence tests; *practical* intelligence, which is involved in everyday life and tasks, such as managerial work; and *creative* intelligence.

a. & b. Verbal and performance intelligence are both measured by standard intelligence tests such as the WAIS and would be included in Sternberg and Wagner's academic intelligence.

c. Academic intelligence refers to skills assessed by intelligence tests; practical intelligence applies to skills required for everyday tasks and, often, for occupational success.

Intelligence and Creativity

15. creativity; 120

16. convergent; divergent

Creative people tend to have expertise, or a solid base of knowledge; imaginative thinking skills, which allow them to see things in new ways, to recognize patterns, and to make connections; intrinsic motivation, or the tendency to focus on the pleasure and challenge of their work; and a venturesome personality that tolerates ambiguity and risk and seeks new experiences. Creative people also have generally benefited from living in creative environments.

Research suggests that you can boost your creativity by developing your expertise in an area you care about and enjoy; allow time for a problem to incubate (sleep on it!); set aside time for your mind to roam freely; and experience other cultures and ways of thinking, which will expose you to multiple perspectives and facilitates flexible thinking.

17. **c.** is the answer.
a. Beyond an intelligence score of about 120, creativity and intelligence scores are not correlated.
b. Just the opposite is true of creative people.
d. This may or may not be true, but most likely it isn't.

Emotional Intelligence

18. academic; social

19. emotional intelligence; perceive; understand; manage; use

20. recognize; predict; express; adaptive

Emotionally intelligent people are both socially and self-aware. They can manage their emotions and they can delay gratification. They handle others' emotions skillfully. They also exhibit modestly better job performance.

21. emotional

22. emotional intelligence

Is Intelligence Neurologically Measurable?

23. volume; MRI; .33

24. frontal; parietal

25. gray matter; white matter; efficient communication between brain centers

26. parietal; mathematical; spatial

27. frontal lobe; left; on both sides of the brain; verbal

28. +.3 to +.5; masking image; inspection

29. genetic influence

Progress Test

Multiple-Choice Questions

1. **d.** is the answer. Up to an intelligence score of about 120, there is a positive correlation between intelligence and creativity. But beyond this point the correlation disappears, indicating that factors other than intelligence are also involved.
   a. The ability to think imaginatively and intelligence are *both* components of creativity.
   b. Creativity, the capacity to produce ideas that are novel and valuable, is related to and depends in part on intelligence but cannot be considered simply a kind of intelligence.
   c. Beyond an intelligence score of about 120 there is no correlation between intelligence scores and creativity.

2. **d.** is the answer. That people with savant syndrome excel in one area but are intellectually disabled in others suggests that there are multiple intelligences.
   a. The ability to adapt defines the capacity we call intelligence.
   b. & c. A general intelligence (*g*) factor was hypothesized by Spearman to underlie each specific factor of intelligent behavior, but its existence is controversial and remains to be proved.

3. **a.** is the answer.

4. **d.** is the answer.

5. **c.** is the answer.
   a. Performance ability and intellectual ability are separate traits.
   b. This has been argued by some, but certainly not most, experts.
   d. Although many experts believe that there are multiple intelligences, this would not be the same thing as diverse acquired skills.

6. **d.** is the answer.
   a. Contemporary researchers emphasize the different aspects of intelligence.
   b. & c. Contemporary researchers see intelligence as the product of both heredity and learning.

7. **c.** is the answer.
   a. Charles Spearman proposed the existence of an underlying general intelligence, which he called *g*.
   b. Howard Gardner proposed that intelligence consists of eight autonomous abilities.
   d. Sandra Scarr believes that parents who try to turn their children into geniuses at a young age are wasting their time.

Matching Items

1. a   4. f
2. b   5. e
3. c   6. d

True–False Items

1. T   3. T
2. F

Terms and Concepts to Remember

1. Most experts define **intelligence** as a mental quality consisting of the ability to learn from experience, solve problems, and use knowledge to adapt to new situations.

2. **Intelligence tests** measure people's mental aptitudes and compare them with those of others, using numerical scores.

3. **General intelligence (*g*)**, according to Spearman and others, is a general intelligence factor that underlies each of the more specific mental abilities identified through factor analysis.

4. **Factor analysis** is a statistical procedure that identifies *factors,* or clusters of related items, that seem to define a common ability.

5. A person with **savant syndrome** has a very low intelligence score, yet possesses one exceptional ability, for example, in music or drawing.

6. Most experts agree that **creativity** refers to an ability to produce novel and valuable ideas. People with high IQs may or may not be creative, which indicates that intelligence is only one component of creativity.

7. **Emotional intelligence** is the ability to perceive, manage, understand, and use emotions.

Assessing Intelligence

MODULE OVERVIEW

Module 30 describes the historical origins of intelligence tests and discusses several important issues concerning their use. These include the methods by which intelligence tests are constructed and whether such tests are valid and reliable. The module also explores the stability of intelligence.

NOTE: Answer guidelines for all Module 30 questions begin on page 262.

MODULE REVIEW

First, skim each section, noting headings and boldface items. After you have read the section, review each objective by answering the fill-in and essay-type questions that follow it. In some cases, Study Tips explain how best to learn a difficult concept and Applications help you to know how well you understand the material. As you proceed, evaluate your performance by consulting the answers beginning on page 262. Do not continue with the next section until you understand each answer. If you need to, review or reread the section in the textbook before continuing.

The Origins of Intelligence Testing

Objective 30-1: Discuss the history of intelligence testing.

1. The early Greek philosopher _____ concluded that individuals differed in their natural endowments.

2. Although Francis Galton's search for a simple intelligence measure failed, he gave us some _____ techniques that we still use, as well as the phrase "_____ and _____ ."

3. The French psychologist who devised a test to predict the success of children in school was _____ . Predictions were made by comparing children's chronological ages with their _____ ages, which were determined by the test. This test _____ (was/was not) designed to measure inborn intelligence; Binet and his collaborator, _____ , leaned toward an _____ explanation of intelligence.

4. Lewis Terman's revision of Binet's test is referred to as the _____ - _____ . From this test, _____ derived the famous _____ _____ , or _____ .

Give the original formula for computing IQ, and explain any items used in the formula.

5. Today's tests compute _____ (IQ/ an intelligence test score) by comparing the individual's performance to the average performance of people of _____ (the same/different) age(s). These tests are designed so that a score of _____ is considered average.

6. The much-criticized movement called _____ proposed measuring human traits and using the results to determine who should be allowed to reproduce.

7. When given intelligence tests in the early 1900s, immigrants arriving in the United States often scored _____ (above/below) average. This is because the tests were based on a particular _____ background.

Modern Tests of Mental Abilities

Objective 30-2: Distinguish between aptitude and achievement tests.

8. Tests designed to measure what you already have learned are called _____ tests. Tests designed to predict your ability to learn something new are called _____ tests.

9. The most widely used intelligence test is the

_____ _____

_____ _____ .

Consisting of 15 subtests, it provides not only a general intelligence score but also separate scores for _____ _____ ,

_____ _____ ,

_____ _____ ,

and _____

_____ .

APPLICATIONS:

10. Before becoming attorneys, law students must pass a special licensing exam, which is an _____ test. Before entering college, high school students must take the SAT Reasoning Test, which is an _____ test.

11. Benito was born in 1937. In 1947, he scored 130 on an intelligence test. Using the original IQ formula, Benito's mental age when he took the test was _____ .

12. If asked to guess the intelligence score of a stranger, your best guess would be _____ .

13. Amelia recently took a test that assessed her ability to perform at the university level. The test she took was the
    a. WAIS.
    b. WISC.
    c. SAT Reasoning Test.
    d. None of these tests, because they are all achievement tests.

14. According to the text, what can be concluded from early intelligence testing in the United States?
    a. Most European immigrants were "feeble-minded."
    b. Army recruits of other than West European heritage were intellectually deficient.
    c. The tests were biased against people who did not share the culture assumed by the test.
    d. None of these things could be concluded.

Principles of Test Construction

Objective 30-3: Explain the meaning of standardization, and describe the normal curve.

15. One requirement of a good test is the process of defining meaningful scores relative to a pretested comparison group, which is called

_____ .

16. When scores on a test are compiled, they generally result in a bell-shaped pattern, or _____ distribution.

Describe the normal curve, and explain its significance in the standardization process.

17. The Stanford-Binet and the Wechsler Scales _____ (are/are not) periodically restandardized, thereby keeping the average score near _____ .

18. During the 1960s and 1970s, college entrance aptitude scores showed a steady _____ (increase/decline). At the same time, intelligence test performance

_____ (improved/decreased). This phenomenon is called the

_____ _____ .

19. Although the actual cause of this effect is unknown, one explanation is that it results from improved _____ . Although the recent performance gains on the WAIS that resulted from this improvement were greatest among _____-class children, intelligence performance gains were greater among _____-class children.

Objective 30-4: Explain the meanings of reliability and validity.

20. If a test yields consistent results, it is said to be

_____ .

21. When a test is administered more than once to the same people, the psychologist is determining its _____-_____ reliability.

22. When a person's scores for the odd- and even-numbered questions on a test are compared,

_____-_____

reliability is being assessed.

23. The Stanford-Binet, WAIS, and WISC have reliabilities of about _____ .

24. The degree to which a test measures or predicts what it is supposed to is referred to as the test's

_____ .

25. The degree to which a test measures the behavior it was designed to measure is referred to as the test's _____ _____ .

26. The degree to which a test predicts future performance of a particular behavior, called the test's _____ , is referred to as the test's

_____ _____ .

Choose a specific example and use it to illustrate and explain the concept of criterion and its relationship to predictive validity.

27. Generally speaking, the predictive validity of general aptitude tests _____ (is/is not) as high as their reliability. The predictive validity of these tests _____ (increases/diminishes) as individuals move up the educational ladder.

APPLICATIONS:

28. If you wanted to develop a test of musical aptitude in North American children, which would be the appropriate standardization group?
    a. children all over the world
    b. North American children
    c. children of musical parents
    d. children with known musical ability

29. Jack takes the same test of mechanical reasoning on several different days and gets virtually identical scores. This suggests that the test has
    a. high content validity.
    b. high reliability.
    c. high predictive validity.
    d. been standardized.

30. You would not use a test of hearing ability as an intelligence test because it would lack
    a. content reliability.
    b. predictive reliability.
    c. predictive validity.
    d. content validity.

31. A school psychologist found that 85 percent of those who scored above 115 on an aptitude test were A students and 75 percent of those who scored below 85 on the test were D students. The psychologist concluded that the test had high
    a. content validity because scores on it correlated highly with the criterion behavior.
    b. predictive validity because scores on it correlated highly with the criterion behavior.
    c. reliabiity because the test yielded inconsistent results.
    d. reliability because the test yielded consistent results.

The Dynamics of Intelligence

Objective 30-5: Describe the stability of intelligence scores over the life span.

32. For the first half of the twentieth century, psychologists were convinced that intelligence gradually _____ (increased/decreased) during late adulthood. This was based

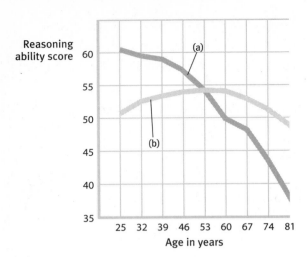

on research using (a) _____-_____ studies, in which people of various _____ are tested at _____ (the same time/different times).

Briefly explain why cross-sectional research can sometimes yield a misleading picture of adult development.

33. A group of people born about the same time constitutes a _____ . In (b) _____ studies, such a group is retested over a period of years. Results of such studies show that, until late in life, intelligence _____ (increases/decreases/remains stable).

Explain why longitudinal findings may be misleading.

34. Intelligence _____ (is/is not) a single trait.

35. The accumulation of knowledge and verbal skills is referred to as _____ intelligence.

36. The ability to reason speedily and abstractly is referred to as _____ intelligence.

37. During adulthood, _____ intelligence declines beginning in the _____ and _____ , slowly until about age _____ , and then more rapidly, especially after about age _____ .

38. Traditional intelligence tests before age _____ predict future aptitudes only modestly.

39. During childhood, the stability of intelligence scores _____ (increases/decreases) with age. A long-term study of mental ability in Scottish children revealed that intelligence _____ (does/does not) stabilize through late adulthood.

40. More intelligent children and adults live _____ and _____ . Give four possible reasons for this relationship.

   a. _____

   b. _____

   c. _____

   d. _____

APPLICATIONS:

41. At age 16, Angel's intelligence score was 110. What will her score probably be at age 32?
   a. 125
   b. 110
   c. 115
   d. There is no basis for predicting an individual's future IQ.

42. A psychologist who is looking at a student's intelligence score finds a jump of 30 points between the earliest score at age 2 and the most recent at age 17. The psychologist's knowledge of testing would probably lead her to conclude that such a jump
   a. indicates that different tests were used, creating an apparent change in intelligence level, although it actually remained stable.
   b. signals a significant improvement in the child's environment over this period.

c. is unsurprising, since intelligence scores do not become stable until late adolescence.

d. is mainly the result of the age at which the first test was taken.

Objective 30-6: Describe the traits of those at the low and high intelligence extremes.

43. Individuals whose intelligence scores fall below 70 and who have difficulty adapting to life may be labeled _____

_____ .

44. An intellectual disability sometimes has a physical basis, such as _____

_____ , a genetic disorder caused by an extra chromosome.

45. The current view is that people with an intellectual disability might be better able to live independently today because, as a result of the

_____ _____ , tests have been _____ and those individuals suddenly lost 6 IQ points.

46. At the high extreme, Lewis Terman's "gifted children" turned out to be _____ ,

well-_____ , and unusually successful _____ .

Discuss criticisms of programs that sort children into gifted and nongifted tracks.

APPLICATION:

47. Twenty-two-year-old Dan has an intelligence score of 63 and the academic skills of a fourth-grader, and is unable to live independently. Dan *probably*

a. suffers from stereotype threat.

b. has savant syndrome.

c. is intellectually disabled.

d. will eventually achieve self-supporting social and vocational skills.

PROGRESS TEST

Multiple-Choice Questions

Circle your answers to the following questions and check them with the answers beginning on page 264. If your answer is incorrect, read the explanation for why it is incorrect and then consult the text.

1. A 6-year-old child has a mental age of 9. The child's IQ is
   a. 96.
   b. 100.
   c. 125.
   d. 150.

2. Standardization refers to the process of
   a. determining the accuracy with which a test measures what it is supposed to.
   b. defining meaningful scores relative to a representative pretested group.
   c. determining the consistency of test scores obtained by retesting people.
   d. measuring the success with which a test predicts the behavior it is designed to predict.

3. Down syndrome is normally caused by
   a. an extra chromosome in the person's genetic makeup.
   b. a missing chromosome in the person's genetic makeup.
   c. malnutrition during the first few months of life.
   d. prenatal exposure to an addictive drug.

4. Which of the following is NOT a requirement of a good test?
   a. reliability
   b. standardization
   c. aptitude
   d. validity

5. Which of the following statements is true?
   a. The predictive validity of intelligence tests is not as high as their reliability.
   b. The reliability of intelligence tests is not as high as their predictive validity.
   c. Modern intelligence tests have extremely high predictive validity and reliability.
   d. The predictive validity and reliability of most intelligence tests is very low.

6. Sorting children into gifted and nongifted educational groups
   a. creates a self-fulfilling prophecy.
   b. increases social isolation between the groups.
   c. promotes racial segregation and prejudice.
   d. has all of these effects.

7. Most of the evidence for an age-related decline in intelligence came from
    a. cross-sectional research.
    b. longitudinal research.
    c. standardized research.
    d. random sampling.

8. The bell-shaped distribution of intelligence scores in the general population is called a
    a. *g* distribution.
    b. standardization curve.
    c. bimodal distribution.
    d. normal distribution.

9. The major flaw in cross-sectional research is the virtual impossibility of
    a. selecting participants who are similar in every aspect except age.
    b. tracking all participants over a number of years.
    c. finding volunteers with high IQs.
    d. testing concept mastery.

10. Which of the following is most likely to DECREASE with age?
    a. vocabulary
    b. accumulated knowledge
    c. speed of processing
    d. practical intelligence

11. The basic mental abilities that go into learning and understanding any subject have been classified as
    a. crystallized intelligence.
    b. plastic intelligence.
    c. fluid intelligence.
    d. rote memory.

12. Some psychologists contend that intelligence consists of fluid intelligence, which _____ during adulthood, and crystallized intelligence, which

    _____ .
    a. remains stable; declines
    b. declines; remains stable
    c. increases; declines
    d. declines; increases

13. The test created by Alfred Binet was designed specifically to
    a. measure inborn intelligence in adults.
    b. measure inborn intelligence in children.
    c. predict school performance in children.
    d. identify intellectually disabled children so that they could be institutionalized.

14. If a test designed to indicate which applicants are likely to perform the best on the job fails to do so, the test has
    a. low reliability.
    b. low content validity.
    c. low predictive validity.
    d. not been standardized.

15. The formula for the intelligence quotient was devised by
    a. Francis Galton.   c. Lewis Terman.
    b. Alfred Binet.   d. William Stern.

16. Current intelligence tests compute an individual's intelligence score as
    a. the ratio of mental age to chronological age multiplied by 100.
    b. the ratio of chronological age to mental age multiplied by 100.
    c. the amount by which the test-taker's performance deviates from the average performance of others the same age.
    d. the ratio of the test-taker's verbal intelligence score to his or her nonverbal intelligence score.

17. The accumulation of knowledge that comes about with education and experience has been classified as
    a. crystallized intelligence.
    b. plastic intelligence.
    c. fluid intelligence.
    d. rote memory.

18. The Flynn effect refers to the fact that
    a. White and Black infants score equally well on measures of infant intelligence.
    b. Asian students outperform North American students on math achievement tests.
    c. The IQ scores of today's better-fed and better-educated population exceed that of the 1930s population.
    d. Individual differences within a race are much greater than between-race differences.

19. In his study of children with high intelligence scores, Terman found that
    a. the children were more emotional and less healthy than a control group.
    b. the children were ostracized by classmates.
    c. the children were healthy and well-adjusted, and did well academically.
    d. later, as adults, they nearly all achieved great vocational success.

20. Originally, IQ was defined as
- **a.** mental age divided by chronological age and multiplied by 100.
- **b.** chronological age divided by mental age and multiplied by 100.
- **c.** mental age subtracted from chronological age and multiplied by 100.
- **d.** chronological age subtracted from mental age and multiplied by 100.

21. Tests of _____ measure what an individual can do now, whereas tests of _____ predict what an individual will be able to do later.
- **a.** aptitude; achievement
- **b.** achievement; aptitude
- **c.** reliability; validity
- **d.** validity; reliability

22. Research indicates that during adulthood declines occur in
- **a.** crystallized intelligence.
- **b.** fluid intelligence.
- **c.** both crystallized and fluid intelligence.
- **d.** neither crystallized nor fluid intelligence.

23. Which of the following is a drawback of longitudinal studies of intelligence?
- **a.** They are especially prone to the distortion of cohort effects.
- **b.** People who remain in the study may be the healthiest and most well-educated.
- **c.** The biases of the experimenter are more likely to distort the results than is true of other research methods.
- **d.** All of these are drawbacks.

24. Over the past 80 years, college aptitude test scores have _____ and WAIS scores have _____ .
- **a.** declined; remained stable
- **b.** remained stable; declined
- **c.** risen; declined
- **d.** declined; risen

Matching Items

Match each term with its definition or description.

Terms

_____ **1.** intelligence test score
_____ **2.** aptitude test
_____ **3.** achievement test
_____ **4.** Stanford-Binet
_____ **5.** criterion
_____ **6.** content validity
_____ **7.** reliability
_____ **8.** fluid intelligence
_____ **9.** crystallized intelligence

Definitions or Descriptions

- **a.** a test designed to predict a person's ability to learn something new
- **b.** a test designed to measure current knowledge
- **c.** the consistency with which a test measures performance
- **d.** the degree to which a test measures what it is designed to measure
- **e.** Terman's revision of Binet's original intelligence test
- **f.** the behavior that a test is designed to predict
- **g.** a person's score on an intelligence test based on performance relative to the average performance of people the same age
- **h.** the ability to reason abstractly and quickly
- **i.** accumulated knowledge and verbal skills

True–False Items

Indicate whether each statement is true or false by placing *T* or *F* in the blank next to the item.

_____   1. In the current version of the Stanford-Binet intelligence test, one's performance is compared only with the performance of others the same age.

_____   2. Intelligence scores in the United States have been dropping over the past 50 years.

_____   3. Most of the major aptitude tests have higher validity than reliability.

_____   4. The Stanford-Binet test and the Wechsler scales are periodically restandardized.

_____   5. To date, cross-sectional research has shown a gradual increase in intellectual ability.

_____   6. Longitudinal research usually shows that intelligence in most abilities increases throughout early and middle adulthood.

_____   7. By age 60, most people decline in even the most basic cognitive abilities.

Essay Question

You have been asked to devise a Psychology Achievement Test (PAT) that will be administered to freshmen who declare psychology as their major. What steps will you take to ensure that the PAT is a good intelligence test? (Use the space below to list the points you want to make, and organize them. Then write the essay on a separate sheet of paper.)

TERMS AND CONCEPTS TO REMEMBER

Using your own words, write on a separate piece of paper a brief definition or explanation of each of the following terms.

1. intelligence test

2. mental age

3. Stanford-Binet

4. intelligence quotient (IQ)

5. achievement test

6. aptitude test

7. Wechsler Adult Intelligence Scale (WAIS)

8. standardization

9. normal curve

10. reliability

11. validity

12. content validity

13. predictive validity

14. cohort

15. crystallized intelligence

16. fluid intelligence

17. intellectual disability

18. Down syndrome

ANSWERS

Module Review

The Origins of Intelligence Testing

1. Plato

2. statistical; nature; nurture

3. Alfred Binet; mental; was not; Théodore Simon; environmental

4. Stanford-Binet; William Stern; intelligence quotient; IQ

In the original formula for IQ, measured mental age is divided by chronological age and multiplied by 100. "Mental age" refers to the chronological age that most typically corresponds to a given level of performance.

5. an intelligence test score; the same; 100

6. eugenics

7. below; cultural

Modern Tests of Mental Abilities

8. achievement; aptitude

9. Wechsler Adult Intelligence Scale; verbal comprehension; perceptual organization; working memory; processing speed

10. achievement; aptitude

11. 13. At the time he took the test, Benito's chronological age (CA) was 10. Knowing that IQ = 130 and CA = 10, solving the equation for mental age yields a value of 13.

12. 100. Modern intelligence tests are periodically restandardized so that the average remains near 100.

13. **c.** is the answer.
a. & b. The WAIS is a general aptitude test, and the WISC is for children.
d. None of these tests are achievement tests; they are all aptitude tests.

14. **c.** is the answer. Although at the time the tests were administered some individuals reached these conclusions, they were, of course, misled.

Principles of Test Construction

15. standardization

16. normal

The normal curve describes the distribution of many physical phenomena and psychological attributes (including intelligence test scores), with most scores falling near the average and fewer near the extremes. When a test is standardized on a normal curve, individual scores are assigned according to how much they deviate above or below the distribution's average.

17. are; 100

18. decline; improved; Flynn effect

19. nutrition; lower; upper

20. reliable

21. test-retest

22. split-half

23. +.9

24. validity

25. content validity

26. criterion; predictive validity

The criterion is the particular behavior a predictive test, such as an aptitude test, is intended to predict. For example, performance in a relevant job situation would be the criterion for a test measuring managerial aptitude. The criterion determines whether a test has predictive validity. For example, the on-the-job success of those who do well on a job aptitude test would indicate the test has predictive validity.

27. is not; diminishes

28. **b.** is the answer. A standardization group provides a representative comparison for the trait being measured by a test. Because this test will measure musical aptitude in North American children, the standardization group should be limited to North American children but should include children of all degrees of musical aptitude.

29. **b.** is the answer.

30. **d.** is the answer. Because the hearing acuity test would in no way sample behaviors relevant to intelligence, it would not have content validity as a test of intelligence.
a. & b. There is no such thing as content reliability or predictive reliability.
c. There is nothing to indicate that, used to test hearing, this test would lack predictive validity.

31. **b.** is the answer.
a. Content validity is the degree to which a test measures what it claims to measure. The question gives no indication as to the nature of the questions.
c. & d. Reliability is the degree to which a test yields consistent results. There is no indication in the question as to whether the test's results are consistent or inconsistent.

The Dynamics of Intelligence

32. decreased; cross-sectional; ages; the same time

Cross-sectional research may be misleading because each cohort has its own unique history of life experiences and because in each generation, academic intelligence increases as a result of improved education.

33. cohort; longitudinal; remains stable

The participants in a longitudinal study may be bright, healthy people whose intelligence is least likely to decline.

34. is not

35. crystallized

36. fluid

37. fluid; twenties; thirties; 75; 85

38. 3

39. increases; does

40. longer; healthier

a. Intelligence facilitates more education, better jobs, and a healthier environment.

b. Intelligence encourages healthy living: less smoking, better diet, more exercise.

c. Prenatal events or early childhood illnesses might have influenced both intelligence and health.

d. A "well-wired body," as evidenced by fast reaction speeds, perhaps fosters both intelligence and longevity.

41. **b.** is the answer. Intelligence scores become quite stable during adolescence.

42. **d.** is the answer. It is not until after age 4 that intelligence-test performance begins to predict adolescent and adult scores.

a. Nothing in the question suggests the use of different intelligent tests. Also, intelligence doesn't begin to become stable until after age 4.

b. No such conclusion is possible, because intelligence-test performance before age 4 does not predict later aptitude.

c. Stability in intelligence scores is generally established by late adolescence.

43. intellectually disabled

44. Down syndrome

45. Flynn effect; restandardized

46. healthy; adjusted; academically

Critics of ability tracking contend that it sometimes creates self-fulfilling prophecies and that it promotes racial segregation and prejudice. Denying lower-ability students opportunities for enriched education widens the achievement gap between ability groups.

47. **c.** is the answer. To be labeled intellectually disabled a person must have a test score below 70 and experience difficulty adapting to the normal demands of living independently.

a. Stereotype threat occurs when a person performs poorly because he or she expects to be evaluated negatively.

b. There is no indication that Dan possesses one extraordinary skill, as do people with savant syndrome.

d. The text does not suggest that intellectually disabled people eventually become self-supporting.

Progress Test

Multiple-Choice Questions

1. **d.** is the answer. If we divide 9, the measured mental age, by 6, the chronological age, and multiply the result by 100, we obtain 150.

2. **b.** is the answer.

a. This answer refers to a test's content validity.

c. This answer refers to test-retest reliability.

d. This answer refers to predictive validity.

3. **a.** is the answer.

b. Down syndrome is normally caused by an extra, rather than a missing, chromosome.

c. & d. Down syndrome is a genetic disorder that is manifest during the earliest stages of prenatal development, well before malnutrition and exposure to drugs would produce their harmful effects on the developing fetus.

4. **c.** is the answer. Aptitude is a measure of your capacity to learn new information.

5. **a.** is the answer.

c. & d. Most modern tests have high reliabilities of about +.9; their validity scores are much lower.

6. **d.** is the answer.

7. **a.** is the answer.

b. Although results from this type of research may also be misleading, longitudinal studies often demonstrate age-related increases in intelligence.

c. Standardized research is not a category of research.

d. Random sampling refers to the selection of subjects for a research study.

8. **d.** is the answer.

a. *g* is Spearman's term for "general intelligence"; there is no such thing as a "*g* distribution."

b. There is no such thing.

c. A bimodal distribution is one having two (bi-) modes, or averages. The normal distribution has only one mode.

9. **a.** is the answer.

b. This is a problem in longitudinal research.

c. & d. Neither of these is particularly troublesome in cross-sectional research.

10. **c.** is the answer.

a., b., & d. These often increase with age.

11. **c.** is the answer.

a. Crystallized intelligence is the accumulation of knowledge and verbal skills that comes with education and experience.

b. Although intelligence is characterized by plasticity, "plastic intelligence" is not discussed as a specific type of intelligence.

d. Rote memory is memory that is based on the conscious repetition of to-be-remembered information.

12. d. is the answer.

13. c. is the answer. French compulsory education laws brought more children into the school system, and the government didn't want to rely on teachers' subjective judgments to determine which children would require special help.

a. & b. Binet's test was intended for children, and Binet specifically rejected the idea that his test measured inborn intelligence, which is an abstract capacity that cannot be quantified.

d. This was not a purpose of the test, which dealt with children in the school system.

14. c. is the answer. Predictive validity is the extent to which tests predict what they are intended to predict.

a. Reliability is the consistency with which a test samples the particular behavior of interest.

b. Content validity is the degree to which a test measures what it is designed to measure.

d. Standardization is the process of defining meaningful test scores based on the performance of a representative group.

15. d. is the answer.

16. c. is the answer.

a. This is William Stern's original formula for the intelligence quotient.

b. & d. Neither of these formulas is used to compute the score on current intelligence tests.

17. a. is the answer.

b. Although intelligence is characterized by plasticity, "plastic intelligence" is not discussed as a specific type of intelligence.

c. Fluid intelligence is the ability to reason speedily and abstractly.

d. Rote memory is based on the conscious repetition of to-be-remembered information.

18. c. is the answer.

19. c. is the answer.

a. & b. There was no evidence of either in the individuals studied by Terman.

d. Vocational success in adulthood varied.

20. a. is the answer.

21. b. is the answer.

c. & d. Reliability and validity are characteristics of good tests.

22. b. is the answer.

a., c., & d. Crystallized intelligence typically increases during adulthood.

23. b. is the answer.

a. This is a drawback of cross-sectional research.

c. Longitudinal studies are no more sensitive to experimenter bias than other research methods.

24. d. is the answer. College aptitude tests are complex tests that are not periodically restandardized. The WAIS, a more basic test that is periodically restandardized so that the average is always 100, also reflects the performance of a more diverse group.

Matching Items

1. g	**4.** e	**7.** c
2. a	**5.** f	**8.** h
3. b	**6.** d	**9.** 1

True–False Items

1. T	**4.** T	**7.** F
2. F	**5.** F	
3. F	**6.** F	

Essay Question

The first step in constructing the test is to create a valid set of questions that measure psychological knowledge and therefore give the test content validity. If your objective is to predict students' future achievement in psychology courses, the test questions should be selected to measure a criterion, such as information faculty members expect all psychology majors to master before they graduate.

To enable meaningful comparisons, the test must be standardized. That is, the test should be administered to a representative sample of incoming freshmen at the time they declare psychology to be their major. From the scores of your pretested sample you will then be able to assign an average score and evaluate any individual score according to how much it deviates above or below the average.

To check your test's reliability you might retest a sample of people using the same test or another version of it. If the two scores are correlated, your test is reliable. Alternatively, you might split the test in half and determine whether scores on the two halves are correlated.

Terms and Concepts to Remember

1. **Intelligence tests** measure people's mental aptitudes and compare them with those of others, using numerical scores.

2. A concept introduced by Binet, **mental age** is the chronological age that most typically corresponds to a given level of performance.

3. The **Stanford-Binet** is Lewis Terman's widely used revision of Binet's original intelligence test.

4. The **intelligence quotient (IQ)** was defined originally as the ratio of mental age to chronological age multiplied by 100. Contemporary tests of intelligence assign a score of 100 to the average performance for a given age and define other scores as deviations from this average.

5. **Achievement tests** measure a person's current knowledge.

6. **Aptitude tests** are designed to predict future performance. They measure your capacity to learn new information, rather than measuring what you already know.

7. The **Wechsler Adult Intelligence Scale (WAIS)** is the most widely used intelligence test. It is individually administered, contains 15 subtests, and yields separate scores for verbal comprehension, perceptual organization, working memory, and processing speed, as well as an overall intelligence score.

8. **Standardization** is the process of defining meaningful scores by comparison with a pretested standardization group.

9. The **normal curve** is a bell-shaped curve that represents the distribution (frequency of occurrence) of many physical and psychological attributes. The curve is symmetrical, with most scores near the average and fewer near the extremes.

10. **Reliability** is the extent to which a test produces consistent results.

11. **Validity** is the degree to which a test measures or predicts what it is supposed to.

12. The **content validity** of a test is the extent to which it samples the behavior that is of interest.

13. **Predictive validity** is the extent to which a test predicts the behavior it is designed to predict; also called *criterion-related validity*.

14. A **cohort** is a group of people from a given time period.

15. **Crystallized intelligence** is the accumulated knowledge and verbal skills that comes with education and experience.

16. **Fluid intelligence** is the ability to reason speedily and abstractly.

17. The two criteria that designate **intellectual disability** are an IQ below 70 and difficulty adapting to the normal demands of independent living; formerly called *mental retardation*.

18. A condition of mild to severe intellectual disability and associated physical disorders, **Down syndrome** is usually the result of an extra chromosome in the person's genetic makeup.

Genetic and Environmental Influences on Intelligence

MODULE OVERVIEW

Module 31 discusses the relative contributions to intelligence of heredity and environment, including the effects of early deprivation and intervention.

The second section describes research results regarding differences in intelligence test scores between the genders and among ethnicities. The module concludes with the controversial issue of whether intelligence tests are biased.

NOTE: Answer guidelines for all Module 31 questions begin on page 271.

MODULE REVIEW

First, skim each section, noting headings and bold-face items. After you have read the section, review each objective by answering the fill-in and essay-type questions that follow it. In some cases, Study Tips explain how best to learn a difficult concept and Applications help you to know how well you understand the material. As you proceed, evaluate your performance by consulting the answers on page 271. Do not continue with the next section until you understand each answer. If you need to, review or reread the section in the textbook before continuing.

Twin and Adoption Studies

Objective 31-1: Discuss the evidence for a genetic influence on intelligence, and explain what is meant by heritability.

1. The intelligence scores of identical twins reared together are _____ (more/no more) similar than those of fraternal twins. Brain scans also reveal that identical twins have similar volume to their brain's _____ and _____ matter, and those areas

associated with _____ and _____ intelligence.

2. The amount of variation in a trait within a group that is attributed to genetic factors is called its _____ . For intelligence, estimates range from _____ to _____ percent.

3. Identical twins exhibit substantial similarity (and _____) in specific talents.

4. Because intelligence is influenced by many genes, it is said to be _____ .

5. Where environments differ widely, as they do among children of _____-_____ parents, environmental differences are _____ (more/less) predictive of intelligence scores.

6. Studies of adopted children and their adoptive and biological families demonstrate that with age, genetic influences on intelligence become _____ (more/less) apparent. Thus, children's intelligence scores are more like those of their _____ (biological/adoptive) parents than their _____ (biological/adoptive) parents.

STUDY TIP: Heritability is a difficult concept to grasp in part because it is often confused with genetic determination, which refers to what causes a characteristic to develop. The number of toes on your feet is genetically determined because your genes cause five toes to develop on each foot. Heritability, on the other hand, is what causes differences in a characteristic. To say that the heritability of intelligence is 50 percent does not mean that half of an individual's intelligence is inherited. Rather, it means that we can attribute to heredity 50 percent of the variation of intelligence among those studied. A good way to keep the two concepts straight is to remember that while the concept of genetic determination makes sense in the case of a single person, heritability does not. Genetic determination is biological; heritability is a statistical measure. Heritability only makes sense relative to differences among groups of people. It doesn't make sense to ask, "What's the heritability of my intelligence?"

APPLICATIONS:

7. Raoul and Fidel are identical twins separated at birth. Because they have similar heredity and different environments, heritability for their intelligence is likely to be _____ (high/low). Ramona was adopted by Francesa's parents when she was 2 months old. The heritability for their intelligence is likely to be _____ (high/low).

8. If you compare the same trait in people of similar heredity who live in very different environments, heritability for that trait will be _____ ; heritability for the trait is most likely to be _____ among people of very different heredities who live in similar environments.
   a. low; high
   b. high; low
   c. environmental; genetic
   d. genetic; environmental

Environmental Influences

Objective 31-2: Discuss the evidence for hereditary and environmental influences on intelligence.

9. Studies indicate that neglected children _____ (do/do not) show signs of recovery in intelligence and behavior when placed in more nurturing environments. Although normal brain development can be retarded by _____ , _____ deprivation, and _____ _____ , there is no sure environment that will transform a normal baby into a genius.

10. Although the aptitude benefits of programs for disadvantaged children, such as the government-funded _____ _____ program, _____ (increase/decrease) over time, some believe that there _____ (are/are not) long-term benefits.

Group Differences in Intelligence Test Scores

Objective 31-3: Describe how and why the genders differ in mental ability scores.

11. Girls tend to outscore boys on _____ tests and are more _____ fluent. They also have an edge in _____ and _____ objects, in sensation, and in _____-detecting ability.

12. Although boys and girls hardly differ in math _____ , boys score higher in _____ _____ and complex _____ _____ .

13. Working from an _____ perspective, some theorists speculate that these gender differences in spatial manipulation helped our ancestors survive.

14. According to many, boys' and girls' interests and abilities are shaped in large part by _____ _____ and divergent opportunities. The mental ability scores of males tend to vary _____ (less/more) than those of females.

Objective 31-4: Describe how and why racial and ethnic groups differ in mental ability scores.

15. Group differences in intelligence scores _____ (do/do not) provide an accurate basis for judging individuals. Individual differences within a race are _____ (greater than/less than) between-race differences.

Explain why heredity may contribute to individual differences in intelligence but not necessarily contribute to group differences.

16. Under the skin, the races _____ (are/are not) alike. Race _____ (is/is not) a neatly defined biological category.

17. Although Asian students on the average score _____ (higher/lower) than North American students on math tests, this difference may be due to the fact that _____ _____ _____ .

18. The intelligence test performance of today's population exceeds that of the 1930s population because they are better-_____ , better-_____ , and more _____-_____ .

APPLICATION:

19. The contribution of environmental factors to racial gaps in intelligence scores is indicated by
   a. evidence that individual differences within a race are much greater than differences between races.
   b. evidence that white and black infants score equally well on certain measures of infant intelligence.
   c. the fact that Asian students outperform North American students on math achievement and aptitude tests.
   d. all of this evidence.

The Question of Bias

Objective 31-5: Discuss whether intelligence tests are inappropriately biased.

20. In the sense that they detect differences caused by cultural experiences, intelligence tests probably _____ (are/are not) biased.

21. Most psychologists agree that, in terms of predictive validity, the major aptitude tests _____ (are/are not) racially biased.

22. When women and members of ethnic minorities are led to expect that they won't do well on a test, a _____ _____ may result, and their scores may actually be lower.

PROGRESS TEST

Multiple-Choice Questions

Circle your answers to the following questions and check them with the answers beginning on page 271. If your answer is incorrect, read the explanation for why it is incorrect and then consult the text.

1. Studies of adopted children and their biological and adoptive families demonstrate that with age, genetic influences on intelligence
   a. become more apparent.
   b. become less apparent.
   c. become more difficult to disentangle from environmental influences.
   d. become easier to disentangle from environmental influences.

2. Which of the following is NOT true?
   a. In math grades, the average girl typically equals or surpasses the average boy.
   b. The gender gap in math and science scores is increasing.
   c. Women are better than men at detecting emotions.
   d. Males score higher than females on tests of spatial abilities.

3. Most psychologists believe that racial gaps in test scores
   a. have been exaggerated when they are, in fact, insignificant.
   b. indicate that intelligence is in large measure inherited.
   c. are in large measure caused by environmental factors.
   d. are increasing.

4. First-time parents Geena and Brad want to give their baby's intellectual abilities a jump-start by providing a super enriched learning environment. Experts would suggest that the new parents should
   a. pipe stimulating classical music into the baby's room.
   b. hang colorful mobiles and artwork over the baby's crib.
   c. take the child to one of the new "superbaby" preschools that specialize in infant enrichment.
   d. relax, since there is no surefire environmental recipe for giving a child a superior intellect.

5. Which of the following provides the strongest evidence of the role of heredity in determining intelligence?
   a. The IQ scores of identical twins raised separately are more similar than those of fraternal twins raised together.
   b. The intelligence scores of fraternal twins are more similar than those of ordinary siblings.
   c. The intelligence scores of identical twins raised together are more similar than those of identical twins raised apart.
   d. The intelligence scores of adopted children show relatively weak correlations with scores of adoptive as well as biological parents.

6. Reported racial gaps in average intelligence scores are most likely attributable to
   a. the use of biased tests of intelligence.
   b. the use of unreliable tests of intelligence.
   c. genetic factors.
   d. environmental factors.

7. To say that the heritability of a trait is approximately 50 percent means
   a. that genes are responsible for 50 percent of the trait in an individual, and the environment is responsible for the rest.
   b. that the trait's appearance in a person will reflect approximately equal genetic contributions from both parents.
   c. that of the variation in the trait within a group of people, 50 percent can be attributed to heredity.
   d. all of these things.

8. Which of the following provides the strongest evidence of environment's role in intelligence?
   a. Adopted children's intelligence scores are more like their adoptive parents' scores than their biological parents'.
   b. Children's intelligence scores are more strongly related to their mothers' scores than to their fathers'.
   c. Children moved from a deprived environment into an intellectually enriched one show gains in intellectual development.
   d. The intelligence scores of identical twins raised separately are no more alike than those of siblings.

9. J. McVicker Hunt found that institutionalized children given "tutored human enrichment"
   a. showed no change in intelligence test performance compared with institutionalized children who did not receive such enrichment.
   b. responded so negatively as a result of their impoverished early experiences that he felt it necessary to disband the program.
   c. thrived intellectually and socially on the benefits of positive caregiving.
   d. actually developed greater intelligence than control subjects who had lived in foster homes since birth.

10. Prenatal hormones have an influence on
    a. verbal reasoning.
    b. spatial abilities.
    c. overall intelligence.
    d. all of these aspects of intelligence.

11. Which of the following statements most accurately reflects the text's position regarding the relative contribution of genes and environment in determining intelligence?
    a. Except in cases of a neglectful early environment, each individual's basic intelligence is largely the product of heredity.
    b. Except in those with genetic disorders such as Down syndrome, intelligence results primarily from environmental experiences.
    c. Both genes and life experiences significantly influence performance on intelligence tests.
    d. Because intelligence tests have such low predictive validity, the question cannot be addressed until psychologists agree on a more valid test of intelligence.

True–False Items

Indicate whether each statement is true or false by placing *T* or *F* in the blank next to the item.

_____ 1. The gap in intelligence scores between Black and White children is increasing.

_____ 2. The intelligence scores of adopted children are more similar to those of their adoptive parents than their biological parents.

_____ 3. The consensus among psychologists is that most intelligence tests are extremely biased.

_____ 4. Most psychologists agree that intelligence is mainly determined by heredity.

_____ 5. The variation in intelligence scores within a racial group is much larger than that between racial groups.

_____   **6.** Telling students they are unlikely to succeed often erodes their performance on aptitude tests.

TERMS AND CONCEPTS TO REMEMBER

Using your own words, write on a separate piece of paper a brief definition or explanation of each of the following terms.

1. heritability

2. stereotype threat

ANSWERS

Module Review

Twin and Adoption Studies

1. more; gray; white; verbal; spatial

2. heritability; 50; 80

3. heritability

4. polygenic

5. less-educated; more

6. more; biological; adoptive

7. low; high

8. **a.** is the answer. If everyone has nearly the same heredity, then heritability—the variation in a trait attributed to heredity—must be low. If individuals within a group come from very similar environments, environmental differences cannot account for variation in a trait; heritability, therefore, must be high.

Environmental Influences

9. do; malnutrition; sensory; social isolation

10. Head Start; decrease; are

Group Differences in Intelligence Test Scores

11. spelling; verbally; remembering; locating; emotion

12. computation; spatial ability; math problems

13. evolutionary

14. social expectations; more

15. do not; greater than

Because of the impact of environmental factors such as education and nutrition on intelligence test performance, even if the heritability of intelligence is high within a particular group, differences in intelligence among groups may be environmentally caused. One

group may, for example, thrive in an enriched environment while another of the same genetic predisposition may falter in an impoverished one.

16. are; is not

17. higher; Asian students have a longer school year and spend more time studying math

18. fed; educated; test-prepared

19. **d.** is the answer. These reasons, along with other historical and cross-cultural reasons, all argue for the role of environment in creating and perpetuating the gap.

The Question of Bias

20. are

21. are not

22 . stereotype threat

Progress Test

Multiple-Choice Questions

1. **a.** is the answer.

   c. & d. Separating genetic from environmental influences is difficult *at any age.*

2. **b.** is the answer. As social expectations have changed, the gender gap in math and science scores is narrowing.

3. **c.** is the answer.
   a. On the contrary, many *group* differences are highly significant, even though they tell us nothing about specific *individuals.*
   b. Although heredity contributes to individual differences in intelligence, it does not necessarily contribute to group differences.
   d. In fact, the difference has diminished somewhat in recent years.

4. **d.** is the answer.

5. **a.** is the answer. Identical twins who live apart have the same genetic makeup but different environments; if their scores are similar, this is evidence for the role of heredity.
   b. Because fraternal twins are no more genetically alike than ordinary siblings, this could not provide evidence for the role of heredity.
   c. That twins raised together have more similar scores than twins raised apart provides evidence for the role of the environment.
   d. As both sets of correlations are weak, little evidence is provided either for or against the role of heredity.

6. **d.** is the answer. Findings from a range of studies—including studies related to the Flynn

effect and adoption studies—have led experts to focus on the influence of environmental factors.

a. Most experts believe that in terms of predictive validity, the major tests are not racially biased.

b. The reliability of the major tests is actually very high.

c. The bulk of the evidence on which experts base their findings points to the influence of environmental factors.

7. **c.** is the answer. Heritability is a measure of the extent to which a trait's variation within a group of people can be attributed to heredity.

a. & b. Heritability is *not* a measure of how much of an *individual's* behavior is inherited, nor of the relative contribution of genes from that person's mother and father. Further, the heritability of any trait depends on the context, or environment, in which that trait is being studied.

8. **c.** is the answer.

a., b., & d. None of these is true.

9. **c.** is the answer. Enrichment led to dramatic results and thereby testified to the importance of environmental factors.

a. & d. The study involved neither intelligence tests nor comparisons with control groups.

b. The children showed a dramatic positive response.

10. **b.** is the answer.

11. **c.** is the answer.

a. & b. Studies of twins, family members, and adopted children point to a significant hereditary contribution to intelligence scores. These same studies, plus others comparing children reared in neglectful or enriched environments, indicate that life experiences also significantly influence test performance.

d. Although the issue of how intelligence should be defined is controversial, intelligence tests generally have predictive validity, especially in the early years.

True–False Items

1.	F	**4.**	F
2.	F	**5.**	T
3.	F	**6.**	T

Terms and Concepts to Remember

1. **Heritability** is the proportion of variation among individuals that can be attributed to genes.

2. **Stereotype threat** is the phenomenon in which a person's concern that he or she will be evaluated based on a negative stereotype (as on an aptitude test, for example) is actually followed by lower performance.

Basic Motivational Concepts and Hunger

MODULE OVERVIEW

Motivation is the study of forces that energize and direct our behavior. Module 32 discusses various motivational concepts and looks closely at the hunger motive. Research on hunger points to the fact that our biological drive to eat is strongly influenced by psychological and social-cultural factors.

NOTE: Answer guidelines for all Module 32 questions begin on page 279.

MODULE REVIEW

First, skim each section, noting headings and bold-face items. After you have read the section, review each objective by answering the fill-in and essay-type questions that follow it. In some cases, Study Tips explain how best to learn a difficult concept and Applications help you to know how well you understand the material. As you proceed, evaluate your performance by consulting the answers beginning on page 279. Do not continue with the next section until you understand each answer. If you need to, review or reread the section in the textbook before continuing.

Introduction and Motivational Concepts

Objective 32-1: Define *motivation* as psychologists use the term, and identify four perspectives useful for studying motivated behavior.

1. Motivation is defined as _____

   _____

   _____ .

2. Four perspectives on motivation are
   _____ theory (which has
   been replaced by the _____

perspective), _____ -

_____ theory,

_____ theory, and the

_____ of needs proposed by

_____ .

3. As a result of Darwin's influence, many complex behaviors were classified as rigid, unlearned behavior patterns that are characteristic of a species, called _____ . Although early instinct theory_____ (did/ did not) explain human motives, the underlying assumption that _____ predispose species-typical behavior remains strong.

4. According to another view of motivation, organisms may experience a physiological _____ , which creates a state of arousal that _____ the organism to reduce the need.

5. The aim of drive reduction is to maintain a constant internal state, called _____ .

6. Behavior is often not so much pushed by our drives as it is pulled by _____ in the environment.

7. Rather than reduce a physiological need, some motivated behaviors actually _____ arousal. This demonstrates that human motives _____ (do/do not) always satisfy some biological need.

8. Human motivation aims not to eliminate _____ but to seek

   _____ _____

   of arousal.

9. Starting from the idea that _____-_____ needs such as the need for water take precedence over others, Maslow constructed a hierarchy of needs.

10. According to Maslow, the _____ needs are the most pressing, whereas the highest-order needs relate to _____ and _____ .

11. A criticism of Maslow's theory is that the sequence is _____ and not _____ fixed.

12. Surveys of life satisfaction reveal that _____ satisfaction is strongly predictive of subjective well-being in poorer nations, whereas _____-_____ satisfaction matters more in wealthy nations and _____ in individualist nations.

APPLICATIONS:

13. Mary loves hang-gliding. It would be most difficult to explain Mary's behavior according to
    a. incentives.
    b. achievement motivation.
    c. drive-reduction theory.
    d. Maslow's hierarchy of needs.

14. For two weeks, Orlando has been on a hunger strike to protest his country's involvement in what he perceives as an immoral war. Orlando's willingness to starve himself to make a political statement conflicts with the theory of motivation advanced by
    a. Masters.   c. Johnson.
    b. Murray.   d. Maslow.

15. Which of the following is NOT an example of homeostasis?

    a. perspiring to restore normal body temperature
    b. feeling hungry and eating to restore the level of blood glucose to normal
    c. feeling hungry at the sight of an appetizing food
    d. All of these are examples of homeostasis.

Hunger

Objective 32-2: Describe the physiological factors that produce hunger.

16. Researchers observed that men became preoccupied with thoughts of food when they underwent _____ .

17. Cannon and Washburn's experiment using a balloon indicated that there is an association between hunger and _____ _____ .

18. When rats had their stomachs removed, hunger _____ (did/did not) continue.

19. (Use art as clues to lettered blanks) Increases in the hormone (a) _____ diminish blood _____ , partly by converting it to stored fat, which causes hunger to _____ .

20. The brain area that plays a role in hunger and other bodily maintenance functions is the _____ . One area called the _____ _____ has a center that secretes appetite-stimulating hormones and another center that secretes appetite-suppressing hormones.

21. The hunger-arousing hormone secreted by an empty stomach is (b) _____ .

22. When a portion of an obese person's stomach is surgically sealed off, the remaining stomach produces _____ (more/less) of this hormone. Other appetite hormones include (c) _____ , which is secreted by fat cells and decreases hunger; (d) _____ , which is secreted by the hypothalamus and triggers hunger; and (e) _____ from the digestive tract, which decreases hunger.

23. The weight level at which an individual's body is programmed to stay is referred to as the body's

_____ _____ .

A person whose weight goes beyond this level will tend to feel _____
(more/less) hungry than usual and expend _____ (more/less) energy.

24. The rate of energy expenditure in maintaining basic functions when the body is at rest is the

_____ _____

rate. When food intake is reduced, the body compensates by _____ (raising/lowering) this rate.

25. The concept of a precise body set point that drives hunger _____ (is accepted/is not accepted) by all researchers. Some researchers believe that the set point can be altered by _____

_____ ,

and that _____
_____ also sometimes drive our feelings of hunger. In support of this idea is evidence that when people and other animals are given unlimited access to tasty foods, they tend to _____ and _____
_____ . For these reasons, some researchers prefer to use the term

_____ _____ as an
alternative to the idea that there is a fixed set point.

APPLICATIONS:

26. Kenny and his brother have nearly identical eating and exercise habits, yet Kenny is obese and his brother is very thin. The MOST LIKELY explanation for the difference in their body weights is that they differ in
   a. their bone structure.
   b. amygdala activity.
   c. their set points and their metabolic rates.
   d. their differing exposure to carbohydrate-laden foods.

27. Lucille has been sticking to a strict diet but can't seem to lose weight. What is the most likely explanation for her difficulty?
   a. Her body has a very low set point.
   b. Her prediet weight was near her body's set point.
   c. Her weight problem is actually caused by an increase in basal metabolic rate.
   d. Lucille is influenced primarily by external factors.

Objective 32-3: Discuss psychological, cultural, and situational factors that influence hunger.

28. Research with amnesia patients indicates that part of knowing when to eat is our

_____ of our last meal.

29. Carbohydrates boost levels of the neurotransmitter _____ , which
_____ (calms/arouses) the body.

30. Taste preferences for sweet and salty are
_____ (genetic/learned). Other influences on taste include _____
and _____ .

31. We have a natural dislike of many foods that are
_____ ; this _____
was probably adaptive for our ancestors, and protected them from toxic substances.

32. Because of _____ facilitation, people tend to eat _____
(less/more) when they are with other people. The phenomenon of _____
_____ is the tendency to mindlessly eat more when portions are larger. Another factor that stimulates eating is food

_____ .

APPLICATION:

33. Randy, who has been under a lot of stress lately, has intense cravings for sugary junk foods, which tend to make him feel more relaxed. Which of the following is the most likely explanation for his craving?
   a. Randy feels that he deserves to pamper himself with sweets because of the stress he is under.
   b. The extra sugar gives Randy the energy he needs to cope with the demands of daily life.
   c. Carbohydrates boost levels of serotonin, which has a calming effect.
   d. The extra sugar tends to lower blood insulin level, which promotes relaxation.

Objective 32-4: Discuss the factors that predispose some people to become and remain obese.

34. Being slightly overweight _____
(poses/does not pose) serious health risks. In the United States, _____ percent of adults are obese. Significant obesity increases the risk of _____

_____ .

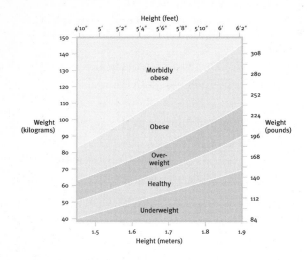

35. Obesity has also been linked in women to their risk of late-life _____ disease and brain tissue loss.

36. Obese people are often stereotyped as
_____ , _____ , and _____ .

37. One study found that obese women earned _____ (more/less) than a control group of nonobese women and were less likely to be _____ .

38. In one experiment, job applicants were rated as less worthy of hiring when they were made to appear _____ .

39. The energy equivalent of a pound of fat is approximately _____ calories.

40. Fat tissue has a _____ (higher/lower) metabolic rate than lean tissue. The result is that fat tissue requires _____ (more/less) food energy to be maintained.

Explain why, metabolically, many obese people find it so difficult to become and stay thin.

41. Studies of adoptees and twins _____ (do/do not) provide evidence of a genetic influence on obesity. A particular variant of the gene

called _____ has been shown to nearly double a person's risk of becoming obese.

42. Also contributing to the problem of obesity are _____ factors. For example, adults who suffer from _____ _____ are more vulnerable to obesity. Also, people are _____ (less/more) likely to become obese when a friend becomes obese, thus demonstrating _____ influence as a factor in obesity.

43. Global increases in the prevalence of obesity are most common in _____ (developed/developing) nations. Two reasons are changing _____ _____ and _____ _____ .

(Close-Up) State several pieces of advice for those who want to lose weight.

APPLICATIONS:

44. Owen is on a diet. After an initial _____ (slow/rapid) weight loss, he loses weight _____ (more slowly/more rapidly). This slowdown occurs because his metabolism rate has _____ (increased/decreased).

45. (Close-Up) Which of the following would be the WORST piece of advice to offer to someone trying to lose weight?
   a. "To treat yourself to one 'normal' meal each day, eat very little until the evening meal."
   b. "Reduce your consumption of saturated fats."
   c. "Boost your metabolism by exercising regularly."
   d. "Begin only if you feel motivated and self-disciplined."

PROGRESS TEST

Multiple-Choice Questions

Circle your answers to the following questions and check them with the answers beginning on page 280. If your answer is incorrect, read the explanation for why it is incorrect and then consult the text.

1. Motivation is best understood as a state that
   a. reduces a drive.
   b. aims at satisfying a biological need.
   c. energizes an organism to act.
   d. energizes and directs behavior.

2. Which of the following is a difference between a drive and a need?
   a. Needs are learned; drives are inherited.
   b. Needs are physiological states; drives are psychological states.
   c. Drives are generally stronger than needs.
   d. Needs are generally stronger than drives.

3. One problem with the idea of motivation as drive reduction is that
   a. because some motivated behaviors do not seem to be based on physiological needs, they cannot be explained in terms of drive reduction.
   b. it fails to explain any human motivation.
   c. it cannot account for homeostasis.
   d. it does not explain the hunger drive.

4. Increases in insulin will
   a. lower blood sugar and trigger hunger.
   b. raise blood sugar and trigger hunger.
   c. lower blood sugar and trigger satiety.
   d. raise blood sugar and trigger satiety.

5. One shortcoming of the instinct theory of motivation is that it
   a. places too much emphasis on environmental factors.
   b. focuses on cognitive aspects of motivation.
   c. applies only to animal behavior.
   d. does not explain human behaviors; it simply names them.

6. The text suggests that a *neophobia* for unfamiliar tastes
   a. is more common in children than in adults.
   b. protected our ancestors from potentially toxic substances.
   c. may be an early warning sign of obesity.
   d. only grows stronger with repeated exposure to those tastes.

7. The brain area known as the arcuate nucleus is notable in the study of motivation because it
   a. secretes hormones that affect appetite.
   b. secretes hormones that affect the sex drive.
   c. is enlarged in heterosexuals.
   d. is enlarged in homosexuals.

8. Instinct theory and drive-reduction theory both emphasize _____ factors in motivation.
   a. environmental   c. psychological
   b. cognitive   d. biological

9. Few human behaviors are rigidly patterned enough to qualify as
   a. needs.   c. instincts.
   b. drives.   d. incentives.

10. In their study of men on a semistarvation diet, researchers found that
    a. the metabolic rate of the men increased.
    b. the men eventually lost interest in food.
    c. the men became obsessed with food.
    d. the men's behavior directly contradicted predictions made by Maslow's hierarchy of needs.

11. Research on genetic influences on obesity reveals that
    a. the body weights of adoptees correlate with that of their biological parents.
    b. the body weights of adoptees correlate with that of their adoptive parents.
    c. identical twins usually have very different body weights.
    d. the body weights of identical twin women are more similar than those of identical twin men.

12. Research on obesity indicates that
    a. pound for pound, fat tissue requires more calories to maintain than lean tissue.
    b. given an obese parent, boys are more likely than girls to be obese.
    c. one pound of weight is lost for every 3500-calorie reduction in diet.
    d. when weight drops below the set point, hunger increases.

13. Which of the following influences on hunger motivation does NOT belong with the others?
    a. set/settling point
    b. attraction to sweet and salty tastes
    c. reduced production of ghrelin after stomach bypass surgery
    d. memory of time elapsed since your last meal

14. Homeostasis refers to
    a. the tendency to maintain a steady internal state.
    b. the tendency to seek external incentives for behavior.
    c. the setting of the body's "weight thermostat."
    d. a theory of the development of sexual orientation.

15. The tendency to overeat when food is plentiful
    a. is a recent phenomenon that is associated with the luxury of having ample food.
    b. emerged in our prehistoric ancestors as an adaptive response to periods when food was scarce.
    c. is greater in developed, than in developing, societies.
    d. is stronger in women than in men.

16. Unit bias refers to the research finding that people tend to
    a. eat more when a portion of food is supersized.
    b. avoid unfamiliar tasting foods.
    c. overeat during celebrations with other people.
    d. do all of these things.

17. According to Maslow's theory
    a. the most basic motives are based on physiological needs.
    b. needs are satisfied in a specified order.
    c. the highest motives relate to self-transcendence.
    d. all of these statements are true.

18. Which of the following is INCONSISTENT with the drive-reduction theory of motivation?
    a. When body temperature drops below 98.6° Fahrenheit, blood vessels constrict to conserve warmth.
    b. A person is driven to seek a drink when his or her cellular water level drops below its optimum point.
    c. Monkeys will work puzzles even if not given a food reward.
    d. A person becomes hungry when body weight falls below its biological set point.

19. Which of the following is NOT necessarily a reason that obese people have trouble losing weight?
    a. Fat tissue has a lower metabolic rate than lean tissue.
    b. Once a person has lost weight, it takes fewer calories to maintain his or her current weight.
    c. The tendency toward obesity may be genetically based.
    d. Obese people tend to lack willpower.

20. Beginning with the most basic needs, which of the following represents the correct sequence of needs in the hierarchy described by Maslow?
    a. safety; physiological; esteem; belongingness and love; self-fulfillment
    b. safety; physiological; belongingness and love; esteem; self-fulfillment
    c. physiological; safety; esteem; belongingness and love; self-fulfillment
    d. physiological; safety; belongingness and love; esteem; self-fulfillment

Matching Items

Match each term with its definition or description.

Terms

_____ 1. set point
_____ 2. incentive
_____ 3. homeostasis

Definitions or Descriptions

a. the body's tendency to maintain a balanced internal state
b. environmental stimulus that motivates behavior
c. the body's weight-maintenance setting

_____ 3. An increase in insulin increases blood glucose levels and triggers hunger.
_____ 4. Obesity is often a sign of social status and affluence in developing countries.

True–False Items

Indicate whether each statement is true or false by placing *T* or *F* in the blank next to the item.

_____ 1. When body weight rises above set point, hunger increases.
_____ 2. All taste preferences are conditioned.

Essay Question

Differentiate the three major theories of motivation, discuss their origins, and explain why they cannot fully account for human behavior. (Use the space below to list the points you want to make, and organize them. Then write the essay on a separate sheet of paper.)

TERMS AND CONCEPTS TO REMEMBER

Using your own words, write on a separate piece of paper a brief definition or explanation of each of the following terms.

1. motivation

2. instinct

3. drive-reduction theory

4. homeostasis

5. incentive

6. hierarchy of needs

7. glucose

8. set point

9. basal metabolic rate

ANSWERS
Module Review

Introduction and *Motivational Concepts*

1. a need or desire that energizes behavior and directs it toward a goal

2. instinct; evolutionary; drive-reduction; arousal; hierarchy; Abraham Maslow

3. instincts; did not; genes

4. need; drives

5. homeostasis

6. incentives

7. increase; do not

8. arousal; optimum levels

9. lower-level

10. physiological; self-actualization; self-transcendence

11. arbitrary; universally

12. financial; home-life; self-esteem

13. **c.** is the answer. Drive-reduction theory maintains that behavior is motivated when a biological need creates an aroused state, driving the individual to satisfy the need. It is difficult to believe that Mary's hang-gliding is satisfying a biological need.
    a., b., & d. Mary may enjoy hang-gliding because it is a challenge that "is there" (incentive), because it satisfies a need to accomplish something challenging (achievement), or because it increases her self-esteem and sense of fulfillment in life (Maslow's hierarchy of needs).

14. **d.** is the answer. According to Maslow's theory, physiological needs, such as the need to satisfy hunger, must be satisfied before a person pursues loftier needs, such as making political statements.
    a. & c. Masters and Johnson were concerned with sexual behavior.
    b. Murray was concerned with achievement motivation.

15. **c.** is the answer. This is an example of salivating in response to an incentive rather than to maintain a balanced internal state.
    a. & b. Both examples are behaviors that maintain a balanced internal state (homeostasis).

Hunger

16. semistarvation

17. stomach contractions

18. did

19. insulin; glucose; increase

20. hypothalamus; arcuate nucleus

21. ghrelin

22. less; leptin; orexin; PYY

23. set point; less; more

24. basal metabolic; lowering

25. is not accepted; slow, sustained changes in body weight; psychological factors; overeat; gain weight; settling point

26. **c.** is the answer. Individual differences in metabolism and set point explain why it is possible for two people to have very different weights despite similar patterns of eating and exercise.

27. **b.** is the answer. The body acts to defend its set point, or the weight to which it is predisposed. If Lucille was already near her set point, weight loss would prove difficult.
    a. If the weight level to which her body is predisposed is low, weight loss upon dieting should not be difficult.
    c. An increase in basal metabolic rate would help her to lose weight.
    d. People influenced by external factors might have greater problems losing weight because they tend to respond to food stimuli, but this can't be the explanation in Lucille's case because she has been sticking to her diet.

28. memory

29. serotonin; calms

30. genetic; conditioning; culture

31. unfamiliar; neophobia

32. social; more; unit bias; variety

33. **c.** is the answer. Serotonin is a neurotransmitter that is elevated by the consumption of carbohydrates and has a calming effect.
    a. & b. These answers do not explain the feelings of relaxation that Randy associates with eating junk food.
    d. The consumption of sugar tends to elevate insulin level rather than lower it.

34. does not pose; 34; diabetes, high blood pressure, heart disease, gallstones, arthritis, and certain types of cancer

35. Alzheimer's

36. slow; lazy; undisciplined

37. less; married

38. overweight

39. 3500

40. lower; less

Obese persons have higher set-point weights than nonobese persons. During a diet, metabolic rate drops to defend the set-point (or settling-point) weight. The dieter therefore finds it hard to progress beyond an initial weight loss. When the diet is concluded, the lowered metabolic rate continues, so that relatively small amounts of food may prove fattening. Also, some people have lower metabolic rates than others.

41. do; FTO

42. environmental; sleep loss; more; social

43. developed; food consumption; activity levels

Begin only if you are motivated and self-disciplined. Minimize exposure to tempting food cues. Eat healthy foods. Don't starve all day and eat one big meal at night. Beware of binge eating. Be realistic and moderate. Boost your metabolism through exercise. Connect to a support group.

44. rapid; more slowly; decreased

45. **a.** is the answer. Dieting, including fasting, lowers the body's metabolic rate and reduces the amount of food energy needed to maintain body weight.
    b., c., & d. Each of these strategies would be a good piece of advice to a dieter.

Progress Test

Multiple-Choice Questions

1. **d.** is the answer.
   a. & b. Although motivation is often aimed at reducing drives and satisfying biological needs, this is by no means always the case, as achievement motivation illustrates.
   c. Motivated behavior not only is energized but also is directed at a goal.

2. **b.** is the answer. A drive is the psychological consequence of a physiological need.
   a. Needs are unlearned states of deprivation.
   c. & d. Because needs are physical and drives psychological, their strengths cannot be compared directly.

3. **a.** is the answer. The curiosity of a child or a scientist is an example of behavior apparently motivated by something other than a physiological need.
   b. & d. Some behaviors, such as thirst and hunger, are partially explained by drive reduction.
   c. Drive reduction is directly based on the principle of homeostasis.

4. **a.** is the answer. Increases in insulin increase hunger indirectly by lowering blood sugar, or glucose.

5. **d.** is the answer.
   a. & b. Instinct theory emphasizes biological factors rather than environmental or cognitive factors.
   c. Instinct theory applies to both humans and other animals.

6. **b.** is the answer.
   a. Neophobia for taste is typical of all age groups.
   c. Neophobia for taste is *not* an indicator of obesity.
   d. With repeated exposure, our appreciation for a new taste typically *increases*.

7. **a.** is the answer.

8. **d.** is the answer.

9. **c.** is the answer.
a. & b. Needs and drives are biologically based states that stimulate behaviors but are not themselves behaviors.
d. Incentives are the external stimuli that motivate behavior.

10. **c.** is the answer. The deprived men focused on food almost to the exclusion of anything else.
a. To conserve energy, the men's metabolic rate actually *decreased*.
b. & d. Far from losing interest in food, the men came to care only about food—a finding consistent with Maslow's hierarchy, in which physiological needs are at the base.

11. **a.** is the answer.

12. **d.** is the answer.

13. **d.** is the answer. Memory of the time of the last meal is an example of a psychological influence on hunger motivation.
a., b., & c. Each of these is a biological influence on hunger motivation.

14. **a.** is the answer.
b. This describes extrinsic motivation.
c. This describes set point.
d. Homeostasis has nothing to do with sexual orientation.

15. **b.** is the answer.
c. If anything, just the opposite is true.
d. Men and women do not differ in the tendency to overeat.

16. **a.** is the answer.
b. This is an example of neophobia.
c. This is an example of social facilitation.

17. **d.** is the answer.

18. **c.** is the answer. Such behavior, presumably motivated by curiosity rather than any biological need, is inconsistent with a drive-reduction theory of motivation.
a., b., & d. Each of these examples is consistent with a drive-reduction theory of motivation.

19. **d.** is the answer. Most researchers today discount the idea that people are obese because they lack willpower.

20. **d.** is the answer.

Matching Items

1. c
2. b
3. a

True–False Items

1.	F	**3.**	F
2.	F	**4.**	T

Essay Question

Under the influence of Darwin's evolutionary theory, it became fashionable to classify all sorts of behaviors as instincts. Instinct theory fell into disfavor for several reasons. First, instincts do not explain behaviors, they merely name them. Second, to qualify as an instinct, a behavior must have a fixed and automatic pattern and occur in all people, regardless of differing cultures and experiences. Apart from a few simple reflexes, however, human behavior is not sufficiently automatic and universal to meet these criteria. Although instinct theory failed to explain human motives, the underlying assumption that genes predispose many behaviors is as strongly believed as ever.

Instinct theory was replaced by drive-reduction theory and the idea that biological needs create aroused drive states that motivate the individual to satisfy these needs and preserve homeostasis. Drive-reduction theory failed as a complete account of human motivation because many human motives do not satisfy any obvious biological need. Instead, such behaviors are motivated by environmental incentives.

Arousal theory emerged in response to evidence that some motivated behaviors *increase*, rather than decrease, arousal.

Terms and Concepts to Remember

1. **Motivation** is a need or desire that energizes and directs behavior.

2. An **instinct** is a complex behavior that is rigidly patterned throughout a species and is unlearned.

3. **Drive-reduction theory** attempts to explain behavior as arising from a physiological need that creates an aroused tension state (drive) that motivates an organism to satisfy the need.

4. **Homeostasis** refers to the body's tendency to maintain a balanced or constant internal state.

5. An **incentive** is a positive or negative environmental stimulus that motivates behavior.

6. Maslow's **hierarchy of needs** proposes that human motives may be ranked from the basic, physiological level through higher-level needs for safety, love, esteem, self-actualization, and self-transcendence; until they are satisfied, the more

basic needs are more compelling than the higher-level ones.

7. **Glucose**, or blood sugar, is the major source of energy for body tissues. Elevating the level of glucose in the body will reduce hunger.

8. **Set point** is an individual's regulated weight level, which is maintained by adjusting food intake and energy output.

9. **Basal metabolic rate** is the body's base rate of energy expenditure when resting.

Sexual Motivation and the Need to Belong

MODULE OVERVIEW

Sexual motivation in men and women is triggered less by physiological factors and more by external incentives. Even so, research studies demonstrate that sexual orientation is neither willfully chosen nor easily changed.

The module also includes a section on the need to belong, a major influence in motivating human behavior. Social bonds boosted our ancestors' survival rates. We experience our need to belong when feeling the gloom of loneliness or joy of love, and when seeking social acceptance.

NOTE: Answer guidelines for all Module 33 questions begin on page 288.

MODULE REVIEW

First, skim each section, noting headings and bold-face items. After you have read the section, review each objective by answering the fill-in and essay-type questions that follow it. In some cases, Study Tips explain how best to learn a difficult concept and Applications help you to know how well you understand the material. As you proceed, evaluate your performance by consulting the answers beginning on page 288. Do not continue with the next section until you understand each answer. If you need to, review or reread the section in the textbook before continuing.

The Physiology of Sex

Objective 33-1: Describe the physiological factors that affect human sexual behavior, and identify disorders that disrupt the sexual response cycle.

1. The two researchers who identified a four-stage sexual response cycle are _____

and _____ . In order, the stages of the cycle are the _____ phase, the _____ phase, _____ , and the _____ phase.

2. During resolution, males experience a

_____ _____ , during which they are incapable of another orgasm.

3. Problems that consistently impair sexual functioning are called _____ _____ . Examples of such problems include _____ _____ , _____ _____ , and _____ .

4. In most mammals, females are sexually receptive only during ovulation, when the hormones, called _____ (such as _____), have peaked.

5. The importance of the hormone _____ to male sexual arousal is confirmed by the fact that sexual interest declines in animals if their _____ are removed. In women, low levels of the hormone _____ may cause a waning of sexual interest.

6. Normal hormonal fluctuations in humans have _____ (little/significant) effect on sexual motivation. In later life, frequency of intercourse _____ (increases/decreases) as sex hormone levels _____ (increase/decline).

The Psychology of Sex

Objective 33-2: Discuss the impact of external and internal stimuli on human sexual motivation.

7. Research has shown that erotic stimuli _____ (are/are not) nearly as arousing for women as for men.

8. Brain scans reveal more activity in the _____ among _____ (women/men) who are viewing erotica.

9. With repeated exposure, the emotional response to an erotic stimulus often _____ .

Explain some of the possible harmful consequences of sexually explicit material.

10. Most women and men _____ (have/ do not have) sexual fantasies. Compared with women's fantasies, men's sexual fantasies are more _____ _____ .

Sexual fantasies _____ (do/do not) indicate sexual problems or dissatisfaction.

Adolescent Sexuality

Objective 33-3: Discuss the factors that influence teen pregnancy and risk of sexually transmitted infections.

11. Sexual expression varies widely from one _____ to another and with the passage of _____ . Rates of teen intercourse are roughly similar in _____ _____ and _____ _____ but much lower in _____ and _____ countries and among North Americans of _____ descent.

12. Compared with European teens, American teens have _____ (higher/lower) rates of teen pregnancy.

State four factors that contribute to the high rate of unprotected sex among teenagers.

13. (Close-Up) An APA report points to the increasing _____ of girls, which harms their _____ and leads to unhealthy _____ _____ . This occurs when girls (a) are led to value themselves in terms of their _____ _____ ; (b) compare themselves with narrowly defined _____ _____ ; and (c) see themselves as _____ _____ .

14. Unprotected sex has led to an increase in adolescent rates of _____ _____ _____ .

Teenage girls, because of their not yet fully mature biological development and lower levels of protective _____ , may be especially vulnerable to STIs.

State several predictors of sexual restraint (reduced teen sexuality and pregnancy).

APPLICATIONS:

15. Which of the following was NOT identified as a contributing factor in the high rate of unprotected sex among adolescents?
    a. alcohol use
    b. thrill-seeking
    c. mass media sexual norms
    d. guilt

16. Which of the following teens is most likely to delay the initiation of sex?
    a. Jack, who has below-average intelligence
    b. Jason, who is not religiously active
    c. Ron, who regularly volunteers his time in community service
    d. It is impossible to predict.

Sexual Orientation

Objective 33-4: Summarize what research has taught us about sexual orientation.

17. A person's sexual attraction toward members of a particular gender is referred to as

    _____ _____ .

18. Most homosexuals begin thinking of themselves as gay or lesbian _____ (age).

19. Studies in Europe and the United States indicate that approximately _____ percent of men and _____ percent of women are exclusively homosexual. This finding suggests that popular estimates of the rate of homosexuality are _____ (high/low/accurate).

20. Sexual orientation _____ (is/is not) an indicator of mental health.

21. Some homosexuals struggle with their sexual orientation and are at increased risk of _____ attempts.

22. A person's sexual orientation _____ (does/does not) appear to be voluntarily chosen. Several research studies reveal that sexual orientation among _____ (women/men) tends to be less strongly felt and potentially more changeable than among the other gender. This phenomenon has been called the gender difference in _____

    _____ .

23. Childhood events and family relationships _____ (are/are not) important factors in determining a person's sexual orientation. Also, homosexuality _____ (does/does not) involve a fear of the other gender that leads people to direct their sexual desires toward members of their own gender.

24. Sex hormone levels _____ (do/do not) predict sexual orientation.

25. As children, most homosexuals _____ (were/were not) sexually victimized.

26. Homosexual and bisexual people appear more often in certain populations, including

    _____ , _____

    _____ , _____ ,

    and _____ .

27. Men who have older brothers are somewhat _____ (more/less) likely to be gay. This phenomenon, which has been called the _____ _____-

    _____ _____ ,

    may represent a defensive maternal _____ response to substances produced by _____ (male/female) fetuses.

28. One theory proposes that people develop a homosexual orientation if they are segregated with _____ (their own/the other) gender at the time their sex drive matures. The fact that early homosexual behavior _____ (does/does not) make people homosexual _____ (supports/conflicts with) this theory.

29. Same-sex attraction _____ (does/does not) occur among animals.

30. Researcher Simon LeVay discovered a cluster of cells in the

    _____

    that is larger in _____ men than in all others. Gays and lesbians differ from their straight counterparts in their preference for sex-related

    _____ .

31. Studies of twins suggest that genes probably _____ (do/do not) play a role in homosexuality. Research has confirmed that homosexual men have more homosexual relatives on their _____ (mother's/father's) side than on their _____ (mother's/father's) side.

32. In animals and some exceptional human cases, sexual orientation has been altered by abnormal _____ conditions during prenatal development. In humans, prenatal exposure to hormone levels typical of _____ , particularly between _____ and _____ months after conception, may predispose an attraction to males.

33. Gays and lesbians may have certain physical traits that fall midway between straight males and females, including _____ _____ counts, greater odds of being _____ (right/left)-handed, and anatomical traits of the _____ within the hearing system. Gay men's scores on tests of _____ _____ resemble those of straight women.

34. The consistency of brain, genetic, and prenatal findings suggests that _____ plays the larger role in predisposing sexual orientation, which explains why sexual orientation is _____ (difficult/relatively easy) to change. Those who believe that sexual orientation is determined by _____ express more accepting attitudes toward homosexual persons.

APPLICATION:

35. Summarizing his presentation on the origins of homosexuality, Dennis explains that the fraternal birth-order effect refers to the fact that
    a. men who have younger brothers are somewhat more likely to be gay.
    b. men who have older brothers are somewhat more likely to be gay.
    c. women with older sisters are somewhat more likely to be gay.
    d. women with younger sisters are somewhat more likely to be gay.

Sex and Human Values

Objective 33-5: Discuss whether scientific research on sexual motivation is value free.

36. The study of sexual behavior and what motivates it _____ (can/cannot) be free of values.

37. Researchers' values _____ (should/should not) be openly stated.

The Need to Belong

Objective 33-6: Describe the evidence that points to our human need to belong.

38. The philosopher _____ referred to humans as the _____ animal. From an evolutionary standpoint, social bonds in humans boosted our ancestors' _____ rates. As adults, those who formed _____ were more likely to _____ and co-nurture their offspring to maturity.

39. When asked what makes life meaningful, most people mention _____ _____ .

    People experience a deep sense of well-being when their need for relatedness is satisfied along with two other basic psychological needs: _____ and _____ .

40. Feeling accepted and loved by others boosts our _____ .

41. Much of our _____ behavior aims to increase our belonging. For most people, familiarity leads to _____ (liking/disliking).

42. After years of placing individual refugee and immigrant families in _____ communities, U.S. policies today encourage _____ _____ .

43. _____ (Throughout the world/ Only in certain cultures do) people use social exclusion, or _____ , to control social behavior. Researchers have found that social exclusion elicits increased activity in brain areas, such as the _____ _____ _____ , that also activate in response to _____ .

44. Researchers have found that people who are rejected are more likely to engage in _____ behaviors, to

underperform on _____ _____ , and to act in disparaging or _____ ways.

Objective 33-7: Describe how social networking influences us.

45. History's most rapidly adopted technology are _____ _____ .

46. Phone talking is being displaced by the greater use of _____ and _____ .

47. People who are _____ tend to spend greater-than-average time online.

48. People who are active in _____ _____ are less likely to know their real-world neighbors.

49. Texting and e-mailing can stimulate healthy _____ but an even better predictor of life satisfaction is _____ _____ .

50. Generally speaking, social networks _____ (reveal/do not reveal) people's real personalities.

51. People who are overly self-important, self-focused, and self-promoting are said to be _____ . People who score high on this trait tend to be _____ (especially active/less active) on social networking sites.

APPLICATIONS:

52. Summarizing her report on the need to belong, Rolanda states that
   a. "Cooperation amongst our ancestors was uncommon."
   b. "Social bonding is not in our nature; it is a learned human trait."
   c. "Because bonding with others increased our ancestors' success at reproduction and survival, it became part of our biological nature."
   d. "Our male ancestors were more likely to bond than were females."

53. Right after dinner, Dennis goes to his room, turns on his computer, and begins chatting with friends on Facebook. Which of the following is true, according to the most recent research?
   a. His connections with friends have been strengthened.
   b. He is more willing to disclose personal thoughts and feelings, which deepens his friendships.
   c. He reveals his true personality to friends and others online.
   d. All of these statements are true.

PROGRESS TEST

Multiple-Choice Questions

Circle your answers to the following questions and check them with the answers beginning on page 289. If your answer is incorrect, read the explanation for why it is incorrect and then consult the text.

1. Some scientific evidence makes a preliminary link between homosexuality and
   a. late sexual maturation.
   b. the age of an individual's first erotic experience.
   c. atypical prenatal hormones.
   d. early problems in relationships with parents.

2. The correct order of the stages of Masters and Johnson's sexual response cycle is
   a. plateau; excitement; orgasm; resolution.
   b. excitement; plateau; orgasm; resolution.
   c. excitement; orgasm; resolution; refractory.
   d. plateau; excitement; orgasm; refractory.

3. Which of the following is NOT true regarding sexual orientation?
   a. Sexual orientation is neither willfully chosen nor willfully changed.
   b. Some homosexuals struggle with their sexual orientation.
   c. Men's sexual orientation is potentially more fluid and changeable than women's.
   d. Women, regardless of sexual orientation, respond to both female and male erotic stimuli.

4. When asked what makes life meaningful, most people first mention
   a. good health.
   b. challenging work.
   c. satisfying relationships.
   d. serving others.

5. Castration of male rats results in
   a. reduced testosterone and sexual interest.
   b. reduced testosterone, but no change in sexual interest.
   c. reduced estradiol and sexual interest.
   d. reduced estradiol, but no change in sexual interest.

6. It has been said that the body's major sex organ is the brain. With regard to sex education
   a. transmission of value-free information about the wide range of sexual behaviors should be the primary focus of the educator.
   b. transmission of technical knowledge about the biological act should be the classroom focus, free from the personal values and attitudes of researchers, teachers, and students.
   c. the home, not the school, should be the focus of all instruction about reproductive behavior.
   d. people's attitudes, values, and morals cannot be separated from the biological aspects of sexuality.

7. Exposure of a fetus to the hormones typical of females between _____ and _____ months after conception may predispose the developing human to become attracted to males.
   a. 1; 3   c. 4; 7
   b. 2; 5   d. 6; 9

8. Which of the following statements concerning homosexuality is true?
   a. Homosexuals have abnormal hormone levels.
   b. As children, most homosexuals were molested by an adult homosexual.
   c. Homosexuals had a domineering opposite-sex parent.
   d. Research indicates that sexual orientation may be at least partly physiological.

9. Sexual orientation refers to
   a. a person's tendency to display behaviors typical of males or females.
   b. a person's sense of identity as a male or female.
   c. a person's enduring sexual attraction toward members of a particular gender.
   d. all of these.

10. According to Masters and Johnson, the sexual response of males is most likely to differ from that of females during
    a. the excitement phase.
    b. the plateau phase.
    c. orgasm.
    d. the resolution phase.

True–False Items

Indicate whether each statement is true or false by placing *T* or *F* in the blank next to the item.

_____ 1. According to Masters and Johnson, only males experience a plateau period in the cycle of sexual arousal.

_____ 2. Testosterone affects the sexual arousal of the male only.

_____ 3. Unlike men, women tend not to be aroused by sexually explicit material.

_____ 4. Separated or divorced people are half as likely as married people to say they are happy.

_____ 5. One's sexual orientation is not voluntarily chosen.

_____ 6. Eighty percent of people in the United States think homosexuality is never justified.

TERMS AND CONCEPTS TO REMEMBER

Using your own words, write on a separate piece of paper a brief definition or explanation of each of the following terms.

1. sexual response cycle

2. refractory period

3. sexual disorder

4. estrogens

5. testosterone

6. sexual orientation

ANSWERS
Module Review

The Physiology of Sex

1. Masters; Johnson; excitement; plateau; orgasm; resolution

2. refractory period

3. sexual disorders; premature ejaculation; erectile dysfunction; orgasmic dysfunction

4. estrogens; estradiol

5. testosterone; testes; testosterone

6. little; decreases; decline

The Psychology of Sex

7. are

8. amygdala; men

9. habituates

Erotic material may increase the viewer's acceptance of the false idea that women enjoy rape, may increase men's willingness to hurt women, may lead people to devalue their partners and relationships, and may diminish people's satisfaction with their own sexual partners.

10. have; frequent, physical, and less romantic; do not

Adolescent Sexuality

11. culture; time; Western Europe; Latin America; Asian; Arab; Asian

12. higher

Among the factors that contribute to unprotected sex among adolescents are (1) minimal communication about birth control, (2) guilt related to sexual activity, (3) alcohol use that influences judgment, and (4) mass media norms of unprotected promiscuity.

13. sexualization; self-image; sexual development; sexual appeal; beauty standards; sexual beings for others' use

14. sexually transmitted infection (STI); antibodies

Teens with high intelligence test scores, those who are actively religious, those whose father is present, and those who participate in service learning programs more often delay sex. Trends toward commitment show declining teen birth rates.

15. b. is the answer.

16. c. is the answer.
a., b., & d. Teens with high rather than average intelligence (therefore, not a.), and those who are religiously active (therefore, not b.) are most likely to delay sex.

Sexual Orientation

17. sexual orientation

18. in their teens or twenties

19. 3; 1 or 2; high

20. is not

21. suicide

22. does not; women; erotic plasticity

23. are not; does not

24. do not

25. were not

26. poets; fiction writers; artists; musicians

27. more; fraternal birth-order effect; immune; male

28. their own; does not; conflicts with

29. does

30. hypothalamus; heterosexual; odors

31. do; mother's; father's

32. hormone; females; 2; 5

33. fingerprint ridge; left; cochlea; spatial abilities

34. biology; difficult; biology

35. b. is the answer.

Sex and Human Values

36. cannot

37. should

The Need to Belong

38. Aristotle; social; survival; attachments; reproduce

39. close, satisfying relationships with family, friends, or romantic partners; autonomy; competence

40. self-esteem

41. social; liking

42. isolated; chain migration

43. Throughout the world; ostracism; anterior cingulate cortex; pain

44. self-defeating; aptitude tests; aggressive

45. cell phones

46. e-mail; texting

47. lonely

48. social networking

49. self-disclosure; eye-to-eye conversation

50. reveal

51. narcissistic; especially active

52. c. is the answer.

53. d. is the answer.

Progress Test

Multiple-Choice Questions

1. c. is the answer.
a., b., & d. None of these is linked to homosexuality.

2. b. is the answer.

3. **c.** is the answer. Research studies suggest that women's sexual orientation is potentially more fluid and changeable than men's.

4. **c.** is the answer.

5. **a.** is the answer.
   c. & d. Castration of the testes, which produce testosterone, does not alter estrogen levels.

6. **d.** is the answer. Sex is much more than just a biological act, and its study therefore inherently involves values, attitudes, and morals, which should thus be discussed openly.

7. **b.** is the answer. The time between the middle of the second and fifth months after conception may be a critical period for the brain's neuro-hormonal control system. Exposure to abnormal hormonal conditions at other times has no effect on sexual orientation.

8. **d.** is the answer. Researchers have not been able to find any clear differences, psychological or otherwise, between homosexuals and heterosexuals. Thus, the basis for sexual orientation remains unknown, although recent evidence points more to a physiological basis.

9. **c.** is the answer.

10. **d.** is the answer. During the resolution phase males experience a refractory period.
    a., b., & c. The male and female responses are very similar in each of these phases.

True–False Items

1. F   4. T
2. F   5. T
3. F   6. F

Terms and Concepts to Remember

1. The **sexual response cycle** described by Masters and Johnson consists of four stages of bodily reaction: excitement, plateau, orgasm, and resolution.

2. The **refractory period** is a resting period after orgasm, during which a male cannot be aroused to another orgasm.

3. A **sexual disorder** is a problem—such as erectile dysfunction, premature ejaculation, and orgasmic dysfunction—that consistently impairs sexual arousal or functioning.

4. **Estrogens** are sex hormones, such as estradiol, secreted in greater amounts by females than by males and contributing to female sex characteristics. In mammals other than humans, estrogen levels peak during ovulation and trigger sexual receptivity.

5. **Testosterone** is a sex hormone secreted in greater amounts by males than by females. In males, higher testosterone levels stimulate the prenatal growth of the male sex organs and the development of the male sex characteristics during puberty.

6. **Sexual orientation** refers to a person's enduring attraction to members of either the same or the opposite gender.

Motivation at Work

MODULE OVERVIEW

People who view their work as a meaningful calling, those working in jobs that optimize their skills, and those who become absorbed in activities that result in flow find work satisfying and enriching. Effective leaders recognize this and develop management styles that focus on workers' strengths and adapt their leadership style to the situation. Research on achievement motivation underscores the importance of self-discipline and persistence in achieving one's goals. Human factors psychologists focus on developing ways of making machines and work settings user-friendly.

NOTE: Answer guidelines for all Module 34 questions begin on page 295.

MODULE REVIEW

First, skim each section, noting headings and bold-face items. After you have read the section, review each objective by answering the fill-in and essay-type questions that follow it. In some cases, Study Tips explain how best to learn a difficult concept and Applications help you to know how well you understand the material. As you proceed, evaluate your performance by consulting the answers beginning on page 295. Do not continue with the next section until you understand each answer. If you need to, review or reread the section in the textbook before continuing.

Introduction

Objective 34-1: Explain the concept of "flow," and identify three subfields of industrial-organizational psychology.

1. People who view their work as an unfulfilling but necessary way to make money see it as a

_____ . Those who see it as an opportunity to advance from one position to a better one view work as a _____ . People who view their work as a _____ report the greatest satisfaction.

2. Psychologist Mihaly Csikszentmihalyi formulated the concept of _____ , which is defined as a focused state of _____ and diminished awareness of _____ and time. People who experience this state also experience increased feelings of

_____ , _____ , and _____ .

3. In many nations, the nature of work has changed, from _____ to _____ to _____ .

4. The sense of mutual obligations between workers and employers is called the

_____ _____ .

5. The field of _____-_____ psychology applies psychology's principles to the workplace. The subfield of _____ psychology focuses on employee recruitment, training, appraisal, and development. Another subfield, _____ psychology, examines how work environments and _____ styles influence worker motivation, satisfaction, and productivity. A third subfield,

_____ _____

psychology, focuses on the design of appliances, machines, and work environments.

APPLICATION:

6. Which of the following individuals would be characterized as experiencing flow?
   a. Sheila, who, despite viewing her work as merely a job, performs her work conscientiously
   b. Larry, who sees his work as an artist as a calling
   c. Arnie, who views his present job as merely a stepping stone in his career
   d. Montel, who often becomes so immersed in his writing that he loses all sense of self and time

Personnel Psychology

Objective 34-2: Describe how personnel psychologists help organizations with employee selection, work placement, and performance appraisal.

7. Researchers note that the first step to a stronger organization is to institute a

   _____-_____

   selection system, which matches strengths to work.

8. (Close-Up) Satisfied and successful people devote less time to _____

   _____ than to

   _____ _____ .

9. Interviewers tend to _____ (feel confident/lack confidence) in their ability to predict job performance from unstructured interviews. These impressions tend to be highly _____ (accurate/error-prone).

10. The best predictor of long-term job performance for most jobs is _____

    _____ _____ .

    Interviewers tend to _____ (over/under) estimate their interviewing skills and intuition—a phenomenon labeled the

    _____ _____ .

State four effects that fuel this phenomenon.

11. A more disciplined method of collecting information from job applicants is the

    _____ _____ ,

    which asks the same questions of all applicants. This method enhances the _____ accuracy and _____ of the interview process.

12. Performance appraisal has several purposes, including helping organizations decide

    _____ ,

    how to appropriately _____

    _____ ,

    and how to better harness employees'

    _____ . Performance appraisal methods include _____ ,

    _____ _____ scales,

    and _____ _____ scales.

13. Some organizations practice _____-

    _____ feedback, in which employees not only rate themselves but are also rated by their supervisors and other colleagues.

14. Performance appraisal is subject to bias. When the overall evaluation of an employee biases ratings of work-related behaviors, a

    _____ _____

    has occurred. The tendency to be too easy or too harsh results in _____ and

    _____ errors, respectively. When raters focus on easily remembered recent behavior, they are committing the

    _____ error.

Organizational Psychology: Motivating Achievement

Objective 34-3: Define *achievement motivation*, and describe the role of organizational psychologists.

15. Psychologists refer to the desire for significant accomplishments, for mastering skills or ideas, for control, and for attaining a high standard as

    _____ _____ .

16. Research has shown that _____ is a better predictor of school performance than

    _____ _____ have been. Extremely successful individuals

differ from equally talented peers in their
_____ , their passionate dedication to a long-term goal.

17. Positive moods at work contribute to worker
_____ , _____ , and
_____ .

Researchers have also
found a positive correla-
tion between measures of
organizational success and
employee _____ , or the extent of
workers' involvement, satisfaction, and
enthusiasm.

STUDY TIP: Research studies have shown that people who possess a low need for achievement tend to
prefer situations and tasks that are either very easy
or impossibly hard. Conversely, people with a high
need for achievement tend to prefer tasks that are
moderately difficult. Why do you think this might be?
Which types of tasks (e.g., college courses) do you
prefer?

APPLICATIONS:

18. During a meeting with the parents of a struggling high school student, the guidance counselor notes which of the following as the best
predictor of school performance?

   a. attendance
   b. intelligence scores
   c. talent
   d. self-discipline

19. Darren, a sales clerk at a tire store, enjoys his
job, not so much for the money as for its challenge and the opportunity to interact with
a variety of people. The store manager asks
you to recommend a strategy for increasing
Darren's motivation. Which of the following is
most likely to be effective?

   a. Create a competition among the salespeople
   so that whoever has the highest sales each
   week receives a bonus.
   b. Put Darren on a week-by-week employment
   contract, promising him continued employment only if his sales increase each week.
   c. Leave Darren alone unless his sales drop and
   then threaten to fire him if his performance
   doesn't improve.
   d. Involve Darren as much as possible in company decision making and use rewards to in-
   form him of his successful performance.

Objective 34-4: Describe some effective leadership
techniques.

20. The best managers help people to
_____ , match
tasks to _____ , care how their
people feel about their work, and
_____ positive behaviors.

21. Higher worker achievement is motivated by a
leader who sets _____ ,
_____ goals. When people state
goals together with _____ and
_____ _____ , they
become more focused in their work.

22. Managers who are directive, set clear standards,
organize work, and focus attention on specific
goals are said to employ _____
_____ . More democratic manag-
ers who aim to build teamwork and mediate
conflicts in the work force employ
_____ _____ .

23. Effective leaders tend to exude a self-confident
_____ that is a mix of a
_____ of some goal, an ability to
_____ the goal clearly, and
enough optimism to _____ oth-
ers to follow. Leadership that inspires others to
transcend their own self-interests for the sake of
the group is called _____
leadership.

24. The most effective style of leadership
_____ (varies/does not vary)
with the situation and/or the person.

25. Effective managers _____
(rarely/often) exhibit a high degree of both task
and social leadership. The _____
effect occurs when people respond more positively to managerial decisions on which they
have voiced an opinion.

STUDY TIP: Think about several leaders you know.
These might be group leaders, employers, teachers, and relatives. Of these people, whose leadership
skills do you admire the most? Why? What type of
leadership style (e.g., social leadership, task leadership) best characterizes this person?

The Human Factor

Objective 34-5: Describe human factors psychologists' work to create user-friendly machines and work settings.

26. Human factors psychologists help to design machines and work settings that fit our

    _____ .

    They also work to devise ways to reduce the _ _____ , _____ , and _____ that contribute to traffic accidents.

27. One example of good design is the use of

    _____ _____ that broadcast sound directly through a person's own hearing aid. This is an example of an effective _____ _____ technology.

PROGRESS TEST

Multiple-Choice Questions

Circle your answers to the following questions and check them with the answers on page 296. If your answer is incorrect, read the explanation for why it is incorrect and then consult the text.

1. The best predictor of on-the-job performance for all but less-skilled jobs is
   a. age.
   b. general mental ability.
   c. motivation.
   d. stated intentions.

2. To increase employee productivity, industrial-organizational psychologists advise managers to
   a. adopt a directive leadership style.
   b. adopt a democratic leadership style.
   c. instill competitiveness in each employee.
   d. deal with employees according to their individual motives.

3. For as long as she has been the plant manager, Juanita has welcomed input from employees and has delegated authority. Bill, in managing his department, takes a more authoritarian, iron-fisted approach. Juanita's style is one of _____ leadership, whereas Bill's is one of _____ leadership.
   a. task; social
   b. social; task
   c. directive; democratic
   d. democratic; participative

4. Dr. Iverson conducts research focusing on how management styles influence worker motivation. Dr. Iverson would most accurately be described as a(n)
   a. motivation psychologist.
   b. personnel psychologist.
   c. organizational psychologist.
   d. human factors psychologist.

5. Which of the following is NOT an aspect of Murray's definition of achievement motivation?
   a. the desire to master skills
   b. the desire for control
   c. the desire to gain approval
   d. the desire to attain a high standard

6. Which of the following was NOT identified as a contributing factor in the interviewer illusion?
   a. The fact that interviews reveal applicants' intentions but not necessarily their habitual behaviors.
   b. The tendency of interviewers to think that interview behavior only reflects applicants' enduring traits.
   c. The tendency of interviewers to more often follow the successful careers of applicants they hired rather than those who were not hired.
   d. The tendency of most interviewers to rely on unstructured rather than structured interviews.

7. Munson is conducting his annual appraisal of employees' performance. Which of the following is NOT a type of appraisal method?
   a. graphic rating
   b. behavior rating
   c. checklist
   d. unstructured interview

8. Because Brent believes that his employees are intrinsically motivated to work for reasons beyond money, Brent would be described as a(n) _____ manager.
   a. directive
   b. social-oriented
   c. task-oriented
   d. charismatic

9. Jack works for a company that requires employees to periodically rate their own performance and to be rated by their managers, other colleagues, and customers. This type of assessment is called
   a. 360-degree feedback.
   b. multifactorial evaluation.
   c. analytical performance review.
   d. human resource management.

Matching Items

Match each term with its definition or description.

Terms

_____ 1. human factors psychology
_____ 2. personnel psychology
_____ 3. organizational psychology
_____ 4. flow
_____ 5. task leadership
_____ 6. social leadership
_____ 7. industrial-organizational psychology

TERMS AND CONCEPTS TO REMEMBER

Writing Definitions

Using your own words, write on a separate piece of paper a brief definition or explanation of each of the following terms.

1. flow
2. industrial-organizational psychology
3. personnel psychology
4. organizational psychology
5. human factors psychology
6. structured interviews
7. achievement motivation
8. task leadership
8. social leadership

ANSWERS
Module Review

Introduction

1. job; career; calling
2. flow; consciousness; self; self-esteem, competence, well-being
3. farming; manufacturing; knowledge work
4. psychological contract
5. industrial-organizational; personnel; organizational; management; human factors
6. **d.** is the answer.

Definitions or Descriptions

a. state of focused consciousness
b. studies issues related to optimizing behavior in workplaces
c. seeks to optimize person-machine interactions
d. applies psychological methods and principles to the selection and evaluation of workers
e. goal-oriented leadership that sets standards, organizes work, and focuses attention on goals
f. seeks to maximize worker satisfaction and productivity
g. group-oriented leadership that builds teamwork, mediates conflict, and offers support

Personnel Psychology

7. strengths-based
8. correcting deficiencies; accentuating strengths
9. feel confident; error-prone
10. general mental ability; over; interviewer illusion
    Four effects that fuel the interviewer illusion are
    a. Interviews disclose the interviewees' good intentions, which are less revealing than their typical behaviors.
    b. Interviewers tend to follow the successful careers of people they hired and lose track of those they did not hire.
    c. Interviewers mistakenly presume that *how* interviewees present themselves reflects only their enduring traits.
    d. Interviewers' preconceptions and moods influence their perceptions of job applicants.
11. structured interview; predictive; reliability
12. whom to retain; reward and pay workers; strengths; checklists; graphic rating; behavior rating
13. 360-degree
14. halo error; leniency; severity; recency

Organizational Psychology: Motivating Achievement

15. achievement motivation
16. self-discipline; intelligence scores; grit
17. creativity; persistence; helpfulness; engagement
18. **d.** is the answer.
19. **d.** is the answer. Because Darren appears to resonate with the principle that people are intrinsically motivated to work for reasons beyond money, giving him feedback about his work and

involving him in decision making are probably all he needs to be very satisfied with his situation.

a., b., & c. Creating competitions and using controlling, rather than informing, rewards may have the opposite effect and actually undermine Darren's motivation.

20. identify and measure their talents; talent; reinforce

21. specific; challenging; subgoals; implementation intentions

22. task leadership; social leadership

23. charisma; vision; communicate; inspire; transformational

24. varies

25. often; voice

The Human Factor

26. natural perceptions and inclinations; distractions; fatigue; inattention

27. loop systems; assistive listening

Progress Test

Multiple-Choice Questions

1. **b**. is the answer.

2. **d**. is the answer. As different people are motivated by different things, to increase motivation and thus productivity, managers are advised to learn what motivates individual employees and to challenge and reward them accordingly.
   a. & b. The most effective management style will depend on the situation.
   c. This might be an effective strategy with some, but not all, employees.

3. **b**. is the answer.
   a. Bill's style is one of task leadership, whereas Juanita's is one of social leadership.
   c. Juanita's style is democratic, whereas Bill's is directive.
   d. Participative is another term used to refer to the social or group-oriented style of leadership.

4. **c**. is the answer.

5. **c**. is the answer.

6. **d**. is the answer. Although unstructured interviews *are* more prone to bias than structured interviews, the text does not suggest that they are used more often.

7. **d**. is the answer.

a., b., & c. These are all performance appraisal methods used by supervisors.

8. **b**. is the answer.
   a. & c. Directive, or task-oriented, managers are likely to assume that worker motivation is low.
   d. The most effective leaders are generally charismatic, which has nothing to do with whether they are directive or democratic leaders.

9. **a**. is the answer.

Matching Items

1. c	5. e
2. d	6. g
3. f	7. b
4. a	

Terms and Concepts to Remember

1. **Flow** is a completely involved, focused state of consciousness on a task that optimally engages a person's skills, accompanied by a diminished awareness of self and time.

2. **Industrial-organizational (I/O) psychology** is a profession that applies psychological concepts and methods to optimizing human behavior in workplaces.

3. **Personnel psychology** is a subfield of I/O psychology that applies psychological methods and principles to the selection and evaluation of workers.

4. **Organizational psychology** is a subfield of I/O psychology that explores how work environments and management styles affect worker motivation, satisfaction, and productivity.

5. **Human factors psychology** is a branch of psychology that explores how people and machines interact and how physical environments can be made safer and easier to use.

6. A **structured interview** is one in which an interviewer asks the same job-relevant questions of all interviewees, who are then rated on established evaluation scales.

7. **Achievement motivation** is a desire for significant accomplishment; for mastery of things, people, or ideas; and for rapidly attaining a high standard.

8. **Task leadership** is goal-oriented leadership that sets standards, organizes work, and focuses attention on goals.

9. **Social leadership** is group-oriented leadership that builds teamwork, mediates conflict, and offers support.

Introduction to Emotion

MODULE OVERVIEW

Emotions are responses of the whole individual, involving physiological arousal, expressive behaviors, and conscious experience. Module 35 discusses several theoretical controversies concerning the relationship and sequence of the components of emotion, primarily regarding whether the body's response to a stimulus causes the emotion that is felt and whether thinking is necessary to and must precede the experience of emotion. It also examines the physiological changes that accompany emotions, explaining how they may differ from one emotion to another.

NOTE: Answer guidelines for all Module 35 questions begin on page 303.

MODULE REVIEW

First, skim each section, noting headings and boldface items. After you have read the section, review each objective by answering the fill-in and essay-type questions that follow it. In some cases, Study Tips explain how best to learn a difficult concept and Applications help you to know how well you understand the material. As you proceed, evaluate your performance by consulting the answers beginning on page 303. Do not continue with the next section until you understand each answer. If you need to, review or reread the section in the textbook before continuing.

Cognition and Emotion

Objective 35-1: Describe how arousal and expressive behaviors interact in emotion.

1. Emotions have three components: _____ _____ , _____ _____ , and _____ _____ .

2. According to the James-Lange theory, emotional states _____ (precede/follow) bodily responses.

Describe two problems that Walter Cannon identified with the James-Lange theory.

3. Cannon proposed that emotional stimuli in the environment are routed simultaneously to the _____ , which results in awareness of the emotion, and to the _____ nervous system, which causes the body's reaction. Because another scientist concurrently proposed similar ideas, this theory has come to be known as the _____-_____ theory.

Objective 35-2: Explain whether we can experience emotions without consciously interpreting and labeling them.

4. The two-factor theory of emotion proposes that emotion has two components: _____ arousal and a _____ label. This theory was proposed by _____ and _____ .

5. The *spillover effect* refers to occasions when our _____ response to one event carries over into our response to another event.

6. Schachter and Singer found that physically aroused college men told that an injection would cause arousal _____ (did/did not) become emotional in response to an accomplice's aroused behavior. Physically aroused volunteers not expecting arousal _____ (did/did not) become emotional in response to an accomplice's behavior.

7. Arousal _____ emotion; cognition _____ emotion.

8. Robert Zajonc believes that the feeling of emotion _____ (can/cannot) precede our cognitive labeling of that emotion.

Cite two pieces of evidence that support Zajonc's position.

9. A pathway from the _____ via the (a) _____ to the (b) _____ enables us to experience emotion before _____ . For more complex emotions, sensory input is routed through the (c) _____ for interpretation.

10. The researcher who disagrees with Zajonc and argues that most emotions require cognitive processing is _____ . According to this view, emotions arise when we _____ an event as beneficial or harmful to our well-being.

11. Complex emotions are affected by our _____ , _____ , and _____ .

Express some general conclusions that can be drawn about cognition and emotion.

STUDY TIP/APPLICATION: The theories of emotion discussed in this chapter seem so similar that it's often hard to tell them apart. As you think about the theories, remember: The theories differ in the order of importance they assign to the three components of emotions: physical arousal (increased heart rate, for example), the expression of the emotion (feeling angry, for example), and the importance of cognitive appraisal of the situation in which the emotion has occurred. To help ensure your understanding of the theories, see if you can fill in the missing information in the chart below for a common emotional experience: Hearing the screeching of a car's tires. For example, the first response might be a physical reaction such as increased heart beat or an emotional expression of fear, or it might be the opposite.

12. Theory	Stimulus Event	First Response	Second Response	Third Response
James-Lange	Screeching tires			
Cannon-Bard	Screeching tires			
Schachter-Singer	Screeching tires			

APPLICATIONS:

13. You are on your way to school to take a big exam. Suddenly, you feel nervous and you notice that your pulse is racing and you are sweating. This fits with the _____-_____ theory of emotion.

14. Two years ago, Maria was in an automobile accident in which her spinal cord was severed, leaving her paralyzed from the neck down. Today, Maria finds that she experiences emotions less intensely than she did before her accident. This tends to support the _____-_____ theory of emotion.

15. After hitting a grand-slam home run, Mike noticed that his heart was pounding. Later that evening, after nearly having a collision while driving on the freeway, Mike again noticed that his heart was pounding. That he interpreted this reaction as fear, rather than as ecstasy, can best be explained by the _____-_____ theory of emotion.

Embodied Emotion

Objective 35-3: Describe the link between emotional arousal and the autonomic nervous system, and discuss the relationship between arousal and performance.

16. Describe the major physiological changes that each of the following undergoes during emotional arousal

   a. heart: _____

   b. liver: _____

   c. respiration: _____

   d. digestion: _____

   e. pupils: _____

   f. blood: _____

   g. skin: _____

17. The responses of arousal are activated by the _____ nervous system. In response to its signal, the _____ glands release the stress hormones _____ and _____ .

18. When the need for arousal has passed, the body is calmed through activation of the _____ nervous system.

Objective 35-4: Discuss whether different emotions activate different physiological and brain-pattern responses.

19. The various emotions are associated with _____ (similar/different) forms of physiological arousal. In particular, the emotions of _____ , _____ , and _____ are difficult to distinguish physiologically.

20. A neural center in the brain called the _____ is activated when we experience lust, pride, and _____ .

21. The emotions _____ and _____ are sometimes accompanied by differing _____ temperatures and _____ secretions.

22. The emotions _____ and _____ stimulate different facial muscles.

23. The brain circuits underlying different emotions
_____ (are/are not) different. For example, seeing a fearful face elicits greater activity in the _____ than seeing a(n) _____ face. People who have generally negative personalities, and those who are prone to _____ , show more
_____ _____
lobe activity.

24. When people experience positive moods, brain scans reveal more activity in the
_____ _____
_____ .

25. Individuals with more active _____ (right/left) _____ lobes tend to be more cheerful than those in whom this pattern of brain activity is reversed.

Objective 35-5: Discuss the effectiveness of polygraphs in using body states to detect lies.

26. (Thinking Critically) The technical name for the "lie detector" is the _____ .

(Thinking Critically) Explain how lie detectors supposedly indicate whether a person is lying.

27. (Thinking Critically) How well the lie detector works depends on whether a person exhibits _____ while lying.

28. (Thinking Critically) Those who criticize lie detectors feel that the tests are particularly likely to err in the case of the _____ (innocent/guilty), because different _____ all register as
_____ .

29. (Thinking Critically) By and large, experts _____ (agree/do not agree) that lie detector tests are highly accurate.

30. (Thinking Critically) A test that assesses a suspect's knowledge of details of a crime that only the guilty person should know is the
_____ _____
_____ .

APPLICATIONS:

31. A student participating in an experiment concerned with physical responses that indicate emotions reports that her mouth is dry, her heart is racing, and she feels flushed. Can the emotion she is experiencing be determined?
   a. Yes, it is anger.
   b. Yes, it is fear.
   c. Yes, it is ecstasy.
   d. No, it cannot be determined from the information given.

32. Julio was extremely angry when he came in for a routine EEG of his brain activity. When he later told this to the doctor, she was no longer concerned about the
   a. increased electrical activity in Julio's right hemisphere.
   b. increased electrical activity in Julio's left hemisphere.
   c. decreased electrical activity in Julio's amygdala.
   d. increased electrical activity in Julio's amygdala.

33. As part of her job interview, Jan is asked to take a lie-detector test. Jan politely refuses and points out the problems with the test, which are that
   a. _____
   b. _____

34. Nine-month-old Nicole's left frontal lobe is more active than her right frontal lobe. We can expect that, all other things being equal, Nicole
   a. may suffer from mild depression for most of her life.
   b. may have trouble "turning off" upsetting feelings later in her life.
   c. may be more cheerful than those with more active right frontal lobes.
   d. may have trouble expressing feelings later in her life.

PROGRESS TEST

Multiple-Choice Questions

Circle your answers to the following questions and check them with the answers beginning on page 304. If your answer is incorrect, read the explanation for why it is incorrect and then consult the text.

1. Which division of the nervous system is especially involved in bringing about emotional arousal?
   a. somatic nervous system
   b. peripheral nervous system
   c. sympathetic nervous system
   d. parasympathetic nervous system

2. Concerning emotions and their accompanying bodily responses, which of the following appears to be true?
   a. Each emotion has its own bodily response and underlying brain circuit.
   b. All emotions involve the same bodily response as a result of the same underlying brain circuit.
   c. Many emotions involve similar bodily responses but have different underlying brain circuits.
   d. All emotions have the same underlying brain circuits but different bodily responses.

3. The Cannon-Bard theory of emotion states that
   a. emotions have two ingredients: physical arousal and a cognitive label.
   b. the conscious experience of an emotion occurs at the same time as the body's physical reaction.
   c. emotional experiences are based on an awareness of the body's responses to an emotion-arousing stimulus.
   d. emotional ups and downs tend to balance in the long run.

4. Which of the following was NOT raised as a criticism of the James-Lange theory of emotion?
   a. The body's responses are too similar to trigger the various emotions.
   b. Emotional reactions occur before the body's responses can take place.
   c. The cognitive activity of the cortex plays a role in the emotions we experience.
   d. People with spinal cord injuries at the neck typically experience less emotion.

5. (Thinking Critically) Current estimates are that an innocent person taking a polygraph test would have been declared guilty approximately _____ of the time.
   a. three-fourths   c. one-third
   b. one-half   d. one-fourth

6. In the Schachter-Singer experiment, which college men reported feeling an emotional change in the presence of the experimenter's highly emotional confederate?
   a. those receiving epinephrine and expecting to feel physical arousal
   b. those receiving a placebo and expecting to feel physical arousal
   c. those receiving epinephrine but not expecting to feel physical arousal
   d. those receiving a placebo and not expecting to feel physical arousal

7. Emotions consist of which of the following components?
   a. physiological reactions
   b. behavioral expressions
   c. conscious feelings
   d. all of these components

8. (Thinking Critically) Law enforcement officials sometimes use a lie detector to assess a suspect's responses to details of the crime believed to be known only to the perpetrator. This is known as the
   a. inductive approach.
   b. deductive approach.
   c. guilty knowledge test.
   d. screening examination.

9. In laboratory experiments, fear and joy
   a. result in an increase in heart rate.
   b. stimulate different facial muscles.
   c. increase heart rate and stimulate different facial muscles.
   d. result in a decrease in heart rate.

10. Research with subliminally flashed stimuli supports Robert Zajonc's view that
   a. the heart is always subject to the mind.
   b. emotional reactions involve deliberate rational thinking.
   c. cognition is not necessary for emotion.
   d. responding to a subliminal stimulus is a learned skill.

11. Which of the following most accurately describes emotional arousal?
   a. Emotions prepare the body to fight or flee.
   b. Emotions are voluntary reactions to emotion-arousing stimuli.
   c. Because all emotions have the same physiological basis, emotions are primarily psychological events.
   d. Emotional arousal is always accompanied by cognition.

12. Schachter's and Singer's two-factor theory emphasizes that emotion involves both
   a. the sympathetic and parasympathetic divisions of the nervous system.
   b. verbal and nonverbal expression.
   c. physical arousal and a cognitive label.
   d. universal and culture-specific aspects.

13. Which theory of emotion emphasizes the simultaneous experience of the body's response and emotional feeling?
   a. James-Lange theory
   b. Cannon-Bard theory
   c. two-factor theory
   d. catharsis theory

14. (Thinking Critically) The polygraph measures
   a. lying.
   b. brain rhythms.
   c. chemical changes in the body.
   d. physiological indexes of arousal.

15. People who are exuberant and persistently cheerful show increased activity in the brain's
   _____ .
   a. right frontal lobe
   b. left frontal lobe
   c. amygdala
   d. thalamus

16. Which theory of emotion implies that every emotion is associated with a unique physiological reaction?
   a. James-Lange theory
   b. Cannon-Bard theory
   c. two-factor theory
   d. Zajonc's theory

17. Which of the following was NOT presented in the text as evidence that some emotional reactions involve no deliberate, rational thinking?
   a. Some of the neural pathways involved in emotion are separate from those involved in thinking and memory.
   b. Emotional reactions are sometimes quicker than our interpretations of a situation.
   c. People can develop an emotional preference for visual stimuli to which they have been unknowingly exposed.
   d. Arousal of the sympathetic nervous system will trigger an emotional reaction even when artificially induced by an injection of epinephrine.

18. In an emergency situation, emotional arousal will result in
   a. increased rate of respiration.
   b. increased blood sugar.
   c. a slowing of digestion.
   d. all of these events.

19. Several studies have shown that physical arousal can intensify just about any emotion. For example, when people who have been physically aroused by exercise are insulted, they often misattribute their arousal to the insult. This finding illustrates the importance of
   a. cognitive labels of arousal in the conscious experience of emotions.
   b. a minimum level of arousal in triggering emotional experiences.
   c. the simultaneous occurrence of physical arousal and cognitive labeling in emotional experience.
   d. all of these things.

20. (Thinking Critically) Many psychologists are opposed to the use of lie detectors because
   a. they represent an invasion of a person's privacy and could easily be used for unethical purposes.
   b. there are often serious discrepancies among the various indicators such as perspiration and heart rate.
   c. polygraphs cannot distinguish the various possible causes of arousal.
   d. they are accurate only about 50 percent of the time.

Matching Items

Match each definition or description with the appropriate term.

Definitions or Descriptions

_____ 1. emotions consist of physical arousal *and* a cognitive label

_____ 2. an emotion-arousing stimulus triggers cognitive and body responses simultaneously

_____ 3. the division of the nervous system that calms the body following arousal

_____ 4. the division of the nervous system that activates arousal

_____ 5. a device that measures the physiological correlates of emotion

_____ 6. we are sad because we cry

Terms

a. two-factor theory
b. sympathetic nervous system
c. James-Lange theory
d. polygraph
e. Cannon-Bard theory
f. parasympathetic nervous system

True–False Items

Indicate whether each statement is true or false by placing *T* or *F* in the blank next to the item.

_____ 1. The sympathetic nervous system triggers physiological arousal during an emotion.

_____ 2. Physical arousal can intensify emotion.

_____ 3. All emotions involve conscious thought.

_____ 4. The two-factor theory states that emotions are given a cognitive label before physical arousal occurs.

TERMS AND CONCEPTS TO REMEMBER

Using your own words, on a separate piece of paper write a brief definition or explanation of each of the following terms.

1. emotion
2. James-Lange theory
3. Cannon-Bard theory
4. two-factor theory
5. polygraph

ANSWERS

Module Review

Cognition and Emotion

1. bodily arousal; expressive behaviors; conscious experience

2. follow

Cannon argued that the body's responses were not sufficiently distinct to trigger the different emotions and, furthermore, that bodily changes occur too slowly to trigger sudden emotion.

3. cortex; sympathetic; Cannon-Bard

4. physical; cognitive; Stanley Schachter; Jerome Singer

5. arousal

6. did not; did

7. fuels; channels

8. can

First, experiments on subliminal perception indicate that although stimuli are not consciously perceived, people later prefer those stimuli to others they have never been exposed to. Second, there is some separation of the neural pathways involved in emotion and cognition.

9. eye or ear; thalamus; amygdala; cognition; cortex

10. Richard Lazarus; appraise

11. interpretations; expectations; memories

It seems that some emotional responses—especially simple likes, dislikes, and fears—involve no conscious thinking. Other emotions are greatly affected by our interpretations and expectations.

12. Answers are given in order: first response, second response, third response.
    James-Lange theory: physical arousal, expressed emotion, cognitive appraisal is unimportant
    Cannon-Bard theory: physical arousal and cognitive appraisal occur simultaneously, expressed emotion
    Two-factor theory: physical arousal, cognitive appraisal, expressed emotion

13. James-Lange. The James-Lange theory proposes that the experienced emotion is an awareness of a prior body response: Your pulse races, and so you feel nervous.

14. James-Lange. According to the James-Lange theory, Maria's emotions should be greatly diminished because her brain is unable to sense physical arousal.

15. two-factor. According to the two-factor theory, it is cognitive interpretation of the same general physiological arousal that distinguishes the two emotions.

Embodied Emotion

16. **a.** Heart rate increases.
    b. The liver pours extra sugar into the bloodstream.
    c. Respiration rate increases.
    d. Digestion slows.
    e. Pupils dilate.
    f. If wounded, blood tends to clot more rapidly.
    g. Skin perspires.

17. sympathetic; adrenal; epinephrine (adrenaline); norepinephrine (noradrenaline)

18. parasympathetic

19. similar; fear; anger; sexual arousal

20. insula; disgust

21. fear; rage; finger; hormone

22. fear; joy

23. are; amygdala; angry; depression; right frontal

24. left frontal lobe

25. left; frontal

26. polygraph

The polygraph measures several of the physiological responses that accompany emotion, such as changes in breathing, pulse rate, blood pressure, and perspiration. The assumption is that lying is stressful, so a person who is lying will become physiologically aroused.

27. anxiety

28. innocent; emotions; arousal

29. do not agree

30. guilty knowledge test

31. **d.** is the answer.

32. **a.** is the answer. As people experience negative emotions, such as anger, the right hemisphere becomes more electrically active.
    c. & d. The EEG measures electrical activity on the surface of the cortex, not at the level of structures deep within the brain, such as the amygdala.

33. **a.** Our physiological arousal is much the same from one emotion to another.
    b. Many innocent people respond with heightened tension to the accusations implied by the critical questions.

34. **c.** is the answer.
    a. Individuals with more active right frontal lobes tend to be less cheerful and are more likely to be depressed.
    b. In fact, just the opposite is true: people with greater left frontal activity tend to be better able to turn off upsetting feelings.
    d. The text does not suggest that greater left or right frontal activity influences a person's ability to express his or her feelings.

Progress Test

Multiple-Choice Questions

1. **c.** is the answer.
   a. The somatic division of the peripheral nervous system carries sensory and motor signals to and from the central nervous system.
   b. The peripheral nervous system is too general an answer, since it includes the sympathetic and parasympathetic divisions, as well as the somatic division.
   d. The parasympathetic nervous system restores the body to its unaroused state.

2. **c.** is the answer. Although many emotions have the same general body arousal, resulting from activation of the sympathetic nervous system, they appear to be associated with different brain circuits.

3. **b.** is the answer.
   a. This expresses the two-factor theory.
   c. This expresses the James-Lange theory.
   d. This theory was not discussed.

4. **d.** is the answer. The finding that people whose brains can't sense the body's responses experience considerably less emotion in fact supports the James-Lange theory, which claims that experienced emotion follows from the body's responses.

a., b., & c. All these statements go counter to the theory's claim that experienced emotion is essentially just an awareness of the body's response.

5. **c.** is the answer.

6. **c.** is the answer. The men who received epinephrine without an explanation felt arousal and experienced this arousal as whatever emotion the experimental confederate in the room with them was displaying.

a. Epinephrine recipients who expected arousal attributed their arousal to the drug and reported no emotional change in reaction to the confederate's behavior.

b. & d. In addition to the two groups discussed in the text, the experiment involved placebo recipients; these subjects were not physically aroused and did not experience an emotional change.

7. **d.** is the answer. These are the three components of emotions identified in the text.

8. **c.** is the answer. If the suspect becomes physically aroused while answering questions about details only the perpetrator of the crime could know, it is presumed that he or she committed the crime.

9. **c.** is the answer. Both fear and joy increase heart rate but stimulate different facial muscles.

10. **c.** is the answer.

a. & b. These answers imply that cognition *always* precedes emotion.

d. These responses are unconscious and automatic and so are not learned.

11. **a.** is the answer. Emotional arousal activates the sympathetic nervous system, causing the release of sugar into the blood for energy, pupil dilation, and the diverting of blood from the internal organs to the muscles, all of which help prepare the body to meet an emergency.

b. Being autonomic responses, most emotions are *involuntary* reactions.

c. All emotions do *not* have the same physiological basis.

d. Some emotions occur without cognitive awareness.

12. **c.** is the answer. According to Schachter and Singer, the two factors in emotion are (1) physical arousal and (2) conscious interpretation of the arousal.

13. **b.** is the answer.

a. The James-Lange theory states that the experience of an emotion is an awareness of one's physical response to an emotion-arousing stimulus.

c. The two-factor theory states that to experience emotion one must be physically aroused and attribute the arousal to an emotional cause.

d. Zajonc proposed that some emotional reactions do not involve cognition.

14. **d.** is the answer. No device can literally measure lying. The polygraph measures breathing, cardiovascular activity, and perspiration for changes indicative of physiological arousal.

15. **b.** is the answer.

16. **a.** is the answer. If, as the theory claims, emotions are triggered by physiological reactions, then each emotion must be associated with a unique physiological reaction.

b. According to the Cannon-Bard theory, the same general body response accompanies many emotions.

c. The two-factor theory states that the cognitive interpretation of a general state of physical arousal determines different emotions.

d. Zajonc proposed that some emotional reactions do not involve cognition.

17. **d.** is the answer. As the Schachter-Singer study indicated, physical arousal is not always accompanied by an emotional reaction. Only when arousal was attributed to an emotion was it experienced as such. The results of this experiment, therefore, support the viewpoint that conscious interpretation of arousal must precede emotion.

a., b., & c. Each of these was presented as a supporting argument in the text.

18. **d.** is the answer.

19. **a.** is the answer. That physical arousal can be misattributed demonstrates that it is the cognitive interpretation of arousal, rather than the intensity or specific nature of the body's arousal, that determines the conscious experience of emotions.

b. & c. The findings of these studies do not indicate that a minimum level of arousal is necessary for an emotional experience nor that applying a cognitive label must be simultaneous with the arousal.

20. **c.** is the answer. As heightened arousal may reflect feelings of anxiety or irritation rather than of guilt, the polygraph, which simply measures arousal, may easily err.

a. Misuse and invasion of privacy are valid issues, but researchers primarily object to the use of lie detectors because of their inaccuracy.

b. Although there are discrepancies among the various measures of arousal, this was not what Lykken objected to.

d. The lie detector declares an innocent person guilty about one-third of the time and about one-fourth of the guilty innocent.

Matching Items

1. a
2. e
3. f
4. b
5. d
6. c

True–False Items

1. T
2. T
3. F
4. F

Terms and Concepts to Remember

1. **Emotion** is a response of the whole organism involving three components: (1) bodily arousal, (2) expressive behaviors, and (3) conscious experience.

2. The **James-Lange theory** states that emotional experiences are based on an awareness of the body's responses to emotion-arousing stimuli: a stimulus triggers the body's responses that in turn trigger the experienced emotion.

3. The **Cannon-Bard theory** states that the subjective experience of an emotion occurs at the same time as the body's physical reaction.

4. The **two-factor theory** of emotion proposes that emotions have two ingredients: physical arousal and a cognitive label. Thus, physical arousal is a necessary, but not a sufficient, component of emotional change. For an emotion to be experienced, arousal must be attributed to an emotional cause.

5. The **polygraph**, or lie detector, is a device that measures several of the physiological responses accompanying emotion.

Expressed Emotion

MODULE OVERVIEW

Module 36 discusses the various ways in which emotions are expressed, noting that nonverbal expressions are often important signs of emotion. Of particular interest are the discussions of cultural and gender differences in body and facial expressions in emotion and the effect of facial expressions on emotions.

NOTE: Answer guidelines for all Module 36 questions begin on page 309.

MODULE REVIEW

First, skim each section, noting headings and boldface items. After you have read the section, review each objective by answering the fill-in and essay-type questions that follow it. In some cases, Study Tips explain how best to learn a difficult concept and Applications help you to know how well you understand the material. As you proceed, evaluate your performance by consulting the answers beginning on page 309. Do not continue with the next section until you understand each answer. If you need to, review or reread the section in the textbook before continuing.

Detecting Emotion in Others

Objective 36-1: Describe our ability to perceive and communicate emotions nonverbally.

1. Most people are especially good at interpreting nonverbal _____ . Although we are good at detecting emotions, we find it difficult to detect _____ expressions.

2. Introverts are _____ (better/worse) at reading others' emotions, whereas extraverts are themselves _____ (easier/harder) to read.

3. The absence of nonverbal cues to emotion is one reason that communications sent as _____ are easy to misread.

Gender, Emotion, and Nonverbal Behavior

Objective 36-2: Discuss gender differences in the ability to communicate nonverbally.

4. Women are generally _____ (better/worse) than men at detecting nonverbal signs of emotion. Women possess greater emotional _____ than men, as revealed by the tendency of men to describe their emotions in _____ terms. This gender difference may contribute to women's greater emotional _____ . Although women are _____ (more/less) likely than men to describe themselves as empathic, physiological measures reveal a much _____ (smaller/larger) gender difference. Women are _____ (more/less) likely than men to express empathy.

APPLICATION:

5. Pat is very accurate at reading others' nonverbal behavior and is more likely to express empathy. Based on body responses, Alex seems to feel almost as much empathy. Pat is _____ (male/female); Alex is _____ (male/female).

Culture and Emotional Expression

Objective 36-3: Discuss the culture-specific and culturally universal aspects of nonverbal expressions of emotion.

6. Gestures have _____ (the same/ different) meanings in different cultures.

7. Studies of adults indicate that in different cultures facial expressions have _____ (the same/different) meanings. Studies of children indicate that the meaning of their facial expressions _____ (varies/does not vary) across cultures. The emotional facial expressions of blind children _____ (are/are not) the same as those of sighted children.

8. According to _____ , human emotional expressions evolved because they helped our ancestors communicate before language developed. It has also been adaptive for us to _____ faces in particular _____ .

9. Cultures that encourage _____ display mostly visible emotions. In cultures such as that of Japan people _____ emotions from the surrounding context. This points to the importance of realizing that emotions are not only biological and psychological but also _____-_____ .

APPLICATION:

10. Who is the LEAST likely to display personal emotions openly?
    a. Paul, a game warden in Australia
    b. Niles, a stockbroker in Belgium
    c. Deborah, a physicist in Toronto
    d. Yoko, a dentist in Japan

The Effects of Facial Expressions

Objective 36-4: Describe whether facial expressions influence our feelings.

11. Darwin believed that when an emotion is accompanied by an outward facial expression, the emotion is _____ (intensified/ diminished).

12. In one study, students who were induced to _____ reported feeling a little angry.

13. The _____ _____ effect occurs when expressions amplify our emotions by activating muscles associated with specific states.

14. Studies have found that imitating another person's facial expressions _____ (leads/does not lead) to greater empathy with that person's feelings.

15. Similarly, moving our body as we would when experiencing a particular emotion causes us to feel that emotion. This is the _____ _____ effect.

APPLICATIONS:

16. The candidate stepped before the hostile audience, panic written all over his face. It is likely that the candidate's facial expression caused him to experience
    a. a lessening of his fear.
    b. an intensification of his fear.
    c. a surge of digestive enzymes in his body.
    d. increased body temperature.

17. Children in New York, Nigeria, and New Zealand smile when they are happy and frown when they are sad. This suggests that
    a. the Cannon-Bard theory is correct.
    b. some emotional expressions are learned at a very early age.
    c. the two-factor theory is correct.
    d. facial expressions of emotion are universal and biologically determined.

PROGRESS TEST

Multiple-Choice Questions

Circle your answers to the following questions and check them with the answers on page 310. If your answer is incorrect, read the explanation for why it is incorrect and then consult the text.

1. Research on nonverbal communication has revealed that
    a. it is easy to hide your emotions by controlling your facial expressions.
    b. facial expressions tend to be the same the world over, while gestures vary from culture to culture.
    c. most authentic expressions last between 7 and 10 seconds.

d. most gestures have universal meanings; facial expressions vary from culture to culture.

2. With regard to emotions, Darwin believed that
   a. the expression of emotions helped our ancestors to survive.
   b. all humans express basic emotions using similar facial expressions.
   c. human facial expressions of emotion retain elements of animals' emotional displays.
   d. all of these statements are true.

3. Which of the following is true regarding gestures and facial expressions?
   a. Gestures are universal; facial expressions, culture-specific.
   b. Facial expressions are universal; gestures, culture-specific.
   c. Both gestures and facial expressions are universal.
   d. Both gestures and facial expressions are culture-specific.

True–False Items

Indicate whether each statement is true or false by placing *T* or *F* in the blank next to the item.

_____ 1. Men are generally better than women at detecting nonverbal emotional expression.
_____ 2. When one imitates an emotional facial expression, the body may experience physiological changes characteristic of that emotion.

Essay Question

Discuss biological and cultural influences on emotions. (Use the space below to list the points you want to make, and organize them. Then write the essay on a separate sheet of paper.)

ANSWERS

Module Review

Detecting Emotion in Others

1. threats; deceiving
2. better; easier
3. e-mail

Gender, Emotion, and Nonverbal Behavior

4. better; literacy; simpler; responsiveness; more; smaller; more
5. female; male

Culture and Emotional Expression

6. different
7. the same; does not vary; are
8. Charles Darwin; interpret; contexts
9. individuality; infer; social-cultural
10. **d.** is the answer. In Japan and China, cultures that encourage people to adjust to others, personal emotional displays are less visible.
    a., b., & c. In cultures that encourage individuality, as in Western Europe, Australia, and North America, personal emotions are displayed openly.

The Effects of Facial Expressions

11. intensified
12. frown
13. facial feedback
14. leads
15. behavior feedback
16. **b.** is the answer. Expressions may amplify the associated emotions.
    a. Laboratory studies have shown that facial expressions *intensify* emotions.
    c. Arousal of the sympathetic nervous system, such as occurs when one is afraid, slows digestive function.
    d. Increased body temperature accompanies anger but not fear.
17. **d.** is the answer.
    a. & c. The Cannon-Bard and two-factor theories of emotion do not address the universality of emotional expressions.
    b. Even if it is true that emotional expressions are acquired at an early age, this would not necessarily account for the common facial expressions of children from around the world. If anything, the different cultural experiences of the children

might lead them to express their feelings in very *different* ways.

Progress Test

Multiple-Choice Questions

1. **b.** is the answer.
   a. The opposite is true; relevant facial muscles are hard to control voluntarily.
   c. Authentic facial expressions tend to fade within 4 or 5 seconds.
   d. Facial expressions are generally universal; many gestures vary from culture to culture.

2. **d.** is the answer.

3. **b.** is the answer. Whereas the meanings of gestures vary from culture to culture, facial expressions seem to have the same meanings around the world.

True–False Items

1. F
2. T

Essay Question

All emotions involve some degree of physiological arousal of the sympathetic nervous system. Although the arousal that occurs with different emotions is in most ways undifferentiated, there may be subtle differences in the brain pathways and hormones associated with different emotions. Other examples of the influence of biological factors on emotion are the universality of facial expressions of emotion.

Unlike facial expressions of emotion, the meaning of many gestures is culturally determined. Culture also influences how people express their feelings. In cultures that encourage individuality, for example, personal emotions are displayed openly. In cultures that emphasize human interdependence, the display of personal emotions is discouraged.

Experienced Emotion

MODULE OVERVIEW

Module 37 discusses the experience of emotion, beginning with Izard's identification of 10 basic emotions and other researchers' views regarding the naming of emotions. The module focuses on two emotions: anger and happiness. Particular attention is paid to the relationship between happiness and previous experience and happiness and other people's attainments.

NOTE: Answer guidelines for all Module 37 questions begin on page 315.

MODULE REVIEW

First, skim each section, noting headings and boldface items. After you have read the section, review each objective by answering the fill-in and essay-type questions that follow it. In some cases, Study Tips explain how best to learn a difficult concept and Applications help you to know how well you understand the material. As you proceed, evaluate your performance by consulting the answers beginning on page 315. Do not continue with the next section until you understand each answer. If you need to, review or reread the section in the textbook before continuing.

Objective 37-1: Name some basic emotions, and describe two dimensions psychologists use to differentiate them.

1. Carroll Izard believes that there are _____ basic emotions, most of which _____ (are/are not) present in infancy. Although others claim that emotions such as pride and love should be added to the list, Izard contends that they are _____ of the basic emotions.

2. Throughout the world, people place emotions along two dimensions: _____ , which refers to whether a feeling is _____ or _____ , and high versus low _____ .

Anger

Objective 37-2: Identify the causes and consequences of anger.

3. Most people become angry when another person's act seems _____ , _____ , and _____ .

4. The belief that expressing pent-up emotion is adaptive is most commonly found in cultures that emphasize _____ . This is the _____ hypothesis. In cultures that emphasize _____ , such as those of _____ or _____ , expressions of anger are less common.

5. Psychologists have found that when anger has been provoked, retaliation may have a calming effect under certain circumstances. List the circumstances.
   a. _____
   b. _____
   c. _____

Identify some potential problems with expressing anger.

6. List two suggestions offered by experts for handling anger.

   a. _____

   b. _____

7. Researchers have found that students who mentally rehearsed the times they _____ someone who had hurt them had lower bodily arousal than when they thought of times when they did not.

APPLICATIONS:

8. Who will probably be angrier after getting a parking ticket?

   a. Bob, who has just awakened from a nap
   b. Veronica, who has just finished eating a big lunch
   c. Dan, who has just completed a tennis match
   d. Alicia, who has been reading a romantic novel

9. Marysol was so mad at her brother that she exploded at him when he entered her room. That she felt less angry afterward is best explained by

   a. the behavior feedback effect.
   b. physiological arousal.
   c. the two-factor theory.
   d. catharsis.

10. Expressing anger can be adaptive when you

    a. retaliate immediately.
    b. have mentally rehearsed all the reasons for your anger.
    c. count to 10, then blow off steam.
    d. first wait until the anger subsides, then deal with the situation in a civil manner.

Happiness

Objective 37-3: Identify the causes and consequences of happiness.

11. Happy people tend to perceive the world as _____ and live _____ and more energized and satisfied lives.

12. Happy people are also _____ (more/less) willing to help others. This is called the _____-_____, _____-_____ phenomenon.

13. An individual's self-perceived happiness or satisfaction with life is called his or her _____ _____ .

14. Using web science, social psychologists have found that the most positive moods days of the week are _____ and _____ .

15. Positive emotions _____ (rise/fall) in the early to middle part of most days. The gloom of stressful events usually _____ (is gone by/continues into) the next day.

16. After experiencing tragedy or dramatically positive events, people generally _____ (regain/do not regain) their previous degree of happiness.

17. Most people tend to _____ (underestimate/overestimate) the duration of emotions and _____ (underestimate/overestimate) their resiliency and capacity to adapt.

18. Researchers have found that, after people achieve a certain level of income, money _____ (does/does not) increase their feelings of happiness.

19. During the last 50 years, buying power in the United States has almost tripled; personal happiness has _____ (increased/decreased/remained almost unchanged). This is partly because of the _____ _____ phenomenon.

20. Research has demonstrated that people generally experience a higher quality of life and greater well-being when they strive for _____ _____ _____ than when they strive for _____ .

21. The idea that happiness is relative to one's recent experience is stated by the _____-_____ phenomenon.

Explain how this principle accounts for the fact that, for some people, material desires can never be satisfied.

22. The principle that one feels worse off than others is known as _____
_____ . This helps to explain why the middle- and upper-income people who compare themselves with the relatively poor are _____ (more/less/equally) satisfied with life.

23. List six factors that have been shown to be positively correlated with feelings of happiness. .

_____

_____

_____

_____

_____

_____

24. List four factors that are evidently unrelated to happiness.

_____

_____

_____

_____

25. Research studies of identical and fraternal twins have led to the estimate that _____ percent of the variation in people's happiness ratings is heritable.

(Close-Up) State several research-based suggestions for increasing your satisfaction with life.

APPLICATIONS:

26. As elderly Mr. Hooper crosses the busy intersection, he stumbles and drops the packages he is carrying. Which passerby is most likely to help Mr. Hooper?
    a. Drew, who has been laid off from work for three months
    b. Leon, who is on his way to work
    c. Bonnie, who earned her doctoral degree the day before
    d. Nancy, whose father recently passed away

27. Cindy was happy with her promotion until she found out that Janice, who has the same amount of experience, receives a higher salary. Cindy's feelings are BEST explained according to the
    a. adaptation-level phenomenon.
    b. two-factor theory.
    c. catharsis hypothesis.
    d. principle of relative deprivation.

28. When Professor Simon acquired a spacious new office, he was overjoyed. Six months later, however, he was taking the office for granted. His behavior illustrates the
    a. relative deprivation principle.
    b. adaptation-level phenomenon.
    c. two-factor theory.
    d. optimum arousal principle.

PROGRESS TEST

Multiple-Choice Questions

Circle your answers to the following questions and check them with the answers on page 316. If your answer is incorrect, read the explanation for why it is incorrect and then consult the text.

1. Which of the following is true regarding happiness?
    a. People with less education tend to be happier.
    b. Beautiful people tend to be happier than plain people.
    c. Women tend to be happier than men.
    d. People who are socially outgoing or who exercise regularly tend to be happier.

2. Catharsis will be most effective in reducing anger toward another person if
    a. you wait until you are no longer angry before confronting the person.
    b. the target of your anger is someone you feel has power over you.
    c. your anger is directed specifically toward the person who angered you.
    d. the other person is able to retaliate by also expressing anger.

3. Research suggests that people generally experience the greatest well-being when they strive for
   a. wealth.
   b. modest income increases from year to year.
   c. slightly higher status than their friends, neighbors, and co-workers.
   d. intimacy and personal growth.

4. Research indicates that a person is most likely to be helpful to others if he or she
   a. is feeling guilty about something.
   b. is happy.
   c. recently received help from another person.
   d. recently offered help to another person.

5. A graph depicting the course of positive emotions over the hours of the day since waking would
   a. start low and rise steadily until bedtime.
   b. start high and decrease steadily until bedtime.
   c. remain at a stable, moderate level throughout the day.
   d. rise over the early hours and fall during the day's last several hours.

6. When students studied others who were worse off than themselves, they felt greater satisfaction with their own lives. This is an example of the principle of
   a. relative deprivation.
   b. adaptation level.
   c. behavioral contrast.
   d. opponent processes.

7. Izard believes that there are _____ basic emotions.
   a. 3   c. 7
   b. 5   d. 10

8. Concerning the catharsis hypothesis, which of the following is true?
   a. Expressing anger can be temporarily calming if it does not leave one feeling guilty or anxious.
   b. The arousal that accompanies unexpressed anger never dissipates.
   c. Expressing one's anger always calms one down.
   d. Psychologists agree that under no circumstances is catharsis beneficial.

9. When he asked people how they handled anger, James Averill found that they often recalled
   a. reacting hurtfully.
   b. walking away from the situation.
   c. reacting assertively.
   d. internalizing the anger.

10. Which of these factors have researchers NOT found to correlate with happiness?
   a. age
   b. high self-esteem
   c. religious faith
   d. opimism

Matching Items

Match each definition or description with the appropriate term.

Definitions or Descriptions

_____ 1. the tendency to react to changes on the basis of recent experience

_____ 2. an individual's self-perceived happiness

_____ 3. emotional release

_____ 4. the tendency to evaluate our situation negatively against that of other people

_____ 5. the tendency of people to be helpful when they are in a good mood

Terms

a. adaptation-level phenomenon
b. catharsis
c. relative deprivation principle
d. feel-good, do-good phenomenon
e. subjective well-being

TERMS AND CONCEPTS TO REMEMBER

Using your own words, on a separate piece of paper write a brief definition or explanation of each of the following terms.

1. catharsis

2. feel-good, do-good phenomenon

3. subjective well-being

4. adaptation-level phenomenon

5. relative deprivation

ANSWERS

Module Review

1. 10; are; combinations

2. valence; pleasant (positive valence); unpleasant (negative valence); arousal

Anger

3. willful; unjustified; avoidable

4. individuality; catharsis; interdependence; Tahiti; Japan

5. **a.** Retaliation must be directed against the person who provoked the anger.
   b. Retaliation must be justifiable.
   c. The target of the retaliation must not be someone who is intimidating.

One problem with expressing anger is that it breeds more anger, in part because it may trigger retaliation. Expressing anger can also magnify anger and reinforce its occurrence.

6. **a.** Wait to calm down.
   b. Deal with anger in a way that involves neither chronic anger nor sulking and rehearsing your grievances.

7. forgave

8. **c.** is the answer. Because physical arousal tends to intensify emotions, Dan (who is likely to be physically aroused after playing tennis) will probably be angrier than Alicia, Bob, or Veronica, who are in more relaxed states.

9. **d.** is the answer. In keeping with the catharsis hypothesis, Jane feels less angry after releasing her aggression.
   a. Behavior feedback refers to the phenomenon that when we behave as another person does, we feel that person's emotions.
   b. This is not a specific theory.

   c. The two-factor theory states that emotions involve cognitive appraisal and physical arousal.

10. **d.** is the answer.
    a. Venting anger immediately may lead you to say things you later regret and/or may lead to retaliation by the other person.
    b. Going over the reasons for your anger merely prolongs the emotion.
    c. Counting to 10 may give you a chance to calm down, but "blowing off steam" may rekindle your anger.

Happiness

11. safer; healthier

12. more; feel-good, do-good

13. subjective well-being

14. Friday; Saturday

15. rise; is gone by

16. regain

17. overestimate; underestimate

18. does not

19. remained almost unchanged; diminishing returns

20. intimacy, personal growth, and contribution to the community; wealth

21. adaptation-level

If we acquire new possessions, we feel an initial surge of pleasure. But we then adapt to having these new possessions, come to see them as normal, and require other things to give us another surge of happiness.

22. relative deprivation; more

23. high self-esteem; satisfying marriage or close friendships; active religious faith; optimistic outgoing personality; good sleeping habits and regular exercise; having work and leisure that engage our skills

24. age; gender; parenthood; physical attractiveness

25. 50

Realize that happiness doesn't come from financial success. Take control of your time. Act happy. Seek work and leisure that engage your skills. Engage in regular aerobic exercise. Get plenty of sleep. Give priority to close relationships. Focus beyond self. Be grateful. Nurture your spiritual self.

26. **c.** is the answer. People who are in a good mood are more likely to help others. Bonnie, who is probably pleased with herself for earning a Ph.D., is likely to be in a better mood than Drew, Leon, or Nancy.

27. **d.** is the answer. Cindy is unhappy with her promotion because she feels deprived relative to Janice.

a. The adaptation-level phenomenon would predict that Cindy's raise would cause an increase in her happiness, since her most recent experience was to earn a lower salary.

b. The two-factor theory has to do with the cognitive labeling of physical arousal.

c. The catharsis hypothesis maintains that venting one's anger may relieve aggressive urges.

28. **b.** is the answer. Professor Simon's judgment of his office is affected by his recent experience: When that experience was of a smaller office, his new office seemed terrific; now, however, it is commonplace.

a. Relative deprivation is the sense that one is worse off than those with whom one compares oneself.

c. The two-factor theory has to do with the cognitive labeling of physical arousal.

d. This is the idea that there is an inverse relationship between the difficulty of a task and the optimum level of arousal. It is not discussed in this module.

Progress Test

Multiple-Choice Questions

1. **d.** is the answer. Education level, parenthood, gender, and physical attractiveness seem unrelated to happiness.

2. **c.** is the answer.

a. This would not be an example of catharsis because catharsis involves releasing, rather than suppressing, aggressive energy.

b. Expressions of anger in such a situation tend to cause the person anxiety and thus tend not to be effective.

d. One danger of expressing anger is that it will lead to retaliation and an escalation of anger.

3. **d.** is the answer.

4. **b.** is the answer.

a., c., & d. Research studies have not found these factors to be related to altruistic behavior.

5. **d.** is the answer.

6. **a.** is the answer. The principle of relative deprivation states that happiness is relative to others'

attainments. This helps explain why those who are relatively well off tend to be slightly more satisfied than the relatively poor, with whom the better-off can compare themselves.

b. Adaptation level is the tendency for our judgments to be relative to our prior experience.

c. This phenomenon has nothing to do with the interpretation of emotion.

d. Opponent processes are not discussed in the text in relation to emotion.

7. **d.** is the answer.

8. **a.** is the answer.

b. The opposite is true. Any emotional arousal will simmer down if you wait long enough.

c. Catharsis often magnifies anger, escalates arguments, and leads to retaliation.

d. When counterattack is justified and can be directed at the offender, catharsis may be helpful.

9. **c.** is the answer.

10. **a.** is the answer.

Matching Items

1. a
2. e
3. b
4. c
5. d

Terms and Concepts to Remember

1. **Catharsis** is emotional release; according to the catharsis hypothesis, "releasing" aggressive energy (through action or fantasy) relieves aggressive urges.

2. The **feel-good, do-good phenomenon** is the tendency of people to be helpful when they are in a good mood.

3. **Subjective well-being** refers to a person's sense of satisfaction with his or her life.

4. The **adaptation-level phenomenon** refers to our tendency to judge things relative to a neutral level defined by our prior experience.

5. The principle of **relative deprivation** is the perception that we are worse off relative to those with whom we compare ourselves.

Stress and Health

MODULE OVERVIEW

Behavioral factors play a major role in maintaining health and causing illness. Module 38 addresses a key topic in health psychology, a subfield of the inter-disciplinary field of behavioral medicine: stress—its nature, its effects on the body, psychological factors that determine how it affects us, and how stress contributes to infectious diseases, cancer, and heart disease. Specifically, health psychology focuses on questions such as: How do our perceptions of a situation determine the stress we feel? How do our emotions and personality influence our risk of disease? How can psychology contribute to the prevention of illness?

NOTE: Answer guidelines for all Module 38 questions begin on page 322.

MODULE REVIEW

First, skim each section, noting headings and bold-face items. After you have read the section, review each objective by answering the fill-in and essay-type questions that follow it. In some cases, Study Tips explain how best to learn a difficult concept and Applications help you to know how well you understand the material. As you proceed, evaluate your performance by consulting the answers beginning on page 322. Do not continue with the next section until you understand each answer. If you need to, review or reread the section in the textbook before continuing.

Stress: Some Basic Concepts

Objective 38-1: Identify events that provoke stress responses, and describe how we respond and adapt to stress.

1. The field that integrates behavioral and medical knowledge relevant to health and disease is _____ _____ . The subfield of psychology that contributes to behavioral medicine is called _____ psychology.

2. Stress is not merely a _____ or a _____ . Rather, it is the _____ by which we perceive and respond to environmental threats and challenges.

3. This definition highlights the fact that stress arises less from the events than from how we _____ them and that stressors can have _____ (only negative/both positive and negative) effects, depending on how they are perceived.

STUDY TIP/APPLICATION: The words *stress* and *stressor* are so similar it's easy to think that they mean the same thing. To understand the difference, remember that *stress* is the process by which we appraise and cope with challenging environmental events (the *stressors*). But they are different concepts describing different aspects of a behavior. It may help you to see the difference between these concepts if you realize that stressors can be external events, such as having your flight cancelled, or internal events, such as worrying about an upcoming term paper assignment, and that stress includes those events plus your response to them. To make sure you understand the differences between stress and stressors, see if you can come up with examples of each as you complete the chart on the next page. The first example has already been filled in.

| Appraisal | Response | | Response | |
4. Stressor (Stressful Event)	Threat	Challenge	Threat	Challenge
Getting cut off by a driver on the freeway	"I'm going to be in an accident"	"I need to watch more carefully"	Heart races; hit the brakes hard	Heart races; swerve out of the way

5. Catastrophic events, such as floods, hurricanes, and fires, usually result in significant damage to _____ and _____ health.

6. Research studies have found that people who have recently been widowed, fired, or divorced are _____ (more/no more) vulnerable to illness than other people.

7. Another source of stress comes from _____ _____ , such as rush-hour traffic and family frustration. The stresses that accompany poverty and unemployment, for example, often compounded by _____ , drive up _____ _____ levels among African-Americans.

8. In the 1920s, physiologist _____ began studying the effect of stress on the body. He discovered that the hormones _____ and _____ are released into the bloodstream in response to stress. This and other bodily changes due to stress are mediated by the _____ nervous system, thus preparing the body for _____ _____ _____ .

9. Physiologists have discovered that in response to stress the cerebral cortex, via the _____ and the _____ gland, triggers the outer part of the _____ _____ to release _____ stress hormones such as _____ .

10. In studying animals' reactions to stressors, Hans Selye referred to the bodily response to stress as the _____ _____ _____ .

11. During the first phase of the GAS—the _____ reaction—the person is in a state of shock due to the sudden arousal of the _____ nervous system.

12. This is followed by the stage of _____ , in which the body's resources are mobilized to cope with the stressor.

13. If stress continues, the person enters the stage of _____ . During this stage, a person is _____ (more/less) vulnerable to disease.

14. One study found that women who suffered enduring caregiver stress had especially short _____ , which are pieces of _____ at the ends of _____ that are important in allowing cells to _____ .

15. A common response to stress among women has been called "_____ _____ _____ ," which refers to the increased tendency to _____ . This tendency in women may in part due to _____ , a stress-moderating hormone.

APPLICATIONS:

16. Each semester, Bob does not start studying until just before midterms. Then he is forced to work around the clock until after final exams, which makes him sick, probably because he is in the _____ phase of the _____ .
   a. alarm; general adaptation syndrome
   b. resistance; general adaptation syndrome
   c. exhaustion; general adaptation syndrome
   d. depletion; general adaptation syndrome

17. Connie complains to the campus psychologist that she has too much stress in her life. The psychologist tells her that the level of stress people experience depends primarily on
   a. how many activities they are trying to do at the same time.
   b. how they appraise the events of life.
   c. their physical hardiness.
   d. how predictable stressful events are.

18. Karen and Kyumi attend different universities, but both have rooms in on-campus dorms. Karen's dorm is large, roomy, with only two students to a suite. Kyumi attends a city school, where the dorms are small, overcrowded, and noisy, with five students to a room, which makes study very difficult. Which student is probably under more stress?
   a. Karen
   b. Kyumi
   c. There should be no difference in their levels of stress.
   d. It is impossible to predict stress levels in this situation.

Stress and Illness

Objective 38-2: Describe how stress makes us more vulnerable to disease.

19. In _____ illnesses, physical symptoms are produced by psychological causes.

20. Examples of such illnesses are _____ and some _____ . Such illnesses appear to be linked to _____ .

21. The term _____ was once used to describe such illness. However, this term implied that symptoms were _____ .

22. The new field of _____ investigates how psychological, neural, and endocrine systems together affect the immune system and health.

23. The body's system of fighting disease is the _____ system. This system includes two types of white blood cells, called _____ : the _____ , which fight bacterial infections, and the _____ , which form in the _____ and attack viruses, cancer cells, and foreign substances.

24. Two other immune agents are the _____ , which pursues and ingests foreign substances, and _____ cells, which pursue diseased cells.

25. Responding too strongly, the immune system may attack the body's tissues and cause _____ or an _____ reaction. Or it may _____ , allowing a dormant herpes virus to erupt or _____ cells to multiply.

26. _____ (Women/Men) are the immunologically stronger gender. This makes them less susceptible to _____ but more susceptible to _____ diseases such as _____ and _____ _____ .

27. Stress can suppress the lymphocyte cells, resulting in a(n) _____ (increase/decrease) in disease resistance. Stress diverts energy from the _____ _____ to the _____ and _____ , mobilizing the body for action and making us more vulnerable to disease.

28. Worldwide, the fourth leading cause of death is _____ , caused by the _____ _____ , which is spread primarily through the exchange of _____ and _____ .

29. Stressful life circumstances _____ (have/have not) been shown to accelerate the progression of this chronic disease.

30. Educational initiatives, support groups, and other efforts to control stress _____ (have/have not) been shown to have positive consequences on HIV-positive individuals.

31. Stress _____ (does/does not) create cancer cells. However, some studies find that people are at increased risk for cancer within a year after experiencing

    _____ , _____ ,

    or _____ .

32. When rodents were inoculated with _____ cells or given _____ , tumors developed sooner in those that were also exposed to _____ stress.

APPLICATIONS:

33. A white blood cell that is formed in the thymus and that attacks cancer cells is
    a. a macrophage.
    b. a B lymphocyte.
    c. a T lymphocyte.
    d. any of these cells.

34. When would you expect that your immune responses would be WEAKEST?
    a. during summer vacation
    b. during exam weeks
    c. just after receiving good news
    d. Immune activity would probably remain constant during these times

Objective 38-3: Explain why some of us are more prone than others to coronary heart disease.

35. The leading cause of death in North America is

    _____ _____

    _____ . List several risk factors for developing this condition: _____

    _____

    _____ .

36. Friedman, Rosenman, and their colleagues discovered that tax accountants experience an increase in blood _____ level and blood-_____ speed during tax season. This showed there was a link between coronary warning indicators and

    _____ .

Friedman and Rosenman, in a subsequent study, grouped people into Type A and Type B personalities. Characterize these types, and indicate the difference that emerged between them over the course of this nine-year study.

37. The Type A characteristic that is most strongly linked with coronary heart disease is

    _____ _____ ,

    especially _____

    _____ .

38. When a _____ (Type A/Type B) person is angered, bloodflow is diverted away from the internal organs, including the liver, which is responsible for removing _____ and fat from the blood. Thus, such people have elevated levels of these substances in the blood.

39. Another toxic emotion is _____ ; researchers have found that _____ are more than twice as likely to develop heart disease as _____ .

40. Depression _____ (increases/has no effect on) one's risk of having a heart attack or developing other heart problems.

41. Heart disease and depression may both result when chronic _____ triggers persistent _____ .

APPLICATION:

42. Jill is an easygoing, noncompetitive person who is happy in her job and enjoys her leisure time. She would PROBABLY be classified as
    a. Type A.
    b. Type B.
    c. Type C.
    d. There is too little information to tell.

PROGRESS TEST

Multiple-Choice Questions

Circle your answers to the following questions and check them with the answers beginning on page 323. If your answer is incorrect, read the explanation for why it is incorrect and then consult the text.

1. Researchers Friedman and Rosenman refer to individuals who are very time-conscious, supermotivated, verbally aggressive, and easily angered as
   a. ulcer-prone personalities.
   b. cancer-prone personalities.
   c. Type A.
   d. Type B.

2. During which stage of the general adaptation syndrome is a person especially vulnerable to disease?
   a. alarm reaction   c. stage of exhaustion
   b. stage of resistance   d. stage of adaptation

3. The leading cause of death in North America is
   a. lung cancer.
   b. AIDS.
   c. coronary heart disease.
   d. alcohol-related accidents.

4. Genuine illnesses that are caused by stress are called _____ illnesses.
   a. psychophysiological   c. psychogenic
   b. cathartic   d. psychotropic

5. Stress has been demonstrated to place a person at increased risk of
   a. cancer.
   b. progressing from HIV infection to AIDS.
   c. bacterial infections.
   d. all of these conditions.

6. *Stress* is defined as
   a. unpleasant or aversive events that cannot be controlled.
   b. situations that threaten health.
   c. the process by which we perceive and respond to challenging or threatening events.
   d. anything that decreases immune responses.

7. Behavioral and medical knowledge about factors influencing health form the basis of the field of
   a. health psychology.
   b. holistic medicine.
   c. behavioral medicine.
   d. osteopathic medicine.

8. The stress hormones epinephrine and norepinephrine are released by the _____ gland(s) in response to stimulation by the _____ branch of the nervous system.
   a. pituitary; sympathetic
   b. pituitary; parasympathetic
   c. adrenal; sympathetic
   d. adrenal; parasympathetic

9. In order, the sequence of stages in the general adaptation syndrome is
   a. alarm reaction, stage of resistance, stage of exhaustion.
   b. stage of resistance, alarm reaction, stage of exhaustion.
   c. stage of exhaustion, stage of resistance, alarm reaction.
   d. alarm reaction, stage of exhaustion, stage of resistance.

10. AIDS is a disorder that causes a breakdown in the body's
    a. endocrine system.
    b. circulatory system.
    c. immune system.
    d. respiratory system.

11. *Tend and befriend* refers to
    a. the final stage of the general adaptation syndrome.
    b. the health-promoting impact of having a strong system of social support.
    c. an alternative to the fight-or-flight response that may be more common in women.
    d. the fact that spiritual people typically are not socially isolated.

12. Which of the following statements concerning Type A and Type B persons is true?
    a. Even when relaxed, Type A persons have higher blood pressure than Type B persons.
    b. When stressed, Type A persons redistribute bloodflow to the muscles and away from internal organs.
    c. Type B persons tend to suppress anger more than Type A persons.
    d. Type A persons tend to be more outgoing than Type B persons.

13. The disease- and infection-fighting cells of the immune system are
    a. B lymphocytes.
    b. T lymphocytes.
    c. macrophages.
    d. all of these types of cells.

14. One effect of stress on the body is to
   a. suppress the immune system.
   b. facilitate the immune system response.
   c. increase disease resistance.
   d. increase the growth of B and T lymphocytes.

15. Compared with men, women
   a. have stronger immune systems.
   b. are less susceptible to infections.
   c. are more susceptible to self-attacking diseases such as multiple sclerosis.
   d. have all these characteristics.

16. Allergic reactions and arthritis are caused by
   a. an overreactive immune system.
   b. an underreactive immune system.
   c. the presence of B lymphocytes.
   d. the presence of T lymphocytes.

17. Research on cancer patients reveals that
   a. stress affects the growth of cancer cells by weakening the body's natural resources.
   b. patients' attitudes can influence their rate of recovery.
   c. cancer occurs slightly more often than usual among those widowed, divorced, or separated.
   d. all of these statements are true.

18. The component of Type A behavior that is the most predictive of coronary disease is
   a. time urgency.   c. high motivation.
   b. competitiveness.   d. anger.

19. The field of health psychology is concerned with
   a. the prevention of illness.
   b. the promotion of health.
   c. the treatment of illness.
   d. all of these things.

True–False Items

Indicate whether each statement is true or false by placing *T* or *F* in the blank next to the item.

_____ 1. Stressors tend to increase activity in the immune system and in this way make people more vulnerable to illness.

_____ 2. Events are most stressful when perceived as both negative and controllable.

_____ 3. Type A persons are more physiologically reactive to stress than are Type B persons.

TERMS AND CONCEPTS TO REMEMBER

Using your own words, on a separate piece of paper write a brief definition or explanation of each of the following terms.

1. health psychology
2. stress
3. general adaptation syndrome (GAS)
4. tend and befriend
5. psychophysiological illness
6. psychoneuroimmunology
7. lymphocytes
8. coronary heart disease
9. Type A
10. Type B

ANSWERS

Module Review

Stress Some Basic Concepts

1. behavioral medicine; health
2. stimulus; response; process
3. appraise; both positive and negative
4. Many answers will complete the table. Just think about stressful events in your life—an upcoming exam, a first date, a job interview. For each one, consider how you would appraise it (as a subject beyond your ability or as a task to be completed with extra work), then ask yourself how you would respond (if beyond your ability, you might go out with friends the night before the exam; as a challenge, you would stay home and study hard).
5. emotional; physical
6. more
7. daily hassles; racism; blood pressure
8. Walter Cannon; epinephrine (adrenaline); norepinephrine (noradrenaline); sympathetic; fight or flight
9. hypothalamus; pituitary; adrenal glands; glucocorticoid; cortisol
10. general adaptation syndrome
11. alarm; sympathetic
12. resistance

13. exhaustion; more

14. telomeres; DNA; chromosomes; divide

15. tend and befriend; seek and give support; oxytocin

16. **c.** is the answer. According to Selye's general adaptation syndrome, diseases are most likely to occur in this final stage.
    a. & b. Resistance to disease is greater during the alarm and resistance phases because the body's mobilized resources are not yet depleted.
    d. There is no such thing as the "depletion phase." Moreover, the post-traumatic stress syndrome refers to the haunting nightmares and anxiety of those who have suffered extreme stress, such as that associated with combat.

17. **b.** is the answer.
    a., c., & d. Each of these is a factor in coping with stress, but it is how an event is perceived that determines whether it is stressful.

18. **b.** is the answer. Living under crowded conditions contributes to feeling a lack of control, which is the situation in Kyumi's case.

Stress and Illness

19. psychophysiological

20. hypertension; headaches; stress

21. psychosomatic; unreal

22. psychoneuroimmunology

23. immune; lymphocytes; B lymphocytes; T lymphocytes; thymus

24. macrophage; natural killer (NK)

25. arthritis; allergic; underreact; cancer

26. Women; infections; self-attacking; lupus; multiple sclerosis

27. decrease; immune system; brain; muscles

28. AIDS; human immunodeficiency virus (HIV); blood; semen

29. have

30. have

31. does not; depression; helplessness; bereavement

32. tumor; carcinogens; uncontrollable

33. **c.** is the answer.
    a. Macrophages are immune agents that search for and ingest harmful invaders.
    b. B lymphocytes form in the bone marrow and release antibodies that fight bacterial infections.

34. **b.** is the answer. Stressful situations, such as exam weeks, decrease immune responses.

35. coronary heart disease; smoking, obesity, high-fat diet, physical inactivity, elevated cholesterol level, stress responses, personality traits

36. cholesterol; clotting; stress

Type A people are reactive, competitive, hard-driving, supermotivated, impatient, time-conscious, verbally aggressive, and easily angered. Type B people are more relaxed and easygoing. In the Friedman and Rosenman study, heart attack victims came overwhelmingly from the Type A group.

37. negative emotions; the anger associated with an aggressively reactive temperament

38. Type A; cholesterol

39. pessimism; pessimists; optimists

40. increases

41. stress; inflammation

42. **b.** is the answer.
    a. Type A persons are hard-driving and competitive.
    c. There is no such thing as a "Type C" person.

Progress Test

Multiple-Choice Questions

1. **c.** is the answer.
   a. & b. Researchers have not identified such personality types.
   d. Individuals who are more easygoing are labeled Type B.

2. **c.** is the answer.
   a. & b. During these stages, the body's defensive mechanisms are at peak function.
   d. This is not a stage of the GAS.

3. **c.** is the answer. Coronary heart disease is followed by cancer, stroke, and chronic lung disease. AIDS is the world's fourth leading cause of death.

4. **a.** is the answer.
   b. Catharsis refers to the release of emotion.
   c. *Psychogenic* means "originating in the mind." One's reaction to stress is partially psychological, but this term is not used to refer to stress-related illness.
   d. There is no such term in psychology.

5. **d.** is the answer. Because stress depresses the immune system, stressed individuals are prone to all of these conditions.

6. **c.** is the answer.
   a., b., & d. Whether an event is stressful depends on how it is appraised.

7. **c.** is the answer.
   a. Health psychology is a subfield of behavioral medicine.
   b. Holistic medicine is an older term that refers to medical practitioners who take more of an interdisciplinary approach to treating disorders.

d. Osteopathy is a medical therapy that emphasizes manipulative techniques for correcting physical problems.

8. **c.** is the answer.
   a., b., & d. The pituitary does not produce stress hormones nor is the parasympathetic division involved in arousal.

9. **a.** is the answer.

10. **c.** is the answer.

11. **c.** is the answer.
    a. The final stage of the general adaptation syndrome is exhaustion.
    b. & d. Although both of these are true, neither has anything to do with "tend and befriend."

12. **b.** is the answer. The result is that their blood may contain excess cholesterol and fat.
    a. Under relaxed situations, there is no difference in blood pressure.
    c. Anger, both expressed and suppressed, is more characteristic of Type A people.
    d. The text doesn't indicate that Type A persons are more outgoing than Type B persons.

13. **d.** is the answer. B lymphocytes fight bacterial infections; T lymphocytes attack cancer cells, viruses, and foreign substances; and macrophages ingest harmful invaders.

14. **a.** is the answer. A variety of studies have shown that stress depresses the immune system, increasing the risk and potential severity of many diseases.

15. **d.** is the answer.

16. **a.** is the answer.
    b. An *under*reactive immune system would make an individual more susceptible to infectious diseases or the proliferation of cancer cells.
    c. & d. Lymphocytes are disease- and infection-fighting white blood cells in the immune system.

17. **d.** is the answer.

18. **d.** is the answer. The crucial characteristic of Type A behavior seems to be a tendency to react with negative emotions, especially anger; other aspects of Type A behavior appear not to predict heart disease, and some appear to be helpful to the individual.

19. **d.** is the answer. This chapter deals with the topics of health psychology, namely, preventing illness, by developing better ways to cope with stress; treating illness, by improving the ways in which people notice and explain symptoms; and promoting health, for example, through nutrition and weight control.

True–False Items

1. F
2. F
3. T

Terms and Concepts to Remember

1. **Health psychology** is a subfield of psychology that provides psychology's contribution to behavioral medicine.

2. **Stress** refers to the process by which we perceive and respond to events, called *stressors*, that we perceive as threatening or challenging.

3. The **general adaptation syndrome (GAS)** is the three-stage sequence of bodily reaction to stress outlined by Hans Selye.

4. **Tend and befriend** refers to the tendency of some people (especially women) to provide support (tend) and seek support from others (befriend) when under stress.

5. A **psychophysiological illness** is any genuine illness such as hypertension and some headaches that is apparently linked to stress rather than caused by a physical disorder.

   Memory aid: Psycho- refers to mind; *physio-* refers to body; a **psychophysiological illness** is a mind-body disorder.

6. **Psychoneuroimmunology** is the study of how psychological, neural, and endocrine processes affect the immune system and resulting health.

7. **Lymphocytes** are the two types of white blood cells of the immune system that fight bacterial infections *(B lymphocytes)* and viruses, cancer cells, and foreign substances in the body *(T lymphocytes)*.

8. The leading cause of death in North America today, **coronary heart disease** results from the clogging of the vessels that nourish the heart muscle.

9. **Type A** is Friedman and Rosenman's term for the coronary-prone behavior pattern of competitive, hard-driving, impatient, verbally aggressive, and anger-prone people.

10. **Type B** is Friedman and Rosenman's term for the coronary-resistant behavior pattern of easygoing, relaxed people.

Promoting Health

MODULE OVERVIEW

Module 39 discusses the physical and psychological factors that promote good health. For example, research has shown that social support can improve one's chances of surviving a major illness such as cancer. A Thinking Critically box explores the growing market for complementary and alternative medicine.

NOTE: Answer guidelines for all Module 39 questions begin on page 329.

MODULE REVIEW

First, skim each section, noting headings and boldface items. After you have read the section, review each objective by answering the fill-in and essay-type questions that follow it. In some cases, Study Tips explain how best to learn a difficult concept and Applications help you to know how well you understand the material. As you proceed, evaluate your performance by consulting the answers beginning on page 329. Do not continue with the next section until you understand each answer. If you need to, review or reread the section in the textbook before continuing.

Coping With Stress

Objective 39-1: Identify ways that people cope with stress, and describe how a perceived lack of control can affect health.

1. People learn to _____ with stress by finding _____ , _____ , or _____ ways to alleviate it.

2. When we cope directly with a stressor, we are using _____-_____ coping.

3. When we attempt to alleviate stress by avoiding it and attending to emotional needs, we are using _____-_____ coping.

4. People tend to use _____-_____ coping when they feel a sense of _____ over a situation. They turn to _____-_____ coping when they cannot or believe they cannot _____ a situation.

5. Negative situations are especially stressful when they are appraised as _____ .

6. With higher economic status comes lower risks of infant _____ , a low _____ _____ , smoking, and _____ .

7. In animals and humans, sudden lack of control is followed by a drop in immune responses, a(n) _____ (increase/decrease) in blood pressure, and a rise in the levels of _____ _____ .

STUDY TIP/APPLICATION: Two basic strategies for coping with stressors are problem-focused coping and emotion-focused coping. *Problem-focused coping* is an action-oriented strategy in which we attempt to reduce stress by changing the stressor or the way we interact with that stressor. In contrast, with *emotion-focused coping* we focus on our feelings and try to change how we think about stressors. Think about how you typically cope with stress. Do you more often rely on problem-focused coping or emotion-focused coping? Now complete the chart below. For each stressor, write down one example of a problem-focused strategy and one example of an emotion-focused strategy.

8. Stressor	Emotion-Focused Strategy	Problem-Focused Strategy
You are worried about the amount of reading needed to prepare for an exam.	To take your mind off things, you go to a movie.	You divide the reading into manageable, daily sessions, and get started!
a. You get into an argument with your roommate.		
b. Your car muffler falls off.		
c. You develop a cold sore on your lip the day of an important dance.		

APPLICATIONS:

9. Ricardo has been unable to resolve a stressful relationship with a family member. To cope, he turns to a close friend for social support. Ricardo's coping strategy is an example of
   a. problem-focused coping.
   b. emotion-focused coping.
   c. managing rather than coping.
   d. general adaptation.

10. To help him deal with a stressful schedule of classes, work, and studying, Randy turns to a regular program of exercise and relaxation training. Randy's strategy is an example of
    a. problem-focused coping.
    b. emotion-focused coping.
    c. managing rather than coping.
    d. general adaptation.

Objective 39-2: Discuss the links among basic outlook on life, social support, stress, and health.

11. People who have an optimistic outlook on life expect to have more _____ , to _____ better with stressful events, and to enjoy better _____ .

12. Another buffer against the effects of stress is _____ support.

13. People whose marriages are characterized by low levels of _____ live longer, healthier lives than people who are

    _____ .

14. Longitudinal research reveals that a

    _____ _____ at age 50 predicts healthy aging better than

    _____ _____ at the same age.

State some possible reasons for the link between health and social support.

15. (Close-Up) Some research studies suggest that the presence of _____ may help some people handle stress.

16. James Pennebaker has found that emotional _____ can adversely affect our physical health.

17. Health can be improved by _____ about personal traumas in a diary. Another way to reduce stress is to talk about it. In another study by Pennebaker, Holocaust survivors who were the most _____ had the most improved health.

APPLICATIONS:

18. You have just transferred to a new campus and find yourself in a potentially stressful environment. According to the text, which of the following would help you cope with the stress?
    a. believing that you have some control over your environment
    b. having a friend to confide in
    c. feeling optimistic that you will eventually adjust to your new surroundings
    d. All of these behaviors would help.

19. Which of the following would be the best piece of advice to offer a person who is trying to minimize the adverse effects of stress on his or her health?
    a. "Avoid challenging situations that may prove stressful."
    b. "Learn to play as hard as you work."
    c. "Maintain a sense of control and a positive approach to life."
    d. "Keep your emotional responses in check by keeping your feelings to yourself."

Reducing Stress

Objective 39-3: Discuss the advantages of aerobic exercise as a way to manage stress and improve well-being.

20. Sustained exercise that increases heart and lung fitness is known as _____ exercise.

21. Regular exercise in later life also predicts better

    _____

    functioning and reduced risk of _____ and Alzheimer's disease. By one estimate, moderate exercise adds _____ (how many?) years to one's life expectancy.

22. Experiments _____ (have/have not) been able to demonstrate conclusively that such exercise reduces anxiety, depression, and stress.

23. Exercise increases the body's production of mood-boosting neurotransmitters such as

    _____ , _____ ,

    and the _____ . It also may foster _____ .

Objective 39-4: Describe how relaxation and meditation might influence stress and health.

24. A system for recording a physiological response and providing information concerning it is called _____ . The instruments used in this system _____ (provide/do not provide) the individual with a means of monitoring physiological responses. Most recently, researchers have found that this system works best on _____

    _____ .

25. Simple relaxation procedures have been shown to help alleviate _____ ,

    _____ , _____ ,

    and _____ . Lowered blood pressure, heart rate, and oxygen consumption have been found to be characteristic of people who regularly practice _____ . The _____ response is a state of calm resulting from sitting quietly, with closed eyes, while breathing deeply.

26. Brain scans of experienced meditators reveal decreased activity in the _____ lobe and increased activity in the _____ lobe.

APPLICATION:

27. Philip's physician prescribes a stress management program to help Philip control his headaches. The physician has apparently diagnosed Philip's condition as a _____ illness.
    a. psychogenic
    b. biopsychosocial
    c. psychophysiological
    d. biofeedback

Objective 39-5: Define complementary and alternative medicine, and explain how it is best assessed through scientific research.

28. (Thinking Critically) Acupuncture, massage therapy, homeopathy, and similar treatments comprise the growing health care market called

    _____ _____

    _____ _____ .

    In China, _____ therapies have flourished for centuries, as have acupuncture and acupressure therapies that claim to correct imbalances in the flow of the energy called

    _____ .

29. (Thinking Critically) Critics of alternative medicine point out that such treatments seem especially effective with _____ diseases such as arthritis and _____ , as well as with diseases that disappear naturally—a phenomenon called

_____ _____ .

Critics also argue that the seeming effectiveness of alternative medicine is due to a _____ effect.

APPLICATION:

30. (Thinking Critically) Andrew, who is convinced that an expensive herbal remedy "cured" his arthritis, has decided to turn to homeopathy and herbal medicine for all of his health care. You caution him by pointing out that
    a. arthritis is a cyclical disease that often improves on its own.
    b. botanical herbs have never been proven effective in controlled experiments.
    c. alternative medicine is a recent fad in this country that has few proponents in other parts of the world.
    d. all of these statements are true.

Objective 39-6: Describe what is meant by the faith factor, and offer some possible explanations for this link.

31. Several recent studies demonstrate that religious involvement _____ (predicts/ does not predict) health and longevity.

State two possible intervening variables that might account for the *faith factor* in health.

APPLICATIONS:

32. Concluding her presentation on spirituality and health, Maja notes that
    a. historically, religion and medicine joined hands in caring for the sick.
    b. religious involvement predicts health and longevity.
    c. people who attend religious services weekly have healthier lifestyles.
    d. all of these statements are true.

PROGRESS TEST

Multiple-Choice Questions

Circle your answers to the following questions and check them with the answers beginning on page 330. If your answer is incorrect, read the explanation for why it is incorrect and then consult the text.

1. Attempting to alleviate stress directly by changing a stressor or how we interact with it is an example of
   a. problem-focused coping.
   b. emotion-focused coping.
   c. managing rather than coping with stress.
   d. catharsis.

2. A study in which Holocaust survivors spent time recalling their experiences found that
   a. most did not truthfully report feelings and events.
   b. all survivors experienced a sustained increase in blood pressure until they finished talking about their experiences.
   c. those who were most self-disclosing later had the most improved health.
   d. all the survivors denied undergoing concentration camp horrors.

3. Which of the following was NOT mentioned in the text as a potential health benefit of exercise?
   a. Exercise can increase ability to cope with stress.
   b. Exercise can lower blood pressure.
   c. Exercise can reduce stress, depression, and anxiety.
   d. Exercise improves functioning of the immune system.

4. Social support _____ our ability to cope with stressful events.
   a. has no effect on
   b. usually increases
   c. usually decreases
   d. has an unpredictable effect on

5. Research has demonstrated that as a predictor of health and longevity, religious involvement
   a. has a small, insignificant effect.
   b. is more accurate for women than men.
   c. is more accurate for men than women.
   d. equals nonsmoking and exercise.

6. Which of the following is true of biofeedback training?
   a. A person is given sensory feedback for a subtle body response.
   b. Biological functions controlled by the autonomic nervous system may come under conscious control.
   c. The accompanying relaxation is much the same as that produced by other, simpler methods of relaxation.
   d. All of these statements are true.

7. Which of the following was NOT suggested as a possible explanation of the faith factor in health?
   a. Having a coherent worldview is a buffer against stress.
   b. Religious people tend to have healthier lifestyles.
   c. Those who are religious have stronger networks of social support.
   d. Because they are more affluent, religiously active people receive better health care.

8. (Thinking Critically) Acupuncture, aromatherapy, and homeopathy are forms of
   a. psychophysiological medicine.
   b. complementary and alternative medicine.
   c. Chi therapy.
   d. psychosomatic medicine.

True–False Items

Indicate whether each statement is true or false by placing *T* or *F* in the blank next to the item.

_____ 1. Optimists cope more successfully with stressful events than do pessimists.
_____ 2. People with few social and community ties are more likely to die prematurely than are those with many social ties.

Essay Question

Discuss several factors that enhance a person's ability to cope with stress. (Use the space below to list the points you want to make, and organize them. Then write the essay on a separate sheet of paper.)

TERMS AND CONCEPTS TO REMEMBER

Using your own words, on a separate piece of paper write a brief definition or explanation of each of the following terms.

1. coping
2. problem-focused coping
3. emotion-focused coping
4. aerobic exercise
5. complementary and alternative medicine (CAM)

ANSWERS

Module Review

Coping With Stress

1. cope; emotional; cognitive; behavioral
2. problem-focused
3. emotion-focused
4. problem-focused; control; emotion-focused; change
5. uncontrollable
6. mortality; birth weight; violence
7. increase; stress hormones
8. a. Emotion-focused: You go next door to be comforted by another close friend.

   Problem-focused: You talk with your roommate about resolving your disagreement.

   b. Emotion-focused: You call a friend but keep driving, leaving the muffler where it is and listening to the loud noises of the car.

   Problem-focused: You immediately drive to the nearest muffler shop to have a new muffler put on.

   c. Emotion-focused: You start crying, saying you can't possibly go to the dance.
   Problem-focused: You go to the local drug store to find out what kind of cream you can buy to get rid of the cold sore.
9. b. is the answer. Ricardo is attempting to address his emotional needs, since he has been unable to alleviate stress directly.
10. c. is the answer.
11. control; cope; health
12. social
13. conflict; unmarried
14. good marriage; low cholesterol

Close relationships provide the opportunity to confide painful feelings, which may mitigate physical reactions to stressful events. Environments that foster our need to belong also foster stronger immune functioning. Social support calms us and reduces blood pressure and stress hormones.

15. pets
16. suppression
17. writing; self-disclosing
18. **d.** is the answer.
19. **c.** is the answer.

    a. This is not realistic.

    b. & d. These might actually increase the health consequences of potential stressors.

Reducing Stress

20. aerobic
21. cognitive; dementia; two
22. have
23. norepinephrine; serotonin; endorphins; neurogenesis
24. biofeedback; provide; tension headaches
25. headaches; hypertension; anxiety; insomnia; meditation; relaxation
26. parietal; frontal
27. **c.** is the answer.

    a. The text does not discuss any such thing as a "psychogenic" illness.

    b. Biopsychosocial refers to the approach that incorporates biological, psychological, and social-cultural levels of analysis.

    d. Biofeedback is a system for recording information regarding a subtle physiological state, such as blood pressure.

28. complementary and alternative medicine; herbal; Qi or Chi
29. cyclical; allergies; spontaneous remission; placebo
30. **a.** is the answer.
31. predicts

Religiously active people have healthier lifestyles. They also tend to have stronger networks of social support and are more likely to be married.

32. **d.** is the answer.

Progress Test

Multiple-Choice Questions

1. **a.** is the answer.
   b. In emotion-focused coping, we attempt to alleviate stress by avoiding or ignoring it.
   c. This is an example of coping rather than managing stress because it involves an attempt to actually alleviate a stressor.
   d. Catharsis refers to the release of emotion.

2. **c.** is the answer. The finding that talking about grief leads to better health makes a lot of sense in light of this physiological finding.
   a., b., & d. The study by Pennebaker did not find these to be true.

3. **d.** is the answer. Regular aerobic exercise has been shown to increase ability to cope with stress, lower blood pressure, and reduce depression and anxiety. The text does not cite evidence that exercise enhances immune function.

4. **b.** is the answer.

5. **d.** is the answer.
   b. & c. The text does not indicate that a gender difference exists in the "faith factor" in health.

6. **d.** is the answer. In biofeedback training, people are given sensory feedback about autonomic responses. Although biofeedback may promote relaxation, its benefits may be no greater than those produced by simpler, and less expensive, methods.

7. **d.** is the answer. As a group, religiously active people are no more affluent than other people.

8. **b.** is the answer.
   a. There is no such subfield of medicine.
   c. Chi is an alleged form of energy, imbalances of which Chinese herbal therapies and acupuncture are intended to treat.
   d. The term psychosomatic was once used to describe psychologically caused symptoms. Many forms of alternative medicine, including acupuncture, are intended to treat a full range of symptoms and diseases.

True–False Items

1. T
2. T

Essay Question

When potentially stressful events occur, a person's appraisal is a major determinant of their impact. Catastrophes, significant life events, and daily hassles are especially stressful when appraised as negative and uncontrollable and when the person has a pessimistic outlook on life. Under these circumstances, stressful events may suppress immune responses and make the person more vulnerable to disease. If stressors cannot be eliminated, aerobic exercise, biofeedback, relaxation, and spirituality can help the person cope. Aerobic exercise can reduce stress, depression, and anxiety, perhaps by increasing production of mood-boosting neurotransmitters. During biofeedback training, people enjoy a calm, relaxing experience that can be helpful in reducing stress. Research demonstrates that people who regularly practice relaxation techniques enjoy a greater sense of tranquility and have lower blood pressure and stronger immune responses. People with strong social ties eat better, exercise more, and smoke and drink less. Social support may also help people evaluate and overcome stressful events. In addition, confiding painful feelings to others has been demonstrated to reduce the physiological responses linked to stress.

Terms and Concepts to Remember

1. **Coping** refers to any effort to alleviate stress using emotional, cognitive, or behavioral methods.

2. **Problem-focused coping** involves attempting to alleviate stress directly by changing a stressor or how we interact with it.

3. **Emotion-focused coping** involves attempting to alleviate stress by avoiding or ignoring a stressor and attending to the emotional reactions it triggers.

4. **Aerobic exercise** is any sustained activity such as running, swimming, or cycling that promotes heart and lung fitness and may help alleviate depression and anxiety.

5. **Complementary and alternative medicine (CAM)** is a collection of health care remedies and treatments that have not been accepted by medical science or verified by controlled research trials.

Psychodynamic Theories

MODULE OVERVIEW

Personality refers to each individual's characteristic pattern of thinking, feeling, and acting. Module 42 describes and then evaluates the contributions, shortcomings, and significance of psychodynamic theories. Freud's psychoanalytic theory emphasizes the unconscious and irrational aspects of personality. Neo-Freudians and psychodynamic theorists adhere to many of Freud's beliefs but focus more on social influences than sexual and aggressive impulses. In addition, the module includes a brief description of some of the techniques used by psychodynamic theorists in analyzing personality. It concludes with an evaluation of Freud's psychoanalytic perspective and a discussion of the concept of the unconscious mind in psychology today.

NOTE: Answer guidelines for all Module 40 questions begin on page 340.

MODULE REVIEW

First, skim each section, noting headings and boldface items. After you have read the section, review each objective by answering the fill-in and essay-type questions that follow it. In some cases, Study Tips explain how best to learn a difficult concept and Applications help you to know how well you understand the material. As you proceed, evaluate your performance by consulting the answers beginning on page 340. Do not continue with the next section until you understand each answer. If you need to, review or reread the section in the textbook before continuing.

Introducing Personality

1. Personality is defined as an individual's characteristic pattern of _____ , _____ , and _____ .

2. The psychoanalytic perspective on personality was proposed by _____ . A second, historically significant perspective was the _____ approach, which focused on people's capacities for _____ and _____ .

Freud's Psychoanalytic Perspective: Exploring the Unconscious

Objective 40-1: Explain how Freud's treatment of psychological disorders led to his study of the unconscious mind.

3. Freud's perspective is an example of a _____ theory in that it views human behavior as an interaction between the _____ and _____ minds.

4. Sigmund Freud was a medical doctor who specialized in _____ disorders.

5. Freud developed his theory in response to his observation that many patients had disorders that did not make _____ sense.

Objective 40-2: Describe Freud's view of personality.

6. At first, Freud thought _____ would unlock the door to the unconscious.

7. The technique later used by Freud, in which the patient relaxes and says whatever comes to mind, is called _____ _____ .

8. Freud called his theory and associated techniques, whereby painful unconscious memories are exposed, _____ .

9. According to this theory, many of a person's thoughts, wishes, and feelings are hidden in a large _____ region. Some of the thoughts in this region can be retrieved at will into consciousness; these thoughts are said to be _____ . Many of the memories of this region, however, are blocked, or _____ , from consciousness.

10. Freud believed that a person's _____ wishes are often reflected in his or her beliefs, habits, symptoms, and _____ of the tongue or pen. Freud called the remembered content of dreams the _____ _____ , which he believed to be a censored version of the dream's true _____ _____ .

11. Freud believed that all facets of personality arise from conflict between our _____ internalized urges and the _____ controls over them.

12. According to Freud, personality consists of three interacting structures: the (a) _____ , the (b) _____ , and the (c) _____ .

13. The id is a reservoir of psychic energy that is primarily _____ (conscious/unconscious) and operates according to the _____ principle.

14. The ego develops _____ (before/after) the id and consists of perceptions, thoughts, and memories that are mostly _____ (conscious/unconscious). The ego operates according to the _____ principle.

Explain why the ego is considered the "executive" of personality.

15. The personality structure that reflects moral values is the _____ , which Freud believed began emerging at about age _____ .

16. A person with a _____ (strong/weak) superego may be self-indulgent; one with an unusually _____ (strong/weak) superego may be virtuous but guilt-ridden.

STUDY TIP/APPLICATION: Each of Freud's three interacting systems—the id, the ego, and the super-ego—has a different role in our conscious and unconscious thought processes. To help you understand the systems and how they differ, try completing the table on the next page. It includes three real-life conflicts and asks you to explain how each system would respond in each situation.

17. Conflict	The Id's Response	The Ego's Response	The Superego's Response
a. The driver ahead of you is driving 10 miles/hour below the speed limit.			
b. You have pledged a charitable donation but now need money to buy a new sweater.			
c. You've procrastinated about completing a term paper and a friend suggests buying one online.			

18. A psychoanalyst would characterize a person who is impulsive and self-indulgent as possessing a strong _____ and a weak _____ .
    a. id and ego; superego   c. ego; superego
    b. id; ego and superego   d. id; superego

19. According to the psychoanalytic perspective, a child who frequently "slips" and calls her teacher "Mom" PROBABLY
    a. has some unresolved conflicts concerning her mother.
    b. is fixated in the oral stage of development.
    c. is ruled by the pleasure principle.
    d. has a superego that overrides her id.

Objective 40-3: Identify Freud's developmental stages.

20. According to Freud, personality is formed as the child passes through a series of _____ stages, each of which is focused on a distinct body area called an _____ _____ .

21. The first stage is the _____ stage, which takes place during the first 18 months of life. During this stage, the id's energies are focused on behaviors such as _____ .

22. The second stage is the _____ stage, which lasts from about age _____ months to _____ months.

23. The third stage is the _____ stage, which lasts roughly from ages _____ to _____ years. During this stage, the id's energies are focused on the _____ . Freud also believed that during this stage children develop sexual desires for the _____ (same/opposite)-sex parent. Freud referred to these feelings as the _____ _____ in boys. Some psychoanalysts in Freud's era believed that girls experience a parallel _____ _____ .

24. Freud believed that _____ with the same-sex parent is the basis for what psychologists now call _____ _____ .

Explain how this complex of feelings is resolved through the process of identification.

25. During the next stage, sexual feelings are repressed: this phase is called the _____ stage and lasts until puberty.

26. The final stage of development is called the

_____ stage.

27. According to Freud, it is possible for a person's development to become blocked in any of the stages; in such an instance, the person is said to be _____ .

APPLICATIONS:

28. Jill has a biting, sarcastic manner. According to Freud, she is

a. projecting her anxiety onto others.
b. fixated in the oral stage of development.
c. fixated in the anal stage of development.
d. identifying with her mother.

29. Song Yi works in a smoke-free office. So, she frequently has to leave work and go outside to smoke a cigarette. Freud would probably say that Song Yi is _____

at the _____ stage of development.

Objective 40-4: Describe Freud's views on how people defended themselves against anxiety.

30. The ego attempts to protect itself against anxiety through the use of _____

_____ . The process underlying each of these mechanisms is _____ .

APPLICATIONS:

38. Match each defense mechanism in the following list with the proper example of how it could show itself.

Defense Mechanisms

_____	**1.**	displacement
_____	**2.**	projection
_____	**3.**	reaction formation
_____	**4.**	rationalization
_____	**5.**	regression
_____	**6.**	denial

31. All defense mechanisms function

_____ and _____ .

32. Dealing with anxiety by returning to an earlier stage of development is called

_____ .

33. When a person reacts in a manner opposite that of his or her true feelings, _____

_____ is said to have occurred.

34. When a person attributes his or her own feelings to another person, _____ has occurred.

35. When a person offers a false, self-justifying explanation for his or her actions, _____ has occurred.

36. When impulses are directed toward an object other than the one that caused arousal,

_____ has occurred.

37. When a person refuses to believe or even perceive a painful reality, he or she is experiencing

_____ .

Example

a. nail biting or thumb sucking in an anxiety-producing situation
b. overzealous crusaders against "immoral behaviors" who don't want to admit to their own sexual desires
c. saying you drink "just to be sociable" when in reality you have a drinking problem
d. a parent will not admit that his child could cheat on a test
e. thinking someone hates you when in reality you hate that person
f. a child who is angry at his parents and vents this anger on the family pet, a less threatening target

39. Suzy bought a used, high-mileage automobile because it was all she could afford. Attempting to justify her purchase, she raves to her friends about the car's attractiveness, good acceleration, and stereo. According to Freud, Suzy is using the defense mechanism of

   a. displacement.   **c.** rationalization.
   b. reaction formation.   **d.** projection.

Neo-Freudian and Psychodynamic Theorists

Objective 40-5: Identify which of Freud's ideas were accepted or rejected by his followers.

40. The theorists who established their own, modified versions of psychoanalytic theory are called

   _____-_____ .

   These theorists typically place _____ (more/less) emphasis on the conscious mind than Freud did and _____ (more/less) emphasis on sex and aggression.

Briefly summarize how each of the following theorists departed from Freud.

   a. Adler _____

   _____

   b. Horney _____

   _____

   c. Jung _____

   _____

41. Today's psychologists _____ (accept/reject) the idea of inherited experiences, which _____ (which theorist?) called a _____ _____ , a reservoir of images, or _____ .

42. More recently, some of Freud's ideas have been incorporated into _____ theory. Unlike Freud, the theorists advocating this perspective do not believe that _____ is the basis of personality. They do agree, however, that much of mental life is _____ , that _____ shapes personality, and that we often struggle with _____ _____ .

Assessing Unconscious Processes

Objective 40-6: Describe projective tests and how they are used, and discuss some criticisms of them.

43. Tests that provide test-takers with ambiguous stimuli for interpretation are called _____ tests.

44. The most widely used projective test is the _____ , in which people are shown a series of _____ . Critics contend that these tests have _____ (little/significant) validity and reliability.

APPLICATION:

45. Teresa is taking a personality test that asks her to describe random patterns of dots. This is a _____ test.

Evaluating Freud's Psychoanalytic Perspective and the Modern Unconscious Mind

Objective 40-7: Summarize how contemporary psychologists view Freud's psychoanalytic perspective.

46. Contrary to Freud's theory, research indicates that human development is _____ (fixed in childhood/life-long), children gain their gender identity at a(n) _____ (earlier/later) age, and the presence of a same-sex parent _____ (is/is not) necessary for the child to become strongly masculine or feminine.

47. Research also disputes Freud's belief that dreams disguise _____ and that defense mechanisms disguise _____ and _____ impulses. Another Freudian idea that is no longer widely accepted is that psychological disorders are caused by _____ _____ .

48. Criticism of psychoanalysis as a scientific theory centers on the fact that it provides _____-_____-_____ explanations and does not offer _____ _____ .

49. Psychoanalytic theory rests on the assumption that the human mind often _____ painful experiences. Many of today's researchers think that this process is much _____ (more common/rarer) than Freud believed. They also believe that when it does occur, it is a reaction to terrible _____ .

Objective 40-8: Describe the modern view of the unconscious.

50. Today's psychologists agree with Freud that we have limited access to all that goes on in our minds. However, they believe that the unconscious involves the _____ that control our perceptions and interpretations, the _____ of stimuli not consciously attended, and our _____ memories, for example.

51. An example of the defense mechanism that Freud called _____ is what researchers today call the _____ _____ effect. This refers to our tendency to _____ the extent to which others share our beliefs and behaviors.

52. Another Freudian idea that has received support is that people defend themselves against _____ . According to _____-_____ theory, when people are faced with a threatening world, they act to enhance their _____ and may adhere more strongly to the _____ that create meaning in their lives.

State several of Freud's ideas that have endured.

PROGRESS TEST

Multiple-Choice Questions

Circle your answers to the following questions and check them with the answers on page 342. If your answer is incorrect, read the explanation for why it is incorrect and then consult the text.

1. The text defines *personality* as
   a. the set of personal attitudes that characterizes a person.
   b. an individual's characteristic pattern of thinking, feeling, and acting.
   c. a predictable set of responses to environmental stimuli.
   d. an unpredictable set of responses to environmental stimuli.

2. Which of the following is the correct order of psychosexual stages proposed by Freud?
   a. oral; anal; phallic; latency; genital
   b. anal; oral; phallic; latency; genital
   c. oral; anal; genital; latency; phallic
   d. anal; oral; genital; latency; phallic

3. According to Freud, defense mechanisms are methods of reducing
   a. anger.   **c.** anxiety.
   b. fear.   **d.** lust.

4. Neo-Freudians such as Adler and Horney believed that
   a. Freud placed too great an emphasis on the conscious mind.
   b. Freud placed too great an emphasis on sexual and aggressive instincts.
   c. the years of childhood were more important in the formation of personality than Freud had indicated.
   d. Freud's ideas about the id, ego, and superego as personality structures were incorrect.

5. Which of Freud's ideas would NOT be accepted by most contemporary psychologists?
   a. Development is essentially fixed in childhood.
   b. Sexuality is a potent drive in humans.
   c. The mind is an iceberg with consciousness being only the tip.
   d. Repression can be the cause of forgetting.

6. Projective tests such as the Rorschach inkblot test have been criticized because
   a. their scoring system is too rigid and leads to unfair labeling.
   b. they were standardized with unrepresentative samples.

c. they have low reliability and low validity.

d. it is easy for people to fake answers in order to appear healthy.

7. Id is to ego as _____ is to _____ .

a. reality principle; pleasure principle

b. pleasure principle; reality principle

c. conscious forces; unconscious forces

d. conscience; "personality executive"

8. Recent research has provided more support for defense mechanisms such as _____ than for defense mechanisms such as _____ .

a. displacement; reaction formation

b. reaction formation; displacement

c. displacement; regression

d. displacement; projection

9. According to Freud's theory, personality arises in response to conflicts between

a. our unacceptable urges and our tendency to become self-actualized.

b. the process of identification and the ego's defense mechanisms.

c. the collective unconscious and our individual desires.

d. our biological impulses and the social restraints against them.

Matching Items

Match each definition or description with the appropriate term.

Definitions or Descriptions

_____ 1. redirecting impulses to a less threatening object

_____ 2. test consisting of a series of inkblots

_____ 3. the conscious executive of personality

_____ 4. disguising an impulse by imputing it to another person

_____ 5. switching an unacceptable impulse into its opposite

_____ 6. the unconscious repository of instinctual drives

_____ 7. personality structure that corresponds to a person's conscience

_____ 8. providing self-justifying explanations for an action

10. The Oedipus and Electra complexes have their roots in the

a. anal stage.   c. latency stage.

b. oral stage.   d. phallic stage.

11. Which of the following was NOT mentioned in the text as a criticism of Freud's theory?

a. The theory is sexist.

b. It offers few testable hypotheses.

c. There is no evidence of anything like an "unconscious."

d. The theory ignores the fact that human development is lifelong.

12. According to Freud, _____ is the process by which children incorporate their parents' values into their _____ .

a. reaction formation; superegos

b. reaction formation; egos

c. identification; superegos

d. identification; egos

13. Which of the following refers to the tendency to overestimate the extent to which others share our beliefs?

a. the spotlight effect

b. projection

c. rationalization

d. the false consensus effect

Terms

a. id

b. ego

c. superego

d. reaction formation

e. rationalization

f. displacement

g. projection

h. Rorschach

Matching Items

Match each term with the appropriate definition or description.

Terms

_____ 1. projective test
_____ 2. identification
_____ 3. collective unconscious
_____ 4. reality principle
_____ 5. psychosexual stages
_____ 6. pleasure principle
_____ 7. Oedipus complex
_____ 8. preconscious

TERMS AND CONCEPTS TO REMEMBER

Using your own words, on a separate piece of paper write a brief definition or explanation of each of the following terms.

1. personality
2. psychodynamic theories
3. free association
4. psychoanalysis
5. unconscious
6. id
7. ego
8. superego
9. psychosexual stages
10. Oedipus complex
11. identification
12. fixation
13. defense mechanisms
14. repression
15. collective unconscious
16. projective tests
17. Rorschach inkblot test
18. terror-management theory

ANSWERS
Module Review

Introducing Personality

1. thinking; feeling; acting
2. Sigmund Freud; humanistic; growth; self-fulfillment

Definitions or Descriptions

a. the id's demand for immediate gratification
b. a boy's sexual desires toward his mother
c. information that is retrievable but currently not in conscious awareness
d. stages of development proposed by Freud
e. personality test that provides ambiguous stimuli
f. the repository of universal memories proposed by Jung
g. the process by which children incorporate their parents' values into their developing superegos
h. the process by which the ego seeks to gratify impulses of the id in nondestructive ways

Freud's Psychoanalytic Perspective: Exploring the Unconscious

3. psychodynamic; conscious; unconscious
4. nervous
5. neurological
6. hypnosis
7. free association
8. psychoanalysis
9. unconscious; preconscious; repressed
10. unconscious; slips; manifest content; latent content
11. biological; social
12. id; ego; superego
13. unconscious; pleasure
14. after; conscious; reality

The ego is considered the executive of personality because it directs our actions as it intervenes among the impulsive demands of the id, the reality of the external world, and the restraining demands of the superego.

15. superego; 4 or 5
16. weak; strong
17. There are no right or wrong answers. Here's a sample answer to a. Complete b. and c. on your own.
    a. The id's response: "I'm so angry; the driver is extremely thoughtless. I think I'll speed up and tailgate."
    The ego's response: "I'll relieve my frustration by mentioning the other driver to my friend in the car, then wait for a safe opportunity to pass."

The superego's response: "The driver may be going way below the speed limit because he or she is an elderly person or is sick or having car trouble."

18. **d.** is the answer. Impulsiveness is the mark of a strong id; self-indulgence is the mark of a weak superego. Because the ego serves to mediate the demands of the id, the superego, and the outside world, its strength or weakness is judged by its decision-making ability, not by the character of the decision—so the ego is not relevant to the question asked.

19. **a.** is the answer. Freud believed that dreams and such slips of the tongue reveal unconscious conflicts.

20. psychosexual; erogenous zone

21. oral; sucking (also biting, chewing)

22. anal; 18; 36

23. phallic; 3; 6; genitals; opposite; Oedipus complex; Electra complex

24. identification; gender identity

Children eventually cope with their feelings for the opposite-sex parent by repressing them and by identifying with the rival (same-sex) parent. Through this process children incorporate many of their parents' values, thereby strengthening the superego.

25. latency

26. genital

27. fixated

28. **b.** is the answer. Sarcasm is said to be an attempt to deny the passive dependence characteristic of the oral stage.
   a. A person who is projecting attributes his or her own feelings to others.
   c. Such a person might be either messy and disorganized or highly controlled and compulsively neat.
   d. Identification involves incorporating the parent's values into one's superego.

29. fixated; oral. Song Yi was probably orally deprived (weaned too early) as an infant, so she is fixated at the oral stage. Smoking satisfies her id's needs.

30. defense mechanisms; repression

31. indirectly; unconsciously

32. regression

33. reaction formation

34. projection

35. rationalization

36. displacement

37. denial

Matching Items

38. **1.** f **4.** c
   2. e **5.** a
   3. b **6.** d

39. **c.** is the answer. Suzy is trying to justify her purchase by generating (inaccurate) explanations for her behavior.
   a. Displacement is the redirecting of impulses toward an object other than the one responsible for them.
   b. Reaction formation is the transformation of unacceptable impulses into their opposites.
   d. Projection is the attribution of one's own unacceptable thoughts and feelings to others.

Neo-Freudian and Psychodynamic Theorists

40. neo-Freudians; more; less
   a. Adler emphasized the social, rather than the sexual, tensions of childhood and said that much of behavior is driven by the need to overcome feelings of inferiority.
   b. Horney questioned the male bias in Freud's theory, such as the assumptions that women have weak egos and suffer "penis envy." Like Adler, she emphasized social tensions.
   c. Jung emphasized an inherited collective unconscious.

41. reject; Jung; collective unconscious; archetypes

42. psychodynamic; sex; unconscious; childhood; inner conflicts

Assessing Unconcious Processes

43. projective

44. Rorschach; inkblots; little

Evaluating Freud's Psychoanalytic Perspective and the Modern Unconscious Mind

45. projective

46. lifelong; earlier; is not

47. wishes; sexual; aggressive; sexual suppression

48. after-the-fact; testable predictions

49. represses; rarer; trauma

50. schemas; priming; implicit

51. projection; false consensus; overestimate

52. anxiety; terror-management; self-esteem; worldviews

Freud drew attention to the unconscious and the irrational, to human defenses against anxiety, to the importance of human sexuality, and to the tension between our biological impulses and our social well-being.

Progress Test

Multiple-Choice Questions

1. **b.** is the answer. Personality is defined as patterns of response—of thinking, feeling, and acting—that are relatively consistent across a variety of situations.

2. **a.** is the answer.

3. **c.** is the answer. According to Freud, defense mechanisms reduce anxiety unconsciously, by disguising one's threatening impulses.
   a., b., & d. Unlike these specific emotions, anxiety need not be focused. Defense mechanisms help us cope when we are unsettled but are not sure why.

4. **b.** is the answer.
   a. According to most neo-Freudians, Freud placed too great an emphasis on the *unconscious* mind.
   c. Freud placed great emphasis on early childhood, and the neo-Freudians basically agreed with him.
   d. The neo-Freudians accepted Freud's ideas about the basic personality structures.

5. **a.** is the answer. Developmental research indicates that development is lifelong.
   b., c., & d. To varying degrees, research has partially supported these Freudian ideas.

6. **c.** is the answer. As scoring is largely subjective and the tests have not been very successful in predicting behavior, their reliability and validity have been called into question.
   a. This is untrue.
   b. Unlike empirically derived personality tests, projective tests are not standardized.
   d. Although this may be true, it was not mentioned as a criticism of projective tests.

7. **b.** is the answer. In Freud's theory, the id operates according to the pleasure principle; the ego operates according to the reality principle.
   c. The id is presumed to be unconscious.
   d. The superego is, according to Freud, the equivalent of a conscience; the ego is the "personality executive."

8. **b.** is the answer.
   a., c., & d. The evidence supports defenses that defend self-esteem, rather than those that are tied to instinctual energy.

9. **d.** is the answer.
   a. Self-actualization is a concept of the humanistic perspective.
   b. Through identification, children *reduce* conflicting feelings as they incorporate their parents' values.

c. Jung, rather than Freud, proposed the concept of the collective unconscious.

10. **d.** is the answer.

11. **c.** is the answer. Although many researchers think of the unconscious as information processing without awareness rather than as a reservoir of repressed information, they agree with Freud that we do indeed have limited access to all that goes on in our minds.

12. **c.** is the answer.
    a. & b. Reaction formation is the defense mechanism by which people transform unacceptable impulses into their opposites.
    d. It is the superego, rather than the ego, that represents parental values.

13. **d.** is the answer.

Matching Items

1. f		**5.** d	
2. h		**6.** a	
3. b		**7.** c	
4. g		**8.** e	

Matching Items

1. e		**5.** d	
2. g		**6.** a	
3. f		**7.** b	
4. h		**8.** c	

Terms and Concepts to Remember

1. **Personality** is an individual's characteristic pattern of thinking, feeling, and acting.

2. **Psychodynamic theories** view human behavior as a dynamic interaction between the conscious and unconscious minds. They stress the importance of childhood experiences.

3. **Free association** is the Freudian technique in which the person is encouraged to say whatever comes to mind as a means of exploring the unconscious.

4. **Psychoanalysis** is Freud's theory of personality that attributes thoughts and actions to unconscious motives and conflicts; also, the techniques used in treating psychological disorders by seeking to expose and interpret the tensions within a patient's unconscious.

5. In Freud's theory, the **unconscious** is the reservoir of mostly unacceptable thoughts, wishes, feelings, and memories. According to contemporary psychologists, it is a level of information processing of which we are unaware.

6. In Freud's theory, the **id** is the unconscious system of personality, consisting of basic sexual and aggressive drives, that supplies psychic energy to personality. It operates on the *pleasure principle*.

7. In psychoanalytic theory, the **ego** is the largely conscious, "executive" division of personality that attempts to mediate among the demands of the id, the superego, and reality. It operates on the *reality principle*.

8. In Freud's theory, the **superego** is the division of personality that represents internalized ideals and provides standards for judgment (the conscience) and for future aspirations.

9. Freud's **psychosexual stages** are developmental periods children pass through during which the id's pleasure-seeking energies are focused on different erogenous zones.

10. According to Freud, boys in the phallic stage develop a collection of feelings, known as the **Oedipus complex**, that center on sexual attraction to the mother and resentment of the father. Some psychologists believe girls have a parallel *Electra complex*.

11. In Freud's theory, **identification** is the process by which the child's superego develops and incorporates the parents' values. Freud saw identification as crucial, not only to resolution of the Oedipus complex, but also to the development of what psychologists now call *gender identity*.

12. In Freud's theory, **fixation** occurs when development becomes arrested, due to unresolved conflicts, in an earlier psychosexual stage.

13. In psychoanalytic theory, **defense mechanisms** are the ego's methods of unconsciously protecting itself against anxiety by distorting reality.

14. The basis of all defense mechanisms, **repression** is the unconscious exclusion of anxiety-arousing thoughts, feelings, and memories from consciousness.

15. The **collective unconscious** is Jung's concept of an inherited unconscious shared by all people and deriving from our species' history.

16. **Projective tests**, such as the Rorschach, present ambiguous stimuli onto which people supposedly *project* their own inner feelings.

17. The **Rorschach inkblot test**, the most widely used projective test, consists of 10 inkblots that people are asked to interpret; it seeks to identify people's inner feelings by analyzing their interpretations of the blots.

18. **Terror-management theory** focuses on people's emotional and behavioral responses to reminders of their mortality.

Humanistic Theories

MODULE OVERVIEW

Module 41 describes and then evaluates the contributions, shortcomings, and significance of humanistic theories. Humanistic theories draw attention to the concept of self and to human potential for healthy growth. In addition, the module includes a brief description of the techniques used by humanistic theorists in analyzing personality. It concludes with a discussion of the contributions of humanistic theory and some drawbacks of this point of view.

NOTE: Answer guidelines for all Module 41 questions begin on page 347.

MODULE REVIEW

First, skim each section, noting headings and bold-face items. After you have read the section, review each objective by answering the fill-in and essay-type questions that follow it. In some cases, Study Tips explain how best to learn a difficult concept and Applications help you to know how well you understand the material. As you proceed, evaluate your performance by consulting the answers on page 347. Do not continue with the next section until you understand each answer. If you need to, review or reread the section in the textbook before continuing.

Abraham Maslow and Carl Rogers

Objective 41-1: Describe how humanistic psychologists view personality, and explain their goal in studying personality.

1. Two influential theories of humanistic psychology were proposed by _____ and _____ . These theorists offered a _____-_____

perspective that emphasized human

_____ .

2. According to Maslow, humans are motivated by needs that are organized into a _____ . Maslow refers to the process of fulfilling one's potential as _____ and the process of finding meaning, purpose, and communion beyond the self as _____ . Many people who fulfill their potential have been moved by

_____ _____

that surpass ordinary consciousness.

List some of the characteristics Maslow associated with those who fulfilled their potential.

3. According to Rogers, a person nurtures growth in a relationship by being _____ , _____ , and _____ .

4. People who are accepting of others offer them _____ _____ _____ . By so doing, they enable others to be _____ without fearing the loss of their esteem.

5. For both Maslow and Rogers, an important feature of personality is how an individual perceives himself or herself; this is the person's

_____ .

Assessing the Self

Objective 41-2: Explain how humanistic psychologists assessed a person's sense of self.

6. Humanistic psychologists sometimes use _____ to assess personality, that is, to evaluate the _____ .

7. One questionnaire, inspired by Carl Rogers, asked people to describe themselves both as they would _____ like to be and as they _____ are. When these two selves are alike, the self-concept is

_____ .

8. Some humanistic psychologists feel that questionnaires are _____ and prefer to use _____ to assess personality.

Evaluating Humanistic Theories

Objective 41-3: Describe how humanistic theories have influenced psychology, and discuss the criticisms they have faced.

9. Humanistic psychologists have influenced such diverse areas as _____ , _____ , _____ , _____ , and _____ . They have also had a major impact on today's _____ psychology.

10. Critics contend that the concepts of humanistic theory are _____ and _____ .

11. Another criticism of humanistic theory is that it encourages _____ , which can lead to _____ .

12. A third criticism of humanistic theory is that it is _____ , and fails to appreciate the human capacity for _____ .

APPLICATIONS:

13. Professor Minton believes that people are basically good and are endowed with self-actualizing tendencies. Evidently, Professor Minton is a proponent of
    a. psychoanalysis.
    b. psychodynamic theory.
    c. the humanistic perspective.
    d. self theory.

14. Andrew's grandfather, who has lived a rich and productive life, is a spontaneous, loving, and self-accepting person. Maslow might say that he
    a. is fixated at the latency stage.
    b. has a collective unconscious.
    c. has resolved all the conflicts of the psychosexual stages.
    d. is a self-actualizing person.

15. The school psychologist believes that having a positive self-concept is necessary before students can achieve their potential. Evidently, the school psychologist is working within the _____ perspective.
    a. psychoanalytic   c. humanistic
    b. psychodynamic   d. neo-Freudian

16. Wanda wishes to instill in her children an accepting attitude toward other people. Maslow and Rogers would probably recommend that she
    a. teach her children first to accept themselves.
    b. use discipline sparingly.
    c. be affectionate with her children only when they behave as she wishes.
    d. exhibit all of these behaviors.

PROGRESS TEST

Multiple-Choice Questions

Circle your answers to the following questions and check them with the answers on page 347. If your answer is incorrect, read the explanation for why it is incorrect and then consult the text.

1. Humanistic theories of personality
    a. emphasize the driving force of unconscious motivations in personality.
    b. emphasize the growth potential of "healthy" individuals.
    c. emphasize the importance of interaction with the environment in shaping personality.
    d. describe personality in terms of scores on various personality scales.

2. According to Rogers, three conditions are necessary to promote growth in personality. These are
   a. honesty, sincerity, and empathy.
   b. high self-esteem, honesty, and empathy.
   c. high self-esteem, genuineness, and acceptance.
   d. genuineness, acceptance, and empathy.

3. For humanistic psychologists, many of our behaviors and perceptions are ultimately shaped by whether our _____ is _____ or _____ .
   a. ego; strong; weak
   b. locus of control; internal; external
   c. personality structure; introverted; extraverted
   d. self-concept; positive; negative

4. Which of the following is a common criticism of the humanistic perspective?
   a. Its concepts are vague and subjective.
   b. The emphasis on the self encourages selfishness in individuals.
   c. Humanism fails to appreciate the reality of evil in human behavior.
   d. All of these are common criticisms.

5. In promoting personality growth, the person-centered perspective emphasizes all but
   a. empathy.   c. genuineness.
   b. acceptance.   d. altruism.

TERMS AND CONCEPTS TO REMEMBER

Using your own words, on a separate piece of paper write a brief definition or explanation of each of the following terms.

1. humanistic theories
2. self-actualization
3. unconditional positive regard
4. self-concept

ANSWERS
Module Review

Abraham Maslow and Carl Rogers

1. Abraham Maslow; Carl Rogers; third-force; potential
2. hierarchy; self-actualization; self-transcendence; peak experiences

For Maslow, such people were self-aware, self-accepting and open, spontaneous, loving and caring, not paralyzed by others' opinions, secure, and problem-centered rather than self-centered.

3. genuine; accepting; empathic
4. unconditional positive regard; spontaneous
5. self-concept

Assessing the Self

6. questionnaires; self-concept
7. ideally; actually; positive
8. depersonalizing; interviews

Evaluating Humanistic Theories

9. counseling; education; child rearing; management; popular
10. vague; subjective
11. individualism; self-indulgence, selfishness, and an erosion of moral restraints
12. naive; evil
13. c. is the answer.
    b., c., & d. None of these theories or perspectives offers any particular explanation of this tendency.
14. d. is the answer.
    a. & c. These are concepts used by Freud rather than humanistic theorists such as Maslow.
    b. This reflects Jung's viewpoint.
15. c. is the answer.
    a., b., & d. The self-concept is not relevant to psychodynamic theories.
16. a. is the answer.
    b. The text does not discuss the impact of discipline on personality.
    c. This would constitute conditional, rather than unconditional, positive regard and would likely cause the children to be less accepting of themselves and others.

Progress Test

Multiple-Choice Questions

1. b. is the answer.
   a. This is true of the psychodynamic perspective.
   c. This is true of the social-cognitive perspective.
   d. This is true of the trait perspective.

2. d. is the answer.

3. d. is the answer.
   a. & c. Personality structure is a concern of the psychoanalytic perspective.
   b. Locus of control is a major focus of the social-cognitive perspective.

4. d. is the answer.

5. d. is the answer.

Terms and Concepts to Remember

1. **Humanistic theories** of personality focus on our potential for healthy personal growth.

2. In Maslow's theory, **self-actualization** describes the process of fulfilling one's potential and becoming spontaneous, loving, creative, and self-accepting. Self-actualization becomes active only after the more basic physical and psychological needs have been met.

3. According to Rogers, **unconditional positive regard** is an attitude of total acceptance toward another person.

4. **Self-concept** refers to one's personal awareness of "who I am." In the humanistic perspective, the self-concept is a central feature of personality; life happiness is significantly affected by whether the self-concept is positive or negative.

Trait Theories, Social-Cognitive Theories, and the Self

MODULE OVERVIEW

Module 42 examines the trait and social-cognitive perspectives on personality as well as current research on the concept of self. Trait theory led to advances in techniques for evaluating and describing personality. The text first describes and then evaluates the contributions and shortcomings of the trait and social-cognitive perspectives. In addition, it includes a brief description of some of the techniques used by these perspectives in analyzing personality.

The module concludes with a discussion of the current emphasis on the concept of self. Although humanistic psychology focused on the self, it did not instigate much scientific research. Renewed interest in the self has prompted a wealth of scientific studies.

NOTE: Answer guidelines for all Module 42 questions begin on page 356.

MODULE REVIEW

First, skim each section, noting headings and boldface items. After you have read the section, review each objective by answering the fill-in and essay-type questions that follow it. In some cases, Study Tips explain how best to learn a difficult concept and Applications help you to know how well you understand the material. As you proceed, evaluate your performance by consulting the answers beginning on page 356. Do not continue with the next section until you understand each answer. If you need to, review or reread the section in the textbook before continuing.

Trait Theories

Objective 42-1: Explain how psychologists use traits to describe personality.

1. Gordon Allport developed trait theory, which defines personality in terms of people's stable and enduring _____ and _____ . Unlike Freud, he was generally less interested in _____ individual traits than in _____ them.

2. The _____-_____ _____ _____ classifies people according to Carl Jung's personality types. Although recently criticized for its lack of predictive value, this test has been widely used in _____ and _____ counseling.

3. To reduce the number of traits to a few basic ones, psychologists use the statistical procedure of _____ _____ . The Eysencks think that two or three personality dimensions are sufficient; these include (a) _____ – _____ and (b) emotional _____ – _____ .

Moody
Anxious
Rigid
Sober
Pessimistic
Reserved
Unsociable
Quiet
(a)
Passive
Careful
Thoughtful
Peaceful
Controlled
Reliable
Even-tempered
Calm
(b)

(b)
Touchy
Restless
Aggressive
Excitable
Changeable
Impulsive
Optimistic
Active
(a)
Sociable
Outgoing
Talkative
Responsive
Easygoing
Lively
Carefree
Leadership

4. Some researchers believe that extraverts seek stimulation because their level of _____ _____ is relatively low. PET scans reveal an area of the brain's _____ lobe that is less active in _____ (extraverts/introverts) than in _____ (extraverts/introverts). Dopamine and dopamine-related neural activity tend to be higher in _____ (extraverts/introverts).

5. Research increasingly reveals that our _____ play an important role in defining our _____ and _____ style.

6. Jerome Kagan attributes differences in children's _____ and _____ to autonomic nervous system reactivity.

7. Personality differences among dogs, birds, and other animals _____ (are/are not) stable.

APPLICATIONS:

8. Isaiah is sober and reserved; Rashid is fun-loving and affectionate. The Eysencks would say that Isaiah _____ and Rashid _____ .

   a. has an overactive id; has an overactive super-ego
   b. has a negative self-concept; has a positive self-concept
   c. is an extravert; is an introvert
   d. is an introvert; is an extravert

9. Because you have a relatively low level of brain arousal, a trait theorist would suggest that you are an _____ who would naturally seek _____ .

   a. introvert; stimulation
   b. introvert; isolation
   c. extravert; stimulation
   d. extravert; isolation

10. Nadine has a relatively high level of brain arousal. Trait theorists would probably predict that she is an _____ .

Objective 42-2: Describe personality inventories, and discuss their strengths and weaknesses as trait-assessment tools.

11. Questionnaires that categorize personality traits are called _____

_____ .

12. The most widely used of all such personality tests is the _____ _____ _____ _____ ; its questions are grouped into _____ (how many?) clinical scales.

13. This test was developed by testing a large pool of items and selecting those that differentiated particular individuals; in other words, the test was _____ derived.

(Thinking Critically) Explain several techniques used by astrologers to persuade people to accept their advice.

APPLICATION:

14. A psychologist at the campus mental health center administered an empirically derived personality test to diagnose an emotionally troubled student. Which test did the psychologist MOST LIKELY administer?

   a. the MMPI
   b. the Narcissism Index
   c. the Rorschach
   d. the Eysenck Personality Questionnaire

Objective 42-3: Identify the traits that seem to provide the most useful information about personality variation.

15. Researchers have arrived at a cluster of five factors that seem to describe the major features of personality. List and briefly describe the Big Five.

   a. _____
   b. _____
   c. _____
   d. _____
   e. _____

16. While some traits wane a bit during early and middle adulthood, others increase. For example, as young adults mature and learn to manage their commitments, _____ increases. From the thirties through the sixties, _____ increases.

17. In adulthood, the Big Five are quite _____ (stable/variable), with heritability estimated at _____ percent or more for each dimension. Moreover, these traits _____ (do/do not) predict other attributes.

APPLICATION:

18. For his class presentation, Bruce plans to discuss the Big Five personality factors used by people throughout the world to describe others or themselves. Which of the following is NOT a factor that Bruce will discuss?
    a. extraversion   **c.** independence
    b. openness   **d.** conscientiousness

Objective 42-4: Discuss whether research supports the consistency of personality traits over time and across situations.

19. Human behavior is influenced both by our inner _____ and by the external _____ . The issue of which of these is the more important influence on personality is called the _____-_____ controversy.

20. To be considered a personality trait, a characteristic must persist over _____ and across _____ . Research studies reveal that personality trait scores _____ (correlate/do not correlate) with scores obtained seven years later. The consistency of specific behaviors from one situation to the next is _____ (predictably consistent/not predictably consistent).

21. An individual's score on a personality test _____ (is/is not) very predictive of his or her behavior in any given situation.

Explain the apparent contradiction between behavior in specific situations and average behavior patterns.

22. People's expressive styles, which include their _____ , manner of _____ , and _____ , are quite _____ (consistent/inconsistent), which _____ (does/does not) reveal distinct personality traits.

Social-Cognitive Theories

Objective 42-5: Identify the psychologist who first proposed the social-cognitive perspective, and describe how these theorists view personality development.

23. Social-cognitive theory, which focuses on how the individual and the _____ interact, was proposed by _____ .

24. Social-cognitive theorists propose that personality is shaped by the mutual influence of our internal _____ , our _____ , and _____ factors, as reflected in the _____ approach to personality. This is the principle of _____ _____ .

Describe three different ways in which the environment and personality interact.

25. In studying how we interact with our environment, social-cognitive theorists point to the importance of our sense of _____ _____ . Individuals who believe that they control their own destinies are said to perceive an _____ _____ _____ . Individuals who believe

that their fate is determined by outside forces are said to perceive an _____

_____ _____

_____ . Self-control, which is the ability to control _____ and _____ gratification, predicts good _____ , better _____ , and _____ success.

26. Seligman found that exposure to inescapable punishment produced a passive resignation in behavior, which he called _____

_____ .

27. People become happier and show improved health and morale when they are given _____ (more/less) control over what happens to them.

28. One measure of a person's feelings of effectiveness is his or her degree of _____ . Our characteristic manner of explaining negative and positive events is called our

_____ _____ .

29. Our natural positive-thinking bias can sometimes promote an _____ _____ about future life events that can be unhealthy.

30. (Close-Up) During its first century, psychology focused primarily on understanding and alleviating _____ _____ . Today, however, thriving Western cultures have an opportunity to create a more _____ psychology, focused on three pillars:

   a. _____

   b. _____

   c. _____

APPLICATION:

31. (Close-Up) During a class discussion, Trevor argues that positive psychology is sure to wane in popularity because it suffers from the same criticisms as humanistic psychology. You counter his argument by pointing out that, unlike humanistic psychology, positive psychology
   a. focuses on advancing human fulfillment.
   b. is rooted in science.
   c. is not based on the study of individual characteristics.
   d. has all of these characteristics.

Objective 42-6: Describe how social-cognitive researchers explore behavior, and state the criticism they have faced.

32. People tend to be most overconfident of their abilities in areas where they are, in fact, most _____ (competent/incompetent).

33. It follows from the social-cognitive perspective that the best means of predicting people's future behavior is their _____

_____ .

34. The major criticism of the social-cognitive perspective is that it fails to appreciate a person's

_____ _____ .

APPLICATIONS:

35. Ramona identifies with her politically conservative parents. At college, most of her friends also held conservative views. After four years in this environment Ramona's politics have become even more conservative. According to the social-cognitive perspective, in this case Ramona's parents (_____ factor) helped shape her political beliefs (_____ factor), which influenced her choice of college (also a _____ factor) and created an _____ that fostered her already formed political attitudes.

36. In high school, Chella and Nari were best friends. They thought they were a lot alike, as did everyone else who knew them. After high school, they went on to very different colleges, careers, and life courses. Now, at their twenty-fifth reunion, they are shocked at how little they have in common. Bandura would suggest that their differences reflect the interactive effects of environment, personality, and behavior, which he refers to as _____

_____ .

37. Dayna is not very consistent in showing up for class and turning in assignments when they are due. Research studies would suggest that Dayna's inconsistent behavior
   a. indicates that she is emotionally troubled and may need professional counseling.
   b. is a sign of learned helplessness.
   c. is not necessarily unusual.
   d. probably reflects a temporary problem in another area of her life.

Exploring the Self

Objective 42-7: Explain why psychology has generated so much research on the self, and discuss the importance of self-esteem to human well-being.

38. One of Western psychology's most vigorously researched topics today is the _____ .

39. Hazel Markus and colleagues introduced the concept of an individual's _____ _____ to emphasize how our aspirations motivate us through specific goals.

40. Our tendency to overestimate the extent to which others are noticing and evaluating us is called the _____ _____ .

41. According to self theorists, personality development hinges on our feelings of self-worth, or _____ . People who feel good about themselves are relatively _____ (dependent on/independent of) outside pressures.

42. In a series of experiments, researchers found that people who were made to feel insecure were _____ (more/less) critical of other persons or tended to express heightened _____ _____ .

APPLICATION:

43. The behavior of many people has been described in terms of a *spotlight effect*. This means that they
    a. tend to see themselves as being above average in ability.
    b. perceive that their fate is determined by forces not under their personal control.
    c. overestimate the extent to which other people are noticing them.
    d. do all of these things.

Objective 42-8: Discuss some evidence for self-serving bias, and contrast defensive and secure self-esteem.

44. Research has shown that most people tend to have _____ (low/high) self-esteem.

45. The tendency of people to judge themselves favorably is called the _____ bias.

46. Responsibility for success is generally accepted _____ (more/less) readily than responsibility for failure.

47. Most people perceive their own behavior and traits as being _____ (above/below) average.

48. Bushman and Baumeister found that students with unrealistically _____ (low/high) self-esteem were most likely to become exceptionally aggressive after criticism. Some psychologists believe that today's new generation expresses more _____ than earlier generations.

Identify some of the attitudes and behaviors that seem to be on the rise in *Generation Me*.

49. Some researchers distinguish _____ self-esteem, which is fragile and sensitive to _____ , from _____ self-esteem, which is less focused on _____ evaluations.

APPLICATION:

50. James attributes his failing grade in chemistry to an unfair final exam. His attitude exemplifies
    a. internal locus of control.
    b. unconditional positive regard.
    c. self-serving bias.
    d. reciprocal determinism.

PROGRESS TEST

Multiple-Choice Questions

Circle your answers to the following questions and check them with the answers beginning on page 358. If your answer is incorrect, read the explanation for why it is incorrect and then consult the text.

1. Research on locus of control indicates that internals are _____ than externals.
   a. more dependent
   b. more intelligent
   c. better able to cope with stress
   d. more sociable

2. Which two dimensions of personality have the Eysencks emphasized?
   a. extraversion–introversion and emotional stability–instability
   b. internal–external locus of control and extraversion–introversion
   c. internal–external locus of control and emotional stability–instability
   d. melancholic–phlegmatic and choleric–sanguine

3. With regard to personality, it appears that
   a. there is little consistency of behavior from one situation to the next and little consistency of traits over the life span.
   b. there is little consistency of behavior from one situation to the next but significant consistency of traits over the life span.
   c. there is significant consistency of behavior from one situation to the next but little consistency of traits over the life span.
   d. there is significant consistency of behavior from one situation to the next and significant consistency of traits over the life span.

4. Regarding high self-esteem, psychologists who study the self have found that self-affirming thinking
   a. is generally maladaptive to the individual because it distorts reality by overinflating self-esteem.
   b. is generally adaptive to the individual because it reduces shyness, anxiety, and loneliness.
   c. tends to prevent the individual from viewing others with compassion and understanding.
   d. tends *not* to characterize people who have experienced unconditional positive regard.

5. A major criticism of trait theory is that it
   a. places too great an emphasis on early childhood experiences.
   b. overestimates the consistency of behavior in different situations.
   c. underestimates the importance of heredity in personality development.
   d. places too great an emphasis on positive traits.

6. In studying personality, a trait theorist would MOST LIKELY
   a. use a projective test.
   b. observe a person in a variety of situations.
   c. use a personality inventory.
   d. use the method of free association.

7. Which of the following is the major criticism of the social-cognitive perspective?
   a. It focuses too much on early childhood experiences.
   b. It focuses too little on the inner traits of a person.
   c. It provides descriptions but not explanations.
   d. It lacks appropriate assessment techniques.

8. Some contemporary researchers are focusing their work on
   a. basic dimensions of personality.
   b. promoting positive aspects of life.
   c. classic theories of behavior.
   d. negative states.

9. Seligman has found that humans and animals who are exposed to aversive events they cannot escape may develop
   a. an internal locus of control.
   b. a reaction formation.
   c. learned helplessness.
   d. neurotic anxiety.

10. The _____ classifies people according to Carl Jung's personality types.
    a. Myers-Briggs Type Indicator
    b. MMPI
    c. Locus of Control Scale
    d. Kagan Temperament Scale

11. Research has shown that individuals who are made to feel insecure are subsequently
    a. more critical of others.
    b. less critical of others.
    c. more likely to display self-serving bias.
    d. less likely to display self-serving bias.

12. An example of self-serving bias described in the text is the tendency of people to

    a. see themselves as average on nearly any desirable dimension.

    b. accept more responsibility for successes than failures.

    c. be overly critical of other people.

    d. exhibit heightened racial prejudice.

13. The Minnesota Multiphasic Personality Inventory (MMPI) is a(n)

    a. projective personality test.

    b. empirically derived and objective personality test.

    c. personality test developed mainly to assess job applicants.

    d. personality test used primarily to assess locus of control.

14. Trait theory attempts to

    a. show how development of personality is a lifelong process.

    b. describe and classify people in terms of their predispositions to behave in certain ways.

    c. determine which traits are most conducive to individual self-actualization.

    d. explain how behavior is shaped by the interaction between traits, behavior, and the environment.

15. With which of the following statements would a social-cognitive psychologist agree?

    a. People with an internal locus of control achieve more in school.

    b. "Externals" are better able to cope with stress than "internals."

    c. "Internals" are less independent than "externals."

    d. A social-cognitive psychologist would agree with all of these statements.

16. Which of the following statements about self-esteem is NOT correct?

    a. People with low self-esteem tend to be negative about others.

    b. People with high self-esteem are less prone to drug addiction.

    c. People with low self-esteem tend to be nonconformists.

    d. People with high self-esteem suffer less from insomnia.

17. In studying personality, a social-cognitive theorist would MOST LIKELY make use of

    a. personality inventories.

    b. projective tests.

    c. observing behavior in different situations.

    d. factor analyses.

18. The Big Five personality factors are

    a. emotional stability, openness, introversion, sociability, locus of control.

    b. neuroticism, extraversion, openness, emotional stability, sensitivity.

    c. neuroticism, gregariousness, extraversion, impulsiveness, conscientiousness.

    d. emotional stability, extraversion, openness, agreeableness, conscientiousness.

19. Which of the following refers to the tendency to overestimate the extent to which others share our beliefs?

    a. the spotlight effect

    b. projection

    c. rationalization

    d. the false consensus effect

20. Research on the Big Five personality factors provides evidence that

    a. some tendencies decrease during adulthood, while others increase.

    b. these traits only describe personality in Western, individualist cultures.

    c. the heritability of individual differences in these traits generally runs about 25 percent or less.

    d. all of these statements are true.

Matching Items

Match each definition or description with the appropriate term.

Definitions or Descriptions

_____   1. the most widely used personality inventory with questions grouped into 10 scales

_____   2. a statistical technique that identifies clusters of personality traits

_____   3. the ability to control impulses and delay gratification

_____   4. questionnaire used to assess personality traits

_____   5. the two-way interactions of behavior with personal and environmental factors

_____   6. developed by testing a pool of items and then selecting those that discriminate the group of interest

Terms

a. factor analysis
b. self-control
c. MMPI
d. empirically derived test
e. reciprocal determinism
f. personality inventory

TERMS AND CONCEPTS TO REMEMBER

Using your own words, on a separate piece of paper write a brief definition or explanation of each of the following terms.

1. trait
2. personality inventory
3. Minnesota Multiphasic Personality Inventory (MMPI)
4. empirically derived test
5. social-cognitive perspective
6. reciprocal determinism
7. personal control
8. external locus of control
9. internal locus of control
10. self-control
11. learned helplessness
12. positive psychology
13. self
14. spotlight effect
15. self-esteem
16. self-serving bias
17. narcissism

ANSWERS

Module Review

Trait Theories

1. behaviors; motives; explaining; describing
2. Myers-Briggs Type Indicator; business; career
3. factor analysis; extraversion–introversion; stability–instability
4. brain arousal; frontal; extraverts; introverts; extraverts
5. genes; temperament; behavioral
6. shyness; inhibition
7. are
8. **d.** is the answer.
   a. This refers to psychoanalytic concepts.
   b. This refers to humanistic concepts.
9. **c.** is the answer.
   a. & b. According to this theory, introverts have relatively high levels of arousal, causing them to crave solitude.
   d. Isolation might lower arousal level even further.
10. introvert
11. personality inventories
12. Minnesota Multiphasic Personality Inventory; 10
13. empirically

Astrologers use a "stock spiel" that includes information that is generally true of almost everyone. The willingness of people to accept this type of phony information is called the "Barnum effect." A second technique used by astrologers is to "read" a person's clothing, features, reactions, etc. and build their advice from these observations.

14. **a.** is the answer.
     b. There is no such test.
     c. The Rorschach is a projective test that was not empirically derived.
     d. A personality test that measures personality traits would not be helpful in identifying troubled behaviors.

15. **a.** Emotional stability: on a continuum from calm to anxious; secure to insecure
     b. Extraversion: from sociable to retiring
     c. Openness: from preference for variety to routine
     d. Agreeableness: from soft-hearted to ruthless
     e. Conscientiousness: from disciplined to impulsive

16. conscientiousness; agreeableness

17. stable; 50; do

18. **c.** is the answer.

19. traits (or dispositions); situation (or environment); person-situation

20. time; situations; correlate; not predictably consistent

21. is not

At any given moment a person's behavior is powerfully influenced by the immediate situation, so that it may appear that the person does not have a consistent personality. But averaged over many situations a person's outgoingness, happiness, and carelessness, for instance, are more predictable.

22. animation; speaking; gestures; consistent; does

Social-Cognitive Theories

23. environment; Albert Bandura

24. cognition; behaviors; environmental; biopsychosocial; reciprocal determinism

Different people choose different environments partly on the basis of their dispositions. Our personality shapes how we interpret and react to events. It also helps create the situations to which we react.

25. personal control; internal locus of control; external locus of control; impulses; delay; adjustment; grades; social

26. learned helplessness

27. more

28. optimism; attributional style

29. unrealistic (illusory) optimism

30. negative states; positive
     a. positive emotions
     b. positive character
     c. positive groups, communities, and cultures

31. **b.** is the answer.
     a. Both positive psychology and humanistic psychology focus on advancing human fulfillment.
     c. Both perspectives focus, at least partly, on individual characteristics.

32. incompetent

33. past behavior in similar situations

34. inner traits

35. situational; internal; situational; environment. This shows the interaction of internal and situational factors, using the social-cognitive view of how personality develops.

36. reciprocal determinism. This shows how the interaction of behavior, internal personal factors, and environment can change behavior.

37. **c.** is the answer.

Exploring the Self

38. self

39. possible selves

40. spotlight effect

41. self-esteem; independent of

42. more; racial prejudice

43. **c.** is the answer.
     a. This describes self-serving bias.
     b. This describes external locus of control.

44. high

45. self-serving

46. more

47. above

48. high; narcissism

Narcissism correlates with materialism, the desire to be famous, inflated expectations, more hookups with fewer committed relationships, more gambling, and more cheating, all of which have been on the rise.

49. defensive; criticism; secure; external

50. **c.** is the answer.
     a. A person with an internal locus of control would be likely to accept responsibility for a failing grade.
     b. Unconditional positive regard is an attitude of total acceptance directed toward others.
     d. Reciprocal determinism refers to the mutual influences among personality, environment, and behavior.

Progress Test

Multiple-Choice Questions

1. **c.** is the answer.
   a. & d. In fact, just the opposite is true.
   b. Locus of control is not related to intelligence.

2. **a.** is the answer.
   b. & c. Locus of control is emphasized by the social-cognitive perspective.
   d. This is how the ancient Greeks described personality.

3. **b.** is the answer. Studies have shown that people do not act with predictable consistency from one situation to the next. But, over a number of situations, consistent patterns emerge, and this basic consistency of traits persists over the life span.

4. **b.** is the answer. Psychologists who study the self emphasize that for the individual, self-affirming thinking is generally adaptive. People with high self-esteem have fewer sleepless nights, succumb less easily to pressures to conform, and are just plain happier.

5. **b.** is the answer. In doing so, it underestimates the influence of the environment.
   a. The trait perspective does not emphasize early childhood experiences.
   c. This criticism is unlikely since trait theory does not seek to explain personality development.
   d. Trait theory does not look on traits as being "positive" or "negative."

6. **c.** is the answer.
   a. & d. A psychodynamic theorist would be most likely to use a projective test or free association.
   b. This would most likely be the approach taken by a social-cognitive theorist.

7. **b.** is the answer. The social-cognitive theory has been accused of putting so much emphasis on the situation that inner traits are neglected.
   a. Such a criticism has been made of the psychodynamic perspective but is not relevant to the social-cognitive perspective.
   c. Such a criticism might be more relevant to the trait perspective; the social-cognitive perspective offers an explanation in the form of reciprocal determinism.
   d. There are assessment techniques appropriate to the theory, namely, questionnaires and observations of behavior in situations.

8. **b.** is the answer.

9. **c.** is the answer. In such situations, passive resignation, called learned helplessness, develops.

   a. This refers to the belief that one controls one's fate; the circumstances described lead to precisely the opposite belief.
   b. Reaction formation is a defense mechanism in which unacceptable impulses are channeled into their opposites.
   d. Seligman did not specify that neurotic anxiety occurs.

10. **a.** is the answer.

11. **a.** is the answer. Feelings of insecurity reduce self-esteem, and those who feel negative about themselves tend to feel negative about others.

12. **b.** is the answer.

13. **b.** is the answer. The MMPI was developed by selecting from many items those that differentiated between the groups of interest; hence, it was empirically derived. That it is an objective test is shown by the fact that it can be scored by computer.
    a. Projective tests present ambiguous stimuli for people to interpret; the MMPI is a questionnaire.
    c. Although sometimes used to assess job applicants, the MMPI was developed to assess emotionally troubled people.
    d. The MMPI does not focus on control but, rather, measures various aspects of personality.

14. **b.** is the answer. Trait theory attempts to describe behavior and not to develop explanations or applications. The emphasis is more on consistency than on change.

15. **a.** is the answer. "Internals," or those who have a sense of personal control, have been shown to achieve more in school. Relative to externals, they also cope better with stress and are more independent.

16. **c.** is the answer. In actuality, people with *high* self-esteem are generally more independent of pressures to conform.

17. **c.** is the answer. In keeping with their emphasis on interactions between people and situations, social-cognitive theorists would most likely make use of observations of behavior in relevant situations.
    a. & d. Personality inventories and factor analyses would more likely be used by a trait theorist.
    b. Projective tests would more likely be used by a psychologist working within the psychodynamic perspective.

18. **d.** is the answer.

19. **d.** is the answer.

20. **a.** is the answer. Neuroticism, extraversion, and openness tend to decrease, while agreeableness and conscientiousness tend to increase.

b. The Big Five dimensions describe personality in various cultures reasonably well.

c. Heritability generally runs 50 percent or more for each dimension.

Matching Items

1. c   4. f
2. a   5. e
3. b   6. d

Terms and Concepts to Remember

1. A **trait** is a characteristic pattern of behavior or a disposition to feel and act.

2. **Personality inventories**, associated with the trait perspective, are questionnaires used to assess personality traits.

3. Consisting of 10 clinical scales, the **Minnesota Multiphasic Personality Inventory (MMPI)** is the most widely researched and clinically used personality inventory.

4. An **empirically derived test** is one developed by testing many items to see which best distinguish between groups of interest.

5. According to the **social-cognitive perspective,** behavior is the result of interactions between people's traits (including their thinking) and their social context.

6. According to the social-cognitive perspective, personality is shaped through **reciprocal determinism,** or the interacting influences of behavior, internal cognition, and environment.

7. **Personal control** refers to the extent to which people perceive control over their environment.

8. **External locus of control** is the perception that your fate is determined by forces not under personal control.

9. **Internal locus of control** is the perception that, to a great extent, you control your own destiny.

10. **Self-control** is the ability to control impulses and delay gratification.

11. **Learned helplessness** is the passive resignation and perceived lack of control that a person or animal develops from repeated exposure to inescapable aversive events.

12. Focusing on positive emotions, positive character traits, and enabling institutions, **positive psychology** is the scientific study of optimal human functioning.

13. In contemporary psychology, the **self** is the organizer of our thoughts, feelings, and actions.

14. The **spotlight effect** is the tendency of people to overestimate the extent to which other people are noticing and evaluating their appearance, performance, and blunders.

15. **Self-esteem** refers to an individual's feeling of self-worth.

16. **Self-serving bias** is the tendency to perceive oneself favorably.

17. **Narcissism** is excessive self-love and self-absorption.

Social Thinking

MODULE OVERVIEW

Module 43 examines the process by which we decide whether to attribute behavior to the person or to the situation. It focuses on the fundamental attribution error, which is our tendency to attribute other people's behavior to their personalities while attributing our own behavior to the situation. The module concludes with a discussion of the reciprocal relationship between attitudes and actions.

NOTE: Answer guidelines for all Module 43 questions begin on page 364.

MODULE REVIEW

First, skim each section, noting headings and bold-face items. After you have read the section, review each objective by answering the fill-in and essay-type questions that follow it. In some cases, Study Tips explain how best to learn a difficult concept and Applications help you to know how well you understand the material. As you proceed, evaluate your performance by consulting the answers on page 364. Do not continue with the next section until you understand each answer. If you need to, review or reread the section in the textbook before continuing.

Introduction and The Fundamental Attribution Error

Objective 43-1: Identify what social psychologists study, and discuss how we tend to explain others' behavior and our own.

1. Psychologists who study how we think about, influence, and relate to one another are called

   _____ _____ .

2. Fritz Heider's theory of how we explain others' behavior is the _____ theory. According to this theory, we attribute behavior

either to an internal cause, which is called a

_____ _____ ,

or to an external cause, which is called a

_____ _____ .

3. Most people tend to_____ (overestimate/underestimate) the extent to which people's actions are influenced by social situations because their _____ is focused on the person. This tendency is called the

_____ _____

_____ . When explaining our own behavior, or that of someone we know well, this tendency is _____ (stronger/weaker). When observers view the world from others' perspectives, attributions are _____ (the same/reversed).

Give an example of the practical consequences of attributions.

STUDY TIP: To drive home the concept of the fundamental attribution error, think about a recent embarrassing moment. Perhaps you made an unkind remark that you later regretted. In explaining your behavior, you likely would say, "I was caught up in the moment," or "It was the people I was with." These are *external* (situational) attributions. Now think about how you would explain the same type of behavior in another person, especially someone you have just met. If you committed the fundamental attribution error, you would be less likely to "forgive" the person by making an external attribution. Instead, you would attribute it to personality and expect the person to behave similarly in the future.

APPLICATION:

4. Professor Washington's students did very poorly on the last exam. The tendency to make the fundamental attribution error might lead her to conclude that the class did poorly because
   a. the test was unfair.
   b. not enough time was given for students to complete the test.
   c. students were distracted by some social function on campus.
   d. students were unmotivated.

Attitudes and Actions

Objective 43-2: Explain whether what we think affects what we do, and whether what we do affects what we think.

5. Feelings, often based on our beliefs, that predispose our responses are called _____ . When people focus on an issue and respond favorably to an argument, _____ _____ _____ has occurred. Persuasion may also occur through the _____ (slower/faster) _____ _____ as people respond to incidental cues such as a speaker's appearance.

6. Many research studies demonstrate that our attitudes are strongly influenced by our _____ . One example of this is the tendency for people who agree to a small request to comply later with a larger one. This is the _____-_____-_____-_____ phenomenon.

7. When you follow the social prescriptions for how you should act as, say, a college student, you are adopting a _____ .

8. Taking on a set of behaviors, or acting in a certain way, generally _____ (changes/does not change) people's attitudes.

9. According to _____ _____ theory, thoughts and feelings change because people are motivated to justify actions that would otherwise seem hypocritical. This theory was proposed by _____ .

10. Dissonance theory predicts that people induced (without coercion) to behave contrary to their true attitudes will be motivated to reduce the resulting _____ by changing their _____ .

STUDY TIP/APPLICATION: Cognitive dissonance theory and the foot-in-the-door phenomenon are two powerful examples of our attitudes following our actions. Think about these examples as you complete the following exercises.

11. a. Using the foot-in-the-door technique, how might you persuade a friend to take on an important, time-consuming task such as becoming treasurer of a ski club?

    b. Suppose your roommate thinks climate change is nothing more than a hoax foisted by politicians on a gullible public. Using cognitive dissonance theory, how might you go about changing your roommate's attitude?

APPLICATIONS:

12. Which of the following is an example of the foot-in-the-door phenomenon?
    a. To persuade a customer to buy a product, a store owner offers a small gift.
    b. After agreeing to wear a small "Enforce Recycling" lapel pin, a woman agrees to collect signatures on a petition to make recycling required by law.
    c. After offering to sell a car at a ridiculously low price, a car salesperson is forced to tell the customer the car will cost $1000 more.
    d. All of these are examples.

13. Which of the following situations should produce the GREATEST cognitive dissonance?
    a. A soldier is forced to carry out orders he finds disagreeable.
    b. A student who loves animals has to dissect a cat in order to pass biology.
    c. As part of an experiment, a subject is directed to deliver electric shocks to another person.
    d. A student volunteers to debate an issue, taking the side he personally disagrees with.

14. Before she gave a class presentation favoring gun control legislation, Wanda opposed it. Her present attitude favoring such legislation can best be explained by
   a. attribution theory.
   b. cognitive dissonance theory.
   c. reward theory.
   d. evolutionary psychology.

PROGRESS TEST

Multiple-Choice Questions

Circle your answers to the following questions and check them with the answers beginning on page 364. If your answer is incorrect, read the explanation for why it is incorrect and then consult the text.

1. According to cognitive dissonance theory, dissonance is most likely to occur when
   a. a person's behavior is not based on strongly held attitudes.
   b. two people have conflicting attitudes and find themselves in disagreement.
   c. an individual does something that is personally disagreeable.
   d. an individual is coerced into doing something that he or she does not want to do.

2. Which of the following phenomena is best explained by cognitive dissonance theory?
   a. the fundamental attribution error
   b. the foot-in-the-door phenomenon
   c. peripheral route persuasion
   d. central route persuasion

3. Two neighboring nations are each stockpiling weapons. Each sees its neighbor's actions as an act of aggression and its own actions as self-defense. Evidently, these nations are victims of
   a. prejudice.
   b. groupthink.
   c. self-serving bias.
   d. the fundamental attribution error.

4. When male students in an experiment were told that a woman to whom they would be speaking had been instructed to act in a friendly or unfriendly way, most of them subsequently attributed her behavior to
   a. the situation.
   b. the situation *and* her personal disposition.
   c. her personal disposition.
   d. their own skill or lack of skill in a social situation.

5. Which of the following is true?
   a. Attitudes and actions rarely correspond.
   b. Attitudes predict behavior about half the time.
   c. Attitudes are excellent predictors of behavior.
   d. Attitudes predict behavior under certain conditions.

6. Which theory describes how we explain others' behavior as being due to internal dispositions or external situations?
   a. cognitive dissonance theory
   b. reward theory
   c. two-factor theory
   d. attribution theory

Matching Items

Match each term with the appropriate definition or description.

Terms

_____ 1. peripheral route persuasion
_____ 2. attribution
_____ 3. foot-in-the-door phenomenon
_____ 4. cognitive dissonance
_____ 5. central route persuasion

Definitions or Descriptions

a. a causal explanation for someone's behavior
b. responding favorably to arguments as a result of systematic thinking about an issue
c. tendency for people who agree with a small request to comply later with a larger request
d. responding favorably to arguments as a result of more superficial and incidental cues
e. feeling of discomfort when our behavior conflicts with what we think and feel

True–False Items

Indicate whether each statement is true or false by placing *T* or *F* in the blank next to the item.

_____ 1. When explaining another's behavior, we tend to underestimate situational influences.

_____ 2. When explaining our own behavior, we tend to underestimate situational influences.

_____ 3. Counterattitudinal behavior (acting contrary to our beliefs) often leads to attitude change.

_____ 4. Peripheral route persuasion allows for fast responding to an issue.

TERMS AND CONCEPTS TO REMEMBER

Using your own words, on a separate piece of paper write a brief definition or explanation of each of the following terms.

1. social psychology

2. attribution theory

3. fundamental attribution error

4. attitudes

5. peripheral route persuasion

6. central route persuasion

7. foot-in-the-door phenomenon

8. role

9. cognitive dissonance theory

ANSWERS

Module Review

Introduction and *The Fundamental Attribution Error*

1. social psychologists

2. attribution; dispositional attribution; situational attribution

3. underestimate; attention; fundamental attribution error; weaker; reversed

Our attributions—to individuals' dispositions or to situations—have important practical consequences. A hurtful remark from an acquaintance, for example, is more likely to be forgiven if it is attributed to a temporary situation than to a mean disposition.

4. **d.** is the answer. The fundamental attribution error refers to the tendency to underestimate situ-

ational influences in favor of this type of dispositional attribution when explaining the behavior of other people.

a., b., & c. These are situational attributions.

Attitudes and Actions

5. attitudes; central route persuasion; faster; peripheral route

6. actions (or behavior); foot-in-the-door

7. role

8. changes

9. cognitive dissonance; Leon Festinger

10. dissonance; attitudes

11. No single answer is correct. A possible answer for a. is to ask the friend to check some figures from the monthly expenses. For b., you might get your roommate to debate the issue and have him or her argue that climate change is a major concern.

12. **b.** is the answer. In the foot-in-the-door phenomenon, compliance with a small initial request, such as wearing a lapel pin, later is followed by compliance with a much larger request, such as collecting petition signatures.

13. **d.** is the answer. In this situation, the counterattitudinal behavior is performed voluntarily and cannot be attributed to the demands of the situation.

    a., b., & c. In all of these situations, the counterattitudinal behaviors should not arouse much dissonance because they can be attributed to the demands of the situation.

14. **b.** is the answer. Dissonance theory focuses on what happens when our actions contradict our attitudes.

    a. Attribution theory holds that we give causal explanations for others' behavior, often by crediting either the situation or people's dispositions.

    c. Reward theory maintains that we continue relationships that maximize benefits and minimize costs. This has nothing to do with relationships.

    d. This is not a theory of social influence.

Progress Test

Multiple-Choice Questions

1. **c.** is the answer. Cognitive dissonance is the tension we feel when we are aware of a discrepancy between our thoughts and actions, as would occur when we do something we find distasteful.

    a. Dissonance requires strongly held attitudes, which must be perceived as not fitting behavior.

b. Dissonance is a personal cognitive process.

d. In such a situation the person is less likely to experience dissonance, since the action can be attributed to "having no choice."

2. **b.** is the answer.

a. The fundamental attribution error is our tendency to underestimate the impact of situations on the behavior of others.

c. & d. Peripheral and central route persuasion refer the ways in which people are inflluenced either by superficial cues or by systematic thinking about an issue.

3. **d.** is the answer. In this case, each nation has mistakenly attributed the other's action to a *dispositional* trait, whereas its own action is viewed as a *situational* response.

4. **c.** is the answer. In this example of the fundamental attribution error, even when given the situational explanation for the woman's behavior, students ignored it and attributed her behavior to her personal disposition.

5. **d.** is the answer. Our attitudes are more likely to guide our actions when other influences are minimal, especially when the attitude is stable, specific to the behavior, and easily recalled. The presence of other people would more likely be an outside factor that would lessen the likelihood of actions being guided by attitude.

6. **d.** is the answer.

Matching Items

1. d   4. e
2. a   5. b
3. c

True–False Items

1. T   3. T
2. F   4. T

Terms and Concepts to Remember

1. **Social psychology** is the scientific study of how we think about, influence, and relate to one another.

2. **Attribution theory** deals with our causal explanations of behavior. We attribute behavior to the individual's disposition or to the situation.

3. The **fundamental attribution error** is our tendency to underestimate the impact of situations and to overestimate the impact of personal dispositions on the behavior of others.

4. **Attitudes** are feelings, often influenced by our beliefs, that may predispose us to respond in particular ways to objects, people, and events.

5. **Peripheral route persuasion** occurs when people are influenced by more superficial and incidental cues, such as a speaker's appearance.

6. **Central route persuasion** occurs when people respond favorably to arguments as a result of engaging in systematic thinking about an issue.

7. The **foot-in-the-door phenomenon** is the tendency for people who agree to a small request to comply later with a larger request.

8. A **role** is a set of explanations (norms) about how people in a specific social position ought to behave.

9. **Cognitive dissonance theory** refers to the theory that we act to reduce the psychological discomfort we experience when our behavior conflicts with what we think and feel, or more generally, when two of our thoughts are inconsistent. This is frequently accomplished by changing our attitude rather than our behavior.

Memory aid: *Dissonance* means "lack of harmony."
Cognitive dissonance occurs when two thoughts, or cognitions, are at variance with one another.

Social Influence

MODULE OVERVIEW

Module 44 demonstrates the powerful influences of social situations on the behavior of individuals. Central to this topic are research studies on conformity, obedience, and group and cultural influences. The social principles that emerge help us to understand how individuals are influenced by advertising, political candidates, and the various groups to which they belong. Although social influences are powerful, it is important to remember the significant role of individuals in choosing and creating the social situations that influence them.

Although there is some terminology for you to learn in this module, your primary task is to absorb the findings of the many research studies discussed. The module headings, which organize the findings, should prove especially useful to you here. In addition, you might, for each main topic (conformity, group influence, etc.), ask yourself the question, "What situational factors promote this phenomenon?" The research findings can then form the basis for your answers.

NOTE: Answer guidelines for all Module 44 questions begin on page 371.

MODULE REVIEW

First, skim each section, noting headings and bold-face items. After you have read the section, review each objective by answering the fill-in and essay-type questions that follow it. In some cases, Study Tips explain how best to learn a difficult concept and Applications help you to know how well you understand the material. As you proceed, evaluate your performance by consulting the answers beginning on page 371. Do not continue with the next section until you understand each answer. If you need to, review or reread the section in the textbook before continuing.

Conformity: Complying With Social Pressures

Objective 44-1: Describe automatic mimicry, and explain how conformity experiments reveal the power of social influence.

1. People take on the _____ tones of others around them. This natural tendency is called _____ _____ . The *chameleon effect* refers to our natural tendency to unconsciously _____ others' expressions, postures, and voice tones. This helps us to feel what they are feeling, referred to as _____ . It also helps explain why studies of British nurses and accountants have revealed _____ _____—sharing up and down moods.

2. The term that refers to the tendency to adjust one's behavior to coincide with an assumed group standard is _____ .

3. The psychologist who first studied the effects of group pressure on conformity is

   _____ .

4. In this study, when the opinion of other group members was contradicted by objective evidence, research participants _____ (were/were not) willing to conform to the group opinion.

1   2   3

List the conditions under which we are more likely to conform.

5. One reason that people comply with social pressure is to gain approval or avoid rejection; this is called _____

_____ _____ .

Understood rules for accepted and expected behavior are called social _____ .

6. Another reason people comply is that they have genuinely been influenced by what they have learned from others; this type of influence is called _____

_____ _____ .

APPLICATION:

7. Maria recently heard a speech calling for a ban on aerosol sprays that endanger the earth's ozone layer. Maria's subsequent decision to stop using aerosol sprays is an example of
   a. informational social influence.
   b. normative social influence.
   c. the foot-in-the-door phenomenon.
   d. cognitive dissonance.

Obedience: Following Orders

Objective 44-2: Describe what we learned about the power of social influence from Milgram's obedience experiments.

8. The classic social psychology studies of obedience were conducted by

_____ .

When ordered by the experimenter to electrically shock the "learner," the majority of participants (the "teachers") in these studies _____ (complied/refused). More recent studies have found that women's compliance rates in similar situations were _____ (higher than/lower than/similar to) men's.

List the conditions under which obedience was highest in Milgram's studies.

Objective 44-3: Discuss what we learned from the Asch and Milgram studies.

9. In getting people to administer increasingly larger shocks, Milgram was in effect applying the

_____-_____-

_____-_____

technique.

10. The Asch and Milgram studies demonstrate that strong _____ influences can make _____ people _____ to falsehoods and commit cruel acts.

APPLICATIONS:

11. José is the one student member on his school's board of trustees. At the board's first meeting, José wants to disagree with the others on several issues but in each case decides to say nothing. Studies on conformity suggest all except one of the following are factors in José's not speaking up. Which one is NOT a factor?
    a. The board is a large group.
    b. The board is prestigious and most of its members are well known.
    c. The board members are already aware that José and the student body disagree with them on these issues.
    d. Because this is the first meeting José has attended, he feels insecure and not fully competent.

12. Twenty-year-old Marge belonged to a sorority. During pledge week, she was ordered to force potential members to strip in front of their friends. Although Marge disapproved of asking fellow students to embarrass themselves, she did it anyway. She respected the sorority officers, and all her fellow sisters were also hazing the pledges. How would Milgram explain Marge's behavior?

Group Influence

Objective 44-4: Describe how our behavior is affected by the presence of others.

13. The tendency to perform a task better when other people are present is called _____ _____ . In general, people become aroused in the presence of others, and arousal enhances the correct response on a(n) _____ (easy/difficult) task. Later research revealed that arousal strengthens the response that is most _____ in a given situation.

14. Researchers have found that the reactions of people in crowded situations are often _____ (lessened/amplified).

15. Researchers found that people worked _____ (harder/less hard) in a team tug-of-war than they had in an individual contest. This phenomenon has been called _____ _____ .

16. The feeling of anonymity and loss of self-restraint that an individual may develop when in a group is called _____ .

STUDY TIP: To help solidify the idea of social facilitation in your mind, think about sports you play—or don't play (because you don't do well). Think about your friends in similar situations, your children if you are a parent. Then think about professional athletes. Does the same hold true for the performing arts (acting, playing a musical instrument, dancing)? What about your everyday activities?

APPLICATIONS:

17. Which of the following would most likely be subject to social facilitation?
    a. proofreading a page for spelling errors
    b. typing a letter with accuracy
    c. playing a difficult piece on a violin
    d. running quickly around a track

18. Concluding her presentation on deindividuation, Renée notes that deindividuation is less likely in situations that promote
    a. anonymity.
    b. decreased self-awareness.
    c. increased self-awareness.
    d. the fundamental attribution error.

Objective 44-5: Explain group polarization and groupthink, and discuss the power of the individual.

19. Over time, the initial differences between groups usually _____ (increase/decrease).

20. The enhancement of each group's prevailing tendency over time is called _____ _____ . Electronic discussions in _____ groups provide a medium for this tendency.

21. When the desire for group harmony overrides realistic thinking in individuals, the phenomenon known as _____ has occurred.

22. In considering the power of social influence, we cannot overlook the interaction of _____ _____ (the power of the situation) and _____ _____ (the power of the individual).

23. The power of one or two individuals to sway the opinion of the majority is called _____ _____ .

24. A minority opinion will have the most success in swaying the majority if it takes a stance that is _____ (unswerving/flexible).

APPLICATION:

25. Jane and Sandy were best friends in their first year of university. Jane joined a sorority; Sandy didn't. By the end of their last year, they found that they had less in common with each other than with their current friends. Which of the following phenomena most likely explains this?
    a. group polarization   c. deindividuation
    b. groupthink   d. social facilitation

PROGRESS TEST

Multiple-Choice Questions

Circle your answers to the following questions and check them with the answers beginning on page 372. If your answer is incorrect, read the explanation for why it is incorrect and then consult the text.

1. In his study of obedience, Stanley Milgram found that the majority of participants
    a. refused to shock the learner even once.
    b. complied with the experiment until the "learner" first indicated pain.
    c. complied with the experiment until the "learner" began screaming in agony.
    d. complied with all the demands of the experiment.

2. Which of the following statements is true?
   a. Groups are almost never swayed by minority opinions.
   b. Group polarization is most likely to occur when group members frequently disagree with one another.
   c. Groupthink provides the consensus needed for effective decision making.
   d. A group that is like-minded will probably not change its opinions through discussion.

3. Conformity increased under which of the following conditions in Asch's studies of conformity?
   a. The group had three or more people.
   b. The group had high status.
   c. Individuals were made to feel insecure.
   d. All of these conditions increased conformity.

4. The phenomenon in which individuals lose their identity and relinquish normal restraints when they are part of a group is called
   a. groupthink.   c. empathy.
   b. cognitive dissonance. d. deindividuation.

5. Subjects in Asch's line-judgment experiment conformed to the group standard when their judgments were observed by others but not when they were made in private. This tendency to conform in public demonstrates
   a. social facilitation.
   b. overjustification.
   c. informational social influence.
   d. normative social influence.

6. Based on findings from Milgram's obedience studies, participants would be LESS likely to follow the experimenter's orders when
   a. they hear the "learner" cry out in pain.
   b. they merely administer the test while someone else delivers the shocks.
   c. the "learner" is an older person or mentions having some physical problem.
   d. they see another person disobey instructions.

7. Which of the following most accurately states the effects of crowding on behavior?
   a. Crowding makes people irritable.
   b. Crowding sometimes intensifies people's reactions.
   c. Crowding promotes altruistic behavior.
   d. Crowding usually weakens the intensity of people's reactions.

8. Research has found that for a minority to succeed in swaying a majority, the minority must
   a. make up a sizable portion of the group.
   b. express its position as consistently as possible.
   c. express its position in the most extreme terms possible.
   d. be able to convince a key majority leader.

9. Which of the following conclusions did Milgram derive from his studies of obedience?
   a. Even ordinary people, without any particular hostility, can become agents in a destructive process.
   b. Under the proper circumstances, most people can suppress their natural aggressiveness.
   c. The need to be accepted by others is a powerful motivating force.
   d. He reached all of these conclusions.

10. Which of the following best summarizes the relative importance of personal control and social control of our behavior?
    a. Situational influences on behavior generally are much greater than personal influences.
    b. Situational influences on behavior generally are slightly greater than personal influences.
    c. Personal influences on behavior generally are much greater than situational influences.
    d. Situational and personal influences interact in determining our behavior.

11. Which of the following is important in promoting conformity in individuals?
    a. whether an individual's behavior will be observed by others in the group
    b. whether the individual is male or female
    c. the size of the group's meeting room
    d. whether the individual is of a higher status than other group members

12. Which of the following is most likely to promote groupthink?
    a. The group's leader fails to take a firm stance on an issue.
    b. A minority faction holds to its position.
    c. The group consults with various experts.
    d. Group polarization is evident.

Matching Items

Match each term with the appropriate definition or description.

Terms

_____ 1. social facilitation
_____ 2. social loafing
_____ 3. conformity
_____ 4. normative social influence
_____ 5. informational social influence
_____ 6. group polarization

Definitions or Descriptions

a. people work less hard in a group
b. performance is improved by an audience
c. the effect of social approval or disapproval
d. adjusting one's behavior to coincide with a group standard
e. group discussion enhances prevailing tendencies
f. the effect of accepting others' opinions about something

TERMS AND CONCEPTS TO REMEMBER

Using your own words, on a separate piece of paper write a brief definition or explanation of each of the following terms.

1. conformity
2. normative social influence
3. informational social influence
4. social facilitation
5. social loafing
6. deindividuation
7. group polarization
8. groupthink

True–False Items

Indicate whether each statement is true or false by placing _T_ or _F_ in the blank next to the item.

_____ 1. An individual is more likely to conform when the rest of the group is unanimous.
_____ 2. The tendency of people to conform is influenced by their culture.
_____ 3. Group polarization tends to prevent groupthink from occurring.
_____ 4. Crowded conditions usually subdue people's reactions.
_____ 5. When individuals lose their sense of identity in a group, they often become more uninhibited.

Essay Question

The Panhellenic Council on your campus has asked you to make a presentation on the topic "Social Psychology" to all freshmen who have signed up to "rush" a fraternity or sorority. In a fit of cynicism following your rejection last year by a prestigious fraternity or sorority, you decide to speak on the negative influences of groups on the behavior of individuals. What will you discuss? (Use the space below to list the points you want to make, and organize them. Then write the essay on a separate sheet of paper.)

ANSWERS

Module Review

Conformity: Complying With Social Pressures

1. emotional; automatic mimicry; mimic; empathy; mood linkage
2. conformity
3. Solomon Asch
4. were

We are more likely to conform when we are made to feel incompetent or insecure, when the group has at least three people, when everyone else in the group agrees, when we admire the group's status and attractiveness, when we have not made a prior commitment to any response, when others will observe our behavior, and when our culture encourages respect for social standards.

5. normative social influence; norms
6. informational social influence

7. **a.** is the answer. As illustrated by Maria's decision to stop buying aerosol products, informational social influence occurs when people have genuinely been influenced by what they have learned from others.
   b. Had Maria's behavior been motivated by the desire to avoid rejection or to gain social approval (which we have no reason to suspect is the case), it would have been an example of normative social influence.
   c. The foot-in-the-door phenomenon is the tendency for people who agree to a small request to comply later with a larger request.
   d. Cognitive dissonance is the psychological discomfort we experience when our behavior conflicts with what we think and feel.

Obediance: Following Orders

8. Stanley Milgram; complied; similar to
   Obedience was highest when the person giving the orders was close at hand and perceived to be a legitimate authority figure, the authority figure was supported by a prestigious institution, the victim was depersonalized, and when there were no role models for defiance.

9. foot-in-the-door

10. social; ordinary; conform

11. **c.** is the answer. Prior commitment to an opposing view generally tends to work against conformity. In contrast, large group size, prestigiousness of a group, and an individual's feelings of incompetence and insecurity all strengthen the tendency to conform.

12. Milgram would say that Marge's behavior was a product of the situation, not her personal traits. She respected the officers of the sorority and everyone else was participating in the hazing.

Group Influence

13. social facilitation; easy; likely

14. amplified

15. less hard; social loafing

16. deindividuation

17. **d.** is the answer. Social facilitation, or better performance in the presence of others, occurs for easy tasks but not for more difficult ones. For tasks such as proofreading, typing, playing an instrument, or giving a speech, the arousal resulting from the presence of others can lead to mistakes.

18. **c.** is the answer. Deindividuation involves the loss of self-awareness and self-restraint in group situations that involve arousal and anonymity, so (a.) and (b.) cannot be right.

19. increase

20. group polarization; Internet

21. groupthink

22. social control; personal control

23. minority influence

24. unswerving

25. **a.** is the answer. Group polarization means that the tendencies within a group—and therefore the differences among groups—grow stronger over time. Thus, because the differences between the sorority and nonsorority students have increased, Jane and Sandy are likely to have little in common.
   b. Groupthink is the tendency for realistic decision making to disintegrate when the desire for group harmony is strong.
   c. Deindividuation is the loss of self-restraint and self-awareness that sometimes occurs when one is part of a group.
   d. Social facilitation refers to improved performance of a task in the presence of others.

Progress Test

Multiple-Choice Questions

1. **d.** is the answer. In Milgram's initial experiments, 63 percent of the subjects complied fully with the experiment.

2. **d.** is the answer. In such groups, discussion usually strengthens prevailing opinion; this phenomenon is known as group polarization.
   a. Minority opinions, especially if consistently and firmly stated, can sway the majority in a group.
   b. Group polarization, or the strengthening of a group's prevailing tendencies, is most likely in groups where members agree.
   c. When groupthink occurs, there is so much consensus that decision making becomes less effective.

3. **d.** is the answer.

4. **d.** is the answer.
   a. Groupthink refers to the mode of thinking that occurs when the desire for group harmony overrides realistic and critical thinking.

b. Cognitive dissonance refers to the discomfort we feel when two thoughts (which include the knowledge of our *behavior*) are inconsistent.
c. Empathy is feeling what another person feels.

5. **d.** is the answer. Normative social influence refers to influence on behavior that comes from a desire to look good to others. Subjects who were observed conformed because they didn't want to look like oddballs.
a. Social facilitation involves performing tasks better or faster in the presence of others.
b. Overjustification occurs when a person is rewarded for doing something that is already enjoyable.
c. Informational social influence is the tendency of individuals to accept the opinions of others, especially in situations where they themselves are unsure.

6. **d.** is the answer. Role models for defiance reduce levels of obedience.
a. & c. These did not result in diminished obedience.
b. This "depersonalization" of the victim resulted in increased obedience.

7. **b.** is the answer.
a. & c. Crowding may amplify irritability or altruistic tendencies that are already present. Crowding does not, however, produce these reactions as a general effect.
d. In fact, just the opposite is true. Crowding often intensifies people's reactions.

8. **b.** is the answer.
a. Even if they made up a sizable portion of the group, although still a minority, their numbers would not be as important as their consistency.
c. & d. These aspects of minority influence were not discussed in the text; however, they are not likely to help a minority sway a majority.

9. **a.** is the answer.

10. **d.** is the answer. The text emphasizes the ways in which personal and social controls interact in influencing behavior. It does not suggest that one factor is more influential than the other.

11. **a.** is the answer. As Solomon Asch's experiments demonstrated, individuals are more likely to conform when they are being observed by others in the group. The other factors were not discussed in the text and probably would not promote conformity.

12. **d.** is the answer. Group polarization, or the enhancement of a group's prevailing attitudes, promotes groupthink, which leads to the disintegration of critical thinking.

a. Groupthink is more likely when a leader highly favors an idea, which may make members reluctant to disagree.
b. A strong minority faction would probably have the opposite effect: It would diminish group harmony while promoting critical thinking.
c. Consulting experts would discourage groupthink by exposing the group to other opinions.

Matching Items

1. b   4. c
2. a   5. f
3. d   6. e

True–False Items

1. T   4. F
2. T   5. T
3. F

Essay Question

Your discussion might focus on some of the following topics: normative social influence; conformity, which includes suggestibility; obedience; group polarization; and groupthink.

As a member of any group with established social norms, individuals will often act in ways that enable them to avoid rejection or gain social approval. Thus, a fraternity or sorority pledge would probably be very suggestible and likely to eventually conform to the attitudes and norms projected by the group—or be rejected socially. In extreme cases of pledge hazing, acute social pressures may lead to atypical and antisocial individual behaviors—for example, on the part of pledges complying with the demands of senior members of the fraternity or sorority. Over time, meetings and discussions will probably enhance the group's prevailing attitudes (group polarization). This may lead to the unrealistic and irrational decision making that is groupthink. The potentially negative consequences of groupthink depend on the issues being discussed, but may include a variety of socially destructive behaviors.

Terms and Concepts to Remember

1. **Conformity** is the tendency to change one's thinking or behavior to coincide with a group standard.

2. **Normative social influence** refers to the pressure on individuals to conform to avoid rejection or gain social approval.
Memory aid: *Normative* means "based on a norm, or pattern, regarded as typical for a specific

group." **Normative social influence** is the pressure groups exert on the individual to behave in ways acceptable to the group standard.

3. **Informational social influence** results when one is willing to accept others' opinions about reality.

4. **Social facilitation** is stronger performance of simple or well-learned tasks that occurs when other people are present.

5. **Social loafing** is the tendency for individual effort to be diminished when one is part of a group working toward a common goal.

6. **Deindividuation** refers to the loss of self-restraint and self-awareness that sometimes occurs in group situations that foster arousal and anonymity.

   Memory aid: As a prefix, *de-* indicates reversal or undoing. To **deindividuate** is to undo one's individuality.

7. **Group polarization** refers to the enhancement of a group's prevailing tendencies through discussion, which often has the effect of accentuating the group's differences from other groups.

   Memory aid: To *polarize* is to "cause thinking to concentrate about two poles, or contrasting positions."

8. **Groupthink** refers to the unrealistic thought processes and decision making that occur within groups when the desire for group harmony overrides a realistic appraisal of alternatives.

   Example: The psychological tendencies of self-justification, conformity, and group polarization foster the development of the "team spirit" mentality known as **groupthink**.

Antisocial Relations

MODULE OVERVIEW

Module 45 discusses how people relate to one another in a negative fashion—developing prejudice, behaving aggressively, and provoking conflict.

Although there is some terminology for you to learn in this module, your primary task is to absorb the findings of the many research studies discussed. The module headings, which organize the findings, should prove especially useful to you here. In addition, you might, for each main topic, ask yourself the question, "What situational factors promote this phenomenon?" The research findings can then form the basis for your answers.

NOTE: Answer guidelines for all Module 45 questions begin on page 380.

MODULE REVIEW

First, skim each section, noting headings and bold-face items. After you have read the section, review each objective by answering the fill-in and essay-type questions that follow it. In some cases, Study Tips explain how best to learn a difficult concept and Applications help you to know how well you understand the material. As you proceed, evaluate your performance by consulting the answers beginning on page 380. Do not continue with the next section until you understand each answer. If you need to, review or reread the section in the textbook before continuing.

Prejudice

Objective 45-1: Define *prejudice*, and identify its social and emotional roots.

1. Prejudice is an _____ and usually _____ attitude toward a group that involves overgeneralized beliefs known as _____ .

2. Like all attitudes, prejudice is a mixture of _____ , _____ , and predispositions to _____ .

3. Prejudice is a negative _____ , and _____ is a negative _____ .

4. Americans today express _____ (less/the same/more) racial and gender prejudice than they did 50 years ago.

5. (text and Close-Up) Blatant forms of prejudice _____ (have/have not) diminished. However, even people who deny holding prejudiced attitudes may carry negative _____ about race.

6. (Close-Up) Studies of prejudice indicate that it is often an unconscious, or _____ , action. Research has shown that _____ people with a flashed Black rather than White face makes them _____ (more/less) likely to perceive a flashed tool as a gun.

7. (Close-Up) Today's biopsychosocial approach has stimulated neuroscience studies that have detected implicit prejudice in people's _____-muscle responses and in the activation of their brain's _____ .

8. Worldwide, _____ (women/men) are more likely to live in poverty. People tend to perceive women as being more _____ and _____ and less _____ than men.

9. For those with money, power, and prestige, prejudice often serves as a means of _____ social inequalities.

10. The belief that people get what they deserve—that the good are rewarded and the bad punished—is expressed in the

    _____ - _____

    phenomenon.

11. Discrimination increases prejudice through the tendency of people to _____ victims for their plight.

12. Through our _____

    _____ , we associate ourselves with certain groups and contrast ourselves with others.

13. Prejudice is also fostered by the

    _____ _____ , a tendency to favor groups to which one belongs—called the _____—while excluding others, or the _____ .

14. That prejudice derives from attempts to blame others for one's frustration is proposed by the _____ theory.

15. People who feel loved and supported become more _____ to and _____ of those who differ from them.

16. Prejudice is also nourished by _____ emotions.

Objective 45-2: Identify the cognitive roots of prejudice.

17. Research suggests that prejudice may also derive from _____ , the process by which we attempt to simplify our world by classifying people into groups. One by-product of this process is that people tend to _____ the similarity of those within a group. One manifestation of this is the

    _____ - _____

    _____ , the tendency to recall faces of one's own race more accurately than those of other races.

18. Another factor that fosters the formation of group stereotypes and prejudice is the tendency to _____ from vivid or memorable cases.

19. The belief that people get what they deserve is

based in part on _____

_____ , the tendency to believe that one would have foreseen how something turned out.

APPLICATIONS:

20. Students at State University are convinced that their school is better than any other; this most directly illustrates

    a. an ingroup bias.
    b. prejudice and discrimination.
    c. the scapegoat effect.
    d. the just-world phenomenon.

21. Alexis believes that all male athletes are self-centered and sexist. Her beliefs are an example of

    a. in-group bias.
    b. groupthink.
    c. stereotypes.
    d. the fundamental attribution error.

22. Ever since their cabin lost the camp softball competition, the campers have become increasingly hostile toward one camper in their cabin, blaming her for every problem in the cabin. This behavior is best explained in terms of

    a. the ingroup bias.
    b. prejudice.
    c. the scapegoat theory.
    d. catharsis.

23. Given the tendency of people to categorize information according to preformed schemas, which of the following stereotypes would Juan, a 65-year-old political liberal and fitness enthusiast, be most likely to have?

    a. "People who exercise regularly are very extraverted."
    b. "All political liberals are advocates of a reduced defense budget."
    c. "Young people today have no sense of responsibility."
    d. "Older people are lazy."

Aggression

Objective 45-3: Explain how psychology's definition of *aggression* differs from everyday usage, and identify the biological factors that make us more prone to hurt one another.

24. Aggressive behavior is defined by psychologists

    as _____

    _____ .

    Thus, psychologists _____ (do/do not) consider assertive salespeople to be aggressive.

25. Like other behaviors, aggression emerges from the interaction of _____ and _____ .

26. Today, most psychologists _____ (do/do not) consider human aggression to be instinctive.

27. In humans, aggressiveness _____ (varies/does not vary) greatly from culture to culture, era to era, and person to person.

28. That there are genetic influences on aggression can be shown by the fact that many species of animals have been _____ for aggressiveness.

29. Twin studies suggest that genes _____ (do/do not) influence human aggression. One genetic marker of those who commit the most violence is the _____ chromosome. Studies of violent criminals reveal diminished activity in the brain's _____ _____ , which play an important role in controlling _____ .

30. In humans and animals, aggression is facilitated by _____ systems, which are in turn influenced by _____ , alcohol, and other substances in the blood.

31. The aggressive behavior of animals can be manipulated by altering the levels of the hormone _____ . When this level is _____ (increased/decreased), aggressive tendencies are reduced.

32. High levels of testosterone correlate with _____ , low tolerance for _____ , _____ , and _____ . Among teenage boys and adult men, high testosterone also correlates with _____ , hard _____ _____ , and aggressive-bullying responses to _____ . Although testosterone heightens aggressiveness, aggression _____ (increases/ decreases) testosterone level.

33. One drug that unleashes aggressive responses to provocation is _____ .

Objective 45-4: Outline psychological and social-cultural triggers of aggression.

34. According to the _____-_____ principle, inability to achieve a goal leads to anger, which may generate aggression.

35. Other aversive stimuli can provoke hostility, including _____ _____ .

36. Aggressive behavior can be learned through _____ , as shown by the fact that people use aggression where they've found it pays, and through _____ of others.

37. Parent-training programs often advise parents to avoid _____ violence by screaming and hitting. One _____-_____ program with juvenile offenders and gang members and their parents has been successful in bringing down the youths' re-arrest rates.

38. Crime rates are higher in countries in which there is a large disparity between those who are _____ and those who are _____ . High violence rates also are typical of cultures and families in which there is minimal _____ _____ .

39. Repeatedly viewing on-screen violence may create _____ _____ to which people respond when they are in new situations or are uncertain how to act.

40. The "rape myth" is the mistaken idea that _____ . Most rapists _____ (accept/do not accept) this myth.

Comment on the impression of women that pornography frequently conveys and the effects this impression has on attitudes and behavior.

Summarize the findings of the study in which undergraduates viewed either sexually explicit films or nonerotic films.

41. Experiments have shown that, among other factors, depictions by the media of _____ _____ most directly affect men's acceptance and performance of aggression against women.

42. Violence on television tends to _____ people to cruelty and _____ them to respond aggressively when they are provoked.

43. Kids who play a lot of violent video games see the world as more _____ , get into more _____ and _____ , and get worse _____ .

44. Research studies of the impact of violent video games _____ (confirm/disconfirm) the idea that we feel better if we "blow off steam" by venting our emotions. Playing violent video games _____ (increases/decreases) aggressive thoughts, emotions, and behaviors.

45. Many factors contribute to aggression, including _____ factors, such as an increase in testosterone; _____ factors, such as frustration; and _____-_____ factors, such as deindividuation.

APPLICATIONS:

46. Summarizing his report on the biology of aggression, Sam notes that
  a. biology does not significantly influence aggression.
  b. when one identical twin has a violent temperament, the other member of the twin pair rarely does.
  c. hormones and alcohol influence the neural systems that control aggression.
  d. testosterone reduces dominance behaviors in animals.

47. After waiting in line for an hour to buy concert tickets, Teresa is told that the concert is sold out. In her anger she pounds her fist on the ticket counter, frightening the clerk. Teresa's behavior is best explained by
  a. evolutionary psychology.
  b. deindividuation.
  c. reward theory.
  d. the frustration-aggression principle.

PROGRESS TEST

Multiple-Choice Questions

Circle your answers to the following questions and check them with the answers beginning on page 381. If your answer is incorrect, read the explanation for why it is incorrect and then consult the text.

1. Violent criminals often have diminished activity in the _____ of the brain, which play(s) an important role in _____ .
  a. occipital lobes; aggression
  b. hypothalamus; hostility
  c. frontal lobes; controlling impulses
  d. temporal lobes; patience

2. *Aggression* is defined as behavior that
  a. hurts another person.
  b. is intended to hurt another person.
  c. is hostile, passionate, and produces physical injury.
  d. has all of these characteristics.

3. Which of the following is true about aggression?
  a. It varies too much to be instinctive in humans.
  b. It is just one instinct among many.
  c. It is instinctive but shaped by learning.
  d. It is the most important human instinct.

4. Research studies have found a positive correlation between aggressive tendencies in animals and levels of the hormone
  a. estrogen.   **c.** noradrenaline.
  b. adrenaline.   **d.** testosterone.

5. Research studies have indicated that the tendency of viewers to misperceive normal sexuality, devalue their partners, and trivialize rape is
   a. increased by exposure to pornography.
   b. not changed after exposure to pornography.
   c. decreased in men by exposure to pornography.
   d. decreased in both men and women by exposure to pornography.

6. Which of the following was NOT mentioned in the text discussion of the roots of prejudice?
   a. people's tendency to overestimate the similarity of people within groups
   b. people's tendency to assume that exceptional, or especially memorable, individuals are unlike the majority of members of a group
   c. people's tendency to assume that the world is just and that people get what they deserve
   d. people's tendency to discriminate against those they view as "outsiders"

7. The belief that those who suffer deserve their fate is expressed in the
   a. just-world phenomenon.
   b. phenomenon of ingroup bias.
   c. scapegoat theory.
   d. frustration-aggression principle.

8. (Close-Up) Which of the following is an example of implicit prejudice?
   a. Jake, who is White, gives higher evaluations to essays he believes to be written by Blacks than to White-authored essays.
   b. Carol believes that White people are arrogant.
   c. Brad earns more than Jane, despite having the same job skills, performance level, and seniority.
   d. In certain countries, women are not allowed to drive.

9. We tend to perceive the members of an ingroup as _____ and the members of an outgroup as
   _____ .
   a. similar to one another; different from one another
   b. different from one another; similar to one another
   c. above average in ability; below average in ability
   d. below average in ability; above average in ability

10. Regarding the influence of alcohol and testosterone on aggressive behavior, which of the following is true?
    a. Consumption of alcohol increases aggressive behavior; injections of testosterone reduce aggressive behavior.
    b. Consumption of alcohol reduces aggressive behavior; injections of testosterone increase aggressive behavior.
    c. Consumption of alcohol and injections of testosterone both promote aggressive behavior.
    d. Consumption of alcohol and injections of testosterone both reduce aggressive behavior.

11. Research studies have shown that frequent exposure to sexually explicit films
    a. makes a woman's friendliness seem more sexual.
    b. diminishes the attitude that rape is a serious crime.
    c. may lead individuals to devalue their partners.
    d. may produce all of these effects.

12. Most researchers agree that
    a. media violence is a factor in aggression.
    b. there is a negative correlation between media violence and aggressiveness.
    c. paradoxically, watching excessive pornography ultimately diminishes an individual's aggressive tendencies.
    d. media violence is too unreal to promote aggression in viewers.

13. People with power and status may become prejudiced because
    a. they tend to justify the social inequalities between themselves and others.
    b. those with less status and power tend to resent them.
    c. those with less status and power appear less capable.
    d. they feel proud and are boastful of their achievements.

Matching Items

Match each term with the appropriate definition or description.

Terms

_____ 1. ingroup bias
_____ 2. stereotype
_____ 3. social script

Definitions or Descriptions

a. a generalized belief about a group of people
b. the tendency to favor one's own group
c. a culturally specific model of how to act in a given situation

TERMS AND CONCEPTS TO REMEMBER

Using your own words, on a separate piece of paper write a brief definition or explanation of each of the following terms.

1. prejudice
2. stereotype
3. discrimination
4. just-world phenomenon
5. ingroup
6. outgroup
7. ingroup bias
8. scapegoat theory
9. other-race effect
10. aggression
11. frustration-aggression principle
12. social script

ANSWERS

Module Review

Prejudice

1. unjustifiable; negative; stereotypes
2. beliefs; emotions; action
3. attitude; discrimination; behavior
4. less
5. have; associations
6. implicit; priming; more
7. facial; amygdala
8. women; nurturant; sensitive; aggressive
9. justifying
10. just-world
11. blame

12. social identities
13. ingroup bias; ingroup; outgroup
14. scapegoat
15. open; accepting
16. negative
17. categorization; overestimate; other-race effect
18. overgeneralize
19. hindsight bias

20. **a.** is the answer.
    b. Prejudices are unjustifiable and usually negative attitudes toward other groups. They may result from an ingroup bias, but they are probably not why students favor their own university.
    c. Scapegoats are individuals or groups toward which prejudice is directed as an outlet for the anger of frustrated individuals or groups.
    d. The just-world phenomenon is the tendency for people to believe that others "get what they deserve."

21. **c.** is the answer.
    a. The ingroup bias is the tendency to favor one's own group.
    b. Groupthink refers to the unrealistic thought processes and decision making that occur within groups when the desire for group harmony becomes paramount.
    d. The fundamental attribution error is our tendency to underestimate the impact of situations and to overestimate the impact of personal dispositions on the behavior of others.

22. **c.** is the answer. According to the scapegoat theory, when things go wrong, people look for someone on whom to take out their anger and frustration.
    a. These campers are venting their frustration on a member of their *own* cabin group (although this is not always the case with scapegoats).
    b. Prejudice refers to an unjustifiable and usually negative attitude toward another group.
    d. Catharsis is the idea that releasing aggressive energy relieves aggressive urges.

23. **c.** is the answer. People tend to overestimate the similarity of people within groups other than their own. Thus, Juan is not likely to form stereotypes of fitness enthusiasts (a.), political liberals (b.), or older adults (d.), because these are groups to which he belongs.

Aggression

24. any physical or verbal behavior intended to hurt or destroy; do not

25. biology; experience

26. do not

27. varies

28. bred

29. do; Y; frontal lobes; impulses

30. neural; hormones

31. testosterone; decreased

32. irritability; frustration; assertiveness; impulsiveness; delinquency; drug use; frustration; increases

33. alcohol

34. frustration-aggression

35. physical pain, personal insults, foul odors, hot temperatures, cigarette smoke, crowding

36. rewards; observation (or imitation)

37. modeling; aggression-replacement

38. rich; poor; father care

39. social scripts

40. some women invite or enjoy rape; accept

Pornography tends to portray women as enjoying being the victims of sexual aggression, and this perception increases the acceptance of coercion in sexual relationships. Repeatedly watching X-rated films and Internet pornography also makes one's partner seem less attractive, makes a woman's friendliness seem more sexual, and makes sexual aggression seem less serious.

The study found that after viewing sexually explicit films for several weeks, undergraduates were more likely to recommend a lighter prison sentence for a convicted rapist than were those who viewed nonerotic films.

41. sexual violence

42. desensitize; prime

43. hostile; arguments; fights; grades

44. disconfirm; increases

45. biological; psychological; social-cultural

46. **c.** is the answer.

   a. & b. Biology is an important factor in aggressive behavior. This includes genetics, which

means identical twins would have similar temperaments.

   d. Just the opposite is true.

47. **d.** is the answer. According to the frustration-aggression principle, the blocking of an attempt to achieve some goal—in Teresa's case, buying concert tickets—creates anger and can generate aggression.

   a. Evolutionary psychology maintains that aggressive behavior is a genetically based drive. Teresa's behavior clearly was a reaction to a specific situation.

   b. Deindividuation refers to loss of self-restraint in group situations that foster arousal. Teresa's action has only to do with her frustration.

   c. Reward theory views behavior as an exchange process in which people try to maximize the benefits of their behavior by minimizing the costs. Teresa's behavior likely brought her few benefits while exacting some costs, including potential injury, embarrassment, and retaliation by the clerk.

Progress Test

Multiple-Choice Questions

1. **c.** is the answer.

2. **b.** is the answer. Aggression is any behavior, physical or verbal, that is intended to hurt or destroy.

   a. A person may accidentally be hurt in a nonaggressive incident; aggression does not necessarily prove hurtful.

   c. Verbal behavior, which does not result in physical injury, may also be aggressive. Moreover, acts of aggression may be cool and calculated, rather than hostile and passionate.

3. **a.** is the answer. The very wide variations in aggressiveness from culture to culture indicate that aggression cannot be considered an unlearned instinct.

4. **d.** is the answer.

5. **a.** is the answer.

6. **b.** is the answer. In fact, people tend to overgeneralize from vivid cases, rather than assume that they are unusual.

   a., c., & d. Each of these is an example of a cognitive (a. & c.) or a social (d.) root of prejudice.

7. **a.** is the answer.

   b. Ingroup bias is the tendency of people to favor their own group.

c. With the scapegoat theory, we blame someone else as an outlet for our anger.

d. The frustration-aggression principle states that people behave aggressively when their attempts to reach a goal are blocked.

8. **a.** is the answer.
   b. This is an example of overt prejudice.
   c. & d. These are examples of discrimination.

9. **b.** is the answer.
   a. We are keenly sensitive to differences within our group, less so to differences within other groups.
   c. & d. Although we tend to look more favorably on members of the ingroup, the text does not suggest that ingroup bias extends to evaluations of abilities.

10. **c.** is the answer.

11. **d.** is the answer.

12. **a.** is the answer.

13. **a.** is the answer. Such justifications arise as a way to preserve inequalities. The just-world phenomenon presumes that people get what they deserve. According to this view, someone who has less must deserve less.

Matching Items

1. b
2. a
3. c

Terms and Concepts to Remember

1. **Prejudice** is an unjustifiable (and usually negative) attitude toward a group and its members.

2. A **stereotype** is a generalized (sometimes accurate but often overgeneralized) belief about a group of people.

3. **Discrimination** is unjustifiable negative behavior toward a group and its members.

4. The **just-world phenomenon** is a manifestation of the commonly held belief that good is rewarded and evil is punished. The logic is indisputable: "If I am rewarded, I must be good."

5. The **ingroup** refers to the people and groups with whom we share a common identity.

6. The **outgroup** refers to the people and groups that are excluded from our ingroup.

7. The **ingroup bias** is the tendency to favor our own group.

8. The **scapegoat theory** proposes that prejudice provides an outlet for anger by finding someone to blame.

9. The **other-race effect** is our tendency to recall the faces of our own race more accurately than those of other races.

10. **Aggression** is any physical or verbal behavior intended to hurt or destroy.

11. The **frustration-aggression principle** states that aggression is triggered when people become angry because their efforts to achieve a goal have been blocked.

12. A **social script** is a culturally specific model of how to behave in various situations.

Prosocial Relations

MODULE OVERVIEW

Module 46 discusses how people relate to one another a positive fashion—being attracted to people who are nearby and/or similar, behaving altruistically, and resolving conflicts through peaceful means. The module concludes with a discussion of techniques that have been shown to promote conflict resolution.

Although there is some terminology for you to learn in this module, your primary task is to absorb the findings of the many research studies discussed. The module headings, which organize the findings, should prove especially useful to you here. In addition, you might, for each main topic (attraction, altruism, peacemaking), ask yourself the question, "What situational factors promote this phenomenon?" The research findings can then form the basis for your answers.

NOTE: Answer guidelines for all Module 46 questions begin on page 387.

MODULE REVIEW

First, skim each section, noting headings and bold-face items. After you have read the section, review each objective by answering the fill-in and essay-type questions that follow it. In some cases, Study Tips explain how best to learn a difficult concept and Applications help you to know how well you understand the material. As you proceed, evaluate your performance by consulting the answers beginning on page 387. Do not continue with the next section until you understand each answer. If you need to, review or reread the section in the textbook before continuing.

Attraction

Objective 46-1: Explain why we befriend or fall in love with some people but not with others.

1. A prerequisite for, and perhaps the most powerful predictor of, attraction is _____ .

2. (Close-up) Compared with relationships formed in person, Internet-formed relationships are _____ (more/less) likely to last beyond two years. Studies of people who engage in _____ dating reveal that observers can read a _____ (woman's/man's) level of romantic interest more accurately than a _____ (woman's/man's).

3. When people are repeatedly exposed to unfamiliar stimuli, their liking of the stimuli _____ (increases/decreases). This phenomenon is the _____ _____ effect. This phenomenon was _____ for our ancestors, for whom the unfamiliar was often dangerous. One implication of this is that _____ against those who are culturally different may be a primitive, _____ emotional response.

4. Our first impression of another person is most influenced by the person's _____ .

5. In a sentence, list several of the characteristics that physically attractive people are judged to possess: _____
_____ .

6. A person's attractiveness _____
(is/is not) strongly related to his or her self-esteem or happiness.

7. Cross-cultural research reveals that men judge women as more attractive if they have a _____ appearance, whereas women judge men who appear
_____ , _____ ,
_____ , and _____
as more attractive. People also seem to prefer physical features that are neither unusually _____ nor _____ .
Average faces, which tend to be _____ , are judged to be more sexually attractive.

8. Compared with strangers, friends and couples are more likely to be similar in terms of
_____
_____ .

Explain what a reward theory of attraction is and how it can account for the three predictors of liking—proximity, attractiveness, and similarity.

APPLICATIONS:

9. Ahmed and Monique are on a blind date. Which of the following will probably be MOST influential in determining whether they like each other?
   a. their personalities
   b. their beliefs
   c. their social skills
   d. their physical attractiveness

10. Having read the chapter, which of the following is best borne out by research on attraction?
    a. Birds of a feather flock together.
    b. Opposites attract.
    c. Familiarity breeds contempt.
    d. Absence makes the heart grow fonder.

Objective 46-2: Describe how romantic love typically changes as time passes.

11. Hatfield has distinguished two types of love: _____ love and _____ love.

12. According to the two-factor theory, emotions have two components: physical _____ and a _____ label.

13. When college men were placed in an aroused state, their feelings toward an attractive woman _____ (were/were not) more positive than those of men who had not been aroused.

14. Companionate love is promoted by _____—mutual sharing and giving by both partners. Another key ingredient of loving relationships is the revealing of intimate aspects of ourselves through _____ . A third key to enduring love is _____ .

APPLICATION:

15. Opening her mail, Joan discovers a romantic greeting card from her boyfriend. According to the two-factor theory, she is likely to feel the most intense romantic feelings if, prior to reading the card, she has just
    a. completed her daily run.
    b. finished reading a chapter in her psychology textbook.
    c. awakened from a nap.
    d. finished eating lunch.

Altruism

Objective 46-3: Identify the times when people are most—and least—likely to help.

16. An unselfish regard for the welfare of others is called _____ .

Give an example of altruism.

17. According to Darley and Latané, people will help only if a three-stage decision-making process is completed: Bystanders must first _____ the incident, then _____ it as an emergency, and finally _____ _____ for helping.

18. When people who overheard a seizure victim calling for help thought others were hearing the same plea, they were _____ (more/less) likely to go to his aid than when they thought no one else was aware of the emergency.

19. In a series of staged accidents, Latané and Darley found that a bystander was _____ (more/less) likely to help when more people shared responsibility for helping, that is, when there was a _____ _____ _____ . This phenomenon has been called the _____ _____ .

Identify the circumstances in which a person is most likely to offer help during an emergency.

STUDY TIP: As with other concepts, altruism is best understood by relating it to your own experiences. Can you think of instances of altruism in your home town? At school? Have you personally stopped to help a person who seemed to be in need—for example, an older woman struggling to carry groceries to her car? What are some other examples of truly altruistic behavior?

Objective 46-4: Discuss how social exchange theory and social norms explain helping behavior.

20. The idea that social behavior aims to maximize rewards and minimize costs is proposed by the _____ _____ theory.

21. One rule of social behavior tells us to return help to those who have helped us; this is the _____ norm.

22. Another rule tells us to help those who need our help; this is the _____-_____ norm.

Peacemaking

Objective 46-5: Explain how social traps and mirror-image perceptions fuel social conflict.

23. A perceived incompatibility of actions, goals, or ideas is called _____ . This perception can take place between _____ at war, _____ groups feuding within a society, or _____ sparring in a relationship.

24. Situations in which conflicting parties become caught in mutually destructive behavior by pursuing their own self-interests are called _____ _____ .

25. The distorted images people in conflict form of each other are called _____-_____ perceptions.

26. In most situations, establishing contact between two conflicting groups _____ (is/is not) sufficient to resolve conflict.

27. In Muzafer Sherif's study, two conflicting groups of campers were able to resolve their conflicts by working together on projects in which they shared _____ goals. Shared _____ breed solidarity, as demonstrated by a surge in the use of the word _____ in the weeks after 9/11.

Objective 46-6: Discuss how we can transform feelings of prejudice, aggression, and conflict into attitudes that promote peace.

28. When conflicts arise, a third-party _____ may facilitate communication and promote understanding.

29. Charles Osgood has advanced a strategy of conciliation called GRIT, which stands for _____ and _____ in _____-_____ . The key to this method is each side's offering of a small _____ gesture in order to increase mutual trust and cooperation.

APPLICATIONS:

30. Mr. and Mrs. Samuels are constantly fighting, and each perceives the other as hard-headed and insensitive. Their conflict is being fueled by
   a. self-disclosure.
   b. stereotypes.
   c. a social norm.
   d. mirror-image perceptions.

31. Which of the following strategies would be MOST likely to foster positive feelings between two conflicting groups?
   a. Take steps to reduce the likelihood of mirror-image perceptions.
   b. Separate the groups so that tensions diminish.
   c. Increase the amount of contact between the two conflicting groups.
   d. Have the groups work on a superordinate goal.

PROGRESS TEST

Multiple-Choice Questions

Circle your answers to the following questions and check them with the answers beginning on page 388. If your answer is incorrect, read the explanation for why it is incorrect and then consult the text.

1. Increasing the number of people that are present during an emergency tends to
   a. increase the likelihood that people will cooperate in rendering assistance.
   b. decrease the empathy that people feel for the victim.
   c. increase the role that social norms governing helping will play.
   d. decrease the likelihood that anyone will help.

2. The mere exposure effect demonstrates that
   a. familiarity breeds contempt.
   b. opposites attract.
   c. birds of a feather flock together.
   d. familiarity breeds fondness.

3. In one experiment, college men were physically aroused and then introduced to an attractive woman. Compared with men who had not been aroused, these men
   a. reported more positive feelings toward the woman.
   b. reported more negative feelings toward the woman.
   c. were ambiguous about their feelings toward the woman.

   d. were more likely to feel that the woman was "out of their league" in terms of attractiveness.

4. The deep affection that is felt in long-lasting relationships is called _____ love; this feeling is fostered in relationships in which _____ .
   a. passionate; there is equity between the partners
   b. passionate; traditional roles are maintained
   c. companionate; there is equity between the partners
   d. companionate; traditional roles are maintained

5. Which of the following is associated with an increased tendency on the part of a bystander to offer help in an emergency situation?
   a. being in a good mood
   b. having recently needed help and not received it
   c. observing someone as he or she refuses to offer help
   d. being a female

6. Most people prefer mirror-image photographs of their faces. This is best explained by
   a. the principle of equity.
   b. the principle of self-disclosure.
   c. the mere exposure effect.
   d. mirror-image perceptions.

7. Research studies indicate that in an emergency situation, the presence of others often
   a. prevents people from even noticing the situation.
   b. prevents people from interpreting an unusual event as an emergency.
   c. prevents people from assuming responsibility for assisting.
   d. leads to all of these behaviors.

8. Which of the following factors is the MOST powerful predictor of friendship?
   a. similarity in age
   b. common racial and religious background
   c. similarity in physical attractiveness
   d. physical proximity

9. Which of the following BEST describes how GRIT works?
   a. The fact that two sides in a conflict have great respect for the other's strengths prevents further escalation of the problem.
   b. The two sides engage in a series of reciprocated conciliatory acts.

c. The two sides agree to have their differences settled by a neutral, third-party mediator.

d. The two sides engage in cooperation in those areas in which shared goals are possible.

Matching Items

Match each term with the appropriate definition or description.

Terms

_____   **1.** bystander effect
_____   **2.** altruism
_____   **3.** mere exposure effect

Definitions or Descriptions

a. unselfish regard for others
b. the tendency that a person is less likely to help someone in need when others are present
c. the increased liking of a stimulus that results from repeated exposure to it

TERMS AND CONCEPTS TO REMEMBER

Using your own words, on a separate piece of paper write a brief definition or explanation of each of the following terms.

1. mere exposure effect
2. passionate love
3. companionate love
4. equity
5. self-disclosure
6. altruism
7. bystander effect
8. social exchange theory
9. reciprocity norm
10. social-responsibility norm
11. conflict
12. social trap
13. mirror-image perceptions
14. superordinate goals
15. GRIT

ANSWERS

Module Review

Attraction

1. proximity
2. more; speed; man's; woman's
3. increases; mere exposure; adaptive; prejudice; automatic
4. appearance

5. Attractive people are perceived as healthier, happier, more sensitive, more successful, and more socially skilled.
6. is not
7. youthful; mature; dominant; masculine; affluent; large; small; symmetrical
8. attitudes, beliefs, interests, religion, race, education, intelligence, smoking behavior, economic status, and age

A reward theory of attraction says that we are attracted to, and continue relationships with, those people whose behavior provides us with more benefits than costs. Proximity makes it easy to enjoy the benefits of friendship at little cost, attractiveness is pleasing, and similarity is reinforcing to us.

9. **d.** is the answer. Hundreds of experiments indicate that first impressions are most influenced by physical appearance.
10. **a.** is the answer. Friends and couples are much more likely than randomly paired people to be similar in views, interests, and a range of other factors.
   b. The opposite is true.
   c. The mere exposure effect demonstrates that familiarity tends to breed fondness.
   d. This is unlikely, given the positive effects of proximity and intimacy.
11. passionate; companionate
12. arousal; cognitive
13. were
14. equity; self-disclosure; positive support
15. **a.** is the answer. According to the two-factor theory, physical arousal can intensify whatever emotion is currently felt. Only in the situation described in (a.) is Joan likely to be physically aroused.

Altruism

16. altruism

An example of altruism is giving food and shelter to people displaced by a hurricane or other major disaster without expectation of reward.

17. notice; interpret; assume responsibility

18. less

19. less; diffusion of responsibility; bystander effect

People are most likely to help someone when they have just observed someone else being helpful; when they are not in a hurry; when the victim appears to need and deserve help; when they are in some way similar to the victim; when the person is a woman; when in a small town or rural area; when feeling guilty; when not preoccupied; and when in a good mood.

20. social exchange

21. reciprocity

22. social-responsibility

Peacemaking

23. conflict; nations; cultural; partners

24. social traps

25. mirror-image

26. is not

27. superordinate; predicaments; "we"

28. mediator

29. Graduated; Reciprocated Initiatives; Tension-Reduction; conciliatory

30. **d.** is the answer. The couple's similar, and presumably distorted, feelings toward each other fuel their conflict.
a. Self-disclosure, or the sharing of intimate feelings, fosters love.
b. Stereotypes are overgeneralized ideas about groups.
c. A social norm is an understood rule for expected and accepted behavior.

31. **d.** is the answer. Sherif found that hostility between two groups could be dispelled by giving the groups superordinate, or shared, goals.
a. Although reducing the likelihood of mirror-image perceptions might reduce mutually destructive behavior, it would not lead to positive feelings between the groups.
b. Such segregation would likely increase ingroup bias and group polarization, resulting in further group conflict.
c. Contact by itself is not likely to reduce conflict.

Progress Test

Multiple-Choice Questions

1. **d.** is the answer. This phenomenon is known as the bystander effect.
a. This answer is incorrect because individuals are less likely to render assistance at all if others are present.
b. Although people are less likely to assume responsibility for helping, this does not mean that they are less empathic.
c. This answer is incorrect because norms such as the social responsibility norm encourage helping others, yet people are less likely to help with others around.

2. **d.** is the answer. Being repeatedly exposed to novel stimuli increases our liking for them.
a. For the most part, the opposite is true.
b. & c. The mere exposure effect concerns our tendency to develop likings on the basis, not of similarities or differences, but simply of familiarity, or repeated exposure.

3. **a.** is the answer. This result supports the two-factor theory of emotion and passionate attraction, according to which arousal from any source can facilitate an emotion, depending on how we label the arousal.

4. **c.** is the answer. Deep affection is typical of companionate love, rather than passionate love, and is promoted by equity, whereas traditional roles may be characterized by the dominance of one sex.

5. **a.** is the answer.
b. & c. These factors would most likely decrease a person's altruistic tendencies.
d. There is no evidence that one sex is more altruistic than the other.

6. **c.** is the answer. The mere exposure effect refers to our tendency to like what we're used to, and we're used to seeing mirror images of ourselves.
a. Equity refers to equality in giving and taking between the partners in a relationship.
b. Self-disclosure is the sharing of intimate feelings with a partner in a loving relationship.
d. Although people prefer mirror images of their faces, mirror-image perceptions are often held by parties in conflict. Each party views itself favorably and the other negatively.

7. **d.** is the answer.

8. **d.** is the answer. Because it provides people with an opportunity to meet, proximity is the most powerful predictor of friendship, even though, once a friendship is established, the other factors mentioned become more important.

9. **b.** is the answer.
   a. GRIT is a technique for reducing conflict through a series of conciliatory gestures, not for maintaining the status quo.
   c. & d. These measures may help reduce conflict but they are not aspects of GRIT.

Matching Items

1. b
2. a
3. c

Terms and Concepts to Remember

1. The **mere exposure effect** refers to the fact that repeated exposure to an unfamiliar stimulus increases our liking of it.

2. **Passionate love** refers to an aroused state of intense positive absorption in another person, especially at the beginning of a relationship.

3. **Companionate love** refers to a deep, enduring, affectionate attachment to those with whom we share our lives.

4. **Equity** refers to the condition in which there is mutual giving and receiving between the partners in a relationship.

5. **Self-disclosure** refers to a person's revealing intimate aspects of oneself to others.

6. **Altruism** is unselfish regard for the welfare of others.

7. The **bystander effect** is the tendency of a person to be less likely to offer help to someone if there are other people present.

8. **Social exchange theory** states that our social behavior revolves around exchanges, in which we try to minimize our costs and maximize our benefits.

9. The **reciprocity norm** is the expectation that people will help, not hurt, those who have helped them.

10. The **social-responsibility norm** is the expectation that people will help those who depend on them.

11. **Conflict** is a perceived incompatibility of actions, goals, or ideas between individuals or groups.

12. A **social trap** is a situation in which conflicting parties become caught in mutually destructive behaviors because each persists in pursuing its own self-interest.

13. **Mirror-image perceptions** are the negative, mutual views that conflicting people often hold about one another.

14. **Superordinate goals** are mutual goals that require the cooperation of individuals or groups otherwise in conflict.

15. **GRIT** (Graduated and Reciprocated Initiatives in Tension-Reduction) is a strategy of conflict resolution based on the defusing effect that conciliatory gestures can have on parties in conflict.

Introduction to Psychological Disorders

MODULE OVERVIEW

Although there is no clear-cut line between normal and abnormal behavior, we can characterize as abnormal those behaviors that are deviant, distressful, and dysfunctional. Module 47 introduces the Diagnostic and Statistical Manual of Mental Disorders (DSM-IV-TR). Although this classification system follows a medical model, most psychologists today advocate a biopsychosocial approach. Thus, psychoanalytic theory, learning theory, social-cognitive theory, and other psychological perspectives are drawn on when relevant. The module concludes with a discussion of the incidence of serious psychological disorders in society today.

NOTE: Answer guidelines for all Module 47 questions begin on page 395.

MODULE REVIEW

First, skim each section, noting headings and bold-face items. After you have read the section, review each objective by answering the fill-in and essay-type questions that follow it. In some cases, Study Tips explain how best to learn a difficult concept and Applications help you to know how well you understand the material. As you proceed, evaluate your performance by consulting the answers on page 395. Do not continue with the next section until you understand each answer. If you need to, review or reread the section in the textbook before continuing.

Defining Psychological Disorders

Objective 47-1: Discuss how we draw the line between normality and disorder.

1. Mental health workers label thoughts, feelings, and actions disordered when they are

   _____ , _____ ,

   and _____ .

2. This definition emphasizes that standards of acceptability for behavior _____ (are constant/vary) by _____ , by _____ , and with

   _____ .

STUDY TIP: To be considered evidence of a psychological disorder, a behavior pattern must be deviant, distressful, *and* dysfunctional. Most people sometimes behave in ways that fit one or two of these criteria yet fall short of being clinically significant. For example, a deviant behavior is simply one that does not occur in most other people in a specific culture. The remarkable skills of a professional rodeo athlete, for example, while deviant from most of us, are not distressful or dysfunctional. Think about your own behavior patterns and see if you can think of examples that fit one or two of the three criteria that characterize psychological disorders.

APPLICATION:

3. Kitty has agreed to appear on the TV show *Fear Factor.* Her test involves eating roaches, a practice that disgusts most North Americans. Although Kitty's task is _____ and possibly briefly _____ , it is not _____ and so is not disordered.

Objective 47-2: Discuss the controversy over the diagnosis of attention-deficit hyperactivity disorder.

4. (Thinking Critically) ADHD, or

   _____-_____

   _____ _____ ,

   plagues children who display one or more of three key symptoms: extreme

   _____ , _____ ,

   and _____ .

5. (Thinking Critically) ADHD is diagnosed more often in _____ (boys/girls). In the past two decades, the proportion of American children being treated for this disorder _____ (increased/decreased) dramatically. Experts _____ (agree/do not agree) that ADHD is a real disorder.

6. (Thinking Critically) ADHD _____ (is/is not) thought by some to be heritable, and it _____ (is/is not) caused by eating too much sugar or poor schools. ADHD is often accompanied by a _____ disorder or with behavior that is _____ or temper-prone.

APPLICATION:

7. (Thinking Critically) Thirteen-year-old Ronald constantly fidgets in his seat at school, frequently blurts out answers without being called, and is extremely distractible. A psychiatrist might diagnose Ronald with _____-

_____ _____

_____ .

Understanding Psychological Disorders

Objective 47-3: Contrast the medical model with the biopsychosocial approach to psychological disorders.

8. The view that psychological disorders are sicknesses is the basis of the _____ model. According to this view, psychological disorders are viewed as mental _____ , or _____ , diagnosed on the basis of _____ and cured through _____ .

9. One of the first reformers to advocate this position and call for providing more humane living conditions for the mentally ill was _____ .

10. Today's psychologists recognize that all behavior arises from the interaction of _____ and _____ . To presume that a person is "mentally ill" attributes the condition solely to a "_____" that must be identified and cured.

11. Major psychological disorders such as _____ and

_____ are universal; others, such as _____ _____ and _____ _____ , are culture-bound. These culture-bound disorders may share an underlying _____ , such as _____ , yet differ in their _____ .

12. Most mental health workers today take a _____ approach, whereby they assume that disorders are influenced by

_____ _____ and _____ _____ , inner _____ _____ , and _____ and _____ circumstances (see art below for clues to answers).

_____ influences:
• evolution
• individual genes
• brain structure and chemistry

_____ influences:
• stress
• trauma
• learned helplessness
• mood-related perceptions and memories

Psychological disorder

_____ - _____ influences:
• roles
• expectations
• definitions of *normality* and *disorder*

STUDY TIP: Think about the implications of the medical model and biopsychosocial models of psychological disorders. If a behavior pattern that is deviant, distressful, and dysfunctional is caused by a brain abnormality, for example, how would you answer the following questions?

1. How should this behavior be diagnosed?
2. How should this behavior be treated in efforts to cure it?
3. How will people view people who are diagnosed with this disorder? For example, are they to blame for their plight?

Now think about a disordered behavior that is caused by a person's environment, thinking patterns, and habits. Would your answers to these questions change for this type of behavior? Why or why not?

APPLICATION:

13. Haya, who suffers from *taijin-kyofusho,* is afraid of direct eye contact with another person. A therapist who believes in the medical model would say that her problem has a _____ basis. A biopsychosocial therapist would want to look into the interaction

of her _____ , _____ ,
and _____-_____
environment.

Classifying Psychological Disorders

Objective 47-4: Describe how and why clinicians classify psychological disorders.

14. The most widely used system for classifying psychological disorders is the American Psychiatric Association manual, commonly known by its abbreviation, _____ . It was developed in coordination with the World Health Organization's _____ _____ of _____ .This manual _____ (does/does not) explain the cause of a disorder; rather, it _____ the disorder.

15. Independent diagnoses made with the current manual generally _____ (show/do not show) agreement.

Labeling Psychological Disorders

Objective 47-5: Explain why some psychologists criticize the use of diagnostic labels.

16. One criticism of DSM-IV-TR is that as the number of disorder categories has _____ (increased/decreased), the number of adults who meet the criteria for at least one psychiatric ailment has _____ (increased/ decreased).

17. Studies have shown that labeling has _____ (little/a significant) effect on our interpretation of individuals and their behavior.

Outline the pros and cons of labeling psychological disorders.

18. (Thinking Critically) Most people with psychological disorders _____ (are/are not) violent. Most people whose _____ defense is accepted are nonetheless institutionalized, often for as long as those convicted of crimes.

Rates of Psychological Disorders

Objective 47-6: Discuss the prevalence of psychological disorders, and summarize the findings on the link between poverty and serious psychological disorders.

19. Research reveals that approximately _____ percent of adult Americans suffered a clinically significant mental disorder during the prior year.

20. The incidence of serious psychological disorders is _____ (higher/lower) among those below the poverty line.

21. In terms of age of onset, most psychological disorders appear by _____ (early/middle/late) adulthood. Some, such as the _____ _____ and _____ , appear during childhood.

PROGRESS TEST

Multiple-Choice Questions

Circle your answers to the following questions and check them with the answers beginning on page 395. If your answer is incorrect, read the explanation for why it is incorrect and then consult the text.

1. The criteria for classifying behavior as psychologically disordered
   a. vary from culture to culture.
   b. vary from time to time.
   c. vary by culture and with time.
   d. have remained largely unchanged over the course of history.

2. Most mental health workers today take the view that disordered behaviors
   a. are usually genetically triggered.
   b. are organic diseases.
   c. arise from the interaction of nature and nurture.
   d. are the product of learning.

3. The view that all behavior arises from the interaction of heredity and environment is referred to as the _____ approach.
   a. biopsychosocial
   b. psychodynamic
   c. medical
   d. conditioning

4. Evidence of environmental effects on psychological disorders is seen in the fact that certain disorders, such as _____ , are universal, whereas others, such as _____ , are culture-bound.
   a. schizophrenia; depression
   b. depression; schizophrenia
   c. antisocial personality; neurosis
   d. depression; anorexia nervosa

5. The diagnostic reliability of DSM-IV-TR
   a. is unknown.
   b. depends on the age of the patient.
   c. is very low.
   d. is relatively high.

6. (Thinking Critically) The term *insanity* refers to
   a. legal definitions.
   b. psychotic disorders only.
   c. personality disorders only.
   d. both psychotic disorders and personality disorders.

7. Which of the following is true concerning abnormal behavior?
   a. Definitions of abnormal behavior are culture-dependent.
   b. A behavior cannot be defined as abnormal unless it is considered harmful to society.
   c. Abnormal behavior can be defined as any behavior that is distressful.
   d. Definitions of abnormal behavior are based on physiological factors.

8. The fact that disorders such as schizophrenia are universal and influenced by heredity, whereas other disorders such as anorexia nervosa are culture-bound provides evidence for the _____ model of psychological disorders.
   a. medical   c. social-cultural
   b. biopsychosocial d. psychodynamic

9. Our early ancestors commonly attributed disordered behavior to
   a. "bad blood."   c. brain injury.
   b. evil spirits.   d. laziness.

10. Which of the following statements concerning the labeling of disordered behaviors is NOT true?
   a. Labels interfere with effective treatment of psychological disorders.
   b. Labels promote research studies of psychological disorders.
   c. Labels may create preconceptions that bias people's perceptions.
   d. Labels may influence behavior by creating self-fulfilling prophecies.

11. Which of the following is true of the medical model?
   a. In recent years, it has been in large part discredited.
   b. It views psychological disorders as sicknesses that are diagnosable and treatable.
   c. It emphasizes the role of psychological factors in disorders over that of physiological factors.
   d. It focuses on cognitive factors.

12. Behavior is classified as disordered when it
   a. is deviant.
   b. is distressful.
   c. is dysfunctional.
   d. has all of these characteristics.

13. Most practitioners find the DSM-IV-TR a helpful and practical tool despite its
   a. failure to emphasize observable behaviors in the diagnostic process.
   b. learning theory bias.
   c. medical model bias.
   d. psychoanalytic bias.

Essay Question

Clinical psychologists label people disordered if their behavior is (1) deviant, (2) distressful, and (3) dysfunctional. Demonstrate your understanding of the classification process by giving examples of behaviors that might be considered deviant, distressful, or dysfunctional but, because they do not fit all three criteria, would not necessarily be labeled disordered. (Use the space below to list the points you want to make, and organize them. Then write the essay on a separate piece of paper.)

TERMS AND CONCEPTS TO REMEMBER

Using your own words, on a separate piece of paper write a brief definition or explanation of each of the following terms.

1. psychological disorder

2. attention-deficit hyperactivity disorder (ADHD)

3. medical model

4. DSM-IV-TR

ANSWERS

Module Review

Defining Psychological Disorders

1. deviant; distressful; dysfunctional

2. vary; context; culture; time

3. deviant; distressful; dysfunctional

4. attention-deficit hyperactivity disorder; inattention; hyperactivity; impulsivity

5. boys; increased; do not agree

6. is; is not; learning; defiant

7. attention-deficit hyperactivity disorder

Understanding Psychological Disorders

8. medical; sickness; psychopathology; symptoms; therapy

9. Philippe Pinel

10. nature; nurture; sickness

11. depression; schizophrenia; anorexia nervosa; bulimia nervosa; dynamic; anxiety; symptoms

12. biopsychosocial; genetic predispositions; physiological states; psychological dynamics; social; cultural

13. biological; biology; psychology; social-cultural. Haya's behavior is directed by a specific situation. Because it does not interfere with her everyday life, it is not considered disordered.

Classifying Psychological Disorders

14. DSM-IV-TR; Internal Classification; Diseases; does not; describes

15. show

Labeling Psychological Disorders

16. increased; increased

17. a significant

Psychological labels may be arbitrary. They can create preconceptions that bias our perceptions and interpretations and they can affect people's self-images. Moreover, labels can change reality, by serving as self-fulfilling prophecies. Despite these drawbacks, labels are useful in describing, treating, and researching the causes of psychological disorders.

18. are not; mental disorders

Rates of Psychological Disorders

19. 26

20. higher

21. early; antisocial personality; phobias

Progress Test

Multiple-Choice Questions

1. **c.** is the answer.

2. **c.** is the answer. Most clinicians agree that psychological disorders may be caused by both psychological (d.) and physical (a. and b.) factors.

3. **a.** is the answer.

4. **d.** is the answer. Although depression is universal, anorexia nervosa and bulimia are rare outside of Western culture.
   a. & b. Schizophrenia and depression are both universal.
   c. The text mentions only schizophrenia and depression as universal disorders. Furthermore, neurosis is no longer a category of diagnosis.

5. **d.** is the answer.
   b. The text does not mention DSM-IV-TR's reliability in terms of a person's age.

6. **a.** is the answer.

7. **a.** is the answer. Different cultures have different standards for behaviors that are considered acceptable and normal.
   b. Some abnormal behaviors are simply maladaptive for the individual.
   c. Many individuals who are deviant, such as Olympic gold medalists, are not considered abnormal. There are other criteria that must be met in order for behavior to be considered abnormal.
   d. Although physiological factors play a role in the various disorders, they do not define abnormal behavior. Rather, behavior is said to be abnormal if it is deviant, distressful, and dysfunctional.

8. **b.** is the answer. The fact that some disorders are universal and at least partly genetic in origin implicates biological factors in their origin. The

fact that other disorders appear only in certain parts of the world implicates sociocultural and psychological factors in their origin.

9. **b.** is the answer.

10. **a.** is the answer. In fact, just the opposite is true. Labels are useful in promoting effective treatment of psychological disorders.

11. **b.** is the answer.
    a. This isn't the case; in fact, the medical model has gained credibility from recent discoveries of genetic and biochemical links to some disorders.
    c. & d. The medical perspective tends to place more emphasis on physiological factors.

12. **d.** is the answer.

13. **c.** is the answer. DSM-IV-TR was shaped by the medical model.
    a. In fact, just the opposite is true. DSM-IV-TR was revised to improve reliability by basing diagnoses on observable behaviors.
    b. & d. DSM-IV-TR does not reflect a learning or a psychoanalytic bias.

Essay Question

There is more to a psychological disorder than being different from other people. Gifted artists, athletes, and scientists have deviant capabilities, yet are not considered psychologically disordered. Also, what is deviant in one culture may not be in another, or at another time. Homosexuality, for example, was once classified as a psychological disorder, but it is no longer. Similarly, nudity is common in some cultures and disturbing in others. Deviant behaviors are more likely to be considered disordered when judged as distressful and dysfunctional to the individual. Prolonged feelings of depression or the use of drugs to avoid dealing with problems are examples of deviant behaviors that may signal a psychological disorder if the person is unable to function, to perform routine behaviors (becomes dysfunctional).

Terms and Concepts to Remember

1. To be classified as a **psychological disorder**, behavior must be deviant, distressful, and dysfunctional.

2. **Attention-deficit hyperactivity disorder (ADHD)** is a psychological disorder characterized by the appearance by age 7 of one or more of three symptoms: extreme inattention, hyperactivity, and impulsivity.

3. The **medical model** holds that psychological disorders are illnesses that can be diagnosed, treated, and, in most cases, cured, often through treatment in a psychiatric hospital.

4. **DSM-IV-TR** is a short name for the American Psychiatric Association's *Diagnostic and Statistical Manual of Mental Disorders* (*Fourth Edition, Text Revision*), which provides a widely used system of classifying psychological disorders.

Anxiety Disorders

MODULE OVERVIEW

Module 48 discusses types of anxiety disorders, as classified by the Diagnostic and Statistical Manual of Mental Disorders (DSM-IV-TR). After a brief description of generalized anxiety disorder, phobias, obsessive-compulsive disorder, and post-traumatic stress disorder, the module presents psychoanalytic, learning, and biological explanations for these disorders.

NOTE: Answer guidelines for all Module 48 questions begin on page 401.

MODULE REVIEW

First, skim each section, noting headings and boldface items. After you have read the section, review each objective by answering the fill-in and essay-type questions that follow it. In some cases, Study Tips explain how best to learn a difficult concept and Applications help you to know how well you understand the material. As you proceed, evaluate your performance by consulting the answers beginning on page 401. Do not continue with the next section until you understand each answer. If you need to, review or reread the section in the textbook before continuing.

Introduction

Objective 48-1: Identify the different anxiety disorders.

1. Anxiety disorders are psychological disorders characterized by _____ _____ .

2. Five anxiety disorders discussed in the text are

_____ _____

_____ , _____

_____ , _____ ,

_____ - _____

_____ , and _____ -

_____ _____

_____ .

Generalized Anxiety Disorder and Panic Disorder

3. When a person is continually tense, apprehensive, and physiologically aroused for no apparent reason, he or she is diagnosed as suffering from a

_____ _____

disorder. In Freud's term, the anxiety is

_____ - _____ .

4. Generalized anxiety disorder can lead to physical problems, such as _____

_____ _____ .

In some instances, anxiety may intensify dramatically and unpredictably and be accompanied by heart palpitations or choking, for example; people with these symptoms are said to have

_____ _____ . This

anxiety may escalate into a minutes-long episode of intense fear, or a _____ .

_____ .

5. People who _____ have at least a doubled risk of a first-time _____

_____ because _____

is a stimulant.

Phobias

6. When a person has an irrational fear of a specific object, activity, or situation, the diagnosis is a _____ . Although in many situations, the person can live with the problem, some _____ _____ , such as a fear of thunderstorms, are incapacitating.

7. When a person has an intense fear of being scrutinized by others, the diagnosis is a

_____ _____ .

People who fear situations in which escape or help might not be possible when panic strikes suffer from _____ .

Obsessive-Compulsive Disorder

8. When a person cannot control repetitive thoughts and actions, an _____-_____ disorder is diagnosed. Older people are _____ (more/less) likely than teens and young adults to suffer from this disorder.

Post-Traumatic Stress Disorder

9. Traumatic stress, such as that associated with witnessing atrocities or combat, can produce

_____-_____ _____ disorder. The symptoms of this disorder include _____

_____ , _____ ,

_____ _____ ,

_____ _____ ,

and _____ .

10. People who have a sensitive _____

_____ are more vulnerable to this disorder. Brain scans reveal an aberrant and persistent _____

_____ _____

activation in these patients. Research with identical twins indicates that _____ may also play a role.

11. Researchers who believe this disorder may be overdiagnosed point to the _____ _____ of most people who suffer trauma. Also, suffering can lead to

_____-_____

_____ , in which people experience an increased appreciation for life, more meaningful relationships, changed priorities, and a richer spiritual life.

APPLICATIONS:

12. Irene occasionally experiences unpredictable episodes of intense dread accompanied by heart palpitations and a sensation of smothering. Since her symptoms have no apparent cause, they would probably be classified as indicative of
   a. schizophrenia.
   b. generalized anxiety disorder.
   c. depression.
   d. panic attack.

13. Han has an intense, irrational fear of snakes. He is suffering from
   a. generalized anxiety disorder.
   b. obsessive-compulsive disorder.
   c. a phobia.
   d. a panic attack.

14. Isabella is continually tense, jittery, and apprehensive for no specific reason. She would probably be diagnosed as suffering from
   a. a phobia.
   b. post-traumatic stress disorder.
   c. obsessive-compulsive disorder.
   d. generalized anxiety disorder.

15. Jason is so preoccupied with staying clean that he showers as many as 10 times each day. Jason would be diagnosed as suffering from
   a. schizophrenia.
   b. generalized anxiety disorder.
   c. agoraphobia.
   d. obsessive-compulsive disorder.

16. Although she escaped from war-torn Bosnia two years ago, Zheina still has haunting memories and nightmares. Because she is also severely depressed, her therapist diagnoses her condition as
   a. panic disorder.
   b. obsessive-compulsive disorder.
   c. generalized anxiety disorder.
   d. post-traumatic stress disorder.

Understanding Anxiety Disorders

Objective 48-2: Describe how the learning and biological perspectives explain anxiety disorders.

17. Freud assumed that anxiety disorders are symptoms of submerged mental energy that derives from intolerable impulses that were _____ during childhood.

18. Learning theorists, drawing on research in which rats are given unpredictable electric shocks, link general anxiety with _____ conditioning of _____ .

19. Some fears arise from _____ _____ , such as when a person who fears heights after a fall also comes to fear airplanes.

20. Phobias and compulsive behaviors reduce anxiety and thereby are _____ . Through _____ learning, someone might also learn fear by seeing others display their own fears.

21. Humans probably _____ (are/ are not) biologically prepared to develop certain fears. Compulsive acts typically are exaggerations of behaviors that contributed to our species' _____ .

22. The anxiety response probably _____ (is/is not) genetically influenced. There may be anxiety _____ that affect brain levels of the neurotransmitter _____ , which influences mood, as well as the neurotransmitter _____ , which regulates the brain's alarm centers.

23. fMRI scans of persons with obsessive-compulsive disorder reveal excessive activity in a brain region called the _____

_____ cortex. Some antidepressant drugs dampen fear-circuit activity in the _____ , thus reducing this behavior.

STUDY TIP: Phobias are persistent fears of certain objects, activities, or situations. They are irrational because they are much stronger than the actual danger. Also, many *specific phobias* may be unrelated to a direct, negative experience with the feared object. Are there any specific objects, activities, or situations that you find particularly frightening? How do you think you acquired these fears? Can you remember a bad experience? Did you see someone else have a problem? Does your fear ever interfere with your daily life?

APPLICATIONS:

24. Julia's psychologist believes that Julia's fear of heights can be traced to a conditioned fear she developed after falling from a ladder. This explanation reflects a _____ perspective.
   a. medical   **c.** social-cognitive
   b. psychoanalytic **d.** learning

25. Before he can study, Rashid must arrange his books, pencils, paper, and other items on his desk so that they are "just so." The campus counselor suggests that Rashid's compulsive behavior may help alleviate his anxiety about failing in school, which reinforces the compulsive actions. This explanation of obsessive-compulsive behavior is most consistent with which perspective?
   a. learning   **c.** humanistic
   b. psychoanalytic **d.** social-cognitive

26. After falling from a ladder, Joseph is afraid of airplanes, although he has never flown. This demonstrates that some fears arise from

   _____ .

27. To which of the following is a person MOST likely to acquire a phobia?
   a. heights
   b. being in public
   c. being dirty
   d. All of these are equally likely.

PROGRESS TEST

Multiple-Choice Questions

Circle your answers to the following questions and check them with the answers on page 402. If your answer is incorrect, read the explanation for why it is incorrect and then consult the text.

1. Because of some troubling thoughts, Carl recently had a PET scan of his brain that revealed excessive activity in the anterior cingulate area. Carl's psychiatrist believes that Carl suffers from
   a. schizophrenia.
   b. a mood disorder.
   c. a personality disorder.
   d. obsessive-compulsive disorder.

2. Which of the following was presented in the text as evidence of biological influences on anxiety disorders?
   a. Identical twins often develop similar phobias.
   b. Brain scans of persons with obsessive-compulsive disorder reveal unusually high activity in the anterior cingulate cortex.
   c. Drugs that dampen fear-circuit activity in the amygdala also alleviate OCD.
   d. All of these findings were presented.

Matching Items

Match each term with the appropriate definition or description.

Terms

_____ 1. agoraphobia
_____ 2. post-traumatic growth
_____ 3. obsessive-compulsive disorder
_____ 4. panic attack
_____ 5. social phobia

TERMS AND CONCEPTS TO REMEMBER

Using your own words, on a separate piece of paper write a brief definition or explanation of each of the following terms.

3. The psychodynamic perspective would most likely view phobias as
   a. conditioned fears.
   b. displaced responses to incompletely repressed impulses.
   c. biological predispositions.
   d. manifestations of self-defeating thoughts.

4. Which of the following provides evidence that human fears have been subjected to the evolutionary process?
   a. Compulsive acts typically exaggerate behaviors that contributed to our species' survival.
   b. Most phobias focus on objects that our ancestors also feared.
   c. It is easier to condition some fears than others.
   d. All of these provide evidence.

5. Psychodynamic and learning theorists both agree that anxiety disorders are symptoms that represent the person's attempt to deal with
   a. unconscious conflicts.
   b. anxiety.
   c. unfulfilled wishes.
   d. unpleasant responsibilities.

Definitions or Descriptions

a. a sudden escalation of anxiety often accompanied by a sensation of choking or other physical symptoms
b. fear or avoidance of situations in which escape might be difficult or help unavailable when panic strikes
c. intense fear of being scrutinized by others
d. a disorder characterized by repetitive thoughts and actions
e. positive psychological changes stemming from dealing with an extreme crisis

1. anxiety disorders

2. generalized anxiety disorder

3. panic disorder

4. phobia

5. obsessive-compulsive disorder (OCD)

6. post-traumatic stress disorder (PTSD)

7. post-traumatic growth

ANSWERS

Module Review

Introduction

1. distressing, persistent anxiety or dysfunctional behaviors that reduce anxiety

2. generalized anxiety disorder; panic disorder; phobias; obsessive-compulsive disorder; post-traumatic stress disorder

Generalized Anxiety Disorder and *Panic Disorder*

3. generalized anxiety; free-floating

4. high blood pressure; panic disorder; panic attack

5. smoke; panic attack; nicotine

Phobias

6. phobia; specific phobias

7. social phobia; agoraphobia

Obsessive-compulsive Disorder

8. obsessive-compulsive; less

Post-Traumatic Stress Disorder

9. post-traumatic stress; haunting memories; nightmares; social withdrawal; jumpy anxiety; insomnia

10. limbic system; right temporal lobe; genes

11. survivor resiliency; post-traumatic growth

12. **d.** is the answer.
    a. Baseless physical symptoms rarely play a role in schizophrenia.
    b. Generalized anxiety disorder is continually tense, apprehensive state.
    c. There is no indication that she is depressed.

13. **c.** is the answer. An intense fear of a specific object is a phobia.
    a. His fear is focused on a specific object, not generalized.
    b. In this disorder a person is troubled by repetitive thoughts and actions.
    d. A panic attack does not involve a specific object, such as a snake.

14. **d.** is the answer.
    a. In phobias, anxiety is focused on a specific object.
    b. Post-traumatic stress disorder is tied to a specific traumatic experience.
    c. The obsessive-compulsive disorder is characterized by repetitive and unwanted thoughts and/or actions.

15. **d.** is the answer. Jason is obsessed with cleanliness; as a result, he has developed a compulsion to shower.
    a. Schizophrenia does not involve repetititve behaviors that reduce anxiety.
    b. Generalized anxiety disorder does not have a specific focus.
    c. Agoraphobia is fear or avoidance of situations in which escape might not be possible.

16. **d.** is the answer.
    a. There is no evidence that Zheina is having panic attacks.
    b. Zheina shows no signs of being obsessed with certain thoughts or behaviors.
    c. Zheina's haunting memories are not free-floating; they are tied to real events.

Understanding Anxiety Disorders

17. repressed

18. classical; fears

19. stimulus generalization

20. reinforced; observational

21. are; survival

22. is; genes; serotonin; glutamate

23. anterior cingulate; amygdala

24. **d.** is the answer. In the learning perspective, a phobia, such as Julia's, is seen as a conditioned fear.
    a. Because the fear is focused on a specific stimulus, the medical model does not easily account for the phobia. In any event, it would presumably offer an internal, biological explanation.
    b. The psychoanalytic view of phobias would be that they represent incompletely repressed anxieties that are displaced onto the feared object.
    c. The social-cognitive perspective would emphasize a person's conscious, cognitive processes, not reflexive conditioned responses.

25. **a.** is the answer. According to the learning view, compulsive behaviors are reinforced because they reduce the anxiety created by obsessive thoughts. Rashid's obsession concerns failing, and his desk-arranging compulsive behaviors apparently help him control these thoughts.
    b. The psychoanalytic perspective would view obsessive thoughts as a symbolic representation of forbidden impulses. These thoughts may prompt the person to perform compulsive acts that counter these impulses.
    c. & d. The text does not offer explanations of obsessive-compulsive behavior based on the humanistic or social-cognitive perspectives. Presumably, however, these explanations would emphasize growth-blocking difficulties in the

person's environment (humanistic perspective) and the reciprocal influences of personality and environment (social-cognitive perspective), rather than symbolic expressions of forbidden impulses.

26. **stimulus generalization.** Joseph's fear has generalized from ladders to airplanes.

27. **a.** is the answer. Humans seem biologically prepared to develop a fear of heights and other dangers that our ancestors faced.

Progress Test

Multiple-Choice Questions

1. **d.** is the answer. These areas show increased activity during compulsive behaviors.

2. **d.** is the answer.

3. **b.** is the answer.
   a. This answer reflects the learning perspective.
   c. Although certain phobias are biologically predisposed, this could not fully explain phobias, nor is it the explanation offered by psychodynamic theory.
   d. Social-cognitive theorists propose self-defeating thoughts as a cause of depression.

4. **d.** is the answer.

5. **b.** is the answer. The psychodynamic explanation is that these disorders are a manifestation of incompletely repressed impulses over which the person is anxious. According to the learning perspective, the troubled behaviors that result from these disorders have been reinforced by anxiety reduction.
   a. & c. These are true of the psychodynamic, but not the learning, perspective.

Matching Items

1. b   4. a
2. e   5. c
3. d

Terms and Concepts to Remember

1. **Anxiety disorders** involve distressing, persistent anxiety or maladaptive behaviors that reduce anxiety.

2. In the **generalized anxiety disorder**, the person is continually tense, apprehensive, and in a state of autonomic nervous system arousal for no apparent reason.

3. A **panic disorder** is an episode of intense dread accompanied by chest pain, dizziness, or choking. It is essentially an escalation of the anxiety associated with generalized anxiety disorder.

4. A **phobia** is an anxiety disorder in which a person has a persistent, irrational fear and avoidance of a specific object, activity, or situation.

5. **Obsessive-compulsive disorder (OCD)** is an anxiety disorder in which the person experiences uncontrollable and repetitive thoughts (obsessions) and actions (compulsions).

6. **Post-traumatic stress disorder (PTSD)** is an anxiety disorder characterized by haunting memories, nightmares, social withdrawal, jumpy anxiety, and/or insomnia lasting four weeks or more following a traumatic experience.

7. **Post-traumatic growth** refers to positive psychological changes that may result from dealing with extremely challenging circumstances and life crises.

Mood Disorders

MODULE OVERVIEW

Module 49 discusses the mood disorders, which include major depressive disorder, the "common cold" of psychological disorders, and bipolar disorder, which is characterized by extreme mood swings. Suicide and non-suicidal self-injury are featured in a Close-Up box. This module focuses on the various explanations for mood disorders, particularly those provided by the biological and social-cognitive perspectives.

NOTE: Answer guidelines for all Module 49 questions begin on page 407.

MODULE REVIEW

First, skim each section, noting headings and bold-face items. After you have read the section, review each objective by answering the fill-in and essay-type questions that follow it. In some cases, Study Tips explain how best to learn a difficult concept and Applications help you to know how well you understand the material. As you proceed, evaluate your performance by consulting the answers beginning on page 407. Do not continue with the next section until you understand each answer. If you need to, review or reread the section in the textbook before continuing.

Major Depressive Disorder and Bipolar Disorder

Objective 49-1: Define *mood disorders,* and contrast major depressive disorder and bipolar disorder.

1. Mood disorders are psychological disorders characterized by _____ _____ . They come in two forms: The experience of prolonged depression with no

discernible cause is called _____ _____ disorder. When a person's mood alternates between depression and the hyperactive state of _____ , a _____ disorder is diagnosed.

2. Although _____ are more common, _____ is the number one reason that people seek mental health services. It is also the leading cause of disability worldwide.

3. The possible signs of depression include _____ _____ .

4. Major depression occurs when its signs last _____ _____ or more with no apparent cause.

5. Depressed persons usually _____ (can/cannot) recover without therapy.

6. Symptoms of mania include _____ _____ .

7. Bipolar disorder is less common among creative professionals who rely on _____ and _____ than among those who rely on _____ expression and vivid _____ .

APPLICATIONS:

8. For the past six months, Haeji has complained of feeling isolated from others, dissatisfied with life, and discouraged about the future. Haeji could be diagnosed as suffering from

   a. bipolar disorder.
   b. major depressive disorder.
   c. generalized anxiety disorder.
   d. panic disorder.

9. On Monday, Delon felt optimistic, energetic, and on top of the world. On Tuesday, he felt hopeless and lethargic, and thought that the future looked very grim. Delon would MOST likely be diagnosed as having

   a. bipolar disorder.
   b. major depressive disorder.
   c. schizophrenia.
   d. panic disorder.

Understanding Mood Disorders

Objective 49-2: Describe how the biological and social-cognitive perspectives explain mood disorders.

10. The commonality of depression suggests that its _____ must also be common.

11. Compared with men, women are _____ (more/less) vulnerable to major depression. In general, women are most vulnerable to disorders involving _____ states, such as

_____

_____ .

12. Men's disorders tend to be more _____ and include _____

_____ .

13. Most people suffering major depression _____ (do/do not) eventually return to normal even without professional help. It usually _____ (is/is not) the case that a depressive episode has been triggered by a stressful event. An individual's vulnerability to depression also increases following, for example, _____ .

14. With each new generation, the rate of depression is _____ (increasing/decreasing) and the disorder is striking _____ (earlier/later). In North America, today's young adults are _____ (how many?) times more likely than their grandparents to suffer depression.

15. Mood disorders _____ (tend/do not tend) to run in families. Studies of _____ also reveal that genetic influences on mood disorders are _____ (weak/strong).

16. To determine which genes are involved in depression, researchers use

_____ _____ , in which they examine the _____ of both affected and unaffected family members.

17. The brains of depressed people tend to be _____ (more/less) active, especially in an area of the _____ _____ lobe and an adjacent brain _____ _____ . In severely depressed patients, this brain area may also be _____ (smaller/larger) in size. The brain's _____ , which is important in processing _____ , is vulnerable to stress-related damage.

18. Depression may also be caused by _____ (high/low) levels of two neurotransmitters, _____ and _____ . Most people with a history of depression also were habitual _____ .

19. Drugs that alleviate mania reduce _____ ; drugs that relieve depression increase _____ or _____ supplies by blocking either their _____ or their chemical _____ .

20. According to the social-cognitive perspective, depression may be linked with _____ beliefs and a _____ _____ style. Such beliefs may arise from _____ _____ , the feeling that can arise when the individual repeatedly experiences uncontrollable, painful events.

21. Gender differences in responding to _____ help explain why women have been twice as vulnerable to depression. According to Susan Nolen-Hoeksema, when trouble strikes, men tend to _____ and women tend to _____ .

Describe how depressed people differ from others in their explanations of failure and how such explanations tend to feed depression.

22. According to Martin Seligman, depression is more common in Western cultures that emphasize _____ and that have shown a decline in commitment to _____ and family.

23. Depression-prone people respond to bad events in an especially _____ way.

24. Being withdrawn, self-focused, and complaining tends to elicit social _____ (empathy/rejection).

Outline the vicious cycle of depression.

APPLICATIONS:

25. Connie's therapist has suggested that her depression stems from unresolved anger toward her parents. Evidently, Connie's therapist is working within the _____ perspective.
    a. learning
    b. social-cognitive
    c. biological
    d. psychoanalytic

26. Ken's therapist suggested that his depression is a result of his self-defeating thoughts and negative assumptions about himself, his situation, and his future. Evidently, Ken's therapist is working within the _____ perspective.
    a. learning
    b. social-cognitive
    c. biological
    d. psychoanalytic

27. Alicia's doctor, who thinks that Alicia's depression has a biochemical cause, prescribes a drug that
    a. reduces norepinephrine.
    b. increases norepinephrine.
    c. reduces serotonin.
    d. increases acetylcholine.

28. Complete the following flow chart comparing how a depressed person and a person who is not depressed would deal with this situation.

Objective 49-3: Discuss the factors that affect suicide and self-injuring, and identify important warning signs to watch for in suicide prevention efforts.

(Close-Up) Identify several group differences in suicide rates.

29. (Close-Up) Factors that affect suicide are _____ dependence and social _____ . For the elderly, it may be an alternative to current or future _____ . People who engage in non-suicidal self-injury do so to gain relief from intense _____ _____ , to ask for help and gain _____ , to relieve _____ , or to get others to change their negative behavior.

30. (Close-Up) Important warning signs to watch for in suicide prevention efforts include

_____ _____ , giving _____ _____ , or _____ and _____ .

PROGRESS TEST

Multiple-Choice Questions

Circle your answers to the following questions and check them with the answers on page 408. If your answer is incorrect, read the explanation for why it is incorrect and then consult the text.

1. Gender differences in the prevalence of depression may partly result from the fact that when stressful experiences occur
   a. women tend to act, while men tend to think.
   b. women tend to think, while men tend to act.
   c. women tend to distract themselves by drinking, while men tend to delve into their work.
   d. women tend to delve into their work, while men tend to distract themselves by drinking.

2. Which of the following is the most pervasive of the psychological disorders?
   a. depression
   b. schizophrenia
   c. bipolar disorder
   d. generalized anxiety disorder

3. Which of the following is NOT true concerning depression?
   a. Depression is more common in women than in men.
   b. Most depressive episodes appear not to be preceded by any particular factor or event.
   c. With each new generation, depression is striking earlier.
   d. Most people recover from depression without professional therapy.

4. According to the social-cognitive perspective, a person who experiences unexpected aversive events may develop helplessness and manifest a(n)
   a. obsessive-compulsive disorder.
   b. dissociative disorder.
   c. personality disorder.
   d. mood disorder.

5. In treating depression, a psychiatrist would probably prescribe a drug that would
   a. increase levels of acetylcholine.
   b. decrease levels of dopamine.
   c. increase levels of norepinephrine.
   d. decrease levels of serotonin.

6. In general, women are more vulnerable than men to
   a. external disorders such as anxiety.
   b. internal disorders such as depression.
   c. external disorders such as antisocial conduct.
   d. internal disorders such as alcohol dependence.

7. Which neurotransmitter is present in overabundant amounts during the manic phase of bipolar disorder?
   a. dopamine   c. epinephrine
   b. serotonin   d. norepinephrine

8. Social-cognitive theorists contend that depression is linked with
   a. negative moods.
   b. maladaptive explanations of failure.
   c. self-defeating beliefs.
   d. all of these characteristics.

9. Which of the following is NOT true of mood disorders, according to the biological perspective?
   a. Activity in the left frontal lobe is increased during a depressed state.
   b. Norepinephrine is scarce during depression.
   c. Brain reward centers are less active during a depressed state.
   d. The hippocampus, which is linked with the brain's emotion circuitry, is vulnerable to stress-related damage.

TERMS AND CONCEPTS TO REMEMBER

Using your own words, on a separate piece of paper write a brief definition or explanation of each of the following terms.

1. mood disorders

2. major depressive disorder

3. mania

4. bipolar disorder

ANSWERS

Module Review

Major Depressive Disorder and *Bipolar Disorder*

1. emotional extremes; major depressive; mania; bipolar

2. phobias; depression

3. lethargy, feelings of worthlessness, and loss of interest in family, friends, and activities

4. two weeks

5. can

6. euphoria, hyperactivity, and a wildly optimistic state

7. precision; logic; emotional; imagery

8. b. is the answer. The fact that this woman has had these symptoms for more than two weeks indicates that she is suffering from major depressive disorder.

9. a. is the answer. Delon's alternating states of the hopelessness and lethargy of depression and the energetic, optimistic state of mania are characteristic of bipolar disorder.
   b. Although he was depressed on Tuesday, Delon's manic state on Monday indicates that he is not suffering from major depressive disorder.

c. Delon was depressed, not detached from reality.
d. That Delon is not exhibiting episodes of intense dread indicates that he is not suffering from panic disorder.

Understanding Mood Disorders

10. causes

11. more; internal; depression, anxiety, and inhibited sexual desire

12. external; alcohol abuse, antisocial conduct, and lack of impulse control

13. do; is; a family member's death, loss of a job, a marital crisis, or a physical assault

14. increasing; earlier; three

15. tend; twins; strong

16. linkage analysis; DNA

17. less; left frontal; reward center; smaller; hippocampus; memories

18. low; norepinephrine; serotonin; smokers

19. norepinephrine; norepinephrine; serotonin; reuptake; breakdown

20. self-defeating; negative explanatory; learned helplessness

21. stress; act; overthink (ruminate)

Depressed people are more likely than others to explain failures or bad events in terms that are stable (it's going to last forever), global (it will affect everything), and internal (it's my fault). Such explanations lead to feelings of hopelessness, which in turn feed depression.

22. individualism; religion

23. self-blaming

24. rejection

Depression is often brought on by negative, stressful experiences. Depressed people brood over such experiences with maladaptive explanations that produce self-blame and amplify their depression, which in turn triggers other symptoms of depression. In addition, being withdrawn and complaining tends to elicit social rejection and other negative experiences.

25. d. is the answer. Freud believed that the anger once felt toward parents was internalized and would produce depression.
   a. & b. The learning and social-cognitive perspectives focus on environmental experiences, conditioning, and self-defeating attitudes in explaining depression.

c. The biological perspective focuses on genetic predispositions and biochemical imbalances in explaining depression.

26. **b.** is the answer.

27. **b.** is the answer. Norepinephrine, which increases arousal and boosts mood, is scarce during depression. Drugs that relieve depression tend to increase norepinephrine.
c. Increasing serotonin, which is sometimes scarce during depression, might relieve depression.

d. This neurotransmitter is involved in motor responses but has not been linked to psychological disorders.

28. There are no right or wrong answers to this. Possible responses of a depressed person might be "I'll never be able to pass this course (stable)," "I'm never going to do well in any college courses (global)," and "It's my fault; I didn't study hard enough (internal)."

Suicide rates are higher among White Americans, the rich, older people, the nonreligious, and those who are single, widowed, or divorced. Although women more often attempt suicide, men are more likely to succeed. Suicide rates also vary widely around the world.

29. alcohol; suggestion; suffering; negative thoughts; attention; guilt

30. verbal hints; possessions away, withdrawal; preoccupation with death

Progress Test

Multiple-Choice Questions

1. **b.** is the answer.
c. & d. Men are more likely than women to cope with stress in these ways.

2. **a.** is the answer.

3. **b.** is the answer. Depression is often preceded by a stressful event related to work, marriage, or a close relationship.

4. **d.** is the answer. Learned helplessness may lead to self-defeating beliefs, which in turn are linked with depression, a mood disorder.

5. **c.** is the answer. Drugs that relieve depression tend to increase levels of norepinephrine.
a. Acetylcholine is a neurotransmitter involved in muscle contractions.
b. It is in certain types of schizophrenia that decreasing dopamine levels is helpful.
d. On the contrary, it appears that a particular type of depression may be related to *low* levels of serotonin.

6. **b.** is the answer.
a. Anxiety is an internal disorder.
d. Alcohol dependence is an external disorder.

7. **d.** is the answer. In bipolar disorder, norepinephrine appears to be overabundant during mania and in short supply during depression.
a. There is an overabundance of dopamine receptors in some schizophrenia patients.
b. Serotonin sometimes appears to be scarce during depression.
c. Epinephrine has not been implicated in psychological disorders.

8. **d.** is the answer.

9. **a.** is the answer. Just the opposite is true.

Terms and Concepts to Remember

1. **Mood disorders** are characterized by emotional extremes.

2. **Major depressive disorder** is the mood disorder that occurs when a person exhibits the lethargy, feelings of worthlessness, or loss of interest in family, friends, and activities characteristic of depression for more than a two-week period and for no discernible reason. Because of its relative frequency, depression has been called the "common cold" of psychological disorders.

3. **Mania** is the wildly optimistic, euphoric, hyperactive state that alternates with depression in the bipolar disorder.

4. **Bipolar disorder** is the mood disorder in which a person alternates between depression and the euphoria of a manic state.
Memory aid: *Bipolar* means having two poles, that is, two opposite qualities. In **bipolar disorder,** the opposing states are mania and depression.

Schizophrenia

MODULE OVERVIEW

Module 50 discusses schizophrenia, including the general symptoms and the different types. The major portion of this module is devoted to exploring the possible causes of schizophrenia, both psychological and physiological.

NOTE: Answer guidelines for all Module 50 questions appear on page 412.

MODULE REVIEW

First, skim each section, noting headings and bold-face items. After you have read the section, review each objective by answering the fill-in and essay-type questions that follow it. In some cases, Study Tips explain how best to learn a difficult concept and Applications help you to know how well you understand the material. As you proceed, evaluate your performance by consulting the answers on page 412. Do not continue with the next section until you understand each answer. If you need to, review or reread the section in the textbook before continuing.

Symptoms of Schizophrenia

Objective 50-1: Describe the patterns of thinking, perceiving, feeling, and behaving that characterize schizophrenia.

1. Schizophrenia, or "split mind," refers not to a split personality but rather to a split from _____ . This disorder is an example of a _____ because it is marked by _____ and _____ .

2. Three manifestations of schizophrenia are disorganized _____ , disturbed _____ , and inappropriate _____ and _____ .

3. The distorted, false beliefs of schizophrenia patients are called _____ .

4. Many psychologists attribute the disorganized thinking of schizophrenia to a breakdown in the capacity for _____ _____ .

5. The disturbed perceptions of people suffering from schizophrenia may take the form of _____ , which usually are _____ (visual/auditory).

6. Some victims of schizophrenia lapse into a zombielike state of apparent apathy, or _____ _____ ; others, who exhibit _____ , may remain motionless for hours and then become agitated.

Onset and Development of Schizophrenia

Objective 50-2: Distinguish the five subtypes of schizophrenia, and contrast chronic and acute schizophrenia.

7. People with schizophrenia who display inappropriate behavior are said to have _____ , while those with toneless voices and expressionless faces are said to have _____ .

8. Schizophrenia is a cluster of disorders, including five subtypes: preoccupation with delusions or hallucinations, called _____ ;

disordered speech or behavior, or

_____ ; immobility, or

_____ ; many and varied symp-

toms, or _____ ; and withdrawal,

or _____ .

9. When schizophrenia develops slowly (called

_____ schizophrenia), recovery

is _____ (more/less) likely than

when it develops rapidly in reaction to particular

life stresses (called _____

schizophrenia).

APPLICATION:

10. Claiming that she heard a voice commanding
her to warn other people that eating is harmful,
Sandy attempts to convince others in a restaurant not to eat. The psychiatrist to whom she is
referred finds that Sandy's thinking and speech
are often fragmented and incoherent. In addition,
Sandy has an unreasonable fear that someone is
"out to get her" and consequently trusts no one.
Her condition is most indicative of
_____ symptoms of
schizophrenia.

Understanding Schizophrenia

Objective 50-3: Discuss how brain abnormalities and
viral infections help explain schizophrenia.

11. The brain tissue of schizophrenia patients has
been found to have an excess of receptors for the
neurotransmitter _____ . Drugs
that block these receptors have been found to
_____ (increase/decrease)
schizophrenia symptoms.

12. Brain scans have shown that many people suffering from schizophrenia have abnormally
_____ (high/low) brain activity
in the _____ lobes.

13. Enlarged, _____-filled areas
and a corresponding _____ of
cerebral tissue is also characteristic of schizophrenia. Schizophrenia patients also have a smaller-
than-normal _____ , which may

account for their difficulty in filtering

_____ _____

and focusing _____ .

14. Some scientists contend that the brain abnormalities of schizophrenia may be caused by a prenatal
problem, such as _____

_____ _____ ,

maternal _____ , older

_____ age, and

_____ _____

during delivery. Another possible culprit is a

mid-pregnancy _____

_____ .

List several pieces of evidence for the fetal-virus idea.

Objective 50-4: Discuss the evidence for genetic influences on schizophrenia, and describe some factors
that may be early warning signs of schizophrenia in
children.

15. Twin studies _____
(support/do not support) the contention that
heredity plays a role in schizophrenia.

16. The role of the prenatal environment in schizophrenia is demonstrated by the fact that identical
twins who share the same _____ ,
and are therefore more likely to experience the
same prenatal _____ , are more
likely to share the disorder.

17. Adoption studies _____
(confirm/do not confirm) a genetic link in the
development of schizophrenia.

18. It appears that for schizophrenia to develop there
must be both a _____ predisposi-
tion and other factors such as those listed earlier
that "_____" the
_____ that predispose this
disease.

Identify several of the possible early warning signs for schizophrenia.

APPLICATIONS:

19. Wayne has been diagnosed with schizophrenia. His doctor attempts to help Wayne by prescribing a drug that blocks receptors for

_____ .

20. Janet, whose class presentation is titled "Current Views on the Causes of Schizophrenia," concludes her talk with the statement
  a. "Schizophrenia is caused by intolerable stress."
  b. "Schizophrenia is inherited."
  c. "Genes may predispose some people to react to particular experiences by developing schizophrenia."
  d. "As of this date, schizophrenia is completely unpredictable and its causes are unknown."

PROGRESS TEST

Multiple-Choice Questions

Circle your answers to the following questions and check them with the answers on page 412. If your answer is incorrect, read the explanation for why it is incorrect and then consult the text.

1. Which of the following is NOT true regarding schizophrenia?
  a. It occurs more frequently in people born in winter and spring months.
  b. It occurs less frequently as infectious disease rates have declined.
  c. It occurs more frequently in lightly populated areas.
  d. It usually appears during adolescence or early adulthood.

2. The effect of drugs that block receptors for dopamine is to
  a. alleviate schizophrenia symptoms.
  b. alleviate depression.
  c. increase schizophrenia symptoms.
  d. increase depression.

3. Most of the hallucinations of schizophrenia patients involve the sense of
  a. smell.   **c.** hearing.
  b. vision.   **d.** touch.

4. Hearing voices would be a(n) _____ ; believing that you are Napoleon would be a(n)

_____ .
  a. obsession; compulsion
  b. compulsion; obsession
  c. delusion; hallucination
  d. hallucination; delusion

5. When schizophrenia is slow to develop, called _____ schizophrenia, recovery is _____ .
  a. reactive; unlikely   **c.** process; unlikely
  b. process; likely   **d.** reactive; likely

6. Many psychologists believe the disorganized thoughts of people with schizophrenia result from a breakdown in
  a. selective attention.   **c.** motivation.
  b. memory storage.   **d.** memory retrieval.

7. Research evidence links the brain abnormalities of schizophrenia to _____ during prenatal development.
  a. maternal stress
  b. a viral infection contracted
  c. abnormal levels of certain hormones
  d. the weight of the unborn child

8. Among the following, which is generally accepted as a possible cause of schizophrenia?
  a. an excess of endorphins in the brain
  b. being a twin
  c. extensive learned helplessness
  d. a genetic predisposition

TERMS AND CONCEPTS TO REMEMBER

Using your own words, on a separate piece of paper write a brief definition or explanation of each of the following terms.

1. schizophrenia

2. psychosis

3. delusions

ANSWERS

Module Review

Symptoms of Schizophrenia

1. reality; psychosis; irrationality; lost contact with reality
2. thinking; perceptions; emotions; actions
3. delusions
4. selective attention
5. hallucinations; auditory
6. flat affect; catatonia

Onset and Development of Schizophrenia

7. positive symptoms; negative symptoms
8. paranoid; disorganized; catatonic; undifferentiated; residual
9. chronic (or process); less; acute (or reactive)
10. positive

Understanding Schizophrenia

11. dopamine; decrease
12. low; frontal
13. fluid; shrinkage; thalamus; sensory input; attention
14. low birth weight; diabetes; paternal; oxygen deprivation; viral infection

Risk of schizophrenia increases for those who undergo fetal development during a flu epidemic, or simply during the flu season. People born in densely populated areas and those born during winter and spring months are at increased risk. The months of excess schizophrenia births are reversed in the Southern Hemisphere, where the seasons are the reverse of the Northern Hemisphere's. Mothers who were sick with influenza during their pregnancy may be more likely to have children who develop schizophrenia. Blood drawn from pregnant women whose children develop schizophrenia have higher-than-normal levels of viral infection antibodies.

15. support
16. placenta; viruses
17. confirm
18. genetic; turn on; genes

The possible early warning signs for schizophrenia include a mother whose schizophrenia was severe and long-lasting; birth complications, often involving oxygen deprivation and low birth weight; separation from parents; short attention span and poor muscle coordination; disruptive or withdrawn behavior; emotional unpredictability; and poor peer relations and solo play.

19. dopamine
20. c. is the answer.

Progress Test

Multiple-Choice Questions

1. c. is the answer.
2. a. is the answer.
   b. & d. Thus far, only norepinephrine and serotonin have been implicated in depression and bipolar disorder.
   c. Schizophrenia has been associated with an excess of dopamine receptors. Blocking them alleviates schizophrenia symptoms.
3. c. is the answer.
4. d. is the answer. Hallucinations are false sensory experiences; delusions are false beliefs.
   a. & b. Obsessions are repetitive and unwanted thoughts. Compulsions are repetitive behaviors.
5. c. is the answer.
6. a. is the answer. Schizophrenia sufferers are easily distracted by irrelevant stimuli, evidently because of a breakdown in the capacity for selective attention.
7. b. is the answer.
8. d. is the answer. Risk for schizophrenia increases for individuals who are related to a schizophrenia victim, and the greater the genetic relatedness, the greater the risk.
   a. Schizophrenia victims have an overabundance of the neurotransmitter dopamine, not endorphins.
   b. Being a twin is, in itself, irrelevant to developing schizophrenia.
   c. Although learned helplessness has been suggested by social-cognitive theorists as a cause of self-defeating depressive behaviors, it has not been suggested as a cause of schizophrenia.

Terms and Concepts to Remember

1. **Schizophrenia** refers to the group of severe disorders whose symptoms may include disorganized and delusional thinking, inappropriate emotions and actions, and disturbed perceptions.

2. **Psychosis** refers to a psychological disorder in which a person experiences irrational ideas, distorted perceptions, and a loss of contact with reality.

3. **Delusions** are false beliefs that often are symptoms of psychotic disorders.

Dissociative, Personality, and Eating Disorders

MODULE OVERVIEW

Module 51 discusses dissociative disorders, focusing on the controversial and unique dissociative identity disorder, personality disorders, and eating disorders. Although the dissociative identity disorder has received much attention, some critics are skeptical; they note that it may be a construct of therapists looking to explain certain behaviors. Personality disorders, on the other hand, are widely accepted; the antisocial personality in particular is thought to be a product of genetic and environmental factors. Psychological influences on eating disorders are evident in those who are motivated to be abnormally thin.

NOTE: Answer guidelines for all Module 51 questions begin on page 416.

MODULE REVIEW

First, skim each section, noting headings and boldface items. After you have read the section, review each objective by answering the fill-in and essay-type questions that follow it. In some cases, Study Tips explain how best to learn a difficult concept and Applications help you to know how well you understand the material. As you proceed, evaluate your performance by consulting the answers beginning on page 416. Do not continue with the next section until you understand each answer. If you need to, review or reread the section in the textbook before continuing.

Dissociative Disorders

Objective 51-1: Describe the symptoms of dissociative disorders, and discuss why they are controversial.

1. In _____ disorders, a person experiences a sudden loss of _____ or change in _____ .

2. Dissociation means to become _____ from painful memories, thoughts, and feelings.

3. Dissociation itself _____ (is/is not so) rare.

4. A person who develops two or more distinct personalities is suffering from

   _____ _____

   disorder.

5. Nicholas Spanos has argued that such people may merely be playing different

   _____ .

6. Those who accept this as a genuine disorder point to evidence that differing personalities may be associated with distinct _____ and _____ states.

Identify two pieces of evidence brought forth by those who do not accept dissociative identity disorder as a genuine disorder.

7. The psychoanalytic and learning perspectives view dissociative disorders as ways of dealing with _____ . Others view them as a protective response to histories of

_____ _____ .

Skeptics claim these disorders are sometimes contrived by _____-_____ people and sometimes constructed out of the _____-_____ interaction.

APPLICATIONS:

8. Multiple personalities have long been a popular subject of films and novels. For example, Dr. Jekyll, whose second personality was Mr. Hyde, had _____ _____ disorder.

9. As a child, Monica was criticized severely by her mother for not living up to her expectations. This criticism was always followed by a beating with a whip. As an adult, Monica is generally introverted and extremely shy. Sometimes, however, she acts more like a young child, throwing tantrums if she doesn't get her way. At other times, she is a flirting, happy-go-lucky young lady. Most likely, Monica is suffering from
   a. a phobia.
   b. dissociative schizophrenia.
   c. dissociative identity disorder.
   d. bipolar disorder.

Personality Disorders

Objective 51-2: Contrast the three clusters of personality disorders, and describe the behaviors and brain activity that characterize the antisocial personality disorder.

10. Personality disorders exist when an individual has character traits that are enduring and impair _____ _____ .

11. A fearful sensitivity to rejection may predispose the _____ personality disorder. Eccentric behaviors, such as emotionless disengagement, are characteristic of the _____ personality disorder. The third cluster exhibits dramatic or _____ behaviors, such as the _____ or _____ personality disorders.

12. An individual who seems to have no conscience, lies, steals, is generally irresponsible, and may be criminal is said to have an _____ personality. Previously, this person was labeled a _____ .

13. Studies of biological relatives of those with antisocial and unemotional tendencies suggest that there _____ (is/is not) a biological predisposition to such traits.

14. Antisocial adolescents tended to have been _____ , _____ , unconcerned with _____ _____ , and low in _____ .

15. PET scans of murderers' brains reveal reduced activity in the _____ _____ , an area of the cortex that helps control _____ .

16. As in other disorders, in antisocial personality, genetics _____ (is/is not) the whole story. Rather, genes _____ some children to be more sensitive to _____ influences such as _____ .

APPLICATION:

17. Ming has never been able to keep a job. He's been in and out of jail for charges such as theft, sexual assault, and spousal abuse. Ming would most likely be diagnosed as having
   a. a dissociative identity disorder.
   b. major depressive disorder.
   c. schizophrenia.
   d. an antisocial personality.

Eating Disorders

Objective 51-3: Explain how anorexia nervosa, bulimia nervosa, and binge-eating disorder demonstrate the influence of psychological forces.

18. The disorder in which a person becomes significantly underweight and yet feels fat is known as _____ _____ .

19. A more common disorder is

_____

_____ , which is characterized

by repeated _____-.

_____ episodes and by feelings

of depression or anxiety. When bouts of excessive

eating followed by remorse are not accompanied

by purging or fasting, the _____-

_____ disorder may be

diagnosed.

20. The families of bulimia patients have a high inci-

dence of childhood _____

and _____ self-evaluation.

The families of anorexia patients tend to be

_____ , _____-

_____ , and _____ .

21. Genetic factors _____

(may/do not) influence susceptibility to eating

disorders.

22. Vulnerability to eating disorders

_____ (increases/does not

increase) with greater body dissatisfaction.

23. In impoverished areas of the world, where thin-

ness can signal poverty, _____

is better. In _____ cultures, how-

ever, the rise in eating disorders has coincided

with an increasing number of women having a

poor _____

_____ .

24. When young women were shown pictures of

unnaturally thin models, they felt more

_____ , _____ , and

_____ with their own bodies.

APPLICATION:

25. Of the following individuals, who might be most
prone to developing an eating disorder?

a. Jason, an adolescent boy who is somewhat
overweight and is unpopular with his peers

b. Jennifer, a teenage girl who has a poor self-
image and a fear of not being able to live up
to her parents' high standards

c. Susan, a 35-year-old woman who is a "worka-
holic" and devotes most of her energies to her
high-pressured career

d. Bill, a 40-year-old man who has had problems
with alcoholism and is seriously depressed
after losing his job of 20 years

PROGRESS TEST

Multiple-Choice Questions

Circle your answers to the following questions and
check them with the answers on page 417. If your
answer is incorrect, read the explanation for why it is
incorrect and then consult the text.

1. When expecting to be electrically shocked, people
with an antisocial personality disorder, as compared with normal people, show

a. less fear and greater arousal of the autonomic
nervous system.

b. less fear and less autonomic arousal.

c. greater fear and greater autonomic arousal.

d. greater fear and less autonomic arousal.

2. Which of the following is true concerning eating
disorders?

a. Genetic factors may influence susceptibility.

b. Cultural pressures for thinness strongly influence teenage girls.

c. Family background is a significant factor.

d. All of these statements are true.

3. (Thinking Critically) Nicholas Spanos considers
dissociative identity disorder to be

a. a genuine disorder.

b. merely role-playing.

c. a disorder that cannot be explained according
to the learning perspective.

d. a biological phenomenon.

4. Although the cause of eating disorders is still
unknown, proposed explanations focus on all the
following, EXCEPT

a. metabolic factors.

b. genetic factors.

c. family background factors.

d. cultural factors.

5. Psychodynamic and learning theorists both agree
that dissociative disorders are symptoms that
represent the person's attempt to deal with

a. unconscious conflicts.

b. anxiety.

c. unfulfilled wishes.

d. unpleasant responsibilities.

6. Women in _____ consider "bigger" to be the
ideal body shape.

a. Western cultures

b. countries such as Africa, where thinness can
signal poverty,

c. the United States

d. Australia, New Zealand, and England

Matching Items

Match each term with the appropriate definition or description.

Terms

_____ 1. dissociative disorder
_____ 2. anorexia nervosa
_____ 3. bulimia nervosa
_____ 4. dissociative identity disorder
_____ 5. antisocial personality
_____ 6. schizoid personality
_____ 7. avoidant personality

Definitions or Descriptions

a. a disorder in which conscious awareness becomes separated from previous memories, feelings, and thoughts
b. an individual who seems to have no conscience
c. an individual who exhibits eccentric behaviors, such as social disengagement
d. a person with a fearful sensitivity to rejection
e. a disorder formerly called multiple personality disorder
f. disorder in which the person restricts food intake to become significantly underweight but still feels fat
g. disorder characterized by episodes of overeating, followed by purging or fasting.

TERMS AND CONCEPTS TO REMEMBER

Using your own words, on a separate piece of paper write a brief definition or explanation of each of the following terms.

1. dissociative disorders

2. dissociative identity disorder (DID)

3. anorexia nervosa

4. bulimia nervosa

5. binge-eating disorder

6. personality disorders

7. antisocial personality disorder

ANSWERS

Module Review

Dissociative Disorders

1. dissociative; memory; identity
2. separated
3. is not so
4. dissociative identity
5. roles
6. brain; body

Skeptics point out that the recent increase in the number of reported cases of dissociative identity disorder indicates that it has become a fad. The fact that the disorder is much less prevalent outside North America also causes skeptics to doubt the disorder's genuineness.

7. anxiety; childhood trauma; fantasy-prone; therapist-patient
8. dissociative identity
9. **c.** is the answer.
   a. Phobias focus anxiety on a specific object, activity, or situation.
   b. There is no such disorder.
   d. In this mood disorder, a person alternates between feelings of hopeless depression and overexcited mania.

Personality Disorders

10. social functioning
11. avoidant; schizoid; impulsive; histrionic; narcissistic
12. antisocial; psychopath (or sociopath)
13. is
14. impulsive; uninhibited; social rewards; anxiety
15. frontal lobe; impulses
16. is not; predispose; environmental; maltreatment
17. **d.** is the answer. Repeated wrongdoing and aggressive behavior are part of the pattern associated with the antisocial personality disorder, which may also include marital problems and an inability to keep a job.
    a. Although dissociative identity disorder may involve an aggressive personality, there is nothing in the example to indicate a dissociation.
    b. Nothing in the question indicates that Ming is passive and resigned and having the self-defeating thoughts characteristic of depression.

c. Ming's behavior does not include the disorganized thinking and disturbed perceptions typical of schizophrenia.

Eating Disorders

18. anorexia nervosa
19. bulimia nervosa; binge-purge; binge-eating
20. obesity; negative; competitive; high-achieving; protective
21. may
22. increases
23. bigger; Western; body image
24. ashamed; depressed; dissatisfied
25. **b.** is the answer. Adolescent females with low self-esteem and high-achieving families seem especially prone to eating disorders such as anorexia nervosa.
    a. & d. Eating disorders occur much more frequently in women than in men.
    c. Eating disorders usually develop during adolescence, rather than during adulthood.

Progress Test

Multiple-Choice Questions

1. **b.** is the answer. Those with an antisocial personality disorder show less autonomic arousal in such situations, and emotions, such as fear, are tied to arousal.

2. **d.** is the answer.

3. **b.** is the answer.
   c. Playing a role is most definitely a learned skill.
   d. Role playing, being completely learned, is not biologically based.

4. **a.** is the answer. The text does not indicate whether their metabolism is higher or lower than most.
   b., c., & d. Genes, family background, and cultural influence have all been proposed as factors in eating disorders.

5. **b.** is the answer. The psychodynamic explanation is that these disorders are a manifestation of incompletely repressed impulses over which the person is anxious. According to the learning perspective, the troubled behaviors that result from these disorders have been reinforced by anxiety reduction.
   a. & c. These are true of the psychodynamic, but not the learning, perspective.

6. **b.** is the answer.

Matching Items

1. a
2. f
3. g
4. e
5. b
6. c
7. d

Terms and Concepts to Remember

1. **Dissociative disorders** involve a separation of conscious awareness from previous memories, thoughts, and feelings.
   Memory aid: To *dissociate* is to separate or pull apart. In the **dissociative disorders** a person becomes dissociated from his or her memories and identity.

2. The **dissociative identity disorder (DID)** is a dissociative disorder in which a person exhibits two or more distinct and alternating personalities; formerly called *multiple personality disorder.*

3. **Anorexia nervosa** is an eating disorder, most common in adolescent females, in which a person restricts food intake to become significantly underweight and yet still feels fat.

4. **Bulimia nervosa** is an eating disorder characterized by episodes of overeating followed by purging (by vomiting or laxative use) or fasting.

5. **Binge-eating** disorder is characterized by episodes of overeating, followed by distress, but without the purging or fasting that marks bulimia nervosa.

6. **Personality disorders** are characterized by inflexible and enduring maladaptive character traits that impair social functioning.

7. The **antisocial personality disorder** is a personality disorder in which the person is aggressive, ruthless, and shows no sign of a conscience that would inhibit wrongdoing.

The Psychological Therapies

MODULE OVERVIEW

Module 52 discusses the major psychotherapies for maladaptive behaviors. The various psychotherapies all derive from personality theories, namely, the psychoanalytic, humanistic, behavioral, and cognitive theories. The module groups the therapies by perspective. The last section discusses the advantages of group and family therapy.

NOTE: Answer guidelines for all Module 52 questions begin on page 427.

MODULE REVIEW

First, skim each section, noting headings and bold-face items. After you have read the section, review each objective by answering the fill-in and essay-type questions that follow it. In some cases, Study Tips explain how best to learn a difficult concept and Applications help you to know how well you understand the material. As you proceed, evaluate your performance by consulting the answers beginning on page 427. Do not continue with the next section until you understand each answer. If you need to, review or reread the section in the textbook before continuing.

Treating Psychological Disorders

Objective 52-1: Discuss how *psychotherapy, biomedical therapy,* and an *eclectic approach* to therapy differ.

1. Mental health therapies are classified as either _____ therapies or _____ therapies.

2. Some therapists blend several psychotherapy techniques and so are said to take an _____ approach.

Psychoanalysis and Psychodynamic Therapy

Objective 52-2: Discuss the goals and techniques of psychoanalysis, and describe how they have been adapted in psychodynamic therapy.

3. The goal of Freud's psychoanalysis, which is based on his personality theory, is to help the patient gain _____ .

4. Freud assumed that many psychological problems originate in childhood impulses and conflicts that have been _____ .

5. Psychoanalysts attempt to bring _____ feelings into _____ awareness where they can be dealt with.

6. Freud's technique in which a patient says whatever comes to mind is called _____ _____ .

7. When, in the course of therapy, a person omits shameful or embarrassing material, _____ is occurring. Insight is facilitated by the analyst's _____ of the meaning of such omissions, of dreams, and of other information revealed during therapy.

8. When strong feelings, similar to those experienced in other important relationships, are developed toward the therapist, _____ has occurred.

9. Today, psychoanalysis _____ (is/is not) commonly practiced in the United States. Critics point out that psychoanalysts' interpretations are hard to _____ _____ and that therapy takes a long time and is very _____ .

10. Therapists who are influenced by Freud's psycho-analysis but who talk to the patient face to face are _____ therapists. In addition, they work with patients only _____ (how long?) and for only a few weeks or months. These therapists focus on _____ across important relationships.

11. A brief alternative to psychodynamic therapy that has proven effective with _____ patients is _____ _____ .

12. While this approach aims to help people gain _____ into the roots of their difficulties, it focuses on _____ _____ rather than on past hurts.

APPLICATIONS:

13. During a session with his psychoanalyst, Jamal hesitates while describing a highly embarrassing thought. In the psychoanalytic framework, this is an example of
    a. transference.   c. mental repression.
    b. insight.   d. resistance.

14. During psychoanalysis, Jane has developed strong feelings of hatred for her therapist. The analyst interprets Jane's behavior in terms of a _____ of her feelings toward her father.
    a. projection   c. regression
    b. resistance   d. transference

15. Ernesto is seeing a psychodynamic therapist. Unlike a psychoanalyst, his therapist does not talk about _____ , _____ , and _____ , but rather about themes across important _____ .

16. Isadora's psychoanalyst would be most likely to interpret her fear of intimate relationships in terms of _____ _____ .

Humanistic Therapies

Objective 52-3: Identify the basic themes of humanistic therapy, and describe the specific goals and techniques of Rogers' client-centered approach.

17. Humanistic therapies attempt to help people meet their potential for _____ . Like psychodynamic therapies, humanistic therapies attempt to reduce inner conflicts by providing clients with new _____ .

List several ways that humanistic therapy differs from psychodynamic therapy.

18. The humanistic therapy based on Rogers' theory is called _____-_____ therapy, which is described as _____ therapy because the therapist _____ (interprets/does not interpret) the person's problems.

19. To promote growth in clients, Rogerian therapists exhibit _____ , _____ , and _____ .

20. Rogers' technique of echoing, restating, and clarifying what a person is saying is called _____ _____ . Given a nonjudgmental environment that provides _____ _____ _____ , patients are better able to accept themselves as they are and to feel valued and whole.

21. Three tips for listening more actively in your own relationships are to _____ , _____ _____ , and _____ _____ .

Behavior Therapies

Objective 52-4: Explain how the basic assumption of behavior therapy differs from those of psychodynamic and humanistic therapies, and describe the techniques used in exposure therapies and aversive conditioning.

22. Behavior therapy applies principles of _____ to eliminate troubling behaviors.

Contrast the assumptions of the behavior therapies with those of psychodynamic and humanistic therapies.

23. One cluster of behavior therapies is based on the principles of _____ _____ , as developed in Pavlov's experiments. This technique, in which a new, incompatible response is substituted for a maladaptive one, is called _____ . Two examples of this technique are

_____ _____

and _____ _____ .

24. The most widely used types of behavior therapies are the _____ _____ developed by _____ . In systematic desensitization, he assumed that one cannot simultaneously be _____ and relaxed.

25. The first step in systematic desensitization is the construction of a _____ of anxiety-arousing stimuli. The second step involves training in _____ _____ . In the final step, the person is trained to associate the _____ state with the _____-arousing stimuli.

26. For those who are unable to visually imagine an anxiety-arousing situation, or too afraid or embarrassed to do so,

_____
_____
_____

therapy offers a promising alternative.

27. In aversive conditioning, the therapist attempts to substitute a _____ (positive/negative) response for one that is currently

_____ (positive/negative) to a harmful stimulus. In this technique, a person's unwanted behaviors become associated with _____ feelings. In the long run, aversive conditioning _____ (does/does not) work.

APPLICATIONS:

28. To help Sam quit smoking, his therapist blew a blast of smoke into Sam's face each time Sam inhaled. Which technique is the therapist using?
   a. exposure therapy
   b. behavior modification
   c. systematic desensitization
   d. aversive conditioning

29. To help him overcome his fear of flying, Duane's therapist has him construct a hierarchy of anxiety-triggering stimuli and then learn to associate each with a state of deep relaxation. Duane's therapist is using the technique called
   a. systematic desensitization.
   b. aversive conditioning.
   c. transference.
   d. free association.

Objective 52-5: State the main premise of therapy based on operant conditioning principles, and describe the views of proponents and critics.

30. Reinforcing desired behaviors and withholding reinforcement for undesired behaviors are key aspects of _____

_____ .

31. Therapies that influence behavior by controlling its consequences are based on principles of _____ conditioning. One application of this form of therapy to institutional settings is the _____ _____ , in which desired behaviors are rewarded.

State two criticisms of behavior modification.

State some responses of proponents of behavior modification.

conditioning is based on the formation of a learned association between two stimulus situations or events. Operant conditioning is based on the use of reinforcement and punishment to modify the future likelihood of behaviors.

Several problem behaviors are described in the chart below. Test your understanding of behavior therapy by completing the chart and explaining how you would treat the problem behavior using one of the behavior therapies. Be sure to identify any reinforcers, conditioned stimuli, and unconditioned stimuli that you would use. The first example is completed for you.

STUDY TIP: Each type of behavior therapy discussed is derived from principles of either classical conditioning or operant conditioning. Classical

32. Situation	Type of Conditioning	Procedure
A friend is trying to quit smoking	Aversive conditioning, a type of counterconditioning (classical conditioning)	Each time your friend puffs the cigarette, the taste of the cigarette (conditioned stimulus) is paired with a blast of hot air delivered to his/her face (unconditioned stimulus).
a. A relative has a fear of flying (Hint: use imagined situations)		
b. The parents of a sloppy teenager want to get him to clean up his room		
c. A child is terrified of dogs (Hint: use real situations)		

Cognitive Therapies

Objective 52-6: Discuss the goals and techniques of cognitive therapy and of cognitive-behavioral therapy.

33. Therapists who teach people new, more constructive ways of thinking are using _____ therapy. One such therapy, created by _____ and called _____ - _____ _____ therapy, vigorously challenges people's illogical, self-defeating attitudes.

34. One variety of cognitive therapy attempts to reverse the _____ beliefs often associated with _____ by helping clients see their irrationalities. This therapy was developed by _____ .

35. Training people to restructure their thinking in stressful situations is the goal of _____ _____ training. Students trained to _____ their negative thoughts are less likely to experience future depression.

36. An integrative therapy that combines an attack on negative thinking with efforts to modify behavior is known as _____ - _____ therapy.

37. This type of therapy is an effective treatment program for anxiety and mood disorders, because they share a common problem: _____ _____ .

APPLICATIONS (review of all psychotherapies):

38. Given that Don Carlo's therapist attempts to help him by offering genuineness, acceptance, and empathy, she is probably practicing _____ therapy.

39. To help Sam lose weight by eating fewer sweets, his therapist laced a batch of cookies with a nausea-producing drug. Which technique is the therapist using?

_____ _____

40. B.J.'s therapist interprets her psychological problems in terms of repressed impulses. Which type(s) of therapy is she using? _____

41. Leota is startled when her therapist says that she needs to focus on eliminating her problem behavior rather than gaining insight into its underlying cause. Most likely, Leota has consulted a _____ therapist.

    a. behavior   **c.** cognitive
    b. humanistic   **d.** psychoanalytic

42. Ben is a cognitive-behavioral therapist. Compared with Rachel, who is a behavior therapist, Ben is more likely to

    a. base his therapy on principles of operant conditioning.
    b. base his therapy on principles of classical conditioning.
    c. address clients' attitudes as well as behaviors.
    d. focus on clients' unconscious urges.

43. A patient in a hospital receives poker chips for making her bed, being punctual at meal times, and maintaining her physical appearance. The poker chips can be exchanged for privileges, such as television viewing, snacks, and magazines. This is an example of the

    a. psychodynamic therapy technique called systematic desensitization.
    b. behavior therapy technique called token economy.
    c. cognitive therapy technique called token economy.
    d. humanistic therapy technique called systematic desensitization.

44. After Darnel dropped a pass in an important football game, he became depressed and vowed to quit the team because of his athletic incompetence. The campus psychologist used gentle questioning to reveal to Darnel that his thinking was irrational: his "incompetence" had earned him an athletic scholarship. The psychologist's response was most typical of a _____ therapist.

    a. behavior   **c.** client-centered
    b. psychodynamic **d.** cognitive

Group and Family Therapies

Objective 52-7: Discuss the aims and benefits of group and family therapy.

List several advantages of group therapy.

45. Although _____ therapy does not provide the same degree of therapist involvement with each client, it does save time and money and permits therapeutic benefits from _____ interaction.

46. The type of group interaction that focuses on the fact that we live and grow in relation to others is _____ _____ .

47. In this type of group, therapists focus on improving _____ within the family.

48. Many people also participate in _____ - _____ and _____ groups. One such group is _____ _____ .

STUDY TIP/APPLICATION: To organize your thinking about the modern psychological therapies discussed in this module, complete the chart on the next page. For each category of therapy, state the assumed underlying cause of psychological disorders, the overall goal of therapy, and the role of the therapist. To help you get started, the first example is already filled in.

49. Type of Psychotherapy	Assumed Cause of Psychological Disorder	Goal of Therapy	Role of Therapist
Psychodynamic Therapies	Unconscious conflicts from childhood	Self-insight	Interpreting patients' memories and feelings
Humanistic Therapies			
Behavior Therapies			
Cognitive Therapies			
Cognitive-Behavioral Therapy			
Group and Family Therapies			

PROGRESS TEST

Multiple-Choice Questions

Circle your answers to the following questions and check them with the answers beginning on page 429. If your answer is incorrect, read the explanation for why it is incorrect and then consult the text.

1. The technique in which a person is asked to report everything that comes to his or her mind is called _____ ; it is favored by_____ therapists.
   a. active listening; cognitive
   b. spontaneous remission; humanistic
   c. free association; psychoanalytic
   d. systematic desensitization; behavior

2. Of the following categories of psychotherapy, which is known for its nondirective nature?
   a. psychoanalysis   c. behavior therapy
   b. humanistic therapy   d. cognitive therapy

3. Which of the following is NOT a common criticism of psychoanalysis?
   a. It emphasizes the existence of repressed memories.
   b. It provides interpretations that are hard to disprove.
   c. It is generally a very expensive process.
   d. It gives therapists too much control over patients.

4. Which of the following is NOT necessarily an advantage of group therapies over individual therapies?
   a. They tend to take less time for the therapist.
   b. They tend to cost less money for the client.
   c. They are more effective.
   d. They allow the client to test new behaviors in a social context.

5. Cognitive-behavioral therapy aims to
   a. alter the way people act.
   b. make people more aware of their irrational negative thinking.
   c. alter the way people think and act.
   d. countercondition anxiety-provoking stimuli.

6. An eclectic psychotherapist is one who
   a. takes a nondirective approach in helping clients solve their problems.
   b. views psychological disorders as usually stemming from one cause, such as a biological abnormality.
   c. uses one particular technique, such as psychoanalysis or counterconditioning, in treating disorders.
   d. uses a variety of techniques, depending on the client and the problem.

7. The technique in which a therapist echoes and restates what a person says in a nondirective manner is called
   a. active listening.
   b. free association.
   c. systematic desensitization.
   d. transference.

8. Unlike traditional psychoanalytic therapy, interpersonal psychotherapy
   a. helps people gain insight into the roots of their problems.
   b. offers interpretations of patients' feelings.
   c. focuses on current relationships.
   d. does all of these things.

9. The technique of systematic desensitization is based on the premise that maladaptive symptoms are
   a. a reflection of irrational thinking.
   b. conditioned responses.
   c. expressions of unfulfilled wishes.
   d. all of these things.

10. The operant conditioning technique in which desired behaviors are rewarded with points or poker chips that can later be exchanged for various rewards is called
    a. counterconditioning.
    b. systematic desensitization.
    c. a token economy.
    d. exposure therapy.

11. One variety of _____ therapy is based on the finding that depressed people often attribute their failures to _____ .
    a. humanistic; themselves
    b. behavior; external circumstances
    c. cognitive; external circumstances
    d. cognitive; themselves

12. Carl Rogers was a _____ therapist who was the creator of _____ .
    a. behavior; systematic desensitization
    b. psychoanalytic; insight therapy
    c. humanistic; client-centered therapy
    d. cognitive; cognitive therapy for depression

13. Using techniques of classical conditioning to develop an association between unwanted behavior and an unpleasant experience is known as
    a. aversive conditioning.
    b. systematic desensitization.
    c. transference.
    d. electroconvulsive therapy.

14. Which type of psychotherapy emphasizes the individual's inherent potential for self-fulfillment?
    a. behavior therapy
    b. psychodynamic therapy
    c. humanistic therapy
    d. biomedical therapy

15. Which type of psychotherapy focuses on changing unwanted behaviors rather than on discovering their underlying causes?
    a. behavior therapy
    b. cognitive therapy
    c. humanistic therapy
    d. psychodynamic therapy

16. The techniques of counterconditioning are based on principles of
    a. observational learning.
    b. classical conditioning.
    c. operant conditioning.
    d. behavior modification.

17. In which of the following does the client learn to associate a relaxed state with a hierarchy of anxiety-arousing situations?
    a. cognitive therapy
    b. aversive conditioning
    c. counterconditioning
    d. systematic desensitization

18. Principles of operant conditioning underlie which of the following techniques?
    a. counterconditioning
    b. systematic desensitization
    c. stress inoculation training
    d. the token economy

19. Which of the following is NOT a common criticism of behavior therapy?
    a. Clients may rely too much on extrinsic rewards for their new behaviors.
    b. Behavior control is unethical.
    c. Outside the therapeutic setting, the new behavior may disappear.
    d. All of these are criticisms of behavior therapy.

20. Which type of therapy focuses on eliminating irrational thinking?
    a. EMDR
    b. client-centered therapy
    c. cognitive therapy
    d. behavior therapy

21. Family therapy differs from other forms of psychotherapy because it focuses on
    a. using a variety of treatment techniques.
    b. conscious rather than unconscious processes.
    c. the present instead of the past.
    d. how family tensions may cause individual problems.

22. One reason that aversive conditioning may only be temporarily effective is that
    a. for ethical reasons, therapists cannot use sufficiently intense unconditioned stimuli to sustain classical conditioning.
    b. patients are often unable to become sufficiently relaxed for conditioning to take place.
    c. patients know that outside the therapist's office they can engage in the undesirable behavior without fear of aversive consequences.
    d. most conditioned responses are elicited by many nonspecific stimuli and it is impossible to countercondition them all.

Matching Items

Match each term with the appropriate definition or description.

Terms

_____ 1. cognitive therapy
_____ 2. behavior therapy
_____ 3. systematic desensitization
_____ 4. cognitive-behavioral therapy
_____ 5. client-centered therapy
_____ 6. exposure therapy
_____ 7. aversive conditioning
_____ 8. psychoanalysis
_____ 9. biomedical therapy
_____ 10. counterconditioning
_____ 11. insight therapy

Definitions or Descriptions

a. associates unwanted behavior with unpleasant experiences
b. associates a relaxed state with anxiety-arousing stimuli
c. integrative therapy that focuses on changing self-defeating thinking and unwanted behavior
d. category of therapies that teach people more adaptive ways of thinking and acting
e. the most widely used method of behavior therapy
f. therapy developed by Carl Rogers
g. therapy based on Freud's theory of personality
h. treatment with psychosurgery, electroconvulsive therapy, or drugs
i. classical conditioning procedure in which new responses are conditioned to stimuli that trigger unwanted behaviors
j. category of therapies based on learning principles derived from classical and operant conditioning
k. therapies that aim to increase the client's awareness of underlying motives and defenses

Matching Items

Match each term with the appropriate definition or description.

Terms

_____ 1. active listening
_____ 2. token economy
_____ 3. free association
_____ 4. stress inoculation training

Definitions or Descriptions

a. empathic technique used in person-centered therapy
b. technique of psychoanalytic therapy
c. an operant conditioning procedure
d. cognitive-behavioral therapy in which people are trained to restructure their thinking in stressful situations

Essay Question

Willie has been diagnosed as suffering from major depressive disorder. Describe the treatment he might receive from a psychodynamic therapist and a cognitive therapist. (Use the space below to list points you want to make, and organize them. Then write the essay on a separate sheet of paper.)

TERMS AND CONCEPTS TO REMEMBER

Using your own words, on a separate piece of paper write a brief definition or explanation of each of the following terms.

1. psychotherapy
2. biomedical therapy
3. eclectic approach
4. psychoanalysis
5. resistance
6. interpretation
7. transference
8. psychodynamic therapy
9. insight therapies
10. client-centered therapy
11. active listening
12. unconditional positive regard
13. behavior therapy
14. counterconditioning
15. exposure therapies
16. systematic desensitization
17. virtual reality exposure therapy

18. aversive conditioning
19. token economy
20. cognitive therapy
21. rational-emotive behavioral therapy (REBT)
22. cognitive-behavior therapy
23. group therapy
24. family therapy

ANSWERS

Module Review

Treating Psychological Disorders

1. psychological; biomedical
2. eclectic

Psychoanalysis and Psychodynamic Therapy

3. insight
4. repressed
5. repressed; conscious
6. free association
7. resistance; interpretation
8. transference
9. is not; prove or disprove; expensive
10. psychodynamic; once or twice a week; themes
11. depressed; interpersonal psychotherapy
12. insight; current relationships
13. **d.** is the answer. Resistances are blocks in the flow of free association that hint at underlying anxiety.
   a. In transference, a patient redirects feelings from other relationships to his or her analyst.
   b. The goal of psychoanalysis is for patients to gain insight into their feelings.
   c. Although such hesitation may well involve material that has been repressed, the hesitation itself is a resistance.
14. **d.** is the answer. In transference, the patient develops feelings toward the therapist that were experienced in important early relationships but were repressed.
   a. Projection is a defense mechanism in which a person imputes his or her own feelings to someone else.
   b. Resistances are blocks in the flow of free association that indicate repressed material.
   c. Regression is a defense mechanism in which a person retreats to an earlier form of behavior.

15. id; ego; superego; relationships
16. repressed impulses

Humanistic Therapies

17. self-fulfillment; insights

Unlike psychodynamic therapy, humanistic therapy is focused on the present and future instead of the past, on conscious rather than unconscious processes, on promoting growth and self-fulfillment instead of curing illness, and on helping clients take immediate responsibility for their feelings and actions rather than on uncovering the obstacles to doing so.

18. client-centered; nondirective; does not interpret
19. genuineness; acceptance; empathy
20. active listening; unconditional positive regard
21. paraphrase; invite clarification; reflect feelings

Behavior Therapies

22. learning

Whereas psychoanalysis and humanistic therapies assume that problems diminish as self-awareness grows, behavior therapists doubt that self-awareness is the key. Instead of looking for the inner cause of unwanted behavior, behavior therapy applies learning principles to directly attack the unwanted behavior itself.

23. classical conditioning; counterconditioning; exposure therapy; aversive conditioning
24. exposure therapies; Joseph Wolpe; anxious
25. hierarchy; progressive relaxation; relaxed; anxiety
26. virtual reality exposure
27. negative; positive; unpleasant; does not
28. **d.** is the answer. Aversive conditioning is the classical conditioning technique in which a positive response is replaced by a negative response. (In this example, the US is the blast of smoke, the CS is the taste of the cigarette as it is inhaled, and the intended CR is aversion to cigarettes.)
    a. Exposure therapy exposes someone, in imagination (virtual reality exposure therapy) or actuality, to a feared situation.
    b. Behavior modification applies the principles of operant conditioning and thus, in contrast to the example, uses reinforcement.
    c. Systematic desensitization is used to help people overcome specific anxieties.
29. **a.** is the answer.
    b. Aversive conditioning associates unpleasant states with unwanted behaviors.

c. In psychoanalytic therapy, transference is the patient's redirecting to the analyst emotions from other relationships.
d. Free association is a psychoanalytic technique in which a patient says whatever comes to mind.

30. behavior modification
31. operant; token economy

Behavior modification is criticized because the desired behavior may stop when the rewards are stopped. Also, critics contend that one person should not be allowed to control another.

Proponents of behavior modification contend that some clients request this therapy and that the behaviors will persist if patients are properly weaned from the tokens. Also, control already exists.

32. **a.** Virtual reality exposure therapy, a type of counterconditioning (classical conditioning).
    b. Token economy, based on operant conditioning principles.
    c. Systematic desensitization, an exposure therapy, which is a form of counterconditioning. Specific procedures may vary. Refer to the text for general descriptions.

Cognitive Therapies

33. cognitive; Albert Ellis; rational-emotive behavior
34. catastrophizing; depression; Aaron Beck
35. stress inoculation; dispute
36. cognitive-behavioral
37. emotion regulation
38. humanistic
39. aversive conditioning
40. psychoanalysis
41. **a.** is the answer.
    b. & c. These types of therapists are more concerned with promoting self-fulfillment (humanistic) and healthy patterns of thinking (cognitive) than with correcting specific problem behaviors.
    d. Psychoanalysts see the behavior merely as a symptom and focus their treatment on its presumed underlying cause.
42. **c.** is the answer.
    a. & b. Behavior therapists make extensive use of techniques based on both operant and classical conditioning.
    d. Neither behavior therapists nor cognitive behavioral therapists focus on clients' unconscious urges.
43. **b.** is the answer.
44. **d.** is the answer. Because the psychologist is focusing on Darnel's irrational thinking, this

response is most typical of Beck's cognitive therapy for depression.

a. Behavior therapists treat behaviors rather than thoughts.

b. Psychoanalysts focus on helping patients gain insight into previously repressed feelings.

c. Client-centered therapists attempt to facilitate clients' growth by offering a genuine, accepting, empathic environment.

Group and Family Therapies

Group therapy saves therapists time and clients money. It offers a social laboratory for exploring social behaviors and developing social skills. It enables people to see that others share their problem. It provides feedback as clients try out new ways of behaving.

45. group; social

46. family therapy

47. communication

48. self-help; support; Alcoholics Anonymous

49. Humanistic therapies focus on the present and future, conscious thoughts, and having the person take responsibility for his or her feelings and actions. The goal is self-fulfillment. The therapist is genuine, accepting, and empathic and uses active listening in this nondirective therapy.

Behavior therapies focus on the problem behavior. The goal is to change undesirable behaviors to desirable behaviors. They use techniques based on classical and operant conditioning principles—for example, exposure therapies, aversive conditioning, and token economies.

Cognitive therapies focus on the person's way of thinking about himself or herself. Self-blaming and overgeneralized explanations of bad events cause the problem. The goal is to change the person's negative thinking. They use gentle questioning to reveal the patient's irrational thinking and persuade a depressed person, for example, to adopt a more positive attitude.

Cognitive-behavioral therapy is an integrative therapy that focuses training people to change their self-harmful thoughts and behaviors. Its goal is to make people aware of their irrational negative thinking, to replace it with new ways of thinking, and to apply that to their everyday behavior.

Group and family therapies assume that problems arise from social interactions. They help people to see that others have similar problems and that communication can resolve most problems. During sessions, for example, they try to

guide family members toward positive relationships and improved communication.

Progress Test

Multiple-Choice Questions

1. **c.** is the answer.
   a. Active listening is a Rogerian technique in which the therapist echoes, restates, and seeks clarification of the client's statements.
   b. Spontaneous recovery refers to improvement without treatment.
   d. Systematic desensitization is a process in which a person is conditioned to associate a relaxed state with anxiety-triggering stimuli.

2. **b.** is the answer.

3. **d.** is the answer. This is not among the criticisms commonly made of psychoanalysis. (It would more likely be made of behavior therapies.)

4. **c.** is the answer. Outcome research on the relative effectiveness of different therapies reveals no clear winner; the other factors mentioned are advantages of group therapies.

5. **c.** is the answer.

6. **d.** is the answer. Today, half of all psychotherapists describe themselves as eclectic—as using a blend of therapies.
   a. An eclectic therapist may use a nondirective approach with certain behaviors; however, a more directive approach might be chosen for other clients and problems.
   b. In fact, just the opposite is true. Eclectic therapists generally view disorders as stemming from many influences.
   c. Eclectic therapists, in contrast to this example, use a combination of treatments.

7. **a.** is the answer.

8. **c.** is the answer.

9. **b.** is the answer.
   a. This reflects a cognitive perspective.
   c. This reflects a psychodynamic perspective.

10. **c.** is the answer.
    a. & b. Counterconditioning is the replacement of an undesired response with a desired one by means of aversive conditioning or systematic desensitization.
    d. Exposure therapy exposes a person, in imagination or in actuality, to a feared situation.

11. **d.** is the answer.

12. **c.** is the answer.
    a. This answer would be a correct description of Joseph Wolpe.

b. There is no such thing as insight therapy.
d. This answer would be a correct description of Aaron Beck.

13. **a.** is the answer.
b. In systematic desensitization, a hierarchy of anxiety-provoking stimuli is gradually associated with a relaxed state.
c. Transference refers to a patient's transferring of feelings from other relationships onto his or her psychoanalyst.
d. Electroconvulsive therapy is a biomedical shock treatment.

14. **c.** is the answer.
a. Behavior therapy focuses on behavior, not self-awareness.
b. Psychodynamic therapy focuses on bringing unconscious feelings into awareness.
d. Biomedical therapy focuses on physical treatment through drugs, ECT, or psychosurgery.

15. **a.** is the answer. For behavior therapy, the problem behaviors *are* the problems.
b. Cognitive therapy teaches people to think and act in more adaptive ways.
c. Humanistic therapy promotes growth and self-fulfillment by providing an empathic, genuine, and accepting environment.
d. Psychodynamic therapy focuses on uncovering and interpreting unconscious feelings.

16. **b.** is the answer. Counterconditioning techniques involve taking an established stimulus, which triggers an undesirable response, and pairing it with a new stimulus in order to condition a new, and more adaptive, response.
a. As indicated by the name, counterconditioning techniques are a form of conditioning; they do not involve learning by observation.
c. & d. The principles of operant conditioning are the basis of behavior modification, which, in contrast to counterconditioning techniques, involves use of reinforcement.

17. **d.** is the answer.
a. This is a confrontational therapy, which is aimed at teaching people to think and act in more adaptive ways.
b. Aversive conditioning is a form of counterconditioning in which unwanted behavior is associated with unpleasant feelings.
c. Counterconditioning is a general term, including not only systematic desensitization, in which a hierarchy of fears is desensitized, but also other techniques, such as aversive conditioning.

18. **d.** is the answer.
a. & b. These techniques are based on classical conditioning.
c. This is a type of cognitive therapy.

19. **d.** is the answer.

20. **c.** is the answer.
a. This is an alternative therapy in which the practitioner triggers eye movements in patients who are imagining traumatic events.
b. In this humanistic therapy, the therapist facilitates the client's growth by offering a genuine, accepting, and empathic environment.
d. Behavior therapy concentrates on modifying the actual symptoms of psychological problems.

21. **d.** is the answer.
a. This is true of most forms of psychotherapy.
b. & c. This is true of humanistic, cognitive, and behavior therapies.

22. **c.** is the answer. Although aversive conditioning may work in the short run, the person's ability to discriminate between the situation in which the aversive conditioning occurs and other situations can limit the treatment's effectiveness.
a., b., & d. These are not limitations of the effectiveness of aversive conditioning.

Matching Items

1. d	5. f	9. h
2. j	6. e	10. i
3. b	7. a	11. k
4. c	8. g	

Matching Items

1. a	3. b
2. c	4. d

Essay Question

Psychodynamic therapists assume that psychological problems such as depression are caused by unconscious conflicts from childhood experiences. A psychodynamic therapist would probably attempt to bring these feelings into Willie's conscious awareness and interpret those memories and feelings in order to help him gain insight into his depression.

Cognitive therapists assume that a person's emotional reactions are influenced by the person's thoughts in response to the event in question. A cognitive therapist would probably try to teach Willie new and more constructive ways of thinking in order to reverse his catastrophizing beliefs about himself, his situation, and his future.

Terms and Concepts to Remember

1. **Psychotherapy** is an interaction between a trained therapist and someone who suffers from psychological difficulties or wants to achieve personal growth.

2. **Biomedical therapy** is the use of prescribed medications or medical procedures that act on a person's physiology to treat psychological disorders.

3. With an **eclectic approach**, therapists are not locked into one form of psychotherapy, but draw on whatever combination seems best suited to a client's problems.

4. **Psychoanalysis**, the therapy developed by Sigmund Freud, attempts to give clients self-insight by bringing into awareness and interpreting previously repressed feelings.

   Example: The tools of the **psychoanalyst** include free association, the analysis of dreams and transferences, and the interpretation of repressed impulses.

5. **Resistance** is the psychoanalytic term for the blocking from consciousness of anxiety-laden memories. Hesitation during free association may reflect resistance.

6. **Interpretation** is the psychoanalytic term for the analyst's helping the patient to understand resistances and other aspects of behavior, so that the patient may gain deeper insights.

7. **Transference** is the psychoanalytic term for a patient's redirecting to the analyst emotions from other relationships.

8. Derived from the psychoanalytic tradition, **psychodynamic therapy** seeks to enhance patients' self-insight into their symptoms by focusing on childhood experiences and important relationships in addition to unconscious forces.

9. **Insight therapies** such as psychodynamic and humanistic therapies aim to increase the person's awareness of underlying motives and defenses.

10. **Client-centered therapy** is a humanistic non-directive therapy developed by Carl Rogers, in which growth and self-awareness are facilitated in an environment that offers genuineness, acceptance, and empathy.

11. **Active listening** is a nondirective technique of Rogers' client-centered therapy, in which the listener echoes, restates, and seeks clarification of, but does not interpret, clients' remarks.

12. **Unconditional positive regard** refers to the accepting, nonjudgmental attitude that is the basis of client-centered therapy.

13. **Behavior therapy** is therapy that applies learning principles to the elimination of unwanted behaviors.

14. **Counterconditioning** is a category of behavior therapy in which new responses are classically conditioned to stimuli that trigger unwanted behaviors.

15. **Exposure therapies** treat anxiety by exposing people (in imagination or actual situations) to things they normally fear and avoid. Among these therapies are systematic desensitization and virtual reality exposure therapy.

16. **Systematic desensitization** is a type of exposure therapy in which a state of relaxation is classically conditioned to a hierarchy of gradually increasing anxiety-provoking stimuli.

   Memory aid: This is a form of **counterconditioning** in which sensitive, anxiety-triggering stimuli are *de*sensitized in a progressive, or **systematic**, fashion.

17. **Virtual reality exposure therapy** progressively exposes people to electronic simulations of feared situations to treat their anxiety.

18. **Aversive conditioning** is a form of counterconditioning in which an unpleasant state is associated with an unwanted behavior.

19. A **token economy** is an operant conditioning procedure in which desirable behaviors are promoted in people by rewarding them with tokens, or positive reinforcers, which can be exchanged for privileges or treats. For the most part, token economies are used in hospitals, schools, and other institutional settings.

20. **Cognitive therapy** focuses on teaching people new and more adaptive ways of thinking and acting. The therapy is based on the idea that our feelings and responses to events are strongly influenced by our thinking, or cognition.

21. **Rational-emotive behavior therapy (REBT)** is a confrontational cognitive therapy that challenges people's illogical, self-defeating attitudes and assumptions.

22. **Cognitive-behavioral therapy** is an integrative therapy that focuses on changing self-defeating thinking (cognitive therapy) and unwanted behaviors (behavior therapy).

23. **Group therapy** is therapy conducted with groups rather than individuals.

24. **Family therapy** views problem behavior as influenced by, or directed at, other members of the individual's family. Therapy therefore focuses on relationships and problems among the various members of the family.

Evaluating Psychotherapies

MODULE OVERVIEW

In evaluating the therapies, the module points out that, although people who are untreated often improve, those receiving psychotherapy tend to improve somewhat more, regardless of the type of therapy they receive. This section includes a discussion of two popular alternative therapies.

Because the origins of problems often lie beyond the individual, the module concludes with a discussion of approaches that aim at preventing psychological disorders by focusing on the family or on the larger social environment as possible contributors to psychological disorders.

NOTE: Answer guidelines for all Module 53 questions begin on page 437.

MODULE REVIEW

First, skim each section, noting headings and bold-face items. After you have read the section, review each objective by answering the fill-in and essay-type questions that follow it. In some cases, Study Tips explain how best to learn a difficult concept and Applications help you to know how well you understand the material. As you proceed, evaluate your performance by consulting the answers beginning on page 437. Do not continue with the next section until you understand each answer. If you need to, review or reread the section in the textbook before continuing.

Is Psychotherapy Effective?

Objective 53-1: Discuss whether psychotherapy works as interpreted by clients, clinicians, and outcome research.

1. A majority of psychotherapy clients express _____ (satisfaction/dissatisfaction) with their therapy.

Give three reasons that client testimonials are not persuasive evidence for psychotherapy's effectiveness.

2. Clinicians tend to _____ (overestimate/underestimate) the effectiveness of psychotherapy.

3. One reason clinicians' perceptions of the effectiveness of psychotherapy are inaccurate is that clients justify entering therapy by emphasizing their _____
_____ and justify leaving therapy by emphasizing their _____ .

4. (Thinking Critically) Clients' and therapists' perceptions of therapy's effectiveness may be inflated by their _____ that a treatment works. This phenomenon is called the
_____ _____ .

Another phenomenon that may inflate their perceptions of therapy's effectiveness is the phenomenon called _____
_____ _____
_____ , which is the tendency for _____ events or emotions to return to their _____ state.

5. In hopes of better assessing psychotherapy's effectiveness, psychologists have turned to _____ research studies.

6. The debate over the effectiveness of psychotherapy began with a study by _____ ; it showed that the rate of improvement for those who received therapy _____ (was/was not) higher than the rate for those who did not.

7. In the best studies of the effectiveness of therapy, researchers randomly assign people on a waiting list to therapy or no therapy and later evaluate everyone. These are _____ _____ trials.

8. A statistical technique that makes it possible to combine the results of many different psychotherapy outcome studies is called _____ . Overall, the results of such analyses indicate that psychotherapy is _____ (somewhat effective/ineffective).

The Relative Effectiveness of Different Psychotherapies

Objective 53-2: Describe which psychotherapies are most effective for specific disorders.

9. Comparisons of the effectiveness of different forms of therapy reveal _____ (clear/no clear) differences, that the type of therapy provider _____ (matters greatly/does not matter), and that whether therapy is provided by an individual therapist or within a group _____ (makes a difference/does not make a difference).

10. Some forms of therapy are best for particular problems, though there is often an overlapping— or _____ —of disorders. With phobias, compulsions, and other specific behavior problems, _____ _____ therapies have been the most effective. Other studies have demonstrated that anxiety, post-traumatic stress disorder, and depression may be effectively treated with _____ or _____-_____ therapy.

11. As a rule, psychotherapy is most effective with problems that are _____ (specific/nonspecific).

12. Clinical decision making that integrates research with clinical expertise and patient preferences and characteristics is called _____-_____ _____ .

APPLICATION:

13. Your best friend Armand wants to know which type of therapy works best. You should tell him that
   a. psychotherapy does not work.
   b. behavior therapy is the most effective.
   c. cognitive therapy is the most effective.
   d. no one type of therapy is consistently the most successful.

Evaluating Alternative Therapies

Objective 53-3: Discuss how alternative therapies fare under scientific scrutiny.

14. Today, many forms of _____ _____ are touted as effective treatments for a variety of complaints.

15. Aside from testimonials, there is very little evidence based on _____ research for such therapies.

16. In one popular alternative therapy, a therapist triggers eye movements in patients while they imagine _____ _____ . This therapy, called _____ _____ _____ _____ , has proven _____ (completely ineffective/somewhat effective) as a treatment for nonmilitary _____-_____ _____ . However, skeptics point to evidence that _____ _____ is just as effective as triggered eye movements in producing beneficial results. The key seems to be in the person's _____ traumatic memories and in a _____ effect.

17. For people who suffer from the wintertime form of depression called _____ _____ _____ , timed _____ _____ therapy may be beneficial.

APPLICATION:

18. A close friend who for years has suffered from wintertime depression is seeking your advice regarding the effectiveness of light exposure therapy. What should you tell your friend?

    a. "Don't waste your time and money. It doesn't work."

    b. "A more effective treatment for seasonal affective disorder is eye movement desensitization and reprocessing."

    c. "You'd be better off with a prescription for lithium."

    d. "It might be worth a try. There is some evidence that morning light exposure produces relief."

Commonalities Among All Psychotherapies

Objective 53-4: Describe the three elements shared by all forms of psychotherapy.

19. All forms of psychotherapy offer three benefits: _____ for demoralized people; a new _____ on oneself; and a relationship that is _____ , _____ , and _____ .

20. The emotional bond between therapist and client—the _____ _____—is a key aspect of effective therapy. In one study of depression treatment, the most effective therapists were those who were perceived as most _____ and _____ .

Culture, Gender, and Values in Psychotherapy

Objective 53-5: Discuss how culture, gender, and values influence the therapist-client relationship.

21. Generally speaking, psychotherapists' personal values _____ (do/do not) influence their therapy. This is particularly significant when the therapist and client are from different _____ or are different _____ . Another area of potential value conflict is _____ .

22. In North America, Europe, and Australia, most therapists reflect their culture's _____ .

23. Differences in values may help explain the reluctance of some _____ populations to use mental health services.

Objective 53-6: Identify some guidelines for selecting a therapist.

24. The American Psychological Association suggests that a person should seek help when he or she has feelings of _____ , a deep and lasting _____ , _____ behavior, disruptive _____ , sudden _____ shifts, and _____ rituals, for example.

APPLICATION:

25. Seth enters therapy to talk about some issues that have been upsetting him. The therapist prescribes some medication to help him. The therapist is most likely a

    a. clinical psychologist.

    b. psychiatrist.

    c. psychiatric social worker.

    d. clinical social worker.

Preventing Psychological Disorders

Objective 53-7: Explain the rationale of preventive mental health programs.

26. Lifestyle changes may also help prevent some disorders by building an individual's _____ .

27. Psychotherapies and biomedical therapies locate the cause of psychological disorders within the _____ . An alternative viewpoint is that many psychological disorders are responses to _____ _____ .

28. According to this viewpoint, it is not just the _____ who needs treatment but also the person's _____ .

29. One advocate of _____ mental health, George Albee, believes that many social stresses undermine people's sense of _____ , _____ , and _____ .

These stresses include _____ , work that is _____ , constant _____ , _____ , _____ , and _____ .

30. Albee's views remind us that disorders are not just biological and not just environmental or psychological because we are all an

_____ _____ system.

APPLICATION:

31. A psychotherapist who believes that the best way to treat psychological disorders is to prevent them from developing would be MOST likely to view disordered behavior as

a. maladaptive thoughts and actions.
b. expressions of unconscious conflicts.
c. conditioned responses.
d. an understandable response to stressful social conditions.

PROGRESS TEST

Multiple-Choice Questions

Circle your answers to the following questions and check them with the answers on page 438. If your answer is incorrect, read the explanation for why it is incorrect and then consult the text.

1. The effectiveness of psychotherapy has been assessed both through clients' perspectives and through controlled research studies. What have such assessments found?
   a. Clients' perceptions and controlled studies alike strongly affirm the effectiveness of psychotherapy.
   b. Whereas clients' perceptions strongly affirm the effectiveness of psychotherapy, studies point to more modest results.
   c. Whereas studies strongly affirm the effectiveness of psychotherapy, many clients feel dissatisfied with their progress.
   d. Clients' perceptions and controlled studies alike paint a very mixed picture of the effectiveness of psychotherapy.

2. The results of outcome research on the effectiveness of different psychotherapies reveal that
   a. no single type of therapy is consistently superior.
   b. behavior therapies are most effective in treating specific problems, such as phobias.
   c. cognitive therapies are most effective in treating depressed emotions.
   d. all of these statements are true.

3. Psychologists who advocate a _____ approach to mental health contend that many psychological disorders could be prevented by changing the disturbed individual's _____ .
   a. biomedical; diet
   b. family; behavior
   c. humanistic; feelings
   d. preventive; environment

4. A person can derive benefits from psychotherapy simply by believing in it. This illustrates the importance of
   a. spontaneous recovery.
   b. the placebo effect.
   c. the transference effect.
   d. interpretation.

5. Before 1950, the main mental health providers were
   a. psychologists.   c. psychiatrists.
   b. paraprofessionals.   d. the clergy.

6. Light exposure therapy has proven useful as a form of treatment for people suffering from
   a. bulimia.
   b. seasonal affective disorder.
   c. schizophrenia.
   d. dissociative identity disorder.

7. Which form of therapy is MOST likely to be successful in treating depression?
   a. behavior modification c. cognitive therapy
   b. psychoanalysis   d. humanistic therapy

8. Unusual emotions tend to return to their average state. This phenomenon is called
   a. regression toward the mean.
   b. resistance.
   c. counterconditioning.
   d. systematic desensitization.

9. Among the common ingredients of the psychotherapies is
   a. the offer of a therapeutic relationship.
   b. the expectation among clients that the therapy will prove helpful.
   c. the chance to develop a fresh perspective on oneself and the world.
   d. all of these are common ingredients.

Matching Items

Match each term with the appropriate definition or description.

Terms

_____   **1.** placebo effect
_____   **2.** evidence-based practice
_____   **3.** regression toward the mean
_____   **4.** meta-analysis

TERMS AND CONCEPTS TO REMEMBER

Using your own words, on a separate piece of paper write a brief definition or explanation of each of the following terms.

1. psychotherapy

2. regression toward the mean

3. meta-analysis

4. evidence-based practice

5. therapeutic alliance

ANSWERS

Module Review

Is Psychotherapy Effective?

1. satisfaction

People often enter therapy in crisis. When the crisis passes, they may attribute their improvement to the therapy. Clients, who may need to believe the therapy was worth the effort, may overestimate its effectiveness. Clients generally find positive things to say about their therapists, even if their problems remain.

2. overestimate

3. unhappiness; well-being

4. belief; placebo effect; regression toward the mean; unusual; average

5. controlled

6. Hans Eysenck; was not

7. randomized clinical

8. meta-analysis; somewhat effective

Definitions or Descriptions

a. clinical decision making that integrates research, clinical expertise, and patient characteristics

b. the beneficial effect of a person's expecting that treatment will be effective

c. the tendency for unusual emotions to return toward their average state

d. a procedure for statistically combining the results of many research studies

The Relative Effectiveness of Different Psychotherapies

9. no clear; does not matter; does not make a difference

10. comorbidity; behavioral conditioning; cognitive; cognitive-behavioral

11. specific

12. evidence-based practice

13. **d.** is the answer.
a. Psychotherapy has proven "somewhat effective" and more cost-effective than physician care for psychological disorders.
b. & c. Behavior and cognitive therapies are both effective in treating depression, and behavior therapy is effective in treating specific problems such as phobias.

Evaluating Alternative Therapies

14. alternative therapy

15. controlled

16. traumatic events; eye movement desensitization and reprocessing (EMDR); somewhat effective; post-traumatic stress disorder; finger tapping; reliving; placebo

17. seasonal affective disorder; light-exposure

18. **d.** is the answer.

a. In fact, there is evidence that light exposure therapy can be effective in treating SAD.

b. There is no evidence that EMDR is effective as a treatment for SAD.

c. Lithium is a mood-stabilizing drug that is often used to treat bipolar disorder.

Commonalities Among All Psychotherapies

19. hope; perspective; caring; trusting; empathic

20. therapeutic alliance; empathic; caring

Culture, Gender, and Values in Psychotherapy

21. do; cultures; genders; religion
22. individualism
23. minority
24. hopelessness; depression; self-destructive; fears; mood; compulsive
25. **b.** is the answer. Psychiatrists are physicians who specialize in treating psychological disorders. As doctors they can prescribe medications.
    a., c., & d. These professionals cannot prescribe drugs.

Preventing Psychological Disorders

26. resilience
27. person; a disturbing and stressful society
28. person; social context
29. preventive; competence; personal control; self-esteem; poverty; meaningless; criticism; unemployment; racism; sexism
30. integrated biopsychosocial
31. **d.** is the answer.
    a. This would be the perspective of a cognitive-behavioral therapist.
    b. This would be the perspective of a psychoanalyst.
    c. This would be the perspective of a behavior therapist.

Progress Test

Multiple-Choice Questions

1. **b.** is the answer. Clients' testimonials regarding psychotherapy are generally very positive. The research, in contrast, seems to show that therapy is only *somewhat* effective.
2. **d.** is the answer.
3. **d.** is the answer.
4. **b.** is the answer.
   a. Spontaneous recovery refers to improvement without any treatment.

c. Transference is the psychoanalytic phenomenon in which a client transfers feelings from other relationships onto his or her analyst.
d. Interpretation is the psychoanalytic procedure through which the analyst helps the client become aware of resistances and understand their meaning.

5. **c.** is the answer.
6. **b.** is the answer.
7. **c.** is the answer.
   a. Behavior modification is most likely to be successful in treating specific behavior problems, such as bed wetting.
   b. & d. The text does not single out particular disorders for which these therapies tend to be most effective.
8. **a.** is the answer.
9. **d.** is the answer.

Matching Items

1. b   3. c
2. a   4. d

Terms and Concepts to Remember

1. **Psychotherapy** is an interaction between a trained therapist and someone who suffers from psychological difficulties or wants to achieve personal growth.
2. **Regression toward the mean** is the tendency for extreme or unusual events (or emotions) to return toward their average state.
3. **Meta-analysis** is a procedure for statistically combining the results of many different research studies.
4. **Evidence-based practice** is clinical decision making that integrates the best available research with clinical expertise and patient characteristics and preferences.
5. A **therapeutic alliance** is the bond of trust that develops between a therapist and client working together to overcome the client's problem.

The Biomedical Therapies

MODULE OVERVIEW

The biomedical therapies discussed are drug therapies; brain-stimulation techniques, including electroconvulsive therapy and repetitive transcranial magnetic stimulation; and psychosurgery, which is seldom used. By far the most important of these, drug therapies are being used in the treatment of psychotic, anxiety, and mood disorders.

NOTE: Answer guidelines for all Module 54 questions appear on page 443.

MODULE REVIEW

First, skim each section, noting headings and boldface items. After you have read the section, review each objective by answering the fill-in and essay-type questions that follow it. In some cases, Study Tips explain how best to learn a difficult concept and Applications help you to know how well you understand the material. As you proceed, evaluate your performance by consulting the answers on page 443. Do not continue with the next section until you understand each answer. If you need to, review or reread the section in the textbook before continuing.

Drug Therapies

Objective 54-1: Identify and describe the drug therapies, and explain how double-blind studies help researchers evaluate a drug's effectiveness.

1. As noted earlier, therapy involving changing the brain's functioning is referred to as _____ therapy. The most widely used biomedical treatments are the _____ therapies. Thanks to these therapies, the number of residents in mental hospitals has _____ (increased/ decreased) sharply.

2. The field that studies the effects of drugs on the mind and behavior is _____ .

3. To guard against the _____ effect and normal _____ , neither the patients nor the staff involved in a study may be aware of which condition a given individual is in; this is called a _____- _____ procedure.

4. One effect of _____ drugs such as _____ is to help those experiencing _____ (positive/ negative) symptoms of schizophrenia by decreasing their responsiveness to irrelevant stimuli. Schizophrenia patients who are apathetic and withdrawn may be more effectively treated with atypical antipsychotics such as _____ .

5. The antipsychotic drugs work by blocking the receptor sites for the neurotransmitter _____ .

6. Long-term use of antipsychotic drugs can produce _____ _____ , which involves involuntary movements of the muscles of the _____ , _____ , and _____ .

7. Xanax and Ativan are classified as _____ drugs.

8. These drugs depress activity in the _____ _____ .

9. When used in combination with _____ _____ , these drugs can help people cope with frightening situations.

439

10. Antianxiety drugs have been criticized for merely reducing _____ , rather than resolving underlying _____ . These drugs can also cause _____ _____ .

11. Drugs that are prescribed to alleviate depression are called _____ drugs. They are increasingly being used to treat _____ disorders such as _____-_____ disorder. These drugs work by increasing levels of the neurotransmitters _____ or _____ .

12. One example of this type of drug is _____ , which works by blocking the reabsorption and removal of _____ from synapses and is therefore called a _____-_____-_____ drug. Increased serotonin promotes _____ , the development of new brain cells. Drugs that work by

Sending neuron
Action potential
Synaptic gap
Receiving neuron
Neurotransmitter molecule
Receptors
Reuptake
(a)   (b)   (c)

blocking the reabsorption or breakdown of norepinephrine and serotonin are called _____-_____ drugs. These drugs have _____ (more/fewer) side effects.

13. Also effective in calming anxious people and energizing depressed people is _____ _____ , which has positive side effects. Even better is to use antidepressant drugs, which work _____ (bottom-up/top-down), in conjunction with _____-_____ therapy, which works _____ (bottom-up/top-down).

14. Although people with depression often improve after one month on antidepressants, a large percentage of the effectiveness is due to _____ _____ or a _____ _____ .

15. To treat the emotional highs and lows of _____ disorder, a _____-_____ drug such as the simple salt _____ is often prescribed.

16. Another effective drug in the control of mania was originally used to treat epilepsy; it is _____ .

APPLICATIONS:

17. In an experiment testing the effects of a new antipsychotic drug, neither Dr. Cunningham nor her patients know whether the patients are in the experimental or the control group. This is an example of
  a. outcome research.
  b. within-subjects research.
  c. the double-blind procedure.
  d. the single-blind procedure.

18. Linda's doctor prescribes medication that blocks the activity of dopamine in her nervous system. Evidently, Linda is being treated with an _____ drug.
  a. antipsychotic   c. antidepressant
  b. antianxiety   d. anticonvulsive

19. Abraham's doctor prescribes medication that increases the availability of norepinephrine or serotonin in his nervous system. Evidently, Abraham is being treated with a(n) _____ drug.
  a. antipsychotic
  b. mood-stabilizing
  c. antidepressant
  d. anticonvulsive

20. A psychiatrist has diagnosed a patient as having bipolar disorder. It is likely that she will prescribe
  a. an antipsychotic drug.
  b. lithium.
  c. an antianxiety drug.
  d. a drug that blocks receptor sites for serotonin.

Brain Stimulation and Psychosurgery

Objective 54-2: Describe the use of brain stimulation techniques and psychosurgery in treating specific disorders.

21. The therapeutic technique in which the patient receives an electric shock to the brain is referred to as _____ therapy, abbreviated as _____ .

22. ECT is most often used with patients suffering from severe _____ . Research

evidence _____ (confirms/ does not confirm) ECT's effectiveness with such patients.

23. The mechanism by which ECT works is

_____ .

24. A gentler procedure called _____

_____

_____ aims to treat depression by presenting pulses through a magnetic coil held close to a person's skull above the right eyebrow. Unlike ECT, this procedure produces no

_____ , _____

loss, or other side effects. Although how it works is unclear, one explanation is that it energizes the brain's left _____

_____ , which is relatively inactive in depressed patients.

25. Another treatment being investigated for treatment of patients with depression is

_____-_____

stimulation of a neural hub that bridges the frontal lobes to the limbic system.

26. The biomedical therapy in which a portion of brain tissue is removed or destroyed is called

_____ .

27. In the 1930s, Moniz developed an operation called the _____ . In this procedure, the _____ lobe of the brain is disconnected from the rest of the brain.

28. Today, most psychosurgery has been replaced by the use of _____ or some other form of treatment.

APPLICATION:

29. In concluding her talk titled "Psychosurgery Today," Ashley states that
    a. "Psychosurgery is still widely used throughout the world."
    b. "Electroconvulsive therapy is the only remaining psychosurgical technique that is widely practiced."
    c. "With advances in psychopharmacology, psychosurgery has largely been abandoned."
    d. "Although lobotomies remain popular, other psychosurgical techniques have been abandoned."

Therapeutic Lifestyle Change

Objective 54-3: Describe how, by taking care of themselves with a healthy lifestyle, people might find some relief from depression, and explain how this reflects our being biopsychosocial systems.

30. A recent approach to therapy promotes

_____ _____

change, which includes regular aerobic exercise, adequate sleep, light exposure, social connection, anti-rumination, and nutritional supplementation.

31. The relative success of this _____ approach seems to confirm that everything psychological is also biological and that we are all social creatures.

PROGRESS TEST

Multiple-Choice Questions

Circle your answers to the following questions and check them with the answers on page 443. If your answer is incorrect, read the explanation for why it is incorrect and then consult the text.

1. Electroconvulsive therapy is most useful in the treatment of
   a. schizophrenia.
   b. depression.
   c. personality disorders.
   d. anxiety disorders.

2. Which biomedical therapy is MOST likely to be practiced today?
   a. psychosurgery
   b. electroconvulsive therapy
   c. drug therapy
   d. counterconditioning

3. The antipsychotic drugs appear to produce their effects by blocking the receptor sites for
   a. dopamine.   c. norepinephrine.
   b. epinephrine.   d. serotonin.

4. Antidepressant drugs are believed to work by affecting serotonin or
   a. dopamine.   c. norepinephrine.
   b. lithium.   d. acetylcholine.

5. After many years of taking antipsychotic drugs, Greg's facial muscles sometimes twitch involuntarily. This behavior is called
   a. tardive dyskinesia.
   b. spontaneous recovery.
   c. repetitive transcranial magnetic stimulation.
   d. EMDR.

6. Which of the following is the mood-stabilizing drug most commonly used to treat bipolar disorder?
   a. Ativan   c. Xanax
   b. chlorpromazine   d. lithium

7. The type of drugs criticized for reducing symptoms without resolving underlying problems are the
   a. antianxiety drugs.
   b. antipsychotic drugs.
   c. antidepressant drugs
   d. amphetamines.

8. The lobotomy procedure is not widely used today because
   a. it produces a lethargic, immature personality.
   b. it is irreversible.
   c. calming drugs became available in the 1950s.
   d. of all of these reasons.

Matching Items

Match each term with the appropriate definition or description.

Terms

_____   1. placebo effect
_____   2. lobotomy
_____   3. lithium
_____   4. psychopharmacology
_____   5. double-blind technique
_____   6. Xanax

Definitions or Descriptions

a. type of psychosurgery
b. mood-stabilizing drug
c. the beneficial effect of a person's expecting that treatment will be effective
d. antianxiety drug
e. the study of the effects of drugs on the mind and behavior
f. experimental procedure in which both the patient and staff are unaware of a patient's treatment condition

TERMS AND CONCEPTS TO REMEMBER

Using your own words, on a separate piece of paper write a brief definition or explanation of each of the following terms.

1. biomedical therapy

2. psychopharmacology

3. antipsychotic drugs

4. antianxiety drugs

5. antidepressant drugs

6. electroconvulsive therapy (ECT)

7. repetitive transcranial magnetic stimulation (rTMS)

8. psychosurgery

9. lobotomy

10. resilience

Essay Question

Willie has been diagnosed as suffering from major depressive disorder. Describe the treatment he might receive from a biomedical therapist. (Use the space below to list points you want to make, and organize them. Then write the essay on a separate sheet of paper.)

ANSWERS

Module Review

Drug Therapies

1. biomedical; drug; decreased
2. psychopharmacology
3. placebo; recovery; double-blind
4. antipsychotic; chlorpromazine (Thorazine); positive; clozapine (Clozaril)
5. dopamine
6. tardive dyskinesia; face; tongue; limbs
7. antianxiety
8. central nervous system
9. psychological therapy
10. symptoms; problems; physiological dependence
11. antidepressant; anxiety; obsessive-compulsive; norepinephrine; serotonin
12. fluoxetine (Prozac); serotonin; selective-serotonin-reuptake-inhibitor; neurogenesis; dual-action; fewer
13. aerobic exercise; bottom-up; cognitive-behavioral; top-down
14. spontaneous recovery; placebo effect
15. bipolar; mood-stabilizing; lithium
16. Depakote
17. **c.** is the answer.
    a. This is a statistical technique used to combine the results of many different research studies.
    b. In this design, which is not mentioned in the text, there is only a single research group.
    d. This answer would be correct if the experimenter, but not the research participants, knew which condition was in effect.
18. **a.** is the answer.
19. **c.** is the answer.
20. **b.** is the answer.

Brain Stimulation and Psychosurgery

21. electroconvulsive; ECT
22. depression; confirms
23. unknown
24. repetitive transcranial magnetic stimulation (rTMS); seizures; memory; frontal lobe
25. deep-brain
26. psychosurgery
27. lobotomy; frontal
28. drugs
29. **c.** is the answer.

b. Although still practiced, electroconvulsive therapy is not a form of psychosurgery.

Therapeutic Lifestyle Change

30. therapeutic lifestyle
31. biopsychosocial

Progress Test

Multiple-Choice Questions

1. **b.** is the answer. Although no one is sure how ECT works, one possible explanation is that it increases release of norepinephrine, the neurotransmitter that elevates mood.
2. **c.** is the answer.
   a. The fact that its effects are irreversible makes psychosurgery a drastic procedure, and with advances in psychopharmacology, psychosurgery was largely abandoned.
   b. ECT is still widely used as a treatment of severe depression, but in general it is not used as frequently as drug therapy.
   d. Counterconditioning is not a biomedical therapy.
3. **a.** is the answer. By occupying receptor sites for dopamine, these drugs block its activity and reduce its production.
4. **c.** is the answer.
5. **a.** is the answer.
6. **d.** is the answer. Lithium works as a mood stabilizer.
   a. & c. Ativan and Xanax are antianxiety drugs.
   b. Chlorpromazine is an antipsychotic drug.
7. **a.** is the answer.
8. **d.** is the answer.

Matching Items

1. c
2. a
3. b
4. e
5. f
6. d

Essay Question

Biomedical therapists attempt to treat disorders by altering the functioning of the patient's brain. A biomedical therapist would probably prescribe an antidepressant drug such as fluoxetine to increase the availability of norepinephrine and serotonin in Willie's nervous system. If Willie's depression is especially severe, a *psychiatrist* might treat it with several sessions of electroconvulsive therapy.

Terms and Concepts to Remember

1. **Biomedical therapy** is the use of prescribed medications or medical procedures that act on a person's physiology to treat psychological disorders.

2. **Psychopharmacology** is the study of the effects of drugs on mind and behavior.

   Memory aid: Pharmacology is the science of the uses and effects of drugs. *Psycho*pharmacology is the science that studies the psychological effects of drugs.

3. **Antipsychotic drugs** are used to treat schizophrenia and other severe thought disorders.

4. **Antianxiety drugs** help control anxiety and agitation by depressing activity in the central nervous system.

5. **Antidepressant drugs** treat depression and some anxiety disorders by altering the availability of various neurotransmitters.

6. In **electroconvulsive therapy (ECT)**, a biomedical therapy often used to treat severe depression, a brief electric shock is passed through the brain of an anesthetized patient.

7. **Repetitive transcranial magnetic stimulation (rTMS)** is the delivery of repeated pulses of magnetic energy to stimulate or suppress brain activity.

8. **Psychosurgery** is a biomedical therapy that attempts to change behavior by removing or destroying brain tissue. Since drug therapy became widely available in the 1950s, psychosurgery has been infrequently used.

9. Once used to control violent patients, the **lobotomy** is a form of psychosurgery in which the nerves linking the emotion centers of the brain to the frontal lobes are severed.

10. **Resilience** is a person's ability to cope with stress and recover from adversity and even trauma.